Answer to the Pelagians, III:
Unfinished Work in Answer to Julian

THE WORKS OF SAINT AUGUSTINE
A Translation for the 21st Century

Part I – Books
Volume 25:
Answer to the Pelagians, III
Unfinished Work in Anwer to Julian

THE WORKS OF SAINT AUGUSTINE
A Translation for the 21st Century

Answer to the Pelagians, III:
Unfinished Work in Answer to Julian

I/25

introduction, translation, and notes
Roland J. Teske, S.J.

editor
John E. Rotelle, O.S.A.

New City Press
Hyde Park, New York

Published in the United States by New City Press
202 Cardinal Rd., Hyde Park, New York 12538
©1999 Augustinian Heritage Institute, Inc.

Translation, introduction, and notes by Roland J. Teske, S.J.

Library of Congress Cataloging-in-Publication Data:

Augustine, Saint, Bishop of Hippo.
    The works of Saint Augustine.

    "Augustinian Heritage Institute"
    Includes bibliographical references and indexes.
    Contents: — pt. 1, v .25. Answer to the Pelagians, III
—pt. 3, v. 1. Sermons on the Old Testament, 1-19.
— pt. 3, v. 2. Sermons on the Old Testament, 20-50 — [et al.] — pt. 3,
v. 10 Sermons on various subjects, 341-400.
    1.   Theology — Early church, ca. 30-600.   I. Hill,
Edmund.   II. Rotelle, John E.   III. Augustinian
Heritage Institute.   IV. Title.
BR65.A5E53   1990   270.2   89-28878
ISBN 1-56548-055-4 (series)
ISBN 1-56548-129-1 (pt. 1, v. 25)

Nihil Obstat: Francis J. McAree, S.T.D., Censor Librorum
Imprimatur: + Patrick Sheridan, D.D., Vicar General
                    Archdiocese of New York, October 23, 1998

The Nihil Obstat and *Imprimatur* are official declarations that a book or pamphlet is free
of doctrinal or moral error. No implication is contained therein that those who have
granted the *Nihil Obstat* and *Imprimatur* agree with the contents, opinions or statements
expressed.

Printed in the United States of America

For Mary Ann Wendling Teske

Beloved Second Wife of My Father,

Mother to His Five Sons,

Someone Very Dear

Contents

Book Three

Book Four

Book Five

Book Six

Common Folk Will Be Corrected—608; The Traducianist Is Mani's Heir and Off-spring—608; Like Mani Augustine Accuses God—610; The Incredibly Great Sin of Adam and Eve—612; The Charge That Free Choice Was Lost by Being Used—614; The Insanity of Mixing Choice with the Seeds—616; The Atrocious State of Adam Destined to Fall—618; Freedom as the Possibility of Sinning Or Not Sinning—620; Only an Evil Choice Destroys the Other Possibility—623; Augustine Is Confronted with a Difficult Dilemma—626; Augustine Is Challenged to Show His Difference from Mani—628; Giving the Law Presupposes the Freedom to Observe It—636; The Goodness of Creatures Refutes the Traducianist—639; Augustine Ascribes a Matter of the Will to the Seeds—642; The Monstrous Stories Invented by the Phoenician—645; The Loss and Restoration of Innocence—647; Augustine Extols the Power of the Devil—651; Why Is the First Sin So Different from the Rest?—653; Either All Sins Are Voluntary Or God Is Unjust—656; How Could Adam's Sin Have Caused Such Harm?—661; Inherited Sin Attacks God as Well as Innocence—664; More Sins against Understanding than Syllables—665; The Pains of Childbirth Are Natural, Not Penal—668; Adam Learns of the Comfort of Death's Coming—674; The Need to Interpret the Curse upon the Serpent—685; Julian's Afterthoughts on Childbirth and Labor—686; The Laws of Nature versus the Rewards of Obedience—689; Julian's Interpretation of Our Death in Adam—694; The Full Context of Paul's Statement—696; The Flesh of Christ Is Not Separate from Ours—697; The Presuppositions of Paul's Argument—698; Julian Turns Paul's Argument against Original Sin—700; Adam Revealed Death As Christ Reveals the Resurrection—702; The Destruction of Death, the Last Enemy—707; Baptism on behalf of the Dead—709; Adam Became a Living Soul, but a Mortal One—710; The Earthly Man and the Heavenly Man—711; The Law Which Is the Power of Sin—717

General Introduction

The six books of Augustine's *Unfinished Work in Answer to Julian* were written in reply to the first six books of Julian of Eclanum's eight books, *To Florus*. This huge work of the bishop of Hippo has been somewhat neglected and even disdained. Peter Brown found in it "the cold competence of an old, tired man, who knew only too well how to set about the harsh business of ecclesiastical controversy."[1] Brown goes on to describe Augustine's encounter with Julian as "an unintelligent slogging-match" and points to the tragedy of "a man as great as Augustine" ending "his life so much at the mercy of his own blind-spots."[2] So too, Alberto Pincherle, speaking of Augustine's encounter with Julian, says that his "intransigence . . . became ever more bitter and impatient" and claims that "the pessimism which dominates all his ideas becomes so black as to leave in the reader an impression of dismay as he draws all the consequences from his theology."[3]

On the other hand, the *Unfinished Work in Answer to Julian* contains the fullest exposition of Pelagian theology by its most able and eloquent exponent, Julian of Eclanum, as well as Augustine's detailed replies, paragraph by paragraph, to Julian's work. Though Augustine was in his seventies when he undertook the refutation of Julian's *To Florus*, his argumentative powers and rhetorical eloquence in defense of the grace of God had not, in my opinion, diminished, even if the theology of grace and election which Augustine defended has some sterner aspects which make his thought less attractive than that of the new convert of 387 or of the younger bishop who first entered into conflict with Pelagius and Caelestius in 411 or 412. In no case can Augustine's last answer to Julian be justly labeled as "a work of senility."[4] It is, rather, an eloquent defense of the grace of God and especially of the role of Jesus as the savior of all human beings from their sins, including the newborn little ones.[5]

Historical Background

After Julian of Eclanum and seventeen other bishops refused to accept the letter, *Tractoria*, which was issued by Pope Zosimus in the summer of 418 to condemn the teachings of Pelagius and his disciple, Caelestius, the eighteen rebellious bishops were exiled from Italy.[6] Julian took refuge in the East with Theodore of Mopsuestia from 419 until 428 when Theodore died. After that, Julian moved to Constantinople where he lived along with some of the other deposed Italian bishops, namely, Florus, Orontius, and Fabius. In Constantinople he appealed to the emperor and to Nestorius, the patriarch of the city, in an effort to become reconciled with the Church. Nestorius twice wrote to Pope Celestine, asking whether the deposed bishops were in fact condemned. The response of Celestine on 10 August 430 was clear, confirming the previous sentence and demanding a full correction of the deposed bishops. In the same year the Council of Ephesus confirmed the deposition of Julian and the other Pelagian bishops without entering into the theological questions involved. In 439 Julian tried to reestablish communion with the Church, but Pope Sixtus refused. The stories that Julian took refuge at Lérins with Faustus of Riez and lived in a Sicilian village until the time of Fulgentius of Ruspe cannot be documented.

In the summer of 421 Alypius, Augustine's friend of many years and now bishop of Thagaste, carried to Italy copies of Augustine's *Answer to the Two Letters of the Pelagians* and the second book of *Marriage and Desire*. The former work was a reply to Julian's letter to Pope Boniface and to the joint letter of Julian and his fellow dissident bishops to Rufus, the bishop of Thessalonica. The latter work was a reply to a set of excerpts from Julian's *To Turbantius*. Augustine had written the first book of *Marriage and Desire* when he had heard from Count Valerius, an important official at the imperial court in Ravenna, that Julian had accused Augustine of condemning marriage. Augustine added the second book of *Marriage and Desire* after he had received from Count Valerius the excerpts from Julian's *To Turbantius* which were made by some unidentified person who occasionally changed what Julian had said—a point which was destined to cause considerable bitterness and misunderstanding. Although, after he had received the full text of *To Turbantius*, Augustine wrote the six books of his *Answer to Julian* to refute Julian's four books, Julian's exile in the East after his refusal to accept the *Tractoria* of Zosimus in 418 apparently prevented him from ever seeing Augustine's *Answer to Julian*. It was, in any case, the second book of *Marriage and Desire* which triggered Julian's writing the eight books of *To Florus*, a work he wrote in Cilicia while living with Theodore of Mopsuestia.[7] It is more difficult to pin down the precise date of its composition, but, given the facts that Augustine's second book of *Marriage and Desire* was carried to Italy by Alypius in 421 and that it had to be carried to Constantinople and then forwarded by Florus to Mopsuestia and that Julian's work had to travel to Italy and then to Africa for Augustine to begin his answer to it, it is most likely that *To Florus* was written between 423 and 426.

Alypius received a copy of *To Florus* during this fourth trip to Italy in 427. He had books one through five copied and delivered them to Augustine with the promise of the remaining three. Though busy with the composition of *Revisions*, a critical review of all his books, and of *Heresies*, a work which had been persistently demanded of him by Quodvultdeus, a deacon of Carthage, Augustine set to work on a refutation of Julian's work, devoting his nights to refuting *To*

Florus and his days to the other works.[8] However, before completing this last work against Julian, Augustine died on 28 August 430.

Julian's To Florus

Given the previous problems arising from the excerpts which omitted phrases and even sentences from Julian's *To Turbantius*, it seems certain that the first six books of *To Florus* are preserved in their entirety in Augustine's *Unfinished Work in Answer to Julian*, though the last two books of *To Florus* are completely lost. Augustine's procedure in replying to Julian's work was to quote a passage from *To Florus* and then to add his own response. That procedure permitted Augustine to assure his readers that he was not misrepresenting his opponent's views, and it also guaranteed that we have in Augustine's *Unfinished Work* the most complete extant presentation of the Pelagian theology by its leading and most eloquent theologian, for the writings of Pelagius himself and of Caelestius, his disciple, on the topic of grace are extant only in fragments, most often quoted in other works of Augustine. The bishop of Hippo's procedure also meant that his answer was structured by the order of Julian's work which, though written with a certain classical eloquence, is hardly a model of conciseness and order. Despite the apparently rambling style of Julian's writing which is so often filled with invective and which equally often evoked similar invective from the bishop of Hippo, one can point to the general outline of the issues around which Julian has structured his *To Florus*.

A Synopsis of Julian's To Florus

The first book is divided into an introduction and two principal parts.[9] The introduction contains Julian's dedication of the work to Florus, his announced aim of combating the new Manichees who defend original sin, and his promise to deal fully in the present work with the scriptural arguments which were passed over in *To Turbantius* (chapters 1 to 21). The first part contains Julian's prescriptive argument against original sin, namely, that nothing contained in scripture can establish God's injustice (chapters 22 to 51). He first rebuts the accusations that he has acted with deceit in omitting some of what Augustine had written and turns such charges back against Augustine who omitted part of what Julian had said, since Augustine had access only to the excerpts from *To Turbantius* which were not made by Julian (chapters 22 to 23). The main argument claims that Augustine cannot use scripture, and especially the Letters of Paul, to defend the doctrine of original sin because that doctrine is opposed to justice and scripture can neither teach injustice nor attribute it to God (chapters 24 to 47). As a corollary, Julian argues that Augustine's God, who is an unjust and cruel attacker of innocent little ones, is not the God of the old testament prophets or of the apostolic church (chapters 48 to 51).

The second part (chapters 51 to 141) can be further subdivided into three sections. In turning to the refutation of the second book of *Marriage and Desire* Julian replies to the charges brought against him on the topic of baptismal grace. He first maintains that he is not opposed to the baptism of infants and stresses the many benefits of the sacrament, while firmly rejecting the doctrine of original sin on the grounds that it is a Manichean doctrine which brings accusations against nature and makes human beings and marriage the work of the devil (chapters 52 to 66). The second section takes up the topic of freedom and grace (chapters 67 to 109). Julian argues first that Romans 7:24-25 does not entail a condemnation of human nature and explains that the law of sin in the members is merely a bad habit of committing sins, while concupiscence of the flesh is something entirely natural (chapters 67 to 73). Second, he argues that those on his side, whom he calls the Catholics, do not deny grace, but defend free choice which excludes any necessitating inclination toward evil or toward good. Augustine, he claims, agrees in part with Mani and in part with Jovinian: with Mani on the necessity of sinning before baptism and with Jovinian on the necessity of not sinning after baptism (chapters 74 to 109). The third section takes up the topic of Christ's work of redemption in relation to original sin (chapters 110 to 141). Julian first explains his faith in Christ as redeemer of human beings, but opposes Augustine on the grounds that the latter presents God as the author of human beings who are naturally evil (chapters 110 to 125). He next argues that the image of God as a potter in Romans 9:20 and Isaiah 45:8 does not support Augustine's doctrine of predestination according to which God creates some for salvation and others for damnation (chapters 126 to 141).

The second book begins with Julian's lament over the state of the Church in which the views of the masses have prevailed so that the Pelagians stand alone in defending the truth in face of persecution (chapters 1 to 15). Julian then summarizes his first book and announces the theme of the second book, namely, the content of chapter five of Saint Paul's Letter to the Romans. He recalls his argument that by definition sin must be voluntary, an argument which is meant to undercut any possibility of finding the doctrine of original sin in Saint Paul (chapters 16 to 27). The heart of the book falls into two parts, the first presenting Julian's refutation of Augustine's interpretation of Romans 5:12-18 (chapters 28 to 149), and the second presenting Julian's own exegesis of Romans 5:12-21 (chapters 150 to 236). In the first part Julian accuses Augustine of taking advantage of the ignorance of his followers and of relying upon ambiguities in scripture, while Julian appeals to the judgment of those trained in dialectic, arguing that the doctrine of original sin is absurd in itself and was not taught by the apostle who had no intention of disparaging nature or of condemning the innocent (chapters 28 to 46). Julian then turns to a critique of Augustine's exegesis of

Romans 5:12-14 in which he argues that the apostle did not speak of generation, but of example, that it was not sin, but death which was passed on to Adam's descendants, and that it was not death of the body, but rather the death of the soul which was passed on, though only to those who imitated the example of Adam's transgression by their own sins (chapters 47 to 64). Second, Julian argues that in Romans 5:15-18 Paul taught that the grace of Christ was more efficacious than Adam's sin. However, if the sin of Adam spelled the complete corruption of nature and condemnation of all his descendants, then Adam's transgression was more efficacious than the grace of Christ which, after all, saves only those who believe (chapters 65 to 143). Third, Julian appeals to the parallel which Saint Paul drew between Adam and Christ, arguing that the apostle did not maintain that all descendants of Adam are born as sinners and are subject to the devil and that only some are set free by the grace of Christ (chapters 144 to 149).

The second part of book two contains Julian's interpretation of the fifth chapter of Romans. Julian appeals to the intention of the apostle in writing the letter, namely, that he wanted to subdue the pride of the Jews who thought that because of the law of Moses they had less need of the forgiveness of Christ in comparison with the Gentiles, and to that end, Julian claims, Paul recalls the many sins which they committed since the time of Adam (chapters 150 to 172). Hence, in Romans 5:12 Paul did not speak of an original sin passed on by generation, but of a voluntary sin which was passed on to all who sinned by imitating Adam. Julian accuses Augustine of holding traducianism, Tertullian's view that human souls are generated in the same way that bodies are (chapters 173 to 184). With regard to Romans 5:13-14, Julian argues that Adam prefigured Christ as an antitype or as a model by way of contrast. Even if Adam was not the first to sin, he became the model of sin in being the greatest sinner, just as Christ is the much greater model of righteousness, even if he was not the first righteous member of the human race (chapters 185 to 203). With regard to Romans 5:15-21 Julian argues that the grace of Christ is more abundant than the sin of Adam because it reaches a greater number of human beings (chapters 204 to 221). Finally, Julian argues that in Romans 6:1-19 the apostle exhorts his readers to a life of holiness, thus demonstrating that there is no inborn sin, but that all sins are voluntary and that one can freely hold back from sin (chapters 222 to 235). Hence, Julian concludes his exegesis of Romans with the claim that the apostle had absolutely no thought of original sin in writing that letter (chapter 236).

In the introduction of the third book, having established the hermeneutical principle that the law of God cannot teach anything evil because God is just by nature, Julian undertakes the fulfillment of his promise to prove that the doctrine of original sin is unjust on the basis of a series of scriptural texts (chapters 1 to 20). In the first part of the book (chapters 12 to 100) he produces various scriptural passages which he claims run counter to the doctrine of original sin. For example, Julian first cites Deuteronomy 24:14-18, in which God sets various norms of justice and insists that parents will not die for the sins of their children or children for the sins of their parents. He argues that God would act against his law of justice if he condemned children for the sins of their parents, as the traducianist doctrine of original sin claims (chapters 12 to 30). Second, he singles out the praiseworthy example of King Amaziah who, according to 2 Kings 14:5-6, obeyed the law of God in killing the men who murdered his father, while sparing their children (chapters 31 to 37). Third, he cites the text of Ezekiel 18:1-30 where the prophet foretells the abandonment of the proverb that parents have eaten sour grapes and their children's teeth have been set on edge. Julian argues that God would be acting against his own law in punishing infants for the sins of their parents (chapters 38 to 52). In addition, Julian goes on to argue that, as no text of scripture can be employed in favor of a Marcionite or Manichean doctrine (chapters 53 to 66), so no scriptural arguments can support the doctrine of original sin (chapters 67 to 83). Fourth, Julian takes up a possible objection to his exegesis of Romans 5:12 based on Hebrews 11:8-12 in which the author speaks of Abraham's many descendants being born from one man. Julian had argued that Paul's claim that *through one man sin entered the world* (Rom 5:12) had nothing to do with generation because generation obviously requires two persons, not merely one; hence, he explains that in the Letter to the Hebrews the author could speak of Abraham's descendants coming from one man because he had already eliminated any ambiguity by the explicit discussion of generation and mention of Abraham's wife, Sarah (chapters 84 to 95). Fifth, Julian takes up Augustine's appeal in *Marriage and Desire* to the words of Paul in Romans 9:20-21 about God's acting like a potter and making some vessels for destruction so that some human beings are forced into perdition, not by the choice of their will, but by the power of their maker (chapters 96-100).

The second part of the book is devoted to demonstrating the Manicheism of Augustine. It can be divided into three sections and a concluding summary. In the first section Julian argues that Augustine denies free choice, that he is an enemy of the law of God, and that he believes in an unjust God who is the author of evil. On the other hand, by professing their faith in God the creator, the Pelagians do not deny the necessity of the grace of Christ, whether for the little ones or for all other human beings. But Julian claims that Augustine continues to believe in the Manichean doctrine of natural evil (chapters 101 to 161). In the second section Julian quotes and analyzes a letter of Mani addressed to his daughter, Menoch (chapters 162 to 187). The letter, which was allegedly discovered in Constantinople by Florus and forwarded to Julian, is now not regarded as authentic,[10] though Julian did not know this and used the letter to confirm Augustine's Manicheism. In the third section Julian shows that the Manichean doctrine of an evil nature is explicitly taught in various passages from Augustine's writings (chapters 188 to 206). Finally, Julian adds several final attacks and draws the book to a close with a summation (chapters 207 to 216).

The fourth book begins with Julian's explanation of the division between books three and four. Julian then undertakes the defense of God's works and law against the Manichees, especially with regard to concupiscence of the flesh (chapters 1 to 5). The book falls into two principal parts. The first part runs from chapters 6 to 89. In this part Julian first argues that Augustine's condemnation of concupiscence entails the condemnation of marriage (chapters 6 to 13). Turning to the basic scriptural text on concupiscence of the flesh, namely, the First Letter of John 2:15-16, Julian argues that the words of the apostle do not condemn the natural desire for sexual pleasure, but the sinful desires of human beings who are absorbed in earthly concerns (chapters 14 to 28). Furthermore, shame over one's nakedness is not a proof of the evil of concupiscence (chapters 29 to 37). Julian appeals to the other animals, all of whom experience sexual desire, in order to prove the God-given naturalness of sexual desire in human beings, even though a sense of shame keeps human beings from having sexual intercourse in public (chapters 38 to 45). Julian argues that to deny that Christ had concupiscence amounts to the heresy of Apollinarism, since such a denial deprives Christ of human sensations and, hence, of the fullness of humanity. Moreover, if Christ is to provide us with an example of virtuous conduct, he must, Julian argues, have the same natural desires other human beings have. If he did not have to struggle to be virtuous, he cannot be a model for us. Finally, concupiscence of the flesh cannot be diabolical or cause the transmission of original sin; otherwise, Christ too would have original sin (chapters 45 to 89).

The second part runs from chapters 90 to 136, in which Julian argues against original sin. He first argues that original sin is absurd: If it is natural, it is not voluntary and, therefore, not a sin. On the other hand, if it is voluntary, it is not inborn. Necessity and voluntariness are incompatible (chapters 90 to 104). Furthermore, original sin entails the condemnation of marriage (chapters 105 to 107). Augustine's appeal to the authority of Ambrose of Milan in support of the doctrine of inherited sin fails because the doctrine of inherited sin is Manichean and Ambrose was not a Manichee. Ambiguous or careless expressions found in the works of Ambrose or of Cyprian should be excused, Julian argues, since they were uttered at a time when Manicheism presented no danger (chapters 108 to 122). Julian claims that Augustine's interpretation of Wisdom 12:10-11 is a further proof of his Manicheism. The Book of Wisdom in fact contains an exhortation to moral improvement which implies freedom and is absolutely incompatible with a natural and congenital malice (chapters 123 to 135). Julian draws the book to a close with an insistence upon the consistency and rationality of the Catholic faith (chapter 136).

Book five begins with Julian lamenting the present state of the Church. In the introduction (chapters 1 to 4) he complains that Manicheism has pervaded the Church due to a widespread lack of natural talent and to an element of cowardice; yet, he remains confident that the wise will bring about the correction of the masses. The book is divided into two parts. The first part which runs from chapters 5 to 24 is focused upon concupiscence and marriage. Julian argues that Augustine's belief that concupiscence is diabolical is shown to be false by the fact that scripture portrays it as a gift of God to Abraham. Concupiscence of the flesh and sexual pleasure are, Julian maintains, perfectly natural and intended by God (chapters 5 to 16). Saint Paul also gave his approval to marital intercourse along with sexual desire and sexual pleasure when he spoke of natural relations of a man with a woman in Romans 1:27 (chapters 17 to 20). So too, the parable in Matthew 12:33 of the good tree which bears good fruit and of the bad tree which bears bad fruit upholds the goodness of marriage on the basis of the goodness of children born from it (chapters 21 to 24).

The second part of the book deals with the Manicheism of Augustine (chapters 25 to 64). Julian argues that Augustine is a Manichee because he speaks of natural evil, while, according to Julian, the only evil is sin which is found solely in an evil action arising from the free will of a human being (chapters 25 to 30). As Mani attributes the necessity of evil to the prince of darkness, Augustine attributes the necessity of evil to an eternal nothing (chapters 31 to 40). Julian defines "will" as "an act of the mind with nothing forcing it" and claims that the very definition of will precludes will's having a cause. So too, Julian accepts Augustine's definition of sin drawn from an early anti-Manichean work as "the will to do that which justice forbids and from which one is free to hold back" and insists that the sin must be free and voluntary and cannot be necessary and natural (chapters 41 to 63). Finally, Julian argues that Augustine openly declares that God creates evil human beings (chapter 64).

After a brief introduction, book six deals with three principal topics, namely, the original state of Adam and Eve and the first sin (chapters 7 to 22), the interpretation of the text of the third chapter of Genesis (chapters 23 to 29), and the natural character of death (chapters 30 to 40). Julian begins with an introduction (chapters 1 to 6), in which he accounts for the popularity of the doctrine of inherited sin by the fact that it offers "a pretext of necessity" by which sinners can excuse their sins. Moreover, he maintains that the masses of believers have supposed that the traducianists and the Catholics, by whom he means the Pelagians, were in agreement. Julian, however, is adamant that Augustine's arguments have made it clear that the God of the traducianists is not the God whom Christians worship. The traducianist is, rather, the heir and offspring of Mani for he maintains that sins are natural, that the necessity of evil comes from the eternal nothing out of which human beings were created, and that desire implanted in our senses pollutes even the saints and makes human beings, who are images of God, subject to the devil. Augustine's teaching is, in fact, worse than Mani's insofar as Augustine states that God makes and creates evil, that is, sin. Hence, Julian insists that no believer has ever had better reasons for fighting for his faith.

In the first part Julian deals with the original state of human beings and the first sin. According to Augustine, only the first two human beings were created good, but because of original sin all the rest are born with a nature damaged to the point of having lost free choice and the ability to live well (chapters 7-8). Julian, however, argues that it is absurd to suppose that an act of the will is transformed into something natural, for that supposition implies that Adam's nature was very evil if it could be corrupted by the commission of one sin, though it was not bettered by the fact that he observed the divine command over a period of time, as the biblical narrative shows (chapters 9 to 14). Julian constructs an imaginary dialogue between Mani and Augustine in which Augustine is unable to refute Mani's arguments, but is forced to reply in a way that runs counter to Augustine's own views (chapters 15 to 16). Julian's reply to the Manichees exalts the original innocence of Adam and Eve on the basis of the dignity of their creator and ascribes to human beings the freedom to lose that innocence (chapters 17 to 20). In concluding the first part, Julian claims that there is no difference between Augustine and his teacher, Mani (chapters 21 to 22).

The second part deals with the exegesis of Genesis 3. Julian claims that Adam's sin was not as serious as Augustine pretends and was the cause neither of death nor of the other evils which human beings now suffer. Animals suffer in giving birth just as women do, even though they have not sinned. A careful exegesis of the text shows that the punishment which followed the sin of the first couple was imposed upon those two alone and did not damage the natural condition of their descendants. The punishment of Adam and Eve made their natural condition worse without adding anything new (chapters 23 to 29).

In the third part Julian maintains the natural character of death, first, on the basis of various scriptural texts, but especially on the basis of First Corinthians 15:12-28, a passage in which Julian finds no basis for the Manichean idea of inherited sin; rather, the Pauline text indicates the natural condition of mortality of all human beings and declares that Christ is the first to rise from the dead as the first fruits of the resurrection (chapters 31 to 40). Finally, Julian recalls his basic exegetical principle that ambiguous passages of scripture must be interpreted in the light of the truth and of reason so that they are in accord with justice (chapter 40).

Augustine's Answer to Julian

For the previous works in the Pelagian controversy I have attempted to provide a brief description of each work paragraph by paragraph, but the sheer immensity and rambling and repetitive character of the *Unfinished Work in Answer to Julian* precludes or at least counsels against such a procedure. Instead, I have chosen to focus on several topics which are central to Augustine's controversy with Julian as we find it in the *Unfinished Work*, and to present what I take to be the heart of their interchange on these subjects, to a large extent allowing each of the two thinkers to express his own ideas.

Some Philosophical Issues

Though the controversy between Julian and Augustine is hardly a matter of mere philosophical differences, Julian takes a stand on certain views on the justice of God, the goodness of creation, the freedom of the will, and the nature of sin which are based on reason and are meant to preclude the possibility of an inherited original sin and of nature's having suffered damage by Adam's sin so that the human will is no longer free to refrain from sinning without the help of God's grace.

One of Julian's principal tactics involves an appeal to a set of definitions which together constitute a strong argument against the possibility of original sin.[11] Julian, for example, describes justice as "the greatest of all the virtues" and claims that its function involves "restoring to each person what is due without fraud and without favor" (I, 35), where "favor" translates the term "*gratia:* grace." For Julian the term "grace" smacks of partiality and favoritism, precisely the sort of thing which justice excludes. Justice, rather, "recompenses each person's merits" (I, 37). Justice has its origin in God, and without justice God would not be God (I, 38). Justice rewards the good and rightly condemns the evil; justice does not exclude God's mercy toward his own creature, "when he is not forced to be severe," for mercy "is a large part of justice" (I, 39), though it cannot involve favoritism.

Julian adopts Augustine's own definition of sin from his anti-Manichean work, *The Two Souls*, namely, "Sin is the will to do or to keep that which justice forbids and from which we are free to hold back" (I, 44). He adds a definition of will as "the movement of the mind which has in its power either to descend toward evil on the left or to strive toward noble things on the right" (I, 46); will presupposes the age at which one can use reason and at which one is presented with the choice between punishment and glory, but without the necessity of either alternative being imposed on it. Sin, then, is nothing but the will's "departing from the path on which it ought to stay and from which one is free not to turn aside" (I, 47). Given his definitions of sin, will, and freedom, Julian concludes that, since there is no sin without the will, no will without full freedom, and no freedom without the power of choice, there can be no sin in little ones who lack the power of choice. Against Augustine's claim that little ones have no sin of their own, but are weighed down by the sin of another, Julian appeals to justice of God who, if he is just—as God must be—cannot declare little ones guilty on the basis of the sin of others.

Confronted with Julian's claim that justice gives each one what is due, Augustine appeals to the actual sufferings of little ones and asks what sort of justice has recompensed such little ones upon whom there rests so heavy a yoke of misery from the day of their birth.[12] He also asks by what sort of justice one child is adopted in baptism while another is not (I, 35). That is, the facts that infants suffer in all sorts of ways and often die without baptism must also fall under God's justice. Why, Augustine asks, does Julian not admit that God also treats such human beings justly? That is, if their suffering is just, they must have merited it, not by a sin of their own, but by the transgression of Adam. Why, Augustine asks, does Julian want justice to be a matter of human choice rather than divine gift? (I, 37).

Against Julian's definition of justice as excluding fraud or favor, Augustine appeals to the parable of the workers in the vineyard, all of whom received a full day's wage, though not all have worked a full day.[13] Divine justice defrauds no one, but "gives many gifts as favors to those who do not merit them" (I, 38). Certainly, Augustine agrees, God acts justly; hence, a child who dies without baptism is not treated unjustly, though God's judgments are inscrutable (I, 39).[14] When some are rejected, they receive what all justly deserve, and when some are saved, they receive salvation through God's ineffable and inscrutable grace (I, 40).

Augustine acknowledges his earlier definition of sin, but points out that he had in *The Two Souls* defined the sin which is only sin and not the sin which is also the punishment of sin (I, 44). When Adam sinned, he committed a sin which was only sin, for he had nothing evil in him which urged him against his will to do evil so that he might say, *I do not do the good that I will, but I do the evil that I do not will* (Rom 7:19). Augustine insists that Julian must distinguish: 1) the sin which is only sin, 2) the penalty of sin, and 3) the sin which is at the same time also the penalty of sin. Adam's sin exemplified the first; the evil which one suffers without in any way causing it exemplifies the second; the third is exemplified by the evil of which Paul complained in Romans 7:19 as well as by original sin, which in the newborn is both sin and the punishment of sin, though its origin lies in the will of Adam in whom, as Augustine learned from Ambrose, we all existed and in whom we all perished (I, 47). Augustine agrees that little ones do not have their own will by which they choose good or evil, but he argues that, as Levi was in the loins of Abraham when Abraham paid the tithe to Melchizedek and, for that reason, also paid the tithe to him,[15] so we all were present in the loins of Adam and, for this reason, sinned in him. Augustine invokes the authority of Ambrose, whom Pelagius himself had so highly praised, in order to show that we all perished in Adam and that we are all born under the power of sin.[16] To Julian's complaints that God unjustly condemns on account of the sins of others a little one who dies without baptism, Augustine simply replies by comparing such complaints to those of "stupid and ignorant people" who, like Julian, complain that God creates those who he foreknows will be sinners and will be condemned (I, 48).

Julian returns to the definition of sin in book five where he charges Augustine with the inconsistency of having accepted the definition of sin as "the will to keep or to do that which justice forbids and from which we are free to hold back," while maintaining that there is sin in the little ones who have no will (V, 26). Augustine had said in *Marriage and Desire* that the evil will arose in a good nature "not because it was made good by the good God, but because it was made out of nothing" (V, 26). Julian warns that it is foolish to ask about the origin of something whose definition is still unsettled and turns to the question of the existence of evil (V, 27). The frequent occurrence of sins and God's judgment upon them show that sin does exist, and Julian proposes another definition of it, which he regards as equivalent to the first definition, namely, "an inclination of the free will which justice forbids" (V, 28). Sin, then, Julian concludes, comes "from the free will of the one who commits it" (V, 28), and justice imputes only sins which a person commits by free will (V, 29).

Augustine again replies that Julian's definition of sin holds only for that sin which is merely sin; it does not apply to the sin which is also the punishment of sin, the sin of which Saint Paul wrote in Romans 7:20, *But if I do what I do not will, it is no longer I who do it, but the sin that dwells in me* (V, 28). Adam's sin was imputed to him as a sin which he was able to avoid if he had willed to, but his sin so damaged human nature that his descendants need the savior both to remove the guilt present from their origin and to avoid sin once they have attained the use of reason (V, 29).

Julian claims that Augustine and Mani agree that sin is natural and that concupiscence of the flesh is diabolical; moreover, while Mani says that evil comes from the eternal nature of darkness, Augustine says that evil originated from the will of the first human being and then became natural in all others. Augustine admits that he agrees with Mani that concupiscence of the flesh is evil, but points out that Mani attributes this evil to an eternal, alien nature of evil, while Augustine himself attributes it to the sin of Adam (V, 30).

Julian returns to Augustine's statement that evil arose in a good creature of God because the creature was made out of nothing, a nothing which always existed; hence, Julian claims that Augustine makes this eternal nothing a cause of evil, not unlike the Manichean prince of darkness (V, 32). Augustine explains that a rational creature can sin because it is made out of nothing, not because nothing is able to do anything, but because to be made out of nothing means only not to be of the nature of God who cannot sin (V, 31). Furthermore, he insists that "neither an angel nor a human being can be compelled to sin by some force. And they would not have sinned if they had not willed to sin" (V, 32).

Julian insists that the reason an evil will could arise in a human being is not due to the creature's being made out of nothing, but is due to free choice, the freedom on account of which a human being is said to be made in the image of God and by which human beings surpass other creatures (V, 38). Augustine replies that his statement that a creature can sin because it is made out of nothing indicates the possibility of the creature's sinning, not the necessity of its sinning (V, 38). He also insists that the nature of free choice does not entail the possibility of sinning, for God has free choice in the highest degree and yet cannot sin (V, 38). Julian seems to persist—almost perversely—to misunderstand Augustine's claim and takes him to mean that any creature made out of nothing, including the elements, can sin, and Augustine takes the opportunity to offer Julian some basic lessons in logic (V, 39).

Again, Julian returns to his definition of will as "nothing but the act of the mind without anything forcing it" (V, 40). According to Julian will cannot have anything prior to it from which it takes its origin; hence, Julian insists that the question about where the bad will could come from is a bad question, since will ceases to be will if it has an origin (V, 41). Augustine points out that anything which once was not and now is has an origin and that Adam's evil will which was not and came to be, therefore, had an origin, namely, Adam himself. In claiming that evil cannot come from good, Julian, Augustine points out, lends his support to the Manichees who use that principle to introduce the alien nature of evil (V, 41).

Julian comes close to what contemporaries label as a libertarian view of freedom which, in an attempt to preserve free choice, excludes any cause of the act of the will. Though such a view is meant to exclude causal necessity from the will, it seems to do so at the cost of rationality, for it eliminates any motives or reasons for choice to the point that choice is simply something which occurs in a person rather than an action a person does. Julian divides all things which come to be into necessary ones and the possible ones; what is necessary is compelled or forced to exist, while the possible has no necessity either to exist or not to exist (V, 45). Whatever belongs to creatures as a part of their nature is necessary (V, 46). Thus human beings have freedom as a necessary element of their nature, but the act of willing is something possible. "They cannot not be free, but they cannot be forced into either act of the will" (V, 47); rather "they do both good and evil by their own will," with God providing help, but not a predetermination toward the good (V, 48).

While Julian insists that human beings do the evil they do as something possible, Augustine points to the words of Saint Paul, *I do the evil that I do not will* (Rom 7:19), as evidence that human beings do evil out of a necessity and without willing it. One, of course, does evil out of necessity if one does not will it and yet does it. But if what one does unwillingly is only to have carnal desires without any assent of the mind or action of the members, the concupiscence of the flesh is, nonetheless, an evil, "even if one does not consent to it to do evil" (V, 50).

Julian insists that Saint Paul's blaming the man who does what he does not will cannot have to do with necessity, for "whatever is attributed to necessity strikes at the creator himself." Hence, he claims that "the evil of the will cannot be attributed to nature" (V, 52). Augustine replies that an angel or a human being is a nature and that "a nature wills whatever an angel wills and a nature wills whatever a human being wills" (V, 53). Moreover, at times we will things which are necessary, such as that those people who persevere in goodness will become blessed, and at times we necessarily will things, such as our own happiness.

Julian insists that human nature and freedom of choice are good works of God, both of which come to a human being as necessary, and neither of which is the cause of evil. Rather, he says, "the will comes to be in them, but not from them" (V, 56), a view which seems to make an act of willing something which happens to one rather than something one does. Augustine, on the other hand, insists that the will of a human being comes from his free choice. "Why," Augustine asks Julian, "is a human being condemned on its account, since the evil will of which he is only the recipient, but not the cause, came to be in him without his willing it?" (V, 56). As human beings were created, they had no necessity to sin, and if they had willed not to sin, they would not have sinned. "It was a great good of their nature to be able not to sin, although it is a greater good not to be able to sin," the condition which will be their great reward in the next life (V, 56).

Julian argues that no one is good or evil just because of having free choice, but only by using one's own will (V, 57). Augustine, on the other hand, insists that *God made human beings upright* (Eccl 7:30) and claims that, on Julian's view, "it is not God who made human beings upright, but human beings who could be upright if they willed to be." And yet, on Julian's view, human beings "do not make themselves upright, but are made upright by some chance or other, because the will by which they are made upright comes to be in them, not from them, but from some unknown source and in an unknown way" (V, 57). Again Julian claims that "human nature could not have been capable of its own good, unless it were capable of evil" (V, 58). In reply, Augustine points to the life of the blessed and of the angels who no longer have the possibility of sinning, but who certainly have not lost their capacity for willing the good. According to Julian whatever is natural is necessary, and whatever is necessary excludes the possibility and the freedom which is requisite for sin. Augustine replies by appealing to Romans 7:19 and pointing to the necessity of the one who does not do the good he wills and does the evil he does not will. Catholic teachers, Augustine claims, understand the source of this necessity, namely, the grave sin of the first man in whom we all were present when he sinned (V, 59).

Julian again insists that it is wrong to ask from where the evil will of the first human being came, because the freedom of the will excludes its having an origin or nature. Julian claims that Adam "sinned because he willed to; that is, he had an evil will precisely because he willed to" (V, 60), where "because he willed to" does not indicate a cause of the evil will, but rather a denial of a cause of it. Augustine, on the other hand, insists that the evil will in Adam came from Adam himself who is, of course, a nature. In trying to avoid blaming nature, Julian said that the evil will in Adam arose "from the act of the mind with nothing forcing it," but Augustine points out that "the act of the mind could only have emerged from the mind," which is also a nature (V, 60). If Julian says that the evil act of the mind "arose from itself, not from the mind"—and this seems to be what he intended—then the mind would be blamed for what it did not do, another awkward consequence of Julian's libertarian view of human freedom.

Julian argues that Adam was created with the possibility for good and for evil. He insists that virtue must be voluntary and that, if one is to be responsible for doing good, there must be the possibility of doing evil. Augustine holds, on the other hand, that Adam was created with a good will and began to have an evil will when he freely turned away from God's commandment which he could have observed without difficulty as long as he willed to (V, 61). Now after Adam's transgression human beings are born under the penal necessity of sinning to which Saint Paul referred in Romans 7, a necessity from which one can be set free only by *the grace of God through Jesus Christ our Lord* (Romans 7:25). In trying to defend our damaged nature, Julian rejects the one explanation of its condemnation which upholds the justice of God, namely, that our nature itself produced the evil will in Adam.

Julian sums up his position: "Attribute, then, the possibility of the will to nature, but do not attribute to nature either the good or the evil will" (V, 62). Augustine replies that "both the angel and the human being are natures." Hence, if Julian were correct, neither the angel nor Adam should be praised for a good will or condemned for an evil will. What is ascribed to an angel or to a human being "is ascribed to a nature which was created good by the good God and which was made evil by its own will" (V, 62). The sin of the angel or of Adam is, however, not ascribed to the creator because he did not create the angel or Adam with a necessity to sin, but only with its possibility. But now human beings are under the necessity which Saint Paul points to in Romans 7:19 and from which they can be set free only by *the grace of God through Jesus Christ our Lord* (Rom 7:25), the grace of which, Augustine insists, Julian is an enemy (V, 62).

The Key Scriptural Texts

Augustine had appealed to Romans 5:12 in *Marriage and Desire* II, 27, 45, as containing a clear statement of the doctrine of original sin. In the introductory chapters to *To Florus* Julian admits that in *To Turbantius* he had dealt with this scriptural text only "rapidly and in brief" (I, 23). Hence, Julian promises to deal with the scriptural texts with which he had not dealt in his earlier work. In the second book of *To Florus*, Julian undertakes a refutation of Augustine's interpretation of the text and a presentation of his own quite different interpretation of Paul's Letter to the Romans. Julian, first of all, appeals to the principles established in the first book concerning God's justice, namely, that, since the law of God expresses God's justice, no argument from scripture can prove his injustice and that God's justice is so essential to him that, were he unjust, he would not be God (II, 15). Coupled with the definition of sin, divine justice excludes the presence of any sin in the newborn (II, 18).

Julian turns to Saint Paul's statement in Romans 5:12 that sin entered the world through one man, though in his opinion reason has already established "that no one is born with sin, that God cannot judge the newborn guilty, that for this reason free choice is whole and intact, and that nature is innocent in each of us before the use of our own will" (II, 20). Julian adds a supplementary exegetical principle, namely, that a difficult or ambiguous passage of scripture "must be understood in accord with what is revealed by clear reason and by the light of other passages in which there is no ambiguity" (II, 22).

The excerpts from *To Turbantius* had omitted Augustine's citation of Romans 5:12, a point on which Augustine had accused Julian of acting with deceit, for Augustine insists that Saint Paul's statement in Romans 5:12 is perfectly clear in teaching original sin (II, 24). Julian continues his preemptive argument against the possibility of original sin. According to Julian, only four persons are involved: God the creator, the two parents, and the newborn child, none of whom committed the sin supposedly present in the child (II, 29). Moreover, Adam died so many centuries ago that he can hardly be blamed (II, 30). Augustine appeals to Paul's claim that Christ *died for all* (2 Cor 5:14) and challenges Julian to state openly that little ones have no sin and "have for themselves no need of Christ's death in which they are baptized" (II, 30).

Julian continues to stall in presenting his exegesis of Romans 5:12, pointing out that Augustine has put the blame on sexual desire or concupiscence of the flesh and has called sexual pleasure diabolical (II, 31). Finally, having cited his previous claim that the apostle did not blame the will of the little one, did not blame marriage, and did not blame the action of the parents, Julian cites the passage from Augustine's *Marriage and Desire* which includes Romans 5:12 and rejects Julian's interpretation of it. For Julian had held, Augustine claimed, that Paul meant that "Adam was the first to sin, and thereafter anyone who chose to sin found in him an example for sinning" so that "sin was passed on to all human beings, not by generation from that one man, but by imitation of that one man" (II, 35). Augustine notes that Julian is still looking for dialecticians to interpret Paul's statement rather than for a judge of the Church, such as Ambrose (II, 36). Again Augustine asks Julian to present his own interpretation (II, 37). Julian continues his preemptive argument, insisting that, even when a child results from sinful intercourse, the child inherits the parents' nature, not their sin. Augustine points to the shameful sexual desire which resulted from Adam's sin and is the source from which the child contracts original sin (II, 42). Julian, Augustine argues, fails to distinguish the evil of defects, such as concupiscence, from the goodness of nature (II, 44).

Finally, Julian faces up to Romans 5:12 and claims that "the apostle said nothing which would bring discredit upon human generation, nothing which points to the condemnation of natural innocence, nothing which amounts to an accusation of God's work" (II, 47). Augustine had said that, if the apostle had wanted us to understand imitation in Romans 5:12, he would have mentioned the devil who was the first to sin rather than Adam. Julian insists that scripture often warns against imitating human beings who do evil. Augustine concedes that there are "sins of imitation in the world," but insists that "the sin which sinners would imitate" entered the world "through that one who sinned first by imitating no one," that is, through the devil, but the sin which is contracted by being born entered the world through Adam who first begot a human being (II, 48).

Julian ascribes generation to the sexes and imitation to minds (II, 52), and sin, Julian argues, could only have been passed on by imitation (II, 54), for the apostle said, *through one man* (Romans 5:12). It is, after all, clear that one man could suffice to set a pattern for imitation, but could not suffice for the act of generation (II, 56). Julian, in fact, rests the weight of his scriptural case against sin being passed on by generation on Paul's having said, *through one man*, since one man alone obviously cannot generate children. Augustine, however, claims that the apostle was correct to use the singular in speaking of generation, because "the beginning of generation comes from the man" (II, 56). Moreover, he appeals to the Lord's words that the man and the woman will be *one flesh* (Mt 19:6) as another reason for Paul's saying that sin entered the world *through one man* (II, 57). Julian, on the other hand, appeals to the same words of the Lord as evidence that God instituted sexual pleasure and sexual desire. Augustine argues that, "if only sexual desire could make them to be two in one flesh," Saint Paul could never have applied this image to Christ and the Church, as he did in Ephesians 5:31-32.

Moreover, Julian argues that Paul "certainly did not say that sin was passed on, but that death was passed on" (II, 63). Augustine admits that from the passage itself it may seem "ambiguous whether sin or death or both of them were said to have been passed on to all human beings," but argues that, "if sin had not been passed on, all human beings would not be born with the law of sin which is in the members" and that, "if death had not been passed on, all human beings would not die" (II, 63). In claiming that the death which entered the world through Adam was the guilt of sin leading to endless death, Julian is, Augustine points out, implicitly maintaining that "Adam was created so that he was going to die, whether he sinned or did not sin"—the proposition which Pelagius condemned at Diospolis in order to avoid being condemned himself (II, 66).[17] Julian holds that the sentence of death was passed on insofar as all sinned by free will, but notes that "all" indicates "many" in the customary manner of the scriptures. Augustine, in turn, appeals to Paul's words: *Just as all die, so all will be brought to life in Christ* (1 Cor 15:22) and challenges Julian to maintain that little ones did not die so that they do not need to be brought to life in Christ (II, 68).

Julian turns to the next verses in Romans and argues that Paul's words, *Up to the law sin was in the world* (Rom 5:13) mean that sin was in the world until the law began and then ceased to exist. He points out that what the law was able to remove or at least lessen could not have been natural (II, 70). Augustine insists that, if the law took away sin, then *Christ has died in vain* (Gal 2:21), and Paul lied when he said, *The law entered in so that sin might abound* (Rom 5:20). Julian goes so far as to concede that sin remained in the world up to Christ, but accuses Augustine of maintaining that the law of sin "lives on in the members of the apostles and all the baptized" (II, 71). Augustine distinguishes sin from the desire for sin, which is also called sin because it was produced by sin and can lead to sin. By rebirth Christ takes away the guilt of sin contracted by birth, and by the gift of his Spirit he stops the reign in our mortal bodies of the desire for sin (II, 71).

Julian challenges Augustine to show that original sin was imputed to someone under the law and that it was made known by the law (II, 74). Augustine appeals to the rite of circumcision as signifying that Christ takes away original sin and to the words of the psalmist: *I was conceived in iniquity, and my mother nourished me in the womb amid sins* (Ps 51:7). To Julian's claim that "natural characteristics last from the beginning of a substance up to its end," a claim which was meant to preclude the removal of natural sin, if such sin existed, Augustine points to the fact that we are born mortal, though "mortality will no longer be ours when we live immortally" (II, 76). Behind the two claims there are two quite different concepts of nature. For Augustine "nature" means either the condition in which Adam was created or that in which each human being is born,[18] while for Julian "nature" signifies the immutable essence of a human being.[19] The different concepts of nature underlie many of the differences between Julian and Augustine and were destined to lead to serious controversies in later centuries.[20] For example, in Augustine's first sense of nature, "nature" includes many factors which later theology regarded as "supernatural" or "preternatural" in relation to a more Aristotelian concept of nature.[21]

After a summary of what he believed he has already accomplished, Julian turns to Augustine's interpretation of Paul's claim that God's grace in Jesus Christ *has been much more abundant* (Rom 5:15). Julian's text apparently added: *for more*, so that he maintained that Christ's grace benefitted more people than Adam's sin harmed. Augustine insists that the Pauline text does not say: *for more*, and claims that it is obvious that "there are more in the human race for whom" Christ's grace "did not abound" (II, 85). Julian lists the evils which, according to Augustine, resulted from Adam's sin, namely, that all human beings are born for condemnation, that marriage and sexual desire become the work of the devil, and that free choice is destroyed (II, 87-89). If the grace of Christ is more abundant, it should have restored what, according to Augustine, Adam's sin destroyed (II, 90), but it is clear that grace has not restored what Augustine claims was damaged by Adam's sin. Hence, Julian concludes that none of these factors resulted from Adam's sin (II, 94). Augustine, on the other hand, argues that Julian ought to see "how great that sin was which entered the world through one man and was passed on to all human beings along with death, since even the baptized, though their guilt is forgiven, are not rescued from all the evils of this world with which human beings are born, except after this life" (II, 94). Furthermore, Augustine adds, Christ's grace is more abundant because the penalties of the reborn are temporal, while the benefits they will receive are everlasting (II, 95). Julian persists in his claim that, according to Augustine, the disasters he listed came upon human nature because of Adam's sin, but "not even one of them is healed in those who receive Christ's sacraments" so that, according to Augustine, Adam's sin "has much more power to do harm than the grace of Christ has to heal" (II, 97). Augustine responds that the grace of Christ is more abundant because it removes not only the guilt of original sin, but also the guilt of other sins; furthermore, by the grace of Christ the spirit has desires opposed to the concupiscence of the flesh in this life[22] and both bodies and souls will have eternal life in the world to come.

Julian takes up Augustine's claim that, though Adam brought us a temporal death, the grace of Christ brings eternal life, arguing that, if Adam's sin brought us only bodily death, then Augustine admits that it did not bring us the death of inherited sin (II, 99) and that, if Adam's sin brought both bodily death and eternal death, Augustine in fact accuses the apostle of lying in claiming that the grace of Christ is more abundant (II, 100). Augustine, on the other hand, maintains that Adam's sin brought the human race both deaths, but insists that the resurrection of the blessed takes away both deaths. Julian concludes that, if the grace of Christ is more abundant, the apostle did not blame nature or birth, but the will and depraved morals. Augustine, however, insists that, if birth did us no harm, rebirth offers us no benefit (II, 101).

Julian quotes from *Marriage and Desire* II, 27, 46, where Augustine had cited Paul's words, *Through the sin of the one condemnation comes upon all human beings* (Romans 5:18). Julian here simply complains about Augustine's insulting way of speaking about the Pelagian side and about Augustine's endeavors to prevent the Pelagian side from receiving a judicial hearing (II, 103). Augustine retorts that the Pelagian case had already received a hearing at Diospolis where the heresy was condemned. Julian concludes that "according to the standard of reason already introduced" what the apostle said is opposed to Augustine's "stupid, impure, and impious teaching" for "he said nothing in defense of natural sin" (II, 104). Augustine points to previous Catholic teachers who agreed with him on original sin and to the misery of human life from infancy on as proof that, given the justice of God's judgment, there must be original sin. Julian argues that, on Augustine's view, Paul would have been more logical if he had said that grace sets a human being free after one sin rather than *after many sins* (Romans 5:16), since Adam's sin, on Augustine's view, destroyed freedom of choice and every good desire (II, 105). Augustine replies that original sin alone in a little one suffices for condemnation, but that, once a person has use of the will, other sins are added to that one sin by the use of the will until "the will is restored to its good freedom to produce true righteousness by the help of God's grace." Julian argues that, according to Augustine, natural sin is the cause of all subsequent evils so that the grace of Christ actually pardons only the one sin of Adam, but that, since so many diseases remain after the application of grace, Christ must have lacked the power to cure the ills with which we are born (II, 106). In reply Augustine claims that the victory of grace will be complete only in the next life. Julian interprets Paul's claim to mean that "by the one sin" Adam "provided an example of sinning" (II, 107), and Augustine points out that Julian's position implies that Adam's sin, therefore, harmed Adam alone and not the human race—the proposition Pelagius himself condemned at Diospolis in order to avoid being condemned.[23] For, Augustine argues, human beings could not imitate a sin of which they had no knowledge, and they could not be made sinners by Adam's sin unless that sin was passed on to all future generations.

Julian's mention of the universal effectiveness of grace of baptism in removing various kinds of guilt leads Augustine to claim that Julian divides the grace of Jesus Christ, allowing him to be Christ for the little ones whom he admits to his kingdom, but not allowing him to be Jesus for them, since he finds no sins in them to forgive (II, 108). Julian argues that Paul's mentioning the one sin and the many sins indicates that both Adam's sin and later sins were the same kind, that is, sins committed by the will, so that Paul did not blame the fertility of the seeds (II, 111 and 112). Augustine admits that in its origin Adam's sin was committed by the will, but insists that he "was able to implant that one sin in those who are born, but Christ is able to forgive many sins for those who are reborn."

Julian accuses Augustine of having openly admitted the existence of the Manichean natural sin (II, 113), while Augustine again appeals to Ambrose's teaching and accuses Julian of maintaining that infants who die without baptism find an eternal happiness outside the kingdom of God.[24] Julian challenges Augustine to prove that the little ones "are subject to many serious sins" so that they too can share in the justification which Paul said comes after many sins (II, 114). Augustine simply replies that Jesus saves the little ones from their single original sins.

Julian claims that the grace of baptism "confers equally upon all who share in it the gifts of adoption, sanctification, and elevation, but that grace does not find all who approach the sacraments in a single degree of guilt" (II, 116), for it finds no bad will at all in the innocent little ones. Rather, "grace changes them from good to better," for it finds them in a state of innocence (II, 117). Augustine again appeals to the heavy yoke upon the little ones from the day of their birth and to the fact that a little one who dies without baptism is separated from the kingdom of God through no fault of its own.[25] Julian continues to argue for the different effects of grace in adults and in little ones (II, 120), and Augustine replies that it is one thing to speak of the different effects of grace, but it is something else "to deny to little ones the grace of forgiveness and to maintain that they do not truly undergo the rites of exorcism and exsufflation in the Church of the Truth."

Julian challenges Augustine to explain how he can call sexual union and sexual pleasure "the work and fruit tree of the devil" (II, 122). Augustine labels Julian a fan of sexual desire and argues that the sort of sexual desire against which one must fight in order to avoid sin "did not exist in paradise before the sin." Before Adam's sin, either there was no sexual desire, or it was obedient to the will. As sexual desire now exists, it is an evil of which marriage makes good use. Julian continues to argue from Paul's words of praise for grace, *After many sins there came grace leading to justification* (Rom 5:16), that little ones have neither many sins nor even one sin of their own will, and Augustine insists that "they have, then, no share in the medicine of the savior, and Christ is not Jesus for them" (II, 131). He also points out that, according to Julian's view, a person who has committed just one sin could not "share in this grace which justifies after many sins" (II, 132).

Julian argues from Paul's statement, *Just as through the sin of the one all entered into condemnation, so through the righteousness of the one all human beings attained justification* (Rom 5:18), that he used "all" in place of "many" in accord with the practice of the scriptures (II, 135). Augustine sees that Julian wants to maintain that the words, *in whom all have sinned* (Rom 5:12), should also be understood in the sense that many sinned, but not the little ones; he spells out the implication of Julian's interpretation, namely, that little ones should not be baptized since whoever is baptized is baptized into the death of Christ.[26] Julian pushes his argument, claiming that, "if Christ has saved all, then let Adam be supposed to have harmed all" (II, 136). Augustine replies that Christ sets all free from condemnation in the sense that "it is only he who sets anyone free." So too, Julian argues from the parallel between Christ and Adam that one should admit that Adam's sin is passed on by generation only if one admits that Christ's remedy is passed on through generation (II, 137), and Augustine replies by distinguishing carnal generation from spiritual regeneration.

Julian argues that, given the opinion of inherited sin, "sins did far more harm than grace did good," though Paul said that grace abounded for more (II, 142). Augustine replies that Paul said that "grace was much more abundant for many, not that it abounded for many more" and claims that those who are saved are few in comparison with those who are perishing, but in themselves they are many. Julian concludes this part of his argument with the claim that the apostle's words "teach us to deny that anyone can be condemned for the sin of another and to deny that any sin can be passed on to our descendants by the condition of our nature" (II, 145). In reply, Augustine accuses Julian of wanting "the grace of Christ to consist in his example, not in his gift" so that "people become righteous by imitating him, not that they are brought by the help of the Holy Spirit to imitate him" (II, 146).

In chapter 150 Julian turns to his own interpretation of Romans; he argues that Paul wrote the letter to subdue the Jewish pride in the law and to take from the Gentiles an excuse for their idolatry "in order to teach that Christ's medicine benefitted both peoples equally" (II, 151). Augustine replies that Julian denies that medicine of Christ to the little ones. According to Julian Paul confronted the Jews over their pride in the law of circumcision, but Augustine insists that Paul was dealing with the law of the commandments (II, 152). Julian cites Paul's words regarding the promise made to Abraham that he would be the father of many nations and interprets the righteousness credited to him and to the nations as a reward for their faith, while Augustine insists Abraham's will as well as the will of the nations destined to be his inheritance had to be prepared by the Lord[27] (II, 154). Julian argues that the promise to Abraham was repayment, not for his circumcision, but for his good moral conduct (II, 156), whereas Augustine points out that, if the promise were such a repayment, God with his foreknowledge ought to have predicted rather than to have promised that the Gentiles would come to believe. Julian claims that "the uncircumcised who willed to follow in the footsteps of Abraham should rightly be judged to be the children of Abraham" (II, 157). Augustine replies that "God produces the acts of the will in the minds of human beings—not so that they believe against their will, for that is utterly absurd to say—but so that they become willing from unwilling."

Julian claims that Paul's words, *For, if those who come from the law are heirs, faith has been done away with, and the promise has been destroyed* (Rom 4:14), must be interpreted to mean that those who come from the law are not the sole heirs (II, 158). Augustine answers that the heirs do not come from the law, but "come from the promise because God himself does what he promises." Those, on the other hand, who suppose that "they fulfill the commandments of the law by the choice of their own will without the Spirit of grace want to establish their own righteousness, not to receive the righteousness of God" (II, 158). Julian argues that the promise to Abraham would be destroyed if no one were righteous apart from the law, while Augustine insists that "the promise would be destroyed if anyone were righteous because of the law" (II, 160).

Given Paul's statement, *Where there is no law, there is no transgression* (Rom 4:15), Julian challenges Augustine to show that "the law was given to infants in the womb . . . so that it could prove them guilty of transgression" (II, 161). Augustine cites the law of Christ, *Whoever has not been reborn of water and the Spirit cannot enter the kingdom of God* (Jn 3:5); he insists that "this law includes the little ones too" and argues that the soul of an uncircumcised infant would not perish from its people in accord with Genesis 17:14, unless, "though it has committed no sin in itself, it was held guilty *in the likeness of the transgression of Adam in whom all have sinned*" (Rom 5:14.12).

Julian points out that the apostle said that Jesus *was handed over on account of our sins* (Rom 4:25) to emphasize that Christ "faced death on account of our sins which were both many and ours, not on account of one sin of someone else—a sin of a person long dead!" (II, 163). Augustine explains that Adam's sin can be "said to be the sin of someone else since, when we were not yet born, we did no action of our own, whether good or bad,[28] but we were all in that one who committed this sin when he committed it" (II, 163). Furthermore, Adam's sin was so great that it damaged the whole of human nature. Augustine appeals to Ambrose's teaching that "all of us human beings are born under the power of sin"[29] and to Paul's words, *All, therefore, have died, and he died for all* (2 Cor 5:15), to show that even the little ones have died in Adam. Everyone born in the human race as a descendant of Adam belongs to the first man, just as everyone reborn in Christ belongs to the second man (II, 163). Julian claims that in opposition to Paul who speaks of many sins Augustine teaches the one sin of the Manichees. Augustine, in turn, appeals to Ambrose, Cyprian, and Hilary as agreeing with him and insists that they certainly were not Manichees (II, 164).

Julian interprets the justification through faith of which Paul speaks in Romans 5:1-2 as consisting in the forgiveness of sins. Augustine, however, notes that God also justifies sinners "by bestowing love so that they avoid evil and do good through the Holy Spirit" (II, 165). In commenting on Romans 5:3-5, Julian says that the fact that we do not commit sin is a reward for our virtuous endurance of sufferings. Augustine replies that the reason human beings do not commit sin is not a reward of their merits, but a gift of God's grace (II, 166) and claims that Julian does not include our not sinning among God's gifts (II, 167). Julian cites Romans 5:7-11 and notes the great goodness of Christ "who consented to die for those who merited nothing good" (II, 170). In reply Augustine points out that Christ "died for the wicked and sinners," that is, "for those who merited evil," from whom Julian excludes the little ones, for whom Christ is also Jesus, that is, the savior from their sins. Julian emphasizes the unparalleled virtue of Christ who died for sinners, and Augustine warns him not to exclude the little ones from the sinners for whom Christ died (II, 171). So too, Augustine insists that the reconciliation with God which Christ brought about implies a state of enmity which came about through Adam's sin and that to exclude the little

ones from a share in Adam's sin entails excluding them from reconciliation with
God through Christ (II, 172).

Finally, Julian comes to Romans 5:12 where he claims that Saint Paul mentioned Adam, "not because sin began with him, for it is clear that the woman sinned first, but because by the privilege of his sex he assumed the role of teacher of sin" so that through Adam sin entered the world and eternal death was passed on to his posterity "by imitation, not by generation" (II, 173). Augustine recalls his previous explanation of why Paul did not mention Eve and argues that, if Julian holds that the death found in sin is passed on by imitation, he should openly say that the little ones do not need to be baptized into the death of Christ. Julian interprets the clause, *In whom all have sinned*, to mean: Because all have sinned (II, 174).[30] Augustine argues that "all die in Adam, and if the little ones have not died in him, neither are they brought to life in Christ." Hence, infant baptism turns out to be "a damnable pretense" if the little ones are in fact alive and well.

To avoid the universality of the statement, *all have sinned* (Romans 5:12), Julian points to many passages of scripture in which "all" is used to signify "many" (II, 175), and Augustine appeals to his previous explanation that "many" need not be opposed to "all." To Julian's claim that sin was passed on to Adam's descendants "only by imitation" (II, 177), Augustine replies that at times parents pass on to their children even physical defects, such as gout. Julian addresses Augustine's claim in *The Punishment and Forgiveness of Sins* I, 11, 13, that Adam's sin was passed on "when all human beings were that one man" (II, 178) and accuses Augustine of teaching the transmission of souls or the Tertullianist doctrine of traducianism. Julian claims that, if all human beings were in Adam, they were there body and soul. Augustine replies by showing that one can call the body alone a human being and claims with Ambrose that all of us existed in Adam,[31] though he confesses his ignorance of whether all were in Adam "only in terms of the body or in terms of both parts of the human being."

Julian appeals to the righteousness of Abel as evidence that his parents' sin did him no harm (II, 180), though Cain sinned by murdering his brother (II, 181). Augustine insists that Abel was born in sinful flesh and that sin was passed on to all human beings so that infants are rescued from the power of darkness by baptism. Saint Paul had said that *death reigned from Adam up to Moses even over those who did not sin in the likeness of the transgression of Adam* (Rom 5:13-14). Julian finds in this passage merely a distinction between sin and transgression. Augustine, however, argues that, if Paul was speaking of death's reign, that reign could not have been just except on account of original sin. He adds that, if one understands that death reigned over all who sinned, but that they did not sin in the likeness of Adam, then Julian will find no one, according to his view, because he maintains that all who sinned sinned by following Adam's example (II, 185). Julian understands the death which reigned to be eternal death, not the death which separates the soul from the body, while Augustine argues that the latter "death itself is a punishment, although divine grace puts it to good use" (II, 186). Julian holds that the people before the law did not sin in the likeness of Adam's transgression, but were not free from sin (II, 187). Augustine replies that, if they did not sin "by reason of the example of the first human being," then death was passed on "not by imitation, but by generation." Julian explains that "the incarnation of Christ did not offer the first pattern of righteousness, but the greatest" (II, 188), a statement in which Augustine finds Pelagius' doctrine that the righteous of the old testament did not live from a faith in Christ's incarnation. So too, Julian finds Adam to have been the greatest pattern of sin, though Augustine argues that Julian has no reason to make such a claim unless he admits that Adam's sin was easier to avoid when human nature was not yet corrupted (II, 189). Julian argues that Paul mentioned Adam rather than Eve because, as the male, he was more worthy of imitation, and in reply Augustine argues that Paul was not contrasting "imitation with imitation, but rebirth with birth" (II, 190). As those who are reborn share in the righteousness of Christ, so those who are born, including the little ones, "are born with the sin passed on by Adam, though they cannot as yet commit any sin." Julian argues that, if Paul were talking of natural sin in Romans 5:12, he would not have gone on to speak of those *who did not sin in the likeness of the transgression of Adam* (Rom 5:14). In reply Augustine points out that Paul would not have said that death reigned over these people unless they contracted some sin from the transgression of Adam (II, 191). Julian points out that the distinction which Paul draws runs counter to the doctrine of natural sin which would have bound all equally, but Augustine replies that original sin does bind all equally "if divine grace had not through Christ come to their rescue" (II, 193).

Julian cites Paul's words, *And in that way death was passed on to all human beings* (Rom 5:12), which he takes to imply that sin was not passed on, but only its punishment (II, 195 and 196). Augustine replies that *in that way* means: "with sin or through sin," and asks how Adam can be the antitype of Christ unless, as Christ gives righteousness to the little ones who are reborn, so Adam gives sin to those who are born. Julian interprets the Latin of *in whom all have sinned* (Rom 5:12) in the causal sense: *inasmuch as all have sinned*, an interpretation of the Greek, ἐφ᾽ ᾧ, which is in fact commonly accepted by contemporary exegetes, so that Paul referred to the actions of sinners (II, 197). Augustine appeals to Paul's statement, *But as all die in Adam, so all will be brought to life in Christ* (1 Cor 15:22), interpreting it to mean that, "as no one comes to death save through Adam, so no one rises to life save through Christ."

Julian claims that Paul's words that sin reigned up to the law showed that "the reign of sin collapsed when the law was given" (II, 198). Augustine challenges Julian to state openly that we could be justified by nature or by the law and that

Christ has, therefore, died in vain.[32] After all, only the Lamb of God *takes away the sin of the world* (Jn 1:29). Julian argues that, since generation remains even after the law and after the coming of Christ, if generation were the source of sins, sin would still be in the world, though Paul said, *Up to the law sin was in the world* (Rom 5:13). Augustine replies with a battery of texts to show that righteousness does not come through the law (II, 199). So too, Julian claims that Paul's words, *But sin is not imputed when the law does not exist* (Rom 5:13), destroys the traducianist position. Augustine argues that God imputes sins when there is no law, even if human beings do not (II, 200). Julian concludes that, if natural sin was not imputed before the law and did not exist after the law, it had no time in which it could exist (II, 201), while Augustine appeals to the need for circumcision and the offering of a sacrifice for sin at the birth of an infant. The apostle, then, Julian argues, "had no idea of natural sin which cannot exist and which is dreamed up by the Manichees" (II, 202). Augustine replies by citing Ambrose and by presenting an interpretation of death's reign in the likeness of Adam's transgression, namely, that those over whom death reigned "had a share in that sin through which death entered the world, for they contracted the likeness of the transgression . . . by being born of the transgressor by whom the whole of human nature was corrupted."

Julian again returns to his claim that the grace of Christ *abounded for more* (Rom 5:15) to which Augustine replies that he has already responded to Julian's misinterpretation (II, 204-211). The exchange between the two continues over the remaining verses of Romans 5 and over most of the following chapter, but adds little to the discussion of the scriptural grounding of original sin. In bringing the book to a close, Augustine pleads with Julian to cease from his praise of the nature of infants and to allow them "to come to Christ the deliverer in order to be set free" and to "allow the second man to heal the wretched nature which the first man corrupted" (II, 236)

In the first eighty-four chapters of book three Julian takes up one scriptural passage after another in order to defend his version of God's justice according to which divine justice neither permits nor tolerates the punishment of children for the sins of their parents. Augustine, on the other hand, replies with other texts which initially seem to contradict the texts which Julian mustered and explains how the apparent contradiction can be resolved. Because, however, Julian rested his claim that Paul could not have meant that sin was passed on through generation upon the phrase *through one man* (Rom 5:12), Julian has to deal with the words in the Letter to the Hebrews that Abraham's descendants *were born from the one man* (Heb 11:12) and that Christ and those he sanctifies *are all from the one* (Heb 2:11). Julian argues that Hebrews could speak of Abraham's descendants as *born from the one man* without any ambiguity after Sarah had been mentioned and could do so to order to increase the praise of God's power (III,

85). Augustine responds by pointing out that Julian has found—or has received as an objection—"a perfectly clear testimony" which "says without any ambiguity that countless persons were born from one, though they had, of course, two parents." Julian interprets the statement that Christ and those he sanctifies *are all from the one* as referring to God rather than to Adam, but then argues that, even if there are scriptural passages in which generation is attributed to one person, "the doctrine of hereditary sin will derive no advantage" (III, 87). Julian argues that in a context of the generation of children no one is misled by an improper expression attributing the generation to one parent, but when one is dealing with sin, sin "is said most improperly to have been passed on by one," if sin is supposed to have been transmitted by generation which requires two parents (III, 90). Hence, Julian accuses Augustine of "acting with intolerable impudence" in claiming that *through one man* (Rom 5:12) involves a figure of speech favoring the traducianist side (III, 91).

Augustine replies that, if he is a traducianist because he accepts Paul's statement in Romans 5:12, then Julian is too as Paul himself was, for all three admit that sin was transmitted somehow (III, 91). Julian continues to complain about Augustine's having abandoned the proper sense of words and of using equivocal statements "to support obscene doctrines that even attack the justice of God," while admitting that the statements support his view only in their borrowed meaning (III, 92). In reply Augustine insists that in Paul's statement, *Through one man sin entered the world* (Rom 5:12), "the words are not used figuratively, but properly." In fact, Augustine claims that, in speaking of Abraham's descendants, the author of the Letter to the Hebrews should have mentioned both parents, unless it were true in the proper sense that his descendants *were born from the one man* (Heb 11:12) on account of the father who is the source of the seed (III, 93). Julian then argues that Paul did not by his statement in Romans 5:12 "form an alliance with the Manichees" (III, 94) and "did not claim that nature was damaged and destroyed by one man through generation, but only that the will of sinners was damaged" (III, 95). Augustine replies that, because he refuses to attribute the defects with which human beings are born to original sin, Julian can only reply to the Manichees that human beings would have been born with bodily defects and subject to death even in paradise—an idea which Augustine finds outrageous.

Concupiscence of the Flesh

Julian's fourth book focuses upon concupiscence of the flesh. In *To Turbantius* Julian had attributed to God the sexual differentiation of human bodies, human fecundity, the union of the sexes, marriage, and children. Hence, he had asked, "What does the devil recognize as his own in the sexes as a result of which," as Augustine claimed, "he rightfully owns their fruit?"[33] Julian had argued that it cannot be the bodies which God made, the differences of the sexes, their union, or fecundity, and Augustine had conceded that the devil recognizes none of these as his own, but had noted that Julian refused "to mention the concupiscence of the flesh which does not come from the Father, but from the world" (IV, 5).[34] Augustine insists that Julian's question was deceitful, for it implied that the devil recognizes nothing as his own in the sexes, and Augustine insists that, though all the good elements which Julian listed would have existed even in paradise if no one had sinned, there would not have existed there the concupiscence of the flesh by which the flesh has desires opposed to the spirit (IV, 10).[35] Even chaste spouses must resist the motions of concupiscence, which Augustine insists is an evil (IV, 17). Julian accuses Augustine of using "the words of Mani himself" when he claims that "concupiscence of the flesh was not made by God, but created by the world, the world of which you say the devil is the prince" (IV, 18). Augustine replies that the Lord himself said that the devil is *the prince of this world* (Jn 12:31). He points out, however, that scripture speaks of the world in two senses: in a good sense as heaven and earth and every creature in them and in a bad sense as sinful human beings. Concupiscence of the flesh, then, belongs to the world in the bad sense.

Julian admits that John spoke of concupiscence, but he calls it "marital" and insists that the apostle did not mean what Mani meant (IV, 19). In reply Augustine accuses Julian of trying "to clothe your shameful darling with the honorable name of marriage" and argues that marital concupiscence could have existed in paradise, even if no one had sinned, but would never have had desires opposed to the spirit. Julian claims that John was challenging the faithful to the pursuit of virtue and holiness and meant by the world which one should not love "all the stimuli of present goods and pleasures" (IV, 20)—even "all the elements." Augustine replies that the apostle called the world in his Letter the life by which human beings live in a merely human way and challenges Julian to show that scripture ever spoke of concupiscence of the flesh in a good sense. Julian uses the Prologue to John's Gospel as proof that John knew that God created the whole world, but claims that John had used the term "world" in his Letter "to signify immoderate desire" (IV, 21). Augustine points out in reply that Julian considers concupiscence of the flesh to be something good so that "to use immoderate concupiscence is . . . to make bad use of a good," as one might make an immoderate or bad use of a good like wine, while Augustine holds that concupiscence of the flesh is an evil, since it *does not come from the Father* (1 Jn 2:16), even though it can be used well, that is, within marriage for having children. Julian adds that by "the world" John meant "the conduct of human beings who have no idea that there is anything after this life as well as the various displays and sexual misconduct of mortals" (IV, 22). In reply Augustine points out that Julian's "fair darling" certainly is included there and points out the inconsistency on Julian's part of calling "sexual misconduct an evil and the desire for sexual misconduct a good." Julian argues that John "did not attack the nature of reality by the term 'world,' but the vices of wills," but that Mani and Augustine believe that "concupiscence of the flesh was created, not by God, but by the devil" (IV, 23). Augustine admits that both he and Mani call concupiscence of the flesh something evil, but claims that Mani does not understand the source of this evil, namely, Adam's transgression, and that, by denying that source, Julian makes Mani seem correct in attributing it to the nature of evil coeternal to God.

Julian claims that John does not blame genus of concupiscence which becomes a vice only in its forbidden and voluntary excess (IV, 24), while Augustine points out that, according to Julian, concupiscence remains a good even when it is used to excess. Julian holds that *the concupiscence of the flesh, the concupiscence of the eyes, and the pride of life* (1 Jn 2:16) are blameworthy only in their excess, not within their licit limit (IV, 25). Augustine, however, holds out that concupiscence of the flesh is an evil for, if one obeys its impulses, one does evil and, if one fights against it, one does good. Julian claims that Adam had concupiscence of the flesh even before he sinned, while Augustine insists that what Adam had was not that concupiscence by which the flesh has desires opposed to the spirit (IV, 26). While Julian links concupiscence with the senses of the flesh, Augustine distinguishes sensation from the movements of carnal concupiscence (IV, 27). In fact, Julian sees concupiscence as having nothing to do with sex and claims that the apostle did not condemn sexual pleasure in his Letter. Augustine admits that concupiscence of the flesh can be found in "whatever sense of the body the flesh has desires opposed to the spirit" (IV, 28). Julian, then, concludes that neither Augustine nor Mani has been able to prove that concupiscence, namely, "the sensation by which the body of those united sexually is affected," is diabolical (IV, 29). In reply, Augustine distinguishes between sensation and concupiscence, for example, between sight which is a good sense of the flesh and concupiscence which is an evil desire of the flesh.

In *Marriage and Desire* II, 9, 22, Augustine seized upon Julian's statement in *To Turbantius* that in saying that husband and wife *will be two in one flesh* (Gn 2:24), the sacred writer "came close to endangering modesty." Julian points to Augustine's inconsistency in claiming "that there is nothing to be ashamed of in the works of God, but that the activity of the sexual organs is something to be ashamed of, and that it cannot, therefore, be ascribed to God" (IV, 31). Julian further claims that Augustine "does not want God to have created the punishment which he says God imposes," that is, concupiscence or the law of sin in our members (IV, 32). In reply, Augustine insists that one must distinguish God's works from God's judgments and claims that the concupiscence of the flesh in opposition to the spirit is an evil and a punishment of sin. Julian claims that there is no cause for shame in God's works, while Augustine insists that the deformity by which the flesh has desires opposed to the spirit is reason for shame and is a punishment for sin (IV, 33). While Julian claims that Augustine has invented the idea that God imposed the punishment of sexual desire, a desire over which one should be ashamed, Augustine argues that God "causes the sinner to receive in recompense what God himself did not create" (IV, 34). Julian argues that, according to Augustine, God imposed a punishment, namely, the law of sin in the members, "which would be an enticement and incentive toward sin," so that he produced the necessity of sinning instead of the punishment of sin (IV, 35). Augustine, in turn, points to scriptural examples of sins which are also punishment of sins.

Citing Paul's words on *our more shameful* or *less honorable members* having *greater honor* (1 Cor 12:23), Julian argues that the reason why people do not perform natural acts of eating or of evacuation in public and do not walk about naked is not that there is something shameful in God's works (IV, 36 and 37). Augustine points out that modesty conceals some members because they cause disgust and others because they cause desire and insists that the first couple covered their genitals in shame over the resistance they experienced in the flesh to the spirit's governance. Julian points to the existence of sexual desire in animals, a desire created in them by God, and argues that such passion "is not unworthy of the works of God" and that, therefore, concupiscence in human beings "has been defended by the example of the animals" and "by the dignity of its author" (IV, 38). In reply Augustine claims that "concupiscence of the flesh is a punishment for human beings, but not for other animals, in which the flesh never has desires opposed to the spirit." Julian goes on to argue that the flesh marks our unity with the animals, but adds that, "in accord with the merits of the rational mind," it will receive an eternal reward or punishment (IV, 39). Augustine retorts that Julian should recognize that, if the image of God had not been deformed by sin, the flesh as it was originally created would have remained incorruptible for eternity and that concupiscence of the flesh would have been perfectly obedient to the mind.

Again Julian claims that God does not blame the genus or the limit in sexual desire, but only the excess, and Augustine asks why, then, sexual desire resists the spirit in human beings so that it does not remain within the limit set by God unless it is held in check (IV, 41). Julian draws the conclusion which he thinks follows from Augustine's position, namely, that "one should not cover out of modesty whatever is believed to be good" (IV, 42) and contends that, on Augustine's principles, one ought to have sexual intercourse in public (IV, 43). Augustine replies by pointing out that Julian would not set the animals and human beings on a par with regard to sexual desire if he "did not believe that those first parents of the human race . . . were destined to die, even if they had not sinned." For before the sin "by which human nature was changed for the worse," there was not the discord between the flesh and the spirit which is now reason for shame. Julian points to reasons why human beings are appropriately or unappropriately clothed or unclothed according to various activities, places, customs, and peoples (IV, 44). Augustine, on the other hand, points to the nakedness of Adam and Eve before their sin over which they *were not ashamed* (Gn 2:25) and argues that they as yet did not have "the disobedience of their own flesh" over which they were later ashamed.

Julian charges that Augustine declared in *Marriage and Desire* II, 5, 14 that "Christ, whom the Catholic faith confesses to be a true man in all respects, did not have in his flesh the concupiscence of the flesh of which the apostle John speaks" (IV, 45). Given his understanding of concupiscence, Julian takes Augustine to have meant that Christ's body lacked normal human sensations and accuses Augustine of Apollinarism in the sense that Christ did not have the senses of the body (IV, 47). Augustine replies that he has never heard that Apollinaris claimed that "Christ did not have the senses of the body and was incapable of suffering," but condemns such a view as well as the view that "the flesh of Christ has desires opposed to the spirit." Julian, then, works out the implications of his accusation, namely, that Christ avoided sin because "he could not experience the desire for sins" (IV, 48), that Christ could not be for us an example for avoiding sin and practicing virtue (IV, 49), and that Christ's teaching us to follow his example involves a fraud (IV, 50). Augustine replies that Christ "refused to have an evil desire," though he could have felt such a desire if he had chosen to have it. So too, Augustine insists that Christ had the senses of the human body and had "the ability to father children, if he had willed, and yet his flesh never had desires opposed to the spirit." Augustine insists that, since on Julian's view virtue is more praiseworthy to the extent that virtue overcomes contrary desires, Christ "ought to have been most filled with desires in his flesh" (IV, 49). Julian suddenly withdraws his charge of Apollinarism and settles for Manicheism because Augustine separates "the nature of Christ from the community of human beings, in accord with the Manichees" (IV, 51). Augustine, on the other hand, again appeals to the common ground he shares with Ambrose and Paul.

Julian says that he showed in *To Turbantius* that, if one holds original sin, one must hold that Christ "contracted guilt from the flesh of Mary" and was placed under the power of the devil (IV, 51), while Augustine simply refers to his fifth book of his *Answer to Julian*, which Julian seems never to have seen. Julian accuses Augustine of having made Christ a eunuch, though Augustine explains that Christ's flesh had the power to father children, but did not have the desire for sin. His lack of sinful desires was not due to "the inability of the flesh," but to "the peak and perfection of virtue" (IV, 52). Julian insists upon the full reality of the masculinity of Christ "whole in his organs, whole in his body, a true human, a complete man" (IV, 53). Augustine admits the reality of Christ's members, but denies that he had concupiscence of the flesh, pointing out that, because Julian regards concupiscence of the flesh as something good, he has to maintain that

Christ has this good and had more concupiscence of the flesh in proportion to his greater chastity.

Julian argues that without sexual organs Christ could not serve as a model for us (IV, 54). Augustine, of course, admits that Christ had sexual organs, but denied that "Christ's sexual organs were at times aroused by sexual desire, even against his will" and that "that part of his holy body became erect for some forbidden uses against his holy choice." Julian argues that Paul taught the reality of Christ's flesh and the holiness of his spirit and also foresaw the rise of Manicheism with its doctrine of natural sin and condemnation of marital intercourse (IV, 55), while Augustine again appeals to Ambrose's teaching that Christ was born free from sin because he was not born from the union of a man and a woman. Julian claims that Mani is more logical, for he holds that all the animals "were defiled by diabolical evil," but Augustine holds that only the image of God was so defiled (IV, 56). Augustine explains that "human beings cannot be born free from sin," though other animals can.

Julian returns to Christ and extols the integrity of his chastity, while Augustine accuses Julian of holding that chastity does not have integrity in a person who does not have desires for forbidden acts and insists that Christ desired nothing forbidden because he "did not have the discord between the flesh and the spirit," which has become our nature as a result of Adam's transgression (IV, 57). Julian argues that, if Christ did not have concupiscence, as Augustine claims, his not having it does not amount to a condemnation of it, just as he did not condemn marriage by not taking a wife (IV, 58). Augustine replies that, if Christ had concupiscence, he would have been aroused in his dreams and ejaculated and that, if Julian does not want to believe this about the flesh of Christ, he ought to hold that Christ did not have concupiscence of the flesh. Moreover, Julian's argument that Christ's not having concupiscence does not entail a condemnation of it does not hold, since concupiscence of the flesh is an evil, though marriage is not. Julian argues that "the body of the savior had nothing less of the nature of human beings" (IV, 59), that our nature can have no sin "because in him in whom that nature was whole, no iniquity was found" (IV, 60), and that "sexual concupiscence" is not evil, whether Christ had it or not (IV, 61). Augustine replies that Christ came to restore our nature to its integrity, accuses Julian of making "the flesh of Christ equal to the flesh of other human beings," that is, making it sinful flesh rather than the likeness of sinful flesh, and claims that "concupiscence of the flesh is evil, even if one does not consent to it to do evil."

Julian claims that Augustine held that "concupiscence of the flesh which is seen in sexual arousal" is the only cause of shame (IV, 62) and argues that Christ, therefore, "ought to have presented himself in public naked" (IV, 63). Augustine replies that Christ "could cover his members, not for the reason that others do, but to conform to those who cover their genitals, though he had nothing to be ashamed of."

Julian continues to defend what he calls "natural concupiscence" as a good common to human beings and animals by appealing to the dignity of their creator (IV, 67). Augustine points out that, by calling concupiscence of the flesh "natural concupiscence," Julian sets it on a par with the desire for beatitude which is a natural concupiscence, though scripture speaks of concupiscence of the flesh only as an evil. So too, Julian calls concupiscence of the flesh "a natural sense of the body" on account of which, on Augustine's view, the prince of darkness has dominion over the image of God (IV, 69), while Augustine again distinguishes between the senses of the body and concupiscence of the flesh. For by the latter "we desire indifferently illicit and licit things, which are differentiated, not by desire, but by intellect."

After a series of chapters of repetition and invective, Julian returns to Christ and Augustine's claim that he had "no sin, neither the sin which we contract by being born, nor the sin which we add as we continue to live" (IV, 78). Julian challenges Augustine to show that Christ denied having the former sort of sin, but Augustine insists on the right "to understand what he did not say" from what he did say. Julian argues that the devil would have found sin in the savior "if any sin were contracted from the condition of the flesh" (IV, 79). In reply Augustine claims that Christ was conceived without concupiscence of the flesh and, hence, was born in the likeness of sinful flesh without the sin which all sinful flesh contracts. Julian insists that, if there were any natural sin, the devil would have found that sin in Christ and that Christ would either have been guilty or not human (IV, 80). Augustine replies that Christ was both human and sinless.

Julian points out that Mani maintained that natural evil exists in the flesh and denied that Christ had flesh (IV, 81). Augustine replies that the Pelagians try to "make sinful flesh equal to the flesh of Christ," while Catholics distinguish the likeness of sinful flesh from sinful flesh. Julian claims that the prince of this world found nothing to blame in Christ, because "he could not disparage the nature whose will he had not bent toward sins" (IV, 82), while Augustine retorts that "he found no sin, neither the sin that is contracted by one who is born because he is conceived in iniquity, nor the sin which is added as one lives because he was led astray by temptation." Julian adds that the devil tempted even Christ's will, because he "could damage no one by creation" (IV, 83). Augustine replies that the devil creates no one and that it is not surprising that he tempted Christ if he tempted Adam and Eve who also did not have sinful flesh.

Christ's righteousness, Julian argues, "came, not from the difference of his nature, but from his voluntary action" (IV, 84). Augustine protests that the fact that Christ "was born of a virgin so that he was now not only the Son of Man, but also the Son of God" surely contributes to the excellence of his righteousness. Moreover, Augustine claims that Julian defends free choice to the point that he says that "even the mediator himself merited by his will to be the only Son of God." Julian argues that Christ has no sin because, as Saint Peter says, *he com-*

mitted no sin (1 Pt 2:22) and that, if there were a natural sin, "Peter's statement would be misguided" (IV, 85). Augustine replies that, when Peter was proposing Christ as an example for others to follow, there was no need to mention original sin for no one could avoid being born with it by imitating Christ. Julian again argues that "the idea of natural sin would not only remove all zeal for discipleship, but would accuse of fraud the praise offered" to Christ (IV, 87); if Christ's nature was different from ours, then he could not offer us an example to imitate. Augustine points to other ways in which Christ's nature differs from ours and to the fact that Christ proposed even his Father for our imitation.

The Grace of Baptism

Central to the whole Pelagian controversy is the question of whether the grace of baptism always involves the forgiveness of sin. Augustine, though often labeled as the tormenter of infants because of his insistence upon the presence of original sin in the newborn, in fact held their salvation as a central concern.[36] In the first book Julian takes up the question of the baptism of infants. Augustine had accused him of being afraid of the reaction of the faithful who rush to bring their children to the bath of rebirth, if these people should hear that the Pelagians "say that there is no sin in little ones to be washed away by rebirth." Julian complains that he is accused of being "opposed to the grace of God," while he accuses Augustine of Manicheism (I, 52). Augustine appeals to the writings of Cyprian, Hilary, Ambrose, Gregory, Basil, and John Chrysostom, all of whom he claims held the doctrine of original sin, though none of them was a Manichee.

Julian quotes his own words from *To Turbantius* in which he said that "the grace of baptism is useful for all ages" and that "we strike with an eternal anathema all those who say that it is not necessary also for little ones." He states in *To Florus* how the grace of baptism is manifold in its gifts, explaining that "this grace, which gives pardon to the guilty, gives to other mortals spiritual enlightenment, adoption as children of God, citizenship in the heavenly Jerusalem, sanctification, transformation into members of Christ, and possession of the kingdom of heaven" (I, 53). Augustine notes that Julian does not want pardon of sins to pertain to the little ones, "for you deny that little ones contract any guilt from Adam." Augustine asks why God denies the other gifts which Julian mentioned to so many little ones who die without baptism since the little ones have no opposite will which fends off from them such a benefit, and he insists that the justice of God "would not deny it to countless little ones who die without it, if in his hidden judgment they merited no punishment." Hence, Augustine urges Julian to "allow Christ to be Jesus" for the little ones, so that he may "bestow on them that on account of which he received this name," namely, salvation from their sins.[37]

Julian, then, does not deny baptism to little ones and maintains that "the sacraments Christ instituted must be administered at absolutely every age with the same words which have been handed down to us." He holds that "sinners are changed from evil to completely good, but that innocents who have no evil from their own will are changed from good to better, that is, to the very best" (I, 54). Infants, then, have "no merit from their acts, but only hold what they got from the gift of so great a maker." In reply Augustine asks why on Julian's view infants are weighed down by such sufferings from birth and why they have to be taught even with beatings. Julian says that, if infancy is accused through the sacrament of renewal, it brings disgrace upon justice (I, 55). Augustine asks what the old state is from which the infant is renewed by the grace of Christ and accuses Julian of failing to recognize the evils in infants which have been produced by Adam's sin. While Julian insists that the oneness of baptism does not prove infants guilty, Augustine asks why they undergo the rite of exsufflation (I, 56). Pelagius had said, "If the sin of Adam harmed even those who do not sin, then Christ's righteousness can also benefit those who do not believe."[38] Augustine argues that, if Christ's righteousness can benefit those who in baptism believe through others, then the sin of Adam could harm those who sinned through him, and Augustine, of course, holds that infants do believe through the faith of those who bring them to baptism.

Julian argues that it involves a contradiction to maintain that "God is so merciful that he pardons the personal sins of everyone who confesses them and so cruel that he imposes upon an innocent the sins of others" (I, 57). Augustine counters by claiming that Julian brings accusations of injustice against both God and the Church: against God because infants are burdened and afflicted without deserving it and against the Church because she makes them undergo the rite of exsufflation when they are not subject to the devil. He insists, moreover, that, though the forgiveness of sins bestowed by baptism is true in all cases, the sins of all who receive the sacrament are not equally grave. He also argues that original sins in little ones are sins of others in the sense that the little ones do not sin by their own will, but that they are the sins of the little ones because they contracted them by birth. Julian concludes that he had not omitted any of Augustine's words out of fear and insists that what Augustine holds is not the faith which has been handed down from antiquity (I, 58 and 59). Again Augustine appeals to his list of the Fathers who taught the doctrine of original sin, but especially to Ambrose whose faith Pelagius has praised very highly.

Julian maintains that human beings without a will or assent of their own have no sin and points out that even Augustine agrees that little ones have no will; hence, he concludes that they have no sin and are not brought to baptism to have their good name attacked (I, 60). Augustine replies that their good name is not attacked when they undergo exsufflation and that "they need as their savior the creator by whose work they were born." Julian argues that, if original sin is contracted from generation, it can condemn marriage which God instituted, but it cannot be removed because what is inborn remains until the end of the substance in which it inheres (I, 61). Augustine replies that original sin "does not condemn marriage because marriage is not its cause" and that "it is removed by that almighty one who was able to be born even as human without it." Julian argues that original sin does condemn marriage because "marriage never exists without sexual union" and because, according to Augustine, "whatever is born of that union belongs to the devil" (I , 62). Augustine replies that marriage would have existed even in paradise along with that bodily union, but without the evil of concupiscence of which marital chastity makes good use. Julian maintains that Augustine clearly declares "that nature is diabolical" because there is found in nature "that on account of which a human being is the property of the devil" (I, 63). Augustine again pleads with Julian, "Allow the little ones to be rescued from the power of darkness so that they may be transferred into the kingdom of Christ."[39] In keeping them from the mercy of the savior, Augustine charges, Julian is only making the anger of God to remain over them and keeping away from the image of God "the mercy of the savior who came to seek what was lost."[40] Augustine, on the other hand, does not deny that the devil claims as his own little ones who have not received baptism because of the original sin they contracted from birth.

Julian again accuses Augustine of holding contradictory propositions, namely, "that human beings who are born of marriage, that is, from males and females, are the work of God" and that, as he said in *Marriage and Desire* I, 1, 1, "those who are born from such a union contract original sin" and "are under the power of the devil unless they are reborn in Christ" (I, 64). In reply Augustine appeals to Paul's words that God *rescued us from the power of darkness and transferred us into the kingdom of his beloved Son* (Col 1:13) and argues that, if the little ones are not rescued from the power of darkness through baptism, they have not died. And, "if they have not died, Christ has not died for them," but "Christ has died for them," for the apostle said, *One has died for all; all, therefore, have died* (2 Cor 5:14).

Julian repeats his charge that Augustine has contradicted himself and claims that the coupling of the man and the woman—the very essence of marriage—is what, according to Augustine, places the newborn under the jurisdiction of the devil (I, 65). Augustine points out that, if the coupling constitutes the essence of marriage, then marriage and adultery have the same essence, and insists that marriage also has as its goods: "the fidelity of the marriage bed, the care to have children in an orderly way, and . . . the good use of an evil, that is, the good use of concupiscence of the flesh, the evil of which adulterers make bad use." Julian charges Augustine with trying to show that this coupling is "something so abominable" that he wants us "to think that Christ chose to be born of a virgin mother, not on account of the splendor of the miracle, but in order to condemn the union of the sexes" (I, 66). Julian claims that, according to Augustine, God and the devil divide humanity between them with the devil owning whatever marriage has produced and God owning only what the virgin produced. Augustine replies that Julian fails to distinguish natures or substances from their defects and insists that God is the creator of natures, while he permits defects to exist in natures under his just ordering of things. The Manichees claim that defects are natures and substances, but Augustine insists that "they are evils which can only exist as a result of what is good and only in what is good." Furthermore, all the angels and all the human beings remain under God's power, even if God has made some subject to the devil "in such a way that they cannot be apart from the power of God under which the devil himself has been placed."

Other Issues

The huge *Unfinished Work in Answer to Julian* deals with other issues which this introduction will pass over with only a brief mention. The last part of the first book takes up the relation of freedom and grace, a topic which has been touched on in passing and of which an adequate treatment would add greatly to the length of this already long introduction. The issue of Augustine's relation to Manicheism is the explicit subject of the second half of book three and the second half of book five, though it has come up incidentally in the treatment of other issues in this introduction; it too would needlessly extend the length of the introduction.[41] In the second half of book four Julian presents a refutation of original or natural sin, though most of his arguments have already been presented along with Augustine's response to them in parts of the work which have been dealt with in this introduction. The first half of book five returns to the topic of concupiscence in its relation to marriage; again, the topic has already been sufficiently treated in this introduction. Book six deals with three principal topics, namely, the original state of Adam and Eve and their sin, an exegesis of the third chapter of Genesis, and a discussion of the naturalness of death, topics which are best encountered first hand by a reading of the text or which have been treated tangentially in other parts of the introduction.

Text and Translations

The translation of books one to three is based on the critical edition by Dr. Michaela Zelzer in CSEL 85/1. The translation of books four to six is based on the Latin text found in PL 45, columns 1337-1608. For the first three books I have incorporated almost all of the emendations and conjectures which Dr. Adolph Primmer made in his articles on the text of the CSEL edition.[42] The translation of all six books has been checked by Dr. Dorothea Weber of the

Kirchenväterkommission in Vienna. I am deeply grateful to her for her great patience and for the many necessary corrections and very many helpful suggestions and conjectures, especially regarding Julian's very difficult Latin. Though I have not explicitly acknowledged each of her corrections, suggestions, and conjectures, they have been very many, very helpful, and almost always followed. In any case I accept ultimate responsibility for the final version.

I also wish to thank Dr. Michaela Zelzer, who is completing the critical edition of the last three books for the CSEL, for supplying me with the paragraph numbers of books four through six which she will use in her forthcoming edition.

The subtitles for various chapters were added to provide some indication of the content of the individual chapters or clusters of chapters and to break up the text; they were composed from the viewpoint of Julian rather than that of Augustine, partly because it is Julian's *To Florus* which provides the structural framework of Augustine's response and partly because doing so provided a consistent point of view.

The *Opus imperfectum contra Iulianum* has been translated into Spanish by Luis Arras in BAC 36 and 37 (Madrid: Biblioteca de Autores Cristianos, 1985). It has been translated into Italian by Italo Volpi in NBA XIX, 1 and 2 (Rome: Città Nuova Editrice, 1992 and 1993). The work has never previously been translated into English.

Notes

1. Peter Brown, *Augustine of Hippo: A Biography* (Berkeley: University of California Press, 1969), 384.

2. Ibid, p. 385.

3. Alberto Pincherle, *Vita di Sant'Agostino* (Rome: Laterza, 1980), 425; my translation.

4. Nello Cipriani's Introduction to the work cites a sixteenth century author, P. Marandino who in *Guiliano di Aeclan*um describes it as "a work of senility" (*Sant' Agostino: Polemica con Giuliano*. II/1. *Opera incompuita*. Introduzione e Note Nello Cipriani, Traduzione Italo Volpi (Rome: Città Nuova Editrice, 1992), VII.

5. See William Harmless, "Christ the Pediatrician: Infant Baptism and Christological Imagery in the Pelagian Controversy," *Augustinian Studies* 28/2 (1997): 7-34. Harmless says, "Augustine's Christ, far from being a persecutor of newborns, was the Great Physician whose potent medicine of baptism was the one best hope for rescuing infants from the infernal genetics of original sin" (page 8).

6. For the historical background to the controversy with Julian, see Flavio G. Nuvolone, "Pélage et Pélagianisme," in *Dictionnaire de spiritualité* (Paris: Beauchesne, 1937-1967), XI, columns 2902-2908.

7. In his *Memorandum against the Heresy of Pelagius and Caelestius or also of Julian* (*Commonitorium adversus haeresim Pelagii et Caelestii vel etiam Iuliani*) 9, 3-4: PL 48, 161-163, Marius Mercator explicitly mentions that Julian wrote the eight books of *To Florus* while staying with Theodore of Mopsuetia.

8. See Letter 224 to Quodvultdeus in which Augustine tells Quodvultdeus of his plan to continue his answer to Julian's *To Florus*, while starting *Heresies*, working on the one by day and the other by night.

9. For the contents and structure of Julian's *To Florus*, I have loosely followed the fairly detailed outline by Nello Cipriani in the general introduction to the *Unfinished Work in Answer to Julian* found in the NBA edition, pages XV-XIX. At times I have simply translated what is found there, while at other times I have modified or amplified Cipriani's outline. I am grateful to the editors of the NBA edition for their permission to follow and adapt this outline.

10. See G. J. D. Alders, "L'epître à Menoch attribué à Mani," *Vigiliae Christianae* 14 (1960): 245-249.

11. It is difficult to pin down sources for Julian's philosophical ideas, though François Refoulé has argued for the predominantly Aristotelian rather Stoic character of Julian's thought, especially in his doctrine of justice and the other virtues and in his view of nature. See F. Refoulé, "Julien d'Éclane: théologien et philosophe," *Recherches de science religieuse* 52 (1964) 42-84 and especially 233-247. Also see François-Joseph Thonnard, "L'aristotélianisme de Julien d'Éclane et saint Augustin," *Revue des études augustiniennes* 11 (1965): 296-304, for critical assessment of Refoulé's claims about Julian's Aristotelianism and his anticipation of the work of Saint Thomas Aquinas.

12. See Sir 40:1.

13. See Mt 20:1-16.

14. See Rom 11:33.

15. See Heb 7:9-11.

16. See Ambrose, *Penance* (*De paenitentia*) 1, 3, 14: Sc 179, 62 and *Commentary on the Gospel of Luke* (*Expositio Euangelii secundum Lucam*) 7, 234: CCL 14, 204.

17. For the errors condemned by the Synod of Diospolis at which Pelagius himself was found innocent, see *The Deeds of Pelagius* 35, 65; the proposition in question was one of the statements of Caelestius condemned at the Council of Carthage in 411 or 412.

18. See *Free Will* III, 19, 54 for Augustine's view which he repeats in *Revisions* I, 10 (9).

19. Julian's view of nature as immutable or of natural characteristics as neither gained nor lost aligns his view with a more philosophical or Aristotelian view of nature. See F. Refoulé, "Julien d'Éclane," pp. 238-239

20. For some of the later theological problems, see Henri de Lubac, *Surnaturel: Études historiques* (Paris: Aubier, 1946), as well as *Le mystère du surnaturel* (Paris: Aubier, 1965); translated by Rosemary Sheed as *The Mystery of the Supernatural* (New York: Herder and Herder, 1967).

21. See F.-J. Thonnard, "La notion de *nature* chez saint Augustin: Ses progrès dans la polémique antipélagienne," *Revue des études augustiniennes* 11 (1965) 239-265.

22. See Gal 5:17.

23. See *The Deeds of Pelagius* 35, 65, for the list of propositions condemned at the synod; the proposition in question was one of the statements of Caelestius which was condemned at the Council of Carthage in 411 or 412.

24. The Church would much later develop a doctrine of a *limbus puerorum* as a place where infants who die without baptism suffer the pain of loss, but not the pain of fire, while at the same time insisting in the Synod of Pistoia (1794) that limbo is not a place "free from guilt and punishment between the kingdom of God and eternal damnation of the sort the Pelagians imagined" (DS 2626).

25. See Sir 40:1 and Jn 3:5.

26. See Rom 6:3.

27. See Prv 8:35.

28. See Rom 9:11.

29. Ambrose, *Penance* (*De paenitentia*) I, 3, 13: SC 179, 62.

30. Julian's interpretation of the crucial Greek clause: ἐφ᾽ ᾧ πάντες ἥμαρτον in a causal sense accords better with modern exegesis, but Augustine's case for original sin did not rest exclusively on the translation of the Latin: "in quo omnes peccaverunt" as: "in whom all have sinned."

31. See Ambrose, *Commentary on the Gospel of Luke (Expositio Euangelii secundum Lucam)* 7, 234: CCL 14, 195.

32. See Gal 2:21.

33. A quotation from *To Turbantius*, cited in *Marriage and Desire* II, 4, 13.

34. See 1 Jn 2:16.

35. See Gal 5:17.

36. The charge that Augustine was a persecutor of infants goes back as far as Julian who said of Augustine: "he is the persecutor of the newborn; . . . he hands over to eternal fire little ones whom he knows could not have either a good or a bad will" (I, 48). Augustine in fact held that infants who die without baptism will "suffer the lightest punishment of all" (*Answer to Julian* V, 11, 44).

37. See Mt 1:21.

38. Pelagius, *Commentary on the Letter to the Romans (Expositio in epistulam ad Romanos)* 5, 15: PLS I, 1137.

39. See Col 1:13.

40. See Lk 19:10.

41. See Yves de Montcheuil, "La polémique de saint Augustin contre Julian d'Éclane d'après L'*Opus imperfectum*," *Recherches de science religieuse* 44 (1956) 193-218, for an insightful treatment of Julian's charge of Manicheism and Augustine's response.

42. A. Primmer, "Textvorschläge zu Augustins 'Opus imperfectum,'" in *Latinität und alte Kirche* (Wien, 1977), 235-250; id., "Rhythmus- und Textproblme in IUL. Aug. op. imperf. 1-3," *Wiener Studien* N.F. 9 (1975) 186-212 and N.F. 11 (1977) 192-218.

BOOK ONE

Preface

(1) I wrote a book against the Pelagian heretics who say that, even if Adam had not sinned, he would have died a bodily death and that the human race was not damaged in him. As a logical consequence of this view of theirs, they maintain that death and deadly diseases and all the evils which we see that even little ones suffer would have existed in paradise even if no one had sinned. The title of the book is *Marriage and Desire*; I wrote it for Count Valerius because I had learned that it was reported to him that the Pelagians say that we condemn marriage. Hence, in that book I distinguished by the best arguments I could the good of marriage from the evil of carnal concupiscence, of which marital chastity makes good use. (2) After receiving that book, the illustrious man I mentioned sent to me in a document some statements excerpted from the work of Julian, the Pelagian heretic.[1] In that work Julian thought that he answered with his four books that one book of mine, the one I said I wrote on marriage and desire. The excerpts had been sent to Valerius by someone one or other who had the selections made, as he thought best, from Julian's first book, and the same Valerius asked me to reply to them as quickly as possible. And so it came about that I also wrote a second book under the same title, and against it Julian with his excessive wordiness wrote another eight books. I am now replying to these, first quoting his words and then adding my reply to them for the individual passages, as I thought that I should refute them. For in six books I already amply and clearly refuted his previous four books after they came into my hands.[2]

Book One

The Occasion of Julian's Work

1. JUL(IAN). Though, as I regarded the state of the churches in this tempest, I was hindered by many troubles which were inflicted upon me in part by indignation, in part by pity, I did not cast aside the commitment to my promise, namely, that I who had placed myself under a debt by my promise should also take care to free myself from it by paying the debt. For in the books which I wrote against the writings of Augustine for our brother, Bishop Turbantius, a man renowned for the great glory of his virtues, I promised that, if no trouble arose which would prevent these activities, I would immediately refute all the arguments of those who in accord with the views of the Manichees[3] defend the inheritance of sin, that is, natural evil. Up until now I have been kept from this task by various unavoidable demands.

AUG(USTINE). After those writings of yours and after these praises of yours in which you say that he was a man renowned for the great glory of his virtues, I wish that you would imitate Turbantius who has been set free from your error! I have replied to your books, and I have shown you the brilliant Catholic lights in the exposition of the holy scriptures which you try to dim with this insult, namely, by calling them Manichees.

2. JUL. But as soon as I was allowed to catch my breath, it was my plan to fulfill my promise briefly—to the extent that the nature of this topic permitted—if you, my blessed father Florus, had not wanted that I take up again with more energy the task assigned me. Since you enjoy such respect for your sanctity that I would regard it as an impiety to obey your commands in a sluggish fashion, you have easily won from me that I should extend the brief shortcut I had chosen into a longer road. You will, therefore, show favor to the work undertaken at your instigation, and I have inserted your name into it, mainly so that my pen may walk along with more security and joy under the protection of so great a directive. I had in mind a plan suited for brevity. For in those four books the truth of the Catholic faith, armed both by invincible arguments and by the testimonies of the sacred law, had crushed out almost all those ideas which were invented by the Manichees and uttered against us by the lips of Augustine. On behalf of that faith and along with that faith we have earned the hatred of the fickle world. And there would be almost nothing left to say if we had impartial judges.

AUG. I wrote six books against those four books of yours. I first listed the Catholic teachers whom you present as Manichees when you raise as objections to me what they learned and taught in the Catholic Church, and I did this in the first two volumes. Then I devoted the following four books to your four, one to each. I refuted the darkness of your heresy by the light of Catholic truth; by abandoning it you rage blindly and, as a new heretic, you ask for impartial judges for a matter over which there never was a controversy in the Church of Christ, as if any judges could seem impartial to you, except those whom you have led astray by your error. But what better judge than Ambrose could you find? Your teacher, Pelagius, said of him that not even an enemy dared to find fault with his faith and his utterly flawless interpretation of the scriptures.[4] Did Ambrose, then, by his utterly flawless interpretation embrace the teaching of the most impure Manichee when he said,"We are all born under the power of sin, and our very origin lies in guilt"?[5] Judge, therefore, how flawed your interpretation is since by it you find fault with this Catholic doctrine, and do not delay to correct yourself with Ambrose as your judge.

3. JUL. I had, nonetheless, omitted some testimonies from the scriptures by which they think that they can achieve something against us. And I had promised to interpret them and so to teach that certain ambiguous words of the law which our enemies often use cannot count against the clear truth, but must be understood in a way that is supported by the absolute authority of sacred scripture and by invincible reason. For how untrained and impious an interpreter of the law of God one is can be seen from the very fact that a person supposes that something which justice cannot uphold is defended by the sanction of the law.

AUG. What you say, rather, cannot be defended by any sense of justice. For the misery of the human race from which we find that no human being is a stranger from birth to death is not part of the just judgment of the Almighty if there is no original sin.

4. JUL. For, if the law of God is the fountain and teacher of justice, the impartiality of God can be also bolstered, but cannot be attacked by help from it. The nature of things permits no support for injustice to be drawn from the strength of that scripture, for it had this one reason for its promulgation, namely, that injustice be wiped out by its testimonies, remedies, threats, and punishments.

AUG. Its testimonies declare that *human beings have become like a vanity, and their days pass like a shadow* (Ps 144:4), and not only truthful scripture which laments over them, but also the laborious and painful care by which they are raised, shows that they are born with that vanity. Among its remedies we read that sacrifice is to be offered for sin, even when a little one is born.[6] Among its threats we read that the soul of a little one will perish if he is not circumcised on the eighth day.[7] Among its punishments we read that even little ones were ordered to be killed when their parents provoked God to anger, so that they were destroyed by extermination in war.[8]

Scripture Can Never Prove God Unjust

5. JUL. Nothing, then, can be accomplished by the law of God against God, the author of the law. By that single shortcut there is, of course, excluded whatever those in error were accustomed to raise as objections. But to teach how rich is the truth which we believe, we are accustomed to bring the light of explanation also to those passages of scripture which veil the understanding of their sense by the complexity of their expressions. In that way, once unlocked, they possess the dignity of their origin and are not separated from the sacred family tree as illegitimate or degenerate.

AUG. You in fact try to obscure the lights of the holy scriptures which shine with certain truth by the complexity of your evil arguments. After all, what is clearer than what I just said: *Human beings have become like a vanity; their days pass like a shadow* (Ps 144:4)? That surely would not have happened, if they had remained in the likeness of God in which they were created. What is clearer than the statement: *As in Adam all die, so too in Christ all will be brought to life* (1 Cor 15:22)? What is clearer than the words: *Who, after all, is clean from filth? Not even an infant whose life has lasted a single day on earth* (Jb 14:4-5 LXX)? And there are many other passages which you try to wrap in your darkness and twist to your perverse meaning by your empty chatter.

6. JUL. According to our custom, then, I was planning to do just this one thing, namely, to free from the interpretations of the traducianists[9] the parts of the law which were subject to insult, by showing that those passages are correct because they are divine.

AUG. With insulting lips you call traducianists Cyprian, Ambrose, Gregory,[10] and the rest of their companions who admit original sin. But it is not surprising that new heretics give a new name to the Catholics from whom they departed. Others have also done this when they too departed.

7. JUL. Because you have demanded it with insistence and in fact have obliged me by your paternal authority to refute the book of the Punic commentator which Alypius, a slave boy of that man's errors, recently brought to Count Valerius, my response has become rather lengthy.[11]

AUG. This Punic debater is a great punishment for you, and long before you were born the Punic Cyprian was raised up as a great punishment for your heresy.[12]

8. JUL. He has, after all, given us examples of his talents and of his faith which are understood with great effort, explained with great difficulty, and scarcely listened to without horror, but they are refuted with great ease, slain with great vigor, and handed over to oblivion, once exterminated, out of a reverence of moral goodness.

AUG. The readers do not judge as you want.

Julian's Complaints about Marriage and Desire

9. JUL. His first book,[13] which was published alone before this one, charges that we are new heretics because we fight against the opinion which, under the pretext of praise for baptism, belches forth the filth of the Manichees and natural sin. And in that way it defiles the sacraments of the Catholic Church which were pure up to now. This opinion is like a whitened sepulcher that according to the statement of the gospel is clothed with a clean color on the outside, but is filled with filth and wickedness.[14]

AUG. The ancient Catholic faith which was proclaimed by most illustrious teachers who lived before us and which you have now begun to attack proves that you are new heretics. But we should not reply to all your statements which are abuse rather than accusations. With impudent effrontery and unbridled tongue you hurl them not just at me, but also at Ambrose, Hilary, Gregory, Cyprian,[15] and other most renowned teachers of the Church.

10. JUL. He praises a man of power because that man blocked our petitions by the weight of his influence. We were only asking that judges be assigned to such an important case so that what was clearly done by a miscarriage of justice might be corrected by a hearing rather than punished. But he did not permit that either a time or a place be assigned to the debate. Whether the man to whom he wrote acted as unjustly as this praise bears witness is his concern. The honorable mention of that name inserted in my little work reveals that we thought much better of him. But that book of his may perhaps speak falsely of its patron. It does, however, reliably show what its author wants, namely, to fight with wild force and blind impotence against reason, against the faith, and against the holiness of doctrine and morals.

AUG. Heaven forbid that the Christian authorities of the earthly commonwealth should doubt the ancient Catholic faith and, for this reason, offer a time and a place for a hearing to its attackers. Rather, certain and solidly grounded in it, they should impose the discipline of coercion upon such enemies of it as you are. The wild mobs of the Donatists made it necessary to do what was done on account of them for they did not know what had been previously settled, and it had to be shown to them.[16] May God prevent that you have such mobs; by his mercy you do not have them at present.

11. JUL. After having done this in the first parts of the book, he went on to the distinction between marriage and concupiscence, as he had promised by the title of the work. And he thereafter gave proof of his skill and power through the whole work. Desperately trapped between the denial of what he admitted and the admission of what he denied, he made public the bitter pangs of his bad conscience.

AUG. Insult me as much as you can. After all, what insulting lout cannot do that?

Julian's Strategy in Writing to Florus

12. JUL. I replied to the first book in four volumes with the ability that the truth provided. I said in the introduction that I would pass over those arguments which appeared to carry no weight for the teaching of that man and which could bring against me the accusation of wordiness if I had followed up every weak and silly argument. And yet, if I had been allowed to observe this rule as was proper—by that I mean that they did not merit even an attack because of their inept statements—I would have had to scorn almost all his arguments with public silence. But things are going from bad to worse, and that is a sign of the world coming to its end. Even in the Church of God stupidity and shamefulness have attained power. But *we serve as ambassadors of Christ* (2 Cor 5:20), and to the best of our ability we bring to the defense of the Catholic religion as much help as we can. Nor do we hesitate to put into writing the remedies which we have devised against the venom of error.

AUG. Stupidity and shamefulness gave you birth, and if these had attained power in the Church, they would, of course, have kept you in it.

13. JUL. I had, of course, declared, as I said, that I would not argue against all the forms of defending inherited sin in the first work and that I would not reply to everything which that book contained, but that I would do battle with those points in which he placed the very essence of his teaching. Any careful readers of the two works, even if they are biased, will see that I faithfully carried out my promise. Confident in the uprightness of my conscience, I exhort and urge our enemy, if he thinks that I passed over some argument which he brought forth and which he himself considers to be of any importance, to bring it into the open and to prove me guilty of fear and deceit.

AUG. I do not believe that you regarded those things which you passed over as unimportant, and yet if I grant that you had thought so, I do not believe that intelligent and Catholic readers will find that such is the case, if they have that one book of mine and those four of yours and read them carefully.

14. JUL. I, of course, explained some testimonies of the scriptures at greater length and others more briefly, because I promised that I would do this fully in my next work. Not a single one, therefore, of all the arguments and claims of Augustine has remained intact; I have carried out everything as I promised. I have shown that many points in his claims are false, that many are stupid, and that many are sacrilegious.

AUG. This is what you say, but it is you who say it. Those readers with understanding do not say this, if they are not Pelagians.

15. JUL. By this claim we need not fear a reputation for arrogance, because we do not maintain that the truth was defended by my talents, but that the feebleness of our talents was aided by the strength of the truth.

AUG. If you wanted to speak the truth, you would have said that your talents were crushed by the strength of truth.

Charges of Interpolation and Falsification

16. JUL. Since it is clear, then, that these matters have been carried out just as I said, I cannot sufficiently marvel at the impudence of this man who in his recent work charged my books with falsity, though he admits that they had not yet come into his hands.[17] It is bad that the habit of sinning produces a love for the sin, but there is nothing worse than when it extinguishes a sense of shame. Though it is agreed that this comes about from evil behavior, the present dangers have taught us this fact even more than any of us could have suspected. For, when would I have believed that the shamelessness of Numidia[18] would have become so brazen that in one work and in one line he would say both that I had made false statements and that he had not read what I said.

AUG. If you did not do it, that fellow did it who excerpted from your books those passages which he thought should be sent to Count Valerius. Since I did not believe that he did that dishonestly, I attributed to the author what was due to the one who made the excerpts. I had not, of course, read your books, but I had read what that fellow had excerpted from them. If you bore in mind that you yourself are a human being, you would see that this could have happened and would by no means look for so odious a slander against another human being on this account.

17. JUL. (1) When writing to the man whom he admired for being a student of his books, though he was busy with the hard labors of the military, he indicates that Alypius delivered to him documents which bore the title: " 'Propositions from a book written by Augustine against which I have drawn a few objections from the books.' Here I see that the person who sent these writings to Your Excellency chose to draw them from some books, though I have no idea which ones. He did this, I suspect, so that he could reply more quickly and could avoid delay in the face of pressure from you. When I considered what books these might be, I suspected that they were those books Julian mentions in his letter which he sent to Rome, a copy of which came into my hands at the same time. There he said: 'They also state that marriage as it now exists was not instituted by God, a statement found in the book of Augustine, to which I have just replied in four books.' "[19] (2) After these words he continues with his own discourse: "It is from those books, I believe, that these statements have been taken. For this reason it would perhaps have been better that our effort be directed to the rebuttal and refutation of that whole work of his, which he developed in four volumes, if I had not been reluctant to postpone a reply, as you did not postpone sending me the writings which require a reply."[20] He clearly shows, therefore, that he sus-

pects that those excerpts were gathered from my work in a hectic manner, but that he does not know the books in their totality, though he dares to say that he was able to reply to them.

AUG. Why should I not have dared, since I certainly had no reason to doubt that you spoke nonsense in them? For in opposition to the truth you could only speak nonsense. Nor did my mind mislead me, for I discovered when I read them that those books of yours were precisely the sort that I presumed they were before I read them.

18. JUL. He also makes mention of a letter which he says that I sent to Rome, but from the words he quoted we could not recognize what text he was speaking about. For I sent two letters on these questions to Zosimus, the former bishop of that city, but I did so at the time when I had not yet begun those books.

AUG. This letter was not meant for Zosimus, but for misleading those at Rome who could be misled by such persuasion. But if you do not recognize it, fine; we will not consider it yours. I wish those books were also not yours, but someone else's, so that you would not become far removed from the truth through them.

19. JUL. (1) But let him use a letter which he received, or pretended to have received, as proof that I developed a reply to the new Manichees in four volumes—for he refuses to be viewed as an old Manichee. Why did he not take care to learn the objections we made? Why did he not strive to know the one with whom he was going to do battle? Rather, aroused by shameful levity, he enters the ultimate combat with his eyes veiled like a blindfolded gladiator. He defends having done this by an allegation of this sort: He says that he wanted to imitate by his hurried reply the haste which his patron had in sending him the pages, as if he could not in perfect honesty convey that he ought to be allowed some time to come to read the published work. He could have said that it is a crime among the learned to fail in the serious task of writing and to attack what you do not know out of an impatience in deliberation. (2) In addition to this, in order to raise up against us a hatred for the cleverness which shortened his series of statements, he gave credence to these excerpts which seem more likely to have been composed by his dishonesty and malice than by the ignorant simplicity of one of ours. But whatever was the intention, whoever was the author of the excerpts, it helps us in two ways. For it was immediately clear how much foolishness and how much weakness there is in the enemy of the truth. For he revealed that, though he ought not to speak, he cannot be silent and that, crushed by a few incomplete sentences torn rather than gathered from my first book alone, he went into retreat so that he might rouse against us the hearts of the common people with almost feminine cries, as will become clear from the rest of our discussion.

AUG. Why are you angry at me because your books happened to come into my hands too late or because, though I looked for them, I could not find them quickly? I could, nonetheless, and I absolutely had to examine with wide open and uncovered eyes those arguments which the document sent to me contained, no matter whose they were and of what sort they were, and to have refuted them without delay so that they were not thought to be invincible. For though I might never have been able to find your books, I had to refute as well as I could those arguments which that person considered important enough that he thought that they should be sent to so distinguished a man, and in that way no one would read them and be led astray by them. You would not, then, raise the objection against me that you did, if it were not you rather who were saying these things—I will not say, with sightless, but certainly with closed eyes. You would in no way say that we roused the hearts of the common people against you, if you did not know that the great number of Christian people of both sexes are well aware of the Christian faith which you are trying to undermine.

Julian Announces His Plan of Action

20. JUL. I give warning here as well, as we did in our earlier work, that I am not going to quote all his words exactly, but only those passages which, once they are destroyed, will wipe out the theory of natural evil.

AUG. Those points which you pass over will perhaps be gathered up either by us or by others so that it will be obvious why you passed them over.

21. JUL. Though it is clear that this was fully accomplished by the first work, nonetheless, because he has now set forth some texts from a single book of mine to be refuted by him, and he accused me, as I have already said, of having extensively truncated the principal parts of his statements which I quoted, I shall first show that I did not do what he blames and that he frequently did the same thing with great impudence in this same book of his. Then I shall prove that he offered no solid responses to these concise and short statements which he cited from my writings which he had attacked. Hence, they remain unrefuted, and he admits that his view is more clearly detestable than our effort had endeavored to explain.

AUG. I have already replied to these points above.

The Offending Text in Marriage and Desire

22. JUL. In astonishment, then, let us listen to what he wrote against me. He said, "From my book which I sent to you and with which you are quite familiar,[21] he cited these words which he tried to refute: 'They keep shouting in a most hateful way that we condemn marriage and the divine work by which God creates human beings from men and women. One of their reasons is that we say that those who are born from such a union contract original sin. Another reason is that we claim that, regardless of the sort of parents from which the children are

born, they are still under the power of the devil, unless they are reborn in Christ.'[22] From these words of mine he omitted the testimony of the apostle which I included, by whose great weight he felt he was being crushed. For, after I said that human beings contract original sin, I immediately added the words of the apostle: (2) *Through one man sin entered the world, and through sin death, and in that way it was passed on to all human beings, in whom all have sinned* (Rom 5:12). Having omitted, as I said, that testimony, he linked together the rest of that passage cited above. He knew, after all, how the hearts of Catholic believers usually interpret these words of the apostle which he omitted. By their dark and twisted interpretations the new heretics undertake to obscure and distort the meaning of these words which are so straightforward and so full of light. Then he added other words of mine where I said, 'They do not notice that the good of marriage cannot be accused because of the original evil which is contracted from it, just as the evil of adulteries and fornications cannot be excused because of the natural good which is born from them. After all, just as sin is the work of the devil whether little ones contract it from the former sort of union or the latter, so human beings are the work of God whether they are born from the former sort of union or the latter.'[23] (3) Here too he omitted those words which he was afraid to have Catholics hear. For, to come to these words, we previously stated, 'We affirm what is contained in the most ancient and most solid rule of the Catholic faith. But these defenders of a novel and perverse doctrine say that there is no sin in little ones to be washed away by the bath of rebirth. Hence, they slander us out of unbelief or out of ignorance, as if we condemn marriage and as if we say that the work of God, that is, the human being who is born from marriage, is the work of the devil.'[24] After the omission of these words of ours, there follows the rest of our words which he cited, as they were set down above."[25]

(4) You who say these things, how long will you continue to mock the simplicity and uneducated ears of religious hearts? How far will your unbridled impudence boast? When you write these things, does not the censure of learned men, does not the fear of the judgment to come, do not the very records of these writings move you at all?[26] Do you not see that your deceit is now exposed and that you cannot hold onto it, now that it has been caught in the act? Do you suppose that any of us are ignorant of what you wrote in your first work or of what you wrote in the second? It was, of course, right and fitting to challenge you with these manners of speaking by which the eloquent consul raged against the murderer of the fatherland.[27]

AUG. You did[28] well to inform us that you took this language from the invective of Cicero and applied it here, lest we perhaps not recognize it. But we do not fear Julian when we see that he has become Tullian. Rather, we grieve over his madness when we see that he has lost the mind of a Christian.[29] For what is more insane than to keep Christ the physician from little ones by saying that they do not have what he came to heal? When Cicero attacked the murderer of the fatherland, he defended the city which its king Romulus founded by gathering sinners from all around. But you shout that so many little ones who are dying without sacred baptism have no sin, and you do not permit them to approach the city of the king in whose image they were made.

23. JUL. You pretend that I passed over the testimony of the apostle, a point which can be of no help to you. It was not passed over by me, but inserted in the order in which you put it there. As I faithfully mentioned it in my first book, so I also explained it in the fourth book of my work, though rapidly and in brief.[30] I also did not pass over the mention you made of the Catholic Church; you did this so that those deceived by you would abandon the Catholic faith and the poor wretches would console themselves with the Catholic name. And though such terms do not have any power of proof, the whole chapter of your statements was cited exactly as you had arranged it. Read my published books; when you see the accuracy of my response which you accuse of deceit, admit that I was speaking the truth all the while. But you, go on and blush if your character allows this. The inexcusable deception has already been revealed; it is always shameful, but becomes more shameful when it assumes the role of a judge and blames another's honor for its own deformity. Answer me: How does the name of the Church or how do the words of the apostle lead to your Manichean ideas so that you charge with such great hatred that they were omitted?

AUG. I have already replied above to this slander of yours by which you reproach me for the inaccuracy of your words which were cited less than fully. But you would not be so happy to attribute to me what the author of the excerpts did, if you did not want to deceive those who read these pages.[31]

24. JUL. This was always the biggest difference between the Manichees and the Catholics. It is a very wide gap which separates the teachings of believers and unbelievers from each other; rather, it is a huge wall dividing our views like the distance of the heaven from the earth. For we ascribe every sin to an evil will, but they ascribe it to an evil nature. They are adherents of various errors, but they flow, as it were, from this fountainhead, and as a consequence of it they come to sacrileges and outrages. But the Catholics, on the other hand, start from a good beginning, grow through good progress, and are carried to the peak of religion which reason and piety protect. You, then, tried to defend a natural evil out of a sacrilegious desire, but with a useless intent you claim as your own the text of the apostle, for I show by that same document that he thought nothing like what you are trying to convince us of. For in your self-contradictory fashion you confess that he is a Catholic, and you think that his statements offer support to Mani.

AUG. Those Catholic teachers who you claim support Mani because they understood from the words of the apostle that little ones contract original sin did not praise nature as healthy in your unhealthy fashion, but rather applied the medicine of Christ to that nature which needed to be healed. If you would consider this with the heart of a Christian, you would blush, you would tremble, you would be silent!

25. JUL. Did not Adimantus and Faustus—the Faustus whom you call your teacher in the books of your *Confessions* —do the same thing in the tradition of the founder of their heresy? They picked up and gnawed on any somewhat obscure ideas either from the gospel or from the letters of the apostles in order to defend their irreligious teaching by the authority of those names. Yet why do I speak only about the Manichees? All heresies use words and statements from the scriptures to defend their innovations by which they have wandered off from piety and the faith.

AUG. They turn obscure ideas into their teaching; you try to obscure clear ones with your teaching. What, after all, is clearer than the statement of the apostle that sin entered this world through one man, and through sin death, and in that way it was passed on to all human beings?[32] If the same apostle were forced to prove that, he would offer the misery of the human race as evidence, for it begins with the wailing of little ones and continues on to the groans of decrepit old age. Under the care of the almighty and just God such great misery would never be imposed upon human nature, if in two human beings our whole nature were not driven from the happiness of paradise into this unhappy state by the merit of sin.

26. JUL. Will the sacred books, then, be shown to be the sources of errors, or will the dignity of the scriptures blot out the grave sins of those who are perishing?

AUG. Ask yourselves those questions.

27. JUL. Let the desire for undisciplined interpretations be extinguished! Let us believe that words achieve nothing against the manifest justice of God. If they are words of a person whom we must respect, let us defend them with an explanation suited to divine justice. But if they are uttered by an author to whom we need not show reverence, let us cast them aside without explanation. We are now discussing the judgment of God of which scripture says, *God is faithful; in him there is no injustice; righteous and holy is the Lord God* (Dt 32:4). Again it says, *The Lord is righteous, and he has loved righteousness; his face sees justice* (Ps 11:8). And again it says, *All your judgments are justice* (Ps 119:172). Countless are the testimonies which proclaim the divine justice in the sacred volumes, and no one from either the pagans or the heretics has doubted this justice except the Manichees and the traducianists.

AUG. Because of this justice *there is a heavy yoke upon the children of Adam from the day they come forth from the womb of their mother* (Sir 40:1), and one who denies original sin claims that this yoke is completely unjust.

God Cannot Both Be God and Unjust

28. JUL. After all, it has been universally inculcated in all human beings by the teaching of nature that God is just so that it is evident that one who has been shown to be unjust is not God. A human being, therefore, can be just, but God cannot but be just.

AUG. Apply this to yourself.

29. JUL. He is the one true God in whom we believe and whom we venerate in the Trinity; he is undoubtedly most just in all respects by reason of his judgment.

AUG. Apply this to yourself, and show how it is just that one who has not contracted original sin is born with such obvious misery or born for such obvious misery.

30. JUL. From his laws, then, what is clearly unjust cannot be approved or defended; if this were possible, his whole divinity would be undermined. Only one who is able to admit that the Trinity in which we believe can be deprived of the glory of divinity will prove that an unjust teaching is supported from the holy scriptures.

AUG. You speak the truth, but apply it to yourselves who are trying to take from Christ the glory of saving little ones.

Both Reason and Piety Oppose Natural Sin

31. JUL. Since neither reason nor any piety supports this, either teach us that it is possible or just that natural sin be ascribed to anyone, or stop defiling the holy scripture whose statements you think sanction what you are forced to admit is unjust.

AUG. You are wrong. It is rather you who are forced to admit that the heavy yoke upon the little ones is unjust if, just as they have no personal sin, they contract no original sin.

32. JUL. But if you will follow neither of these alternatives we mentioned and if you claim to believe in this God whose teachings you think support injustice, recognize that you, a new Manichee, are much worse than the old Mani,[33] because you have the sort of God that Mani devised as an enemy of his God.

AUG. You are more cruel to little ones than the Manichees. In a little one they want at least the soul to be saved through Christ, for they consider it a part of God. But you allow a little one to be saved through Christ in no respect, since you say that it has no evil in its soul or in its flesh. And renowned preachers that you are, you preach Jesus in such a way that you deny that he is Jesus for the little ones. Read in the gospel how he got this name,[34] and do not deny a savior to the little ones who are not saved.

33. JUL. You accuse me of the same evasiveness and the same pillows of lies and stupidity which the prophet Ezekiel attributed to the harlot Jerusalem.[35]

Womanish souls lie down on them, clinging to the names of the mysteries, while they sin against the divinity with evident profanity. Leave aside all your tricks and the crowds of common people whom you often summon, and teach us how the views which you try to uphold through the holy scriptures are just.

AUG. The crowds of the common people whom you mock know the Catholic faith which professes that infants are saved by the savior, and for that reason they detest the error of the Pelagians who deny this.

Julian Appeals to a Definition of Justice

34. JUL. So that the discussion does not run on for endless volumes, let us examine here, right here, the genus, species, difference, limit, and quality of these matters we are discussing. Let us examine even more carefully whether they are, whence they come, where they are, also what they merit, and from whom. In this way, after all, we will not wander for a long time through the winding paths of arguments, and the certitude we ought to hold will be seen clearly.

AUG. You wrote eight books against my one book because you wanted to avoid a long argument with your dialectical short cuts.

35. JUL. The roles, then, of creator and creature, that is, of God and human beings, are under examination here. The former judges; the latter are judged. And so, let us see what is the nature of justice and of guilt. Justice is—as it is usually defined by the learned and as we can understand it—the greatest of all the virtues, if the Stoics allow us to prefer one virtue to another, for it carefully serves the function of restoring to each person what is due without fraud and without favor.[36]

AUG. Tell me then, what sort of justice has recompensed the little ones with a heavy yoke of such great and obvious misery? Tell me, by what justice is one child adopted in baptism, while another dies without such adoption? Why do both not share this honor in common, or why are both not kept from this honor, since both of them have the same condition in common, whether good or bad? You do not reply, because, as someone more a Pelagian than a Christian, you do not understand either the grace of God or the justice of God.

36. JUL. But Zeno[37] may not permit us to call justice the greatest virtue, for he maintains so great a connection and unity of the virtues that, where there is one, he says that all are present and that, where one is missing, he says that all are missing and that true virtue is that which is made up of the union of the four. In that case he will offer us much help when he teaches that one cannot possess prudence or fortitude or temperance without justice. In accord with that truth Ecclesiastes declares, *Whoever sins in one point loses many goods* (Eccl 9:18).

AUG. Listen to the same Ecclesiastes when he says, *Vanity of vanities, and all is vanity. What wealth does a man have from all his work at which he toils un-*

der the sun? (Eccl 1:2-3), and so on. Tell me, why have human beings who were made like the truth also become like a vanity?[38] Or do you exempt little ones from this? We see that, as they grow up and make progress if they are well trained, they lessen the great vanity with which they are born, but they are not completely free of it until all the days of vanity have passed like a shadow.[39]

37. JUL. This august virtue, the virtue which recompenses each person's merits, sparkles in the works of the image of God, that is, of the human soul, in accord with the measure and strength of a creature. But in God himself, the creator out of nothing of everything that is, it is eternally resplendent in its immense and bright fullness. Its origin is divinity; its age is eternity, an eternity that does not know before and after, without either beginning or end. As God is its genus—by that term I want nothing else but its origin to be understood—so its species is seen in the laws it promulgates and the verdicts it comes to.

AUG. If God is the origin of justice, as you say, why do you not admit that justice is given to human beings by God? Why do you want justice to be the choice of the human will rather than the gift of God? In that way you are among those of whom scripture said, *Not knowing the justice of God and wanting to establish their own, they were not subject to the justice of God* (Rom 10:3). Blush with shame at last, I beg you, and ask for justice from him who is, as you were forced to admit, the origin of justice.

Justice's Difference in the Two Testaments

38. JUL. We can without absurdity understand its difference as the varied dispensation in accord with the demands of different times. For example, the old testament ordered the sacrifices of animal victims. To carry out that directive at that time pertained to the reverence owed to the command, but now the announcement of the abandonment of such sacrifices serves the justice that commands it, just as the offering of them once served it. But its limit or state is that it does not impose on any persons more than their strength can bear and that it does not reject mercy. Its quality, however, is understood as that by which it tastes sweet to pious minds. Justice is, then, undoubtedly that without which the deity does not exist; if it did not exist, God would not exist. But God does exist, and justice, therefore, exists beyond all doubt. It is nothing else than a virtue that embraces everything and gives to everyone what is due without fraud and without favor, but it exists most of all in the depth of divinity.

AUG. You have defined justice as a virtue embracing everything and giving to everyone what is due without fraud and without favor. Hence, we see that justice gave a day's wage without fraud to those who worked the whole day in the work of the vineyard. For this was the decision; this was the agreement. They could not deny that they were hired for this pay.[40] But tell me, I beg you, how did justice without favor give the same amount to those who were involved in that work for one hour? Or had it perhaps lost justice? Stop yourself then. Divine justice cheats no one, but it gives many gifts as a favor to those who do not merit them. But as for why it treats this one this way and that one that way, see what you add next. You say with perfect truth that justice exists most of all in the depth of divinity. In this depth lies the fact that *it does not depend on the one who wills or runs, but on God who shows mercy* (Rom 9:16). In this depth lies the fact one child receives the honor of adoption through the bath of rebirth, while another is left in ignominy and will not be admitted to the kingdom, though neither of the two merited anything good or bad by the choice of the will.

39. JUL. As justice merits testimony from its source, so it merits it both from good people and from bad ones, for it rightly exalts the former and rightly condemns the latter. When it permits mercy to be generous to those who by themselves merit nothing either good or bad, it suffers no injury, because the very fact that God is merciful to his own work when he is not forced to be severe is a large part of justice.

AUG. (1) At least pay attention to the name "mercy," and see the root from which it is taken. What need is there for mercy where there is no misery?[41] If you say that there is no misery in little ones, you deny that they should be shown mercy. If you say that there is any misery, you point to their evil merit. For under a just God none can be wretched unless they have merited it. Look, two little ones lie ill; one of them dies after baptism, the other without baptism. To which of them do you say that God was merciful? If to the one, show me the evil merit of the other if you deny original sin. If to both of them, show me any good merit of the baptized child, if you deny grace where there is no partiality toward certain persons.[42] And tell me, if you can, why God did not will to adopt both, since he certainly created both to his own image. Or is he just but not omnipotent if he willed to adopt both, but could not? In this case neither of them was unwilling so you cannot locate the impediment to the divine power in the merit of the human will. Here God cannot say to either of them: I was willing, but you refused. Or if the infant refuses because it cries when it is baptized, both of them should be left, for both of them refuse, and yet one of them is taken and the other left, because the grace of God is great and the justice of God is true. But why was that one taken rather than this one? *The judgments of God are inscrutable* (Rom 11:33).

40. JUL. He made them, after all, because he wanted to, and he does not condemn them unless he is rejected. If, when he is not rejected, he makes them better by consecrating them, he suffers no loss of justice, and he receives honor from the generosity of his mercy.

AUG. Tell me, does he who does not condemn unless he is rejected reject his own image if he is not rejected? If you do not dare to say that he does, tell me why he rejects those little ones whom he does not adopt, since you will not find that they have rejected him unless you find them in Adam. And there you will find that their being rejected was deserved by all through justice, but that not all are rejected on account of his ineffable and inscrutable grace.

Julian Proposes a Definition of Sin

41. JUL. After having explained these divisions of justice which we have set forth, let us examine what is the definition of sin. The writings both of those who philosophize and of those who had been Catholics amply provide for me what we are seeking. But I fear that you will vote against my proposal, and if I summon an assembly of philosophers, you will immediately rouse against me the working folk and all the common people.

AUG. You are contemptuous toward the weak things of the world which God chose in order to confound the mighty.[43] Ultimately they confound those *who place their trust in their own virtue* (Ps 49:7). Why should I say here that you are these people? You are obviously seen to be such people, even if I remain silent, since you do not remain silent.

42. JUL. You shout with women and all the stable hands and tribunes to whom your colleague, Alypius, recently brought eighty and more well fed horses from all of Africa.[44]

AUG. Either you are being slanderous, or you do not know what you are saying. And so, you say these things, either because you are a liar or because you are rash. But what is more wicked than you if you have made these things up yourself? What is more stupid if you have believed those who made them up? Now you have dared to write this, and you were not afraid that your books would arrive in those places which welcomed my colleague, Alypius, as he comes and goes by land or sea. In those places your false statements could not with full openness be read without mockery or rather hatred. To what sort—I do not say: of insolence, but—of madness shall I compare this?

43. JUL. You cry out that you will never accept the views of the educated and, to the second point[45] which suits your intellect, that the apostle said: *God made the wisdom of the world foolish* (1 Cor 1:20). But you say that our teachers can be despised by you because their authority carries no weight with you.

AUG. It is you who despise them since you resist them when they teach original sin. Moreover, you charge them with Manicheism when you name me, but refer to them.

Julian Uses Augustine's Own Definition of Sin

44. JUL. What am I to do then? I shall, of course, give in to you, and I shall abandon all those things I could use as a help, and I shall be content with the definition which slipped from the lips of Your Grace as a proof of the goodness of

nature after contact with the occult teaching of the Manichees. In that book, then, entitled *The Two Souls* or *Against the Two Souls* you speak as follows: "Wait, permit us first to define sin. Sin is the will to do or to keep that which justice forbids and from which we are free to hold back. For, if one is not free, the will cannot be said to be there either, but I have preferred to define it simply rather than in detail."[46]

AUG. There I defined that sin which is only sin, not that sin which is also the punishment of sin. I had to deal with the former when investigating the origin of the sort of evil that was committed by the first human being before every human evil. But either you cannot understand or you are unwilling.

45. JUL. O gold shining in dung! What could anyone, even[47] someone orthodox, say that is more true, more complete? You say, "Sin is the will to do or to keep that which justice forbids and from which we are free to hold back." Ecclesiasticus shows this; he says, *God made human beings and left them in the hands of their own counsel; he set before them life and death, water and fire; whatever they choose will be given them* (Sir 15:14.17-18). And God says through Isaiah, *If you are willing and obey, you will eat the good things of the earth. If you refuse and do not obey, the sword will devour you* (Is 1:19-20). And the apostle says, *Come to your senses, you righteous, and do not sin* (1 Cor 15:34), and again, *Do not be mistaken; God will not be mocked. For human beings will harvest whatever they sow* (Gal 6:7-8).

AUG. These testimonies were given on account of that will by which one does what one wants. If someone does not have it, let it be asked for from him *who also produces in us the will* (Phil 2:13); if one has it, let the works of justice be done, and let thanks be given to him who has produced it.

A Definition of Will

46. JUL. Will then is the movement of the mind which has in its power either to descend toward evil on the left or to strive toward noble things on the right.

AUG. What does it mean then: *Turn not to the right or to the left* (Prv 4:27)?

47. JUL. (1) Will is a movement of that mind which is by reason of its age already able to use the judgment of reason; when punishment and glory or, on the other hand, advantage and pleasure are presented to it, these are offered as a help or occasion, but the necessity of neither alternative is imposed on it. This will, then, which is presented with alternatives, received the origin of its ability in free choice. But it receives the existence of the act from itself, and the will does not exist before it wills, nor can it will before it can refuse to will. It has neither, that is, neither willing nor not willing, in the sense of sin, before it acquires the use of reason.

From all this it is clear that you defined sin with complete truth: "Sin is the will to keep or to do that which justice forbids and from which we are free to hold back." It is agreed, then, that this sin, which is clearly nothing but the will, took its genus, that is, its origin from its own desire. Its species is now found in each of those who are called individuals. But its difference is found in the variety of sins and in the character of the times. (2) The limit is immoderation itself, for, if the limit is to serve one whom you ought to serve, whoever omits this service sins by transgressing the true limit. Here it can be said with a certain subtlety that there is a limit to sin because no one sins more than one can. For, if it is beyond one's strength, one sins with an inefficacious will, but[48] this can only be done by the will. But let us ascribe to the defect the quality which reveals the bitterness which sin produces by dishonor or pain. Sin does exist, then, because if it did not, even you would not make mistakes. But it is nothing else than the will departing from the path on which it ought to stay and from which one is free not to turn aside. It arises from the desire for forbidden things, and it never exists except in the person who both has a bad will and could be without it.

AUG. (1) That definition of ours of which you are fond had Adam himself in mind, when it said, "Sin is the will to keep or to acquire that which justice forbids and from which we are free to hold back." When he sinned, Adam had absolutely nothing evil in him by which he was urged against his will to do evil and on account of which he might say, *I do not do the good that I will, but I do the evil that I do not will* (Rom 7:19). For this reason, when he sinned, he did that which justice forbade and from which he was free to hold back. For the one who said, *I do the evil that I do not will,* was not free to hold back from it. (2) For this reason, if you distinguish these three and realize that sin is one thing, the penalty of sin another, and still other the two of them, that is, sin that is itself also the punishment of sin, you will understand which of these three falls under that definition by which sin is the will to do that which justice forbids and from which we are free to hold back. For it was sin that was defined in this way, not the punishment of sin and not both of them. These three kinds have their species, and it would take too long to discuss them now. If you ask for examples of these three kinds, an example of the first kind unquestionably occurred in Adam. There are, of course, many evil actions which human beings do from which they are free to hold back. But no one is as free as that man was who stood undamaged by any defect before his God who had created him righteous.

(3) An example of the second kind in which there is only the punishment of sin is found in that evil which one in no sense does, but only suffers, for instance, when sinners are killed for their crimes or are tormented by some other bodily punishment. The third kind in which there is[49] the sin and the punishment of sin can be found in the one who says, *I do the evil that I do not want.* To this kind there also belong all the evils which, when they are done, are due to ignorance considered not to be evil or are even considered to be good. For, if blindness of

heart were not a sin, it would be unjust to blame it, but it is justly blamed where scripture says, *You blind Pharisee* (Mt 23:26), and in many other passages of the words of God. (4) Again, if that same blindness were not a punishment of sin, scripture would not say, *For their malice blinded them* (Wis 2:21). If it did not come from the judgment of God, we would not read, *Let their eyes be darkened so that they do not see, and always bend their back* (Ps 69:24). Who is willingly blind of heart since no one wants to be blind even in the body?

Original sin, then, does not belong to that kind which we put in the first place in which there is the will to do an evil from which one is free to hold back. Otherwise, it would not exist in little ones who do not yet have use of the choice of the will. Nor does it belong to that kind which we mentioned second. (5) For we are now dealing with sin, not with the punishment which is not itself sin, although the punishment results from the merit of sin, and little ones suffer it because they have a body dead on account of sin.[50] The death of the body is not, nonetheless, itself sin, nor are any bodily torments.

Original sin belongs to this third kind in which there is sin that it is itself also the punishment of sin. It is present in the newborn, but it begins to be seen in them as they grow up when the foolish need wisdom and those with evil desires need self-control. The origin of this sin, nonetheless, comes from the will of a sinner. "For Adam existed, and we all existed in him; Adam perished, and all perished in him."[51]

48. JUL. (1) Sin deserves a curse from good people and lawful condemnation from that justice whose whole case is under consideration here. With all the curtains removed, at last bring forth into the light why you teach that there is natural sin. Surely we have not above drawn any false conclusion from the praise of divine justice or from the definition of guilt. Show me, then, that these two can be found together in little ones: If there is no sin without the will, if there is no will where there is not full freedom, and if there is no freedom where there is not the faculty of choice through reason, by what indication is sin found in little ones who do not have the use of reason? Therefore, they do not have the faculty of choosing and, for this reason, they do not have will. Since these points have been granted as irrefutable, there is no sin at all. (2) Let us see where you will burst out under pressure from these millstones. You say, "Little ones are not weighed down by any sin of their own, but they are weighed down by the sin of another."[52] It is not yet clear what evil you have in mind. Let us, after all, suppose that you brought forth these points in hatred of someone whose wickedness you, the Punic orator, would express. In whose eyes does another's crime burden undefiled innocence? Who is there who is so mad, so cruel, so forgetful of God and of justice, so treacherous a barbarian as to pronounce these little ones guilty?

We, of course, praise your native intelligence; your learning is evident. You could not produce the person of some judge, or rather tyrant, deserving the hatred of the human race otherwise than by swearing that he did not spare, not only those who committed no sin, but also those who were not able to sin. (3) Before a suspicious mind a good conscience often struggles in its own defense for fear that it may perhaps have sinned because it could sin. But one is completely acquitted of a crime who has as a defense the impossibility of the act. Tell us, then, who is this condemner of innocents? You answer: God.[53] You have utterly stunned us, but since such a great sacrilege scarcely merits belief, we are in doubt about what you meant. For we know that this term can be used in a different sense: *There are many gods and many lords, but we have one God the Father from whom all things are and one Lord Jesus Christ through whom all things are* (1 Cor 8:5.6). Which God then do you accuse of this crime? You, a very pious priest and very learned speaker, breathe forth something more disgusting and horrid than either the valley of Amsanctus or cavern of Avernus,[54] in fact something more criminal than the worship of idols in these places has itself produced. (4) God himself, you say, who *manifests his love in us* (Rom 5:8), who loved us and *did not spare his own Son, but handed him over for us* (Rom 8:32), is such a judge; he is the persecutor of the newborn; with bad will he hands over to eternal fire little ones whom he knows could not have either a good or a bad will. After this statement which is so heinous, so sacrilegious, so lamentable, if we had sound judges, I ought to demand nothing but your excommunication. For with severity that is just and appropriate I would judge you unworthy of further discussion, since you have abandoned religion, learning, and even the common sensibilities to the point that you regard your God as a criminal—something a barbarian would hardly do.

AUG. (1) It is not a great achievement that you see that little ones do not have their own will for choosing good or evil. What I wish that you would see is what that man saw who, when writing to the Hebrews, said that Levi, the son of Israel, was present in the loins of Abraham when Abraham paid the tithe and that Levi, therefore, paid the tithe in him.[55] If you looked on this with the eye of a Christian, you would see by faith, if you cannot by intelligence, that all who were going to be born from Adam through concupiscence of the flesh were present in his loins. After the sin by which his nakedness was revealed to him, he felt that concupiscence, saw it, blushed, and covered it. (2) For this reason Ambrose, my teacher and also a man highly praised by the lips of your teacher, said, "And what is more important, on this interpretation Adam girded himself in those parts where he ought rather to have girded himself by the fruit of chastity. For in the loins which we gird are said to be the seeds of generation. And, therefore, Adam was poorly girded by useless leaves by which he indicated in those parts of the body not the future fruit of future generation, but certain sins."[56] He also correctly says what I mentioned just before: "Adam existed, and we all existed in him; Adam perished, and all perished in him."[57] Because you do not see this, you bark at me in your blindness. But whatever you say against me you, of course, also say against him. (3) I wish, therefore, that I would share in common with that man the reward, just as I hear from you in common with him the abuse. Why do you cry out and say, "If we had sound judges, I ought to demand nothing but your excommunication"? Can I deal with you more generously, more kindly, more liberally than by making that man the judge between us about whom we have the judgment of your teacher, Pelagius? Look, that man is present "who stood out like a beautiful flower among the writers in the Latin language and with whose faith and utterly flawless interpretation of the scriptures not even an enemy has dared to find fault."[58] This is Pelagius' judgment about Ambrose. (4) What then did Ambrose judge about the point at issue between us? I stated above his views on original sin without any obscurity or ambiguity. But if that is not enough, listen further. He said, "We are all born under the power of sin, and our very origin lies in guilt."[59] What is your answer to that? Pelagius made those fine statements about Ambrose, and Ambrose has made these clear statements against you and for me. Blame this man of whom your teacher says that not even an enemy has dared to find fault with him. And you who ask for sound judges, declare that Ambrose is not sound so that you proclaim that you are unsound.[60]

(5) But you, a man of great piety, are angry because, if little ones who have not been reborn die before attaining the choice of their own will, they are said to be condemned on account of the sins of others by him who *manifests his love in us* (Rom 5:8), who loved us and *did not spare his own Son, but handed him over for us* (Rom 8:32). You complain in the same way that stupid and ignorant people like you complain about him when they say: Why does he create those whom he foreknows will be sinners and will be condemned? Why, finally, does he make them live until they attain that sinfulness that deserves condemnation? For he could have taken them from this life before they became such sinners if he loves souls, if he *manifests his love in us* (Rom 5:8), *if he has not spared his own Son, but handed him over for us all* (Rom 8:32). (6) If someone says to them, *Who are you, a human being, to answer back to God?* (Rom 9:20), and *His judgments are inscrutable* (Rom 11:33), they become angry rather than calm down. But *the Lord knows those who belong to him* (2 Tm 2:19). If, then, you want to have sound judges, listen to the sound judge who was particularly praised by your teacher. He says, "Adam existed, and we all existed in him; Adam perished, and all perished in him."[61] But, you say, they certainly ought not to have perished for the sins of others. They are the sins of others, but they are the sins of our parents, and for this reason they are ours by the law of propagation and growth. Who sets us free from this state of being lost but he who *came to seek what was lost* (Lk 19:10)? In those, then, whom he sets free we embrace his mercy, but in those whom he does not set free we acknowledge his judgment which is indeed most hidden, but undoubtedly most just.

The Claim That Augustine Is Worse than Mani

49. JUL. (1) Mani imagined and believed that the God of light fought with the prince of darkness and added that God's substance is held captive in this world. But he tries to explain away such great unhappiness under the cloak of devotion; he claims that, like a good citizen, he fought for his country and sacrificed his members in order not to lose his kingdom. You, a man who had learned these teachings, consider the progress you have made in getting away from them at least for some time. You say that God did not endure the horrors of war, but that he has pronounced an unjust judgment; you do not say that he is subject to dark enemies, but to obvious crimes; you do not, finally, say that he surrendered his substance, but that he violated eternal justice. (2) I leave it to others to judge which of you is worse than the other. One thing is clear: both of you go back to one blasphemous principle. For Mani ascribes injustice to his God when he claims that he will condemn on the last day the members which he surrendered, and you maintain that he is unhappy because he has destroyed the glory for which he was renowned and, by persecuting the innocence which he created, has lost the righteousness by which he was most holy. That God which your teacher devised surpasses this God, which you introduce, to the extent that it is more excusable to have been defeated in battle than to be defeated by sin.

AUG. (1) If you are delighted by the innocence of the little ones, remove from them, if you can, the *heavy yoke* which lies *upon the children of Adam from the day they come forth from the womb of their mother* (Sir 40:1). But I believe that the scripture which said this knew better than you the innocence of the creature and the justice of the creator. Who, however, can fail to see that, if little ones have the innocence which you teach, the justice of God is not found in that heavy yoke of theirs? Since, on the other hand, divine justice is found in their heavy yoke, they do not have the sort of innocence which you teach. Or perhaps a just, but weak God could help you out as you struggle over this question. (2) For God could not come to the aid of his images so that those innocents would not be weighed down by the misery of their heavy yoke. Then you could say that he wanted to because he is just, but that he could not because he is not almighty. And so you would get out of these difficulties only by abandoning the foundation of the faith—the faith by which we profess first of all in the Creed, namely, that we believe in God the Father almighty. In the many and great evils which little ones suffer, your God is, therefore, going to lose his justice or his omnipotence or his very care over human affairs. See what you will be, whichever of these you chose.

50. JUL. (1) Remove yourself, therefore, along with your God from the midst of the churches. He is not the God in whom the patriarchs, the prophets, and the apostles believed; he is not the God in whom the Church of the first Christians, which was written in the heavens,[62] has hoped and continues to hope; he is not

the God which the rational creature believes will be its judge and which the Holy Spirit announces will judge justly.[63] No wise persons would ever have shed their blood for such a lord, for he did not earn the ardor of our love so that he could impose on anyone the obligation of accepting suffering for him. Finally, this God which you introduce, if he ever existed, would be proved to be not God, but a criminal, one who should be judged by my true God, not one who would act as judge in place of God. (2) I want you to know the basic fundamentals of the faith: Our God, the God of the Catholic Church, is unknown to us in his substance and likewise removed from our sight, one *whom no human being has seen or can see* (1 Tm 6:16). As he is eternal without beginning, so he is holy and just without defect; he is most omnipotent, most just, most merciful, known by the splendor of his virtues alone; he is the maker of all things which did not exist, the governor of those which do exist, and the judge of all those who are and will be and have been. He will on the last day change the earth and the sky and all the elements at once; he will raise up ashes and restore bodies, but he will do all these things which I have mentioned only on account of justice.

AUG. (1) If you worship the God of the patriarchs, why do you not believe that circumcision on the eighth day which was imposed upon Abraham was a foreshadowing of rebirth in Christ? For if you would believe this, you would see that the soul of a little one could not justly be lost to its people if it were not circumcised on the eighth day,[64] unless it was subject to some sin? If you worship the God of the prophets, why do you not believe what he[65] so often said through them, *I shall punish the children for the sins of their parents* (Ex 20:5)?[66] If you worship the God of the apostles, why do you not believe that the body is dead on account of sin?[67] If you worship the God in whom the Church of the first Christians, which was written in the heavens,[68] has hoped and continues to hope, why do you not believe that little ones in being baptized are rescued from the power of darkness,[69] since the Church performs the rites of exsufflation and exorcism[70] upon them in order to drive out of them the power of darkness? (2) Give us a text: what third place besides the kingdom for the good and punishment for the evil has that God, whom the rational creature in his holy and faithful people awaits as its judge, prepared for and promised to these innocents of yours who have not been reborn? But how can you say that no wise persons shed their blood for the Lord whom we worship, since the most glorious Cyprian worshiped him and shed his blood for him. That same Cyprian cuts off your breath on this question, when he says that a little one born of Adam according to the flesh contracts the infection of that ancient death by its first birth.[71] Do you not see that you are rather the criminal when you blaspheme against the God of the holy martyrs? (3) You say that you worship the most omnipotent, most just, and most merciful God. But he is most omnipotent so that he undoubtedly could remove from them the heavy yoke by which the children of Adam are weighed down from the day of their birth;[72] in fact, he could bring it about that they were not burdened by any such yoke at all. But he is most just so that he would never impose that yoke or allow it to be imposed on them, if he did not find in them sins with which they were born and whose guilt he himself in his great mercy removes for those who are reborn. If, then, you found delight in the divine justice, you would surely see that the human misery known to us all comes from that justice, and this misery does not, of course, unjustly begin with the little ones. In this misery we spend our lives from the first wails of the newborn up to the last breaths of the dying, for happiness has been promised to the holy and faithful people alone, but only in the next life.

51. JUL. I would act more correctly, as[73] I said, in defense of this God of mine, whom all creation and the holy scripture makes known to me as the sort of God I believe him to be, if I held you unworthy of discussion in my books. But since holy men, the saints of our time, have imposed on me in particular this duty of examining the weight of reason that your statements have, it was advantageous first to show that you do not believe in that God who has always been preached and will be preached in the Church of the Catholics wherever it exists until the end of time.

AUG. I have rather shown that you have not shown what you say you have shown, and if you are not blind, I have proved that I believe in that God who has always been preached in the Church of the Catholics.

An Examination of Augustine's Case from Scripture

52. JUL. (1) But now I shall next examine the testimonies by which you try to defend the position that the faith of believers overcomes. I decided to refute the second book of yours which Alypius delivered, and so that the order of the reply may not be confused,[74] I must still reply to a few points before the discussion turns to the testimony of the apostle by which you suppose that you are best protected. To those words of yours, then, which I cited above, you add these which follow, "In these words which he omitted, he was afraid of something that draws all hearts to the Catholic faith. It appeals with a loud voice, as it were, to that faith rooted in antiquity and handed down to us, and it vigorously arouses that faith against them. What he was afraid of is our statement that they 'say that there is no sin in little ones to be washed away by the bath of rebirth.'[75] (2) For all come running to the Church with their little ones for no other reason than to have the original sin in them that was contracted through the generation of their first birth wiped away by the regeneration of their second birth. Then he returns to our previous words; I do not know why he repeats them: 'We say that those who are born from such a union contract original sin,' and 'We claim that, regardless of the sort of parents from which the children are born, they are still under the power of the devil, unless they are reborn in Christ.'[76] He had already cited these

words of ours a little earlier. Then he added what we said about Christ 'who chose not to be born from that union of both sexes.' But he also omitted here the words I used, 'They must be rescued by his grace from the power of darkness and transferred into the kingdom of the one who chose not to be born from that union of both sexes.'[77] (3) Notice, I beg you, the words of ours which he avoided, because he is totally opposed to the grace of God which comes through Jesus Christ our Lord! He knows, after all, that it is most wicked and impious to exclude little ones from that statement of the apostle in which he says of God the Father, *He has rescued us from the power of darkness and transferred us into the kingdom of his beloved Son* (Col 1:13). For this reason he undoubtedly preferred to omit these words rather than cite them."[78] Am I, you most impudent of all men, opposed to the grace of God? I who, in my first book from which you took those sentences torn from their context in order to chatter away about something without any reason, condemned with a pure and full confession your teachings and those of your people drenched in the mysteries of the Manichees?

AUG. (1) Are you going to bring it about that you have a good case by uttering abuse? Tell me what teachings of my people as well as my own teachings you boast of having condemned. You will say: Manichean teachings, but you speak falsely, not truthfully. For I too detest the Manichees and their supporters, among whom you are vying for the first place, and I refute both of them with the Catholic truth by the help and assistance of the Lord our God. I shall show you my people whom you accuse with more wickedness the more clever you are, when you accuse me. For in this case the question at issue is original sin; on account of it you call me a Manichee and think that I deserve the most atrocious insults. In this case Cyprian is one of my people; though he said that a little one committed no sin, he did not pass up saying that it contracted the infection of sin from Adam by its first birth.[79] Hilary is one of my people; when he explained what we read in the psalm, *My soul shall live and praise you* (Ps 119:175), (2) he said: "The psalmist does not suppose that he is living in this life, for he had said, *See, I was conceived in iniquities, and my mother bore me in sins* (Ps 51:7). He knows that he was born from a sinful origin and under the law of sin."[80] Ambrose, who was praised so highly by your teacher, is one of my people; he said, "All of us human beings are born under the power of sin, and our very origin lies in guilt, as you have read where David says, *See, I was conceived in iniquities, and my mother bore me in sins* (Ps 51:7). And so Paul's flesh was the body of death."[81] Gregory is one of my people; when he was speaking of baptism, he said, "Show reverence for the birth by which you were set free from the chains of earthly birth."[82] Basil is one of my people; when he was dealing with fasting, he said, "Because we did not fast, we fell from paradise; let us fast so that we may return to paradise."[83] (3) John of Constantinople is one of my people; he said, "Adam committed that great sin and condemned the whole human race in common."[84] All these and other companions of theirs who hold the same doctrine—it would take too long to mention them all—are mine. If you recognize them, they are yours as well—my teachers, but men who prove you wrong. How then have you condemned my teachings and the teachings of my people, since you yourself are rather condemned by the harmonious and truthful teaching of these men who you see are on my side? Do you dare with darkened mind, impudent countenance, and undisciplined tongue to accuse these lights of the city of God of the crime of Mani? But if you do not dare to do this, why do you dare to accuse me for no other reason than that I say what they say whom you do not dare to accuse?

Two Views of Necessity of Infant Baptism

53. JUL. (1) For I put together there this sequence of words after I had said that God is the author of heaven and of earth and of all the things which are in them and, for this reason, also of human beings, on account of whom all things were made. I said, "It does not escape me when we say these things that people are going to say of us that we do not think that the grace of God is necessary for little ones. This rightly and deeply offends the Christian people. If, nonetheless, they would not suppose that we are the authors of a statement which is obviously wicked, they would in that way avoid committing the crime of believing false statements about their brothers, and they would prove that they are zealous about the love of the faith. We must, then, defend this flank against an attack by vanity, and by a brief profession of faith we must seal the lips of our attackers. (2) We, therefore, profess that the grace of baptism is useful for all ages to the point that we strike with an eternal anathema all those who say that it is not necessary also for little ones. But we believe that this grace is rich with spiritual gifts. Endowed with many gifts and awesome in its powers, it treats persons in accord with their various kinds of illnesses and the differences of human conditions by the one conferral of its remedies and power of its gifts.[85] When it is applied, it need not be changed for different cases, for it dispenses its gifts in accord with the capacity of those who approach it. For none of the arts themselves suffer either increase or decrease in relation with the different materials which they take up to work on, but always remain the same and exist in the same way, though they are graced with many different forms of expression. In the same way, the apostle says, *There is one faith, one baptism* (Eph 4:5). (3) They become many and are diversified in their gifts, but are not changed in the rites of the sacraments. But this grace is not opposed to the righteousness which wipes away the stains of iniquity. It does not produce sins, but washes them away. It absolves the guilty; it does not bring false charges against the innocent. Christ, who is the redeemer of what he has made, increases his benefits toward his image with continual generosity, and those whom he made good by creating them he makes better by renew-

ing and adopting."[86] This grace, which gives pardon to the guilty, gives to other mortals spiritual enlightenment, adoption as children of God, citizenship in the heavenly Jerusalem, sanctification, transformation into members of Christ, and possession of the kingdom of heaven. Anyone who thinks that it should be denied to some deserves the reprobation of all good people.

AUG. (1) Among all these gifts of the grace of God you mentioned, you do not want that gift which you put first to pertain to little ones, namely, that it gives pardon to the guilty, for you deny that little ones contract any guilt from Adam. Why, then, does God deny the other gifts to many little ones who die without this grace at that age? Why, I ask, are they not given spiritual enlightenment, adoption as children of God, citizenship in the heavenly Jerusalem, sanctification, transformation into members of Christ, and possession of the kingdom of heaven? Would God, who holds sovereign power, deny these gifts which are so many and so necessary to so many of his images who have, according to you, no sin, since no opposing will in the little ones fends off from them this benefit? Hence, in order to remove from yourselves this hateful accusation which claims that you deny the grace of baptism to little ones, you said that one who thinks that grace should be denied to some deserves the reprobation of all good people. (2) The justice, therefore, of almighty God would not deny it to countless little ones who under his omnipotence die without it, if in his hidden judgment they merited no punishment. Let all who, in accord with grace, not in accord with what is owed them, are set free from this judgment which all those who come from Adam's lineage deserve, boast, not in their own merits, but in the Lord.[87] If, then, you want to avoid the grounds for reproach which makes you detestable to the Catholic Church, allow Christ to be Jesus for the little ones. But he will not in any sense be Jesus for them, if he does not bestow on them that on account of which he received this name, that is, if he does not save them from their sins.[88] In order, then, that you may avoid the resentment of Christians about which you complain, say about this grace what the learned Catholic teacher, Gregory, said: "Show reverence for the birth by which you have been set free from the chains of earthly birth."[89] You, therefore, in no way acknowledge that little ones have any share in this grace as long as you deny that by their heavenly birth they are set free from the bonds of their earthly birth.

54. JUL. (1) Since I have defended these ideas to the extent that this section inserted here has permitted, let us return to the point from which we digressed; we shall speak more fully on this topic wherever it will be appropriate. See the great clarity of my confession in which I have rejected those who would deny baptism to little ones and you who dare to defile the justice of God by your attack upon it. I have testified that I hold nothing else than that the sacraments Christ instituted must be administered at absolutely every age with the same words which have been handed down to us and ought not to be changed for different cases. I have testified, however, that sinners are changed from evil to completely good,

but that innocents who have no evil from their own will are changed from good to better, that is, to the very best. Thus both groups are made holy and become members of Christ, though the one was found in an evil life, the other in a good nature. (2) The former persons, after all, spoiled the innocence which they received at birth by their bad actions, but the latter, who have neither praise nor blame because of their own wills, have only what they received from God their creator. These latter are happier by reason of the purity of their tender age and could not damage the goodness of their simplicity, since they have no merit from their acts, but only hold what they got from the gift of so great a maker.

AUG. Why, then, is there a heavy yoke upon them from the day they come forth from the womb of their mother?[90] Why is there such great corruption of the body that their souls are weighed down by it?[91] Why is there such great dullness of the mind that their slowness is educated even by beatings? How long, Julian, will you be heavy of heart? How long will you love vanity and look for lies[92] with which to support your heresy? If no one had sinned, if human nature had remained in that good state in which it was created, would human beings even in paradise be born for such miseries—not to mention the others?

55. JUL. When that age is renewed, that is, raised up by the power of the sacrament of renewal, it proclaims the mercy of Christ; in the same way, when it is either accused or weighed down, it proves the judge guilty of injustice and brings disgrace upon justice.

AUG. (1) What is the old state from which that age is said to be renewed, since it is new by birth? These lips of yours are full of deceit. If you come to learn the old state from which the little ones are renewed by the grace of Christ, listen with faith to what the man of God, Reticius, the bishop of Autun, said when he once sat as judge along with Melchiades, the bishop of Rome, and condemned Donatus as a heretic.[93] For when he spoke of Christian baptism, he said, "No one misses the fact that this is the basic pardon in the Church. In it we unburden ourselves of all the weight of the ancient crime and wipe out the first misdeeds of our ignorance; in it we also strip off the old human being with its inborn wrongdoings."[94] (2) Do you hear him speak, not of iniquities committed later, but of the inborn wrongdoings of the old human being? Was this Reticius a Manichee? How, then, do you say without deceit that little ones are renewed in Christian rebirth, if you refuse to acknowledge in the old human being the evils which the weight of the ancient crime produced? Finally, if that age, when weighed down, proves the judge guilty of injustice, as you claim, is it not weighed down by the heavy yoke upon the children of Adam?[95] And yet God is not on this account unjust, and for this reason that age deserves to be weighed down. But this age has merited nothing evil if there is no original sin.

The Guilt or Innocence of the Newborn

56. JUL. The unity of the sacrament, therefore, does not show that infancy is guilty; rather, the truth of God's judgment proves that it is perfectly innocent.

AUG. (1) You think you have found the reason why infants are baptized; tell me why they undergo the rite of exsufflation.[96] Surely the statement of Pelagius, your founder, is held to be important and irrefutable when he says, "If the sin of Adam harmed even those who do not sin, then Christ's righteousness can also benefit even those who do not believe."[97] What, then, do you say about little ones when they are baptized? Do they believe or do they not believe? If you say that they do not believe, how does the righteousness of Christ benefit even those who do not believe so that they possess the kingdom of heaven? Or if it does benefit them, as you are forced to admit, then, the sin of Adam harmed those who do not yet have a will able to sin, just as the righteousness of Christ benefits those who do not yet have a will able to believe. But if you say that they believe through others, in the same way they also sinned through another. (2) And because it is true that they believe through others—for on this account they are also called believers throughout the whole Church—the words of the Lord certainly also apply to them, *But those who do not believe will be condemned* (Mk 16:16). They will, therefore, be condemned if they do not believe through others, since they are incapable of believing on their own. But they could in no way be justly condemned if they were not born under the power of sin and, for this reason, under the power of the prince of sin. On this account, then, they undergo the rite of exsufflation. Remove from them your deceptive vanity; *allow the little ones to come* (Mk 10:14) to Jesus who *saves his people from their sins* (Mt 1:21), for they too are certainly numbered among his people.

57. JUL. (1) And yet, the logical order of reason demands that I pause to explain the state of infants, for logic does not permit that ideas joined by its law be divided. Now the loss of the newborn would be less of a problem if the divine majesty was not jeopardized by it. Excuse God, then, and accuse the little one. Teach that what God who without justice cannot be God does is just and that everything a person suffers is punishment. But now the ideas which you suppose that you have combined without sacrilege are in blatant contradiction with one another. (2) You say, after all, that all people are proven to be criminals because idolaters and parricides receive initiation by the same sacraments as the little ones, and you add something much more absurd, namely, that the author of this sacrament with which we are dealing attributes the sins of others to the innocent. This is what I said is contradictory: The nature of reality does not admit that at one and the same time God is so merciful that he pardons the personal sins of everyone who confesses them and so cruel that he imposes upon an innocent the sins of others. When you grant one of these, you have denied the other. If he

grants pardon to the guilty, he does not falsely accuse the innocent; if he falsely accuses the innocent, he never spares the guilty.

AUG. (1) It is you rather who make God unjust when you think it unjust to punish the children for the sins of their parents—something that he often testifies by words and shows by deeds that he does. It is you, I say, who make God unjust, for when you see little ones weighed down by the heavy yoke of misery under the providence of almighty God, you maintain that they have no sin. In that way you bring accusations against both God and the Church—against God if they are burdened and afflicted without deserving it, but against the Church if they undergo the rite of exsufflation when they are not subject to the devil's dominion. How have you ever imagined that we set the original sins of little ones on a par with idolatry and parricide? The forgiveness of sins, nonetheless, bestowed by the sacraments is true in the case of all sins—both great and little sins, many sins, few sins, or single sins; in the case of no sins is it false, as you say it is in the case of little ones. (2) Original sins, however, are the sins of others because there is in them no choice of our own will, and yet they are, nonetheless, also found to be our sins because of the infection contracted from our origin. Why, then, do you shout and claim that God cannot both forgive personal sins of adults and attribute the sins of others to little ones? Why it is that you refuse to notice that he forgives both kinds of sin only in those reborn in Christ, but forgives neither in those not reborn in Christ? These are the mysteries of the grace of Christ that are hidden from the wise and prudent and revealed to little ones.[98] If only you were among these, you would not, like a big fellow, put your trust in your own virtue;[99] surely you would understand that the injustice of the first man is imputed to little ones when they are born so that they are subject to punishment, just as the righteousness of the second man[100] is imputed to little ones who are reborn so that they attain the kingdom of heaven. And yet, they are found to have imitated by their own will and action neither the former in an evil action nor the latter in a good action.

58. JUL. I have, therefore, omitted none of your words under the pressures, as you say, of fear. What, after all, could I be afraid of in the writings of so fine a mind except perhaps this one thing, namely, that I should be struck with horror at your indecent attack?

AUG. If you bought these insults, I would call you a spendthrift; they are available to you free of charge. Why should you not enjoy these foods with which you feed your foul mind?

Whose Is the Faith Rooted in Antiquity?

59. JUL. Listen to what I say against those things you said in a few words. Those are not Catholic hearts which your discourse addresses, if they are not in

harmony with piety and reason. They violate both of these, since they neither judge correctly about the justice of God, nor do they understand the wisdom and riches of the mysteries which they accuse. This is not the faith which was rooted in antiquity and handed down to us; rather, it is inspired by the devil in the councils of the wicked and preached by Mani, celebrated by Marcion, by Faustus, by Adimantus,[101] and by all their cohorts. And now it is been spit out by you upon Italy. That is what we deeply mourn.

AUG. (1) What a mouth! What a shameless heart! Do you call the agreement of so many Catholics who were teachers of the churches before us a council of the wicked? Suppose that in a council of bishops—the sort of council which you say, not in a wholesome way, but out of pride, ought to be convoked on account of your questions—there were gathered the bishops I mentioned: to omit the others, Cyprian, Hilary, Ambrose, Gregory, Basil, and John of Constantinople. You act as if you would easily find others who are still alive whom you could regard as their equals or even prefer to them in the doctrine of the Church handed down from antiquity. Since they have issued plain and clear statements in opposition to you on original sin—those which I quoted a little before and many others—do you dare to call the agreement of these men in the Catholic truth a council of the wicked? (2) And you ponder what you should say against them and not rather where you should flee if you do not want to agree with them! But since you said that I spit out upon Italy that over which you mourn, I again set before your eyes that same bishop of Italy whom your teacher praised: Ambrose. He said, "All of us human beings are born under the power of sin, and our very origin lies in guilt, as you have read where David says, *See, I was conceived in iniquities, and my mother bore me in sins* (Ps 51:7). And so Paul's flesh was the body of death, as he himself said, *Who will set me free from the body of this death?* (Rom 7:24). Christ's flesh condemned the sin which he did not experience when he was born, but which he crucified when he died so that in our flesh there might be justification through grace where there was previously defilement through sin."[102] This, then, is the faith which I say was rooted in antiquity and handed down to us; you reject it, and you do not see against whom you are struggling. Can you say that the devil inspired him with this faith? Is he Mani? Is he Marcion, Faustus, or Adimantus? Certainly not! Rather, he is very different from them, very opposed to them. Let Pelagius at least say who this man is. He, he is the one with whose faith and utterly flawless interpretation of the scriptures not even an enemy has dared to find fault.[103] What about that, Julian? Do you realize where you are? He with whose faith not even an enemy dared to find fault held this faith with which you find so much fault that you attribute it to the councils of the wicked. (4) Look, it is not the faith of the wicked, but the faith of Ambrose. Because it is true, because it is sound, because it is, as I said, rooted in antiquity and handed down to us, this faith is also my faith. I did not spit it out upon Italy—something over which you say that you mourn. Rather, I received the bath of rebirth from this bishop of Italy who preached and taught this faith. Because this faith is the Catholic faith and yours is not, where, then, do you stand? See, I beg you, and come back. It is to your advantage to see, not to hate; we want you to come back, not to perish.[104]

60. JUL. There is no sin in human beings if they have no will or assent of their own. The whole race of human beings, even those who are only slightly intelligent, undoubtedly agrees with me on this. But you grant that little ones have had no will of their own. It is not I, but reason that concludes that there is, therefore, no sin in them. Hence, they are by no means brought to the Church in order to have their good name attacked—in fact in order to attack the good name of God. Rather, they are brought to Church to praise God who, they testify, is the author of both natural goods and spiritual gifts.

AUG. Their good name is not attacked when they undergo the rite of exsufflation; rather, they are rescued from the power of darkness.[105] Nor do they attack the good name of God; rather, they need as their savior the creator by whose work they were born. And thus by being reborn they are transferred from Adam to Christ. But where you said, "There is no sin in human beings if they have no will or assent of their own," you would have spoken the truth more completely if you had added, "or infection."

Original Sin and the Condemnation of Marriage

61. JUL. But if original sin is contracted from generation at their first birth, it can condemn marriage which God instituted, but it cannot be removed from the little ones, since what is inborn lasts up to the end of that in which it inhered from its initial causes.

AUG. It does not condemn marriage because marriage is not its cause, and it is removed by that almighty one who was able to be born even as human without it.

62. JUL. It is not, therefore, a false accusation we raise against you that you condemn marriage and say that a human being who is born from marriage is the work of the devil. Nor do we raise this objection out of dishonesty or infer it out of ignorance. Rather we carefully and simply look at what is the result of the following statements. For bodily marriage never exists without sexual union. When you say: Whoever is born of that union belongs to the devil, you undoubtedly declare that marriage falls under the devil's dominion.

AUG. We do not say, do we, that, if no one had sinned, marriage could have existed in paradise without bodily union? But there would not have existed in paradise the evil of which marital chastity now makes good use. That evil comes from the wound which was inflicted by the cunning of the devil. Because of it the offspring of mortals are held guilty; because of it the newborn are under the prince of sinners until they are reborn in Christ who had no sin at all and who alone removes the bonds of death because he alone was free among the dead.

The Argument That Nature Is Diabolical

63. JUL. You say that sin is contracted from the condition of our nature, for you want this evil to come upon us from the will of the first human being. Here I postpone my reply by which I will prove that you are a shameless liar. But with regard to the present passage I infer—and I believe the reasoning of wisdom—that you unambiguously declare that nature is diabolical.[106] For, if that on account of which a human being is the property of the devil is found in nature and comes to be through it, there unquestionably belongs to the devil that by which he was able to claim for himself the image of God. In fact, that is not the image of God which by its birth is found in the kingdom of the devil.

AUG. (1) You believe, not the reasoning of wisdom, but the conjectures of stupidity. Allow the little ones to be rescued from the power of darkness so that they may be transferred into the kingdom of Christ.[107] For when you say that they do not have the infection of the ancient sin, you in that way remove them from the mercy of the savior *who saves his people from their sins* (Mt 1:21). This is the reason he is called Jesus. In doing that you only cause the anger of God to remain over them. Job spoke of that anger when he said, *Human beings born of a woman have a short life full of anger, and like the flowers of the field they fall. They flee like shadows and will not stay. Have you not shown your care for them and made them to enter into your sight for judgment? For who will be clean of filth? No one, even if one's life lasts only a single day upon the earth* (Job 14:1-5 LXX). (2) But, you, you pitiful man, show pity toward the image of God, and you say that it is not born in the flesh under the power of sin. Oh how cruel is this foolish mercy of yours which keeps away[108] from that image the mercy of their savior who came to seek what was lost![109] The devil claims for himself the image of God because of that filth from which the man of God says no one is free, *even if one's life lasts only a single day upon the earth*, not because of the substance which God created. For nature has a defect, but is not itself a defect. But you say, "That is not the image of God which by its birth is found in the kingdom of the devil." What if someone else says to you, "That is not the image of God which, though guilty of no sin, does not, nonetheless, enter the kingdom of God?" Is it not true that you will have no answer unless you want to answer with nonsense? And surely a human being is the image of God because of having been made to the likeness of God. (3) Why, then, have human beings become like a vanity so that their days pass like a shadow?[110] You will not, after all, separate the little ones from this vanity since their days pass like a shadow. Finally, will you separate them from the living? Listen, then, to the one who speaks in another psalm,

See, you have made my days old, and my substance is as nothing before you; nonetheless, every living human being is complete vanity (Ps 39:6). Since every living human being is the image of God, tell me why it is that every living human being is also vanity. What are you going to say, since you do not want to recognize that one of these comes from God's creation and the other from the effect of sin? Permit, we beg you, living human beings who were made to the likeness of God to be rescued from the power of darkness under which they were made like a vanity. Let them now be rescued from subjection to guilt, but after this life that is subject to corruption, let them also be rescued from all vanity.

64. JUL. (1) If, then, you would read my work, you would cease to wonder why I returned to your words which I quoted above. For I promised that I would prove from your writings that between the infidelity that you had absorbed and hatred for what you feared, you stated each of these positions as equals: both what the Catholics and what the Manichees are accustomed to claim. Such, therefore, was the sequence of the words given to your chapter, and you now falsely claim with the effrontery of a swindler that it was an alteration. I know that I have promised a lot, namely, that I would prove from the statements of my opponent two things: that those who deny that human beings are the work of God are rightly condemned and that this man himself who makes this claim aims at nothing else than to maintain that whatever comes from the fruitfulness of marriage is the private property of the devil. With this kind of endorsement the opinion of the Manichees will be destroyed by its own principles,[111] but the entire beginning of his book has made this public knowledge. (2) For he says that human beings who are born of marriage, that is, from males and females, are the work of God. By that proposition he undoes everything that he is going to do, and he agrees with us when we say that it is unbelievers who dare to deny this. One side, then, has been taken care of; there remains for me to show that he upholds what he has just attacked. With that said, I returned to the part of your chapter in which you had said, "We say that those who are born from such a union contract original sin" and "regardless of the sort of parents from whom the children are born, they are still under the power of the devil, unless they are reborn in Christ. They must be rescued by his grace from the power of darkness and transferred into the kingdom of the one who chose not to be born from that union of both sexes."[112] (3) Why, then, do you think that you can be excused from the error of the Manichees because you have dared to add one sentence against which you struggle with all the powers of your mind? For this is not a defense of your error, but a proof of singular stupidity. In the manner of Calliphon, you think that virtue and vices, justice and injustice can enter into an alliance in your discourse.[113] As for the words of the apostle, *He rescued us from the power of darkness and transferred us into the kingdom of his beloved Son* (Col 1:13), read the fourth book of my work, and then it will become clear to you what the teacher of the nations meant.

AUG. (1) My sixth book was a response to your fourth book, and now I rather exhort those people who want to know how far you wandered from the truth and how well the truth refuted you to read those books of yours and mine. But with regard to the document in which were gathered some excerpts from your books, you are free to blame me for what that person did who sent it to the man who sent it to me. For in it he cited what he chose from your work, and he omitted what he chose; on this point I replied to you above briefly and sufficiently. Why are you trying to wrap yourself in your obscure statements in opposition to the clear statements of the apostle? In speaking of God, he says, *He rescued us from the power of darkness and transferred us into the kingdom of his beloved Son* (Col 1:13), and you say that he said this, but excluded the little ones. (2) If the little ones, then, are not rescued from the power of darkness, they have not died; if they have not died, Christ has not died for them. But you admit that Christ has also died for them, and the apostle says the same thing: *One has died for all; all, therefore, have died* (2 Cor 5:14). This conclusion of the apostle is irrefutable, and precisely because he has also died for the little ones, the little ones have also surely died. Christ, moreover, died *to render powerless the one who held the power of death, that is, the devil* (Heb 2:14). Therefore, allow the little ones to be rescued from the power of darkness that they may live. (3) Why do you raise as an objection to me the practice or error of Calliphon, when you say that I think virtue and vices, justice and injustice can enter into an alliance in my discourse? Heaven forbid that I should hold this in my heart or argue for it in words. But I am pleased that you have understood this philosopher so well.[114] For because he thought that the good of a human being is to be found in the virtue of the mind and in the pleasure of the body, you say that he wanted to unite virtues and vices, and on this account you judged, as is right, that the desire for bodily pleasure is a vice. The sexual desire which you praise is, therefore, a vice. The truth, therefore, has crept up from all sides upon your faculties so that, if you would only abandon a little the cause of your protégé, you would say what we say.

65. JUL. I, therefore, accused and rightly accused the desperate and feeble wavering by which you have managed first to state that you do not condemn marriage and then to say that human beings are transferred to the jurisdiction of the devil on account of the coupling of man and woman, though it is evident that this coupling comes from the condition and nature of marriage. In fact, the essence of marriage—insofar as our dispute is concerned—is found only in this coupling.

AUG. If the essence of marriage is found only in the coupling of man and woman, then adultery and marriage have the same essence, because in each of them there is that coupling of the two sexes. But if that is utterly absurd, the essence of marriage is not found, as you so madly claim, only in the coupling of man and woman, although without that coupling marriage is not able to produce children. But there are other things that properly belong to marriage by which it is distinguished from adultery, such as the fidelity of the marriage bed, the care to have children in an orderly way, and—this is the biggest difference—the good use of an evil, that is, the good use of concupiscence of the flesh, the evil of which adulterers make bad use.

66. JUL. You have tried to convince us that this coupling is something so abominable that you want us to think that Christ chose to be born of a virgin mother, not on account of the splendor of the miracle, but in order to condemn the union of the sexes. What could anyone ever say more wicked or more impudent than this? It is as if there are two kings fighting under these standards over the ownership of humanity, and you have divided their two kingdoms so that you say that the devil owns whatever marriage has produced, but God owns only what the virgin has borne. What else is this but to show that he who made the virgin pregnant is most impoverished because of the lack of his part in the action and to deny that this same one is the creator of human beings through marriage? Let the careful reader of your words hold on to the list of charges and know that you, a faithful disciple of the Manichees and leader of the traducianist people, have condemned nothing else but the union of lawful marriage.

AUG. (1) You do not have minds trained to separate good from evil. The nature and substance of human beings and of angels, of good ones or of bad ones, exist because God is their creator. But the defects of natures and substances are permitted to exist in them by the just and omnipotent God under his judicial ordering of things. The Manichees say that these defects are natures and substances, though the truth denies this. They are evils which can exist only as a result of what is good and only in what is good. There are, however, in the power of the devil whatever beings the judgment of God makes subject to him, but they are subject to him in such a way that they cannot be apart from the power of God under which the devil himself has been placed. Since, then, all the angels and all human beings are under God's power, all that wordiness of yours is silly by which you say that God and the devil have divided between themselves which of them will have which ones under his own power. (2) Pay a little attention to the man upon whom you vomit from your sick heart these insults upon which you feed. See, here is Ambrose; see what he says about what you are attacking. He says, "He could not alone be righteous, since the whole human race went astray, if it were not that, because he was born of a virgin, he was not held by the law of the guilty race."[115] Listen further; listen and stop the impudent tongue of your effrontery by shedding tears: "For intercourse with a man did not open the gates of the Virgin's womb; rather, the Holy Spirit poured spotless seed into that inviolable womb. For among those born of a woman the holy Lord Jesus was absolutely the only one who did not experience the contagion of earthly corruption because of the new manner of his immaculate birth; rather, he shrugged it off by his celestial majesty."[116] Do you see who it is who says what I say? Do you see against whom you say whatever you say against me? If, after all, I am on this account a disciple of Mani, he is one too. But he who said these things before us is not a disciple of Mani. Whoever says these things is not, therefore, a disciple of Mani, but whoever contradicts this ancient Catholic teaching is an obvious heretic.

67. JUL. (1) But now let us go on to the rest. Writing about me, therefore, you add after those words of yours which I quoted above these words which follow: "After this he quoted our statement in which we said, 'After all, this shameful desire, which the impudent impudently praise, would not exist at all, if human beings had not first sinned, [but marriage would have existed, even if no one had sinned].[117] Children would be conceived without this disease.' He cited my words up to this point, for he was fearful about what I added: 'in[118] the body of that former life, though they cannot now be conceived without it in the body of this death.'[119] Here, he did not complete my sentence, but in a sense amputated it, for he feared the testimony of the apostle where he said, *Wretched man that I am, who will set me free from the body of this death? The grace of God through Jesus Christ our Lord* (Rom 7:24-25). (2) In paradise, after all, before the sin there did not exist the body of this death. On account of it we said that in the body of that former life which existed in paradise, children would be conceived without this disease, though they cannot now be conceived without it in the body of this death."[120]

You consistently hold to your practice, especially in this work; that is, you who speak against the truth do not say anything true, but a multitude of rebukes is hardly sufficient for the numerous mistakes in your learning. Hence, I shall now briefly note here that you are practicing deceit, but you will understand at least after this work that I am a stranger to lying. Claim for yourself, then, total possession of this vice so that you can hear from the gospel—not, of course, as something unjust—that you are a liar from the beginning, just as your father,[121] either the one to whose dominion[122] you say you belonged at birth or the other secondary one who introduced you to those lavish mysteries which cannot be named among decent people. (3) I, therefore, treated in my first work this whole issue which you pretend I omitted, and if you would read the parts almost at the end of the first volume, you would yourself be able to admit the great truth and light with which it is refuted. Therefore, it is not your amputated statement, but your whole statement that is destroyed by a powerful response. But listen now for a moment. When the apostle said, *Wretched man that I am, who will set me free from the body of this death? The grace of God through Jesus Christ our Lord* (Rom 7:24-25), he was not referring to the mortality of our body which the flesh of living beings received with the creation of their nature, but to the habit of sinning. After the incarnation of Christ all who engage in the pursuit of virtue are set free from that guilt through the new testament. (4) In that passage, then, he spoke in the person of the Jews who went astray out of a desire for things that were tempting even after the prohibition of the sacred law, and he showed that there was a single source of help in the storm, if they would believe in Christ.

Christ promised security regarding future actions, just as he pardoned past ones; he did not go after the guilty by using the force of punishment, but embraced them with his loving arms open for everyone running to him. He did not slay with terror those who were downtrodden, but restored by his goodness those who corrected their lives. That goodness was already experienced by the man who said, *It is a statement full of mercy that Christ Jesus came into this world to save sinners, of which I am the first. But I have obtained mercy so that Christ Jesus might in me reveal all his patience as an example for those who are going to believe for eternal life* (1 Tm 1:15-16). (5) He added: that he *might in me reveal all his patience* in order to bring you to understand that this refers to an evil life, not to the nature of human beings so that you would not think that by his coming Christ declared even little ones to be sinners. That is the patience of God about which Paul speaks to the Romans, *Do you not know that the goodness of God is leading you to repentance? But by your hard and unrepentant heart you store up for yourselves anger on the day of anger* (Rom 2:4-5). God practices his patience when he waits a long time for human conversion. But in little ones his patience cannot be manifested. For if there were sins of nature for the savior to attribute to them, it would not be true to call him patient, but would certainly be true to call him cruel. God, however, can only be just and good; such is my God Jesus Christ, and either Paul who was long his persecutor or others in whose name he is speaking have experienced his patience, because God waited long for them, though they were at last set free.

(6) And for this reason the apostle condemns the life of human beings, not their nature. He recommends this grace, therefore, to the Jews because the law punishes the wicked and does not have the same effect of mercy as baptism in which sins are washed away by a brief confession of one's actions. He shows that they ought to run to Christ, implore the help of his pardon, and realize that, while the law threatens moral wounds, grace quickly and effectively heals them. And so, he called, not the flesh, but sins the body of death. For if he had spoken about the wretched state of the members which you think resulted from sin, he would have more correctly called it the death of the body than the body of death. But so that you may know that sins are called members in accord with the custom of the scriptures, read the Letter to the Colossians where the same apostle said, (7) *Put to death your members which are upon the earth: fornication, impurity, and avarice, which is the worship of idols, on account of which the anger of God comes upon the children of unbelief, among whom you once walked when you lived among them* (Col 3:5-7). See how he calls members what he says are sins. But in the Letter to the Romans he speaks of the body of sin itself: *Our old self was nailed to the cross with Christ that the body of sin might be destroyed so that we might no longer be slaves to sin* (Rom 6:6). In this fashion he also cried out here in the person of the Jews, as we have already said: *Wretched man that I am,*

who will set me free from the body of this death? (Rom 7:24). That is, who will set me free from the guilt of my sins which I have committed, though I could have avoided them? These sins the severity of the law does not pardon, but avenges. (8) Who can release me from these members, that is, from the vices which I have gathered by imitation of the wicked so that I built up a body full of sin? Who, I ask? And he answers, as if stirred by a cry from the facts themselves: *The grace of God through Jesus Christ our Lord* (Rom 7:25). The grace of God which causes the righteousness of believers to be accepted without works, in accord with the words of David, *Blessed are those whose iniquities are forgiven and whose sins are covered; blessed are they to whom the Lord does not impute sin* (Ps 32:1-2). He, therefore, who makes human beings blessed, is himself blessed with everlasting righteousness by which he does not pardon a sin unless he could justly impute it. But he could not justly impute it if the person to whom it is imputed could not also avoid it. But no one can avoid what is natural; therefore, no one at all can have sin from the necessity of nature. Let it suffice to have briefly said this.

AUG. (1) By your argument you tried to change the words of the apostle, *Who will set me free from the body of this death?* (Rom 7:24), into your meaning. But the one who sent the document to the illustrious person saw better that you could not do this. And so when he quoted my words, he omitted those of the apostle so that your reply which he expected and which you gave would not be subjected to ridicule. For who would not laugh at this? You thought that you could persuade others of something of which I do not know whether you can persuade yourselves, namely, that the apostle spoke in the person of a Jew who was not yet under the grace of Christ and said, *Wretched man that I am, who will set me free from the body of this death? The grace of Christ through Jesus Christ our Lord* (Rom 7:24-25). Is he then a Jew and not yet a Christian who says: The grace of God will set me free through Jesus Christ our Lord? (2) But I leave that out. Who will put up with the idea that the man said, *Who will set me free from the body of this death?* about his past sins so that they might be forgiven by the grace of Christ who pardons him, since it is clearly evident how he came to these words? Listen; his words are ringing in our ears. Let us see, then, whether he says that he is wretched because of what he did willingly or because of what he does unwillingly. The man cries out: *I do not do what I will, but I do what I hate* (Rom 7:15). He cries out: *It is no longer I who cause that, but the sin that dwells in me. I know, after all, that the good does not dwell in me, that is, in my flesh. For I can will the good, but I find that I cannot bring it to completion. For I do not do the good that I will, but I carry out the evil that I do not will* (Rom 7:17-19).[123] (3) He does not say, "I did," but "I do." He does not say, "I caused," but "I cause." He does not say, "I carried out," but "I carry out," and not "what I will," but "what I do not will." Finally, he takes delight in the law of God in his inner self, but he sees another law in his members that resists the law of his mind.[124] And by that law he is driven to do not the good that he wills, but the evil that he does not will. On this account he cries out, *Wretched man that I am, who will set me free from the body of this death?* (Rom 7:24). And you close your eyes to the perfectly clear truth and you explain his groan, not as it is evident to all, but as it pleases you, when you say that *Who will set me free from the body of this death?* (Rom 7:24) means: "Who will set me free from the guilt of my own sins which I committed?" He said, *I do the evil that I do not will* (Rom 7:19), and you say: "the sins which I committed."

(4) Do you so despair of those who read these pages that you suppose that they will not prefer to listen to him rather than you and to believe him rather than you? Permit him to beg for the grace of God, not only that he may be forgiven because he has sinned, but also that he may be helped so that he does not sin. That is what he does in this passage. For, where he says, *I do the evil that I do not will* (Rom 7:19), it is not the place to say, *Forgive us our debts* (Mt 6:12), but, *Bring us not into temptation* (Mt 6:13). *But each is tempted,* as the apostle James says, *drawn and attracted by one's own concupiscence* (Jas 1:14). This is the evil of which Paul says, *I know that the good does not dwell in me, that is, in my flesh* (Rom 7:18). (5) This evil exists in the body of this death. This evil did not exist in paradise before the sin, because this flesh was not yet the body of this death to which we shall say in the end of time, *Where, death, is your strength?* (1 Cor 15:55). But we shall say this when this corruptible body has put on incorruptibility and this mortal body has put on immortality.[125] Now it is the body of death because the same apostle said, *The body is dead on account of sin* (Rom 8:10). Listen to the Catholic interpreters of the apostle; accept, not my words, but the words of those along with whom I receive your abuse. Listen, not to Pelagius, but to Ambrose. He says, "Even Paul's flesh was the body of death, as he himself said, *Who will set me free from the body of this death?*"[126] (Rom 7:24).

(6) Listen, not to Caelestius,[127] but to Gregory. He says, "We are under attack within ourselves from our own vices and passions, and we are day and night oppressed by the burning temptations of the body of this lowliness and of the body of death. In it the snares of visible things everywhere entice and arouse us at times in a hidden way, at other times quite openly, and the clay of these dregs to which we cling breathes forth the foul odor of its filth through its larger passages. The law of sin which is in our members resists the law of the spirit."[128] You bark at these luminaries of the heavenly city and say, "He called, not the flesh, but sins the body of death." You deny that the apostle applied this to the mortality of our body, and you say, "which the flesh of living beings received with the creation of their nature." (7) You hold the view which Pelagius condemned in the Palestinian court with a heart that was not sincere, namely, that Adam was created mortal so that, whether he sinned or did not sin, he was going to die.[129] And in that way

you are opposed to these men and to other companions of theirs of sound faith, so many and such great teachers, and you are forced to fill paradise, even if no one had sinned, with the pain of women giving birth, the struggle of the newborn, the groans of the sick, the funerals of the dead, and the grief of the mourners. Why, then, is it surprising that you have left this paradise, namely, the Church? For you have made that paradise from which those who sent us into these miseries by sinning the sort of paradise that no human beings—I will not say: no Christians—would dare to imagine unless they were insane.

Ambiguity over the Meaning of Death

68. JUL. In my first work, after all, this was discussed at greater length. And yet, you do not state clearly which death you want us to understand, when you say that its body was not in paradise before the sin. For in the books which you dedicated to Marcellinus, you admitted that Adam was created mortal.[130] When you add that the activity of marriage is a disease, one can listen to this calmly, if you are saying this of your parents alone. For you could perhaps know of some hidden disease of your mother, for in the books of your *Confessions* you indicated that she was called—to use your word—a tippler.[131] But in the marriage of holy people and of all decent people there is absolutely no disease. Nor did the apostle offer a disease instead of a remedy when he protected men of the Church from the disease of fornication by a respect for marriage. In almost the last part of my first volume I showed how this understanding of the text completely destroys the impudence of your teaching, and I explained it in the whole body of my reply, as the various passages provided the occasion.

AUG. (1) Never has your deceit been so clear, and your knowledge condemns your conscience. For you know this; you certainly know it; it is so obvious that one who reads those books cannot fail to know this. You know, I insist, that in those books which I dedicated to Marcellinus I acted vigorously in opposition to your heresy that was beginning to arise at that time so that no one would believe that Adam would have died, whether he sinned or did not sin. But I called him mortal inasmuch as he could die, for he was able to sin. You wanted by your insidious sham to keep this fact from those who have not read those books, or perhaps will not read them, if they should happen to read your books. You pretend that I said: Adam was created mortal so that, whether he sinned or did not sin, he was going to die. (2) For this is the point at issue with you; the whole question between you and us centers on this point: We say that, if Adam had not sinned, he would not have suffered the death of the body, but you say that he would have died bodily death whether he sinned or did not sin. Why is it that you pretend that you do not know what death I want you to understand when I say that its body was not in paradise before the sin? After all, you know what I showed in those books; you know how clearly and plainly I showed that God would not have said to the sinner facing punishment, *You are earth, and you will return to the earth* (Gn 3:19)—which everyone understands was said of the death of the body—if Adam would have had to return to the earth, that is, would have had to die bodily death, even if he committed no sin.

(3) As for your idea that you should also heap abuse upon my mother who harmed you in no way and never said anything against you, you are overwhelmed by the desire to speak evil, and you do not fear the words of scripture: *Those who speak evil will not possess the kingdom of God* (1 Cor 6:10). But why is it a surprise that you prove yourself her enemy as well, since you are an enemy of the grace of God by which I said that she was set free from her childish failing? I, however, regard your parents as good Catholic Christians, and I congratulate them for having died before they saw you a heretic.[132] We do not, however, say that the marital act is a disease, that is, to have intercourse for the sake of procreating children, not for the sake of satisfying sexual desire. You deny that this sexual desire is a disease, though you admit that the remedy of marriage was provided for it. (4) For in order to avoid committing fornication, one opposes, resists, and fights against the sexual desire which you praise. And if the desire goes beyond the limit which was established for procreating children, at least the spouse who yields to it sins in a pardonable way with the other. For the apostle was speaking to married couples when he said, *Do not deprive each other except for a time by mutual consent so that you have time for prayer, and then return to it so that Satan does not tempt you on account of your lack of self-control*; then he immediately adds, *I say this by way of concession, not by way of command* (1 Cor 7:5-6). Marital chastity, then, makes good use of this evil only by the intention to have children; one yields to this evil in a pardonable way with one's spouse, not for the sake of having children, but for the sake of carnal pleasure; (5) one resists this evil so that one does not carry out the desire for sinful pleasure. This evil dwells in the body of this death; on account of its untimely arousal, even when the mind does not give its consent, the apostle says, *I know that the good does not dwell in me, that is, in my flesh* (Rom 7:18). This evil was not present in the body of that life. Then either sexual desire did not exist when even the genital organs obeyed the will, or it was absolutely never aroused against the choice of the will. Those who, before they sinned, were naked and not ashamed,[133] were ashamed of this evil that suddenly appeared. You have also impudently scattered praise for this evil in those four books of yours, to which I was forced to reply by six of mine.

69. JUL. (1) In order to come to this mention of human misery and divine grace, the apostle said above, *I see another law in my members that resists the law of my mind and holds me captive in the law of sin* (Rom 7:23) After these words he cried out, *Who will set me free from the body of this death? The grace of*

God through Jesus Christ our Lord. It is agreed that, after he set forth the words which you cited, the apostle added, *Wretched man that I am, who will set me free from the body of this death? The grace of God through Jesus Christ our Lord* (Rom 7:24-25). But at the present moment we are not asking whether the apostle said this; rather, we are asking about the faith, the meaning, the reason with which he said this. (2) For the law in his members was at the beginning of his conversion rebellious against holy counsels because of a life of wickedness, and he called this law an evil habit which the learned of the world often call a second nature. For just before, he turned to those to whom he was speaking with a re- proach and said: *What I say is only human on account of the weakness of your flesh; for as you offered your members to serve uncleanness and iniquity upon iniquity, so now offer your members to serve righteousness for sanctification* (Rom 6:19). To show that he called the flesh not this body which has its causes in the seeds, but in a loose sense called the flesh its defects, he added some two chapters later, *When we were in the flesh, sinful passions which are revealed through the law were at work in our members to bear fruit for death* (Rom 7:5). (3) Thus he said, *When we were in the flesh* as if he was not in the flesh at the time he was writing. But one who knows the scriptures recognizes this kind of lan- guage. And so, where the sameness of words raises a question, one applies the rule of reason by whose evenness we measure those things which we suspect to have deviated from it. Besides, Faustus, the bishop of the Manichees, your teacher, relies especially upon this testimony of the apostle against us; he says that by his words about the law, namely, the law which dwells in the members and resists counsel, the apostle meant nothing other than the evil nature. Hence, you ought to do nothing less than interpret this passage as they expound it; other- wise, when you follow the same twisted path which Faustus traced, you seem not to argue, but to give us what you passed over.

AUG. (1) Let the Catholic and learned Gregory, and not the Manichean Fau- stus, answer you. He did not "at the beginning of his conversion," to use your words, "call the law in his members that is rebellious against holy counsels be- cause of a life of wickedness an evil habit which the learned of the world often call a second nature." Rather, he clearly and plainly attributed the law of sin which is in our members and that resists the law of the mind to this mortal and earthly body of ours. He said that the law of sin which is in our members resists the law of the Spirit, "as it strives to take captive the royal image which is in us so that all that has been poured into us by the gift of our original and divine creation becomes its booty. (2) From there," he says, "though they govern themselves with a long and uncompromising pursuit of wisdom and gradually recover the nobility of their soul, hardly any summon back and turn back to God the nature of the light which is joined in them to this humble and dark clay. Or if they do this with God's help, they will call both of them back equally, if by long and constant meditation they become used to always looking upwards and to pulling up by tighter reins the matter bound to them that always drags them wrongly downward and weighs them down."[134] Blessed Gregory said these things, not at the beginning of his conversion, but when he was already a bishop and wanted to tell or rather to remind people of what they already knew, namely, the kind and magnitude of the fight with interior defects due to the body that weighs down the soul[135] in which the saints find themselves. (3) This fight would not, of course, have existed in that place of blessed peace, that is, in the paradise of holy delights, if no one had sinned. For in paradise there would not have been the body of this death by the corruptibility of which the soul is weighed down; rather, there would have been the body of that life in which the flesh would not have desires opposed to the spirit so that the spirit would have to have desires opposed to the flesh.[136] Instead, human nature would rejoice in the happy harmony of the two. If, then, you wanted to fight against and not help the Manichees who introduce another nature and substance of evil, you certainly would not deny, along with your companions in deception, these miseries of human life which begin with infancy and are evident to all. Rather you would admit along with Catholic believers and highly renowned teachers the reason why our nature, which was originally created in happiness, has fallen into these miseries.

70. JUL. To sum up what we have done, then, I did not introduce any deception into your statements, nor did you produce something that you could spread about with at least a somewhat faint color of piety—not to mention something that you could prove by testimonies from the scriptures. The apostle did not understand what you think, and there was no other condition of intercourse in paradise than is now found in marriage. God clearly taught that this marriage was instituted by him as much by the creation of the sexes and the character of the members as by his frequent blessing of it. With those points taken care of, it is clear that all those who are deceived by you are more deserving of anger than of mercy, because in order to excuse their serious sins which they commit by an evil will, they blame their birth at your instigation in order to avoid correcting their actions.

AUG. (1) In this life it is a pious action to worship God and by his grace to fight against internal defects, not to give in to them when they urge and push us to forbidden acts, and to ask pardon with a disposition of religious piety when we give in and the help of God so that we do not give in. But in paradise, if no one had sinned, it would not be an act of piety to fight against those defects, because the continuance of happiness would have meant not having defects. That praise of defects which you frequently practice with impudence is not a sign of human beings who truly fight against these defects. And so, Julian, when Ambrose said, "All of us human beings are born under the power of sin, and our very origin lies in guilt,"[137] was he really saying that under my instigation? Or was he blaming his birth to avoid correcting his actions? (2) Gregory said, "Show reverence for the birth by which you have been set free from the chains of earthly birth,"[138] and he said, in speaking of Christ or the Holy Spirit, "He washes away the stains of our first birth by which we are conceived in iniquity and our mothers gave birth to us in sins."[139] Hilary said of King David, "He knows that he was born under the origin of sin and under the law of sin."[140] Were these men blaming their birth to avoid correcting their actions? Will you dare to persuade your heart that the Pelagians' way of acting should be preferred to their way of acting? Pardon me, but we would never believe that you live a better life than they, not even if you did not love concupiscence of the flesh so much that you wanted to locate it even in paradise before the sin with the same character it now has when it has desires opposed to the spirit. (3) For if, as you say, "there was no other condition of intercourse in paradise than is now found in marriage," there was present in paradise even before the sin the carnal desire without which the two sexes cannot now be united. If, then, you reject the idea that in that beatitude the genital organs, which were not yet a cause of shame, could obey the will of the human beings without sexual desire in order to carry out their function of conceiving a child, I still ask you: What sort of sexual desire do you believe that was? It surely would have followed the will when it would be needed. But, even when it was not needed for propagating children, did it arouse their mind and drive them to intercourse, whether just any acts of intercourse that deserve condemnation or those with one's spouse which are pardonable? For if it was then as it is now, it certainly did that, whether they resisted it by self-control or gave in to it by a lack of self-control. (4) And in that way human beings would be forced to obey sexual desire by sinning or to fight against it in an internal war, and you see, if you have any common sense, that one of these is not in accord with moral goodness and the other is not in accord with the peace of that happiness. The conclusion is, then, that, if sexual desire was present there, it was subject to the will so that it neither pulled the upright and peaceful mind toward sin nor challenged it to battle and did not compel the spirit that was obeying God and enjoying God either to sin or to fight. It is not now that sort of desire; rather, it desires even what is permitted with wild longing and without self-control, while in what is not permitted it either drags down the spirit or has desires opposed to it. And so, recognize that this evil was contracted when the integrity of our nature was damaged. The chastity of married couples makes good use of this evil in the act of procreation, and from this evil we derive the bond of our birth in guilt which must be removed by rebirth.

71. JUL. (1) But enough on this point; now I shall take up those words that follow. "In the body of this death, then, of the sort that was certainly not found in paradise before the sin, another law in our members resists the law of the mind, because even when we refuse and when we do not consent and do not offer our members to it to carry out what it desires, it still dwells in them and entices the mind that resists and fights back so that the very conflict is wretched because it

does not allow peace, even if it is not worthy of condemnation, because it does not carry out the iniquity."[141] We teach by the testimony of the whole world that the pleasure of all the senses is natural. But that this pleasure of concupiscence existed in paradise before the sin is shown by the fact that the path to sin lay through concupiscence. For when it tempted the eyes with the beauty of the fruit, it also aroused the hope of a pleasant taste. (2) When this concupiscence does not hold to the proper limit, it is sinful, but when it is held within the boundary of what is permitted, it is a natural and innocent longing. This concupiscence could not; it could not, I say, be the result of sin, for we are taught that it was the occasion of sin, not by reason of its own defect, but by reason of a defect of the will. Read my second book on this point as well; you will find that what we say is able to convince even your mind. You presented a supposedly clever idea, namely, that the law of sin is found in our members, and begins to involve sin when we consent, but that, when we do not consent, it only stirs up a battle and brings about misery by disturbing our peace. Does anyone with wisdom fail to see the contradiction? (3) For if the law of sin, that is, sin and the necessity of sinning is naturally implanted in our members, what good does it do not to consent to it, since it is necessary to undergo punishment on account of its very existence? Or if it is the law of sin, but when I do not consent to it, it does not commit sin, the power of the human will is incalculable, since—if I may be permitted to state the absurdity—it forces sin itself not to sin. But we come back to the point that what you say is inconsistent. For if it does not sin, it is not the law of sin; but if it is the law of sin, it commits sin. But if it sins simply because it exists, how can it be resisted so that sin is not committed, since it cannot be driven away so that it gives up the work of sin?

AUG. (1) I already replied to your second book with my fourth book, and I proved you guilty of speaking nonsense. But let the readers see whether one should answer a man who has advanced to such great madness that, though he admits that sin is evil, he says that the desire for sins is good. And yet we are compelled to answer, because we do not want to abandon the slower minds of those to whom these writings might find their way. What is it, then, that you say, though you do not know what you are saying? Was there, then, already in paradise before the seductive venom of the serpent, before the will was corrupted by his sacrilegious words, a desire for the forbidden food? And—what is more intolerable to say—did it entice toward evil, but was not evil itself? Did these human beings see the fruit of the forbidden tree and desire it, but the concupiscence of the spirit resisted the concupiscence of the flesh so that they did not eat it? And did they live in that place of such great happiness, though they did not have in themselves peace of mind and of body? (2) You are not so deranged that you believe this; you are not so impudent that you say this. Understand this, then, or do not overwhelm with your empty chatter those who do understand. First came the evil will by which they believed the deceitful serpent, and then there followed the evil desire by which they hankered after the forbidden food. In paradise, then, it was not just any desire that struggled against just any will; it was, rather, an evil desire that obeyed an evil will. And so, though both were already evil, the will led the desire, not the desire the will; the desire neither preceded the will nor resisted it. Hence, if the will turned aside from the forbidden action before the commission of the sin, the wrongful desire would have subsided without any difficulty.

(3) Speaking of this, blessed Ambrose says, "When the flesh returns to its nature, it recognizes the source of the nourishment for its strength; then having set aside its bold arrogance, it is wedded to the judgment of the soul that governs it. The flesh was in such a condition when it received the hidden places of paradise as its dwelling, before it was infected with the venom of the deadly serpent and experienced a sacrilegious hunger. Then out of a gluttonous desire it ignored the memory of the divine commandments impressed on the senses of the soul. From this source sin is reported to have flowed forth from the body and soul as from its parents; when the nature of the body is tempted, the soul in its ill health suffers with it. If the soul had held in check the desire of the body, the origin of sin would have been destroyed in its very source."[142] (4) Do you see how the Catholic teacher and a man endowed with Christian wisdom called the very desire for the forbidden food a sacrilegious hunger, though you say that it is innocent if it is not allowed to carry out what it wants? And yet, if by an upright will "the soul had held in check this desire of the body, the origin of sin," he says, "would have been destroyed in its very source." But since the desire for the forbidden food was not suppressed, the sin was committed, and the origin of sin was not destroyed, but flowed into future generations. And so great a discord between the flesh and the spirit ensued that, as the same teacher says in another passage, it became part of our nature by the transgression of the first human being.[143]

(5) But in opposition to these ideas you say that you "teach by the testimony of the whole world that the pleasure of all the senses is natural." You imply that the pleasure of all the senses could not be sufficient for our nature in the body, not of this death, but of that life, so that because of the supreme harmony of the mind and the flesh in possession of virtue we would desire nothing forbidden. How much you are mistaken! From the present corruptibility and weakness of our nature, you form an idea of the holy delights of paradise and of that blessedness! For that immortality in which a human being would not have had to die is one thing; this mortality in which one has to die is another, but that supreme immortality in which one will not be able to die is still another. (6) Why do you fight a battle over concupiscence that itself fights a battle, that is, over the law in the members that resists the law of the mind? It is called the law of sin because it urges and—so to speak—orders us to sin, and if one obeys it with the mind, one sins without excuse. It is called sin because it was produced by sin and it longs to commit sin. Its guilt is removed by rebirth; the conflict with it is left for our test-

ing. It is an evil; that is obvious. Nor do we, as you suppose, resist it by the strength of our will unless we are helped by God. This evil must be defeated, not denied; it must be conquered, not defended. Finally, if you consent to it, recognize its evil in your sinning; if you resist it, recognize its evil in your fighting it.

72. JUL. (1) Or what good does it do to be moderate about some factor whose mere existence brings accusations against itself? See, then, where your clever wits have carried you. First, you say that nature sins without the will—which is impossible. Second, you say that there is sin and that it does not sin, that is, one and the same thing is and is not. Then, when it disturbs the peace, it evokes pity, though it is not punished for the crime of destroying the peace, but when it carries out the sin, it deserves condemnation. But just as the law of sin itself deserves punishment, it excuses the will of a human being. For a law that is compelling and natural and always present certainly cannot be overpowered by the will, and no one can be guilty on account of what one could not avoid. But even the law itself does not sin since it could not do anything else. (2) God, however, ascribes to guilt actions that are unavoidable, nor does anyone force him to do this great evil. With everything else absolved of guilt, he alone is found to be a criminal for with an astounding impudence he imposes necessity upon others, while he himself does wrong without any necessity. Well done, most noble professor of wisdom! In order to praise his gifts you have destroyed judgment by the steps of Punic dialectics. To give the appearance of grace, you have overthrown justice; to speak ill of nature, you have brought charges against the creator of human beings, and you have brought charges against him to the point that your God is seen as more guilty not merely than some sinner, but than the law of sin itself. And after all this, you insult with great sacrilege Catholic priests when you say that they deny the grace of Christ whose justice they defend, for we praise the mercy of his remedies while the justice of his laws stands firm.

AUG. (1) I wish you would acknowledge the Catholic priests who, long before you came to be, said that concupiscence of the flesh corrupted human nature after the sin that was committed in paradise. That concupiscence has desires opposed to the spirit, although the spirit also has desires opposed to it,[144] for it is understood to be the law of sin which resists the law of the mind.[145] As a result of it no one is now born without it, and in holy people the spirit is opposed to it so that they live righteously by fighting against it until it does not exist at all, when the salvation of the human being is complete and the flesh is perfectly in harmony with the spirit. Ambrose says that by the transgression of the first human being the dissension between the flesh and the spirit became part of our nature,[146] and Cyprian—a Punic man in whom, I think, you will not dare to mock Punic dialectics, as you have dared to do with me—points out this dissension as follows. (2) He said, "There is a conflict between the flesh and the spirit, and there is a daily battle because they are at war with each other so that we do not do what we will. While the spirit seeks heavenly and divine things, the flesh desires earthly and worldly things. For this reason we ask that God's help and assistance bring about peace between the two so that the soul that was reborn through him may be saved, as the will of God is carried out in both the spirit and the flesh. The apostle Paul clearly and plainly states this point in his own words. He said, *The flesh has desires opposed to the spirit, and the spirit has desires opposed to the flesh, for these are opposed to each other so that you do not do what you will* (Gal 5:17).[147] You do not even admit that this peace between the flesh and the spirit, which Cyprian says that we ask and pray for from the Lord, existed in paradise before the sin. (3) Or if it was there, why do you not admit that it was lost when our nature was corrupted by the transgression of the first human being and that wretched discord took the place of blessed peace between the soul and body? You are angry at us because we insult with our words supposedly Catholic priests, that is, you people, because we say that you deny the grace of Christ. And yet, with great impudence and sacrilege you insult these truly Catholic priests with these words which in your confused madness you spit out at me who follow and defend their faith. The apostle says, *Walk by the Spirit, and do not carry out the concupiscences of the flesh* (Gal 5:16). I ask you: Why does he mention them if they do not exist? Why does he forbid us to carry them out if they are good? But he even shows the sort of desires they are when he says, *For the flesh has desires opposed to the spirit, and the spirit has desires opposed to the flesh, for these are opposed to each other so that you do not do what you will* (Gal 5:17). To whom did he say: *So that you do not do what you will?* Was it to the Jews who were not yet under the grace of Christ, as your astounding interpretation has it? Or was it to those to whom he had said, *Have you received the Spirit through the works of the law or through the obedience of faith?* (Gal 3:2). He said, then, that believing Christians did not do what they willed because the flesh has desires opposed to the spirit. Why is this but that they wanted their lower part to agree with their higher part, that is, the flesh with the spirit, and they were not able to carry out what they willed? There remained for them not to consent to that defect, but by the spirit to have desires opposed to the flesh. (5) But even if what you suppose was the case with them, namely, that they unwillingly lived bad lives because of a bad habit, why, then, do you say that nature cannot sin without the will since you admit that they sin though they are unwilling to? But we have already explained above why concupiscence of the flesh is called sin or the law of sin.[148] If it is good not to consent to it for acts that are forbidden, it is, of course, something evil by which we desire those forbidden acts, even though they are not carried out by any consent or by any action. Moreover, you destroy the judgments of God when you say that the miseries of the human race that begin with the little ones come about without any sin that merited them, and you do not ask for the gift of God in order that you do not enter into temptation,[149] that is, in order that you do not sin. For you place your confidence in your own virtue,[150] and either in your blindness you do not see that you are censured and condemned in the holy psalm, or in your stupidity you feel no sorrow over it.

Further Questions about Marriage and Desire

73. JUL. (1) But let us now move on to my words which he took from the preface and set forth to be attacked by himself: "I think that I have given sufficient warning that, in order to refute my words, he chose to set them forth in such a way that in some places he split the sentences by removing words in the middle and in others he clipped them off by removing the final words. I hope that I have sufficiently shown why he did this. Now let us look at his own words which he set forth in opposition to our words which he cited as he chose. For there follow his own words. As the person indicated who sent you the document, he first copied part of the preface, undoubtedly, from the books from which he made the few excerpts. (2) It reads as follows: 'Teachers of our time, my blessed brother, and instigators of a rebellion that is still raging, have resolved to obtain through the ruin of the whole Church the dishonor and death of those persons whose holy aspirations are causing them pain. They do not understand the great honor they bestowed upon those persons in showing that they could not destroy their glory without destroying the Catholic religion. For, if any say that there is free choice in human beings or that God is the creator of the newborn, they are called Pelagians or Caelestians. And so, to avoid being called heretics, they become Manichees, and out of fear of a false bad reputation, they rush into a true crime, like beasts surrounded by fans of feathers so that they are driven into the nets. Because they lack reason, they are driven to true destruction out of an empty fear.' "[151]

(3) I recognize my statements, but they are not quoted by you in their entirety, and though the main point of our dispute is not found in them since they are from the preface, I shall, nonetheless, reveal your superficiality. The phrase, "my blessed brother," was not in that place, but in the very first line of my book. So too, when I said, "To obtain the dishonor and death of those persons whose holy aspirations are causing them pain," I added, "because another path did not lie open to them, they decided to get there through the ruin of the whole Church." (4) After that I also said, "Those who confess free choice and God the creator are called Caelestians or Pelagians, and the simple folk are frightened by those bad words and even abandon the sound faith in order to escape from the odium of those names. They will undoubtedly believe that there is no free choice in human beings and that God is not the creator of the newborn when they have abandoned both points which they previously maintained." But you omitted all this. Next there are those lines which you quoted; it will not be a difficult task to prove how true and how irrefutable they are. I have not, therefore, omitted anything from

your statements, but you have not reported even my first chapter as I had presented it. I emphasize this point so that one can see just how serious the Punic author is.

AUG. The person who sent those excerpts from your books which he chose to whom he chose in order that they might be read did what you attribute to me, nor do I think you yourself believe anything else. Nor did I fail, after all, to mention in the preface of that same book of mine against which you are barking the document to which I was forced to reply, but you are looking for something to say by way of abuse, since you see that you have nothing valid to say by way of argument. And yet even in these words of mine which you set forth in order, as you say, to refute them, you could have noticed what I say. For I would not have said, "It is not as you claim, whoever you are who said this," if I had been certain that you had said it and not the person who sent the writing which he chose and to whom he chose—the writing which I undertook to refute after it was sent to me. But thanks be to God that I have with the help of God replied to this whole work of yours, from which that person made the excerpts he wanted as he wanted, so that I have overthrown all your machines of war which you, a new heretic, had raised up against the most ancient Catholic faith.

74. JUL. Let us, then, listen to what you have written in response to those words of mine: "It is not as you claim; whoever you are who said this, it is not as you claim. You are greatly mistaken, or you are trying to lead others into error. We do not deny free choice. Rather, *If the Son sets you free*, the truth says, *then you will truly be free* (Jn 8:36). You begrudge him as deliverer to those captives to whom you attribute a false freedom. *After all, one becomes a slave*, as scripture says, *to one's conqueror* (2 Pt 2:19). And no one is set free from this chain of slavery, from which no human being is exempt, except by the grace of the deliverer. *Through one man sin came into the world, and through sin death, and in that way it was passed on to all human beings, in whom all have sinned* (Rom 5:12).[152] That the importance of our case is immense is indicated by a consideration and evaluation of the points which we defend as well as by your fear. For though you fight against the lives of our people by outlays of money, the bestowal of inheritances, the sending of horses, the incitement of the people, and the corruption of officials, you are ashamed to profess your faith which we attack, and you take refuge in the words of our position from which you have strayed.

AUG. Either you slander us knowingly if you made up these lies, or without knowing what you say, you share the belief of others who make up these lies. But let my previous reply suffice for your folly or for your malice.

75. JUL. (1) The doctrine which the shameful apostasy of Babylon has adopted is so criminal that you deny it when we raise it as an objection, and what we believe is so holy that you desire to hide in its shadow, though your mind is against it. For I stated the main points which were contained here and there in

parts of your argument and compressed the heart of the question into a few words so that the importance and tenor of the cause of dissension in the Church would be revealed without smoke and clouds. I said that you denied free choice and that God is the creator of the newborn, while we defend both of these points. I said that on account of this you rouse an empty clamor in the ears of the uneducated with the names of Catholic men who labor along with us[153] on account of the apostolic faith which we defend. The result is that those who feared being called Caelestians by you lost the glory of the celestial faith and that those who were aghast at being called Pelagians by you cast themselves into the sea of the Manichees.[154] Some of the ignorant supposed that they could not be called Christians, if the traducianists called them Pelagians, while the wise have, on the contrary, decided that they ought to endure any hatred and injury from such names rather than abandon the Catholic faith. (2) But so that you do not boast that your wits have invented this kind of abuse, recall that we are used to receiving different names from all the heretics. But the Synod of Rimini made it strikingly clear what a crime either the ambiguity of a word or the threat of a new term can produce in hearts of lead. For under an Arian emperor, when almost the whole world fell away from the faith of the apostles, Athanasius, the bishop of Alexandria,[155] a man of great constancy and of the soundest faith, withstood the times of unbelief, and for this reason he was forced into exile. Of six hundred and fifty bishops, it is reported, scarcely seven were found who held God's commandments more precious than the king's, that is, so that they did not consent to the condemnation of Athanasius and did not deny the confession of the Trinity. That whole multitude of abject souls—apart from fear of injuries—was led astray chiefly by this threat of being called Athanasians or by the cleverness by which they were questioned.

AUG. The Arians call the Catholics Athanasians or homoousians,[156] but the other heretics do not. You, however, are called Pelagians not only by the Catholics, but also by heretics like yourselves and those who disagree with you, just as the Arians are called Arians not only by the Catholic Church, but also by other heresies. But you alone call us traducianists, as the Arians call us homoousians, as the Donatists call us Macarians,[157] as the Manichees call us Pharisees,[158] and the other heretics call us by different names.

76. JUL. For when the Arians who at that time were in power asked: Do you want to follow the homoousios or Christ? they replied immediately, as if out of reverence for the name, that they follow Christ and repudiate the homoousios.[159] And so they go away rejoicing, for they think they believe in Christ whom they deny, when they deny that he is homoousios, that is, of one substance with the Father.[160] And now, you fashioners of deceit, you terrify the ears of the unlearned in the same way so that, if they do not want to be spattered with disgrace by being named after some men who are toiling for the faith, they deny both free choice and God as the creator of human beings. This objection, then, which I

made in that passage remains valid, and the present discussion will make it clear how correct it is. You replied, therefore, in this way, "We do not deny free choice," and you added nothing else of your own. It would have been logical for you to complete the statement without any attempt to escape and, since you said that you do not deny freedom of choice, to add: "But we confess that freedom of choice which God gave remains in the nature of human beings."

AUG. How does freedom remain in those people who need divine grace so that they may be set free from the slavery by which they were handed over to victorious sin—unless they are in fact free, but free with regard to righteousness? For this reason the apostle said, *When you were slaves of sin, you were free with regard to righteousness* (Rom 6:20).

77. JUL. By those words you would have completed the sentence, and if you had spoken further against it, you would have appeared really impudent. If, however, you had stated everything logically,[161] you could later, but not too late, have appeared quite correct. But you now say that I am being deceitful, though I can prove the correctness of my objection by your own words, and you immediately utter a lie in what you suppose you have logically established. For you say, "We do not deny free choice," and you add the statement from the gospel, "Rather, *If the Son sets you free*, the truth says, *then you will truly be free*" (Jn 8:36), though in that passage our Lord Jesus Christ clearly did not say this regarding free choice. Let us put off for a little while the explanation of this statement and make clear by definitions and distinctions what each of us holds. According to the teaching of all the learned, the beginning of a discussion ought, of course, to start with a definition.

AUG. Were the apostles, then, who did not begin their discussions with a definition, not learned? And yet they were the teachers of the nations and held in contempt the sort of teachers in whom your pride takes delight. You will try to twist the Lord's words, *If the Son sets you free, then you will truly be free* (Jn 8:36), into your meaning, but it will be evident, when you begin to try this, that they will not go along with you.

A Definition of Free Choice

78. JUL. As the famous author says,[162] every discussion which reason undertakes on any question ought to start off from a definition so that one may understand what is the subject under discussion. And so, as we above discussed the definition of justice and sin, let us now also see what definition belongs to freedom of choice so that it may be clear who of us agrees with it and who is against it. Freedom of choice by which a human being has received emancipation from God consists in the possibility of committing sin and of refraining from sin.

AUG. You say that a human being has received emancipation from God, and you do not notice that one who is emancipated no longer belongs to the household of the father.[163]

79. JUL. The rational mortal animal was made capable of virtue and vice so that it is able by the ability granted to it to observe or to transgress the commandments of God or to preserve the law of human society by the teaching of nature. It is free to will one or the other alternative, and in that lies the essence of sin and righteousness. For, when in accord with virtue one squeezes something for the needy from either the fountains of mercy or the breasts of righteousness, righteousness itself carries this out externally after the holy will conceives this righteousness internally and brings it to birth.

AUG. Does it conceive righteousness from its own resources? That is the point at issue with you who do not know the righteousness of God and want to establish your own.[164] For the holy will, of course, conceives righteousness by a holy thought. Scripture says of it, *A holy thought will preserve you* (Prv 2:11 LXX), but the apostle says, *Not that we are sufficient to think something as if by ourselves; rather, our sufficiency comes from God* (2 Cor 3:5). If you would understand this, you would understand that choice that is free in a praiseworthy manner is nothing but choice that has been set free by the grace of God.

80. JUL. So it is. On the other hand, when any unjust or cruel persons decide to act in an evil manner to the injury of others, the action by which they harm others moves out into the external world from the wickedness which the evil will sowed and begot within. But when there is lacking the chance for the power of the hidden will to burst forth upon one's neighbors, the essence of goodness or malice is realized in the will alone which does something either good or bad, not by a sudden impulse, but by thought and desire.

AUG. You understand that the will realizes the essence of either goodness or malice by thought alone. If you would understand in that way what the apostle says in speaking of a good and holy thought, namely, that we are not able to think anything as if from ourselves, but that our sufficiency comes from God,[165] you will be able to be corrected. And you will be able humbly to receive the grace of which pride makes you an enemy as long as you want to be one of those *who place their trust in their own virtue* (Ps 49:7) and not one of those who say, *I love you, Lord, my virtue* (Ps 18:2).

81. JUL. The capability, then, for good and for evil is good because to be able to do good is the hallway to virtue, and to be able to do evil is evidence of freedom.

AUG. God then is not free. Scripture says of him, *He cannot deny himself* (2 Tm 2:13). And you yourself said of him, "God cannot but be just."[166] In another place you said, "But God can only be just and good."[167]

God's Judgment Implies Human Freedom

82. JUL. Human beings, then, are given the ability to have their own good by
that through which they can do evil. The whole fullness of divine judgment,
then, has so linked the actions of human beings with this freedom that a person
who acknowledges one of them acknowledges both of them. As a result, a person who does injury to one of them does injury to both. The freedom of human
choice, then, must be guarded, just as divine justice is guarded. This is the understanding of free choice which makes the theory of the fates, the calculations of
the Chaldeans, and the imagery of the Manichees subject to the Church's truth.
This is the understanding which reveals that you are also separated from Christ
along with those we listed. Freedom of choice, then, is the capability of committing or of avoiding sin, immune from compelling necessity; it has in its own
power which path it will follow of the two that suggest themselves, that is, either
the arduous and difficult paths of the virtues or the low and swampy paths of the
pleasures.

AUG. As long as human beings remained standing in the good will endowed
with free choice, they did not need that grace by which they might be raised up
once they could not rise up by themselves. But now in their fallen state they are
free of righteousness and slaves of sin, and they cannot be slaves of righteousness and free from sin's dominion unless the Son sets them free.[168]

83. JUL. To have done with this quickly, the capability is on watch only for
this: that one is not either impelled toward sin by someone or drawn away from
sin with a captive will. Courage, whose strength has often been glorious in its
contempt for pain both among the pagans and among the Christians, bears witness that the will cannot be taken captive, if it refuses to surrender.

AUG. This is, of course, what your heresy is after. For you also mention the
pagans so that Christians are not thought to be able to do or to have done an act of
noble courage by the grace of God, which belongs only to Christians and is not
common to the Christians and the pagans. Listen, then, to this, and understand:
Worldly desire produces the courage of the pagans; the love of God produces the
courage of the Christians—the love of God which *is poured out in our hearts*,
not by a choice of the will which comes from us, but *by the Holy Spirit who has
been given to us* (Rom 5:5).

84. JUL. If, then, as reason has revealed, freedom of choice banishes necessity so that no one is good or bad who is not free to do the opposite, how could
you have admitted free choice, when you were going to use a testimony which
applies to captives? Or could you have added such a testimony after you had already defended free choice? For you say, "We do not deny free choice. Rather, *if
the Son sets you free,* the truth says, *you will truly be free.*[169] (Jn 8:36). It is evident that in that passage Christ directed those words to a captive conscience
which he showed was not free, but subject to that retribution which condemns

sins committed by a free will. You understand that statement incorrectly; that is, you do not understand it. Or perhaps you do understand it, and you drag it in here contrary to its own nature, and you put it in that place where it clashes with your words by its own whole character. For to juxtapose these very words, that which is being set free is captive; that which is captive is not free; that which is free is not captive.

AUG. Forgiveness of sins in the case of those evils which we have committed is one thing; quite another is the love which makes us free to do the good things which we ought to do. Christ sets us free in both ways because he both takes away sinfulness by forgiving it and gives love by pouring it into us.

85. JUL. At this point simply admit whichever of the two you wish, and stop being evasive. Either say with us that choice is free, and remove the testimony which was appropriately uttered in its own time, or, as you said in those books you just sent to Boniface by means of Alypius,[170] say that the choice, which we say is free, is captive, and stop denying that you are a Manichee.

AUG. The Manichees in their madness mingle the immutable substance of evil with the nature of their God, and they make the same nature of God corruptible instead and want it to be captive under a foreign nature. The Catholic faith, however, says that a good, but mutable creature was changed for the worse by the will and, after its own nature was ruined and vitiated by this, it is held guilty and kept a slave not under a foreign substance, but under its own sin. And for this reason our views concerning the deliverer are also very different from theirs. For the Manichees say that there is need of a deliverer to separate the evil nature from us, but we say that there is need of a deliverer to heal and give life to our own nature. Show us, then, that you are not a helper of the Manichees, if you can. For the human race undoubtedly agrees that human beings are born with human miseries because it undoubtedly experiences them. You refuse to attribute these miseries to the sin of our damaged nature, and so you cause the Manichees to attribute them to a foreign nature mixed in with us.

86. JUL. But these two ideas which you link together, free and not free, that is, free and captive, cannot apply to the topic we are discussing. They bear witness that you possess a singular stupidity, a novel impudence, and an ancient impiety.

AUG. (1) We say that those people are free to do the works of piety to whom the apostle says, *Now you have been set free from sin; having become slaves to God, you have your return in sanctification, but your end as eternal life* (Rom 6:22). This return in sanctification is, of course, charity, and we can in no sense have it and its works from ourselves; rather, we have them *through the Holy Spirit who has been given to us* (Rom 5:5). God our teacher was speaking of this return when he said to the branches that remain in him, *Without me you can do nothing* (Jn 15:5). (2) But you revile us and say that we have a singular stupidity because God is our virtue and we do not place our confidence in our own virtue.

You say that we have a novel impudence because we do not with your effrontery praise the concupiscence of the flesh which has desires opposed to the spirit. You say that we have an ancient impiety because against your novel perversity we defend with our struggle, however slight it may be, the ancient Catholic teachings which those men taught who ruled the Church of Christ before us with true piety in his grace. Recognize then stupidity in yourself; recognize impudence in yourself; recognize impiety in yourself—not an ancient, but a new impiety.

The Sort of Freedom That Jesus Promised

87. JUL. (1) But now is the time to discuss the statement of the gospel. John the evangelist says, *Jesus said to the Jews who believed in him: If you remain in my word, you will truly be my disciples, and you will know the truth, and the truth will make you free* (Jn 8:31-32). That is, our Lord Jesus was saying to those who believed in him that they should not rejoice over any worldly honor or claim for themselves any glory as descendants of Abraham, but should strive to pursue[171] the virtues and to be slaves to no sins after coming to know Christ. For then they would possess true freedom with a joyous conscience, and by the hope of certain, that is, eternal goods they would be released from the desire for all other things, which are frequently called vain and false because of their fragility. (2) Then the Jews replied to him without understanding the freedom Jesus had spoken about: *We are the descendants of Abraham, and we have never been slaves to anyone. How can you say: You will be free?* (Jn 8:33). Freedom, after all, is a term we use in many senses: in this passage it means holiness; it means resurrection in the apostle where he says that creation is being released *from servitude to corruption into the freedom of the glory of the children of God* (Rom 8:21). It means freedom in a more familiar sense in distinction from slavery. But that term is also used for freedom of choice. Let us separate these cases so that the realities which are very different are not confused because of their common name. (3) In this case, then, the Lord is not saying that freedom of choice must be set free, but while that freedom remains intact, he exhorts the Jews to receive forgiveness and to be set free from guilt and to get that freedom which in God's sight is greatest, namely, that they begin to owe nothing to serious sins. Then the evangelist goes on: *Jesus answered them: Truly, truly, I say to you that everyone who commits sin is the slave of sin. But a slave does not remain in the house for eternity; the Son, however, remains for eternity. If, therefore, the Son sets you free, then you will truly be free* (Jn 8:34-36).

AUG. Notice what he said: *Everyone who commits sin.* After all, he did not say: Who committed, but: *Who commits.* And you do not want him to set human beings free from this evil; you do not want him to promise in this passage the freedom by which we do not commit sin, but only that he set us free because we have committed sin.

88. JUL. He showed the servitude about which he was speaking. He said, *Everyone who commits sin is the slave of sin* (Jn 8:34). But see how strong a point this is against your error, for he says that only one who committed sin is the slave of sin, and sin cannot attach itself to anyone unless the one in question committed it in person either by action or by the will alone. He also shows that the whole of the human race cannot now be owned by the devil when he makes a distinction between slaves and children, that is, between the just and the unjust. Here, after all, as Christ separated himself, so he also separated each of his holy people from the condition of slaves, as they were before the old testament and in the old testament, and he declares that they remain in the house of his Father and are happy at his table.[172] This whole kind of exhortation would have been inappropriately spoken, if it did not address human beings with free choice.

AUG. (1) It clearly addressed those who commit sin because they are slaves of sin so that, when they have received the freedom which he promises, they may cease to commit sin. For sin reigned in their mortal body so that they obeyed its desires and offered their members to sin as weapons of iniquity.[173] Against this evil because of which they were committing sin, they were in need of the freedom which he promised. He said, *Everyone*, not who committed sin, but *who commits sin is the slave of sin* (Jn 8:34). Why do you try to obscure these clear words with cloudy arguments? For they simply leap forth and overwhelm your darkness by their brightness despite your opposition. He says, *Everyone who commits sin is the slave of sin* (Jn 8:34). You hear: *who commits sin*, and you do not want to explain it, but to introduce in its place: who committed sin. Let those hear, then, to whom he opens up the meaning so that they understand the scriptures; let them hear: *Everyone who commits sin is the slave of sin* (Jn 8:34). (2) And let them seek to receive the freedom so that they do not sin, crying out to him to whom is said, *Guide my journeys according to your word, and let no iniquity lord it over me* (Ps 119:133). But why do you mock the slower minds and interpret the words of the Lord as if he said that only one who committed sin is the slave of sin? You are acting deceitfully; he did not say this! He did not say: Only one who commits sin is a slave of sin. Rather, he said: *Everyone who commits sin is the slave of sin* (Jn 8:34). For there are slaves to original sin who have not yet committed sin, and they are released from this bond of servitude by rebirth. Not everyone, then, who is a slave of sin commits sin, but everyone who commits sin is a slave of sin, just as not every animal is a horse, but every horse is, nonetheless, an animal. (3) Where is that logic of yours over which you are usually so proud? Why do these points escape someone as learned and clever as yourself? Or why do you set traps for the ignorant and slow if these points do not escape you? Who of us says that the totality of human beings is owned by the devil, when there are so many thousands of holy persons who are not owned by the devil? Rather, we say that only those are not owned by the devil whom the grace of Christ sets free—the grace of which you are enemies. For if you would not attack, but understand this grace, you would see that even before the old testament and during the time of the old testament all the holy people removed from the condition of slavery were set free by the same grace of Christ.

Jesus Blamed Their Conduct, Not Their Nature

89. JUL. Finally, so that you might understand that he does not blame their nature, but their way of life, there follows: *I know that you are children of Abraham* (Jn 8:37). See the dignity of their origin by which they claimed to be free.[174] Now he shows the servitude to which they were subject when he says, *You seek to kill me, because my word finds no place in you. I speak to you what I heard from my Father, and you do what you have seen with your father* (Jn 8:37-38).

AUG. What does it mean: *My word finds no place in you,* if a nature, even such a nature as now needs a deliverer, is already capable of receiving his word, even if his grace does not open up its meaning, as grace opened it up for the apostles so that they understood the scriptures,[175] or as grace opened it up for that seller of purple goods from the city of Thyatira, so that she paid attention to what Paul said?[176]

90. JUL. See what a difference there is between the meaning of nature and the meaning of will. Jesus did not deny that their flesh pertained to the line of Abraham, but he taught them that they went over to their father the devil by the wickedness of their will. The devil is called their father precisely because he is shown to be their instructor in serious sin. The Jews, he said, *answered and said to him: Our father is Abraham. Jesus said to them: If you were children of Abraham, you would do the works of Abraham. But now you seek to kill me, a man who has told you the truth which I heard from God. Abraham did not do that, but you are doing the works of your father* (Jn 8:39-41). Do you see the distinctions that Wisdom makes in his[177] words? He denies that those whom he had previously said were children of Abraham are children of Abraham. But because speaking about nature is different from speaking about will, he shows that the father of the innocent flesh is other than the seducer of the unhappy will.

AUG. You speak the truth, but do so carelessly. In paradise, after all, the devil was the seducer of the happy will, and by seducing it he made it unhappy. Now, however, as you admit, he is the seducer of an unhappy will. From that unhappiness only God sets the will free so that the will is not now more easily seduced by the devil through that unhappiness than it was then seduced to it. To that God the whole Church daily cries, *Bring us not into temptation, but deliver us from evil* (Mt 6:13).

91. JUL. Here, then, where the Lord said, *If the Son sets you free, you will be truly free* (Jn 8:36), he promised pardon to the guilty who as sinners lost not the freedom of their choice, but knowledge of what is just. Free choice, however, is as complete after their sins as it was before their sins, since it is by its effort that many renounce hidden acts of shame[178] and, having cast aside[179] the filth of sins, they are adorned with the emblems of the virtues.

AUG. At least listen to your own words where you say that scripture said on account of the habit of sins: *I do not do what I will, but I do what I hate* (Rom 7:15).[180] How, then, is choice free after sins? For, even if it was not by the inheritance of sins, since you reject that, but at least by the habit of sins, which is all you yield to this necessity when you are defeated and forced, that man lost his freedom. And his groan strikes your ears and hits you in the face when you hear, *I do not do what I will*, and, *I do not do the good which I will, but I do the evil that I do not will* (Rom 7:15.19).

92. JUL. If you have any sense of right or wrong, stop defiling yourself with impiety by explaining the words of Christ so that he seems to have denied free choice. For, unless free choice remains unimpaired, his own judgment cannot be just.

AUG. In fact, *there is a heavy yoke upon the children of Adam from the day they come forth from the womb of their mother* (Sir 40:1), because his judgment could not be just, but would be completely unjust if they did not contract original sin, by which *human beings have become like a shadow* (Ps 144:4).

Jesus on the Power of Human Freedom

93. JUL. (1) At least listen when he reveals the power of human freedom: *I came in the name of my Father, and you did not welcome me; if someone else comes in his own name, you will welcome him* (Jn 5:43). So too, *Either make the tree good and its fruit good, or make the tree bad and its fruit bad* (Mt 12:33). And again, *If you do not want to believe me, believe my works* (Jn 10:38). And even more strongly than all these, he said that his intention was blocked by the human will. He said, *Jerusalem, Jerusalem, how often I willed to gather your children as a hen gathers her chicks under her wings, and you refused* (Mt 23:37). (2) After this there does not follow: But I gathered you against your will. Rather, there follows: *Your house will be left desolate for you* (Mt 23:38), in order to show them that they are being justly punished for their evil action, but that they should not have been recalled from what they intended by any necessity. After all, he also spoke that way through the prophet: *If you are willing and listen to me, you will eat the good things of the earth; if you are not willing and do not listen, the sword will devour you* (Is 1:19-20). How then can you avoid denying

free choice, for you have declared that it is not free—not by your own statement, but by the testimony of the gospel, as you interpret it?

AUG. (1) You are to be pardoned because in a matter quite hidden you are mistaken, as is only human. Heaven forbid that a human being should block the intention of the omnipotent God who foreknows all things! Those people who suppose that the omnipotent God can will something and be unable to do it, if a weak human being stands in his way, do not think enough on so immense a topic, or they are unable to think it through. Just as it is certain that Jerusalem did not want her children to be gathered by him, so it is certain that he gathered whichever of them he willed, even though she was unwilling. For as Ambrose, a man of God, said, "God calls those whom he pleases and makes religious whom he wills."[181] Scripture often exhorts the human will so that, once admonished, people realize either what they do not have or cannot do and so that in their need they call upon him from whom all good things come. For if they are heard in the prayer we are commanded to pray, *Bring us not into temptation* (Mt 6:13), they will certainly not be deceived by any ignorance or conquered by any desire. (2) Hence, God spoke through the prophet, *If you are not willing and do not listen to me, the sword will devour you* (Is 1:20), and other such things, so that, when they discovered in themselves that their desires are winning out, they would know from whom they must demand help to ward off evil. But scripture said, *See, your house will be left desolate for you* (Mt 23:38), because there were many in it whom he judged worthy of becoming hardhearted and of being abandoned by his hidden, though just judgment. For if, as you say, "none ought to be recalled from their own intention," that is, from their evil intention, why is the apostle Paul, when he is still Saul and breathing murder and thirsting for blood, recalled from that most evil intention of his by a sudden bodily blindness and a terrifying voice from above? After being knocked down as the persecutor of that gospel he was attacking, he is raised up to become a preacher of it who worked harder than the others.[182] Recognize grace: God calls one whom he chooses in this way, another in that way, and *the Spirit breathes where he wills* (Jn 8:36).

94. JUL. (1) For in that work which, as I said above, you recently sent to Rome, you disclosed rather boldly what you thought. In the first book, after all, when you likewise faced our objection that you deny free choice, you argue as a most consistent and subtle debater: "Who of us would say that free choice was removed from the human race by the sin of the first human being? Freedom did indeed perish through sin, but it was that freedom which existed in paradise and which consisted in having complete righteousness with immortality. On account of that sin human nature needs God's grace, for the Lord says in his gospel,[183] *If the Son sets you free, then you will truly be free* (Jn 8:36), free, that is, to live good and righteous lives. It is so far from being true that free choice perished in the sinner that by free choice people sin, but in particular all those who sin with a

delight in and with a love for the sin and who choose to do what pleases them. (2) For this reason the apostle also says, *When you were slaves of sin, you were free with regard to righteousness* (Rom 6:20). You see, he shows that they could in no sense have been slaves of sin save by another freedom. They are free from righteousness only by the choice of freedom,[184] but they do not become free from sin except by the grace of the savior. For this reason that admirable teacher chose these words with care. He said, *For when you were slaves of sin, you were free with regard to righteousness. What return, therefore, did you then have from these things of which you are now ashamed? For their end is death. But now having been set free from sin and having become slaves to God, you have your return in sanctification, and the end is eternal life* (Rom 6:20-22). (3) He said that they were 'free,' not 'set free' of righteousness; he did not say that they were 'free' from sin, for fear that they should attribute this to themselves. Rather, he preferred to say, exercising the utmost care, that they were 'set free,' tying this to the statement of the Lord: *If the Son sets you free, then you will truly be free* (Jn 8:36). Since human beings do not live good lives unless they have become children of God, why does this fellow[185] want to attribute to free choice the power to live a good life? This power is, after all, given only by *the grace of God through Jesus Christ our Lord* (Rom 7:25). For the gospel says, *But to as many as accepted him, he gave the power to become children of God"* (Jn 1:12).[186] After a bit the same person says, "The power, then, by which those who believe in him become children of God is a gift.[187] Unless this power is given by God, it cannot arise from free choice, because it will not be free for what is good if the deliverer has not set it free. But people have free choice for what is evil, if either secretly or openly the deceiver has sown in them a delight in evil or if they have persuaded themselves to it.

(4) It is not true, then, as some claim that we say and as this fellow also dares to write, that we hold that 'all are forced,' as if against their will, 'into sin by the constraints of their flesh.'[188] Rather, if they are already at that age at which they can use the choice of their own mind, they are held in sin by their own will and are hurled down from sin to sin by their own will.[189] But this will, which is free for evil actions because it takes delight in evil, is not free for good actions, because it has not been set free. Nor can a person will something good, unless helped by the one who cannot will evil."[190] In all these words of yours which I have quoted, I see the word "grace" linked with the denial of free choice. The result is not so much that the evils of your thought can be defended by the goodness of the terms, but that the dignity of the words is cheapened by their connection with your teachings. (5) You have not, therefore, made yourself respectable by these words, but you have ruined their beauty. But we separate what you have linked together so that the divinity of grace, once set free from foul associations, is unharmed by your reply and is praised by the honesty of the Catholics, not by

the flattery of the Manichees. We admit, therefore, the manifold grace of Christ. Its first benefit is that we have been made out of nothing. Its second is that, as we surpass mere living things by sensation, so we surpass animals by reason which is impressed upon the mind. We are taught that it is the image of the creator and that the freedom of choice which has been granted to it corresponds to this dignity. We also attribute to grace itself the increases of the benefits that it does not cease to offer us. Grace itself *sent the law as a help* (Is 8:20 LXX). (6) It belonged to its task to stimulate by all sorts of instructions the light of reason which bad example and vicious habits dimmed and to comfort those who have followed it. It belonged, then, to the fullness of this grace, that is, of the divine benevolence which provided the reason for all things, that the Word became flesh and dwelled among us.[191] For God, who demands from his image a return of love, revealed how he did everything for us out of incalculable affection so that we would, though late, love him in return. For, in revealing his love to us,[192] *he did not spare his own Son, but handed him over for us* (Rom 8:32), promising that, if we hereafter chose to obey his will, he would grant that we would be coheirs of his Only-Begotten.[193]

AUG. You Pelagian! Love wills what is good, and love comes from God, not through the letter of the law, but through the Spirit of grace. The letter is a help for those who are predestined insofar as, by its commands, not by its help, it admonishes the weak to flee to the Spirit of grace. In that way those for whom it is good, that is, useful, make legitimate use of the law.[194] Otherwise, by itself the letter kills,[195] because by commanding what is good, but without giving love which alone wills what is good, it makes them guilty of transgression.

The Many Effects of the Grace of Baptism

95. JUL. In baptism, then, this grace not only forgives sins, but along with this benefit of pardon raises us up, adopts us,[196] and makes us holy. This grace, I say, changes what the guilty deserve, but does not create free choice. We receive free choice when we are created, but we use it when we attain the ability to distinguish between good and evil. We do not, therefore, deny that countless forms of divine help are available to a good will, but these kinds of help would not restore a freedom of choice which had been destroyed. Nor should anyone be thought to be under a necessity of doing either good or evil because that freedom is excluded for a time. Rather, every help would work along with free choice.

AUG. If grace does not come first to produce the will, but grace works along with the already existing will, how can it be true that *God also produces in you the will* (Phil 2:13)? How can it be true that *the will is prepared by the Lord* (Prv 8:35 LXX)? How can it be true that *love comes from God* (1 Jn 4:7), the love which alone wills the beatific good? Or if knowledge of the law and of God's words produces love in us so that we love, not by a gift of God, but by the choice of our own will, what we know we should love because God teaches us, how can the lesser good come from God and the greater good from ourselves? I mean that we cannot know without God's giving us knowledge, that is, without his teaching us, but we can love without his giving the love which surpasses knowledge.[197] Only the new heretics and fierce enemies of the grace of God think that way.

96. JUL. Catholics, therefore, admit this free choice. Only on account of this free choice does the teacher of the nations write that we will appear before the judgment seat of Christ so that each may receive recompense, whether good or evil, for one's deeds in the body.[198] With a different, but similar sort of impiety you deny free choice not only with Mani, but also with Jovinian,[199] whom you dare to link to us. To make this clearer, let us examine the differences. We say that the sin of a human being does not change the state of nature, but the quality of the merit; that is, we say that there is in sinners the same nature of free choice by which they can stop sinning as was present in them[200] that they could turn away from righteousness.

AUG. (1) We know that you say that sin of a human being does not change the state of nature, precisely because you have abandoned the Catholic faith. That faith says that the first human being was created so that he did not have to die, but that sin changed the state of nature so that it was necessary for human beings to die. This is so necessary that the apostle says even to those who have been reborn and brought to life by the Spirit, *If Christ is in you, the body is, of course, dead on account of sin, but the spirit is life on account of righteousness. If, then, the Spirit of him who has raised up Jesus from the dead dwells in you, he who has raised up Jesus Christ from the dead will bring to life even your mortal bodies through his Spirit who dwells in you* (Rom 8:10-11). (2) He, of course, said, *He will bring to life even your mortal bodies* something we hope for in the resurrection of the flesh, precisely because he had said, *Your body is dead on account of sin.* And you refuse to admit that sin changed the state of nature. When the objection was raised against Pelagius in the Palestinian court that he said that newborn infants were in the same state in which Adam was before he sinned, he denied that he said this and condemned it.[201] And if he had done this sincerely, your heresy would perhaps have already died out, or at least he himself would have been healed of that disease. Next I ask whether sinful nature is free from defect. But if that is absurd, it, therefore, has a defect. If it has a defect, it is undoubtedly injured. How, then, has it not been changed since, though it was healthy, it is now injured. And so, let us leave out of consideration that sin of which John of Constantinople said, "Adam committed that great sin and condemned the whole human race in common."[202] (3) Even if we leave out of consideration that sin from which human nature incurred condemnation at its origin, how can anyone seriously say that that state of nature was not changed in the one who says, *The law is spiritual, but I am carnal, sold under the power of sin. I do not know what I do, for I do what I do not will* (Rom 7:14-15), and other things of this sort? How can anyone say that human nature was not changed, even if this change was not brought about in us by the condition of being born, but by the habit of sinning, as you would have it? Do you see that what you say is nonsense, namely, that the sin of a human being does not change the state of nature, but the quality of merit? Perhaps you mean that sin does not change the nature, but the human being. And what is this but to deny that a human being is a nature? When would you say these things if you considered with a sound mind what you are saying?

97. JUL. (1) Mani says that a bad will is inspired by that nature which cannot will good, but a good will is infused by that nature which cannot will evil. In that way he, of course, imposes on the natures of individual beings the necessity of some action so that their own wills cannot will the opposite. There is surely a great distance between us and him. Let us now see how far you have withdrawn from him. You say that the will is free, but only to do evil and that it is not free to stop doing evil, unless the necessity of willing good is imposed on it by that nature which, to use your words, "cannot will evil."[203] (2) You declare, then, that by free choice the human race does nothing else but sin and can do nothing else but sin. By this you state absolutely that human nature always desires the one, that is, evil, and can never will its contrary, but that the nature of God cannot will what is evil. And so, unless he makes the evil nature of human beings a partaker of his own necessity, there can be no good action in it. After all this, I leave it to God to see in the secret of your heart whether you are not a great fan of Mani. But as is seen from the close similarity of your teachings, you have done nothing but defend the same thing that he held, though in a different order.

AUG. (1) I wish that you would vigorously destroy Mani and not shamefully help him. For, deranged by a great insanity, he does not say that the nature of evil is forced to do good by the other nature of the good which cannot will evil, but that the nature of the good is forced to do evil by that nature of evil which cannot will the good. For this reason, in an amazing madness he wants the nature of evil to be immutable, but the nature of good to be mutable. Hence, it is certain that Mani says that an evil will is inspired by that nature which cannot will the good. But Mani does not say that the good will is infused by the nature which cannot will evil, as you rather benevolently suppose he does. For he by no means believes that the nature of the good is immutable so that it could not will evil; rather, he believes that the evil will is inspired in it by that nature which cannot will good. Therefore, the nature of evil brings it about that the nature of the good wills evil, though he wants the nature of the good to be nothing other than the nature of God. (2) You, therefore, help Mani when you deny that human nature was injured by the sin of the first human being so that Mani attributes to the nature of evil whatever evils he finds in the very obvious misery of little ones. Moreover, since you are displeased that human beings cannot will the good unless they are helped by him who cannot will evil, do you not see that you contradict the one who said, *Without me you can do nothing* (Jn 15:5)? You contradict the scripture where we read, *The will is prepared by the Lord* (Prv 8:35 LXX) and where we read, *It is God, after all, who also produces in you the will* (Phil 2:13) and where we read, *The steps of human beings are guided by the Lord, and they shall choose his way* (Ps 37:23). Here my only wonder is why you say you are Christian when you contradict these many clear words of God.

98. JUL. (1). You are, however, linked to Jovinian in one respect, for he says in the second book of his work that a baptized person cannot sin, but that before baptism one can both sin and not sin.[204] He agrees with you, then, that from the time of baptism human beings are under the necessity of doing good, and that is just as false as your idea that before baptism human beings are under the necessity of doing evil. For when you say, "Human beings cannot will something good unless they are helped by him who cannot will something evil,"[205] you want human beings to attain the possibility of doing good by sharing, of course, in grace and the good nature, and you say that this can come about from the time of baptism. Standing between impiety and fear, you fled to the company of Jovinian, but you have not yet left the brothel of Mani. (2) Jovinian, nonetheless, was more innocent than you to the same extent that Mani was more sacrilegious than Jovinian. For, to sum up more still briefly what we have done, Mani says: In all human beings the nature of darkness which inspires the evil will sins and cannot do anything else. You say: In all human beings the nature which was infected by the darkness of the first sin and is, for this reason, the origin of the evil will sins and cannot will anything good. Jovinian says that the will of human beings sins, but only up to baptism; afterwards, however, it cannot will anything but good. The Catholics, that is, we, say that from the beginning to the end without any compulsion from natural factors the will sins in each individual even before baptism, and that at the same time at which it sins it has the power to refrain from evil and to do good so that the basic character of freedom remains unshaken. (3) The truth agrees with none of your teachings; nonetheless, since you began from one erroneous principle, it would at least be less dishonest if you admitted the consequences. And since with Mani you say that one sins because of an evil nature, that is, a defective freedom, you should say with him that this nature can by no means be purified, a point which you do state elsewhere. But you ought to add what necessarily follows, namely, that one does not need the sacred rites of baptism. Or, if with Jovinian you say that good desires are infused from the time that one accepts the faith, you should say along with him that human nature was good even before baptism. For, though it had the ability to sin, it did not have the necessity of sinning and in that way, once it has been made holy, it attains an undeniable goodness. In that way, after all, you will not go against the teachings of those you follow, though you will go against reason.[206]

AUG. (1) You have forgotten what we say; recall it, please. We are the ones who say, despite your protests, that even the righteous, as long as they are in this life, do not lack grounds for truthfully saying about themselves in their prayer, *Forgive us our debts* (Mt 6:12). For if they say that they do not have sin, they deceive themselves and the truth is not in them.[207] Why do you make the foolish claim that I am an ally of Jovinian insofar as he says that a baptized person cannot sin? Heaven forbid that we should be so deaf and dumb that we do not hear the voice of those who have been baptized or that we do not say with them, *Forgive us our debts*. But from the time human beings begin to use the choice of their will, they can both sin and not sin, but they do not do the second of these unless they are helped by him who said, *Without me you can do nothing* (Jn 15:5). They can, however, do the other one by their own will, led astray either by themselves or by some other deceiver or handed over to sin like slaves. (2) But we know that human beings are helped by the Spirit of God to will the things of God even before baptism, for example, Cornelius,[208] but that some are not helped even after baptism, for example, Simon Magus.[209] The judgments of God, after all, are like a great abyss,[210] and his grace is not the result of our works; otherwise, grace is no longer grace.[211] Therefore, stop abusing us with the names of Mani and Jovinian. If you had eyes, you would see that you abuse in us those whom we follow and that, because we follow them, we cannot deny original sin. And if you had any sense of shame, you would be silent. But you are so filled with slander that you say that I stated elsewhere that human beings cannot be purified from sins, though I say that they can be purified so that they are even brought to the point that in complete blessedness they cannot sin.

The Question of the Necessity of Sinning

99. JUL. Now you are treacherous toward everyone; you say that a necessity of sinning has been produced in the nature of the flesh.

AUG. (1) Deny that the apostle said, *When you were slaves of sin, you were free with regard to righteousness* (Rom 6:20). Or if you do not deny that he said this, prove that he did not speak correctly. But if you do not dare to do that, deny, if you can, that those to whom he said this had free will in their evil actions when they were free from righteousness and that they had free will in good actions when they were slaves of sin. Dare to say that they were set free from this slavery by themselves, not by the grace of God, for the apostle said to them, *But now having been set free from sin, you have become servants of righteousness* (Rom 6:22). (2) But if you say that the grace of God set them free from the guilt of past sins, not from the dominion of sin which keeps each person from being righteous, and that they could themselves, if they wanted, have brought it about that sin did not have dominion over them, and that they did not need the grace of God for this, where will you put that person who said, *I do not do the good that I will, but I do the evil that I do not will* (Rom 7:19)? If someone still under the law, not under grace, says this, deny that he groaned under the heavy weight of necessity. Claim that he was free to live well and to act rightly by the choice of the will, as he shouts at you: You lie, or you are deceived; *I do not do what I will.* But if, in accord with the better opinion of Ambrose,[212] the apostle is saying this of himself, even the righteous in this life do not have such a great freedom of their own will to carry out the good as there will be in that life where one will not say, *I do not do what I will.*

100. JUL. As a result, once the possession of eternity was forfeit, something which, it is clear, the will never had because it was born, the will was bent upon the constant pursuit of evil. And you add, "The will which is free for evil actions is not free for good actions,"[213] calling free,[214] by a statement clearly no less stupid than sacrilegious, that which you say can only will one thing.

AUG. If only that is free which is able to will two things, that is, good and evil, God is not free, since he cannot will evil. You yourself said of him—and you spoke the truth, "God cannot be but just."[215] Are you going to praise God in such a way that you take away his freedom? Or should you not rather understand that there is a certain blessed necessity by which God cannot be unjust?

Augustine Compared to Jovinian

101. JUL. But though it is in no sense accepted, let the wise reader note what you teach. Let us agree that a will can be called free which cannot will the good. But you claim that this will is set free in baptism. I ask: To what extent is it set free? So that it is always forced to will the good and cannot will evil? Or so that it can desire both? Here if you reply: So that it is always forced to will the good, you yourself recognize that you are a Jovinian. But if you say: How can the will be free if it is always forced to will the good? I reply: How was the will previously said to be free if it was forced to will only evil. If, then, you reply that after baptism the will becomes free so that it can both sin and not sin, you declare by this very response that free choice did not exist when it could not do both. You are surrounded on all sides by the snares of your own argument. Choice was free before baptism; it had the ability to do good, just as it had the ability to do evil, and the whole stage of your teaching collapses by which you try to convince us of a natural evil.

AUG. (1) The reader will find that I already replied to you above with regard to Mani and Jovinian. But I leave it to your brilliant mind to see how can you say that a person whose will we say is prepared by the Lord obtains a good will and is forced to will the good. Heaven forbid that we should say this! After all, if one is forced, one does not will, and what is more absurd than to say that, while not willing, one wills the good? Also see what you hold with regard to the nature of God, when you, a human being, say that human beings are forced to will the good if they cannot will evil. After all, is God forced to will the good because he cannot will evil, since he is utterly immutable? (2) But human nature, though mutable, is good in terms of its creation; it was not only made without defect, but it is also capable of the good by which it might be good, even when it is evil by reason of a defect. This true statement destroys the deceitful madness of the Manichees. But in baptism all sins are forgiven in the grace of God, and by that grace a human being is drawn to baptism itself when the will is prepared by God. Thereafter, though the spirit has desires opposed to the flesh so that it does not consent to iniquity, the flesh, nonetheless, has desires opposed to the spirit so that even the spirit does not do what it wills. (3) After all, the spirit wills not to have the concupiscence of the flesh, but cannot be free from it at present. For this reason the spirit still groans in itself, awaiting the adoption, the redemption of its body,[216] when it will have its flesh in such a way that it can no longer sin. Now, therefore, the spirit not only can sin after baptism, but is at times drawn to consent by concupiscence of the flesh, even though it struggles valiantly against it, and it commits some sins, even though slight ones. We always have reason to say in this life, *Forgive us our debts* (Mt 6:12). This Catholic truth also refutes the vanity of Jovinian. But both of these, that is, what we say against Mani and what we say against Jovinian, destroy your heresy and your slanders.

102. JUL. But if choice was not free to do good before baptism, and it became free after baptism so that it could not do evil, then one never had freedom of choice, and one is shown to have sinned without guilt before and to possess the glory of holiness afterwards without a worry.

AUG. Therefore, there is no freedom of choice in God either, because he cannot do evil, since he cannot deny himself.[217] And he will also grant us as our highest reward that, when we are equal not to God himself, but to the angels, we too will be unable to sin. We have to believe that he gave this to them after the fall of the devil as a reward for their good will by which they remained standing in the truth[218] so that afterwards no new devil came to be through free choice.

103. JUL. That said, you are shown to contradict your teaching: you first announce that you do not deny free choice, and you destroy it by the necessity, first, of doing evil and, then, of doing good.

AUG. You are going to say, as I see it, that God is weighed down by necessity so that he cannot sin. He certainly can neither will to sin, nor does he will to be able to sin. Moreover, if that must be called a necessity by which it is necessary that something be or come to be, then this necessity is most blessed by which it is necessary to live in happiness. And in that life it is necessary not to die and necessary not to change for the worse. By this necessity—if it is to be called a necessity—the saints are not weighed down; rather, they enjoy it. But for us it is still to come, not present.

104. JUL. The whole argument, nonetheless, serves for the destruction of your teaching; for, to recall the previous definitions: If sin is nothing but the will to keep or to do what justice forbids and from which one is free to hold back,[219] there exists no sin at all in the world.

AUG. This is the definition of that sin which is only sin, not of that sin which is also the punishment of sin by which the freedom not to sin was lost. From that evil we are set free only by him to whom we say not only, *Forgive us our debts*, but also, *Bring us not into temptation, but deliver us from evil* (Mt 6:12-13).

105. JUL. For if justice does not impute any sin unless one is free to hold back from it, and if before baptism there is a necessity to do evil because, as you said, the will is not free to do good and, for this reason, it cannot do anything but evil, it is defended from blame by the very necessity to do evil under which it suffers. For in the presence of that justice it cannot be weighed down by its own works, since that justice does not impute sin unless one is free to hold back from it. But after baptism, if there is a necessity to do good, there surely cannot be any sin. See, then, how that which reason shows to be sin cannot be found in the seeds, since in accord with your definitions it is not found even in actions.

AUG. (1) You are very much mistaken. You either think that there is no necessity to sin, or you fail to understand that it is the punishment of that sin which was committed with no necessity. For, if there is no necessity to sin—I leave out the force of that evil which is contracted from our origin, for you want this not to exist at all—what was he suffering, I ask you, who according to your view was pressed down by so great a burden of bad habit that he said, *I do not do the good that I will, but I do the evil that I do not will* (Rom 7:19)? Moreover, I think that you are aware of the great labor by which one learns what one should seek and what one should avoid in living this life. But those who do not know this suffer the necessity of sinning as a result of the very ignorance of the good they should seek and of the evil they should avoid. For it is necessary that we sin when we do what we ought not to do, because we do not know what we ought to do. (2) About this kind of sin the psalmist prays to God where he says, *Do not remember the sins of my youth and ignorance* (Ps 25:7). If the just God did not impute this kind of sin, the faithful would not ask to be forgiven for them. For this reason Job, the servant of God, also says, *You have sealed my sins in a sack and have noted if I have done anything against my will* (Jb 14:17). In your last book of those four which you published against my one book, you yourself say that from the emotions and passions of the mind there is produced in human beings an emotional quality and it inheres "so that it is removed either only by great efforts or not at all."[220] What else, then, will whoever sins because of that fearfulness that cannot be removed do but sin with necessity?

(3) But you concede that these sins stem from those sins which are committed with no necessity, at least in case of that man who says, *I do the evil that I do not*

will (Rom 7:19). For those who are weighed down only by the habit of sinning so that they suffer under this necessity were undoubtedly not oppressed by the necessity of the habit before they sinned. And for this reason, even according to you, the necessity to sin from which they are not free to hold back is a punishment of that sin from which they were free to hold back when no weight of necessity urged them on. Why then do you not believe that that ineffably great sin of the first human being was not at least able to produce as much damage for the whole of human nature as a second nature can now produce in a single human being? You thought that we needed to be reminded that the learned speak of habit in that way.[221] (4) We admit that human beings also have those sins which are committed not by necessity, but by will, sins which are only sins and from which one is free to hold back. And the human race is rife with sins that come from the necessity of ignorance and of the emotions—sins which are not only sins, but also the punishments of sins. Why, then, do you say that by our definitions sin is not found even in actions? Listen to what you reject: From all sins whether original or actual—whether sins that have been committed or so that sins may not be committed—only the grace of God through Jesus Christ our Lord sets us free. For in him we have been reborn, and from him we have learned to say in prayer not only: *Forgive us our debts* (Mt 6:12), that is, because we have sinned, but also: *Bring us not into temptation* (Mt 6:13), that is, so that we do not sin.

106. JUL. (1) But now that we have presented this summary of the discussion to the mind of the wise reader, let us examine how your baptism, which you say was given us only on account of the arousal of the genital organs, carries out the function assigned to it. It professes to purify human beings from their sins, but when the case of the will is tried in the court of justice, the will is not to be declared guilty if it could will nothing else. But once you take away the hatefulness of the guilt, you also take away the magnificence of the pardon, because one cannot pardon what one cannot rightfully impute. (2) And for this reason baptism is deprived of the effects that it promises, because it does not find the sins for the forgiveness of which it is praised. Nor does it have people indebted to it for this benefit which removes the chains of sins, because it cannot convict of bad will those who have found sanctuary in necessity. For all of these reasons it is found to be utterly useless. But because the grace which is given us by Christ is not utterly useless, let us uphold the reasonable benefit of baptism by which the will of the sinner is proven guilty, because it both could have willed the good and yet willed evil. The whole figment of necessity has, therefore, disappeared, and for this reason there is no sin due to the condition of nature. Rather, free choice remains in the nature of human beings, and as you deny it with the Manichees, so we confess it with the apostles and all the Catholics.

AUG. (1) It is necessary that people sin if they do not know the demands of righteousness. Therefore, when they come to know the demands of righteousness, should not the sins which they committed out of the necessity of ignorance be forgiven them? Or because they now know how they ought to live, are they to place their trust in themselves to live righteously and not in him to whom we say, *Bring us not into temptation* (Mt 6:13)? The necessity of sinning does not entail being preserved from punishment, but he to whom we pray, *Rescue me from my necessities* (Ps 25:17), grants that this necessity causes no harm. He grants this, however, in two ways: both by forgiving past sinfulness and by helping us not to enter into temptation. We are all, however, tempted, attracted and enticed by our own concupiscence.[222] (2) For this favorite of yours pleases you so much that, when anyone is not drawn by it to consent, you suppose that she should be praised, as if something that draws one toward evil is not evil if one does not give in to it, but resists when pushed. And yet, you argue with great nonsense that, even if one consents to it, we should blame the one who fell, not the one who pushed, the one who was seduced, not the seducer, the one who was enticed, not the one who enticed, for the former makes a bad use of something good, as you define it. You have such an evil spirit that the concupiscence by which the flesh has desires opposed to the spirit seems good to you. (3) You suppose that you have mocked our view of baptism with great eloquence, when you with a great lie claim that we say that baptism was given us only on account of the arousal of the genital organs. We do not say this; rather, we say what you try to undermine with your new and heretical error. We say that God gave us the help of the second spiritual birth which Christ instituted to take place in him, since those born from Adam according to the flesh contract the infection of the ancient death by their first birth.[223] See, I have used the words of the Punic bishop, Cyprian. You bark against him, even though he was a martyr, when you attack the most solidly grounded faith of the Church, the Church for which he shed his blood. (4) After all, as Paul said, *Through one man sin entered the world, and through sin death, and in that way it was passed on to all human beings in whom all have sinned* (Rom 5:12), so the bishop Cyprian, who understood this apostle, confessed that those born from Adam according to the flesh contract the infection of the ancient death by their first birth. Why is it, then, that you use lies to unite yourself to the apostles and all the Catholics, when you deceitfully contradict the apostle and openly contradict the bishop and martyr on what he held along with the Catholic Church in both the East and the West?

Conflicting Views of Freedom and Slavery

107. JUL. (1) The explanation, of course, which you gave to the words of the apostle Paul, ought to be passed over with a laugh if it did not strike terror into those ignorant of the scriptures. The apostle said, *When you were slaves of sin, you were free with regard to righteousness* (Rom 6:20). He could not, of course, have said: "Set free," since this expression "being set free" is correctly and prop-

erly employed when one is set free from harmful things. But to be free from the virtues is used of those people who decide to have nothing to do with the virtues. Persons can be said, then, to be free both from good and from evil if, while serving the one, they strive to have nothing to do with the other. But one can only be said to be set free from evil because this expression "being set free" contains in itself an indication of the trouble which is fended off. What question, then, could be raised for the apostle concerning his words here? For in accord with the custom of the human race he spoke of people free from good, but set free from evil? (2) He said, therefore, *When you were slaves of sin, you were free with regard to righteousness. What return, therefore, did you have then from these things of which you are now ashamed?* (Rom 6:20-21). But so that you do not think that we become slaves to sin by nature, listen to the apostle speaking in these same passages, *Do you not know that, if you hand yourselves over as slaves to someone in obedience, you are slaves of the one you obey, either of sin or of faith leading to righteousness?* (Rom 6:16). He said that you handed yourselves over as slaves to sin so that you would understand that he attributed the sin to the will, not to birth. He said that they were free with regard to righteousness only because they refused to keep his commandments.

AUG. If human beings were said to be free with regard to righteousness only because they refused to keep his commandments, then, before they received the commandments of righteousness which they refused to keep, were they not free with regard to righteousness and slaves of sin? Who would say this? From this necessity of slavery, then, he sets us free who not only gives commandments by the law, but also bestows love by the Holy Spirit so that the delight of sin may be conquered by the delight of that love. Otherwise, it continues to be unconquered and holds onto its slave. *After all, one becomes a slave to one's conqueror* (2 Pt 2:19).

108. JUL. (1) Then he immediately adds that they are slaves of righteousness, as they were previously slaves of sin. On this account you can now say, if you wish, that they are free with regard to sin when they are serving righteousness, just as the apostle said they were free from righteousness when they served sin. You, therefore, brought a slander against the simplicity of the apostle in a most inept fashion. After all, he did not, as you think, teach with great vigilance the point which you suppose; rather, with much sleepiness you looked at what he said. You argue, of course, that he should have preferred to say, "set free," rather than, "free," so that we would understand that by freedom of choice one can do evil, but cannot do good. (2) But the very order of his words is against you. For if he thought the same thing as you, namely, that by freedom one only sins, he ought to have said: You were free with regard to sin, and not: *You were free with regard to righteousness* (Rom 6:20). In that way one would be said to be free with regard to that[224] to which freedom itself leads. For if you wish to weigh the

import of the cases,[225] he said that they were free with regard to this righteousness, not free from this righteousness. We would, therefore, be helped with
greater logic by this statement if we were willing to press even such minor
points. But heaven keep us from this. We understand the meaning of the apostle,
and we are content with the function of his statements which he expressed with
simplicity. The teacher of the nations said nothing else than: You were free with
regard to righteousness; you were not slaves; you have been set free; you have
received forgiveness of sins, while that freedom of choice remains by which
they were able before to obey sin and afterward to obey righteousness.

AUG. By this heretical interpretation you say that grace does not set us free
from sin except when we receive pardon for the past, but not also so that sin does
not lord it over us when we are drawn by our concupiscence to consent. By this
interpretation you are opposed to the prayers of even the saints. After all, why
does one say to God, *Bring us not into temptation* (Mt 6:13), if it lies in the power
of our free choice which was built into our nature that this does not happen? Why
does the apostle say, *But we pray to God that you do no evil* (2 Cor 13:7), if God
sets us free from sins only by granting pardon to our past sins?

Paul's Exhortation to Righteousness

109. JUL. (1) Then he shows what the exhortation to righteousness contains.
He first says, *What I say is only human on account of the weakness of your flesh.
For as you offered your members to serve impurity and iniquity upon iniquity, so
now offer your members to serve righteousness for sanctification. For when you
were slaves of sin, you were free with regard to righteousness* (Rom 6:19-20).
He quite properly says that those people were free with regard to righteousness
whom he had exhorted to maintain their members in all holiness. (2) But we have
delayed here no small time to show that what I said is absolutely certain, namely,
that human beings who were terror-stricken by your words denied free choice
and were plunged into true destruction by an empty fear and that you are the
chief of those who deny free choice. Now let us return to that book which you
dedicated to Valerius in order that we may prove that you first denied that God is
the creator, but that now in one place you deny this, while in another place you
admit it in a much worse way than you denied it. (3) It was, of course, obvious
enough, when it was discussed, how completely you denied in that previous
book of yours that God is the creator of human beings. After all, you said that the
devil rightfully plucks the human race like the fruit from the fruit trees he
planted.[226] And many other things which you said in place of arguments contribute to this error. But in this second book, even though you are aiming at the same
thing in the whole of your teaching, you strive, nonetheless, to correct your statement in a more destructive fashion than you originally uttered it.

AUG. If the apostle means too little to you, though he said, *Through one man sin entered the world, and through sin death, and in that way it was passed on to all human beings, in whom all sinned* (Rom 5:12), Ambrose at least understood the apostle, not as a Manichee—the name with which you brand those who shared his faith—but as a Catholic. And because he understood him, he said, "All of us human beings are born under power of sin, and our very origin lies in guilt."[227] See the fruit tree from which the devil rightfully plucks fruit as if from his own fruit tree—not the nature which God created, but the sin which the devil planted. After all, those who are born under the power of sin cannot but be under the power of the author of sin, unless they are reborn in Christ.

110. JUL. But let us briefly offer the reply which is owed to your chapter which we quoted above.[228] I, therefore, reply firmly and faithfully that we do not begrudge to human beings the Lord Jesus Christ as their deliverer. We urge them not to believe you so that they are not broken by despair of improving their lives and withdraw from the teaching of Christ as if he commanded things which are too much for the nature of mortal beings, which is weighed down by an evil with which we are born.

AUG. But death too is something with which we are born, and he, nonetheless, sets us free from it who gives life to those he wills.[229] To him they ought to take flight who want to be set free from the evil with which we are born. Read in the gospel who draws them to do this.[230]

111. JUL. But they should run to him who cries out, *My yoke is easy, and my burden light* (Mt 11:30). In accord with his incalculable generosity he grants pardon even to an evil will, and by renewal and adoption he makes better the innocence which he creates good.

AUG. These are the human beings to whom you begrudge a deliverer, when you deny that they have anything evil from which they might be set free. How, then, can you reply firmly and faithfully that you do not begrudge to human beings the Lord Jesus Christ as their deliverer, since you rather stubbornly and faithlessly strive to make people believe that little ones are not saved by him, just as he saves his people from their sins? From the words of the gospel we learn that he was called Jesus for this very reason.[231] You cannot, therefore, teach that you do not begrudge to human beings Christ as deliverer, since you can in no way show that little ones are not human beings.

The Source of Subjection to the Devil

112. JUL. I am amazed, therefore, that you have dared to cite the testimony which says, *After all, one becomes a slave to one's conqueror* (2 Pt 2:19). That is obviously in our favor, for we say that none can be subject to the devil unless after a struggle of the will they are overcome in a shameful surrender. But you

ought not to use it, since it is strongly against you who argue that the newborn are in the kingdom of the devil, though they certainly could not either be defeated or sin without a will of their own.

AUG. The newborn whom you say could neither be defeated nor struggle derive their origin from him in whom all sinned, and—what is worse—that man was defeated without a struggle. "For Adam existed, and we all existed in him. Adam perished, and all perished in him."[232] Allow, then, the little ones to be found by him who came to seek what had perished.[233] Otherwise, since they too are human beings, you certainly begrudge to human beings Jesus as deliverer—no matter by how much verbiage you believe that the cruelty of this error of yours should be covered over.

113. JUL. (1) You see that this text has much force against you. It is as if the text itself asked you: Why are little ones in the kingdom of the enemy power, if scripture is believed that each person, when conquered, is then the slave of the conqueror, and if it is clear that without the use of reason and will infancy can neither engage in combat nor surrender? You, of course, add, "*Through one man sin entered the world, and through sin death, and in that way it was passed on to all human beings, in whom all sinned* (Rom 5:12). (2) God, then, is the creator of those who are born, and yet, as the result of the one, all enter into condemnation[234] who do not have the liberator through whom they are reborn. He has been described as a potter who from the same lump makes one vessel for an honorable purpose in his mercy and another for a dishonorable purpose according to his justice.[235] The Church sings of his mercy and justice."[236] You say that through one man sin entered the world, and by that testimony of the apostle you have disturbed the hearts of many of the uneducated. Though I briefly showed in the fourth book how it is to be understood, we shall, nonetheless, explain it more fully in this work with the help of Christ so that in the second book, along with many other points we have passed over, this passage from the apostle may be fully explained in its context.

AUG. In our sixth book you were given an answer to what you claim that you briefly showed in your fourth book.[237] But when you begin to fulfill what you promise in this work, it will then be evident how you have nothing to say.

114. JUL. Here, however, I shall briefly warn you that it cannot help you to maintain that view which all learning, every reason, and the law of God prove most unjust. Let the careful reader, then, notice what you said, namely, that God is the maker of evil human beings and that he creates them such that they all enter into damnation without any merit of their own will.

AUG. I said this because he makes the nature of human beings who are evil because of a defect which he did not make, and from that defect he brings about good, even though the human beings whom he makes are evil. For he makes them insofar as they are human beings, not insofar as they are evil. After all, they would not be made into vessels of dishonor if they were not evil; by the nature, nonetheless, which God makes, they are certainly good, but they are evil in terms of the defect which the enemy planted against their nature, but in their nature, so that as a result of this there is a bad nature, that is, a bad human being. For an evil can only exist in some good, because it can only exist in a nature, but every nature insofar as it is a nature is something good. Pay careful attention to how we say things which seem to contradict each other, but in fact do not, if you have not completely lost your power of sight because of the smoke of proud contentiousness.

Salvation before the Coming of Christ

115. JUL. And so that we might not be ignorant of the time about which you speak, you declare that from Adam, the one who you say we all were, up to the end, all those who have not been baptized are found to be subject to condemnation and to the devil. In that statement you try to cure yourself in a much more harmful way than you previously wounded yourself. For, in order to remove the hatred which was pouring in upon you because you said that the devil is the creator of human beings, you correct yourself and confess that God is the creator, but the creator of the sort of beings which Mani attributes to the prince of darkness.

AUG. "All of us human beings are born under the power of sin, and our very origin lies in guilt."[238] The foul heretic Mani did not say this, but the holy Catholic Ambrose. Moreover, Mani does not say that every nature insofar as it is a nature is good, nor does he say that the nature which he calls evil is able to be healed in any way and become good. But the Catholic faith says this about the human nature of little ones and of adults; it says this in opposition to the Manichees and in opposition to the Pelagians, both of them equally sick, though with different diseases.

116. JUL. Since he believed that human beings are evil by the condition of their birth, he attributed them to that author by whom he might keep the accusation of an evil work away from the good God. And because he was mistaken in the definition of sin so that he thought it was something natural, though it can only be something voluntary, he logically went on next to fabricate an evil artisan of their evil origin. This man showed more reverence toward God, but more contempt for nature. But you say that human beings are born evil and that God is the author of those evil beings. You show more contempt toward God and more reverence for nature. Nature is defended by the majesty of its author, but its author is accused on account of the ugliness of his work.

AUG. Accuse God, then, if you want, on account of the ugliness of his work, for some bodies are born so ugly that some of them are called monsters because of their excessive deformity. For it is not another god, as Mani imagines, or lesser gods, as Plato mistakenly supposes, who create bodies, but the good and righteous God certainly produces even such bodies.[239] If you attribute them to the heavy yoke upon the children of Adam,[240] you will find that he is not an evil god such as Mani used for fashioning bodies, and that he was not conquered, enmeshed in, and mingled with evils, as Mani is not afraid to believe about the good God. Rather, he is clearly just on account of original sin—the sort of sin known by the Catholic faith from which your error has gone astray. After all, if no one had sinned, in paradise bodies would also not be born ugly and monstrous.

Comparisons of Augustine and Mani

117. JUL. You have not feared to attribute to God, you foul criminal, what led Mani to fabricate another creator in order to avoid attributing it to God. Both of you are, of course, enemies of the truth, but before you came along he was thought to be unsurpassable in impiety.

AUG. Before I came along there was Ambrose who was not a Manichee; before him there was Hilary and Gregory; before these there was Cyprian and the others whom it would take too long to mention; they were not Manichees. And they, nonetheless, taught the Church what they learned in the Church, namely, that little ones contract original sin and that they must undergo the rite of exsufflation in exorcisms so that they are rescued from the power of darkness and transferred to the kingdom of their savior and lord.[241] For, if Christ died also for them, as even you are forced to admit, *all have, therefore, died, and he died for all* (2 Cor 5:14-15), as the apostle says. And so, if according to your words even Paul himself is a Manichee, what will you yourself be?

118. JUL. You have made righteous, as the prophet says, your sister, Sodom.[242] Mani will be considered innocent if he is compared with your blasphemies. I boasted in the first book of my work that I was wounded by the same tongue by which the apostles endured injury. But now I am stunned at the greatness of my good fortune; I am upbraided by the same person who brings charges against God.

AUG. You are upbraided by one who preaches along with Ambrose and his other companions Christ as the deliverer of little ones too. You not only accuse Christ of being a liar where he says that he came to save and to seek what was lost,[243] but you also are opposed to his seeking little ones in order to save them.

119. JUL. Why has the honor of such great abuse fallen to my lot? You could have bestowed upon me nothing of the sort by praising me. You say that my ideas must be rejected, but that the works of God must be condemned. You claim that I argue badly, but that God creates wickedly. You shout that I am in error, but that he is cruel. You state that I do not know the law, but that God does not

know justice. You cry out that I am not a Catholic, because I say that Christ calls those whom he would save, but you swear that God creates people to condemn them and creates them for no other reason than that they may all enter into condemnation.

AUG. All this can also be said of the foreknowledge of God which believers, nonetheless, cannot deny, and I think that even you do not deny it. Otherwise, deny that God foreknows that he will condemn many whom he creates so that he does not seem to create people in order to condemn them and— what is even more amazing and inscrutable—that he does not take many from this life so that evil does not corrupt their mind,[244] though he cannot fail to know that they will be evil. Give honor to God; let the noisy collapse of your words, so shining and sharp, but glassy, yield to the depth of his judgments.

120. JUL. Between you and Mani, who first sowed your ideas, I see that a great distance has been produced by the development of your learning. For, though he introduced two authors, he, nonetheless, left hope of salvation from that side on which he said that the good God is completely free from injustice and cruelty. But in speaking of one good God, but making him the creator of evil, you completely remove both reverence for divinity and hope of salvation.

AUG. The Manichees imagine a God who is cruelly weak, who handed over a part of himself, his own substance, the members of his own nature, to be tortured and defiled by his enemies who he saw threatened him with destruction. But you, who do not deny that God is perfectly omnipotent, want people to believe that he is unjust on account of the heavy yoke upon children, since you deny original sin.

121. JUL. There is, after all, no one to help the guilty, when the only one there is, punishes out of a desire to create misery, even those in whom he recognizes nothing other than what he made.

AUG. He also recognizes there what he did not make; he certainly did not make sin. But another person as foolish as you could say that out of a desire to create misery God also creates those whom he could not fail to know that he would condemn—incomparably more than those he foreknew that he would set free.

God's Omnipotence, Justice, and Love

122. JUL. Having seen the depth of your impiety, it seems that nothing more sacrilegious could ever be found, but a brief discussion will show how all this has no force and what may be inferred from the additions you made to it. God who willed to be called by this name is believed to be both fully omnipotent and fully just. If one of these were lacking, neither would be present. As he is believed to be the most loving creator of human beings, so he is believed to be most

just in recompensing merits. Everything he makes is very good. And for this reason no one is naturally evil; rather, any who are guilty are blamed for their morals, not for their origins.

AUG. Why, then, is there a heavy yoke over the origins of little ones under the most powerful and most just God?[245]

123. JUL. Therefore, there is no natural evil, and God cannot create guilty persons or place them in the kingdom of the devil. When these points are added together, you will be shown to be a Manichee, in fact worse than a Manichee, and it is perfectly clear that the entrance of humanity into this world is without sin, that the fruit of fertility is under the dominion of God, not of the devil, and that innocence is natural.

AUG. And so, Ambrose is shown to be a Manichee or worse than a Manichee, as your insults or madness would have it, for he said, "Little ones who have been baptized are restored from evil to the original state of their nature."[246]

124. JUL. Now that this has been duly recorded, notice what results from your line of argument. It is agreed that the prophets and the patriarchs and all the holy men and women of the old testament were without baptism, but that they were created by God and went on to become resplendent with their own virtues. Contrary to the testimony of the law, then, they will be believed to be under the rule of the devil and to be handed over to eternal punishments, because you declare that all descendants of Adam were created for condemnation.

AUG. (1) And he set free those righteous people of the old testament by the same grace against which you have declared war, although they used different sacraments in accord with their time. For they believed what we believe about Christ. *After all, there is one God and one mediator between God and human beings, the man Christ Jesus* (1 Tm 2:5). To them his coming in humility was foretold, while to us it was reported. But his coming in glory which will take place at the end was foretold both to them and to us. (2) And, therefore, we and they have one faith in this one mediator, and the same Spirit of faith was in them and is in us. For this reason the apostle said, *But having the same Spirit of faith, in accord with the words of scripture: I believed; therefore, I have spoken,*[247] we too believe, and therefore we speak (2 Cor 4:13). But with regard to the source of this faith let us listen to the same apostle so that we do not boast as if it came from us. He says, *You were saved by grace through faith, and this does not come from you; rather, it is the gift of God* (Eph 2:8). And in another passage he says, *Peace to the sisters and brothers and love along with faith from God the Father and the Lord Jesus Christ* (Eph 6:23).

125. JUL. If you say this, even your defenders will be able to admit that you are clearly a Manichee. But if you understand that so great an army of the true king is fighting against your view and that you cannot bring any injunction against them, accept the fact that what you have built up has been destroyed and,

for this reason, that not all enter into condemnation because of the one,[248] but only those rebels against God's will who are caught by surprise on the last day without having done penance and without having reformed their lives.

AUG. Add to these those who have been born, if they have not been reborn, because all sinned in the one.[249]

126. JUL. But you ought not to have mentioned at all the passage in which God was said to be *a potter* making *from the same lump of clay one vessel for an honorable purpose and another for a dishonorable one* (Rom 9:21). For, as we shall explain it further on, it is completely against you. After all, when some are said to be made for an honorable purpose and others for a dishonorable purpose, it helps the interpretation of the Catholics which in accord with the differences of the human will also proclaims different outcomes for the vessels.

AUG. Listen to Ambrose; he says, "All of us human beings are born under the power of sin, and our very origin lies in guilt."[250] Along with his fellow students and fellow teachers who were beyond any doubt Catholic, he understood what scripture says about sin and death, namely, that it entered through the one and was passed on to all human beings.[251] And understand that this is the lump of clay from which the vessels are made, whether the former or the latter. For if the solution of this inscrutable question were, as you think, in accord with the merits of their wills, it would be so obvious that the apostle would not be compelled by any difficulty about it to cry out, *Who are you, a human being, to answer back to God?* (Rom 9:20). After all, he was dealing with those not yet born, one of whom God loved and one of whom he hated, not on the basis of their works, but according to his choice. And from here he came to these words so that he spoke of the same lump of clay and the different vessels and the power of the potter.

127. JUL. You previously said that all enter into condemnation. How do you dare to cite the testimony which declares that one enters into honor and another into dishonor?

AUG. But grace sets free from the condemnation of the whole lump those whom it sets free, and because you deny this grace, you are heretics. For, if one considers what our origin merits, all enter into condemnation because of the one,[252] and if one considers grace which is not given in accord with our merits, all those who are set free from this condemnation are called vessels of mercy. But the anger of God which comes from God's just judgment remains over those who are not set free.[253] His judgment does not deserve blame because it is inscrutable, and these are called vessels of anger because God also makes good use even of them to make known the riches of his glory toward the vessels of mercy.[254] For God's mercy pardons these what God's judgment exacts from the others. If you think that the unsearchable ways of the Lord are to be blamed, listen to this: *Who are you, a human being, to answer back to God?* (Rom 9:20).

More Accusations of Inconsistency

128. JUL. Nothing, after all, is so inconsistent as to say, "all" and "not all." You say that all are made for condemnation by God the potter; the apostle says that not all are made for condemnation and not all are made for an honorable purpose. I shall explain the value of this in its proper context. In the very expression of the idea it is clear, nonetheless, that there is a great disagreement between you and that the potter who makes all for condemnation is not the same one who Paul says makes some for an honorable purpose. Nor do you believe in the God who is preached by our wonderful teacher, since your potter fashions all for condemnation, while the potter of the apostle fashions very many for glory.

AUG. When he says that all enter into condemnation because of the one, he refers to the lump from which the potter makes some vessels for an honorable purpose, that is, to be adopted in grace, and others for a dishonorable purpose, that is, to be left to pay the debt. In that way the children of grace may know that they are spared the punishment that would not be unjust, if it were exacted, and so they may boast not in themselves, but in the Lord.[255]

129. JUL. And I would like to say this so that it may immediately be clear that you are either singularly ignorant or singularly impudent, for you use statements which contradict your own as if they support yours. But piety and reason have explained that my God forms no one for a dishonorable purpose.

AUG. If your God forms no one for a dishonorable purpose, he is not the God of the apostle Paul; he, of course, said of the true God, *Who are you, a human being, to answer back to God? Does the clay pot say to the one who formed it, Why did you make me so? Or does not the potter have the power to make from the same lump of clay one vessel for an honorable and another for a dishonorable purpose?* (Rom 9:20-21). But you, of course, great artist that you are, bring forth from your Pelagian workshop a better god who makes no vessel for a dishonorable purpose!

130. JUL. He creates his image, that is, all human beings, good, and he desires to form again by the generosity of his remedies even those who were destroyed by the wickedness of their actions. To him the Church indeed sings of mercy and judgment,[256] because he is both good to those who have not sinned and punishes by his just judgment those who, though created good by God, sinned by their own will and rejected the helps of his mercy. The Church of the Catholics sings of this mercy and of this judgment, but in your church nothing of the sort can be heard, for your church says that God, the creator of evil persons, forms persons whom he punishes without justice, without judgment, and without mercy, and that he punishes them precisely because he himself formed them from Adam.

AUG. (1) I have already replied above to all these points; nonetheless, listen for a moment here too. God does not hold back the good of his forming activity even from the condemned race. But if it displeases you that God creates people to condemn them, say in opposition to him, if you can, that he should not create those who he foreknew would be evil and would persevere in wickedness to the end and would for this reason be undoubtedly condemned. Or suggest to him, if you want, that he should take from this life, while they are innocent and good, so many thousands of unbaptized little ones who he knows will live evil lives and will enter into eternal fire along with the devil,[257] when he himself condemns them. Then, if not in his kingdom, at least in some place of secondary happiness, which your heresy has devised for such little ones, they could have eternal life. (2) You still have something else which you, as God's counselor, might suggest for his children whom he has given rebirth, whom he has adopted, and who he, nonetheless, foresaw will be evil and will be condemned: They should be deprived of the continuation of life itself before they come to a sinful life so that they may belong to his kingdom, not face eternal punishments. After all, when you think that you are saying something odious in saying that God creates persons to condemn them, think of how much more hateful a statement someone else, a fool like you, could make, namely, that God gives rebirth to some in order to condemn them. For it is in the power of his omnipotence to remove them from the temptations of this mortal life before they become worthy of condemnation. (3) But if you cannot say these things and can neither speak against God nor offer your counsel to his wisdom—who, after all, has known the mind of the Lord, or who has been his counselor?[258]—stop presenting us with another potter who does not make vessels for a dishonorable purpose. Restrain yourself from blaming the one who does make them, and recognize who you are. After all, so that you do not become involved in this sacrilege, the apostle says to you, *Who are you, a human being, to answer back to God?* (Rom 9:20).

The Choice of Jacob and Rejection of Esau

131. JUL. (1) But let us now defend the honor of the apostle's statement so that no one supposes that he held even with regard to some persons what you thought he held with regard to all. The apostle Paul, then, was discussing some questions posed by the Jews who, proud of the honor of their ancestry, refused to have believers from the Gentiles made their equals. Paul emphasizes the righteousness and grace of God, arguing that it pertains to the bountifulness of that righteousness and grace that the knowledge of the law had first brought honor to the Jews and that afterwards the preaching of Christ also called the Gentiles. For the one creator of each of the two peoples will judge the former through the law and the latter without the law,[259] for he is not the God only of the Jews, but also of the Gentiles.[260] He gives to each of them their reward without fraud, without favor,[261] (2) that is, without any favoritism—which is what the word "grace" means in the definition of justice. And so, he justly condemns those who come

from the seed of Abraham when they live wicked lives, and he disinherits them, just as he does to the Gentiles he catches in similar activity. And just the opposite, in the case of both peoples he rewards their good wills and true faith and the goodness of their actions with everlasting joys. Hence, the teacher of the nations deflates the swelling pride of the Jews, and he shows that the difference lies not in the seeds of the human race, but in moral conduct so that they recognize that, unless they take pains to be believers, they will not be defended by any prerogative of the circumcised people. For Jacob and Esau were conceived by a single act of intercourse and brought to birth by one travail of their mother; yet they met with very different lots in accord with the difference of their merits.

AUG. (1) If you agreed with the apostle, you would not mention the merits of Jacob in this passage. Here he says that God did not love him on account of his works in order to emphasize grace which is not given according to our merits. Otherwise, *the reward is not given*, as he himself says, *as a grace, but as something owed* (Rom 4:4). What does he show by these words but that grace is not owed, but gratuitous? He was, therefore, emphasizing this grace where he said, *For when they were not yet born and had not done anything good or bad, so that the plan of God might remain in accord with his choice, it was not because of works, but because of his call that scripture said: The older will serve the younger* (Rom 9:11-13). (2) The points which you try to obscure are clear. Remove the smoke; pay attention to the light of the scriptures. Grace certainly comes to a human being first so that one loves God and by that love does good works. John the apostle showed this most clearly where he said, *Let us love because he loved us first* (1 Jn 4:19). It is not, then, that we should be loved because we have loved; rather, we love[262] because we have been loved.

132. JUL. Esau, after all, was an irreligious man and a fornicator who sold his birthright for one meal.[263] He sought the blessing which he had scorned, and he did not obtain it though he begged for it with tears.[264] But Jacob was quiet and meek, obeying the commands of his parents. He made such progress with strong desires for holiness that, as the holy people spoke of the God of Abraham and of Isaac, so they also spoke of the God of Jacob. Since it has, therefore, been established from all these examples that by his just judgment God does not deny his mercy to good souls in any people whatsoever and that he does not permit evil souls to be defended by any nobility of their ancestry, the Jews should understand that they ought not to look down upon the faith of the Gentiles. For, just as membership in the family of Israel does not excuse serious sins, so Gentile origin is also no obstacle to the virtues. This was the whole point that the apostle was making in that conflict. In certain passages to humble the arrogance of the circumcised, he used the term "grace" to provide an example of the power of God.

AUG. Then, to humble the arrogance of the circumcised, the apostle lied in using the term "grace." For then God chooses on the basis of works, not on the basis of grace. Who thinks that way but an heretical enemy of grace and friend of pride? The vessel of election and the preacher of the grace by which he became the man he was cries out that God did not love Jacob on the basis of works, and you point out the works of Jacob on the basis of which you argue that God loved him. In doing this, you think that you are speaking against me, though you are a new antichrist and you clearly speak against him in whom Christ spoke.[265]

The Image of God as the Potter of Clay Vessels

133. JUL. (1) They boasted over the observance of the ceremonies and sacrifices, and for this reason they thought that other peoples who were not sanctified by rites of the law could not and should not immediately be admitted into their society. Paul, nonetheless, wanted to say to them that, even if perfect righteousness were found in those observances, God had it in his power to substitute one people for another so that he rejected those he wanted to reject and adopted those he wanted to adopt. The person representing the Jews replies to this idea that nothing ought to be demanded of the human will, since God *shows mercy to whom he wills and hardens whom he wills* (Rom 9:18). And to this the apostle replies, *Who are you, a human being, to answer back to God?* (Rom 9:20). (2) He introduces the testimony of the prophet Isaiah. He says, *Does the clay pot say to the one who formed it, Why did you make me so?* (Is 45:9; Rom 9:20). And he adds on his own: *Or does not the potter have the power to make from the same lump of clay one vessel for an honorable purpose and another for a dishonorable purpose?* (Rom 9:21). The meaning is as follows: Since I have emphasized the will of God and explained the value of his grace, saying that he shows mercy to whomever he pities, you have, you Jew, stirred up slander against me as if the emphasis which I placed upon the will and power of God amounted to the elimination of his justice. (3) And because I said, "He does what he wills," you have argued that nothing ought to be asked in return from the human will if God does everything in accord with his own will, since the dignity of his person removes any room for questioning. For, if I had said, "God does what he ought in accord with the laws of his own justice which passes judgment on the merits of individuals," you would, of course, have not replied with your present objection. But now because I said, "God does what he wills," you thought that I had stolen something from the dignity of justice. Each of them, therefore, is the same. For when I say of God, "He does what he wills," I say nothing else but, "He does what he ought," for I know that he wills nothing but what he ought. When the will is inseparably united to justice, whichever of them I name, I have indicated both of them.

AUG. (1) No matter how you say that God does what he ought, he owes grace to no one, and to many he does not give the punishment which is owed to their evil works. Rather, he gives the grace which he does not owe to any of their good works. After all, what did he owe to Paul himself when he was still Saul and was persecuting the Church? Was it not punishment? But when he knocked him down with a voice sent from the heavens, blinded him, and drew him so force-fully to the faith which he was destroying, he undoubtedly did this as a grace, not as something owed. As a result, he would be among that remnant of the people of Israel of whom scripture says, *In that way, then, they became at this time the remnant by being chosen by grace. But if it is by grace, then it is not on the basis of works; otherwise, grace is no longer grace* (Rom 11:5-6). (2) What but pun-ishment did he owe even to those to whom he said, *Not on your account do I act, house of Israel, but on account of my holy name which you have profaned among the nations* (Ez 36:22)? He says that he brings about their good actions in them, but on account of his holy name which they have profaned, not on account of those who have profaned it. For if he chose to act on their account, he would give them the punishment they deserved instead of giving them the grace they did not deserve. What he says he will do, after all, is aimed at their becoming good; it is not the result of their having been good, for they profaned his holy name. Then he says with perfect clarity that they will do good actions, but because he causes them to do them. For among other things he says, *And I will make you walk in my ordinances and observe and carry out my decrees* (Ez 36:27). (3) To these works, of course, a reward is assigned as something owed, for a reward is owed if they do them. But grace which is not owed comes first so that they do these ac-tions. A good reward is owed, I say, to the good works of human beings, but grace is not owed which makes good human beings out of bad ones. Finally, you said that God does what he ought and proudly praised human merits. Tell me, please, to what merits of the little ones is the kingdom of heaven owed? Perhaps you will say that he owes this to his grace by the help of which they are reborn. For on account of having received this grace they now merit to enter into his kingdom, but he owes to no merits of theirs whatsoever the very grace which he offers to those who are going to be reborn. For this reason in the episcopal court in Palestine, in order not to be condemned himself, your Pelagius was forced to condemn those who say that the grace of God is given according to our merits.[266] There he undoubtedly condemned both himself and you who have not ceased to say this.

(4) The apostle emphasized this grace, truly grace, that is, gratuitous and owed to no preceding merits, when he said, *For when they were not yet born and had not done anything good or bad, so that the plan of God might remain in ac-cord with his choice* (Rom 9:11). This is the choice of which this too was said, *They became the remnant by being chosen by grace. But if it is by grace, it is no*

longer on the basis of works; otherwise, grace is no longer grace (Rom 11:5-6).
For this reason when he had said, *that the plan of God might remain in accord
with his choice,* he immediately added, *It was not because of works, but because
of his call that scripture said: The older will serve the younger* (Rom 9:11-12).
(5) Against this trumpet of truth you shout back and say, "To humble the arrogance of the circumcised, the apostle Paul used the term 'grace' to provide an example of the power of God."[267] What else do you say here but: To humble the
arrogance of the circumcised the apostle lies, when he says that God did not love
Jacob because of his works, though in fact he did love him because of his works?
He loved him because he was "quiet and meek, obedient to the commands of his
parents," and "with strong desires for holiness." You do not understand that God
loved him, not because he was or would be such a man, but that he became such a
man because God loved him. Shame on you! The apostle does not lie; Jacob was
not loved because of his works; if it is by grace, it is no longer on the basis of
works;[268] rather, he was loved because of grace. And by the action of that same
grace it was necessary that he abound in good works. Have pity on your soul; do
not be an enemy to this grace.

134. JUL. (1) That pride, then, wanted to enjoy its leisure and cloak its laziness under the appearance of necessity so that it cries out against the gospel over
the reception of the Gentiles. That pride hears: Even if it were as you pretend,
you ought to pray to God, not to incite rebellion. By these words the apostle refutes the wickedness of the person who tried, by taking advantage of the ambiguity of the expression, to ascribe to divine necessity the difference in merits that
comes from the character of the will.[269] In that way such a person claims that one
of the two is necessary, that is, either the Gentiles do not come to share in the
promise or, if this were permissible for God, the duties arising from free will are
eliminated. But this ploy was not sufficient for the task, nor should such a
teacher, who so emphasized God's authority, leave God's justice without defense. Hence, he adds most appropriately that the vessels which are made for a
dishonorable purpose and those made for an honorable purpose have this as the
earnings of their own will. (2) *After all, what if God wanted to show his anger
and to make known his power in much patience toward the vessels of anger
which were made for destruction and in order to make known* he says, *the riches
of his mercy toward the vessels of mercy which he prepared for glory, those of us
whom he called not only from the Jews, but also from the Gentiles* (Rom
9:22-24). Here he certainly opened up the point which the preceding discussion
had covered over, namely, that the anger of God is only brought against these
vessels which were made for destruction, but that glory is given to those which
were prepared for it. (3) The words of the apostle himself revealed who it is by
whom such vessels are prepared for the reception of the things we mentioned.
He says, *In a great house there are not only gold and silver vessels, but also*

for honorable purposes, others for dishonorable purposes. If, then, any purify themselves from the latter, they will be vessels of honor, made holy, useful to the Lord, and ready for every good work (2 Tm 2:20-21).

AUG. Do the vessels, therefore, prepare themselves so that scripture said of God to no point, *which he prepared for glory* (Rom 9:23)? After all, you say this most clearly, and you do not understand that it said, *If any purify themselves* (2 Tm 2:21), to point out also the action of human beings through the will. But, you ungrateful enemy of grace, *the will is prepared by the Lord* (Prv 8:35 LXX). Hence, both of these are true: God prepares the vessels for glory, and they prepare themselves. For in order that human beings may do this, God does it, because in order that human beings may love, God first loves them. Read the prophet Ezekiel from whom I above quoted what seemed appropriate.[270] You will find even these very words, that is, that God makes human beings keep his commandments when he takes pity on them, not on account of their merits which in that passage he says are evil, but on account of his name. In that way, when without any merits of their own God makes them keep his commandments, they begin to have the merits of their good actions. This is the grace which you deny—not from the actions they do, but in order that they do them.

135. JUL. There you have the duties arising from free will. Paul says, *If any purify themselves* from the fellowship of dishonorable vessels—the term denotes sins—*they will be vessels of honor, made holy, useful to the Lord, ready for every good work* (2 Tm 2:21). These vessels, then, are prepared by their own efforts either for anger or for glory, but God makes known his power in each of them, either by exercising severity toward the wicked or by bestowing his blessing on the faithful. It has been shown, then, that this statement of the exemplary teacher did not bring aid to the views of the Manichees and has, on the contrary, put weapons into our hands as a result.

AUG. Why do you utter slanders? Why do you bring false charges, and why do you not notice that you bring charges against these great teachers of the Church? I answer you, not with the words of some Manichee, but with those of Saint Ambrose: "God calls those whom he chooses, and he makes religious whom he wills."[271] This is what God does in the truth; this is what Ambrose understood in the truth of the divine scriptures. But the judgment by which he makes some religious and does not make others is hidden. For this reason it is said through a human being to a human being, but not by a human being, *Who are you, a human being, to answer back to God? Does the clay pot say to the one who formed it, Why did you make me so? Or does the potter not have the power to make out of the same lump of clay one vessel for an honorable purpose and another for a dishonorable purpose?* (Rom 9:20-21). Remove your clouds from the clarity of these words. Those words signify God's hidden judgment, but the words themselves are so clear that they do not permit your haze to cloud them over or obscure them.

136. JUL. And for this reason his statement is also strongly opposed to you, when it says that not all are made for the condemnation into which you say that all enter. But you usually argue in a most absurd fashion so that you say: "But these who are afterward set free are not made for condemnation." For even the surface of the apostle's words could not in that way agree with you. When you say, "All are created for condemnation by the law of their birth, but some, though only a very few, are set free from it by the mysteries," you do not say what he says. He preaches not only that some of the condemned are set free, but that not all are made for condemnation, but some for a dishonorable purpose and others for an honorable purpose.

AUG. When the apostle said, *Because of the one all enter into condemnation* (Rom 5:16), he pointed out the lump of clay itself, all of which came from Adam in damaged condition. But when he says that vessels are made from it for an honorable purpose, he stresses the grace by which he also sets free human beings whom he creates. Where, however, he says that vessels are made from it for a dishonorable purpose, he reveals the judgment by which he does not set free human beings although he creates them. You yourselves are forced to admit this in the case of little ones, for you cannot deny that there is one lump of them all, of whatever sort you may think it to be. From it you admit that some are adopted into the kingdom of God, and you undoubtedly grant that they are vessels made for an honorable purpose. But others are not adopted, and unless with intelligence you agree that they are vessels made for a dishonorable purpose, you deny it with impudence. After all, if this is not, as you would have it, the punishment of condemnation, it will certainly be a dishonor for the image of God to be separated from the kingdom of God. But if you continue to deny that grace, you will show that you fall under that judgment which would certainly be unjust in the case of little ones, if there were no original sin.

137. JUL. As it is clear that the apostle said this regarding moral conduct, so it is evident that you labor under a great dearth of testimonies from the law. You seek help against the lightning bolts of reason from the statements which scornfully refuse you; in fact by their nature they cannot help you.

AUG. The apostle says that from the same lump God makes one vessel for an honorable purpose and another for a dishonorable purpose; he does not say that he makes still another vessel for neither an honorable nor a dishonorable purpose, though that is, of course, what he would say if he believed what you believe about the little ones. Against this apostle, therefore, whose words are divine thunder, your reason is not full of lightning, but of smoke.

Isaiah Is Used to Interpret Paul's Words

138. JUL. (1) And with respect to the testimony of the apostle these points are disputed. But in Isaiah from whom Paul took this idea God is so far from stopping his rational creature from a consideration of his judgment that he says through the same prophet, *Stop acting wrongly; learn to do good. Help the oppressed, and come, argue against me, says the Lord* (Is 1:16-18). So too he here graciously discloses the plan of his saving actions in order not to seem to have done anything by sheer power and not by justice. For to the people of the Jews suffering in captivity he announces that the time of redemption is approaching when they will return to their land, and he discloses the cause of their past woes and their coming joys. (2) He says, *Let the heavens feast, and the clouds spread righteousness. Let mercy rise out of the earth, and righteousness arise with it. I am the Lord God who created you, making you better. I prepared you as the clay of a potter. Will the one who plows plow the earth all the day? Does the clay say to the potter, What are you doing because you do not work, because you do not have hands? Does the clay pot say to the one who fashioned it: You have made me wisely? Or does anyone say to a father: Why will you beget a child? And to a mother, Why will you bear a child? For thus says the Lord God, the holy one of Israel, who has made what will be. Question me about my sons and about my daughters, and give me commands about the works of my hands. I made the earth and human beings on it; I made firm the heavens by my hand. I gave commands to all the stars; I raised up a king with justice, and all his ways are right. He will build my city, and he will lead back the captivity of my people, not for a price, not with bribes, said the Lord of hosts* (Is 45:8-13).[272]

AUG. (1) If you understood the words of the prophet, you would understand in that passage that the king about whom is said, *I raised up a king with justice, and all his ways are right*, is the mediator between God and human beings, the man Jesus Christ.[273] But then you would understand it as it ought to be understood. Nor will you dare to say that because of the preceding merits of his works he was made the Son of God from the beginning, that is, from the womb of the virgin. Human beings, then, who are his members are changed from evil to good by the same grace by which that man was made good from the beginning. You do not find anything to say about Christ as man, that is, that the Word was made flesh, that he who was God and remained God also became man, and that this man was never a man in such a way that he was not the only-begotten Son of God on account of the only-begotten Word. (2) Nor did he earn his being such by the merits of his actions coming from his own will. Rather, Ambrose spoke the truth, "Inasmuch as he was born of the Holy Spirit, he refrained from sin."[274] Otherwise, on your view, there would be many like him, if they had willed to be, and that he alone was such lay in the power of human beings who did not will to be such. Notice the great impiety with which these ideas are spoken or believed in silent thought. As you recognize the nature of the Only-Begotten, for *the Word was in the beginning, and the Word was with God, and the Word was God* (Jn 1:1), so also recognize grace, for *the Word was made flesh and dwelled among us* (Jn 1:14). He, then, "calls those whom he chooses and makes religious those he wills"[275] who made the man he willed the mediator between God and human beings without any preceding merits of his human will.

139. JUL. (1) According to historical exegesis, then, this is the meaning contained in this passage: God says to his people, "I did not hand you over into captivity out of hatred, nor have I now removed you from the chains of captivity in Babylon by forgetting judgment. Rather, for my part, though I was ready to surround you with constant good will, I, nonetheless, owed it to my justice that I hand over sinners to their enemies and restore and set free those who are troubled. For those knowledgeable in farming do not spend all their time on one chore so that they only furrow the fields with a plow, but prepare their land in different ways for the desired fruitfulness. So I too vary the methods of my plan of salvation[276] so that I may train your will, now by troubles, now by consolations, for the fruits of righteousness. (2) Finally, I want you to understand the great fairness with which I deal with you. I could have scorned your murmurings in view of my power and even imposed on you the burden of silence, just as a pot cannot say to its potter, 'Why have you made me?' Contrary to these examples I, nonetheless, invite you to question me about my sons and about my daughters, that is, about yourselves and the works of my hands, and to learn that I have done everything with justice and have never done anything with cruelty."

AUG. You say what you want, not what Isaiah said. He speaks of grace; you speak against it.

140. JUL. (1) Both the prophet and the apostle, then, introduced the example of the potter merely in order to present a means of comparison, but not to show that human beings are as worthless in God's eyes as is clay in a furnace or on a potter's wheel. Having completed this explanation which we put first, we point out that in accord with the preceding interpretation something else shines forth in that passage. It says, *Pour down from above your dew, you heavens, and let the clouds rain down the righteous one. Let the earth open and bring forth a savior, and let righteousness spring forth as well. I the Lord have created him* (2) *Woe to those who speak against their maker, shards of the earth from Samos. Does the clay pot say to the potter, What are you doing? and, Your work is without handles?* (Is 45:8-9).[277] Even though as history these words refer to King Cyrus, as prophecy they refer to the incarnation of the savior. Because he was going to be born of a virgin, the stubbornness of the Jews and all unbelievers is addressed in order that they may not be enemies to the trustworthy signs. For after he had said, *Let the earth open and bring forth a savior*, he said, *I the Lord created him.*

AUG. (1) Tell me the works by which the man Jesus Christ merited this, and dare to jabber about the justice of God by which he alone merited this. Or if you do not dare, at last confess the grace apart from merits that not merely forgives sins for human beings, but also produces by the Holy Spirit righteousness in human nature. For it is not true that grace forgave sins for the man Jesus Christ, nor is it true that it was not grace that made him so that he was always good from the beginning, just as he was always the Son of God from the beginning.[278] Moreover, as those who were afflicted in the desert by the deadly bites of serpents were admonished to look upon that serpent which had been raised up as a sign so that they would not die,[279] so those who are poisoned by your arguments must be admonished to look upon Christ and to see in the righteousness of that man, the mediator, grace apart from merits so that they may keep from themselves the venom of your mouth. Finally, in the words of the prophet, even in accord with the previous interpretation which you mentioned in which Christ is more clearly foretold, you have not taken from them anything for your argument, except that he was born of a virgin. For the prophet said, *Let the earth open and bring forth a savior* (Is 45:8). (2) But concerning his righteousness which is foretold here as well, you did not want to say anything though you cited the very words of the prophet where he said, *Pour down from above your dew, you heavens, and let the clouds rain down the righteous one. Let the earth open and bring forth a savior, and let righteousness arise with him* (Is 45:8). Tell me: Which righteous one did the clouds rain down if not Christ whom the prophets and apostles proclaimed and who was born from the womb of the virgin with righteousness? For this reason after he said, *Let the earth open and bring forth a savior* he soon added, *And let righteousness arise with him.* And for this reason those human beings who are reborn in Christ are made righteous by the same grace by which Christ was born a righteous man. (3) As, then, he is an example of life so that we may act righteously by imitating him, so he is an example of grace so that by believing in him we may hope that we will become righteous through him from the same source from which he became the one *who became for us wisdom from God and righteousness and sanctification and redemption so that, as scripture says, the one who boasts may boast in the Lord* (1 Cor 1:30-31). Let all those whom you have bitten with your deadly fang look upon this righteous one, and they will be healed. That is, let them believe that they receive righteousness from the same source from which Christ's righteousness was born with him, and so let them boast, not in their choice and not in their merit, but in the Lord.

The Book Ends on the Mystery of God's Choice

141. JUL. (1) The earth is opened for the plant before it receives the seed by the work of the farmer. This is shown in the childbearing of the virgin; by a gift

she first achieved the function of a mother and excluded that of a wife. Almighty God promises that he will do what was not usual, and he adds, foreseeing the multitude of unbelievers: *Woe to those who speak against their maker, shards of the earth from Samos* (Is 45:9). That is, woe to those who claim that the virgin could not have become pregnant despite God's promise. They themselves are formed in the wombs of their mothers by the intervention of God's power, even though they are formed from so many seeds which God created, and yet they claim with stubbornness that flesh could not be formed from the flesh of the virgin without the help of a man. (2) When you do not think, you obstinate people, that I could have done this and raise objections for me about the difficulty of the task, though you yourselves were clearly made by my hands, it is as if the clay would say to its potter when it is being worked by him: "You have no hands,"[280] though by those hands it was then being formed into a vessel. And so, you who ask who gave the virgin a son without the seed of a man recognize that it is the same one who made you from seed. But since these interpretations of the holy scriptures, though different, both agree in piety and reverence, let the first book come to an end. At its end, nonetheless, let it exhort all to believe that God is the maker of the newborn, the protector of the innocent, the God who rewards the Catholics and condemns the Manichees.

AUG. (1) So that those who read intelligently may know how you tried to obscure the clear words of the apostle and twist his straightforward words, I must reply to this argument of yours on the basis of the same argument of the apostle. Blessed Paul wanted to show that God is also able to do what he promised, and in this we are especially shown the grace of which you are enemies. For it is not in the power of human beings that God fulfills what he promised, but in the power of God who made the promise. Wanting to prove this point, he says, *The word of God cannot fail. For not all the descendants of Israel are Israelites, nor are all the descendants of Abraham his children. But your offspring will take its name from Isaac. That is, it is not those who are children of the flesh who are children of God, but the children of the promise are counted as offspring. For this is the word of the promise: At this time I shall come, and Sarah will have a son* (Rom 9:6-9). (2) Keep in mind the children of the promise for he who made the promise is able to fulfill it.[281] *Not only this, however, but Rebecca was pregnant from sleeping one time with our father, Isaac. For when they were not yet born and had not done anything either good or bad, so that God's plan might stand in accord with his choice, it was not because of works, but because of his call that scripture said, The older will serve the younger* (Rom 9:10-12). Here too keep in mind that the choice is not on the basis of works, as a later prophet in some sense explained.[282] Adding this, the apostle says, *As scripture said, I loved Jacob, but I hated Esau* (Rom 9:13).

(3) Here there arises a question which could disturb those who do not understand the depth of grace. Posing this question to himself, the apostle says, *What then shall we say? Is there injustice in God? Heaven forbid!* (Rom 9:14). And to teach what he meant, he says, *Heaven forbid! For Moses says, I shall take pity on whomever I shall take pity, and I shall show mercy to whomever I shall show mercy. Therefore, it does not depend on the one who wills or runs, but on God who takes pity* (Rom 9:15-16). If you would pay attention to this, you would not praise the merits of the will in opposition to grace when you hear, *It does not depend on the one who wills or runs, but on God who takes pity.* God, then, did not take pity because Jacob willed and ran; rather, Jacob willed and ran because God took pity. (4) *The will is prepared by the Lord* (Prv 8:35 LXX), and *the steps of human beings are guided by the Lord, and he shall will their way* (Ps 37:23). Then, because this general statement was made on account of Jacob: *It does not depend on the one who wills or runs, but on God who takes pity,* the example of Pharaoh is given on account of the words, *But I hated Esau* And the apostle adds, *For scripture says to Pharaoh: I have raised you up for this purpose that I might show my power over you and so that my name might be proclaimed in all the earth* (Rom 9:17). After this, he concludes with regard to both: *Therefore, he takes pity on whom he wills and he hardens whom he wills* (Rom 9:18), but he surely takes pity according to the grace which is given freely, not as a payment for merits. He hardens, however, according to the judgment which is paid back to merits. To make from the condemned lump a vessel for an honorable purpose is an obvious grace, but to make out of it a vessel for a dishonorable purpose is just judgment.

(5) Then he adds the words of those who are displeased by this and says, *You then say to me: Why does he still find fault? For who can resist his will?* (Rom 9:19). He stops them with the words, *Who are you, a human being, to answer back to God? Does the pot say to the one who fashioned it, Why have you made me so? Does not the potter have the power to make out of the same lump of clay one vessel for an honorable purpose and another for a dishonorable purpose?* (Rom 9:20-21). See whether this does not agree with his previous statements and disagree with yours, for you think that this was said in accord with the merits of our wills. You speak in opposition to his words: *For when they were not yet born and had not done anything either good or bad, so that God's plan might stand in accord with his choice, it was not because of works, but because of his call that scripture said, The older will serve the younger* (Rom 9:11-12). (6) You speak in opposition to his words: *Therefore, it does not depend on the one who wills or runs, but upon God who takes pity* (Rom 9:16). You speak not merely in opposition to his previous words, but also in opposition to his subsequent words. He calls vessels of anger those which were made for destruction, and that would be unjust unless there was already condemned the lump of all who after the one en-

ter into condemnation. And he calls vessels of mercy those which he prepared for glory; it belongs to a mercy that is gratuitous, not owed, to prepare from the condemned lump vessels for glory, *not only from the Jews*, as he says, *but also from the Gentiles* (Rom 9:24). And for this reason he quotes the testimony from the prophet Hosea: *I have called those who were not my people "my people"* (Hos 2:24),[283] and the testimony from Isaiah, *On account of Israel a remnant will be saved* (Is 10:22).[284]

(7) By the following testimony from the same prophet he teaches that the fact that a remnant existed was brought about by grace. The prophet says, *If the Lord of hosts had not left us offspring* (Is 1:9; Rom 9:29). Then he shows that the Gentiles attained righteousness through faith, but that Israel did not attain righteousness because they pursued it not through faith, but through works. For faith means what he mentions a little later: *For everyone who calls upon the Lord will be saved* (Rom 10:13). And to that salvation it pertains that we have good works and righteousness from God, not from ourselves. On this account he goes on to speak of those who have tripped, not because of faith, but as if because of works, over the stumbling block. He says, *Brothers and sisters, the good will of my heart and my prayer to God is for their salvation, for I bear witness on their behalf that they have zeal for God, but not in accord with knowledge. For, not knowing the righteousness of God and seeking to establish their own righteousness, they were not subject to the righteousness of God* (Rom 10:1-3). (8) And you do exactly the same thing! You want to establish your own righteousness to which God should give grace according to your merits; you do not want the grace of God to come first and make you have righteousness.

Then by a connected sequence of arguments he comes to the point where he says, *I ask then: Has God rejected his people? Heaven forbid! For I too am an Israelite, a descendant of Abraham, of the tribe of Benjamin. God has not rejected his people whom he foreknew. Do you not know what the scripture says of Elijah, how he pleaded with God against Israel? Lord, they have killed your prophets; they have demolished your altars. I alone am left, and they seek my life.* (9) *But what does God's answer say to him? I have left for myself seven thousand men who have not bent their knees to Baal. So too, in this time a remnant has been produced through the choice of grace. But if it is by grace, then it is not by works. Otherwise, grace is no longer grace* (Rom 11:1-6). Then see what he adds; he says: *What then? Israel has not attained what it sought, but choice has attained it* (Rom 11:7). But look above to see what sort of choice it is where he says, *A remnant has been produced through the choice of grace. But if it is by grace, then it is not by works. Otherwise, grace is no longer grace* (Rom 11:5-6). (10) And refer this to that point from which this discussion began, *For when they were not yet born and had not done anything either good or bad, so that God's plan might stand in accord with his choice, it was not because of works* (Rom 9:11). This is the choice of grace, not because of works. By grace they are made vessels for an honorable purpose so that they do good works, for good works follow upon grace instead of coming first. The grace of God makes us do them. Let us not establish our own righteousness. Rather, let the righteousness of God be in us, that is, the righteousness which God gives us. *But the others were blinded* (Rom 11:7); this is the judgment by which they are made vessels for a dishonorable purpose. On the basis of that judgment scripture said, *I hated Esau* (Rom 9:13). On the basis of that judgment scripture says to Pharaoh, *I have raised you up for this purpose* (Rom 9:17). (11) Hence, it is clear that you who understand the apostle in this way—or rather who do not understand him—want to boast on the basis of works in opposition to grace, and you want to establish your own righteousness and not be subject to the righteousness of God. We proclaim that God is the maker of little ones, but we do not grant a middle place for vessels which are made from the same lump of clay for neither an honorable purpose nor a dishonorable purpose—something that the apostle did not permit. But by doing this you would escape the judgment of God if you could show that he condemns only the Manichees and not all heretics.

Notes

1. The excerpts from Julian's *To Turbantius* were not made by Julian, and they occasionally departed from what Julian had said.

2. In the six books of his *Answer to Julian* Augustine replied to the four books of Julian's *To Turbantius.*

3. When Julian speaks of the Manichees, he means the Augustinian side in the controversy, just as he refers to the Pelagians as the Catholics.

4. Pelagius, *In Defense of Free Choice (Pro libero arbitrio)* 3; see *The Grace of Christ and Original Sin* I, 43, 47.

5. Ambrose, *Penance (De paenitentia)* I, 3, 13: SC 179, 62.

6. See Lv 12:8.

7. See Gn 17:14.

8. See Jos 6:21 and 10:32.

9. Julian labels Augustine as a traducianist because he claims that original sin is inherited. Augustine was not, however, a traducianist in the sense that he held that the soul of an infant was inherited from the soul of the parent.

10. See below 50 and 52, where, in a reprise of book two of *Answer to Julian*, Augustine cites texts from Cyprian of Carthage, Ambrose of Milan, Gregory of Nazianzus, Hilary of Poitiers, and John Chrysostom against the doctrine.

11. Julian uses "Punic: *Poenus*" as a derogatory term for Augustine; it means Phoenician or Carthaginian, but expresses the Italian contempt for Africa. Alypius, who was baptized with Augustine in Milan, became bishop of Thagaste, his and Augustine's hometown. He journeyed back and forth between Africa and Italy, carrying documents from and to Ravenna and Rome.

12. Augustine puns on Julian's derogatory term "Punic: *Poenus*" and "punishment: *poena.*"

13. That is, the first book of *Marriage and Desire.*

14. See Mt 23:27.

15. See below 53, where Augustine appeals to passages from the writings of Hilary of Poitiers, as well as to passages from the other Fathers of the Church mentioned here.

16. Augustine alludes to the Circumcelliones, the bands of assassins in Donatist Africa.

17. See *Marriage and Desire* II, 2, 2.

18. Hippo, the city where Augustine was bishop, was located in the Province of Numidia.

19. *Marriage and Desire* II, 2, 2.

20. *Ibid.*

21. Augustine is referring to the first book of his *Marriage and Desire* which he sent to Count Valerius.

22. *Marriage and Desire* I, 1, 1.

23. *Ibid.*

24. *Ibid.*

25. *Marriage and Desire* II, 2, 3-4.

26. Julian probably refers to his books, *To Turbantius* which Augustine did not have when he wrote *Marriage and Desire.*

27. Julian's language mimics the style of Marcus Tullius Cicero in his First Oration against Catiline, the conspirator against the republic whom Cicero exposed.

28. I have followed Primmer's suggestion based on one manuscript to read "*fecisti*" instead of "*facis.*"

29. In response to Julian's citation from Cicero, Augustine employs a double rhyme: "*Julianum*" and "*Tullianum*" as well as "*insanum*" and "*Christianum*" Thus he counters Julian's appeal to lofty classical rhetoric with a humble figure that Christian rhetoricians had taken up.

30. See *Answer to Julian* VI, 24, 75, for Julian's statement and Augustine's reply.

31. Augustine plays upon the words "excerptor: *decerptor*" and "deceiver: *deceptor.*"

32. See Rom 5:12.

33. The Latin for Mani and for Manichee are the same.

34. See Mt 1:21.

35. See Ez 13:18.

36. Julian uses "*gratia*", the usual term for "grace," which I have translated as "favor" here, because Julian sees "*gratia*" as a form of favoritism before the law.

37. Julian refers to the Stoic philosopher, Zeno of Citium (ca. 362/357-264/259 B.C.), who taught that the virtues imply one another so that a person who has one will have all the virtues.

38. See Ps 144:4.

39. See Ps 144:4.

40. See Mt 20:1-16.

41. The Latin word for "mercy, or compassion: *misericordia*" is a compound of "misery: *miseria*" and "heart: *cor.*"

42. See Rom 2:11.

43. See 1 Cor 1:27.

44. Julian also accuses Augustine of using horses as a bribe below in I, 74 and in III, 35. In his "note complémentaire" on Count Valerius, A. de Veer points out that Augustine treats Julian's accusation as pure slander. See BA 23, 666.

45. I have followed Primmer's suggestion and read "*et ad*" which is found in one manuscript, instead of "*ut addas.*"

46. *The Two Souls* 11, 15.

47. I have followed Primmer's suggestion to read "*vel*" with one manuscript rather than "*velut.*"

48. I have followed Primmer's conjecture and added "*at.*"

49. I have followed Primmer's suggestion to add "*est*" on the basis of one manuscript.

50. See Rom 8:10.

51. Ambrose, *Commentary on the Gospel of Luke* (*Expositio Euangelii secundum Lucam*) 7, 234: CCL 14, 205.

52. See *Marriage and Desire* I, 20, 22.

53. I have followed Primmer's suggestion to read "*respondes*" as is found in one manu-script, instead of "*respondens*" and to end the sentence with "*deus.*"

54. Both of these sites were noted for lakes with foul smells and were regarded as entrance ways to the underworld. See Vergil, *Aeneid* VII, 563-570, and Cicero, *Divination (De divinatione)* I, 79.

55. See Heb 7:9-10.

56. Ambrose, *Paradise (De paradiso)* 13, 67: CSEL 32/1, 325.

57. See above 47. Ambrose, *Commentary on the Gospel of Luke (Expositio Euangelii secundum Lucam)* 7, 234: CCL 14, 205.

58. Pelagius, *In Defense of Free Choice (Pro libero arbitrio)* III; see *The Grace of Christ and Original Sin* I, 43, 47. Pelagius' work is extant only in fragments, most of them from this work of Augustine.

59. Ambrose, *Penance (De paenitentia)* 1, 3, 13: SC 179, 62.

60. Augustine plays upon "*sanus*" and "*insanus*" which describe someone in good or bad health, whether physical or mental.

61. Ambrose, *Commentary on the Gospel of Luke (Expositio Euangelii secundum Lucam)* 7, 234: CCL 14, 205.

62. See Heb 12:23.

63. See Acts 17:31.

64. See Gen 17:12-14.

65. I have followed Primmer's suggestion and omitted "*deus*" on the basis of two manu-scripts.

66. See also Ex 34:7, Dt 5:9, Nm 14:18, and Jer 32:18.

67. See Rom 8:10.

68. See Heb 12:23.

69. See Col 1:13.

70. The rites of exsufflation and exorcism were parts of the ritual for baptism until recent years. Both rites aimed at the expulsion of the devil from the person about to be baptized.

71. Cyprian, Letter 64 (*Epistula ad Fidum*) 5: CSEL 3, 720-721.

72. See Sir 40:1.

73. I have followed Primmer's conjecture and added "*ut.*"

74. I have followed Primmer's suggestion of "*confundatur*" which is found in one manu-script, instead of "*confunderetur.*"

75. *Marriage and Desire* I, 1, 1. The passage is confusing because Julian is here quoting *Marriage and Desire* II, 2, 4-5 where Augustine is quoting the first book of that work where he reported what the Pelagians held.

76. *Marriage and Desire* I, 1, 1.

77. *Ibid.*

78. *Marriage and Desire* II, 2, 4-5.

79. Cyprian, Letter 64 (*Epistula ad Fidum*) 5: CSEL 3, 720-721.

80. Hilary, *Commentary on Psalm 118 (Tractatus in Psalmum CXVIII)* 22, 6: CSEL 22, 543.

81. Ambrose, *Penance (De paenitentia)* I, 3, 13: SC 179, 62.

82. Gregory Nazianzus, *Sermon on the Birth of Christ (Oratio in Christi nativitate)* 38, 17: PG 36, 330; in Rufinus' translation, *The Epiphany or the Birth of the Lord (De epiphaniis sive de natali Domini)* 2, 17: CSEL 46, 105.

83. Basil, *Sermon on Fasting (Sermo de ieiunio)* 1, 4: PG 31, 167.

84. John Chrysostom, *To Olympias (Ad Olympiadem)* 3, 3: PG 52, 574.

85. See Pelagius, *Profession of Faith (Libellus fidei)* 7, 7: PL 45, 1718 or 17: PL 48, 490. Also see *Profession of Faith (Libellus fidei)* 7: PL 45, 1734; this latter profession is attributed to Julian.

86. Julian is quoting his own words from his *To Turbantius*; see Augustine's *Answer to Julian* III, 3, 8-9, where parts of this passage are quoted.

87. 1 Cor 1:31 and 2 Cor 10:17.

88. See Mt 1:21.

89. Gregory Nazianzus, *Sermon on the Birth of Christ* (*Oratio in Christi nativitate*) 38, 17: PG 36, 330; in Rufinus' translation, *The Epiphany or the Birth of the Lord* (*De epiphaniis sive de natali Domini*) 2, 17: CSEL 46, 105.

90. See Sir 40:1.

91. See Wis 9:15.

92. See Ps 4:3.

93. Melchiades, or Miltiades, was pope from 311 to 314. In October of 313, Constantine delegated to him the hearing of the appeal of Donatus against Caecilian. See *Answer to Julian* I, 3, 7, where Augustine mentions that Reticius heard the case along with Melchiades.

94. The work of Reticius of Autun is not extant.

95. See Sir 40:1.

96. As a part of the ritual of baptism, the minister of the sacrament breathed upon the one to be baptized to blow out (*exsufflare*) the devil.

97. Pelagius, *Commentary on the Letter to the Romans* (*Expositio in epistulam ad Romanos*) 5, 15: *PLS* I, 1137. See *The Punishment and Forgiveness of Sins* III, 2, 2 and *The Grace of Christ and Original Sin* II, 21, 24.

98. See Mt 11:25.

99. See Ps 49:7.

100. See 1 Cor 15:47.

101. For Faustus and Adimantus see above, 25. Marcion was a second century heretic who emphasized the dichotomy between the evil creator God of the old testament and the supreme and good God of the new.

102. Ambrose, *Penance* (*De paenitentia*) I, 3, 13: SC 179, 62-64.

103. See *The Grace of Christ and Original Sin* I, 43, 47, where Augustine cites Pelagius' words of praise for Ambrose.

104. The rhymes in Augustine's language: *videre non invidere* and *redire non perire* cannot be reproduced in English.

105. See Col 1:13.

106. It helps to understand Julian's argument to realize that the meanings of "nature: *natura*" include "the conditions of birth" and "the external organs of generation, or the private parts."

107. See Col 1:13.

108. I have followed Primmer's suggestion and read "*ab illa prohibet*" which is found in one manuscript, instead of "*parvulis negat.*"

109. See Lk 19:10.

110. See Ps 144:4.

111. The CSEL text has "*sui*" but I have followed another manuscript reading which has "*suis.*"

112. *Marriage and Desire* I, 1, 1.

113. Augustine below tells us that Calliphon was a philosopher who held that the human good was to be found in both the virtue of the mind and in the pleasure of the body. Julian infers that he tried to combine contradictory views.

114. See Cicero, *The Ends of the Good and the Evil* (*De finibus*) 2, 6, 19; 2, 11, 34-35; and 5, 25, 73, as well as Lactantius, *Divine Institutes* (*Divinae Institutiones*) III, 7. Both authors mention that Calliphon was a great philosopher who linked virtue and pleasure.

115. Ambrose, *Noah* (*De Noe*) 3 bis, 7: CSEL 32, 417. The sentence is not a question in Ambrose, though it is in the CSEL edition of this work. I have followed the reading in Ambrose.

116. Ambrose, *Commentary on the Gospel of Luke* (*Expositio euangelii secundum Lucam*) 2, 56: CCL 14, 55.

117. The words in brackets are found in *Marriage and Desire* but are missing in all the manuscripts.

118. I have followed Primmer's suggestion and omitted "*potest*" from the beginning of this quotation.

119. *Marriage and Desire* I, 1, 1.

120. *Marriage and Desire* II, 2, 6.

121. See Jn 8:44.

122. I have followed Primmer's conjecture of "*dominium*" instead of "*dominum.*"

123. Since Augustine goes on to mention each of the verbs that Paul used, I had to translate them by different English verbs, though elsewhere I did not do so.

124. See Rom 7:22-23.

125. See 1 Cor 15:53-55.

126. Ambrose, *Penance* (*De paenitentia*) I, 3, 13: SC 179, 62-64.

127. Caelestius was a disciple of Pelagius; he was accused of heresy by Paulinus of Milan at the Council of Carthage in 411 or 412. See *The Deeds of Pelagius* 11, 23 for the propositions of Caelestius condemned at Carthage.

128. Gregory Nazianzus, *Sermon in Self-Defense* (*Oratio apologetica*) 2, 91: PG 35, 494; in Rufinus' translation, *Apologeticus* 91: CSEL 46, 67-68.

129. See *The Deeds of Pelagius* 11, 23.

130. See *The Punishment and Forgiveness of Sins* I, 3, 3-4, 4.

131. See *Confessions* IX, 8, 18.

132. Compare this passage with *Confessions* IX, 10, 26, where Monica says that she prayed to see Augustine a Catholic Christian before her death.

133. See Gn 3:7 and 2:25.

134. Gregory Nazianzus, *Sermon in Self-Defense* (*Oratio apologetica*) 2, 91: PG 35, 494; in Rufinus' translation, *Apologeticus* 91: CSEL 46, 68. See also *Answer to Julian* II, 3, 7.

135. See Wis 9:15.

136. See Gal 5:17.

137. Ambrose, *Penance* (*De paenitentia*) I, 3, 13: SC 179, 62.

138. Gregory Nazianzus, *Sermon on the Birth of Christ* (*Oratio in Christi nativitate*) 38, 17: PG 36, 330; in Rufinus' translation, *The Epiphany or the Birth of the Lord* (*De epiphaniis sive de natali Domini*) 2, 17: CSEL 46, 105.

139. Gregory Nazianzus, *Sermon on Pentecost* (*Oratio de Pentecoste*) 41, 14; in Rufinus's translation *Sermon 4: On Pentecost* (*Oratio*) 4: *De Pentecoste* 14: CSEL 46, 158.

140. Hilary, *Commentary on Psalm 118* (*In psalmum 118*) 175: PL 9, 641.

141. *Marriage and Desire* II, 2, 6.

142. Ambrose, *Commentary on the Gospel of Luke* (*Expositio Euangelii secundum Lucam*) 7, 142-143: CCL 14, 264.

143. See Ambrose, *Commentary on the Gospel of Luke* (*Expositio Euangelii secundum Lucam*) 7, 141; CCL 14, 263.

144. See Gal 5:17.

145. See Rom 7:23.

146. Ambrose, *Commentary on the Gospel of Luke* (*Expositio Euangelii secundum Lucam*) 7, 141: CCL 14, 263.

147. Cyprian, *The Lord's Prayer* (*De oratione dominica*) 16: CCL 3A, 99-100.

148. See above, 71.

149. See Mt 26:41.

150. See Ps 49:7.

151. *Marriage and Desire* II, 2, 6-3, 7.

152. *Marriage and Desire* II, 3, 8.

153. I have with Primmer followed the reading in Migne of "*nobiscum*" instead of "*vobiscum.*"

154. Julian plays not merely on "celestial" and "Caelestius" where the wordplay is clear in English, but upon "Pelagius" and the sea, which is "*pelagus*" in the Latin.

155. Athanasius (circa 300-373) was bishop of Alexandria from 328-373; he was the strongest defender of Nicaean orthodoxy during the years following the Council of Nicaea when various Arian Councils were convened. At the Council of Rimini (Ariminum) held in 359, 330 bishops endorsed an Homoian Arian Creed. See the introduction to Augustine's anti-Arian works in *Arianism and Other Heresies* (Hyde Park: New City, 1995). It was of this Council that Jerome said, "The world groaned and was astonished to find itself Arian" (*Dialogus con-*

tra Luciferianos) 19: PL 23, 181). Athanasius was not present at the council, but in hiding in the Egyptian desert from February of 356 to November of 361. The emperor at the time was Constantius who reigned from 350 to 361.

156. "Homoousians" is taken from the Greek "*homoousios*" —which means "of the same substance." It is the key term in the Symbol of Nicaea (325) which affirmed the full divinity of the Word. The Arians with whom Augustine was directly familiar were Homoians, that is, they held that the Son was like the Father or like the Father according to the scriptures, but not the same in substance with the Father.

157. Macarius was one of two imperial notaries sent to Africa by the emperor, Constans, in 348 to establish church unity. Because of his high-handed methods he roused much resentment, and the Donatists referred to the Catholics as "the Macarian party" or as "Macarians."

158. The Manichees apparently called the Catholics Pharisees because they retained the old testament scriptures which the Manichees rejected.

159. I have followed Primmer's suggestion for the punctuation of the sentence and for reading "*repudiare*" which is found in one manuscript, instead of "*repudiavere.*"

160. "*Homoousios*: of the same substance"defined the sameness in divinity of the Father and the Son. The novelty of the term and its non-biblical character made it difficult for many to accept.

161. I have followed Primmer's suggestion and read with two manuscripts "*concinenter*" instead of "*continenter.*"

162. See Cicero, *Duties* (*De officiis*) I, 7. The Latin text does not mention Cicero by name, but simply says, "*ille,*" "that one."

163. "*Emancipatio*" meant: the formal releasing of a son or daughter from the power of the father, for example, into the hands of an adoptive father or husband.

164. See Rom 10:3.

165. See 2 Cor 3:5.

166. See above, 28.

167. See above, 67.

168. See Jn 8:36.

169. See above, 74; Julian cites *Marriage and Desire* II, 3, 8.

170. See *Answer to the Two Letters of the Pelagians* III, 8, 24. Augustine wrote this work for Pope Boniface.

171. I have followed Primmer's conjecture of "*studere*" instead of "*studerent.*"

172. See Lk 13:28-29.

173. See Rom 6:12-13.

174. The Latin word "*liberi*" can mean either "children, that is, sons and daughters," or "free."

175. See Lk 24:27.

176. See Acts 16:14.

177. I have followed Primmer's suggestion and added "*suorum*" on the basis of one manuscript.

178. See 2 Cor 4:2.

179. I have translated "*abjectis*" which is found in one manuscript, instead of "*objectis*" which is found in the CSEL text.

180. See above, 69.

181. Ambrose, *Commentary on the Gospel of Luke* (*Expositio Euangelii secundum Lucam*) 7, 27: CCL 14, 224.

182. See Acts 9:1-22.

183. Julian adds the phrase, "in his gospel."

184. In *Answer to Two Letters of the Pelagians* the text reads: "choice of the will."

185. Augustine refers to Julian with the Latin "*iste,*" a pronoun which often conveys contempt.

186. *Answer to the Two Letters of the Pelagians* I, 2, 5.

187. Julian omits the clause: "since the very fact that they believe in him is a gift."

188. See *Answer to Two Letters of the Pelagians* I, 2, 4.

189. Julian omits the following: "Nor does the one who persuades and deceives them aim at anything else in them but that they commit sin by their own will, whether out of ignorance of the truth or out of delight in iniquity or out of both of these evils, namely, blindness and weakness."

190. *Answer to the Two Letters of the Pelagians* I, 3, 6-7. Julian omits at the end of this sentence the following: "that is, by the grace of God through Jesus Christ our Lord."

191. See Jn 1:14.

192. See Rom 5:8.

193. See Rom 8:17.

194. See 1 Tm 1:8.

195. See 2 Cor 3:6.

196. I have translated *"adoptat"* which is found in Migne, instead of *"optat"* which the CSEL text has.

197. See Eph 3:19.

198. See 2 Cor 5:10.

199. For the heresy of Jovinian, see Augustine, *Heresies* 82.

200. I have followed Primmer's suggestion to read: *"in eo"* which is found in one manuscript, instead of *"ideo."*

201. See *The Deeds of Pelagius* 11, 23-24.

202. John Chrysostom, *To Olympias (Ad Olympiadem)* 3, 3: PG 52, 574.

203. *Answer to the Two Letters of the Pelagians* I, 3, 7.

204. For Jovinian, see Augustine, *Heresies* 82. Jovinian's work is not extant except in some fragments; its title is not known.

205. *Answer to the Two Letters of the Pelagians* I, 3, 7.

206. I have translated *"contravenires"* which is found in Migne, rather than *"convenires"* which is found in the CSEL text.

207. See 1 Jn 1:8.

208. See Acts 10:1-8.

209. See Acts 8, 9-13.18-24.

210. See Ps 36:7.

211. See Rom 11:6.

212. See *Answer to Julian* II, 5, 14, where Augustine cites the lost work of Ambrose, *The Sacrament of Rebirth, or Philosophy (De sacramento regenerationis, sive de philosophia).*

213. See *Answer to the Two Letters of the Pelagians* I, 3, 7; see also above, 94. Julian here shortens what Augustine had said.

214. I have followed Primmer's conjecture of *"uocans"* instead of *"uocas."*

215. See above, 28.

216. See Rom 8:23.

217. See 2 Tm 2:13.

218. See Jn 8:44.

219. See above, 44 and 45.

220. See *Answer to Julian* VI, 18, 54.

221. See above, 69.

222. See Jas 1:14.

223. See Cyprian, Letter 64, 3. This letter of Cyprian is one of Augustine's favorite texts.

224. I have followed Primmer and several manuscripts in reading *"illi"* instead of *"ille."*

225. "With regard to this righteousness" is in the dative case; "from that righteousness" is in the ablative case.

226. See *Marriage and Desire* I, 23, 26.

227. Ambrose, *Penance (De paenitentia)* I, 3, 13: SC 179, 62.

228. See above, 74.

229. See Jn 5:21.

230. See Jn 6:44.

231. See Mt 1:21.

232. Ambrose, *Commentary on the Gospel of Luke* (*Expositio Euangelii secundum Lucam*) 7, 234: CCL 14, 295.

233. See Lk 19:10.

234. See Rom 5:18.

235. See Rom 9:21.

236. *Marriage and Desire* II, 5, 8; also see Ps 101:1.

237. See *Answer to Julian* VI, 24, 75 ff.

238. Ambrose, *Penance* (*De paenitentia*) I, 9, 13: SC 179, 62.

239. I have followed Primmer's suggestion and read "*corpora talia*" which is found in one manuscript, instead of "*corporalia*" which is found in the CSEL edition.

240. See Sir 40:1.

241. See Col 1:13.

242. See Ez 16:51.

243. See Lk 19:10.

244. See Wis 4:11.

245. See Sir 40:1.

246. Ambrose, *Commentary on the Gospel of Luke* (*Expositio Euangelii secundum Lucam*) I, 37: CCL 14, 25.

247. Paul cites Ps 116:10.

248. See Rom 5:16.

249. See Rom 5:12.

250. Ambrose, *Penance* (*De paenitentia*) I, 3, 13: SC 179, 62.

251. See Rom 5:12.

252. See Rom 5:16.

253. See Jn 3:36.

254. See Rom 9:23.

255. See 1 Cor 1:31.

256. See Ps 101:1.

257. See Mt 25:41.

258. See Rom 11:34.

259. I have followed the CSEL which has "*sine lege* " where Migne has "*in lege.*" See Rom 2:12, 3:30-31, and 3:29.

260. See Rom 3:29.

261. Julian uses "*gratia,*" which for Augustine means "grace, or gift," in the sense of favoritism or partiality.

262. I have followed Primmer's suggestion and read "*diligimus*" which is found in two manuscripts, instead of "*diligamus.*"

263. See Heb 12:16.

264. See Heb 12:17.

265. See 2 Cor 13:3.

266. See *The Deeds of Pelagius* 13, 30.

267. See above, 132.

268. See Rom 11:6.

269. This person is the one cast in the role of the Jews in Julian's interpretation of Paul, though Julian through him also alludes to Augustine.

270. See above, 133.

271. Ambrose, *Commentary on the Gospel of Luke* (*Expositio Euangelii secundum Lucam*) 7, 27: CCL 14, 224.

272. The Latin of Isaiah here follows the text of the Septuagint, though below in 140 Julian cites the text of the Vulgate.

273. See 1 Tm 2:5.

274. Ambrose, *Commentary on Isaiah* (*Fragmenta in Esaiam*) I: CCL 14, 405. See also *Marriage and Desire* I, 35, 40.

275. Ambrose, *Commentary on the Gospel of Luke* (*Expositio Euangelii secundum Lucam*) 7, 27: CCL 14, 224.

276. I have followed Primmer's suggestion to stick with the reading in Migne which has "*dispensationum*" instead of "*disputationum.*"

277. Here Julian follows the Vulgate; above in 138 his text is quite different.

278. The sentence is a question in the CSEL edition.

279. See Nm 21:6-9.

280. The Latin text from Isaiah says quite literally, "Your work has no hands"—which I translated above with "handles" in place of "hands," as does the RSV. The Septuagint has, "What are you doing, for you do not work nor do you have hands."

281. See Rom 4:21.

282. See Mal 1:2-3.

283. See Rom 9:25.

284. See Rom 9:27 and 11:5.

BOOK TWO

Book Two

The Issue of Suitable Judges to Hear the Case

1. JUL. The other side would deal fairly if we were given the chance either to defend the cause of truth before learned judges or, since that has been denied for the time being, if we were not pummeled by the shouting of the ignorant.

AUG. You, of course, ask for the sort of judges who could judge about your statements only if they were highly trained experts in the liberal arts and were familiar with the views of the philosophers of this world as well. Ambrose was such a man, and if you do not reject him as a judge, you should not doubt that you have been condemned with perfect justice. For he said, "All of us human beings are born under the power of sin, and our very origin lies in guilt."[1] By these words of his he wanted to show that Christ the savior, that is, Jesus, is necessary for little ones. When you contradict him, you must admit that you want to have learned judges, but you do not wish to have Catholic Christian judges.

2. JUL. And because we suffer the loss of the flag of victory that we wanted to raise up for the salvation of the churches, the flag of victory which the wisdom of the investigating judges would have brought to the good cause with their wonderful support, the agreement of the common folk should at least not be able to contribute anything to our defamation. Of these two classes of human beings I mentioned, the one would benefit us, the other would do us no harm, if either the former obtained power or the latter a sense of shame. But since great confusion reigns on these topics and there is a huge number of stupid people, the rudder of reason has been snatched from the Church so that the belief of the people steers the ship under full sail.

AUG. If what we maintain is the belief of the people, then it is not the belief of the Manichees which you attack in the Christian peoples with your corrupt mind. You, of course, rightly condemn the Manichean madness in a few. But you also have your own madness. And in that madness you use the name of the Manichees to try to make hostile to us those people whom you reject as judges, as if people deceived by your endless chatter could call Ambrose a Manichee or could call Cyprian a Manichee, because they taught the existence of original sin on account of the salvation of the little ones as well. Ambrose did not create such people, but found them. Cyprian himself did not create such people, but found them. Your father also found such people in the Church when you were baptized as a little one, as it is reported.[2] You yourselves, finally, found such Catholic people. Be quiet; we admit that ours is the belief of the people, because we are the people of the one called Jesus because he saves his people from their sins.[3]

When you want to separate the little ones from that people, you separate your-selves instead.

3. JUL. Thus, since you can accomplish very little with the wise, but with the common folk whatever you decide is also acceptable, a decree of the seditious has banned approval of the virtues from the Church. And it discredits us among the common run of people because we refuse to be an accessory to error. I mean the common run of people who weigh the merit of an opinion by its success and judge that opinion to be more true which they see wins the favor of the majority.

AUG. Did the Manichees win the favor of the majority? Are they not, like parricides, few in number and very evil? Do not, then, boast of your small num-bers and—what is even more foolish —say that our teaching wins the favor of the majority and raise as an objection to us the teaching of a detestable few.

4. JUL. Tully said against Epicurus in a clear argument that a view is not ex-pressed with great refinement when people of just any sort declare that it gener-ally wins their favor.[4] These folks suppose in their twisted fashion that this, like everything else, is proof of its wisdom.

AUG. Tully is, however, defeated and refuted on this point by the one who says, *Praise the Lord, all you nations; praise him, all you peoples* (Ps 117:1). You do not seek to teach these nations the truth, but to deceive some of them with your refinement. You seek to add them to your small number by praising the re-finement of the few worldly philosophers and by reproaching us because we do not state our view with refinement and because for this reason people of just any sort declare that it generally wins their favor. You have, nonetheless, said sev-eral times that I aimed at nothing more than to make myself unintelligible. How, then, does the view I defend win the favor of the multitude, unless this multitude is Catholic and your heresy is rightly displeasing to it?

5. JUL. After all, it surely delights minds in heat to denigrate whatever the saints ever did anywhere so that they are not reproached by the examples of their fine deeds.

AUG. Minds in heat, then, rather run after you who praise sexual desire, for chaste souls reproach and bring accusations against that which they are praised for conquering.

6. JUL. It, of course, delights and deeply pleases minds in heat to talk of the feebleness of nature and to say that the flesh is subject to inborn sins and not to attribute the results of conversion to the human will, but to call the functions of the members serious sins of desire and to say that it is the Catholic faith to admit free choice, but a choice by which one is forced to do evil and cannot will the good.

AUG. Why are you angry with us? We desire the results of conversion the more certainly when we beg for it more faithfully from the Lord. In vain do you spread about your inflated language with your proud voice. We, of course, do not want; we certainly do not want to be counted among *those who place their own virtue* (Ps 49:7). Our soul is thirsting for the Lord,[5] and it says to him, *I would love you, Lord, my virtue* (Ps 18:2). Human beings, after all, can will the good, but *the will is prepared by the Lord* (Prv 8:35 LXX). Our damaged nature, however, readily turns toward evil, and on that account it must be healed.

The Accusation of Heresy and Its Grounds

7. JUL. But such minds say that the statements of those persons are foolish and heretical who maintain that the just God created human beings free to do good actions and that it is in the power of each person to pull back from evil and to become resplendent with enthusiasm for virtue so that the sting of worries and fears afflicts those who blame their serious sins on the necessity of nature.

AUG. We do not say that the statements of those persons are foolish and heretical who maintain that the just God created human beings free to do good actions. He did, after all, create Adam as such a human being, and we were all in that man. But by sinning he destroyed himself and all of us in himself. As a result it is not now in the power of his descendants to be set free from evil unless the grace of God gives them the power to become children of God.[6] On this account the sting of worry and fear does not afflict those who, as you say, blame their serious sins on the necessity of nature, but those who pour forth prayers to God so that they may not be brought into temptations to serious sins, and they worry and fear that they might assent to your proud arguments that are most ungrateful to God.

8. JUL. Finally, such minds teach in churches which have great honor and a great crowd of people that the power of sin is so great that before the formation of the members, before the beginning and arrival of the soul, it hovers over the seeds that are sown, enters the womb of the mother, and makes guilty those who are to be born, and at the very moment of birth an older sin awaits its realization. This law of sin then dwells in the members and forces the captive human being to be a slave to sins, deserving, not of chastisement for shameful acts, but rather of pity. For men and women and great bishops in the Church label what we call the sins of an evil will our original affliction.

AUG. The great bishop Ambrose, who was so magnificently praised by the lips of the founder of your heresy,[7] replies to you. He says, "Wretched was the manner in which Eve gave birth; she left to women that sort of child-bearing as their heritage, and each child conceived in the pleasure of concupiscence, poured into the maternal womb, formed in blood, and wrapped in cloths, has experienced the infection of sins before drawing in the gift of the breath of life."[8] Human nature, therefore, must be healed, Julian, by God's mercy, not praised as if it were in good health by your foolish rhetoric.

9. JUL. These harlots of Manichean teaching, then, pander to the ears of the most impure.

AUG. Charge Ambrose, if you dare, with the crime of Manicheism. Notice against whom you say what you want to be thought to say against me, and if you have either any fear of God or any human sense of shame, be quiet. Along with such men I ought to listen to your abuse, not only patiently, but even gladly, but in attacking such men you ought to be ashamed before human judgment and to fear God's.

10. JUL. This nettle aroused our enemies who are found in both sexes. Once it was biting because of the defect of a bad habit, but it was healed by certain ointments of salutary exhortations.

AUG. When the nettle pricks, it causes an itch, but only in one who praises sexual desire. If on account of a bad habit, as you suppose, that man cries out, *I do not do the good that I will, but I do the evil that I do not will* (Rom 7:19), you surely admit that at least in that one the human will lost the ability to do good actions. For unless the help of divine grace comes to the rescue, what good does the copious and elegant words of any exhortation do that person?

11. JUL. But now, after it has begun to be presented for treatment and authority has been added to delight, by the consent of almost the whole world shamefulness revels. She is a queen over minds who has power over their members, an attacker of good morals, and an irresistible jailer of all hearts. And so, for us the cause of defending the truth has become harder to the degree that it is more honorable. For a small number of healers cannot do much by reason[9] against people who are bent on destruction and opposed to its remedies. What then are we to do? At the sight of these people ought we to sound retreat and avenge our injuries in silence and from the harbor of our good conscience laugh at the shipwrecks of others? But there speaks out against such hatred first the love which we owe the human race and then the hope and the faith we have in God. For apart from the fact that he has often raised up the hopeless downfalls of the ages, he repays with an eternal reward the constancy that he wants us to practice right up to the hour of death, even if no results are achieved at present.

AUG. How does God raise up the downfalls of evil wills—on account of which the ages are blamed when they are correctly blamed—except by producing good wills in the hearts of human beings? Or if they can, let them raise themselves up. By thinking such madness, you yourselves have become a great downfall. Hence, we beseech him on your behalf, and would that he would also graciously hear our prayer for you, as he did for our brother Turbantius.[10]

Julian Will Fulfill His Promise

12. JUL. Rejoicing, then, in this consolation of the faith, let us turn to the work we have begun and fulfill what we promised with these discussions. We have no doubt that it is itself the greatest part of our reward that we have taken a stand in the bastion of that teaching which is attacked both by the envy, but especially by error. But it rises above doubtful events so that it is esteemed invincible for possession of victory.

AUG. You award yourself the palm of victory against so many of God's bishops. Drinking and giving others to drink from the fountains of Israel,[11] they learned and they taught before us in the Church of Christ those truths which you attack. What you are doing, then, does not amount to being esteemed for the possession of victory, but to flowing disgracefully into the sewer of despicable arrogance.[12] To be esteemed is to enjoy a good reputation. But how can you enjoy a good reputation for the possession of victory when you try to stain with filth the ancient and invincible Catholic teachings?

13. JUL. For, if, as both the previous discussion revealed and the following one will teach, all reason, all learning, all justice, all piety, and all the sacred testimonies support this teaching which we defend, our enemies achieve nothing else with their whole endeavor than that they are shown to be most impudent toward any who are learned, most contemptuous toward the saints, and most irreverent toward God.

AUG. But what you say is not true! For neither reason nor sound learning nor justice nor piety nor the sacred testimonies support your teaching. In fact, as those judge who understand correctly, all of these destroy your teaching. Reason, of course, sees that it can scarcely attain any truth because the slowness of nature prevents it. Learning encounters the penalty of hard work in the same slowness of nature. Justice cries out that it is not its fault that the children of Adam are weighed down by a heavy yoke from the day they emerge from the womb of their mother[13] without sins that merited this. Piety asks for God's help against this evil; the sacred testimonies admonish the human mind to ask for this help.

Julian Appeals to the Criterion of Reason

14. JUL. As their other writings, so these books which we are refuting testify that the traducianists have nothing to set against the force of reason by which they are being crushed down. These books were dedicated to a military officer,[14] a man, as he himself can admit, occupied with other tasks rather than literary ones, and they ask the help of the powerless against us. On their own behalf they invoke from above and from below decrees of common peoples or of country

folk and of people of the theater, though history does not record that they were promulgated by any council.

AUG. We do not ask the help of the powerless against you. Rather, in order that you may be held back from your sacrilegious daring, we praise the function of Christian power on your behalf. But see how you can call Cyprian and Ambrose country folk and people of the theater—as well as so many learned writers, their companions in the kingdom of God.

15. JUL. We cannot, nonetheless, deny that it wins much favor, as I said, with the masses, filthy though they be, to attribute sins of the will to nature and to defend the moral disorder by blaming the seeds so that none ever try to correct what they hope someone else commits in them.

AUG. Who ever said to you that someone else commits anyone's sin? For even he who says, *It is no longer I who do it, but the sin that dwells in me*, immediately adds, *For I know that the good does not dwell in me, that is, in my flesh* (Rom 7:17-18). He shows that whatever that is it is his own, because the flesh itself also belongs to one who is composed of flesh and spirit. And yet you do not want to agree with Ambrose that this evil because of which the flesh has desires opposed to the spirit was changed into our nature by the transgression of the first human being.[15] But since even you usually say that these words of the apostle express the force of bad habit, why is it that you now wanted to say, "So that none ever try to correct what they know someone else commits in them"? For you certainly want the one who says, *It is no longer I who do it* (Rom 7:20), to correct himself, and you want him to do this by the strength of his own will, though you see that his will is weak, when he says, *I do not do what I will* (Rom 7:19). I beg you, permit this person at least to ask for God's help since you see the choice of his will has failed in his case.

Julian Sums Up the Chief Points of Book One

16. JUL. (1) But the feeble patronage of blind opinion increases sins rather than lessens them. This itch, then, of those who are wretched and gladly ill will not be able to bring anything important to bear against reason itself. They claim, however, that some passages of the scriptures and especially the words of the apostle Paul support the existence of natural sin.[16] I have postponed their explanation to the second volume, and now is the time for giving that explanation. But first—in order that the reader may be better informed—I shall briefly distinguish what has already been done and what still remains to be done. (2) It has, therefore, been shown that the holy scriptures can prove nothing that justice cannot uphold, because if the full ideal of justice is found in the law of God, its opposite, that is, injustice, is not permitted to derive any support from it. And for this reason, authority cannot defend what reason refutes.[17] Secondly, it has been

proved that God is known to us by his virtues. Hence, we must confess his justice as well as his omnipotence, and if the loss of the former is admitted, his whole majesty will begin to topple. For God is just in such a way that, if he were proved not to be just, he would be shown not to be God.[18] The conclusion has been drawn that we reverence the most just God in the Trinity, and we have seen that it is irrefutable that he cannot attribute to little ones the sin of another.

AUG. Why do you not admit that without any sin that merited this the omnipotent and just God could not have placed the heavy yoke upon the children of Adam from the day they emerge from the womb of their mother?[19]

17. JUL. But as we discussed the definition of justice, so we discussed the nature of sin, and sin was seen to be nothing other than a bad will which was free to hold back from what it had wrongly desired.[20]

AUG. This is precisely the sin of the first human being from whom the origin of evil has come down to all human beings. He was, of course, quite free to hold back from what he had wrongly desired because there was not yet the defect because of which the flesh had desires opposed to the spirit. He did not yet say, *I do not do what I will* (Rom 7:19); as not yet existing in sinful flesh, he did not have any need of help from the likeness of sinful flesh.[21]

18. JUL. And by this brilliant testimony we are taught that there is no sin in the newborn, because the use of the will could not be found in them.[22]

AUG. And what is the source of their heavy yoke if not that, though they do not have the use of the will, they have, nonetheless, the bonds of a sinful origin?

19. JUL. It has, however, been shown by a lucid discussion that those who say there are natural sins deny free choice. The African[23] has denied this, not in his own words for fear that it would have less weight, but by the testimony of the gospel, in order to do so with greater authority. But by explaining it we have restored it to the dignity of the gospel.[24] We have also freed the testimony of the apostle Paul from the snares of the slanderer, and by the witness of the prophet we have shown that our God, the potter of good vessels, is the creator of all.[25]

AUG. There we replied to you and showed how far you have wandered from the truth.

Julian Again Delays His Exegesis of Romans

20. JUL. These, then, were the main arguments set forth in the first book, any one of which is amply sufficient for the victory of the truth. Though there is no real need, it remains, nonetheless, for us to discuss the statement of the teacher of the nations in which he said that sin entered the world through one man.[26] We shall find help, when it is necessary, in the definitions which we have set forth, and we shall prove that reason has not lied, but that it is a crime of injustice to ascribe the actions of some persons to the births of others. We shall show by the

testimonies of the law—either in this book or in the following—that what is unjust is displeasing to God, though no one ought to have any doubt about this, and is forbidden by him. From these points the conclusion necessarily follows that we are perfectly correct in the views we are defending, namely, that no one is born with sin, that God cannot judge the newborn guilty, that for this reason free choice is whole and intact, and that nature is innocent in each of us before the use of our own will.

AUG. Show us; state what you are going to say about the testimony of the apostle as foolishly as you stated your previous ideas.

21. JUL. And it follows, however, that the Manichees are in rebellion against both piety and reason, when they suppose that there is sin even before the time of the will—something that the nature of things does not permit. So too, they claim that God exists, but argue that he is unjust. And they bring discredit to the pages of the holy scriptures when they allege that the records of those pages prove the injustice of the divinity. Since none of the three can be shown by reason, that is, that there is sin without the will or that there is injustice in God or that there is perversity in the law, they alone are shown to be stupid, impudent, and impious.

AUG. Shame on you! Ambrose was not a Manichee though he said that human beings experience the infection of sins before drawing in the gift of the breath of life.[27] But even these sins have only come to be as the result of the will from which they took their origin, and so there is no injustice in God who placed a heavy yoke upon the newborn on this account. Nor is there perversity in the law which teaches that this is perfectly true. You yourselves would see this, if it were not rather you who have perverted eyes.

Julian Attacks Book Two of Marriage and Desire

22. JUL. (1) Let this point, then, be especially impressed upon the mind of the wise reader: All the holy scriptures contain only that which Catholics believe for the honor of God, as is shown by the light of many passages. And when a rather difficult expression raises a question, it is, of course, certain that the author of that passage did not express in it something that is unjust. Rather, the passage must be understood in accord with what is revealed by clear reason and by the light of other passages in which there is no ambiguity. Now, then, let us quote the words of that man with whom we are arguing. In that chapter of his allegations which accused his God of being the potter who fashions sinners, against which we battled in the previous book, he casually mentioned that sin entered the world through one human being, but he did not delay over the explanation of the passage.[28] (2) But after he had argued with many words against those excerpts which he confirms were sent to him, he came to a particular passage of my writings which he set forth as an objection for himself as though he was going to at-

tack it. But without saying anything about the point on which he was attacked, he had recourse to this statement of the apostle in which he says that sin entered the world through one man. And he endeavored to explain the context of this passage in accord with his teaching, and for this reason I have passed over other points and rushed to that part in order to fulfill my promise faithfully, since I had promised that I would resolve this question in the second volume and show what his argumentation amounts to.[29] For I do not want to be thought to have acted deceitfully if I omit his interpretation while I introduce that interpretation which we claim is Catholic.

AUG. You are going to introduce the Pelagian, not the Catholic interpretation. The Catholic interpretation is the one that shows that God is just despite so many and such great punishments and torments of little ones which none of them would have experienced in paradise with any justice, if human nature were not damaged by sin and rightly condemned.

23. JUL. I examined, then, in my first work his statement by which he said, "Just as sin is the work of the devil whether little ones contract it from the former sort of union or the latter, so human beings are the work of God whether they are born from the former sort of union or the latter."[30] The passage is, however, here and now reproduced by me as it is contained in my work from which this fellow had stolen the greater part.

AUG. Your argument is true in the same way that it is true that I stole those words. For it was rather the one whose document was sent to me who copied what he wanted and as he wanted from your work, using his own choice and judgment.

24. JUL. (1) I, therefore, replied to you, "Certainly, you are being evasive—I want to say this without showing disrespect for your authority as a teacher. But recognize that the truth has deprived you of the freedom to be vague. For, see, we too admit that sin is the work of an evil will or is the work of the devil. But how does this sin come to be in a little one? Through the will? But there was no will in the little one. Through the formation of the body? But God gave this. Through the soul's entrance into the body? But the soul which is newly created by God owes nothing to the bodily seed. Through marriage? But marriage pertains to the action of the parents, and you already granted that they did not sin in this act. But if your concession was not sincere, as the development of your argument indicates, marriage should be condemned because it produced the cause of sin. (2) But marriage does not have a substance of its own; rather, its name only refers to the action of the persons. The parents, then, who produced the cause of sin by their union, rightfully deserve condemnation. There is, therefore, no way around it: Spouses are destined for eternal punishment, since by their activity the devil has come to exercise dominion over human beings. If you grant this, you will lose that whole point which you seemed to have previously upheld, namely, your claim that a human being is the work of God. Since the origin of children comes

from the union of bodies, if through their origin there is evil in human beings, and if through evil the devil has dominion over human beings, it necessarily follows that the devil is the author of human beings since newborns have their origin from him."[31] (3) After this I again repeated his words, "Just as sin is the work of the devil whether little ones contract it from the former sort of union or the latter, so human beings are the work of God whether they are born from the former sort of union or the latter."[32] And I immediately rose up against him with these words, "When I think of the fearful cry of yours in which you say that marriage is not something evil, I cannot think of those other words of yours without laughing. For if you believe that human beings are made by God and that married couples are innocent, look, it is impossible to maintain that original sin is contracted from these. Surely the newborn child does not sin; the parents do not sin; the creator does not sin. Through what cracks in so many bulwarks of innocence do you imagine that sin entered?"[33]

AUG. It is sufficient that I already replied to these words of yours after I read your books.[34] But I recommend here too that one should listen to the apostle rather than to you, for he did not point out a hidden crack, but a wide open door by which *sin entered the world, and through sin death, and in that way it was passed on to all human beings, in whom all have sinned* (Rom 5:12). As soon as you begin to explain these words of his in accord with your understanding, not in accord with his, it will become clear that you are fighting against the straight truth by your twisted wordiness.

25. JUL. It was this passage, then, that he quoted for himself from my first work in this second book of his, though with some changes. For he passed over out of cunning, I believe, my mentioning the formation of the body and the soul's entrance into it, since both reason and the authority of the sacred law and of the Catholic Church maintain that God creates a new soul in each individual.

AUG. The person who made the excerpts took from the first of your four books what he wanted and as he wanted it, and I replied to them in this book which you are now trying in vain to refute by your wordy nonsense. Those who read my six books by which I refuted your four will find that I replied to you in my third book. They will see that I did not pass over out of cunning the passage you mention, but that the person to whose document I was replying did not want to copy this from your work, whether out of a desire for brevity or because he thought it was not relevant to the issue.

26. JUL. Then he cited the rest, though with some changes in the words. He thought up nothing against these objections of mine by which I might be refuted. Rather, having admitted by the lack of arguments that I had gotten the truth, he says that the apostle answers[35] me on all these points, for he declares that through one man sin entered the world. In this passage would any learned person judge that he has a sound mind, if he does not understand that he ought to pass over those points on which he can find nothing against me? Or he at least ought to

think up some responses to make to the objections, and he should add the words of the apostle to these responses as a confirmation.

AUG. But you are better refuted by the apostle's words than by mine, though you do not yield even to the words of the apostle. Rather, you prefer to misinterpret them instead of correcting yourself.

The Logic of the Pelagian Argument

27. JUL. (1) I investigated, then, quite logically, as all the learned recognize along with me, how sin, which is a work of an evil will and is also called the work of the devil, might come to be in a little one. If through the will, even this fellow with whom we are arguing admits that there was no will in the little one. But if it is through marriage, there is no one who doubts that marriage pertains to the action of the parents, and he had already admitted that they did not sin in their union. Or if our opponent regrets this concession, as the development of the work has indicated, he should admit that the parents are guilty since by their union a kingdom is prepared for the devil in the image of God. And I added by the necessary steps of argumentation that through original sin the devil is declared to be the author of bodies because, if there is evil in human beings from their origin and if the devil has dominion over human beings through evil, the devil is the author of human beings since the newborn have their origin from him. (2) Since this argument caught the traducianists in the cave of the Manichees to confine them there, I turned the key to offer the captives an escape, and I warned that, if he truly believes that human beings are made by God and honestly admits that married couples are innocent, he should understand that original sin cannot be contracted from them. I said, "Certainly the newborn child does not sin; the parents do not sin; the creator does not sin. Through what cracks in so many bulwarks of innocence do you imagine sin entered?"[36] (3) What argument, I ask you, could be put together that is more holy, more true, more lucid, more succinct, and more solid? For, after the three propositions which I adopted when my enemy conceded them, I inferred a fourth on which the whole conclusion rests. For when a third proposition is necessarily linked at times to one other proposition or to two, what law prevents me, once the three are conceded, to infer a fourth connected with them? All this was done in the second discussion, but in the first my adversary conceded five or more points to me from which a legitimate and irrefutable conclusion is drawn.

AUG. See how you wander off in many directions for fear that the words of the apostle might condemn you, if they were heard without your slanted comments, as they have condemned you in the judgment of the Catholic Church. But run off wherever you want; delay as much as you want; multiply your meanderings in whatever direction you want; whenever the ship of your falla-

cies comes to the same words of truth, you will undoubtedly meet with shipwreck.

28. JUL. (1) Let us, then, now turn to my adversary. You granted me that sin is
the work of the will. I could have immediately said as a result: But there is no will
that might sin in little ones; there is, then, no sin in little ones. But in order that
you might be overwhelmed by many witnesses, I asked one by one: How sin
came to be in a little one? Was it perhaps through the will? After this, with your
agreement, I accepted the proposition that there is no awareness of will in a little
one. I added: Did it contract the shape of its members through the first sin? But
you had already conceded that these are formed by God and are for this reason
good. (2) I asked thirdly whether you thought that guilt came through the soul's
entrance into the body. But it was agreed that the soul is newly created and owes
nothing to the seed. I finally asked—since none of these remain for you to refute—whether you would call marriage, that is, the union of bodies, the work of
the devil. But I showed that it pertains to the action of the parents, as you also
agreed. Since all these factors which we mentioned above were found innocent,
your traducianist doctrine makes the parents who were the cause of the sin subject to the devil. After all this, I shoved under your nose the point which was almost in front of you: I said that you believed that the devil is the author of bodies,
since you attribute to him the act of intercourse without which no bodies could
come to be. And this discussion showed the disease from which you are suffering. But that second discussion proved that you are pitiful along with such ideas
and that the Catholics are undefeated, as your fear indicates.

(3) For you grant that human beings are made by God and that spouses are innocent and that little ones do nothing on their own. Given these three premises,
the inference is irrefutable that, since the newborn child does not sin, the parents
do not sin, and the creator does not sin, no crack remained through which one
may teach that sin entered. If,[37] then, you are not satisfied with the conclusion,
deny what you conceded and say either that the parents sinned or that the creator
sinned or that the newborn child sinned. Of these one is insane; the second is
Manichean, and the third is worse than Manichean. It is insane if you say that the
little ones sin; it is Manichean if you accuse the spouses; it is worse than Manichean if you think that God is the author of sin. But if all these points are so far
from the truth that you still are afraid to admit them openly, how can you, the
greatest lunatic of all, persist in such impudence that you deny what we have inferred?

AUG. When you come to the words of the apostle, you will find not a crack,
but a wide open door by which sin has entered the world, and you, of course, will
try to close it. But despite all your wordiness you will be defeated from the lips of
infants and nursing babies. They look for Christ to save them rather than for you
to praise them, and they bear witness much more certainly to their own wretchedness by speechless wailing, not by tortuous arguments. For if the uprightness

and blessedness of the first human being had lasted, they could never have had such wretchedness in paradise.

Four Possible Sources of Original Sin

29. JUL. This case involves four persons: God the creator, the two parents who provide the matter to the creator, and the newborn little one. You claim that sin is found in this group. I ask you who committed it. Is it God? You say, No. Is it the father? Again you say, No. The mother? Again you say, No. The little one? You say, No. And yet you do not think that the conclusion follows that there cannot be found among these four a sin that none of these four has committed.

AUG. Say whatever you want; you will eventually come to the words of the apostle. And those who throughout the individual parts of your arguments recall those words, which we do not want constantly to repeat for fear of boring the reader, reply to you on the basis of their recollection of them.

30. JUL. Of what are you trying to convince us when you reread the scriptures or name accomplices, when you are still not able to define what you hold? How does it help you to teach that Adam sinned, a point which I in no sense reject? Our question is this: Since Adam died so many centuries ago, how can the sin by which the image of God comes under the dominion of the devil be found in a little one?

AUG. Why do you not admit the image of God into the kingdom of God since according to you it has no sin? Why is the blood which was shed from the likeness of sinful flesh for the forgiveness of sins offered to a little one to drink so that it can have life, if it has not entered into death because of its origin in sin?[38] If you do not like this, openly deny Christ to the little ones;[39] openly deny that he died for little ones though *one has died for all*. From this there follows[40] what the apostle says, *All have, therefore, died, and he has died for all* (2 Cor 5:14.15). State openly: Little ones who have no sin have not died; they have for themselves no need of Christ's death in which they are baptized. Now state openly what you secretly think, for you betray well enough by your discussion what you hold. State, I say, that little ones become Christians to no point. But see whether you should call yourself a Christian.

31. JUL. If sin comes though the union of the parents, condemn by a public statement marriage which you condemn by your argument. And spare us the labor of proving that you are a Manichee. But perhaps you do not dare to say this, and in contempt for the rules of reason[41] you are favorably disposed toward those who engage in intercourse. With monstrous arguments that have never before been heard, you perhaps say that sexual desire is something diabolical and that sexual desire which was put in the senses for the pleasure of the parents having intercourse is linked with guilt in the newborn, and in that way you betray your

madness and shamefulness. But I beg you not to claim for yourself so much that you think that we are not free to defend the innocence of the newborn along with the honor of God, though you are permitted and are pleased to acquit the members of those indulging in sexual desire from the guilt, as you call it, of sexual desire, while bringing accusations against God.

AUG. Whatever itch you have to praise sexual desire, that is, concupiscence of the flesh, the apostle John says that it does not come from the Father, but from the world.[42] On its account the devil is rightly said to be the prince of the world,[43] though[44] we know that God made the world. Marital chastity, then, makes good use of this evil of concupiscence of the flesh, and spiritual rebirth removes the guilt of that evil which was contracted by the newborn. As long as you do not hold this, you will not be a Catholic, but a Pelagian, and you will speak against the holy scriptures, no matter how much you think you defend them. And as often as you call me a Manichee on account of what you oppose, you clearly call that man a Manichee who says that a human being poured into the maternal womb and conceived in the pleasure of concupiscence contracts the infection of sins before drawing in the gift of the breath of life.[45] This is Ambrose, Julian; you call Ambrose a Manichee, you madman.

32. JUL. For when you declare that concupiscence of the flesh was implanted in human beings by the prince of darkness and that it is the fruit tree of the devil that brings forth from itself the human race like its own apples, you are completely exposed, because you hold that it is not God, but the devil who is the creator of human beings. And that most wicked teaching condemns both the act of the spouses, that is, the union of the sex organs, and all flesh.

AUG. We do not condemn the flesh, but it should not be praised as though it were in good health in order that, with even your agreement, it might be healed by its creator and savior. For it will undoubtedly be condemned in those who do not receive this healing.

33. JUL. But after this sacrilege you go on to say that you declare that the pleasure of the married couple in begetting a child is diabolical and that the arousal of the sex organs is diabolical, but that the members themselves which are aroused and the couple who experiences the pleasure are not guilty. Rather, instead of all these you accuse the new human beings, that is, the tender product of the deity in the newborn. You do not lay aside any of the impiety of the Manichees; rather, you reveal the tremendous madness of a disturbed head. Accordingly, one would more logically judge that your head needs to be soothed rather than cut off, if the destruction of many, your stubbornness, and the multiplicity of scripture passages did not declare your determined intention in this affair.

AUG. I ought gladly to listen to these insults along with these teachers of the Church; they understand that sin entered the world through one man as the apostle, who was right, stated it, not as Julian, who is most wrongheaded, supposes.

These include—to pass over the others—Cyprian of Africa, Hilary of Gaul, Ambrose of Italy, and Gregory of Greece. These most learned and wise judges—the very sort of judges that you complain in your foolish insolence that you cannot find—condemned your heresy before it began.

34. JUL. Read on this point also the fourth book of my work, and you will understand how much favor you show to the devil whom you call your father and to sexual desire, your mother, under the pretext of bringing accusations against them.

AUG. I did read your fourth book also, and in my sixth book I replied to you on every point in it. But let the believing reader of both judge which of us is the winner.

Julian Again Promises to Explain the Words of Paul

35. JUL. (1) But let us now[46] look at the words of the apostle for you said that he answered me on all the points I set forth above. "On all these points the apostle replied to this man; he did not blame the will of the little one, since the child has as yet no will of its own for sinning. He did not blame marriage as marriage, since it not only was instituted, but was also blessed by God. He did not blame the parents insofar as the parents are joined in a licit and lawful union for the procreation of children. But he said, *Through one man sin entered the world, and through sin death, and in that way it was passed on to all human beings in whom all have sinned* (Rom 5:12). (2) If these people would hear this with Catholic ears and minds, they would not have minds in rebellion against the faith and grace of Christ, and they would not vainly try to twist these perfectly clear and evident words of the apostle to their own heretical sense. They claim that he said this because Adam was the first to sin, and thereafter anyone who chose to sin found in him an example for sinning. In that way sin was passed on to all human beings, not by generation from that one man, but by imitation of that one man. And yet, if the apostle had wanted us to understand imitation in this passage, he would not have said that sin entered the world *through one man*. Rather, he would have said that it entered the world through the devil and was passed on by all human beings. In fact, scripture says of the devil, *But those who are on his side imitate him* (Wis 2:24-25). But he said, *through one man*, from whom the generation of the human race began, so that he might teach that original sin was passed on to all through generation."[47]

AUG. You have quoted the words of my book; now tell us how the words of the apostle which I quoted there are to be interpreted so that you may be more and more revealed as a heretic when you present yourself as one who praises little ones in order to deprive them of their savior.

36. JUL. Any learned readers of our works, whoever they may be, understand that you take advantage of the ignorance of your followers and hide beneath the ambiguity of words. The rest of the common folk of whom the prophet says to God, *You have regarded human beings like the fish of the sea* (Hab 1:14), are deceived by their common inference, and ignorant of sound discernment they suppose that everything which they see linked together in words can be united in reality. But only the most learned and most attentive can judge what follows logically, what is impossible, and what the inexorable and venerable law of logic forces one to infer from which premises.

AUG. (1) You are still wandering about in search of dialecticians while avoiding the Church's judges. State now how one should interpret, *Through one man sin entered the world*, that is, with a better interpretation than he who says, "All die in Adam, because *through one man sin entered this world, and through sin death, and in that way it was passed on to all human beings, in whom all have sinned* (Rom 5:12). His sin, then, was the death of all."[48] (2) And the same man says elsewhere, "Adam existed, and we all existed in him. Adam perished, and all perished in him."[49] That man is Ambrose, not just anyone from the common folk whose ignorant masses you look down upon with your long neck and upturned nose because they cannot evaluate your arguments. It is Ambrose, I say, a man to whom you are in no sense an equal in the worldly literature of which you are so proud. But with regard to the writings of the Church, listen to or read your teacher Pelagius about who Ambrose is, and do not embrace an interpretation foreign to that of this great teacher.

More Charges of Inconsistency against Augustine

37. JUL. And this is the reason why, in feeling so much pity for the ruin of the churches, we call for a trial by men illustrious for their wisdom so that people might see, not what is said, but what is said with logic. For if we were debating before such an assembly, you would certainly not be permitted to affirm what you had denied or to deny what you had affirmed. But in your book which no censure of shame corrects, you heap together what the Catholics say and what the Manichees profess, content with this idea alone that you are said to have replied. You, however, suppose that it is silly even to think of what weight your words have or of their consistency.

AUG. I beg you, tell me now how one should interpret, *Through one man sin entered the world* (Rom 5:12). Why do you still slander us? Why do you insult us? Why are you so evasive? If Cyprian, Hilary, Ambrose, Gregory, Basil, John of Constantinople—not to mention others—sat in the council whose judgment you seem to desire, would you dare to look for more learned, more wise, more honest judges? These men cry out against your teachings; they condemn your writings by their writings. What more do you want? I explained this sufficiently in the first and second of my six books which I published against your four.[50] But look, I am still ready to listen to you. Tell me now how one should interpret the words, *Through one man sin entered the world* (Rom 5:12).

38. JUL. Finally, you granted without hesitation what I demanded, and seeing the conclusion drawn from these premises, you admitted that you were too weak for the argument that we constructed. You said that the apostle Paul refutes everything which we stated. You introduce him, nonetheless, as someone who concedes all the points which you conceded. For you say, "The apostle did not blame the will of the little one, since the child has as yet no will of its own for sinning."[51] If this is granted, it has already been proved that there cannot be any sin in the child since there is, even according to your definition, no other nature of sin than the will to commit that which justice forbids and from which one is free to hold back.[52]

AUG. This is the definition of that sin which is not at the same time the punishment of sin. For in that passage in which you concede[53] that we hear the cries of bad habit and thus choke off the cries of your teaching, tell me, if you dare, how the human will is free to hold back from evil where you hear, *I do not do what I will* (Rom 7:15). Or deny that there is evil where you hear, *I do not do the good that I will, but I do the evil that I do not will* (Rom 7:19). We, of course, acknowledge that this sin is the punishment of sin and that it must, therefore, be distinguished from that definition of sin where the will commits that from which one is free to hold back. Understand what I say, and tell me now, please, how one should interpret, *Through one man sin entered the world* (Rom 5:12).

39. JUL. If, then, the apostle does not accuse in the child its own will which he understood could not even exist, he certainly declares that no sign of a serious sin is found in the child, especially since that justice is presiding which does not impute sin unless one is free to hold back from it. But not content to have granted only this, you add, "The apostle did not blame marriage as marriage, since it not only was instituted, but was also blessed by God."[54] By itself alone this could also suffice for eliminating natural sin. For, if the apostle knows, as he does know, that one should not blame marriage since the union of the sexes which God instituted and blessed, along with the pleasure involved, belongs to the attraction of marriage and to its function and means, marriage cannot produce the property of the devil, nor can the product of marriage be guilty, especially before that justice which does not impute a sin from which one is not free to hold back.

AUG. Do not, I beg you, imagine the union of the spouses in paradise with the sort of pleasure which sexual desire now produces when it does not arise at a sign from the will and entices the minds even of the saints. Even though it can be held in check, it is still troublesome. Heaven forbid that wise believers should think that such was the pleasure of paradise, that such was that peace and happiness.

40. JUL. Let us consider a third point on which your kindness is seen in your readiness to make concessions. "The apostle did not blame the parents insofar as the parents are joined in a licit and lawful union for the procreation of children."[55] Weigh what you said: The apostle did not blame the parents insofar as they are parents. Hence, the parents insofar as they are parents cannot bear fruit for the devil, nor does he declare that something that comes from them insofar as they are parents belongs to the devil. But children belong to the parents only insofar as they are parents. Therefore, they are proven to be neither guilty nor under the power of the devil, nor should they be accused by the devil. In order that what we have said might be made clear by repetition: The union of the sexes involves offspring only to the extent that those who are married become parents, but if they should choose to do something immoral between themselves or to stray into the illicit unions of adulterers, this cannot affect the children who are born from the power of the seeds, not from the filth of the sins.

AUG. Do you now admit that there can be immoral intercourse between spouses? See what your fair protégée is up to. For this does not happen unless one gives in to her when she impels even spouses united for the sake of having children to the immoral behavior which you too reprehend. And she does this not out of any requirement for conceiving a child. You wanted to praise her so much that no one would believe that you would also dare to attack her. You did, in fact, not blush to praise her in such a way that you would like to place her even in the blessedness of paradise, and you are not ashamed of this.

41. JUL. And so, it is not the sins, but the seeds of the parents that are transferred to the offspring. But God created the fruitfulness of the seeds and blessed them, as you are forced to admit.

AUG. God created the seeds, but those who can in our damaged nature distinguish between what is good in it and what is evil so that they do not suppose that nature is something evil or that a defect is a nature can themselves distinguish which of these pertains to God's act of creating and which to his act of healing. But you cannot do this as long as you are Pelagians and not Catholics. Tell me now, I beg you; tell me now how one should interpret the words, *Through one man sin entered the world* (Rom 5:12).

Parents and the Guilt of Their Children

42. JUL. Children, therefore, are not guilty even when their parents sin in begetting them, because parents affect their children only insofar as they are parents. And, therefore, the children are also[56] affected by their parents only insofar as they are their children. It is clear that the offspring share the nature of their parents, not their guilt. But if you declare that the apostle also affirms this, as reason demonstrates, we are right to maintain, with him as our teacher, that the sins

of the parents cannot belong to their children. For all of us—the apostle enlightened by the Holy Spirit and we instructed by the light of reason and you crushed by the weight of the truth which you attack—admit truly and in common that parents insofar as they are parents are not guilty and that they affect their children only insofar as they are parents. And, therefore, the children insofar as they are children, that is, before they do anything by their own will, cannot be guilty.

AUG. Parents are parents because they have children, and children are children because they are born. But neither to have children nor to be born is something evil, for each of these pertains to God's creation, and each of them could have taken place in paradise without shameful sexual desire, if no one had sinned. For if shameful sexual desire had not either arisen from sin or been damaged by sin, it would not be shameful. Either it would not exist at all, and without it the sexual organs would obey the couple begetting a child, just as the hands obey workers, or it would follow upon the will so that it could never tempt anyone who is unwilling. For chastity teaches us that such desire does not now exist; chastity fights against its stirring both in married couples so that they do not with each other indulge immorally in sexual pleasure or slip into adultery and in those who live lives of continence so that they do not fall by consenting to it. There you see the source from which original sin is contracted; there you see the means by which he chose not to be born who came not to bring his own sin, but to take away ours.[57]

43. JUL. Now let all the talents of the Manichean nation[58] go and devise whatever they can, and let them endure the pains of thought as long as they want. I promise, not arrogantly, but with religious conviction, that this structure can never be shaken.

AUG. What you call a structure has fallen in ruins, and it weighed down upon you so that it forced you to praise what you fight against, at least if you have any sort of chastity which would make you fight against what you praise.

44. JUL. How can you have the effrontery to add, "But *through one man sin entered the world, and through sin death, and in that way it was passed on to all human beings, in whom all have sinned*" (Rom 5:12)?[59] And you interpret this so that the apostle says that sin was transmitted by Adam to his descendants by generation. You had granted above that the teacher of the nations did not blame marriage which God blessed, that there is no will for sinning in the newborn, and that parents insofar as they are parents are licitly and lawfully united to each other for procreating children, and now you add in that passage, as if you had said the previous things while asleep, that serious sin is transmitted to the descendants by generation. After all, if they beget children insofar as they are parents, and if they are licitly and lawfully united to each other insofar as they are parents, and if the apostle did not blame this union because God not only instituted it, but blessed it, with what words, by what right, with what effrontery do you maintain that this

procreation of children is the cause of guilt, the root of serious sins, and the instrument of the devil?

AUG. I no longer know how many times you said these things and how many times we replied to them. By your many words you stir up a cloud for yourself, and it does not allow you to distinguish the evil of defects from the goodness of nature. You repeat the same points in the same words to the point of dreadful boredom, but you still do not say how one should interpret the words, *Through one man sin entered the world* (Rom 5:12).

45. JUL. Procreation, then, does not merit the apostle's blame, and it, nonetheless, falls under the devil's dominion. It is instituted by God, and it is, nonetheless, the source of serious sins. You admit, finally, that God blessed it, and you, nonetheless, accuse it of being the devil's fruit tree.

AUG. God blessed marriage, but not the concupiscence of the flesh which is opposed to the spirit and which did not exist before the sin. God did not bless the sin, just as he did not bless that concupiscence which is opposed to the spirit. But if they had not committed the sin which damaged our nature, marriage which God blessed would make use of the sex organs, just as we make use of our other members which obey the will without any passion. Or shameful desire would not be present there, since it would never resist the will; that sort of desire does not now exist, as even you surely experience when you refuse to assent to its temptations and enticements. Marriage is, nonetheless, praiseworthy even now, because it does not create this evil in human beings, but finds it there, and it makes good use of that evil by the intention to have children, even though the newborn contract from it original sin, on account of which they must be reborn.

46. JUL. The learned in all fields of knowledge bear witness that you have achieved nothing against me. But the contradictory character of your statements proves how you struggle against the apostle and rage against God. But now that we have shown that what the real world has divided cannot be united, let us also question the apostle so that no one thinks that his thoughts contain the wild ideas which we have shown are to be found in your statements.

AUG. State now at least what you postponed by so many digressions.

Whether Sin Entered by Imitation or by Generation

47. JUL. I, therefore, hear Paul declare that *through one man sin entered the world, and through sin death, and in that way it was passed on to all human beings, in whom all have sinned* (Rom 5:12). You maintain that he said this, not on account of the example of sin, but on account of generation, and you call us heretics who refer this to bad example. You think that you are helped by that argument you gave. You said, "And yet, if the apostle had wanted us to understand imitation in this passage, he would not have said that sin entered the world

through one man. Rather, he would have said that it entered the world through the devil and was passed on by all human beings. In fact, scripture says of the devil, *But those who are on his side imitate him* (Wis 2:24-25). But he said, *through one man*, from whom the generation of the human race began, so that he might teach that original sin was passed on to all through generation."[60] But I see that the apostle said nothing which would bring discredit upon human generation, nothing which points to the condemnation of natural innocence, nothing which amounts to an accusation of God's work.

AUG. You say "nothing" for quite a while, and when you stop repeating this word, you will still say nothing. Who, after all, will not laugh at you when you try to persuade us that the apostle's words, *Through one man sin entered the world*, have nothing to do with generation, because the man, from whom the rest came by generation, was not himself begotten by someone? But you say that it has to do with bad example because the example of sin which his descendants imitated entered the world only through the one who sinned by imitating no one. For he was the first to sin. Does any Christian not know that the first one who sinned was not Adam, but the devil? What, then, is it that you want but not to be silent and yet to say nothing?

48. JUL. (1) Finally, you try to infer by argument what the words themselves did not say. And you add that, if he were speaking about imitation, he ought to have mentioned the devil, but because he wanted us to understand that he was talking about generation, he chose to mention the man rather than the demon. I ask, then, what reason you had for this opinion. What then? Do you deny that people sin by imitating other human beings? And though an issue which is clear does not need the testimony of the scriptures, listen, nonetheless, to David: *Do not imitate evil-doers, and do not be jealous of those who work iniquity. Do not imitate those who are prosperous in their way* (Ps 37:1.7). (2) Moreover, all the scriptures of the old testament warn Israel not to imitate the worship of the infidel nations. What, then, makes it necessary that, if the apostle wanted us to understand imitation, he should have mentioned the devil rather than the man, since he knows that one can sin by imitating both the devil and human beings? Either prove, then, that it is not possible to sin by imitating human beings and that this is nowhere contained in the law, and in that way claim a scriptural passage in support of your tenuous idea. Or if it is evident that nothing has led to the increase of sins more than the imitation of the vicious persons,[61] you have surely inferred with great ignorance that the apostle would undoubtedly have spoken of the devil if he had wanted us to understand imitation.

AUG. Did I not say before that you would say nothing, you who say nothing with so many words? There are, of course, sins of imitation in the world, since human beings follow the examples of human beings who sin. But the sin which sinners would imitate did not enter the world through those human beings whom any of them imitate, but through that one who sinned first by imitating no one. This is the devil whom all imitate *who are on his side* (Wis 2:25). In that way the sin which is not committed by imitation, but contracted by being born, entered the world through this one who first begot a human being. You, therefore, said nothing, and you refused to be silent only in order to deceive some readers and to tire out others.

49. JUL. It is, then, clear that we speak not only logically, but necessarily of the imitation of evil human beings; hence, it is obvious that this present argument of yours has been knocked down. But you add that scripture said of the devil, *Those who are on his side imitate him* (Wis 2:25), and I agree that this was stated wisely by whoever is the author of this book. But it does you no good that scripture says that some people sin by imitating the devil, unless you show that one cannot sin by imitating human beings.

AUG. The question here is not whether people sin by imitating human beings. Who, after all, can fail to know that people also sin by imitating human beings? The question is what sort of sin entered the world through the one man: a sin that is committed through imitation or one that is contracted by birth. For the sort of sin I mentioned first, that is, the sin which is committed through imitation, entered the world only through the one who, as the first sinner, imitated no one and introduced the example of sinning for the rest to imitate. This is the devil. But the other sort of sin, that is, the one which is contracted by birth, entered the world only through the one who, as the first father, was born of no one and introduced the beginning of their origin for the rest who were to be born. This is Adam. With regard to the imitation of angels and human beings, then, recognize that you said nothing pertinent to the issue, but that you simply refused to be silent. We are, after all, not arguing about just any sinner who sinned in the world at some time or other, but about that sinner through whom sin entered the world. Here if we look for an example to imitate, we find the devil; if we look for the infection from birth, we find Adam. Hence, when the apostle said, *Through one man sin entered the world* (Rom 5:12), he wanted us to understand the sin transmitted by generation. For the sin spread by imitation entered the world, not through one man, but through the devil.

50. JUL. For we are accustomed to say both of these. We say at times that a person hates someone in imitation of the devil and at times that by modeling oneself on a human being one is stained with hatred or the filth of wickedness. Hence, this term "imitation" can apply to both cases, that is, when we speak of a human being and when we speak of the devil. But you chose to make the ridiculously silly claim that the apostle could not have meant Adam if his words are taken in the sense of the imitation.

AUG. Did sin enter the world through just any human being whom another imitates in sinning? Say, if you can, what this means: *Through one man sin entered the world, and through sin death, and in that way it was passed on to all hu-*

man beings (Rom 5:12)—it does not matter whether it was death or sin or, rather, sin along with death. For the sin in imitation of which one sins entered the world only through the devil who, as the first, did not do by imitation what the rest would do by imitating him.

Speaking of Generation as Opposed to Imitation

51. JUL. The discussion rushes on to the remaining points. But this passage must still be pressed so that by segments as short as possible we may offer to the reader an understanding of the matter and a way to remember it. In almost every area we find the presence of homonyms which we call equivocal terms.

AUG. You promised that you would offer to the reader an understanding of the text, and you speak of homonyms and equivocal terms. How will the Pelagians themselves understand you, unless they are first sent to the schools of the logicians, wherever on earth they can be found, for the sake of learning these things? Or are you yourself going to give lectures and explain to them the categories of Aristotle before they read your books? Why should you not do even this, you clever rascal, since you are at leisure and fed by misguided wretches?

52. JUL. (1) But let our discussion now turn to the present issues. Generation is properly attributed to the sexes, but imitation is always a work of minds. This inclination of the mind, then, that imitates what it wills according to its capability either brings blame or praise to the person in accord with the different cases. Hence, in a good sense a person is said to imitate God and the angels and the apostles: God where it says, *Be perfect as your Father is perfect* (Mt 5:48); the angels where it says, *May your will be done on earth as it is in heaven* (Mt 6:10); and the apostles where it says, *Be imitators of me as I am of Christ* (1 Cor 11:1). (2) But in a bad sense we imitate the devil, as scripture says, *Those who are on his side imitate him* (Wis 2:25), and we imitate human beings, for it says, *Do not be sad like the hypocrites who mar their faces* (Mt 6:16), and we imitate animals, for we are commanded, *Do not become like the horse and the mule that do not have understanding* (Ps 32:9). By these words of exhortation and deterrence we are shown the inclination toward imitation which we would not be warned to avoid, if it were not something possible.

AUG. But the sin of imitation, that is, the sin which is committed by imitation, did not enter the world except through one who sinned without imitating anyone in order that others might sin by imitation. And this is certainly not Adam, but the devil. The one who said that sin *entered the world* (Rom 5:12) indicated the beginning of this sin, and it is obvious that this beginning was not brought about by a human being, but by the devil, if we want to focus on the sin which sinners imitate. It remains, then, that the sin which entered the world through one man can be correctly attributed not to imitation, but to generation.

We, of course, give thanks to God that, as if the light of the truth dawned upon you, you spoke out against your own error and admitted that we should attribute the good will by which we imitate good persons, not to the powers of our own free choice, but to the help of God. For you have shown that in order to imitate the angels, we must not put our trust in ourselves, but must ask help from the Lord, since you explain in that way what we pray with the words, *May your will be done on earth as it is in heaven* (Mt 6:10).

53. JUL. But as it is clear that the term "imitation" is commonly used for different things, so "generation" truly and properly indicates only a substance which generates. But it is applied to other activities, not in a proper, but only in an extended sense. And yet, since this is now the way people speak, we recognize what it means, and we do not allow it to interfere with the proper meaning. The devil, therefore, is said to generate sinners in accord with the words of the Lord in his gospel, *You come from your father, the devil* (Jn 8:44). By that expression he called him the father of serious sinners because they were found guilty of imitating his wickedness, and yet it is clearly understood that this name "father" does not attribute sexuality to the devil nor an airy substance to those human beings. Now, then, let me show you what we want to draw from this. If it were never meant[62] in the proper sense that one human being imitates another and if the apostle had said that all sinned through Adam, I would frankly prescribe that the apostle should be defended by the usage of the scriptures. That is, just as the Lord called the devil a father though he could not generate by his substance, so the apostle wrote that a human being can be imitated, and in that way there is no need to believe that he taught anything contrary to reason.

AUG. Was Adam the first one to be imitated in sin so that it would be correct to say that this kind of sin entered the world through him? Did not the devil come before him as someone who could be imitated in sin? The apostle, then, would have said that sin entered the world through the devil, if he wanted us to understand in that passage the sin which others commit by imitation.

54. JUL. But if the terms used in an extended sense in the gospel must not be criticized,[63] for much better reasons the apostle Paul offered no occasion for error, for he said nothing in an improper sense when he declared that the first human sinner set an example for subsequent sinners.

AUG. He ought, then, not to have set before us those two: the one for sin, the other for righteousness, that is, Adam and Christ.[64] After all, if he set forth Adam as the first sinner on account of the sin which the rest imitated, he should, of course, have set forth as the first righteous man to be imitated by the rest on account of the righteousness, not Christ, but Abel. Abel was the first righteous human being who did not imitate another human being, but was someone for the rest to imitate. The apostle, however, knew what he was saying and set forth Adam as the author of sin and Christ as the author of righteousness, because he knew that the first was the origin of our birth and the latter the origin of our rebirth.

55. JUL. And for this reason you have argued in a most stupid fashion that, if the apostle Paul wanted us to understand that sin was passed on through imitation, he would have mentioned the devil rather than Adam, since it is obvious that the sin of the man and of the devil could not be passed on except by imitation. But since the argument you constructed has been pulled down, not by my hands, but by the hands of reason, pay attention to what we now offer you.

AUG. Those who read the words of the two of us will judge that you did not pull down the argument I constructed and that in vain you brought the hands, not of sound reason, but of your vain opinion, against our structure.

Generation Requires Not One, but Two Persons

56. JUL. (1) The apostle showed that he did not mean that sin was passed on by generation when, in mentioning the man, he added, *one*, for one is the first number. And when he explained through whom sin entered, he not only named him, but added a number. He said, *Through one man sin entered this world* (Rom 5:12). But this man, being only one, was sufficient for setting an example to be imitated; he was not sufficient for the act of generation. Sin was passed on, but through one person. It is clear that the passage points to imitation, not to generation which cannot be carried out except by two people. Either show us, then, that generation could have taken place by Adam alone without a woman—for even this is not beyond your lofty talents—or, since you surely see that generation surely can only come about through two persons, admit, even though it is late, that the action of two cannot be accused through the number one. (2) He said, *Through one man sin entered the world* (Rom 5:12). When he said, *Through one*, he did not want us to understand, "Through two." What, I ask you, was the purpose of the apostle's mentioning the number in these teachings so that he mentioned with such great care not only a man, but also *one man*? But the cautious expression of his august counsel is apparent, for under the revelation of the Holy Spirit he anticipated and disarmed the errors of our times so that he would not be thought to have said anything injurious to marriage which God instituted and to the fertility which he blessed. Since the case demanded that he recount the origins of sin, he said that sin was passed on through that number which could not be suited for offspring. And both of the first human beings surely sinned, and they were both rightly called the pattern of sin for their descendants. Why then did the apostle not say that sin was passed on through the two of them, which fitted better the historical truth? (3) But he could have done nothing wiser, for he saw that, if he had mentioned the two who marked the beginning and set the example of transgression and had stated that sin was passed on through them, he

would be giving occasion for error. For people would think that he condemned sexual union and fertility by naming the two. And so, he very wisely preferred to mention one who was not sufficient to mean generation, but was more than sufficient to signify example. In that way he blamed imitation with his accusation, and he did not find fault with fertility by his use of number. To sum up briefly what we have done: the fertility which God instituted in the first human beings can only be realized by two persons; the apostle, however, declares that sin entered, but only through one.

AUG. I already said that you would say nothing, and it is evident to everyone, however slow, that such is the case. Do sinners not imitate Eve, or did the sin of the human race not take its beginning more from her? As scripture says, *The beginning of sin came from the woman, and on her account we all die* (Sir 25:33). Why, then, do you refuse to notice that the apostle preferred to mention one man through whom sin entered the world, because he wanted us to understand not imitation, but generation? After all, as the beginning of sin came from the woman, so that beginning of generation comes from the man. For a man first sows the seed in order for the woman to bear a child, and in that way *through one man sin entered the world* (Rom 5:12), because it entered through the seed of generation which the woman received from the man when she conceived a child. He who alone was born of a woman without sin chose not to be born that way.

57. JUL. It has been irrefutably established that the apostle indicated that this sin was transferred to their descendants by their moral conduct, not by their seed. See, then, what a great falsehood has flowed from your lips: "But the apostle said, *through one man*, from whom the generation of the human race began, so that he might teach that original sin was passed on to all through generation."[65] For the apostle said, *through one man*, precisely so that no one would think that original sin was passed on to all. You are so silly that I can hardly control my laughter; you say that human reproduction began with one human being, though the difference[66] of the sexes and the words of God bear witness that generation could not take place unless there first existed two human beings, that is, a man and a woman.

AUG. Let the readers of this reread my previous reply, or, if they remember it well, let them laugh at the ravings of this fellow. I could have said that the apostle did not say that it was two, but one human being through whom sin entered the world, because scripture said, *They will be two in one flesh* (Gn 2:24). For this reason the Lord said, *They will, therefore, no longer be two, but one flesh* (Mt 19:6), especially when the husband clings to his wife and they have intercourse. But a child is born as a result of intercourse and contracts original sin, since the defect begets a defect, while God creates the nature. Even when the spouses make good use of the defect, they are not able to beget the nature so that it can exist without the defect, but he who was born without defect destroys this defect in little ones, even though Julian does not like it.

58. JUL. Or if you should perhaps reply—since your teaching cannot survive otherwise—that Adam conceived and bore a child by himself, no one has any doubt that the apostle did not hold this view. But you will show what you want to happen to your own sex.

AUG. Have you no fear of the words of scripture, *Nor will slanderers possess the kingdom of God* (1 Cor 6:10)? After all, you would not utter such foul insults that do not help you at all, if it were not for your desire to utter slander.

59. JUL. But let us leave aside these points, and let us remove by the powers of reason the reply which it seems you could make to this passage. If, then, you say that scripture said of this union that they became two in one flesh and that the apostle said, *through one man* (Rom 5:12), in that sense to signify the coupled members of those having intercourse, I shall reply that this point too is against your impious teaching. After all, scripture did not say: They will be two human beings in one human being, but *They will be two in one flesh* (Gn 2:24). And by that expression of oneness we are taught that before the sin God instituted and implanted in bodies the pleasure of those who engage in intercourse and the desire which affects the mind and arouses the members and which, as that wise man understood, longs to become one flesh.

AUG. (1) If only sexual desire could make them to be two in one flesh, we could in no sense apply to Christ and the Church the words: *They will be two in one flesh* (Gn 2:24). Yet you even dare to bestow the possession of paradise on this protégée of yours, namely, such desire as you now both praise and attack, the desire which you admit is shameful and which you yet shamelessly love. After all, you do not wander so far from the path of the truth that you dare to attribute this desire to the union of Christ and the Church. (2) But if Christ and the Church can be two in one flesh without it, the man and his wife could also, if no one had sinned, have been united, not by shameful desire at which even he blushes who does not blush to praise it, but by a love that is rightly to be praised, and they could have been two in one flesh only for the sake of having children. Hence, when the Lord says, *They are, therefore, no longer two, but one flesh* (Mt 19:6), he certainly does not say, They are not two fleshes, but one flesh. To what, then, does *They are no longer two*, refer but to human beings, just as Christ and the Church are not two Christs, but one Christ. For this reason scripture said to us, *You are, then, the offspring of Abraham* (Gal 3:29), since it also said of Abraham, *And to your offspring who is Christ* (Gal 3:16).

60. JUL. And for this reason the devil can claim for himself none of its pleasure or its modesty.

AUG. Why do you say, "of its modesty"? Are you ashamed to mention shame? You say, nonetheless, that even before the sin shameful desire was present in those of whom scripture says, *They were naked and not ashamed* (Gn 2:25).

61. JUL. And yet, if this apostle had had any such idea, he would have said that sin entered through one flesh, not through one man. But generation gives to the offspring only the substance of the flesh, because a soul is not passed on by a soul, but flesh is passed on by flesh. The term "human being," however, refers in the proper sense to both the mind and the body, and for this reason when the apostle mentioned one human being, he did not indicate the activity of reproduction which he knew passes on only the substance of the flesh. And he did not want us to understand two human beings; rather, he put the stress on "one" in order to teach that sin was passed on by imitation, not by generation.

AUG. What, then, does, *They are no longer two, but one flesh* (Mt 19:6), mean but: They are no longer two human beings on account of the one flesh? For the flesh can also refer to a human being, the whole named after a part, just as scripture said: *The Word was made flesh* (Jn 1:14), because he of whom this was said became a man. I think that the apostle also wanted us to understand his words, *The exterior human being is being corrupted* (2 Cor 4:16) as referring to the flesh. For this reason we speak correctly when we say, "The tomb of a human being," although only the flesh is buried there. Nor was she mistaken when she said, *They have taken my Lord from the tomb* (Jn 20:13), though only his flesh was laid to rest there. As long as the most obscure question about the soul remains, one could say, *Through one man sin entered the world* (Rom 5:12), even if only the flesh is involved in reproduction. Pay attention, then, to these points, and see that you have said nothing.

62. JUL. Now I warn the reader to be attentive, though the truth has done its part. I have, then, laid aside much of my rights in the course of this conflict, and I followed where the rashness of my opponent challenged me. I defended the teachings of the true faith so that, even if they were the words of the teacher of the nations to which the traducianist attributed that meaning, it would be clear that he had no idea of natural sin, since in mentioning only one human being he did not blame the generation of sin, but the examples of sin.

AUG. You have given an example, but an example of foolishness on your part, because, if the apostle had taken the example of sin from the first human sinner, that is, Adam, he would surely have taken the example of righteousness from the first righteous human being, namely, Abel.

Not Sin, But Death Was Passed On to All

63. JUL. (1) But it is clear that the words of the apostle do not have the order which our enemy thought. He, of course, argues in this way: "If the apostle," he says, "had wanted us to understand imitation in this passage, he would not have

said that sin entered the world *through one man* (Rom 5:12). Rather, he would have said that it entered the world through the devil and was passed on by all human beings. In fact, scripture says of the devil, *Those who are on his side imitate him* (Wis 2:25). But he said, *through one man*, from whom the generation of the human race began, so that he might teach that original sin was passed on to all through generation."[67] (2) Hence, he lies insofar as he says that blessed Paul declared that through one man sin entered the world and in that way it was passed on to all human beings. This is not, I insist, contained in the words of the teacher of the nations. He certainly did not say that sin was passed on, but that death was passed on. Here, then, is the order of the words: *Just as through one man sin entered the world, and through sin death, and in that way it was passed on to all human beings, in whom all have sinned* (Rom 5:12). (3) The sublime instructor of the Church weighed what he should say; he said, *Through one man sin entered the world*,[68] and through sin death, and in that way it was passed on to all human beings. He had already mentioned death and sin. Why was it necessary to separate death from its connection with sin in what he said was passed on? In this way he explicitly showed that sin entered this world through one man and through sin death. But it was not sin, but death that was passed on to all human beings. Death was imposed by the severity of judgment to punish the transgression, not to go after the seeds of bodies, but to go after the defects of moral conduct. Why was this necessary if not that he was concerned to teach us and forewarn us that we should not suppose that he offered any help to your teaching?

AUG. In the passage in which it says, *Through one man sin entered the world, and through sin death, and in that way it was passed on to all human beings* (Rom 5:12), it seems ambiguous whether sin or death or both of them were said to have been passed on to all human beings. But the facts themselves which are so clear reveal which of these it is. For if sin had not been passed on, every human being would not be born with the law of sin which is in the members. If death had not been passed on, every human being would not die—at least as it pertains to the present condition of mortals. But in the apostle's words, *in whom all have sinned*, "*in whom*" is only taken to mean "in Adam," in whom he says that they also die, because it would not have been just that the punishment should be passed on without the sin. Wherever you turn, you will not in any way overthrow the foundations of the Catholic faith, especially since you contradict yourself. You now say that it was not sin, but death that was passed on, and you said above that the apostle did not speak of two human beings, but of one, in order to teach that sin was passed on by imitation, not by generation. Sin, therefore, was passed on along with death. Why is it that you now say that it was not sin, but death that was passed on?

64. JUL. Notice the big difference between you and Paul. He says, *Through one man*, but you say, Through two, that is, through generation. He states that

both sin and death were found in the first human being, but only death was passed on to his descendants. You, on the other hand, state that both sin and death were transmitted to all.

AUG. I have already replied to that. Let those who want reread what we said above so that I do not needlessly have to repeat the same things again and again.

65. JUL. You, therefore, impudently hide under the shadow of his name, though you say quite different and opposite things. He, after all, blamed the work of human beings; you blame the work of God. He blamed the desires of sinners; you blame the innocent life of the newborn. He blamed the human will; you blame human nature.

AUG. I have replied to all this above. Those who remember it laugh at you. But if those who do not remember it will reread those parts, they will first laugh at your foolish statements and then they will be sorry for you.

66. JUL. According to the apostle, therefore, sin entered this world through one man, and through sin death, because the world saw that he was both guilty and destined for condemnation to endless death. But death was passed on to all human beings, because the one standard of judgment also included any transgressors from the ages to come. This death, however, is not permitted to harm the saints or any who are innocent, but it is passed on to those who it sees imitate the transgression.

AUG. What you say was raised as an objection against the founder of your heresy, Pelagius, in the episcopal court in Palestine, namely, that Adam was created so that he was going to die, whether he sinned or did not sin.[69] You do not want this death by which all of us die to have been passed on from the beginning to all of us as a result of sin, even though scripture says of it, *The beginning of sin came from the woman, and on her account we all die* (Sir 25:33). You do not want to be forced to say that sin was also passed on along with it from the beginning. You, of course, see how unjust it would be that the punishment was passed on without the sin. The teaching which you are trying to attack is, nonetheless, so Catholic that the man to whom, as I said, this objection was raised would certainly have emerged from that court as a condemned man if he had not condemned it. Death, then, both this death by which the spirit is separated from the body and that death which is called the second death, by which the spirit will be tormented along with the body, has been passed on to all human beings—insofar as this pertains to the merit of the human race. But through him who came to remove the reign of death by dying, the grace of God has not allowed death to reign because of that resurrection of which he has already given us an example. This is what the Catholic faith holds. This is what the judges whom Pelagius feared held. This is not what these heretics hold of whom Pelagius is the father.

67. JUL. Though that transgression did not become part of nature, it was the pattern of sin, and for this reason, though it does not weigh down the newborn, it does, nonetheless, bring accusations against those who imitate it.

AUG. Even if you have forgotten the heavy yoke which weighs down the newborn, we do not stop reminding you of it.

68. JUL. The sentence of death was passed on insofar[70] as all have sinned, but sinned by free will. In the customary manner of the scriptures that word, namely, *all*, indicates very many, not absolutely all.

AUG. In vain do you try to twist straightforward words and make clear ones obscure. All sinned in him in whom all died. That is Adam. And if the little ones do not die in him, they will certainly not be brought to life in Christ. But because *just as in Adam all die, so all will also be brought to life in Christ* (1 Cor 15:22). Those, then, who want to twist these words will be themselves destroyed, while the words endure.

In What Sense Sin Existed up to the Law

69. JUL. (1) But now let us move on to the rest of the passage in order that the apostle may show by the development of the sacred text with which teaching he agrees, as has already become clear to a large extent. "What else do the following words of the apostle signify? For, after he had said this, he added, *For up to the law sin was in the world*, that is, because even the law could not remove sin. *But sin was not imputed, when the law did not exist* (Rom 5:13). It existed, then, but it was not imputed because what might be imputed was not yet revealed. After all, as he says in another passage, *Knowledge of sin came through the law* (Rom 3:20). *But death*, he says, *reigned from Adam up to Moses*; that is, as he had said above: *up to the law* (Rom 5:14.13). (2) It did not reign *up to Moses* in the sense that afterward there was no sin. Rather, not even the law given through Moses was able to remove the reign of death which reigns only through sin. But its reign means that it also casts mortal human beings down into the second death, which is everlasting. Over whom did it reign? He says, *Even over these who have not sinned in the likeness of the transgression of Adam who is the symbol of the one to come* (Rom 5:14). Who is the one to come but Christ? And how is he a symbol but by contrast? He expresses this idea elsewhere, *Just as in Adam all die, so in Christ all will be brought to life* (1 Cor 15:22). (3) As there is the one result in Adam, so there is the other result in Christ. The symbol is the same, but not the same in every respect. For this reason the apostle goes on to add here, *But the grace is not like the sin. For, if many have died on account of the sin of the one, the grace of God and the gift in the grace of the one man Jesus Christ has been much more abundant for many* (Rom 5:15). Why has it *been much more abundant*, but because all who are set free through Christ die a temporal death, but on account of Christ himself they will live a life without end?"[71] You claimed that the following words of the apostle teach nothing except original sin, but we

proved from his very starting point that he did not show this, because he indicated that sin was passed on through one, not through two persons.

AUG. I have already replied to this, and you are still mouthing nonsense. Nor is this, after all, a surprise, for you do not know what my answer is. You will be more impudent if, when you do know my answer, you still refuse to abandon your foolishness and embrace the truth.

70. JUL. We must, nonetheless, consider which of the two doctrines that period he passed over might at least imply. He said, *Up to the law sin was in the world* (Rom 5:13). You say that the apostle wanted us to understand this to be natural sin. I ask, then, why, if it existed up to the law, it ceased after the law. For I do not agree that I should understand, *up to the law*, to mean "up to its end" rather than "up to its beginning." The proper sense of the words is on my side. When the apostle says that it existed up to the law, he shows that it does not exist after the law, and whatever was removed in the course of time was not something natural. What the censure of the law weakened, and curtailed to a large extent by weakening it, was obviously acquired by imitation, not by generation.

AUG. Oh mind of a heretic! What else can I say? If the law, then, took away sin, for that is how you want us to understand, *up to the law*, then righteousness came through the law. *If righteousness came through the law, then Christ has died in vain* (Gal 2:21). If, however, the law did not take away sin so that it did not exist—something that you had said before that it did do, and you soon regretted it—but if the law weakened sin, as you corrected yourself, and curtailed it to a large extent, then he lied who said, *The law entered in so that sin might abound* (Rom 5:20). But since he spoke the truth, you are saying nothing, and yet by saying nothing, you contradict him with your heretical stubbornness.

71. JUL. But I do not want to be too much of a stickler in dealing with you. Let us agree that *up to the law* can mean "up to Christ." You grant, then, that this sin which you call original does not exist after Christ. And how can you say that even up to today so many centuries after the coming of Christ the work of the devil, the fruit tree of the enemy power, and the law of sin remain, thrive, and live on in the members of the apostles and in all the baptized?

AUG. I do not say this; you are not saying anything. Sin is one thing; the desire for sin is another. One who through the grace of God does not sin does not consent to this desire, though the very desire for sin is also called sin because it was produced by sin. So too, any writing is called the hand of the one whose hand made it. The one of whom scripture said, *There is the lamb of God; there is the one who takes away the sin of the world* (Jn 1:29), removes by rebirth the guilt of the sin which is contracted by birth. By giving the Spirit he stops sin from reigning in our mortal body so that we obey its desires.[72] By his daily pardon on account of which we say every day, *Forgive us our debts* (Mt 6:12), he mercifully wipes it away, if the desire for sin should lead us to do anything wrong, though we struggle to do what is right by resisting. He raises up penitents crushed by a serious fall. He leads them to his kingdom where it is impossible to sin and makes them to reign there, and then they will say, *Where, death, is your victory? Where, death, is your sting? But the sting of death is sin* (1 Cor 15:55-56). There you see how that lamb of God takes away the sin of the world which the law could not take away.

72. JUL. But let us look at the rest. The apostle says, *But sin was not imputed when the law did not exist* (Rom 5:13); after this you add, "It existed, then, but it was not imputed, as he says in another passage, *Knowledge of sin came through the law* (Rom 3:20)."[73] If, therefore, knowledge of sin was produced through the law and if inherited sin was not imputed before the law, show us that this was imputed under the law. For, if knowledge of sin came through the law, there was ignorance of sin before the law. There is no way around it: the principal cause of promulgating the law was that sin which was previously hidden might be made known and avoided.

AUG. You speak the truth when you say: that sin might be made known. We too say this. That, however, sin might be avoided came not from the law, but from grace, not from the letter, but from the Spirit. For the law entered in, not so that sin might be avoided, but so that sin might abound and that grace might be much more abundant[74] in wiping out sin that has been committed and in avoiding the commission of sin.

73. JUL. Here, then, must be the heart of our disagreement. Either show that original sin was imputed to someone under the law; show that it was made known, and I shall agree that the apostle spoke of this sin.

AUG. I do show what you challenge me to show, but only if you open[75] your eyes to those things which you do not want to see, and you spread clouds of argumentation so that others may not see them. Circumcision of the flesh was commanded by the law.[76] Nothing better could be signified by it than that Christ, the source of rebirth, takes away original sin. Every man, after all, is born with a foreskin, just as one is born with original sin. And the law commands that the flesh be circumcised on the eighth day because Christ rose on the Lord's Day, which is the eighth day after the seventh day of the Sabbath. And a circumcised father produces a son with a foreskin, passing on to the child what he himself lacked, just as a baptized father passes on to the child he begets the guilt of his origin from which the father was released. Finally, in the law the psalm says, *I was conceived in iniquity, and my mother nourished me in the womb amid sins* (Ps 51:7). You certainly would see this, and you would not dare to speak against this, if you had eyes of faith like Cyprian and Ambrose and other such teachers of the Church.

74. JUL. Or, since it is not possible to find this in the law, at least agree, you most impudent fellow, that the apostle is speaking of that sin which is contracted

by imitation, committed by the will, blamed by reason, revealed by the law, and punished with justice.

AUG. Scripture said of every sin which is taken away by Christ, *Sin was in the world up to the law* (Rom 5:13), because the law does not take away either original sin or the sin which is added to it, whether it was the sin which existed before the law or that sin which abounded when the law entered in. But since you say that the apostle is speaking about that sin which is punished with justice, wake up and see that original sin also belongs there. For otherwise the justice of God would not place a heavy yoke upon even the very first days of the life of little ones.[77] Our concern has often led us to mention that yoke in order to break your proud neck if it does not bend. For I showed that this sin is revealed in the law by the commandment of circumcision. If you deny this, explain what personal sin it was by which the soul of a little one perished from its people if it was not circumcised.[78] I know, you cannot explain this, but you refuse to be silent out of your desire to weary us.

75. JUL. But the original sin which you invent cannot be transmitted by one person, because it takes two to have a child.

AUG. I have already replied to this. Read what I said on this point, and you will find that you have spoken nonsense.

76. JUL. Nor could it exist at one time if it could not exist at another time, because natural characteristics last from the beginning of a substance up to its end.

AUG. You could also say this of death, since we are also born with it. For *the body is dead on account of sin* (Rom 8:10). But even if it is not on account of sin, as you foolishly suppose, we are, nonetheless, undoubtedly born mortal, and yet death and mortality will not be ours when we live immortally. Death comes from our origin, and yet it could cease to exist while our nature survives.[79] In the same way original sin both could exist as contracted by birth and can cease to exist when it is removed by rebirth.

77. JUL. Nor was it revealed by the law, nor could it be revealed, because no lawgiver has ever come to such madness as to command anyone: Do not be born in this way or that. And it cannot be just to punish what it was not right to admonish a person to correct.

AUG. Human beings are not commanded how they should be born. The first man was commanded how he should live, and he broke that commandment. From that parent we derive original sin. It was also a commandment that an infant should be circumcised and would be condemned if it were not. And yet, such an infant is not only given no other commandment, but it is not even given circumcision itself as a commandment. And for this reason human beings are not commanded how to be born, and yet no one is clean from the filth of sin, *not even an infant who has lived one day on earth* (Jb 14:4-5). Read the words of saintly Job, and you will find that you are a liar since he whom God declared truthful says this.

78. JUL. And what exists up to the law is shown not to exist after the law; finally, it is shown not to exist after Christ.

AUG. The guilt of this sin is shown not to exist after the removal of sins, just as death will not exist after the resurrection of the body.

79. JUL. And in this way, even according to your argumentation it does not exist for a certain time; according to the testimony of the truth it never existed.

AUG. Oh how I wish you did not exist, you people who both speak and also write your false testimony against the testimony of the truth!

The Definition of Sin and God's Justice

80. JUL. And to impress upon the mind of the reader what we have accomplished: At one point you defined sin and did so very well as "nothing other than the will to commit that which justice forbids and from which one is free to hold back."[80]

AUG. I have already replied that this is a definition of sin, not of that which is also the punishment of sin.[81]

81. JUL. This definition also opened the path to understand the justice of God so that we declare that the justice of the divine judgment would never stand unless it imputed as sin that from which it knew that the person who is punished on account of it was free to hold back.

AUG. Why, then, are little ones punished if they have no sin at all? Could not the omnipotent and just God have kept unjust punishments from so many innocents?

82. JUL. But the teacher of the nations, arming reason with the prerogative of his authority, declared that sin passed into this world through one human being. By that expression he excluded the activity of marriage which cannot be accomplished without the cooperation of two, and we stressed that he mentioned one person precisely so that no one would dare to think of two.

AUG. I have already answered this. It is an endless delight for you to babble nonsense.

83. JUL. And I maintain that the one the apostle mentions was truly one person in order to teach that it was a sin of imitation, not of generation, and I do this with much more logic than the traducianist. By mentioning the one who is said to be the entrance way of sin, he ascribes to the seeds something that pertains to the will—an idea that the nature of things does not admit.

AUG. Stop repeating what we have already refuted. Why do you force us to say the same things over and over in opposition to your great wisdom? For by that wisdom you suppose that scripture did not refer to generation where it said, *Through one man sin entered the world* (Rom 5:12), because generation is carried out by two persons, not by one, as if one person committed that sin which you want to have been passed on, not by generation, but by imitation. Since, then, two committed that sin, why did the apostle say, *Through one man sin entered the world*, if not because generation does not begin with the woman conceiving and bearing a child, but with the man sowing the seed, or because they are no longer two when they became one flesh by intercourse?

84. JUL. Afterward we also came to the law. The apostle wrote that sin, though not revealed, flourished up to its time. But you tried to extend this time to the end of the law, not understanding that you did not accomplish anything by your argument. Then we had to force you to prove that this sin, which you falsely claim Paul spoke about and which you claim reigned until the abolition of the old testament, was imputed or could have been imputed under the law. Or you had at least to admit that it does not reign after Christ so that the statement of the apostle, though twisted violently, might at least sound in harmony with your views. But you can do none of these. The purity of our faith, therefore, rests upon solid rock, for the teachings of reason and the dignity of justice and the thought of the apostle are completely in agreement with it.

AUG. Our reply and you yourself show that you say nothing. The apostle wanted us to understand by his words, *Sin was in the world up to the law* (Rom 5:13), not original sin alone, but all sin. And it existed up to the law because not even the law could take away sin. *Up to the law* was, of course, said in the sense that this statement also included the law, just as the gospel said, *All the generations, then, from Abraham up to David are fourteen* (Mt 1:17). For we arrive at this number, not by excluding David, but by counting him in. Just as, then, when we hear that there were fourteen generations up to David, we do not exclude David, but count him in, so when we hear, *Sin was in the world up to the law*, we ought not to exclude the law, but to count it in. For, as David was not excluded from that number which the gospel said went up to him, so the law was not excluded from the continuation of sin which Paul said had existed up to the law. And for this reason no one takes away the sin which the law, though holy and just and good,[82] could not take away except the one of whom scripture says, *There is the lamb of God; there is the one who takes away the sin of the world* (Jn 1:29). But he takes sin away by forgiving those sins which have been committed, including original sin, and by giving help so that sins are not committed, and by bringing us to that life where it is utterly impossible to sin.

How Grace Abounded More Than the Sin

85. JUL. But let us look at the remaining points. After you said, "The pattern is the same, but not the same in every respect," you add, "For this reason the apostle goes on to add here, *But the grace is not like the sin. For, if many have died on account of the sin of the one, the grace of God and the gift in the grace of*

the one man Jesus Christ has been much more abundant for more" (Rom 5:15). You explain this statement as follows: "What does it has *been much more abundant* mean but that all who are set free through Christ die a temporal death on account of Adam, but on account of Christ they will live a life without end?"[83] The apostle, about whose view we are having this dispute, certainly declared that the grace of the savior works more efficaciously and more bountifully for bringing salvation than the sin of Adam. He wanted to show that Christ did much greater good and benefitted more people and that his grace—to use his expression—*has been abundant for more* than the transgression of the first human being did harm—the one who you say attached sin to the seeds.

AUG. He said, It *has been much more abundant*, not: For many more, that is, not: For more people. After all, who can fail to see that there are more in the human race for whom it did not abound? As a result, we are shown from these more what the whole mass deserved by just judgment if the Spirit did not breathe where it willed[84] and God did not call those whom he chose and made religious whom he willed.[85]

86. JUL. Prove, then, that what the apostle meant is consistent with your teachings.

AUG. Let his words be read by readers who are not perverse, as your followers are, and no other proof will be needed.

The Injuries Inflicted by Adam's Sin

87. JUL. For if by natural sin, as you say, Adam begot all human beings for condemnation, he spilled such a venom from his innards into his offspring that he upset all of God's creation in the nature of human beings.

AUG. When an unclean spirit troubles a little one and afflicts its soul and body and destroys its senses and sanity, is not the whole of its nature which God created upset? But you will not find anything that merited this great evil if you deny original sin. Why do you not see that in this case all of God's creation in the nature of a human being is upset by the venom of the devil? Tell me the reason for this in the child; tell me how a newborn to whom these things happen is guilty, if you refuse to interpret the words of the apostle, as the Catholic Church has interpreted them since its foundation and as nature itself admits them by its evils which are so evident. And yet, if we consider the matter carefully, God's creation is in no sense upset because he established everything with foreknowledge of the future. Nor does he repay to each individual the whole of what the fallen creature merits. Rather, he arranges all things in measure and number and weight,[86] and he allows no one to suffer any evil which one does not deserve, although each individual does not suffer as much as the whole mass deserves.

88. JUL. And as a result, marriage which God created could not exist without the gift of the devil to which you attribute sexual desire. In fact, that former marriage which God established with the dignity of his creation has fled, and this present marriage has lasted whose order involves the movement of the sexual organs, the shame of the spouses having intercourse, the ardor and climax of the members, the pleasure of the senses, and the sinfulness of the newborn—this marriage Adam forced to be and proved to be the work of the devil, not of God.

AUG. If you distinguish the evil of defects which can only exist in something good from the goodness of natures, you will neither excuse the devil nor accuse God. And you will neither excuse the evil of desire nor accuse the good of marriage.

89. JUL. Finally, by the impact of the one sin Adam destroyed freedom of choice so that from then on none would have it in their power to reject their former sins by choosing virtue. Rather, by the one sin all were carried off to condemnation in the torrent of fallen humanity.

AUG. Why are you not rather surprised at such great misery in the whole human race from the first moment of birth? For one attains happiness only from a state of misery, and only after this life are any free from all evils, if the grace of God grants that they are free from them. By wondering over this, you will correct yourself, and you will recognize in the just affliction of the human race the just judgment of God, because sin entered the world through one man.[87]

What the Grace of Christ Ought to Remedy

90. JUL. If, I say, the sinfulness of the first human being brought all these evils upon the image of God, it is evident that the grace of Christ is too feeble in its gifts, since it finds nothing which cures these many massive evils. Or if it finds something, say so. Let us now compare them one by one. If besides the acts of the will Adam overthrew the state of nature itself, Christ ought most of all to restore those things which that man tore down to the same positions, that is, to those positions from which Adam dislodged them.

AUG. He does this, but not in the way you want. *Who, after all, knows the mind of the Lord? Or who was his counselor?* (Is 40:13, Rom 11:34).

91. JUL. That is, no sexual desire would be experienced at all in the marriage of baptized persons, and their sex organs would not be aroused in the way they are in other people.

AUG. Then baptized women ought not to bear children with groans, because this fact—which you cannot deny—is the punishment of the sinful woman.

92. JUL. After the gift of grace the shame of the couple during intercourse would disappear, and no restless disturbance[88] would pass through their members, and their senses would not suffer the burdens of pleasure. Finally, free

choice would be restored to the baptized, and you would admit that through the correction of nature when the law of sin has been driven out, it is just as possible for mortals to be radiant with the splendor of the virtues as to be ugly with the filth of the vices. In fact, those who have received the sacraments ought not to be mortal at all.

AUG. And yet, Julian, you are not ashamed to locate in paradise such a marriage in which you acknowledge the shame of the couple having intercourse. Was there, then, something to be ashamed of in that place where the creator who ought to be praised above all established nothing that ought not to be praised? But who can think and say that except someone unashamed to praise what causes shame?

93. JUL. For if the medicine fights against the wound and if death is said to have resulted from sin, the removal of sin ought to produce the end of death.

AUG. You are still saying that Adam was created so that he would have died, whether he sinned or did not sin. But in the episcopal court in Palestine your teacher, Pelagius himself, condemned you who say this and condemned himself as well, since he did not correct his views.[89] But in this evil world God does not make blessed those of his own whose sins he forgives in this life and upon whom he bestows the pledge of the Spirit of grace. Therefore, he promised to those people who do not make use of the evils of this world, whether they are sources of pleasure or bitter and painful, or who make good use of them, a world to come in which they will suffer no evil. There marriage would also be the sort of marriage which could have existed in that paradise, if no one had sinned, and of which there would be nothing to be ashamed. But there will not even be marriage of that sort because, once the number of the blessed is complete for which marriage is necessary, there will be no reproduction.

94. JUL. But it is agreed that none of these things which we mentioned takes place in the bodies of the baptized. Hence, the truth which is brighter than the sun has shown that by these manners of healing nothing could have been done, that is, ought to have been done otherwise. And so, you must admit either that those changes which we listed did not result from sin and were for that reason not wounds of nature. In that way the meaning of grace is upheld which makes it evident that those conditions are not a departure from the order assigned to them. Or you must surely deny that the mysteries of Christ contain any remedy since, according to you, they were unable to heal even one out of so many diseases.

AUG. On the contrary, you ought from this to recognize, if you lived with a sober mind, how great that sin was which entered the world through one man and was passed on to all human beings along with death, since even the baptized, though their guilt has now been taken away, are not rescued from all the evils of this world with which human beings are born, except after this life during which it is necessary that we still be tried by evils, despite the good things we have been promised. For if we were immediately given the reward of faith, there would no longer be the faith which sees the present evils and bears up under them with piety, because it awaits with faith and patience the promised good things which it does not see.

95. JUL. I have up to this point acted as if the apostle thought that the power of the gifts and of the wounds were equal, though their effects were opposite. But the sublimity of the sound faith which we are defending is undoubtedly increased when we consider that Paul not only did not emphasize the illness of sins over the remedies of grace, but judged that the benefits were also more abundant than the penalties.

AUG. It is true. The penalties of the reborn are temporal, but the benefits will be undoubtedly everlasting. But tell me on what grounds the penalties to which the newborn bear witness by their wailing are imposed under the perfectly just and omnipotent judge, if the newborn contract no sin.

96. JUL. Let the wise reader note what this discussion has also entailed. The apostle said that the gift of Christ has become abundant for the salvation of more people than the sin of Adam harmed.

AUG. He did not say this; rather, he said, *Grace has become much more abundant for many* (Rom 5:15); that is, it has become more abundant, not for many more, that is, not for more people, as I have already replied.[90]

The Power of the Sin and the Power of Grace

97. JUL. You say that those disasters which we listed above came upon human nature because of that sin. But it is evident that not even one of them is healed in those who receive Christ's sacraments. And for this reason you maintain that the sin of the first human being had much more power to do harm than the grace of Christ has to heal. When this conclusion is drawn, we are shown that there is as great a disagreement between you and the apostle Paul as there is between the Catholics and the Manichees.

AUG. (1) The grace of Christ takes away the guilt of original sin, but it takes away something invisible in an invisible way. It also forgives all sins which human beings have added on to it by living bad lives. Judgment, of course, comes after the one sin and leads to condemnation because that one sin which is contracted by those who are born draws them to eternal condemnation if it is not forgiven. But grace does not forgive this sin alone. Otherwise, grace would be equal in power to sin. Rather, it forgives the other sins along with it; hence, it is more powerful. On this account scripture said, *After the one there came judgment leading to condemnation, but after many sins there came grace leading to justification* (Rom 5:16). (2) It is also a gift of grace that the spirit has desires opposed to the concupiscence of the flesh. And if a believer is ever defeated in a pardonable way in this battle, grace forgives these debts when the believer prays for this, and when one is defeated in a way that deserves condemnation, it grants a more humble penance in order that it grant pardon for it. Finally, it gives eternal life to the soul and to the body. Who can imagine the great and wonderful goods there will be in that life? How, then, did the sin of the first human being do more harm than the goodness of the second, that is, of Christ, brought benefit, since the former did temporal harm, while Christ both provides temporal help and also sets us free and makes us blessed for eternity? Since that is so, our position is Catholic, not Manichean, and it is also not Pelagian either, because it is Catholic.

98. JUL. I would have a perfect right to scorn your quite silly interpretation of this passage and to pass it over unrefuted, as something utterly beneath me, if I were not afraid that people would put their faith in your deceits rather than in my logical thinking. You speak as follows: "Why has it *been much more abundant* (Rom 5:15), but because all who are set free through Christ die a temporal death on account of Adam, but on account of Christ himself they will live a life without end?"[91] If you would consider what should be said as the consequence of these words, you would admit that your fortress, namely, the inheritance of sin, has collapsed. You say, after all, that the grace of Christ was much more abundant because it bestows eternal life, while Adam's sin makes us suffer temporal destruction. If, then, Adam introduced only bodily death, while Christ, on the other hand, by a greater gift conferred everlasting life, it is clear that it was not Adam's sin, but death that was passed on to his descendants.

AUG. It is clear that you laughed at what I said—or rather pretended to laugh at it—so that those who do not understand you would think that you have something to say, though you do not say anything. First, I said that Adam harmed by temporal death those whom Christ's grace sets free, since those whom he does not set free by the truth of his hidden, but just judgment are punished with eternal death, even if they die as little ones. How, then, is it clear from this that it was not Adam's sin, but death that was passed on to his descendants, unless you want us to accept the noise of your words, not the logical consequence of mine? For we say that both of them were passed on, and we cry out that both of them are taken away by Christ, that is, the guilt of sin by the fullest forgiveness of sins and death by the most blessed resurrection of the saints. But this resurrection is not immediately given to those who have been reborn so that they may practice their faith by which they hope for what they do not see. For when believers hope for this both in themselves and in their little ones, they are certainly believers. There you have what we say; there is the Catholic truth against which you speak, though you speak against yourselves rather than against it whatever you say with your heretical arguments.

99. JUL. It will be shown with full logic that perpetual death, that is, everlasting punishment, was not passed on to us, and that for this reason there cannot be an inherited sin. In order to make it clear in a few words what one must undoubtedly hold: The apostle exalts Christ's gifts in comparison with the sin of the first

human being. Do you say that one or two deaths were passed on by this sin of yours, that is, by inherited sin? If you say: one death and that bodily death, as you admitted here, it is clear that the grace of Christ is more powerful than the sin of the first human being, and now no one is born a sinner. For if, as you said above, the reign of sin means that human beings are hurled down to the second death, that is, to perpetual punishment, and if you say that Adam brought about only the death of the body, neither sin nor eternal death is transmitted by Adam to his descendants.

AUG. I have already replied to this; you say nothing at all. For the reign of sin also hurls one down to eternal death unless it is forgiven by the grace of Christ. This temporal death, nonetheless, would also not exist if Adam had not lost as punishment for his sin the possibility of not dying. God, after all, foretold this death to the sinner when he said, *You are earth, and you will return to earth* (Gn 3:19). Christ chose to accept this death, though he had no sin, so that by dying he would through that death return to earth, but by rising would raise up earth to heaven. And so, though he destroyed eternal death, he did not take away temporal death for the faithful precisely so that faith in the resurrection would struggle against death in the combat of this life.

100. JUL. If you say that the sin of Adam made sinfulness natural and brought about two deaths, one eternal, the other temporal, but that the grace of Christ now takes away one death, that is, perpetual death, from the person, not from the nature, while temporal death remains, you prove the apostle guilty of a lie, for he said that grace did us much more good than sin did us harm. But the apostle cannot be refuted; hence, you are rightly rejected.

AUG. I said that the one resurrection of the blessed takes away both deaths, this death so that the soul is not without the body and that other death so that the soul is also not weighed down or afflicted by its body. The faithful are, then, left with this latter death for a time so that faith might have support through it, just as afterwards the guilty are deprived of this death so that the fact that they do not depart from their bodies is an increase of their misery. And for this reason it is clear that grace has done more good for those who are reborn in Christ and who depart from this evil world as his elect than that sin did them harm which entered the world through one man and was passed on along with death to all human beings. The apostle, therefore, cannot be refuted because he spoke the truth, but you do not understand, or contrary to what you understand you try to uphold by your heretical argument what is false.

101. JUL. The apostle said that the grace of Christ was more abundant than the sin of Adam. He did not, therefore, blame nature or birth or fertility, but the will, the choice of evil, and the depravity of morals.

AUG. (1) If birth did no harm, rebirth offers no benefit. If nature is not damaged, the little ones do not have Christ as their savior. If all[92] good and bad merit of individuals lies entirely in their own will, what merit does Christ reward when he bestows the kingdom of God on little ones who have used their will neither for good nor for evil? Finally, the apostle mentioned two persons, the one in relation to sin, not the devil, but Adam, and the other in relation to righteousness, not Abel, but Christ. He did this, not so that imitation might correspond to their examples, but so that rebirth might correspond to birth. If Adam does not pass on sin to human beings who are born, Christ does not give righteousness to the little ones who are reborn, because neither as born nor as reborn did the little ones use their own will. (2) Go on now if you want, and cry out if you dare that little ones are not given righteousness and that they will not have righteousness when they dwell in that kingdom where there will be, as scripture says, new heavens and a new earth in which righteousness will dwell.[93] Or rave on as a result of that most potent teaching of yours which has made you intoxicated, and say that little ones will in fact dwell in that kingdom, but by reason of the merits of their own will, not by reason of the generosity of divine grace. But if you do not dare to say that—for you admit that merits are earned here and rewards given there—why do you hesitate to say or refuse to say that they could have sin from Adam without any merits of a bad will of their own, just as they will receive righteousness from Christ without any preceding merits of a good will of their own?

102. JUL. And in this way, if truth still has some place in human affairs and if absolutely the whole world has not gone deaf with the noise of iniquity, it will admit that by the testimony of reason, of argument, of the faith of the apostle, and of his statement, it has been clearly taught that there is as great a difference between the traducianists and the Catholics as between Paul and Mani, between wisdom and folly, between reason and insanity, between steadfastness in language and that vacillation from which you suffer with a hitherto unseen ugliness. For in almost the same lines you deny what you said and affirm what you denied.

AUG. I have already replied to this. I beg you, if you do not have anything to say, be quiet if you can, but what is worse, you cannot be quiet.

103. JUL. (1) Paul says, *The gift is not like the result of the one man's sin. For after the one there came judgment leading to condemnation, but after many sins there came grace leading to justification* (Rom 5:16). To these words of the apostle you apply your explanation which runs as follows: "What then does *after the one* mean but: after the one sin? For there follows: *But after many sins there came grace.* Let these people explain how condemnation followed after one sin, if it was not that even the one original sin sufficed for condemnation, because it was passed on to all human beings. But after many sins grace brought justification, because it removed not only that one sin which is contracted from our origin, but also the rest which each human being adds by the movement of one's own will. (2) *For, if on account of the sin of the one, death reigned through the one, those who receive an abundance of grace and of righteousness will for even greater reason reign in life through the one Jesus Christ. And so, as through the*

sin of the one, condemnation comes upon all human beings, so through the righteousness of the one, righteousness of life comes upon all human beings" (Rom 5:17-18).[94]

After these words of the apostle you speak of us in an insulting manner, as if you had accomplished something, "Let them persist in their vain thoughts, and let them say that the one man did not hand on the lineage of sin, but the example of sin. Why is it, then, that *through the sin of the one* and not through the many sins of each individual *condemnation comes upon all human beings*, except that this sin, although it is only one, is able to lead to condemnation, even without the addition of any others? In fact, it now leads to condemnation little ones who die, if they are born from Adam, but not reborn in Christ. (3) Why then does this man demand from us what he refuses to hear from the apostle, namely, 'How does sin come to be in a little one? Does it come from the will or from marriage or from the parents?'[95] Now let him hear how it comes to be; let him hear how sin comes to be in a little one, and let him be quiet: *Through the sin of the one*, the apostle says, *condemnation comes upon all human beings*" (Rom 5:18).[96] We know that you fear nothing more than detailed examination of your thought and teaching; this is the reason, of course, why you use every resource to obtain from worldly authorities that they refuse us a hearing, for you understand that you must act with force since you are bereft of any help from reason.

AUG. *Do you want to be free from the fear of worldly powers? Do good* (Rom 13:3). It is not, however, something good to assert and defend an heretical view in opposition to the view of the apostle. Why do you people still ask for a hearing, for you have already had one before the Apostolic See?[97] In fact, you already had a hearing in the episcopal court in Palestine where Pelagius, the author of your heresy, would undoubtedly have been condemned if he had not condemned these teachings of yours which you defend.[98] A heresy, then, which has already been condemned does not need to be further examined by the bishops, but to be suppressed by the Christian authorities.

On Whose Side Is the Apostle?

104. JUL. But your opinion will not have such influence among the wise that, though you are "the origin and cause of these evils,"[99] you may withdraw from the midst of the fray with the apostle as your shield and suppose that he should receive the blows instead of you. For we are armed by him most of all as our teacher and leader against you. I want you to recognize what you must say in the future as a result. If there were no disagreement between you and me on this claim that the apostle supported the teaching of the Manichees with natural sin, then you would logically set him over against one seeking your head. But now the reputation of the teacher of the nations remains undamaged in my eyes, and I

do not allow your explanation to do injury to his words. For according to the standard of reason already introduced, I insist that they are opposed to your stupid, impure, and impious teaching, and I prove that he said nothing in defense of natural sin. With what impudence do you, then, claim that the apostle should reply to me instead of you! He was not, after all, questioned since there is no doubt about his wisdom. Or with what impudence do you shout that I refuse to hear from the apostle that which I detest in you because of the sound interpretation that the apostle handed down to us!

AUG. (1) After the words of the apostle which I quoted, should you not have simply been silent? And yet, while saying nothing against them and not saying anything in agreement with them, you will not be silent for me, and among other things you bandy it about that I am "the origin and cause of these evils," as if I were the first to believe or to have argued that there is original sin. Do you believe that such uneducated people will read these writings of yours that they will not know how many renowned teachers of the Church before us have understood and explained these words of the apostle in the same way, just as the whole Catholic Church has understood and believed them from its beginning? If the words of these teachers are evil, as you are not afraid to say, how am I, I ask you, "the origin and cause of these evils," if not because you are the origin of these slanders which you bring against me in your fury? (2) For if with a sound mind you would consider the miseries of human life from the first wails of infants up to the last groans of the dying, you would surely see that neither I nor you, but Adam was "the origin and cause of these evils." Because you do not want to see this, you close your eyes and cry out that God's judgment is just and that there is no original sin. You would undoubtedly see how opposed to each other these two statements are—I will not say: if you were not the origin of these evils, since you certainly are not, but—if you had a sound head which you could have, if by following the Catholic teachers you did not have Pelagius as your head.[100]

Julian and the Implications of Augustine's Position

105. JUL. (1) Let us state the result of your arguments. After Paul said that the grace of the savior was much more abundant for healing than the transgression of the first human being for doing harm, there follows, *The gift is not like the result of the one man's sin. For after the one there came judgment leading to condemnation, but after many sins there came grace leading to justification* (Rom 5:16). You claim that the one sin which suffices for condemnation is original sin, the sin which is passed on to all human beings, but that grace is said to come after many sins for justification, because it removes not only that one which is contracted from our origin, but also the rest which in each human being are added by the act of one's own will.[101] (2) To confirm this you argue a little later that, if the

apostle had meant that this one sin which suffices for condemnation came about by imitation, he ought to have added that all human beings enter into condemnation not by one sin, but by the many sins each of us committed by our own will. In these passages I warn the reader to be attentive, since we must disentangle the words of the apostle from the snares of the Manichees. You claim, then, that in accord with our position which maintains that the first sin provided the pattern for sinners the apostle should have said that death reigned after many sins, just as he said that grace produces justification after many sins. (3) By this argument, however, you are completely at odds with yourself. For I prove that according to your teaching the apostle was illogical in saying, *But after many sins there came grace leading to justification*, since he had said, *After the one sin there came judgment leading to condemnation* (Rom 5:16). For, in order to leave our own grounds and enter your territory, let us suppose that freedom of choice was destroyed by the first sin and remains so crippled thereafter in the whole human race that it cannot do anything but evil. It does not have in its power the choice of the opposite, that is, to withdraw from evil and do good, but is compelled to obey the desire for sins, since it is weighed down by the necessity of sinfulness. (4) Let us suppose that every law of justice is broken and that whatever was voluntary has become natural; let us suppose that the law of sin dwells in the members and has obtained tyrannical power over the image and work of God by the shamefulness and pleasure of marriage; let us suppose that the fruit tree of the devil has been planted in the interior of the body before the soul and grows by natural increases, develops branches, and becomes laden with deadly fruit. Let us suppose, I say, that the one sin of the first human being produced all this, as you maintain. Then, it would be more logical to say that after one sin the race of mortals enters condemnation than that grace sets it free after many sins. In that way we would understand that this grace can be said to set free in a more proper sense from the one sin those whom it does set free. For no other sins are added by the act of a person's own will, if the sin of the first parent, the spoiler of the seeds, produces every evil since freedom of choice is destroyed and the goodness of desire is excluded.

AUG. (1) How can you, a man who tries to pervert the words of the apostle, possibly speak any way but perversely? For when the use of the will, which little ones do not have, is joined to that sin which birth contracts, a tree sprouts into many different desires for many sins. Before this happened, just that one drew the little one to condemnation if it came to the end of its life before it had the use of the will. After all, it does not follow that, because greater punishment is owed to sin that has become great and many, no punishment is owed to sin that is small and not yet grown many. How, then, does rebirth which takes away the sin that has become many by use of the will fail to benefit us more than birth brings us harm? For birth contracts only the beginning of this great and multiple sin, but it has not yet increased and has not yet multiplied. The sin would remain alone without any growth, if we did not acquire the use of the will by which it might be increased and multiplied. (2) But before the will is restored to its good freedom to produce true righteousness by the help of God's grace, it is moved or is not moved to sin by many other causes besides the original defect. As a result, from among those sinners whom grace, which justifies the sinner, either has not yet helped or will never help, some sin more, and others less. *After the one there came judgment leading to condemnation*, because even those are condemned who have contracted only that one sin by birth, *but after many sins there came grace leading to justification* (Rom 5:16), because it takes away not only that one sin with which a human being is born, but also whatever other sins the use of the will has added to that evil. This is the Catholic truth in those words of the apostle, and you do not destroy it by any heretical wordiness, regardless of how much you try us by the complexities of your foolishness and wordiness.

106. JUL. And for this reason, if natural sin is the cause of such great evils, the grace of Christ by no means produces a state of righteousness by pardoning many sins; rather, by pardoning the one sin it carries out its work of mercy. When his grace promises to do this, it will produce confidence in its promises if it cures these evils which are said to have been inflicted by the wound of sin. But if the same series of diabolical diseases remains after the remedies which the grace of Christ brought, we owe gratitude to his desire and pardon to his presumption, because he lacked the power, not the will, to cure the plagues with which we are born.

AUG. I have already given my reply. Understand it, and be quiet. In one way grace makes us fighters and helps us; in another it preserves us victorious in eternal peace without any enemy either external or internal. The former tiresome warfare is our lot in the present world; the latter blessed rest is ours in the world to come. But if you do not wage war in yourself against your carnal vices, shame on you! But if you do, shut up.

107. JUL. What, then, has this discussion shown? That there is no agreement between your views and the apostle's. The apostle, after all, says that many sins are pardoned by the generosity of grace, but your doctrine claims that one natural sin, which you call the law of sin, fashions sinful desires in all human beings. It is perfectly clear, then, that you blame nature which is the work of God, while he blames the will. He ought, however, certainly not to have said anything other than what he did, namely, that condemnation can come after the one sin, because by the one sin that first human being provided an example of sinning, and just as one sin was more than enough for his condemnation, so one sin can also suffice for the guilt of the rest. On this account Ecclesiastes said, *One who sins in one way loses many goods* (Eccl 9:18), and James says, *If you observe the whole law, but offend on one point, you have become guilty of all* (Jas 2:10).

AUG. Did the sin of Adam, then, harm Adam alone and not the human race as well? You will not, after all, be so absurd as to say that his sin harmed or harms those human beings who do not know or believe that it occurred or what it entailed. For, even if human beings imitate something without knowing it, you are extremely foolish to say that they are harmed or are made sinners by that sin which was committed without their knowledge so many thousands of years before, unless you admit that this sin was passed on to all generations. But if Pelagius had not condemned those who say that Adam's sin harmed him alone and not the human race, he would have been condemned by those judges who were certainly not Manichees.[102]

108. JUL. But the grace of our Lord Jesus Christ was not given in such a way that it provided individual remedies of forgiveness for individual sins, as if for individual wounds, and in such a way that it offered pardon to various sins by different baptisms. Rather, in accord with the power of the most efficacious medicine which is applied to serious sins, that is, to the actions of the evil will, it provides help universally so that it wipes away different kinds of guilt by the power of a single consecration.

AUG. (1) However you claim that the grace of the Lord Jesus Christ was given, you exclude from it the little ones who you deny are saved by it. You divide these titles as you choose so that Christ is thought to belong to the little ones on account of the kingdom of God which you concede only the baptized can attain. But Jesus is, of course, kept far from them because he does not produce in them the result for which he got this name. After all, scripture says, *You shall call his name Jesus.* And it immediately adds the reason why they should call him Jesus, *For he will save his people from their sins* (Mt 1:21). When you deny that he does this in the case of little ones, you separate them both from the name Jesus and from his people. And you dare to become angry because it is you, rather, who are separated from that people. (2) But with regard to voluntary sins, just as after many sins judgment leads to condemnation, so after many sins grace leads to justification. Why does scripture say, *After the one there came judgment leading to condemnation, but after many sins there came grace leading to justification* (Rom 5:16), if it is not that that passage does not contrast will with will or imitation with imitation, but rebirth with birth? For as birth has the judgment after the one sin leading to condemnation, so rebirth has the grace after many sins leading to justification. It is clear what the apostle wanted us to understand; if you would open ears willing to listen, you would close your contentious mouths.

109. JUL. Hence, when he was speaking of Adam, he wisely mentioned the one sin which he wanted us to understand to have been the pattern of sin. I repeat, he recalled the one sin and not many because he knew that the story in the law contained only the one sin of Adam. But he praised grace because after many sins grace brings those who receive it to justification, for he did not want any suspicion to arise that the gift was poor. And if he had said: "After the one there

came grace leading to justification," grace might not seem to have done away with all sins, but single sins. The fact that he first mentioned one sin is faithful to the narrative; the fact that he added that after many sins grace leads to justification reveals the generosity and abundance of the mystery.

AUG. But what need was there for him to speak of Adam when he praised the grace of Christ, except that birth comes from the former and rebirth from the latter?

110. JUL. As this explanation is in accord with reason, so it wipes you out. For this very reason, after all, you must admit that in all the words quoted above the apostle did not speak of the Manichean inheritance of sin, when in his tribute to grace he showed that many sins are forgiven.

AUG. It is you who help the Manichees, for you give them room to introduce another nature which is evil when you deny that the cause of misery of the little ones lies in original sin. They would certainly not suffer this misery in paradise, if they were born there when the uprightness and blessedness of human nature still lasted.

The One Sin and the Many Sins

111. JUL. He showed that he had also previously called that one sin a sin of the same kind as the other sins which he taught were many and were all forgiven by grace. But you admit that these many sins are those which are committed by each human being by the act of the person's own will. That one sin is, then, of the same kind... .

AUG. I say that many sins exist along with that one sin, not apart from it. This one can, however, be correctly said to belong to the same kind, if one looks to its origin, because it too stemmed from the will of the first human being when his sin entered the world and was passed on to all human beings.

112. JUL. So that we might understand that each person contracts that sin by the action of one's own will, and he does not lay the blame on the fertility of seeds, but on the depravity of actions. If he had wanted us to understand that one original sin, he certainly would not have said in the following words that there were many sins which he testifies were forgiven by grace.

AUG. Why would he not have said it except that is what the Pelagians want? But the truth does not want it, the truth which refutes the Pelagian audacity and defeats its nonsense. For the many sins after which grace leads to justification are many along with that one, and after that one sin judgment leads to condemnation, even if the others are not added to it. In that way, then, Adam was able to implant the one sin in those who are born, but Christ is able to forgive many sins for those who are reborn, because the latter is shown to have done more good than the former did harm.

113. JUL. (1) And though what we have done is more than sufficient for the defense of the truth, I warn the reader, nonetheless, to pay attention to those points which we are going to introduce. For it will be apparent beyond all refutation that the apostle Paul did not argue in those passages about nature, but about the way mortals live. For, in opposing the power of the grace of Christ to the power of the first sin and in comparing the effects of each of them, he strived to show that the mystery of Christ produced more good than the sin of the first human being did harm. But we have taught that this cannot be maintained in the sense of inherited sin. As with the many sins which he mentioned, so he wanted this one in particular to redound to the praise of grace; he said, *After the one there came judgment leading to condemnation, but after many sins there came grace leading to justification of life* (Rom 5:16). (2) The defender of natural evil explains this as follows: He says, "*After the one there came condemnation*, because that one sin which was contracted at our origin is sufficient to bring one to condemnation, as it does to little ones who are born of Adam, if they are not reborn in Christ, even if they have no other sins. *But after many sins there came grace leading to justification*, because it removed not only that one which is contracted from our origin, but also the rest which in each human being are added by the movement of one's own will."[103] There you openly admitted, though with Manichean impiety, that natural sin in fact exists, even if it is only one sin, on account of which you say the newborn ought to be condemned.

AUG. The one who said, "All of us human beings are born under the power of sin,"[104] was not a Manichee. But tell me what you people are. You separate so many images of God from the kingdom of God without any sin that merits this. You deny they are condemned by God's judgment, and you create two eternal states of happiness, one which is in the kingdom of God, the other which is outside the kingdom of God. Tell me, I beg you: In that state of happiness which is outside the kingdom of God will anyone reign there or will no one? If no one, that state of happiness will undoubtedly enjoy more freedom without any king. But if someone will reign there, who will be the king of the images of God and yet not be God? If it will be a god, you introduce another god, and you call me a Manichee, do you? But if God himself will reign there, the God of whom they are images, these images themselves, then, will also be happy in the kingdom of their true God. And what will happen to the words, *Whoever are not reborn of water and the Spirit cannot enter the kingdom of God* (Jn 3:5)? But at last admit that those little ones who have not been reborn are going to be unhappy outside the kingdom of God. State, then, the cause of this unhappiness, you wordy and contentious people who deny original sin.

114. JUL. Prove, then, that what the apostle attributed to the grace of Christ is realized in them, namely, that it produces justification after many sins, that is, that it confers righteousness all at once by the one forgiveness of many sins. Ei-

ther, then, teach me how little ones are subject to many serious sins so that you convince us that they share in that benefit in which the apostle located the praise of Christ's munificence so that they are shown to have been set free from many sins. Or admit that in these passages Paul said nothing about little ones and that he did not discuss the nature of human beings when he bore witness that those sins which, as you also agree, cannot be found in the newborn are forgiven by the generosity of grace.

AUG. Why do you keep on talking? Why does your wordy nonsense make you deaf so that the most obvious truth does not enter your ears? Certainly Jesus who saves his people from many sins does not forget the single original sins of little ones because these sins too are included in those many sins.

115. JUL. The apostle says, *After many sins there came grace leading to justification* (Rom 5:16). But you say that little ones are subject to no more than one sin. You see, then, that the praise of grace is crippled in their case because it does not find many sins for the forgiveness of which it is praised. The words, therefore, of the apostle Paul, *After many sins there came grace leading to justification* (Rom 5:16), are shown to be completely false in the case of the little ones. How, then, are you going to try to escape from this? You will undoubtedly say—for the previous discussion has shown that this is your idea—that the words of the apostle, *But after many sins there came grace leading to justification* (Rom 5:16), are realized in human beings of an adult age who are found guilty of many sins by the action of their own will. But in little ones you will say that justification is not produced after many sins, but after the one sin.

AUG. (1) It would not have been a big chore for you to understand that it is you rather who remove little ones from this justification which the savior bestows on his own people by the forgiveness of many sins. For you claim that they can be forgiven no sin, but we do not. When we say that through the one sinner all were brought to condemnation, we exempt no age because even human beings of an adult age have this sin. So too, when we say that grace produces justification after many sins, we likewise exempt no age because he who forgives many sins—and by the word "many" we understand all—certainly does not pass over any sins, that is, neither the many sins of the very bad, nor the fewer sins of some, nor the single sins of the little ones. (2) It would not have been a big chore, then, for you to see this if you did not begrudge to little ones Christ the physician and did not, of course, want him to be Jesus for them because of your horrendous impiety, amazing blindness, and blasphemous wordiness. What is more insane than to want the grace of Christ to belong only to those who have many sins? By this reason or rather by this mental blindness you withdraw from this grace not only the little ones who you think contract no guilt from their origin, but absolutely all those who do not have many sins. For you suppose that the words of the apostle, *But after many sins there came grace leading to justification* (Rom

5:16), should be understood in the sense that no one who does not receive forgiveness for many sins has a share in that grace. (3) For this reason, since, as you
suppose, a little one has no sin, when the child grows up and begins to commit
sin—I do not mean if it has committed a few sins, but if it has perhaps committed
only one—and comes to Christ's baptism, it will in no way share in that grace,
because it is not brought to justification after many sins, but after one. I think that
your deafness of heart will not have such power that this great absurdity does not
force you to blush. But if even a person who has one sin forgiven shares in this
grace, then the apostle said, *After many sins there came grace leading to justifi-*
cation (Rom 5:16), in the sense that he wanted us to understand the sins of the
whole people who are justified by it, though some of that people have many, others have fewer, and still others only one sin, for altogether they are certainly
many sins.

The Various Effects of the One Baptism

116. JUL. By such an explanation you will be able neither to distort his[105]
meaning nor to escape from it. But you have destroyed not only your own deceits, but also the false grounds of that hatred which you kindled against us. You
claimed that we acted against the faith in serious fashion, because we say that the
grace of Christ should be dispensed in a uniform way and that his words and laws
should not be attacked. Grace confers equally upon all who share in it the gifts of
adoption, sanctification, and elevation, but that grace does not find all who approach the sacraments in a single degree of guilt. It sets free from guilt and trans-
forms from bad persons to good persons those who have sinned by their own
will, for without the act of the will sin cannot exist. But it accuses innocents who
are in a state of blessedness at their unstained young age of no act of bad will,
since it knows that they had no experience of it.

AUG. Oh, what singular madness! Is this discussion or insanity? Little ones
testify by their wailing that they are born in misery, but you do not want them to
have Christ as Jesus, and you say that they are happy though you do not admit
them to his kingdom. If you would love that kingdom with Christian love, you
would judge it a great misery to be separated from it.

117. JUL. But grace changes them from good to better and carries all whom it
adopts to one peak of sanctity, though it does not find all in same swamp of vices.
Rather, grace finds some in a state of innocence and others in the pursuit of evils.
We make this claim which is defended by the soundness of the faith, by the fortress of reason, and by the piety of understanding. By this claim the grace of
Christ is rightly praised, and no guilt is attributed to God. Because of this you say
that the prestige of the sacrament is toppling, and you claim with a mental keenness more blunt than a pestle that the authority of grace is taken away unless the

sin of slander is ascribed to it, unless it overthrows the principles of justice, unless it imbeds the sin of another conscience in those who do not have knowledge. Finally, you claim that it accomplishes nothing if it is not said to work uniformly in all persons.

AUG. (1) Why is it that you suppose that the mental keenness, not mine, but that of all Catholic teachers with whom I hold as unshakable what you try in vain to tear, down should be compared with a pestle? Is it because you have begun to feel that it crushes you in your fragile condition? You allegedly rest your case on the defense of God's justice in order to overthrow what the whole Church of Christ holds regarding the condemnation of little ones who have not been reborn, but you are never going to explain why the heavy yoke upon little ones is just if they do not contract original sin. Nor do you notice that it is you rather who overthrow the principles of justice, the justice, that is, of almighty God by whom and under whom you say that this punishment is imposed without any merit upon countless thousands of all human beings, that is, of images of God, from the day they emerge from the womb of their mother.[106] (2) Finally, you will never explain how it is just that little ones who have died without baptism through no fault of their own, and generally also through no fault of their parents, are separated from their believing parents and relatives and are not admitted to the kingdom of God. Though without meriting this by any sins, they are not counted among the vessels made for an honorable purpose, like the other little ones who were baptized, but are counted among the vessels made for a dishonorable purpose,[107] for there is no third kind of vessel. Your heretical wisdom is displeased by what the Catholic faith believes, namely, that, after all entered into condemnation because of the one sin, by the unsearchable ways of the Lord, which are all mercy and truth,[108] some receive the mercy of grace, while others remain under the judgment of truth.

118. JUL. It is evident, then, that your whole teaching by which you deceived minds soiled with stupidity has been destroyed by your explanation.

AUG. You have been destroyed, you who refuse to see or to admit that those who have only one sin share in the forgiveness of sins. In that healing grace little ones have no share if they have no sin. You kill them wickedly because you deny them the savior.

119. JUL. The apostle, after all, declares, *But after many sins there came grace leading to justification* (Rom 5:16), and you say that this cannot be the case with little ones, but that this takes place only in those who are already of adult age, because they have by the action of their own will added to that one sin other sins as well. In that way you undoubtedly admit that the operation of grace is different in accord with the difference of those who come to it. In these, of course, who use the action of their own will, grace has grounds for boasting, because it brings those whom it adopts to justification after many serious sins. But in little ones, according to you, it is more meager, more stingy, and more impov-

erished; it acts without great power or the proper medication, and it fails to keep its morality and modesty intact. For it promises to remove that one sin which it ought not to have ascribed to them, and it tries to bring to justification those whom it sets free from this one sin.

AUG. I have already replied to this. You say the same things many times, since you do not find anything to say. When you say that no sin should be ascribed to little ones, you make God unjust, since he has imposed a heavy yoke upon them from the day they emerge from the womb of their mother.[109] But even if scripture did not say this, who is so blind of heart as not to see that the misery of the human race begins with the wailing of little ones? You also make the law of God unjust which condemns the soul of an infant who is not circumcised on the eighth day.[110] You also judge foolish the commandment which orders that sacrifice for sin be offered when an infant is born.[111] But if this guilt from our origin is made known by the holy scripture and if it makes itself known, this sin too is among those many sins after which grace produces justification. This grace also makes little ones blessed after this misery. This blessedness is not realized in the present world because God willed that all of it be punishment from the time that he dismissed the first human beings from the happiness of paradise, but it will be realized in the eternal world to come. As a promise of this world to come Christ now bestows on his members the Holy Spirit.[112]

120. JUL. You have, then, admitted that grace works in one way in adults and in another way in children. Do not suppose that there is any room left for your reply if you say that there is a great difference, but a difference in the forgiveness of sins, so that grace finds something to forgive, even if it is only one sin. You make no headway by this argument, for it makes no difference in what species you locate the various effects of grace, provided you admit that they can be various.

AUG. It is one thing to speak of the various effects of grace, because scripture says that the grace of God has many forms.[113] It is something else to deny to little ones the grace of the forgiveness of sins and to maintain that they do not truly undergo the rites of exorcism and exsufflation in the Church of the Truth if they are not rescued from the power of darkness, for it does great injury to the creator if they do not need the help of the savior to be rescued from the power of the deceiver.

The Munificence of Grace at Different Ages

121. JUL. I, after all, am content with what you were forced to grant me, namely, that what the apostle preached about the bounteousness of grace cannot apply to all ages equally. If you produced something to show that even at their earliest age the newborn receive forgiveness, you have still not removed[114] the

fact that in little ones there is not realized the reason for which the apostle claimed the grace of Christ worthy of praise. For he extolled the healing power of the sacrament over the sin of the first human being who he taught was the pattern for those to come. He said, *After the one sin there came judgment leading to condemnation, but after many sins there came grace leading to justification* (Rom 5:16). The reason, then, for which he extolled grace, namely, that it produces justification after many sins, is not found in little ones, as even you admit, and you are led, though you have resisted, to the point that you admit that grace is not present equally at different ages.

AUG. I have already replied to this; you are speaking nonsense. The grace of God is glorious even when it forgives single sins of certain persons because those single sins also belong to that same multitude of sins after which he who saves his people from their sins[115] makes them righteous. It is perfectly fitting that you do not belong to this people since you refuse to let little ones belong to this people.

122. JUL. Once you accepted that, it was evident that there was no need to incite slanders against human nature merely to avoid saying that the grace of baptism more correctly has various effects in accord with various ages. Now that all semblance of conviction has been removed, if you have any energy, any intelligence, any virtue, try to prove the existence of natural sin which you see has been destroyed by reason, by authority, and by justice. What consideration has deceived you so that you call the union of bodies which God established and the pleasure of sex fostering this union the work and the fruit tree of the devil? Thriving both in human beings and in animals, it shows that its source is the same as the creator of bodies.

AUG. Shame! You are that fan of sexual desire. Shame, I say! This sexual desire which pleases you so much, against which it is necessary to fight if one does not want to commit sin by consenting to its enticements, did not exist in paradise before the sin. Either, then, there was no sexual desire there, or it neither preceded the will of the mind nor went beyond it. Now it is not that way; all human beings experience this in themselves, and you are a human being. Restrain your desire to fight back, and recognize the defect from which original sin is contracted. Marriage found this defect and did not produce it in human beings who are the products of sexual reproduction. They make use of this defect out of necessity; they make good use of it by chastity and, for that reason, are not blamed in any way. In animals it is not something evil precisely because in them the flesh does not have desires opposed to the spirit; in human beings this evil needs to be healed by the goodness of God, not praised by the vanity of human beings.

123. JUL. What was the reason that you first wounded innocence with the serious sin of another and then tried to mingle a matter of conduct with the seed?

AUG. You say the same things in the same words, but what you say is beyond all doubt nonsense. By nature the seeds are good, but the seeds are damaged, and because they were damaged, defects are also propagated. At least let the shape of bodies teach you a lesson; though their maker is supremely good and spoiled by no defect, many bodies are born with defects, and surely if no one had sinned, none would have been born that way in paradise.

124. JUL. Why did you take from baptism its true and proper effect? Why did you ascribe to God who is nothing but justice, to God who can not be God without justice, a crime of obvious injustice?

AUG. It is you rather who do this; for if little ones are weighed down by a heavy yoke without the guilt of any sin, God is unjust. But because he is not unjust, you are slanderous and blind.

125. JUL. Of such obvious injustice, I say, that he himself condemned by the authority of his law this kind of injustice which you falsely claim is found in his judgments.

AUG. In his law it is written that the soul of a little one will be lost from its people if it is not circumcised on the eighth day.[116] By what merit? Tell me, if you can. But you are utterly unable, and still you do not stop denying original sin.

126. JUL. What need, then, was there of so many blasphemies if even this one which you embraced did not exist? It, of course, has no importance, but it seemed like a plank to which you might cling amid so great a shipwreck, and you released it, though a bit late, when your arms gave out. To make the issue clear by repetition, certain ignorant folk considered you a Manichee who should be tolerated for fear that the grace of Christ would be thought not to have a single effect in all people. But in the development of your explanation you have now introduced this point, without any pressure from us. For you say that the statement of the apostle, *But after many sins there came grace leading to justification* (Rom 5:16), can be realized in human beings of an adult age, but not in little ones. In little ones there is, rather, something more humble, more impoverished, more indigent. Though you come up with this, you still never admit that the apostle said it.

AUG. Reread my answer to you so that you may understand that you are not saying anything and that you, nonetheless, cannot be silent, you big mouth. After many sins grace leads to justification because Jesus saves his people from their sins. Among these same many sins he also finds the single sins of little ones. In the same way, even if there were no original sins, he would also find among these same many sins the single sins of older children who are beginning to sin, and they would never be told as they approached Christ's baptism: You cannot be baptized now because you do not as yet have many sins, for after many sins there comes the grace which leads to justification. They would reply with full truth: Our single sins are included in the multitude of sins after which grace produces righteousness; here some have many sins and others fewer, but all of them put together with our single sins are many.

127. JUL. Even according to you, then, the effect of grace is the same at all ages for adoption, but for the forgiveness of sins there is not a single reckoning for everyone. But up to this point I have acted with too much restraint and patience.

AUG. If, when acting with restraint, you said so much that you attacked one book of mine, and not the whole of it, with your eight books, your restraint is far too bountiful and extravagant. But if you have up to this point spoken with restraint, why have you not spared your soul, since you shout against the truth on so many points.[117]

Paul Taught Justification after Many Sins

128. JUL. I was content to prove by the previous argument that you who stirred up a great plot against us on this account said that the forgiveness of sins does not have only a single way and means in all cases. Hence, even if you could persuade us of the existence of this one natural sin, it would still be clear that one has to say that those who come to grace do not always have the same condition and that this statement of the apostle, *After many sins* grace leads *to justification* (Rom 5:16), is realized only at an adult age, but not in the earliest age as well.

AUG. According to your foolish ideas it is not realized at an adult age either. For many adults who happen to come to baptism when they begin to commit sin have single sins, even if they do not, as you hold, have original sins. Some also have very few, but not many. These will not, then, share in this grace of Christ, since it produces justification after many sins, and they do not have many sins. But anyone who thinks this way is unspeakably foolish. Acknowledge Christ who justifies and saves his people from many sins. Understand that these same many sins can include the few or single sins of some persons, and do not remove the lot of little ones from this people. Believe that even they need Jesus who is called this only because he saves his people from their sins,[118] and the little ones are, of course, also included in that people.

129. JUL. But now, as a result, I state that the apostle had no suspicion of Manichean inherited sin; he shows, in fact, that it does serious harm to the sacraments if they are made equal to the sins on every point, that is, if grace did not more effectively produce good than the pattern of sin did harm. The teacher of the nations placed the greatest honor of the Christian faith in his claim that it is superior to sins. For this reason he was concerned to emphasize the effect of the remedy over the old diseases.

AUG. You deny this remedy to little ones when by your false and hostile defense you claim that they are in good health. But their God, who has made perfect the praise of his own remedy from the mouths of infants and nurslings,[119] surely destroys you who apply this hostile defense to them, while he destroys their enemy and defender.

130. JUL. Then he shows that grace is praiseworthy if his words, *After the one there came judgment leading to condemnation, but after many sins there came grace leading to justification* (Rom 5:16), apply to it in every respect. By what right, then, do you deprive the grace of Christ of this praise by which the apostle wanted it to be proclaimed? For you would tear down its title of dignity, the sole honor by which the vessel of election wanted it to be recognized?

AUG. This grace does not reach the little ones if, as you hold, they are not bound by any sin. But because they are bound by sin, grace, which justifies the multitude of its faithful people after many sins, also comes to heal their one sin so that it destroys from the mouths of infants the mouths of their deceiving enemies and defenders.

131. JUL. He said, *After many sins there came grace leading to justification* (Rom 5:16). He extolled the abundance of the medicine over the effect of sin. This interpretation fits the teaching of the Catholics who understand that the forgiveness of sins takes places in those in whom many sins can be found, that is, sins contracted by the act of one's own will. But in those who have no act of their own will, that is, in little ones, there is neither one sin nor many.

AUG. They have, then, no share in the medicine of the savior, and Christ is not Jesus for them. And you who say this dare to call yourself a Christian! Moreover, if, as you state, forgiveness of sins takes place in those in whom many sins can be found, because you interpret in that way the words of the apostle, *After many sins there came grace leading to justification* (Rom 5:16), they do not receive forgiveness of sins who do not, as you suppose, have original sin and come to the bath of rebirth with just one sin or a few sins. See what you say! Are you not ashamed? Have you no fear? Will you not be silent? But if human beings who are beginning to sin and do not as yet have many sins receive, nonetheless, the grace which justifies after many sins, why do you refuse to count among those same many sins the single sins of any persons, except that you would impiously separate the little ones from that grace? And the destructive weight of the worst injustice looms over you in that you say that even older persons who are just beginning to sin, persons who do not as yet have many sins, but have just one sin or a few sins, have no share in that grace.

132. JUL. When the apostle praised grace over sin, he, therefore, strengthened our teaching.

AUG. On the contrary, he destroyed your teaching because this grace which he praised over sin justifies after many sins and, therefore, belongs to the little ones along with the great, nor does he pass over any of the little ones, because he forgives all the sins of all his own, that is, of the little and of the great.

133. JUL. Explain now where the apostle made grace equal to sin in order that, since your faith does not admit remedies superior to the wounds, it may at

least accept remedies that are reduced to a minimum and do not exceed that to which they are compared. But if you find this anywhere in scripture, it will, nonetheless, remain true that Paul did not accept this idea. And to make the whole mind of the apostle clear by a summary, he said, *After many sins there came grace leading to justification* (Rom 5:16). But little ones do not have many sins, even according to you, and according to the apostle they have none.

AUG. According to you those who have just begun to commit sin also do not have many sins, and you cannot, nonetheless, deny that, when they come to baptism, they share in this grace which justifies after many sins. The many sins, then, belong to the whole people in which the little ones are also included. When the grace which justifies after many sins comes to that people of the city of God, it finds there many sins of some people and a few sins of others and single sins of the little ones. All these sins together are many, and by their multitude they refute your many empty words. But if in agreement with the apostle, as you suppose, the little ones have no sin, why, then, have they died, as the apostle said they did? For, even according to you, Christ also died for them: *After all, one died for all; all, therefore, have died, and he died for all* (2 Cor 5:14-15). Julian, it is not Augustine, but the apostle who said this; in fact, Christ himself said it through his apostle. Stop yourself from speaking nonsense, and submit to God.

134. JUL. It is, therefore, established that the teacher of the nations was not speaking about the newborn in that passage, but about those who already have use of the function of their own will.

AUG. Sleep off the intoxication of your quarrelsomeness, and wake up and understand the sin—the one sin of one person—about which the apostle said, *For if many have died on account of the sin of the one* (Rom 5:15). These many are themselves the "all" about whom he says in another passage, *As in Adam all die* (1 Cor 15:22). There you will see the little ones as well because Christ also died for them, as you admit. In fact, when the apostle had said that *one died for all*, he immediately showed what necessarily follows, when he says, *All, therefore, have died, and he died for all* (2 Cor 5:14-15).

Scripture Uses "All" for "Many"

135. JUL. But the addition which the apostle made next, *Just as through the sin of the one all entered into condemnation, so through the righteousness of the one all human beings attained justification* (Rom 5:18), offers as much help to us as it brings destruction to your doctrine. For because Paul used "all" in mutually contradictory parts of the sentence which cannot be combined together, he makes us have recourse to the custom of the scriptures so that we understand that "all" is often said in place of "many." For on their surface the words form a contradiction. How, after all, do all attain justification if all have entered into con-

demnation? Or how do all meet with punishment if all are carried off to glory? The universality of one statement excludes a place for the other.

AUG. (1) Therefore, even where the apostle said, *In whom all have sinned* (Rom 5:12), are we to understand "many," and not "all"? But if that is so, you will be forced to say that not all sinners, but many sinners sinned by imitating that one human being. But if you say that it was not all, but many who sinned by imitation of him, because it was many, not all who sinned, and you want us to understand that those who did not sin are the little ones, I shall answer you that those little ones did not die in him either. And for this reason Christ did not die for them because he died only for those who were dead, as the apostle cries out. In that way, you will turn against yourself, and you will completely exclude the little ones from the grace of Christ, since you are going to say that Christ did not die for them. As a result, you will also deny that they should be baptized in Christ. (2) *For whoever of us have been baptized in Christ*, as the same apostle said, *have been baptized into his death* (Rom 6:3). But those are baptized into the death of Christ for whom Christ has died. In no way, then, will you exempt little ones from original sin unless you separate them at the same time from the grace of Christ's baptism. With regard, however, to your idea that these two statements are mutually contradictory, namely, that all enter condemnation through Adam and that all again attain justification through Christ, you are utterly mistaken. For no human being is brought to condemnation except through Adam, and from that condemnation human beings are set free by the bath of rebirth. And no human being is set free from this condemnation except through Christ. Hence, "all" was said in both parts of the sentence, because no one comes to this condemnation due to birth except through Adam and no one comes to the life due to rebirth except through Christ. In this way the universality of the one statement does not exclude a place for the other because Christ brings to life those whom he wills from these same human beings who all die in Adam. These will not seem mutually contradictory to you if you do not contradict yourself.

Comparing the Roles of Adam and Christ

136. JUL. But in order that you may note how well we are also protected here, understand the role of the one who wounds from the role of the healer. If Christ has saved all, then let Adam be supposed to have also harmed all.

AUG. Are, then, all not brought to condemnation through Adam because Christ sets free from this condemnation those whom he wills? He was said to set all free because it is only he who sets anyone free, just as he is said to enlighten everyone,[120] because it is only he who enlightens anyone.

137. JUL. If Christ changed the functioning of the sex organs, then let Adam be believed to have ruined them. If Christ corrected something in the feelings of

the flesh, then let Adam's sin be judged to have disturbed them. If Christ made the remedy to be passed on through propagation, then let Adam be said to have passed on sin by generation.

AUG. I have already replied to these points, but listen to them briefly once again. If you were a Catholic Christian, it would be obvious to you that Adam transmits sin by generation and Christ remits sin by regeneration. Generation from Adam is through the flesh; regeneration from Christ is through the Spirit. Do not, then, look for carnal offspring in both cases; if you are not stubborn, you recognize that carnal offspring do not pertain to spiritual rebirth. But the grace of Christ has already begun a battle against the weakness of the flesh; it will later bring about its complete health. He has already given us as a guarantee of that future and lasting good health the Holy Spirit[121] through whom the love of God is poured out in our hearts,[122] so that the weakness of the flesh which was left for the present to test us will not conquer us.

138. JUL. But if all these remain in that condition which they receive from nature, the will is attracted to the faith without any imposition of necessity by exhortations, by signs, by examples, and by the promise of rewards and punishments. This will, which is not suppressed, but is expected, free, and challenged, is healed through laws, through the mysteries, and through gifts. It is clear that, even if the whole world with one spirit stands in opposition, roaring and raging, it is the will of each person, not one's birth, that is soiled by one's imitation of sin.

AUG. No matter where you turn, you will not exempt little ones from original sin unless you deny that they have died. But if you do that, you at the same time will deny that Christ died for them. If, however, to avoid denying this you admit that the little ones have died, you will surely not deny that they died in Adam. Or if it was not in him, tell me where it was.

139. JUL. I have up to now acted with too much gentleness. For even if from the time Christ came, all human beings were taught that he had blocked the road to death and bestowed perpetual life so that no one from that day when the Word became flesh would either fall into sin or fear punishment for sin, that condition, nonetheless, which we are taught is one of extreme generosity was not the condition of the former sinfulness. For to the praise of his clemency God can and often does come to the help of those who do not deserve it, but he cannot punish those who do not sin without destroying justice.

AUG. Because, then, little ones have been punished by a heavy yoke from the day they emerge from the womb of their mother,[123] acknowledge their just judge, and admit original sin. For, without destroying justice, he cannot punish those who do not have the guilt of any sin, as you yourself admit.

140. JUL. Notice then what this whole discussion has accomplished. If the grace of Christ and the sin of Adam were judged equal in their different effects so that they were equal at least in the number of their actions, though they differed

in the kind of their actions, it would have been necessary to teach that grace had benefitted us as much as sin had harmed us so that the weights of that scale on which they were weighed would be in balance. The medicine, therefore, ought also to have provided help at least to those places and to those parts in which the illness had settled. That is, if the ancient sin had produced something in the movements of the genital organs, in the feelings of the couple having intercourse, in the indecency of the members, or in the unhappiness of those who are born, the medicine would have brought remedies by changing these conditions we mentioned. Otherwise, it would be a great proof of a feeble and ineffective art not even to have located the place of the illness and not to have applied to wills treatments for their inertia, since their natural powers were languishing and ruined.

AUG. I already replied to you when we spoke about the difference between the present world and the world to come.[124] Here we receive through the pledge of the Spirit the strength both to fight and to win, but there we shall enjoy ineffable and everlasting peace without any external or internal enemy. Those, then, who want to have here all those things which are to be had there show that they do not have faith.

141. JUL. But among these things the truth shows us that, even if the remedy was poured out generally and benefitted mortals and their activities, even those who did not merit it by any desire or any intention, still it would not immediately follow that sin harms the newborn who could offer no assent to it. And for this reason, even if grace and sin were appraised as equal, it would, nonetheless, be clear that even then such a weighing of things does not amount to a proof that anyone is born with guilt.

AUG. With that heavy yoke by which little ones are weighed down, how can God be just if no one is born with guilt?

Did Grace Abound More or for More?

142. JUL. But the apostle not only did not rank grace after sin, but even ranked it before sin, when he said that the benefits abounded for many more people than those whom the losses affected. But from the opinion of inherited sin it is clear that sins did far more harm than grace did good. Hence, it is irrefutably proven that the apostle Paul did not have the inheritance of sin in mind; rather, his statement equally destroyed the traducianists along with their teachers, the Manichees.

AUG. (1) The apostle Paul did not say that "the benefits abounded for many more people than those whom the losses affected." He did not say that. You are certainly deceived, if you are not a deceiver yourself. For he said that grace was much more abundant for many, not that it abounded for many more, but that it was more abundant. For in comparison with those who are perishing those who are saved are few, but apart from comparison with those who are perishing they are themselves many. As for why the perishing are more than the saved, many want to know God's plan, but either only a very few or no human beings at all do know it. As having foreknowledge of all things, however, almighty God could not create any evil persons whom he could fail to know would be evil unless, as most good, he could make the best use of many evil persons. For this reason the apostle taught us a lesson, namely, that God would reveal his anger and his power in those vessels of anger which he endured with much patience and that he would make known the riches of his glory toward the vessels of mercy.[125] (2) But the Pelagians refuse to believe that in the one human being the lump of clay was damaged as a whole and condemned as a whole, and from that damage and condemnation only grace heals and sets anyone free. For why will even a righteous person scarcely be saved?[126] Is it a great effort for God to set free a righteous person? Heaven forbid! But to show the grounds by which our nature was condemned, even the Almighty does not choose too readily to set anyone free from such a great evil. On this account we are inclined toward sins, and righteousness is difficult except for those in love. But the love which makes these persons lovers comes from God.[127]

143. JUL. But because I have spent a rather long time on this point, let us go on to the others.

AUG. You say this as if you were going to spend less time on other points, though you seek with great wordiness how you may cover over with clouds of nonsense the perfectly clear words of the apostle.

144. JUL. (1) "The apostle said that all come to condemnation through Adam and all come to righteousness of life through Christ, though Christ does not, of course, bring all those who die in Adam to life. Rather, he said 'all' in both places, because, just as without Adam no one comes to death, so without Christ no one comes to life. In the same way we say about a teacher of language, if he is the only one in a city, that he teaches language to all in this city, not because all the people learn from him, but because no one learns except from him. Moreover, those whom he called 'all' he later called 'many,' referring to the same people as 'all' and 'many': (2) *As through the disobedience of the one, many were made sinners, so through the obedience of the one, many will be made righteous* (Rom 5:19). He could still ask how sin comes to be in a little one. The sacred pages answer him, *Through one man sin entered this world*" (Rom 5:12).[128] We admit that the pages of the apostle are of course holy, but only because, in conformity with reason, piety, and faith, they teach us to believe in a God of inviolable justice, to defend his good and honorable works, and by his commandments to win for ourselves moderation, prudence, and justice.

AUG. In the case of little ones the justice of God itself refutes you, since it would be a great injustice if the little ones too are weighed down by a heavy yoke without any guilt and without any chain of sin.

The Heart of the Controversy

145. JUL. And in this way they teach us to deny that anyone can be condemned for the sin of another and to deny that any sin can be passed on to our descendants by the condition of our nature. They teach us to believe and to maintain that human beings born from that fecundity which God created are suited to the just laws of free choice so that they can avoid everything that is evil and practice everything that is good. They need not, as you suppose, think that the love and necessity of serious sins are attached to the causes of their substance, that is, to the very seeds. And they need not admit that a statement so stupid, so insane, and so wicked, that is, one that shows contempt for nature, for reason, and for God, is contained in the book of the apostle, because he said that sin entered the world through one man and that death was passed on to all human beings.[129] For he did not allow this to remain obscure for long, but added that those whom he called "all" should be understood as the many who had sinned[130] by imitation, not by generation.

AUG. (1) Can you say that all the nations were not promised to the descendants of Abraham where scripture said, *All the nations will blessed in your descendants* (Gn 22:18), because it called those same nations "many" where we read, *I have set you as the father of many nations* (Gn 17:5)? Can you, I repeat, say this, and in that passage also contradict by your foolish talk the scripture that foretells what we see is fulfilled in the present world? Can you forbid us to understand all nations where nothing else but all nations was promised him? For by your logic you teach that "all" was not used for all nations, but for many nations, which are not all, and that it should be understood this way. (2) Where it says "many," we need not understand "all," but where it says "all," and they are truly all, we can also correctly say "many," so that all of them are not thought to be few. In this way those holy men whom the blazing fire was forbidden to burn all praised God amid the harmless flames, and yet all of them were few, since they were three.[131] What force, then, does your argument have by which you want us to understand that all are not all, because these same ones were said to be many? For those who are truly all are sometimes also said to be many in order to distinguish them from those who, though they are all, are still only a few. All the hairs on a person's head are also many, but all one's fingers are only a few.

146. JUL. Finally, he wrapped up everything that he had done with the words, *For just as through the disobedience of the one, many were made sinners, so through the obedience of the one, many will be made righteous* (Rom 5:19). Just

as none merit the rewards of virtue except those who, after the incarnation of Christ, have, nonetheless, by imitating his holiness, striven after them, so none are held as transgressors in Adam except those who sinned by a transgression of the law, though in imitation of the first human being.[132]

AUG. (1) This is the hidden and horrid poison of your heresy: you want the grace of Christ to consist in his example, not in his gift. You say that people become righteous by imitating him, not that they are brought by the help of the Holy Spirit to imitate him,[133] the Spirit which he poured out in great richness over his own people. You add as if you were being alert, "after his incarnation," on account of the people of former eras who you say were righteous without his grace because they did not have his example. What if, then, even after the incarnation of Christ, some people set before themselves the example of earlier righteous persons and lived righteously without having heard the gospel? What are you going to do? Where do you see yourselves heading? (2) Will these people not merit the rewards of virtue? If righteousness, then, comes from the imitation of righteous persons, Christ has died in vain.[134] For even before him there were righteous persons whom people could imitate if they had willed to be righteous. Also, why is it that the apostle did not say: Be imitators of me as I am, but said, *Be imitators of me as I am of Christ* (1 Cor 11:1)? Did he, then, want to take the place of Christ for them? Do you see the evil results you have if, when the apostle sets before us Adam and Christ, you want to interpret this as imitation in both cases, not as birth and rebirth?

147. JUL. (1) But the grace of Christ also includes the innocents whom Adam's sin did not affect. For this reason he carefully taught, *Much more did the grace of God and the gift of the one man Jesus Christ abound for more* (Rom 5:15). In that way the equalization of grace and sin, as we mentioned above,[135] is a proof that imitation belongs to that age which uses reason in opposite courses of action, while this superiority in the bountifulness of grace shows that the innocents are consecrated and made more perfect. (2) Since this is so, realize that the apostle is against you, not against me; know that he bears arms against you. He would by this one point, if all the others were lacking, forcefully destroy your teaching and that of your mentor, Faustus, by whom you were indoctrinated first hand, as it were.[136] For he says that by the disobedience of the one, many, not all, were made sinners and that through the obedience of the one, not all, but many, were made righteous. In order to suggest with care to the mind of the reader how much this statement is against you, the apostle declares that not all were made sinners, but you say that through Adam absolutely all belong to the dominion of the devil because of natural sin. There can be no doubt about it: there is a great conflict between you and the apostle.

AUG. Paul said "all" and called those same people "many." When he says "many," he does not deny that they were all, and so he does not contradict himself, as you try in your wickedness to deceive others or are yourself deceived in your blindness. After all, because the apostle said both "all" and "many," I showed that these two are not mutually contradictory. For all are also said to be many because at times even a few are said to be all. But by saying that those whom the apostle said were all were not all, you are undoubtedly shown to be opposed to the apostle.

148. JUL. You and Mani say: All are sinners by nature. The apostle, however, says: Many, not all, are sinners. He removes from the seeds the accusation which is aimed like a sword at moral conduct, and he destroys original sin. But let us insist on the point which we have made. The apostle teaches that we should understand that many became sinners through the disobedience of Adam, but that many become righteous through the obedience of Christ. He certainly shows that those who are righteous are distinct from those who are serious sinners. With what impudence do you try to argue in order to prove from these statements the existence of natural sin? After all, when you say that all are born serious sinners because of Adam and, for this reason, belong to the devil, but that some are afterwards set free from him because of Christ, you do not hold what the apostle holds. He says that not all, but many were made sinners through Adam.

AUG. (1) As we have already shown, it is not contradictory that those same people who are all are also many; hence, the apostle says that those same people whom he called "many" are "all." It is not the apostle, but you who say that they are "not all," and in this way you contradict the apostle. What the apostle says, however, is true; therefore, what you say is false. You said above, "The apostle carefully taught, *Much more did the grace of God and the gift of the one man Jesus Christ abound for more*"[137] (Rom 5:15), where you wanted us to understand that he said "more" because God's grace also reaches the little ones to whom the imitation of the first human being does not apply. Either a defective manuscript has deceived to you, or you yourself are lying, or you have been misled by someone else who is mistaken or deceitful or by your own forgetfulness. (2) For the apostle did not say "more" but "many." Look at the Greek text, and you will find πολλοὺς, not πλείστους. He said, then, that grace was much more abundant for many, not for many more, that is, not for more people, as we have already shown.[138] After all, if he had said "more" on account of the little ones who share in grace, though they do not share in the imitation of the first human being, he would have said something false and would be like you. For if all those who imitate Christ after his incarnation, plus the reborn little ones, are compared to the sinners who sin by their will from Adam up to the end of the world, all of whom you want to share in the imitation of the first human being on account of their freedom of choice, one clearly sees which of these groups has many more so that you are defeated even by your false statement.

149. JUL. For if he had held a view like yours, he should, of course, have said: Through the disobedience of the one all were made sinners, but through the obedience of Christ some of these returned to righteousness. He should, after all,

have spoken that way if he had wanted us to understand what you make up. Along with this statement he could, nonetheless, not make that other statement, namely, that the grace of Christ produced much more good than the sinfulness of Adam did harm. Even if we were completely ignorant of the customary expression by which many were said to be made sinners through the disobedience of one human being, it would still remain unshakable that this does not have to do with original sin, since the apostle taught that it belonged to many, not to all.

AUG. (1) We have already replied with regard to "many" and "all." Why does it come as a surprise that the apostle did not speak in the way you say that he ought to have spoken if he wanted to say what we say? For, even if, as you suppose, the apostle said that through the sin of the one many were made sinners so that we could not understand these many to be all, but only those who sinned by their own will through imitating the first human being, he did not say that through the obedience of Christ some of these were justified, which is, nonetheless, true. Why is it, then, that you say: If the apostle held a view like ours, he should have said: "Through the disobedience of the one all were made sinners, but through the disobedience of Christ some of these returned to righteousness"? (2) For you do not deny that some of the transgressors of the law—the only sort of sinners you claim share in the likeness of Adam's transgression—have returned to righteousness through Christ's obedience. We too, then, can say to you: If the apostle held a view like yours, he ought, of course, to have said: Through the disobedience of the one many, of course, but not all, were made sinners, but even some of these have returned to righteousness through the obedience of Christ. Or, if he held such a view, he would have spoken much more clearly so that he said: Many of the Jews, of course, were made sinners through the disobedience of the one human being; after they received the law, they sinned by a similar transgression. But the obedience of Christ made even some of them righteous. (3) But if he did not rule against you by not speaking as I said he ought to have spoken if he held what you hold, he certainly ought not to rule against me because he did not speak as you say that he ought to have spoken if he held what I hold. Since the apostle, then, spoke as he thought he ought to speak, we must see which one of us agrees with him. Is it I who say that his words, *Through the sin of the one all entered condemnation* (Rom 5:18), are true, and his words, *Through the disobedience of the one many were made sinners* (Rom 5:19), are true, since it is not contradictory that those who are many are all and that those who are all are many? Or is it you who say: When he says many, they are many, and when he says all, they are not all?

Julian's Explanation of the Letter to the Romans

150. JUL. Either your ignorance or your impudence has, then, been revealed; you either do not care or are unable to weigh what the apostle said, and the light of the truth itself, which Christ claimed to be,[139] has shown that nothing in the words of the apostle Paul fits with the Manichean, that is, your madness. Now let us devote our energies to an explanation of Paul so that, as we have shown how he cannot be understood, it may become clear how he both ought to and can be understood.

AUG. You are abandoned by the truth, and you are not able to find anything to say against the clear words of the apostle. As a result, you claim that what so many holy and famous teachers, who learned and taught this in the Catholic Church, understood in those words is the teaching of the Manichees. They could not, after all, understand anything else in such clear words since they possessed sound minds. But you are forced to admit that they were not Manichees, no matter how great is the venom of the Pelagian plague which has driven you out of your mind.

151. JUL. (1) He was writing to the Romans at the time when the Jews began to mix with the Gentiles and, therefore, the churches were filling up with both the Jews and the Gentiles. He settles the disturbances in both peoples, teaching that the Gentiles could not on the grounds of their ignorance of the law excuse their impiety by which they changed the glory of God into the likeness of an image of a human being and of birds and animals and serpents.[140] For through the power of their native reason they could from God's creation know God who reveals himself by his works, though he remains hidden in the depths of his substance, even if they could not know the rites of the Jewish ceremonies. (2) Each person's own state of mind makes known the norm of the law insofar as it pertains to moral goodness, namely, that we should not do to our neighbor the sort of thing we would not want to suffer. In that way he shows that the impiety of the Gentiles can be blamed with perfect right. Even if it cannot be blamed on the basis of the law, it can still be blamed on the basis of that justice which established the law. And by the judgment of that law those who sinned without the law will also perish without the law. But with the great power of his arguments he crushes the Jews, about whom he was more concerned, because they were greatly swollen with pride and showed contempt for the Gentiles. They claimed for themselves honor from the purifications of the law, and in this way they judged that the grace of Christ which forgives sins did not benefit them as it did the Gentiles, since they had avoided sins by the institution of the law. The apostle claims that they received more through forgiveness to the extent that without any ignorance they sinned more after being warned by the law. (3) In that way he shows that they were guilty and could have been severely condemned in the tribunal of that justice before which those who sinned under the law will be judged by the law.

For the hearers of the law are not righteous before God, but the doers of the law will be justified (Rom 2:13). Arguing, then, with this aim through the whole book, he checks the pride of the Jews and takes the lame excuse of their idolatry from the Gentiles in order to teach that Christ's medicine benefitted both peoples equally.

AUG. You deny this medicine to the little ones whom the law ordered to be circumcised on the eighth day as a foreshadowing of the grace of the one whose resurrection was revealed on the Lord's day, that is, the eighth day following the seventh day of the Sabbath. You cannot and will not notice that a little one who dies without the grace of Christ will perish, just as scripture said that the soul of an uncircumcised little one perishes from its people.[141] You cannot find any way that it merited to perish in this way as long as you say that little ones do not contract original sin.

152. JUL. Christ also forgave serious sins of the will from which persons were free to hold back, and to those who reformed their lives by imitating him he who was the model and standard of the virtues granted the glory of blessed eternity. Paul confronts both peoples in accord with the time and authority of his book. In these passages in question, nonetheless, he joins battle with the Israelites who dared to look down upon those coming from the uncircumcised peoples to the point that they claimed that they could not enter their company, even with the support of the faith. In opposition to this arrogance he recalls the beginnings of the Jewish people, and by the very source of circumcision he shows that the foreskin is not so important that leaving it makes persons unrighteous or its removal makes them righteous.

AUG. When the apostle said these things, he was not dealing with circumcision or uncircumcision, but with the commandments of the law which include, *You shall not desire* (Ex 20:17; Dt 5:21), as he himself mentioned.[142] Why do you try to escape? You are the first to perish when you spread clouds before the uneducated.[143]

153. JUL. *The promise, therefore, to Abraham that he would be the heir of the world did not come through the law, but through the righteousness of faith. After all, if those who come from the law are heirs, faith has been done away with, and the promise has been destroyed. For the law produces anger, but where there is no law, there is no transgression either. That is why it comes from faith so that the promise might stand firm as grace for every descendant—not only for the descendant that comes from the law, but for the descendant that comes from the faith of Abraham. He is the father of us all—as it is written: "I have made you the father of many nations"—before the God whom he believed, who brings the dead to life and calls into existence those things which are not. He believed in the hope against all hope that he would become the father of many nations in accord with what he was told: "So your descendants shall be." And without wavering in*

his faith, he saw that his body was already lifeless since he was almost one hundred years old and that the womb of Sarah was also lifeless. But he did not hesitate in disbelief over the promise of God, but grew strong in faith and gave glory to God. He knew perfectly well that God is able also to do whatever he promised, and it was credited to him as righteousness (Rom 4:13-22).

AUG. Are you not ashamed to quote these words, you who attack the grace by which these promises are fulfilled? You, after all, speak against God when you say, "We do what God promised he would do." Isaac, of course, who is the son promised to Abraham, prefigured not those who would make themselves righteous, but those whom God would make righteous. For this reason God said to the whole Church through the prophet, *For I am the Lord who made you* (Is 45:8 LXX). For this reason they are called the children of the promise, as the apostle most clearly says, *The word of God, however, cannot fail. For not all those who are descended from Israel are Israel, nor are they all children of Abraham because they are his descendants, but "Through Isaac your offspring will be named." That is, it is not the children of the flesh who are God's children, but the children of the promise are counted as offspring* (Rom 9:6-8). And so, what God promised God does. As all this builds up those whose hope is in God, so it tears down those *who place their trust in their own virtue* (Ps 49:7), and for this reason, as it builds up the Catholic faith, it tears down the Pelagian error.

The Promise Made to Abraham

154. JUL. I discussed in the first work how this passage is entirely opposed to your position, and if anything needs to be recalled from it, it will be stated. But now let us turn to the promise which was made to Abraham as a reward of his faith. The promise which says that he will become the father of many nations showed that he ought not to be upheld as the father of just one people, for God foretold that he would be the father of many nations. Nor did Abraham alone receive the reward of belief in such a way that we should suppose that he excludes from a share in the reward others who likewise believe. The apostle says, *But scripture did not say only on his account that it was credited to him, but also on account of us to whom it will be credited for believing in him who raised up Jesus Christ our Lord from the dead, Jesus who was handed over for our sins and rose on account of our justification* (Rom 4:23-25).

AUG. Tell us, you silly people, not defenders, but exaggerators of free choice. Not knowing the righteousness of God and wanting to establish your own righteousness, you are not subject to the righteousness of God.[144] Tell us, I insist: If the nations had refused to believe and to live righteously, would the promise which was made to Abraham have been done away with? No, you will say. Therefore, in order that Abraham might obtain as the wages of faith the multiplication of his descendants, the will of the nations was prepared by the Lord, and that they willed what they could have also not willed was caused by God who is also able to do what he has promised.

155. JUL. Since Abraham was declared a witness of the faith when he was still uncircumcised and obtained the multiplication of his offspring as a reward of its faith, Paul asks: What rule makes you, a Jew, think that the Gentiles do not have a share in righteousness, since they make the faith of Abraham live again by believing things similar to what he believed about the powers of God?

AUG. You speak well against yourself. Of course, if they have faith in the powers of God, they do not, like you, put their trust in their own power in order that they may be justified, that is, that they may become righteous, but in the power of him who justifies the sinner.

156. JUL. Why do you suppose, he asks, that the nations could not be brought into Abraham's family without the ceremonies of the law since it is clear that the promise made to Abraham came before the law and that it was not repayment for removing the foreskin,[145] but for moral conduct?

AUG. If, as you suppose, human beings produce for themselves this moral conduct which you undoubtedly want us to understand was good, God ought with his foreknowledge to have predicted, not to have promised this. Then scripture would not say of him in this case, *He is also able to do what he promised* (Rom 4:21), but: He is also able to foretell what he foreknew, or: He is also able to make it known. But when human beings say: We do what God has promised, they make themselves powerful by their effort, and they make him a liar by their arrogance.

157. JUL. *For if those who come from the law are heirs, faith has been done away with, and the promise has been destroyed* (Rom 4:14). Unless this statement is understood, it raises a big question. After all, he undoubtedly means by those who come from the law those who he previously said come from the circumcision. He knows that they made such great claims for themselves that they thought that none besides themselves were included in honor of being the offspring of Abraham. And in the previous argument he had concluded that not merely those who come from the circumcision, but also those from the uncircumcised who willed to follow in the footsteps of Abraham should rightly be judged to be the children of Abraham.

AUG. But what if they refused? Would the promise be done away with? I warn you to understand the grace of which you are enemies when you deny that God produces the acts of the will in the minds of human beings—not so that they believe against their will, for that is utterly absurd to say, but so that they become willing from unwilling. He does not act like a human teacher using the word of God to instruct and exhort and to threaten and promise. That is pointless if God does not in his mysterious ways also produce interiorly the willing. For when a teacher plants and waters with words, we can say: Perhaps the hearers believe;

perhaps they do not. But when God gives the increase,[146] they undoubtedly believe and grow. There you have the difference between the law and the promise, between the Spirit and the letter.

158. JUL. Since the apostle, therefore, earlier made us understand that the Gentiles could not be excluded from a share in righteousness, but that they are, because of the same faith, counted along with the children of the circumcision in the family of Abraham, he now introduced the idea that no one from the circumcision has a share in the promise made to Abraham. But unless this is properly understood, it is utterly self-contradictory. He did not, then, make this statement of his, *For if those who come from the law are heirs, faith has been done away with, and the promise has been destroyed* (Rom 4:14), so that we would believe that no one from the Jews becomes an heir of the ancient promise through faith. Rather, there is missing the statement which intelligence supplies, namely, that those who come from the law are not the sole heirs. It is as if it were stated this way: For if they who come from the law are the sole heirs, faith is done away with. The uncircumcised would, after all, really seem to be excluded if the blessing were the heritage of only those who came from the circumcision. Therefore, we must understand the language of the scriptures, namely, that something left unsaid is not necessarily denied, but the effort[147] of intelligence must make up for the missing words.

AUG. (1) Those who do not understand understand that way. Why do you not notice, I ask, that heirs do not come from the law? After all, *the law produces anger. For where there is no law, there is no transgression either* (Rom 4:15). The heirs come from the promise because God himself does what he promises. Those who imagine that they fulfill the commandments of the law by the choice of their own will without the Spirit of grace want to establish their own righteousness, not to receive the righteousness of God. For why does the same apostle say, *That I might be found in him, not having my own righteousness which comes from the law, but the righteousness which comes from faith, the righteousness from God* (Phil 3:9)? (2) Why does he call his own the righteousness which comes from the law and reject that righteousness, but not call his own the righteousness from God which comes from faith? Does not the law come from God? Who but an unbeliever would say that? He calls his own the righteousness from the law, the righteousness by which human beings think that the law is sufficient for them to carry out God's commandments, while they place their trust in their own virtue.[148] But he says that the righteousness from faith comes from God because God gives to each one the measure of faith,[149] and it pertains to faith to believe that God also produces in us the willing,[150] as he produced it in that seller of purple goods whose mind he had opened so that she paid attention to what Paul was saying.[151] And for this reason even the Jews who believed in Christ, among whom Paul was included, were not to be called heirs because of the law, but rather because of the promise. After all, scripture said, *Through Isaac your off-spring will be named*, because *it is not the children of the flesh who are God's children, but the children of the promise are counted as offspring* (Rom 9:7-8).

The Heirs of the Promise and the Law

159. JUL. The apostle, therefore, concluded his argument in this way: If there were no heirs of the blessing except those who come from the law, then, just as it was clear that the uncircumcised were excluded, so it followed that no one who comes from the law is deprived of the blessing. That is, if circumcision were so effective that without it faith was useless, as it was clear that the Gentiles were rejected, so it was shown that no one from the Jews could ever come to perdition.

AUG. How did this follow, you great logician? How did it follow that, if none were heirs of the blessing except those who come from the law, no one who comes from the law is deprived of the blessing? Because none are heirs unless they are baptized, are all who are baptized, therefore, heirs? I wanted to say this, not because the question between us is here at stake, but to show how sharp you are, you who say that I am more blunt than a pestle.[152]

160. JUL. Now, since you admit that the transgressors under the law are not heirs of the blessing because the law produces anger[153] for such persons, it is clear that the promise does not belong to the circumcision, but to faith. But the promise would be destroyed, if no one were righteous apart from the law, since the law was given four hundred and thirty years after the promise,[154] and it would prove that Abraham himself and Isaac and Jacob and all the holy people in the intervening period were deprived of the blessing which could not be given to anyone apart from the law.

AUG. The promise would in fact be destroyed if anyone were righteous because of the law. *For if any are heirs because of the law, faith has been done away with, and the promise has been destroyed, for the law produces anger* (Rom 4:14.15) for this reason, namely, that the grace of God would be sought to escape the anger of God.

161. JUL. This is clearly false. Sinners, of course, merited punishment under the law, and before the law justice and faith were not deprived of the benefits of their reward. It is, then, clear that the glory of that promise belongs not to flesh trimmed with a knife, but to minds bright with goodness. There follows, however, a thunderbolt of a statement against inherited sin; he says, *For the law produces anger, but where there is no law, there is no transgression either* (Rom 4:15). Convince us that the law was given to infants in the womb, that a law could be given to the newborn so that it could prove them guilty of transgression. But in agreement with the apostle who, we maintain, held nothing opposed to reason, we believe that there is no transgression at that age at which there could

not be a law. For *where there is no law, there is no transgression either*, and *the law produces anger* (Rom 4:15), not because of any defect of the law, but because of the wickedness of those who prefer sin to virtue.

AUG: Is this, then, not the law of Christ: *Whoever has not been reborn of water and the Spirit cannot enter the kingdom of God* (Jn 3:5)? You see that this law includes the little ones too. But tell us rather: For what transgression was the little one blamed whose soul perished from its people if it was not circumcised on the eighth day?[155] Why did it suffer so great a punishment if not for the reason that, though it committed no sin in itself, it was held guilty *in the likeness of the transgression of Adam in whom all have sinned* (Rom 5:14.12)? You try by a great, but vain effort to obscure and twist these words of the apostle which are so clear and correct.

162. JUL. The apostle, then, agreed that scripture said not only on account of Abraham that it was credited to him for righteousness, but also on account of us to whom it is undoubtedly credited when we believe in God *who raised Jesus Christ from the dead, who was handed over*, he says, *on account of our sins and rose on account of our justification* (Rom 4:24-25).

AUG. You exclude from this grace the little ones who you claim have no sin contracted from their origin; from this it follows that they do not share in the benefit of Christ's having been handed over on account of our sins, and while you hold and teach such ideas, you dare to call yourselves Catholic Christians!

Our Many Sins versus the One Sin of Adam

163. JUL. How emphatically he teaches that before God the just judge the sins of one person do no harm to others, for in praising the death of Christ he is careful to state that he faced death on account of our sins which were both many and ours, not on account of one sin of someone else—a sin of a person long dead!

AUG. (1) The disobedience of the one human being is, of course, not absurdly said to be the sin of someone else, because when we were not yet born, we did no action of our own, whether good or bad,[156] but we all were in that one who committed this sin when he committed it, and that sin was so great and so powerful that the whole of human nature was damaged by it. The quite obvious misery of the human race is sufficient proof of this. And this sin of someone else becomes ours through the succession of generations subject to it; on this account the Catholic teacher who correctly understood the apostle said, "All of us human beings are born under the power of sin, and our very origin lies in guilt."[157] If you are willing to follow his interpretation and that of his other companions in the Catholic truth, you will not be forced to exclude the little ones from the benefit of the death of him *who was handed over on account of our sins* (Rom 4:25), and *one died for all* (2 Cor 5:14). (2) Here the apostle cries out what follows: *All, therefore, have died, and he died for all* (2 Cor 5:15). But you shout back: The little ones have not died! Shout what follows as well: He, therefore, did not die for them. See whether you do not lie dead, you who deny the death of Christ to the dead so that they are not brought to life. For, as you suppose, the sin of the one man long dead ought not to be ascribed to them. You do not notice that the first man, Adam, had died long ago and that after him the second man is Christ, though so many thousands of human beings were born between that one and this one. And for this reason it is clear that everyone who is born through that series of generations belongs to that first man, just as everyone belongs to the second man who is reborn in him by the gift of grace. As a result, two men, the first and the second, are in a sense the whole human race.

164. JUL. The apostle, then, who speaks of many sins does not have any idea of the one sin of the Manichees, that is, of the inherited sin.

AUG. (1) But, of course, you contentious rascal, there would be many sins which the many people would have from their own will, even if there were only one sin for each of them if they came to the bath of rebirth when they first began to commit sin. According to this twisted idea of yours—I will not call it a reasonable argument—you exclude all of them from this grace which justifies after many sins, because you do not want any people who have just one sin to have a share in it. How many more sins are there, then, when there are added to these the many sins which some have and the fewer sins others have! From all of them, nonetheless, people are set free by this grace of which the apostle said, *After many sins* it leads to *justification* (Rom 5:16). (2) "For Adam existed and we all existed in him; Adam perished, and we all perished in him."[158] Ambrose said this. You slanderer, he was not a Manichee. Cyprian said that little ones contract the infection of the ancient death by their first birth.[159] You slanderer, he was not a Manichee. Hilary said that all sinned in the one Adam.[160] You slanderer, he was not a Manichee. They taught this in the Church. You slanderer, she is not Manichean. And because she was Catholic and remains Catholic, she could not put up with you people who hold views opposed to these and defend them. And in order to remain Catholic, she defended the weakness of her little ones by condemning you.

165. JUL. *Justified, then, on the basis of faith, let us have peace with God through our Lord Jesus Christ, through whom we also have access to this grace in which we stand and boast in the hope of the glory of God* (Rom 5:1-2). Since you, he says, see that justification has been granted you through the forgiveness of sins, maintain unwavering peace, and with like minds praise the gifts of the mediator, by whose favor it has been granted to you that you have entry into this grace. He has restored to freedom those whom justice held guilty because it is not our nature, but our will that made us guilty. He has rescued us from vengeance, and he has offered us who were expecting eternal punishment reason to boast now in the hope of the glory of God.

AUG. This justification is not conferred through the forgiveness of sins alone, except according to your newfangled theory. God, of course, justifies sinners, not only by forgiving the evil deeds they committed, but also by bestowing love so that they avoid evil and do good through the Holy Spirit. The apostle asked the constant help of the Spirit[161] for those to whom he said, *But we pray to God that you may do nothing evil* (2 Cor 13:7). You wage war against this grace not to defend free choice of the will by your words, but to lead it astray by your presumption.

166. JUL. But in order to express more fully the power and the security of this teaching, the apostle continues with what Christian philosophy gives to the faithful: *Not only this, but we also boast in sufferings, knowing that trials produce patience, but patience produces assurance, and assurance produces hope. But hope is not disappointed, because the love of God has been poured out in our hearts by the Holy Spirit who has been given to us* (Rom 5:3-5). That is, these benefits have not only permitted that we may some day rejoice over the extent of the gifts. But even now at present, when we find ourselves in the midst of the heat of sufferings, we are enthusiastic by reason of the possession of that virtue, and we laugh at the fury of our persecutors. We regard the cruelty of the impious as a lesson in patience rather than as a disturbance of our joy. Hence, we not only avoid sin on account of the rewards, but we regard as a reward the very fact that we do not commit sin.

AUG. (1) If the reward is that we do not commit sin, who gives this reward? I suspect that you are not going to say: Human beings give it to themselves, although the perversity of your heresy forces you to say this. If, then, God gives this reward in that human beings do not sin, I see that we should call it a gift rather than a reward so that no merits seem to have preceded it. For even Pelagius condemned those who say that the grace of God is given in accord with our merits.[162] You yourself said a little before how this gift, that is, the gift of not sinning, is given when you cited the words of the apostle, *Because the love of God has been poured out in our hearts by the Holy Spirit who has been given to us* (Rom 5:5). (2) And for this reason, in Christian philosophy it is not due to ourselves that we boast of tribulations, because we have received these too. As a matter of fact, scripture says to those who boast over something of their own as if they got it for themselves by themselves, *What, after all, do you have that you have not received? But if you have received, why do you boast as if you have not received?* (1 Cor 4:7). And yet we boast, not as if we have not received, but we boast in him who has granted us that those of us who boast may boast in the Lord.[163] This is the grace which the Catholic faith preaches. Why, I ask, does your error attack it since it refutes you from your own lips?

167. JUL. Then, since we see that those things which were promised are realized amid temptations,[164] we count all the good and bad things of this life as mere

trifles, judging the trustworthiness of God's promise from the greatness of his love toward us. For no failure to receive eternal goods will stifle our hope since we have as a pledge of future blessedness the love of God which has been poured out in our hearts by the Holy Spirit who has been given to us.[165] That is, through the gifts of the Holy Spirit God has proved his love for the human race.

AUG. You do not want to include among these gifts our not sinning; rather, placing your trust in your virtue,[166] you want to attribute this to yourself. Do not, please, be angry: *Accursed are all who put their hope in a human being* (Jer 17:5).

168. JUL. He will, therefore, faithfully grant everything he promised to believers.

AUG. He will clearly grant this too, namely, that they are believers, for he promised to Abraham the belief of the nations, and a certain great man of faith said, *I obtained mercy so that I might be a believer* (1 Cor 7:25).

169. JUL. *For he who did not spare his own Son, but handed him over for us all*, through whom he consecrated us by the work of the Holy Spirit, undoubtedly *has given us all things with him* (Rom 8:32). *For why did Christ, when we were still weak, die for sinners at the appointed time?* (Rom 5:6).

AUG. You quote the divine testimonies by which your error is destroyed. He did not, after all, say: Christ also died for sinners, but: He died for sinners. As you yourself have admitted elsewhere,[167] he also died for little ones. And yet, with an audacity I fail to understand you deny that the sinfulness of the first human being was passed on to them at their origin. How then do they belong to him who died for sinners?

Reconciliation through the Death of Christ

170. JUL. *One will, after all, hardly die for a righteous person, though one might perhaps venture to die for someone good. But God showed his love for us. For if, when we were still sinners, Christ died for us, how much more shall we be saved through him from the anger, now that we have been justified in his blood. For if when we were enemies, we were reconciled to God through the death of his Son, how much more shall we be saved in his life, now that we have been reconciled. Not only this, but we also boast in God through our Lord Jesus Christ through whom we have now received reconciliation* (Rom 5:7-11). The apostle showed the great goodness with which Christ did all this when he consented to die for those who merited nothing good.

AUG. These words of yours are so balanced that they seem to apply even to little ones, for you concede that they merited nothing good since you admit that they did nothing good. But the apostle did not speak that way; he said that Christ died for the wicked and for sinners. In vain, then, did you suppose that Christ's mercy had to be trimmed down. For he died for those who merited evil, but you exclude from so great a benefit of the savior the little ones because you say that they are in good health. But he says, *Those in good health do not need a physician* (Mt 9:12). The little ones, then, do not need Christ, for according to you he is not Jesus for them. But for those who need him he is undoubtedly Jesus. Away with you, you evil people; the little ones do need him. And he, therefore, saves them from their sins, since he received that name for this reason when the angel said, *You shall call his name Jesus, for he will save his people from their sins* (Mt 1:21).

171. JUL. (1) Sinners trampled upon reason and the law out of a love for serious sins, as they pursued their own desires, and conscience itself, whose power is very great, chastised them. But it was also agreed that the prophets were frequently glorious in their contempt for death on account of justice and that many ran with a peaceful mind to their own destruction for any important causes that shone brilliantly with their inherent glory. So that the singular virtue of Christ might not seem weaker because of such examples, the apostle introduced a means of showing that his love and courage rose to a unique height. I too agree that some, though rarely and though only a few, have chosen to die for good and just persons. (2) For them the nobility of their tasks, that is, the glory of the causes for which they fought, offset the pain of their perils. But Christ had nothing that he might love in the actions of sinners, and he did not refuse to give his life for those who were despicable by reason of their own will. It is clear that he surpassed all others in the virtues because, though he has a few companions in what he endured, he can have none in such a cause. Let us, then, not despair of his generosity, for, if he died for us though we were still sinners, *how much more shall we be saved from the anger through him, now that we have been justified in his blood* (Rom 5:9).

AUG. Do not, then, remove the little ones from those who are sinners, since you admit that Christ also died for them.

172. JUL. And after the reconciliation with God which we have merited to have through the work[168] of the mediator, we ought to perceive with the mind everlasting joys and to look forward not merely to salvation, but also to glory.

AUG. (1) I beg you, pay attention to what the apostle says and why it was that he spoke about the first man. He was discussing the reconciliation from our state of enmity with God, the reconciliation which you also grant was brought about through Christ the mediator. See, here are the words of the apostle: *Justified, then, by faith, let us have peace with God through our Lord Jesus Christ* (Rom 5:1). And a little later he adds, *For if when we were still weak, Christ died for sinners at the appointed time* (Rom 5:6). Again, after a bit he says, *God reveals his love for us since, when we were still sinners, Christ died for us. Much more shall we be saved from the anger through him, now that we have been justified in his blood* (Rom 5:8-9). (2) Notice further: *For if when we were enemies*, he says, *we were reconciled to God through his Son, much more shall we be saved in his life, now that we have been reconciled* (Rom 5:10). This reconciliation which he praised so often he also mentioned in the last verse where he says, *Through whom we have even now received reconciliation* (Rom 5:11), and then he concludes, *For this reason, as through one man sinned entered the world* (Rom 5:12). As through this one there came the state of enmity, so through the one Christ there came reconciliation. Whoever, then, says that little ones are free from that sin which created the state of enmity clearly denies that they have a share in this reconciliation because of which Christ became the mediator. Hence, such a person also separates them from the justification which Christ's blood produces, for, when he taught that we must drink his blood, the reason given for shedding it was precisely the forgiveness of sins.[169] (3) From this it follows that the death of Christ does no good at all for the little ones who have no sins; by this death we were reconciled to God when we were enemies—something that, according to you, the little ones were not. For in order that on account of this reconciliation we might die to the sin in which the enmity consisted, *whoever of us have been baptized*, as the same apostle says, *have been baptized in his death* (Rom 6:3). In order to get to these words, he asks, *For if we have died to sin, how shall we continue to live in it?* (Rom 6:2). And to show immediately that we died to sin, he says, *Do you not know that whoever of us have been baptized in Christ Jesus have been baptized in his death?* (Rom 6:3). Where is the freedom and strength of your mind? Why are you afraid to say what you are not afraid to believe, namely, that little ones ought not to be baptized in Christ, since you say that they do not have the sin to which they might die?

Julian's Interpretation of Romans 5:12

173. JUL. *For this reason, just as through one man sin entered this world, and through sin death, and in that way death was passed on to all human beings, in whom all have sinned* (Rom 5:12).[170] To conquer the pride of the Jews who thought that they did not need pardon for sins as much as the Gentiles, since they claimed holiness for their people on the basis of the lofty character of the law, the apostle inveighs against the ills of human conduct. He recalls the great number of sinners in order that the evidence of sin in ancient times might reveal the extent of sin's dominion in this world. He did this to show the many sins of long ago which the grace of Christ removed, sins which were handed on by the foulness of our ancestors to their descendants through their imitating one another. For this reason he mentions the first man, not because sin began with him, for it is clear that the woman sinned first, but because by the privilege of his sex he assumed the role of teacher of sin. Through this one, then, *sin entered, and through sin*

death, that death undoubtedly which is promised to sinners, that is, eternal death. *And in that way*, he says, *death was passed on to all human beings in whom all have sinned* (Rom 5:12). He, of course, showed how this death was passed on to posterity, namely, by imitation, not by generation.

AUG. (1) I have already given you the answer why he did not mention the woman with whom sin began, but the one man.[171] It was either that she too was understood to be in him on account of the one flesh, or it was that generation begins with the man, and he wanted to show that sin entered the world through generation. But you people who say that the death which is found in sin is passed on to posterity by imitation, not by generation, why do you not clearly state that little ones need not be baptized in Christ Jesus? For if they must be baptized in Christ, they too undoubtedly die to sin, because whoever are baptized in Christ are baptized into his death. The apostle, after all, proved that we have died to sin from the fact that we have been baptized into the death of Christ. (2) For after he said, *If we have died to sin, how shall we continue to live in it?* (Rom 6:2), he immediately added, in order to show that we have died to sin, *Or do you not know that whoever of us have been baptized in Christ Jesus have been baptized into his death?* (Rom 6:3). Whoever, then, has no sin does not have anything to die to in baptism, but whoever does not die to sin when baptized is not baptized into the death of Christ and, for this reason, is not baptized in Christ. Why do you hesitate? Freely open the gates of your hell; freely let those people join you who do not want their little ones who are dead in sin to be brought to life in baptism.

174. JUL. After he had said, *It was passed on to all human beings*, he immediately added, *in whom all have sinned* (Rom 5:12).[172] This clause, *In whom all have sinned*, means nothing but: Because all have sinned, in accord with the words of David, *In what way does a young man correct his way of life?* That is, how does he correct his way of life? *By keeping your commandments* (Ps 119:9). He is, then, said to correct his way of life in that by which he is also corrected. So too, the apostle also said that death was passed on in that in which all sinned by their own will, not so that we would think that this "*in quo*" refers to either Adam or the sin, but so that we would understand "*in quo*" to express "because."

AUG. Open your eyes. All die in Adam, and if the little ones have not died in him, neither are they brought to life in Christ. Why then do you run with them in a damnable pretense to the baptism of the giver of life and of the savior, when you do not want them to be brought to life and healed since you cry out that they are alive and well?

Scripture's Use of "All" for "Many"

175. JUL. But countless examples from the scriptures bear witness that "all" is used for "many" in accord with the words, *All have turned away; they have at*

the same time become useless (Ps 14:3), and there follows after a bit, *They devour my people like bread* (Ps 14:4), where the psalmist shows that this people was separate from the "all" who he had declared did evil. The gospel reports, *All the people cried out: Crucify him! Crucify him!* (Lk 23:21).[173] And yet the universal scope of this word by no means includes the apostles or Nicodemus or the holy women. In the present passage the apostle a little later calls "many" those whom he now said were "all."[174]

AUG. (1) I have already answered that "many" is not opposed to "all," because the all are not few, but many.[175] And the words you quoted from the psalm, *All turned away; they at the same time became useless* (Ps 14:4), are certainly true. The psalmist distinguished the children of men who all turned away from the children of God who did not turn away and whom the former were devouring. For God looked down upon the children of men; all these had turned away, but the children of God were, of course, distinct from these. Among all these children of men who turned away there were, then, all those people who cried out, *Crucify him! Crucify him!* Those who already believed in Christ by no means belonged to these people. (2) Get free, if you can, from the statement that *one died for all*, and dare to say that not all those for whom Christ died were dead, for the apostle immediately closes your mouth and silences your most brazen tongue, when he shows what follows and says, *All, therefore, have died.* Do not praise the apostle in such a way; do not explain his words so that you refuse to hear, *If one has died for all, all, therefore, have died* (2 Cor 5:14). To all these death along with sin was passed on by the one in whom all die. The little ones are also included there, because Christ also died for them; he died for all precisely because all were dead. Whatever arguments you raise, whatever evasions you take, however you try to undo or twist the words of the apostle, you do not show that the little ones are exempt from the death which lies in sin, because you do not dare to deny that Christ has died for them as well.

176. JUL. What we have accomplished, then, should be clear. The apostle used "all" for the very many who he says were subject to death because they sinned by their own will. He, therefore, does not accuse original sin, but voluntary sin, and his words really show nothing else if one weighs their proper and reliable sense. For if he thought that sin was passed on by generation to Adam's descendants, that is, ejaculated by him onto those who were not present there, his statement that all sinned was utterly false.

AUG. I could say to you: How did Adam's descendants follow his example in sinning, since they were not present there and did not see or hear or believe in the sin? But I do not say this. "For Adam existed, and all existed in him; Adam sinned, and all sinned in him,"[176] and on this account all die in him. Listen to the apostle speaking with perfect clarity, not to yourself gossiping in a most convoluted manner.

177. JUL. It is not correct to say that all do what one person does and directs toward the others. For either it was passed on to them and they themselves did not sin, or they sinned, in which case the words express the doing of the action, and it was passed on to them only by imitation.

AUG. If someone makes himself gouty by intemperance and passes this on to his children, as often happens, is it not correct to say that this defect was passed on to them by the parent and that they were intemperate in the parent for, when he did this, they were in him? And in this way they and their parent were still one; they did this, not by the action of human beings, but by reason of the seed.[177] The apostle, therefore, knew that what is sometimes found in the diseases of the body occurred in that ancient and great sin of the one first parent by which the whole of human nature was corrupted. By a perfectly clear statement which you try to obscure, he said, *Through one man sin entered the world, and through sin death, and in that way it was passed on to all human beings, in whom all have sinned* (Rom 5:12). He, of course, intended to praise the grace of Christ, setting up the opposite pattern and comparing the originator of generation to the originator of regeneration.

The Claim That We Were All That Man

178. JUL. (1) The truth, however, destroys without difficulty and exposes to the mockery of anyone who is wise that point which you thought you made either in this book to which I am now replying or in those books which you had written for Marcellinus.[178] I mean your claim that sin was passed on at the time "when all human beings"—to use your own words—"were that one man."[179] For such an argument reveals nothing but your impiety. I mean the impiety by which you believe that there is a transmission of souls, just as there is a transmission of bodies, a view which was already condemned in the profane teaching of Tertullian and Mani.[180] It is so wicked that, when we raised it as an objection to you in that letter which we sent to the East, you tried to dissociate yourself from it by denying it in these books which you recently sent to Boniface.[181] (2) For you write, "But they say that we admit the transmission of souls, though I do not know in whose books they read this,"[182] that is, you would swear that you say nothing of the sort. But to reveal your falsehood by a comparison of your words, how can you say that your position does not include the transmission of souls, a truly godless view, though you claim that all human beings were that one? For if you do not believe that a part of the soul is bound up in the seeds, what do you mean when you write that all human beings were Adam alone, since a human being certainly can only be a soul and a body together?

AUG. (1) You think that one cannot call just the body of a human being a human being, though you know that the only Son of God, our Lord Jesus Christ, was crucified under Pontius Pilate and was buried, as his whole Church confesses and many heresies too, of which yours is one. And yet only the body of Christ was buried. According to you, we ought not to say that Jesus Christ, the only Son of God, our Lord, was buried since Christ, the only Son of God, our Lord, is not the body alone, but the Word of God and the rational soul and the body, and when the confession of faith came to these words: "He was crucified under Pontius Pilate," it ought to have added, "And his body was buried." Nor should scripture have said of the first man who is under discussion, *God formed man from the dust of the earth* (Gn 2:7), because only the human body comes from the earth. (2) Finally, cry out that God was mistaken, when he said to the man, threatening him with death, *You are earth, and you shall return to earth* (Gn 3:19). For he ought rather to have said on the basis of your teaching: "Your body is earth, and it will return to earth." Because, then, "Adam existed, and all of us existed in him,"[183] as Catholic teachers before us learned and taught in the holy Church in accord with the holy scriptures, I said, "All were that one," because even those two, the man and the woman, were then no longer two, but one flesh. And I said about all their offspring that, when the sin was committed, they all were that one. None of them was, of course, as yet poured from him into the womb of the mother by the sowing of the seed, and children are surely poured by the men into the women. (3) In whatever manner and to whatever extent, all who have been born after him were that one, whether only in terms of the body or in terms of both parts of the human being. That is a point which I admit I do not know, and I am not ashamed, as you are, to admit that I do not know what I do not know. I do know, however, that scripture says of every human being, *Human beings have become like a vanity, and their days pass like a shadow* (Ps 144:4), because elsewhere the same holy scripture says, *Every living human being is, nonetheless, utter vanity* (Ps 39:6). That would not be the case under the justice of God the creator, if there were no original sin.

179. JUL. Moreover, even if you apply this only to the flesh, the fatuousness of your interpretation cannot even then be excused. For you say, "All were that one," though at the time when Adam sinned, there were already two human beings, not one, that is, he and his wife, and from their substance, not from their sin, the race of human beings has sprung forth, as God had decreed.

AUG. I have already said, and—see—I say it again. I said, "All were that one" of these persons whom Adam would father, that is, beget; from that one, then, who begot them as their principal source the newborn were going to contract original sin. But the woman, because of whose presence there were two, later conceived and gave birth to what she received, though she sinned first. For this reason the holy scripture also says that the children of Levi were in the loins of Father Abraham and that in him they paid tithes to the priest Melchizedek.[184] Read the Letter to the Hebrews, and correct your way of speaking.

The Righteousness of Abel and the Sin of Cain

180. JUL. Finally, the holiness of Abel which is celebrated in all the scriptures bears witness that the sin of his parents harmed him in no way.

AUG. Why, then, did the apostle not mention him as a model to imitate since he was the first righteous human being? Why, when he was dealing with two human beings, one of whom led to condemnation, the other to justification, did he speak of Adam and Christ? But if Abel did not have in his members the law which resists the law of the mind[185] and which, as a righteous person, he conquered in inner combat, and if his flesh did not have desires opposed to the spirit,[186] the sin of his parents had not harmed him. But whoever says that Abel was such a person should say that he did not have sinful flesh, since Christ the Lord would certainly not have had the likeness of sinful flesh unless the flesh of all other human beings was sinful flesh.

181. JUL. On the other hand, Cain, a man filled with hate and his brother's murderer, who was born with the same nature, but not guided by the same will, was laid low by a fear that racked his soul. The apostle, then, said that sin entered the world through one, and through sin death, and in that way death was passed on to all who sinned. That statement is in harmony with Catholic teaching and offers you no help.

AUG. The apostle showed that death was passed on along with sin when he said, *And in that way it was passed on to all human beings* (Rom 5:12). For this reason even infants are rescued from the power of darkness when they are baptized; otherwise, as we have already said and must say again and again, the image of God undergoes the rites of exorcism and exsufflation with a great injury to God, if in their case that prince of the world,[187] who is cast out, is not exorcised and blown away so that the Holy Spirit may dwell there. But the crime which Cain committed does not pertain to the cause of our origin, because it was committed by his will.

182. JUL. The statement is, after all, formulated with these words which point to the antecedent example and the subsequent action of the one who imitated it.

AUG. I have already told you:[188] Abel, then, should have been set opposite to him, not Christ.

183. JUL. But if he had wanted to show that generation was either infected by sin or subject to sin, he would not have said that sin entered through one human being, but through two.

AUG. I have already replied to this.[189] You say nothing, and you go on and on speaking because you cannot find anything correct to say.

184. JUL. Nor would he have said: *Death was passed on insofar as all have sinned* (Rom 5:12),[190] but: Because they all flowed from the diabolical pleasure and flesh of the first man and first woman. But if he had said this, the apostle

would not have upheld your teaching; rather, he would have destroyed all his own statements. Hence, he accuses the will of sinners and the example of sin, and in this way both reason and Paul fiercely battle against you.

AUG. He ought, then, to have located the example of becoming righteous in Abel, the first righteous human being, just as you suppose that Paul located the example of sin in Adam, the first sinner. After all, why should we hesitate to give you the same answer, since you are not ashamed to repeat the same things so often and without any point?

Death's Reign from Adam to Moses

185. JUL. *For up to the law sin was in this world, but sin was not imputed since the law did not exist, but death reigned from Adam up to Moses even over those who did not sin in the likeness of the transgression of Adam who is the pattern of the one to come* (Rom 5:13-14). He distinguishes the quality of the sin by changing the names in order to show that sin is one thing, but transgression is something else, and he wants at least in this passage to show that every transgression is a sin, but that not every sin is a transgression. In that way the term "transgression" increases the hatefulness of the sin, and those who transgressed the commandments are seen as more guilty than those who without the warning of the law sinned by closing their eyes to the reason with which they were born. Before the law, then, which God gave through Moses and committed to writing, the law whose sanction prescribed a norm of conduct which the people living under it could not fail to know,[191] there was the intervening time between Adam and Moses. The apostle accused of sin, not of transgression, mortals of that era who were polluted by various wicked acts.

AUG. (1) What, then, does it mean: *Death reigned from Adam up to Moses even over those who did not sin in the likeness of the transgression of Adam* (Rom 5:13-14)? However you analyze the statement, you find that the apostle spoke in opposition to you. For if you take it this way: *Death reigned even over those who did not sin*, you will not find how this reign is just unless it is on account of original sin. And, hence, as if someone asked why death reigned even over those who did not sin, he replied: *In the likeness of the transgression of Adam*, that is, not on account of their own personal sins, but because Adam the transgressor begot them in his own likeness. That is the way those Catholic teachers who came before us also explained those words. For, although that one and first sin which entered the world through one man is common to all, for which reason he said, *In whom all have sinned* (Rom 5:12), the little ones do not, nonetheless, have their own personal sins. (2) And so, it could also truthfully be said of them that they did not sin, but that death reigned over them *in the likeness*, as was said, *of the transgression of Adam*. But if you take it this way: *Death reigned from Adam up to Moses even over those who did not sin in the likeness of the transgression of Adam*, that is, even over those who sinned, but did not sin in the likeness of the transgression of Adam, you find no one, according to your view, because you maintain that all who sinned sinned in his likeness, that is, followed his example. The trap, then, is closed for the fox in both directions; there is no way for him to enter and hide, and if he was already hiding there, there is no way to get out and escape.

186. JUL. He wants us to understand that those who did not have the law did not transgress the commandments, but they are found guilty because they paid no attention to reason to which the personal inclinations of each individual bear witness, and in that way they violated the laws of human society or decency. And in that way they are said to have sinned by imitating one another, but not by a transgression of the law which had not yet been given. Up to the law, then, sin existed, but not transgression. After the law, however, there was not only sin, but also transgression. Eternal death, however, reigned, the death which God promised he would impose on Adam if he sinned. That death, then, owed to sin, death as punishment, reigned even before the law over those who sinned. In the same way it reigned over the inhabitants of Sodom and over the people who were destroyed at the time of the flood on account of their sinfulness, which was, nonetheless, voluntary, though they were of various ages. And it reigned after the law was given over those whom it found guilty of transgression.

AUG. You want only eternal death to be a punishment, but if the death which separates the soul from the body is not a punishment, why does that nature which you praise so much that you deny that it is damaged fear it? What reason is there that an infant already fears being killed once it begins to advance a bit past infancy? Why is our mind not ready for death as it is for sleep? Why are they considered heroic who do not fear death, and why are they so few? Why did the apostle who said that he wanted to be dissolved and to be with Christ[192] not want to be stripped, but to be clothed over so that what is mortal might be swallowed up by life?[193] Why was Peter told of his glorious end, *Another will bind you and take you where you do not want to go* (Jn 21:18)? If the fear of death is groundless, the fear itself is a punishment; if, however, the soul naturally does not want to be separated from the body, death itself is a punishment, although divine grace puts it to good use.

187. JUL. For as justice itself judges which does not impute a sin unless one is free to hold back from it, the people who sinned without the law will be judged without the law, and those who sinned under the law will be judged by the law.[194] The words of the apostle, *But death reigned from Adam up to Moses even over those who did not sin in the likeness of the transgression of Adam* (Rom 5:14), reveal what he thought. That is, he stated that the Jews who sinned under the law were transgressors like Adam. For that first human being also received, not in writing, but orally, the law to refrain from tasting the fruit of that tree, and in this

way his obedience was tested. And by eating from it contrary to the command-ment, he committed the crime of transgression. After the law, therefore, which was given by the ministry of Moses, the people who sinned are shown to have sinned in the likeness of the transgression of Adam because they sinned, as he did, by transgressing the law. But in the period between the two laws, the first given, but not in writing, the second both given and written down, those who sinned are shown not to be free from sin; rather, they are said not to have gone astray in the likeness of the transgression of Adam because they had not received the law.

AUG. When you deny the likeness of the transgression of Adam, you refute yourself, for those who sinned without the law are not guilty by reason of the ex-ample of the first human being. It is, then, not by imitation, but by generation that death was passed on to all human beings through sin.[195] For, if this death which entered the world through the sin of the first human being had skipped over the long stretches of time which preceded the law and began to emerge with the Jews who became transgressors of the law, in order to preserve the likeness of the sin of Adam, it would not be said of this death: *Through one man it entered the world and was passed on to all human beings* (Rom 5:12). After all, is there any-one—I will not say: an idiot, but: a fool—whom you will persuade that death en-tered through one man and was passed on to all human beings, but that, as you say, it skipped over so many peoples and centuries and descended upon those who received the law, while the rest were unaffected? For you say that death reigned over those who sinned, not in the likeness of the transgression of Adam, but without transgression because they were without the law. There is obviously no way for you to correct your error unless you return to the Catholic faith which contrasts the first man who is the initiator of generation with the second man who is the initiator of regeneration.

Adam as the Pattern of the One to Come

188. JUL. Adam is said to be the pattern of the one to come, that is, of Christ, but a pattern by way of contrast so that, as the former is believed to be the pattern of sin, so the latter is believed to be the pattern of righteousness. The incarnation of Christ did not offer the first pattern of righteousness, but the greatest. For even before the Word became flesh, the virtues were resplendent in both the prophets and many other holy men and women as a result of faith in God. When, however, the fullness of time came, the perfect norm of righteousness shone forth in Christ, and he who was foretold to be the father of the world to come[196] stood forth as the one to reward the saints, both those before him and those after him.

AUG. We recognize your heresy. Pelagius, after all, stated that the righteous of old did not live from the faith in the incarnation of Christ because, of course,

Christ had not yet come in the flesh, though they certainly would not have fore-told it unless they first believed it. But you have fallen into this absurdity because you maintain that righteousness could have come through nature and the law. If either of these is true, *then Christ has died in vain* (Gal 2:21).

189. JUL. So too, Adam, on the other hand, is said to be not the first pattern of sin, but the greatest.

AUG. Why, then, is he not the first, but the greatest? After all, on account of the beginning of the human race you are not going to deny that he is the first pat-tern, and you are not going to find a reason why you should call him the greatest, unless you admit that Adam sinned more seriously to the extent that it was easier for him not to sin when nature was not yet corrupted and the law of sin in the members did not resist the law of the mind.[197] All human beings are born with that punishment and will be lost for eternity if they are not reborn, and all are lost unless they are sought and found by him who came to seek what was lost.[198]

190. JUL. I say that he was the greatest pattern, not because I deny that the devil was more guilty, but because, when the apostle was looking for an account of sin's origin, it was more appropriate for him to mention a human being whom the following generations of humanity especially looked up to rather than an airy substance. In humanity itself, however, it is clear that the woman sinned first, but because the authority of fathers is more influential and greater in all respects, he said that he was the pattern of sin—not because sin began with him, but because he is shown to have been more worthy of imitation because of the power of the male sex. You see, of course, how the logic of this interpretation testifies that it contains the truth.

AUG. The very pattern of Christ who as the second man is the counterpart of the first man shows that the apostle did not contrast imitation with imitation, but rebirth with birth. If, then, those who are reborn do not share in the righteousness of Christ, those who are born do not share in the sin of Adam, and Christ is not the pattern by way of contrast. But since he is that pattern, just as the reborn come to share in the righteousness of Christ, so too, though the little ones are not yet able to act righteously, even they were beyond all doubt born or are born with the sin passed on by Adam, though they cannot as yet commit any sin. Recognize the pattern, and do not be deformed by contradicting it.[199]

191. JUL. Now look at those words by which the apostle stated that death reigned even over those *who did not sin in the likeness of the transgression of Adam who is the pattern of the one to come* (Rom 5:14), and see how much they, like the other words of the same passage, disagree with your explanation. After all, if he were dealing with the natural sin about which, on your interpretation, he said, *In which all have sinned* (Rom 5:12), who would these people be who he immediately afterward declares are not found guilty, not only in the transgres-sion of Adam, but not even in the likeness of his sin?

AUG. You who do not understand it understand it in this way. The apostle, however, explained why death reigned even over those who did not sin by going on to say: *in the likeness of the transgression of Adam* (Rom 5:14). That is, he showed that death reigned even over those who did not sin, because they contracted a certain pattern of likeness from the transgression of Adam. Those who are born surely put on Adam, as those who are reborn put on Christ.[200]

192. JUL. He says, *Death reigned even over those who did not sin in the likeness of the transgression of Adam* (Rom 5:14). You see that he made a clear distinction between those who went astray like Adam and those who went astray in a different way.

AUG. If they went astray in a different way, what happens, then, to the example they imitated? Make rebirth correspond to birth, not imitation to imitation, and you will find the pattern which the apostle of the truth taught, not that which Pelagius, the source of your error, imagined.

193. JUL. This division cannot fit natural sin; if natural sin did exist, it would, of course, bind them all equally. There would be no one in whom this evil would not be present, and none would be found of whom it could be truly said that they did not sin in the likeness of the sin of that man, since all would have sinned in his real person.

AUG. What you shout while you fight against it is true, and it goes against you: original sin has certainly bound all equally. There would be none in whom this evil would not be present if divine grace had not through Christ come to their rescue. After all, the likeness of the transgression of Adam who is the pattern of the one to come, that is, of Christ, merited that death would reign over those who did not sin, that is, who did not commit personal sins of their own. For, as those who are born put on the first man, so those who are reborn put on the second.[201]

194. JUL. The apostle concludes and states that there are some who sinned like Adam and others who are not touched by even the likeness of the ancient transgression; it is, then, perfectly clear that serious sins are the result of moral conduct, not of the seeds. And in order to repeat in a few words what we have accomplished, the apostle says that through one man sin entered. Reason shows that this fits with imitation, not with generation which is the work of two people.

AUG. How often you say the same thing, and yet you have nothing to say, and you do not see that, if this passage meant that the sin of imitation was begun by the human race, it would say that sin entered through one woman rather than through one man. For she sinned first so that even her husband imitated her. But because the apostle wanted us to understand generation and not imitation, he said, *Through one man sin entered the world* (Rom 5:12). He either included them both under the singular term, for which reason scripture said, *They are, therefore, no longer two, but one flesh* (Mt 19:6), or he mentioned the man as the more important one, since generation begins with him when the seed is sown so that conception follows. We have already said this many times, but we are not going to yield to your repetitiousness. Rather, we also repeat what we have to say, though less frequently.

What Was Passed On: Sin or Death?

195. JUL. He continued, *And in that way death was passed on to all human beings* (Rom 5:12).

AUG. What does, *in that way* it *was passed on*, mean but the way it entered, that is, with sin or through sin?

196. JUL. He divided the sentence so that no one should suppose that sin was passed on, but so that death which pervaded the human race is shown to have by the judgment of justice followed upon the grounds for retribution which it found in each sinner from the acts of a bad will. He showed, therefore, that one should not accuse nature, but actions.

AUG. In vain do you turn this way and that. Look at Adam and Christ. The former is the pattern of the one to come; the latter who gives his righteousness to little ones who are reborn is, therefore, not his counterpart by contrast if the former does not give sin to those who are born.

197. JUL. He added that death reigned, *inasmuch as all have sinned* (Rom 5:12),[202] and by those words he did not express the downfall of the newborn, but the actions of agents. He proved, therefore, that he accuses wickedness and does not wound innocence.

AUG. All have sinned in him in whom all die; his counterpart by contrast is the one in whom all are brought to life. *But as all die in Adam, so all will be brought to life in Christ* (1 Cor 15:22). He said this because, as no one comes to death save through Adam, so no one rises to life save through Christ. You are a fellow who has nothing to say; could you at least be quiet?

198. JUL. After this he adds that sin reigned up to the law, showing that the reign of sin collapsed when the law was given.

AUG. If the reign of sin collapsed when the law was given, then righteousness comes through the law. *If righteousness comes through the law, then Christ has died in vain* (Gal 2:21). This is the apostle's statement, not mine. Now come out into the open, you enemies of the cross of Christ! Why are you afraid of the great people of Christ and not afraid of the great judgment of Christ? Say it openly: We could be justified by nature; we could be justified by the law; Christ has died in vain. But because you are afraid of the great number of Christians, you substitute your Pelagian expression, and when they ask you why Christ has died if nature or the law makes us righteous, you reply: So that this may be done more easily[203]—as if it could still be done, though with more difficulty, either by nature or by the law. O Christ, reply to them, defeat them, and prove them wrong; cry out, *Without me you can do nothing* (Jn 15:5), to silence those who shout:

Though with more difficulty, we could still do it without you. Or if they cannot keep silent, let them withdraw into some place of hiding so that they may not lead others astray. Why, then, does the apostle say, *For up to the law sin was in the world* (Rom 5:13), if not because even the law which God gave could not take away sin, but only the one of whom scripture said, *There is the lamb of God; there is the one who takes away the sin of the world* (Jn 1:29)?

199. JUL. But generation, which began with Adam, remains even after the law; if it were the source of sins and the fruit tree of the devil, as you argue,[204] this grave sin would flourish not only up to the law, but also after the law and after Christ. The sin, therefore, about which the apostle states that it existed up to the law and could not remain after the law, is proved to stem from action, not from birth.

AUG. (1) See, you clearly state that the apostle said, *Up to the law sin was in the world* (Rom 5:13), not because not even the law could take away sin, but because sin could not remain after the law. Have you no fear of the words of God on the lips of the man of God who pointed to Christ and said, *There is the lamb of God; there is the one who takes away the sin of the world* (Jn 1:29)? Why are you so foolish? Why are you so insane? Not nature, not the law, but *there is the one who takes away the sin of the world.* Do you even dare to say that the reign of sin collapsed when the law was given, and after the law sin could not remain? (2) But the apostle says, *If righteousness comes through the law, Christ has, then, died in vain* (Gal 2:21). The apostle says, *No one is justified by the law* (Gal 3:11). The apostle says, *The law entered in so that sin might abound* (Rom 5:20). The apostle said, *If a law were given that could give life, righteousness would surely come from the law, but scripture enclosed everything under sin so that the promise might be given to those who believe because of faith in Jesus Christ* (Gal 3:21-22). If you have ears, shut your mouths; if you want to speak correctly, first open your ears to the words of God. (3) You surely recall that you said that generation began with Adam, though you like to say that generation begins only with two and that for this reason the apostle did not want us to understand generation in the case of that sin which he said entered the world through one man. Who could believe that you have forgotten the false statement which you made so many times? Still you have forgotten it so that you at times speak the truth. Wake up; at least listen to yourself: Generation began with Adam, and for this reason the sin which entered the world through one man entered through generation. After all, you said: "But generation, which began with Adam, remains even after the law." The apostle, then, quite appropriately spoke of one man by whom there entered the world the sin which is contracted by generation rather than of the devil by whom there entered the world that sin which is followed by imitation.

Inherited Sin Could Never Have Existed

200. JUL. He says, *But sin is not imputed when the law does not exist* (Rom 5:13). By this statement, just as by everything he said, he destroyed the traducianist position.

AUG. Clearly sin is not imputed when there is no law, but it is not imputed by human beings who do not know the inscrutable judgments of God. For if God does not impute sin when there is no law, how under the justice of God can it be that *those who sinned without the law will perish without the law* (Rom 2:12).

201. JUL. If before the law the inherited sin was not imputed and after the law it did not exist, the poison never had any time at all to harm the human race. For before the law natural sin was not imputed; under the law it was not imputed, for no passage of the law anywhere teaches that it was revealed or imputed. It is clear, then, that the apostle blames a sin committed by free will before the law and a transgression likewise committed by free will after the law.

AUG. If original sin is not revealed in the law, why, then, does the law say that the soul of an infant not circumcised on the eighth day perishes from its people?[205] Why was a sacrifice for sin offered when a infant was born?[206] Now, please, be quiet; look at the infant, and imitate its silence.[207]

202. JUL. For this reason it is clear that the apostle said nothing about inherited sin, and though these words were enough to prove that the apostle had no idea of natural sin which cannot exist and which is dreamed up by the Manichees, he, nonetheless, also inculcated more than enough this distinction, namely, that not all were polluted by the transgression of Adam, since, even from among those over whom death reigned because of their iniquity, many were found who, we are taught, were unaffected by the transgression of Adam.

AUG. (1) You slanderer, you blabbermouth, the man who said, "All of us human beings are born in sin, and our very origin lies in guilt,"[208] was not a Manichee, but, as the lips of your teacher praised him, he shone forth like a beautiful flower among the Church's writers.[209] How can you say that not all were polluted by the transgression of Adam? And what is worse—you attribute to the apostle your foolish idea. Though he says, *Death reigned from Adam up to Moses even over those who did not sin*, where he wants us to understand the little ones who committed no personal sins, he also adds, *in the likeness of the transgression of Adam* (Rom 5:14), to show why death reigned over them—a point we dealt with sufficiently above. (2) For how is it that *through one man sin entered the world, and through sin death* (Rom 5:12), if death, nonetheless, has reigned over some who do not share in this sin of the one man? For those over whom death reigned share in that sin through which it entered. But how can those who do not share in the sin through which death entered the world share in death by a just sentence? Those who did not sin in the likeness of the transgression of Adam have no share in the sin which entered the world through one man, as you yourself said. Death, therefore, has not reigned over them. (3) What, then, does it mean: *Death reigned even over those who did not sin in the likeness of the transgression of Adam* (Rom 5:14), but that death reigned even over those who did not sin because they committed no personal sins? It reigned, however, in the likeness of the transgression of Adam because, though they committed no personal sins, they still had a share in that sin through which death entered the world, for they contracted the likeness of the transgression, not by committing a transgression by a sin of their own, but by being born of the transgressor by whom the whole of human nature was corrupted.

203. JUL. See, then, whether even you still ought to doubt what we say, namely, that the innocents, that is, before they had the use of their own will, a work fresh from God's hands, did not sin in Adam since by the testimony of the apostle we are taught that there are very many sinners who did not sin in the likeness of the transgression of Adam.

AUG. I have already replied to this. You need to shut up, for you can only utter twisted ideas when you try to distort the words of the apostle. He, after all, said that death, nonetheless, reigned even over those who did not sin, that is, over the little ones who do not have sins of their own, in the likeness of the transgression of Adam who is the pattern of the one to come. For Christ brought them righteousness just as Adam brought them sin. Christ brought them life, just as Adam brought them death. Otherwise, they will be apart from the pattern of Christ and will not be Christians. You, of course, think this, but you are afraid to say it openly.

204. JUL. Let us, however, look at the rest. *But grace was not like the sin, for if many have died in the sin of the one, much more has the grace of God and the gift in the grace of the one man Jesus Christ abounded for more* (Rom 5:15). He says that the evil of sin is surpassed by the abundance of grace and makes the number of those who are saved higher than that of those who he says have perished by transgression.

AUG. We have already said many times: He does not say, "More," but *Many*.[210] And he does not say, "Many more," but *Abounded more*, because those into whom the life of Christ passes will live eternally, while the death passed on to them from Adam harmed them only for a time. There you see how grace abounded for them much more than sin.

205. JUL. If you claim for yourself the truth of the apostle's words and do not impudently suppose that he lied, explain to me how this statement does not impose on him the shame of an open lie if he speaks about natural sin. For if there were an original sin which made absolutely all of human nature to belong to the dominion of the devil, what room was there to equalize the number of the two groups, that is, of those who are saved and those who perish? When in the gospel the Lord disclosed the small number of the blessed, he said, *How straight and*

narrow is the way which leads to life, and there are few who find it! How wide and roomy is the way which leads to destruction, and there are many who enter upon it! (Mt 7:14.13).

AUG. (1) This is a point by which your ideas are overthrown for those who are saved are few in comparison with those who perish. Yet, apart from comparison with them they are by themselves many. The Book of Revelation, in fact, says that no one can count the great number of them.[211] Hence, if Paul had not said that they were "many," but "more," we could not say that they are fewer. "More" is a term of comparison, and the apostle did not use the word that you falsely attribute to him. But not even in this way will your calculation work out. You suppose that you have so cleverly devised that imitation of yours in opposition to the perfectly clear truth of the apostle's words so that all sinners are supposed to have a share in the sin of the first man, not through generation, but through imitation. That imitation claims that many more perish by the sin of the one or on account of the sin of the one than are set free by the grace of the one man, Jesus Christ. (2) Who, after all, can fail to see that there are more sinners than righteous persons? And you say that not some sinners, but all sinners have a share in the sin of the one man, not through generation, but through imitation. But even if you say that not all sinners, but only the transgressors of the law are linked to the sin of the first man by the chain of imitation, even so, from the time that the law of God is preached among many nations, *How wide and roomy is the way which leads to destruction, and there are many* transgressors *who enter upon it! How straight and narrow is the way which leads to life, and there are few who find it* (Mt 7:13-14), in comparison, of course, with the great number who perish, even if the little ones who die after being baptized are added to the few who are set free. (3) How, then, could the apostle say: The grace of God has abounded much more for more? He did not say what you say; rather, he said, *It has abounded much more for many*. For, even if those who are saved, as we said, are few in comparison with those who perish, they are, however, apart from comparison with them, so many that no one can count them.[212] Grace, however, abounds much more for them, because they live for a time in misery and mortality on account of Adam, but they will live in blessedness without end on account of Christ. Your invention has been overturned; let your intention at long last be corrected.

The Superiority of Grace over Sin

206. JUL. The expressions we use, namely, "many" and "few," refer to an indefinite quantity, since in comparing them with each other we find either a great or a small number. And so, when the Lord compared those who are going to be saved with the great number of those who are perishing, he called them "few."

And here, when the apostle compares those saved by the grace of Christ with these who sinned as Adam did, he says that the saved are many more.

AUG. He does not say "more," but "many." He wrote in Greek, and he used the word, πολλοὺς, not πλείστους. Read it, and shut up.

207. JUL. Claim, then, that this fits with the sin of the Manichees, that is, with inherited sin.

AUG. Catholic teachers, not Manichean deceivers, said that all sinned in Adam; those who understood the apostle said this, and you deny it in opposition to the apostle. You, then, are the deceivers, and you, like the Manichees, are sick, though with a different disease.

208. JUL. For if natural sin handed over the whole of what human fecundity has produced to the kingdom of the devil, and if in the last age of the world some are thought to have been set free from it by Christ, what truth or what authority does that teacher have? For he says contrary to such clear testimony of the whole world that righteousness abounded for more than the sin did. Why, then, is he believed when he speaks on complicated points of doctrine if he lies about matters so obvious? Since to think this is sacrilege, though your teaching forces you to say it, may the vileness of the Manichees be crushed by the dignity of the apostle!

AUG. It is you rather who strive to obscure the obvious. You not only do not understand what the apostle said, but you also change it and bring in what he did not say. After all, he did not say, "more," but "many." Those many, nonetheless, are found to be few when they are compared with those who are perishing. You slanderer, you impudent fellow, you blabbermouth, the apostle said the same thing that Ambrose understood, and Ambrose was not a Manichee. He said, "All of us human beings are born under the power of sin, and our origin lies in guilt."[213] Listen to him; your teacher praised him like a beautiful flower. Pluck out from your heart this thorny ugliness, that is, the foul barbs of your evil arguments.

209. JUL. The apostle does not lie; therefore, the grace of Christ has abounded for more than has the sin of Adam, in the imitation of which those who sinned under the law are said to have sinned. Under the law, however, up to Christ only the Jews sinned. The Jewish people were alone made subject to the law, at least at an adult age, and for this reason they sinned in the likeness of the transgression of Adam who sinned after receiving the law. Compare the Jewish people with the thousands from the great number of those peoples who were called by the preaching of the gospel and who are saved by the generosity of grace. Then you will understand that the apostle Paul spoke the truth, namely, that the grace of God and the gift of Jesus Christ has affected more people than the participation in the ancient sin.

AUG. (1) Since the apostle is found to have said not "more," but "many," the whole structure of this argument of yours is brought down, though not only the

Jews, as you would have it, but all are found to be transgressors, and by transgressing the law that was preached with the gospel they become more deserving of condemnation. The world is full of such transgressors along with the Jews so that in comparison with all of them there are few who are set free, even with the addition of the baptized little ones. And I included this in my previous answer. The teacher of the nations clearly cries out against you: *As in Adam all die, so in Christ all will be brought to life* (1 Cor 15:22), and all of them are not few, but many. (2) And for this reason many die in Adam, and many will be brought to life in Christ, but more die in Adam than are brought to life in Christ. More, then, share in the death of Adam, while fewer in comparison with these share in the life of Christ. But by themselves there is a great number of them which no one can count.[214] What, then, does, *All will be brought to life in Christ*, mean but that no one will be brought to life except in him? I gave as an example of this a teacher of literature: If there is only one in a city, all are said to learn from him, not because all learn literature, but because no one learns except from him.[215] You did not even attempt to refute that manner of speaking because you see that it is perfectly correct and known to everyone.

Through One Sinner or through One Sin

210. JUL. Having explained the generosity of grace in the abundance of human beings who are saved, he compares the gift and the sin, and in a most learned manner he turns to the praise of the gift the fact that it cures many wounds by its one power. He says, *And not as through one sin, so was the gift* (Rom 5:16).

AUG. He said, *Through one sinner*, not: "Through one sin." Hence, his next words, *After the one sin there came judgment leading to condemnation* (Rom 5:16), can only be understood to refer to the sin of that one sinner.[216] And that, of course, is something you do not want. But what are you going to do since the apostle said it, even if you do not like it? Correct your view, then, for you have nothing else at this point that you ought to do.

211. JUL. *For after the one there came judgment leading to condemnation, but after many sins there came grace leading to justification* (Rom 5:16). That is, even single sins which are serious can be sufficient to bring accusation and condemnation.

AUG. Why did you say, "serious," a word the apostle did not use, except that you saw that, if the one sin were slight, it would not be sufficient to bring the condemnation he spoke of? This judgment, then, does not result from just any one sin of anyone at all, but from that one sin which was committed by the one sinner, namely, Adam, there came judgment leading to condemnation. Do you still want to distort the correct words of the apostle instead of correcting your own words which are quite mistaken?

212. JUL. Grace, however, is not bestowed in the same way so that it is applied equally to each and every sin and is frequently repeated; rather, it is poured out once and wipes out different serious sins, though they are many, in one surge that sums up its power. For this reason he says, *After many sins leading to justification* (Rom 5:16). That is, it brings human beings who have been set free from many sins to the glory of the justification granted them. He does not, then, mean the one sin of Adam, as you suppose, but adds the numbers "one" and "many" only that they may redound to the praise of grace. For grace is not bestowed as often as sin is committed by any mortal, as if individual baptisms could remedy only individual sins.

AUG. (1) You speak as though the apostle said: But after many sins grace came once leading to justification. He did not say this. Notice what he said, and correct what you said. He says, *After many sins there came grace leading to justification* (Rom 5:16). Why is it relevant here that in baptism all sins are forgiven each person at one and the same time? Does not also that condemnation to which the last judgment leads undoubtedly occur once for all the sins which were not forgiven? And it is more correct that this condemnation takes place once than that the forgiveness of sins through the grace of Christ takes place once, since, if anyone sins after baptism, they are not the same sins, but they are forgiven for the sinners by the same grace, not once, nor seven times, but seventy times seven times.[217] (2) The same grace daily forgives even daily sins of those who pray when they say, *Forgive us our debts*, and sincerely add, *as we also forgive our debtors* (Mt 6:12). After many sins, then, grace brings to justification those[218] it sets free from condemnation, whether it finds just one sin in certain persons or a few in some or very many in others; it does not matter whether they are committed before baptism or are committed afterwards and are healed by doing penance, by prayer, and by almsgiving. All these sins, after all, are many, and grace brings justification after these many. But if grace does not come to the rescue, a person has to face condemnation even after the one sin—not a personal sin that each one commits, for the apostle was not talking about that in this passage, but that sin which entered the world through the one sinner. The apostle, after all, stated this most clearly. For he does not say as you do: "Not as through one sin," as if he wanted us to understand the individual sin of each person. Rather, he said, *Not as through one sinner* (Rom 5:16). Open your eyes, and read, and do not try to substitute one word for another, as if we were blind.

213. JUL. But he was careful to express this. He says: Though individual sins had fatally wounded those guilty of them, by its single power that was conferred once, this grace saved those who were stabbed countless times.

AUG. He said, *Through one sinner* (Rom 5:16), where Adam is understood; he did not say, "Through one sin," where by changing the word and replacing it with a different one, you want us to understand the individual sins of individual people.

Death's Reign through the One

214. JUL. *For if on account of the sin of the one, death reigned through the one, how much more will those who receive the abundance of grace and the gift of righteousness reign in life through the one Jesus Christ* (Rom 5:17). He logically supports what he began to say. For he set forth two sentences and wanted what he added at the end to fit with each of them. He states that death reigns through the one who was the pattern of sin and in whose likeness sinners under the law transgressed and that any who attained the abundance of grace reign in life through the one, since that grace benefits those who imitate virtue. There remained, then, no question about the one, since what was added, namely, that they reign in life who receive the abundance of grace, also explains that first point, namely, that none are forced into death unless they are very fond of the example of the sinner.

AUG. (1) Who was the sinner of whose example they are very fond? The first man, of course. You, after all, say that he is the pattern of sin on account of imitation, not on account of generation. You say, "None are forced into death unless they are very fond of the example of this sinner." Hence, those who did not sin, as you suppose, in the likeness of his transgression are not forced into death. How, then, can you say that death reigned even over those who surely sinned through free choice, but did not sin in the likeness of the transgression of Adam since they sinned without the law? They did not, therefore, sin because of his example since those who do not sin in the likeness of his transgression were not very fond of his example. They are, after all, as far removed from the imitation of this example as they are from this likeness of this sinner. Since death did, therefore, reign even over them, why is it that you say, "None are forced into death unless they are very fond of the example of the sinner," that is, of the one whom you want to have been the pattern of sin on account of imitation? (2) Look, those who did not sin in the likeness of his transgression were not fond of the example of the sinner, and yet death reigned even over them. Or do you want to return to the Catholic truth and admit that death reigned even over those who did not sin by committing personal sins, but who came, as if by an inheritance of misery, under death's reign over the likeness of the transgression of that one from whose line they were born? That was how the teachers of the Church understood the words of the apostle; they saw that they could not be correctly understood unless one understood in them the origin of sin for the guilty generations to come. On this account they said that the little ones born in the flesh after Adam contracted the infection of the ancient death by their first birth[219]—and they were not

Manichees! But they condemned you Pelagians by the Spirit of God who spoke through them.

215. JUL. (1) The life, however, in which the saints are going to reign, is shown to be eternal. Hence, the death which follows upon voluntary sin should also be believed to be eternal. *Therefore, as through the sin of the one all human beings enter into condemnation, so through the righteousness of the one all human beings come to the righteousness of life. For as through the disobedience of the one many were made sinners, so through the obedience of the one many will be made righteous* (Rom 5:18-19). The whole confusion is removed. You impudently stir up a lie about everyone; you most foolishly look for difficulties where none exist.[220] (2) The apostle states that it was not all, but many who learned to sin through the disobedience of the first man and that it is many, not all, who acquired righteousness through the obedience of the second. He says nothing here about the beginning of humanity; he points out human behavior in its different pursuits. By the words "disobedience" and "obedience" he points out the result of these pursuits, not of generation. Surely, if the apostle agreed with you on some point, where more fittingly than in this passage where he was going to sum up the whole of the discussion would he state that all enter into condemnation by being born, but that a few enter into life by believing? He ought, after all, to have said: "As through the disobedience of one man all were made sinners"—or rather: "Not through the disobedience," but: "As through the generation from the first man all were born sinners, so through the obedience of the one righteous man many will be made righteous."

AUG. (1) On the contrary, he ought to have said: "As through their own disobedience many were made sinners, so through their own obedience many will be made righteous." Or if he wanted to teach the imitation which you think you have discovered as a means of escape, after you have been put into such difficulties and have been trapped by the truth which pursues you, he ought to have said: "As through the imitation of the disobedience of one man many were made sinners, so through the imitation of the obedience of the one man many will be made righteous." See, I too have spoken as the apostle ought to have spoken if he wanted to say what you say. Do not think that it is a big achievement to frame words in accord with our own intention rather than to explain what the author intended by his own words. (2) He said, therefore, that through the disobedience of the one man whom he knew to be the source of generation many were made sinners because that disobedience corrupted human nature, and he said that through the obedience of the one man who is the source of rebirth many are made righteous because his obedience heals human nature. For he became obedient even to the death of the cross[221] so that his grace might make righteous even those who could not here be righteous through their own conduct, such as those who pass away immediately after the bath of rebirth, whether at an older age or at that of an infant. (3) For this reason he preferred to put the verb in the future tense and say:

will be made, not: have been made, because with that righteousness which will be without any sin the righteous will live in the eternity of the world to come. But when he spoke of sinners, he did not say: will be made, but: *were made*, using the verb in the past tense to express this world which is passing away, in which human nature was already corrupted. With regard to the many I have already replied to you sufficiently that they are all, but you could only explain those whom the apostle said were all by contradicting him, explaining and saying: They are not all.[222] No necessity would drive you to that, if you had preferred to hold the Catholic rather than the Pelagian view. All are also said to be many in order to distinguish them from those who, though they are all, are nonetheless few.

An Appropriate or Inappropriate Comparison

216. JUL. But if he had advanced this idea, he was teaching a view no less wicked than silly. By it he would have presented a very stupid comparison in the light of the different cases of these persons, since things that are unlike, namely, nature and the will, were brought into the comparison. For in that way the necessity of the seeds was located on the evil side, while on the side of the good there was only the freedom of action. In fact, there was no longer freedom, since the ability to choose good and to avoid evil was not present if there was natural guilt. The apostle, therefore, a wise and learned teacher of the Church, says that through disobedience sin came to be and was passed on and that through obedience justice is being increased.[223]

AUG. (1) Where is your claim that not sin, but death was passed on? Look, you now say that through the disobedience of the one man, as was mentioned, sin not only came to be, but was passed on. Have you perhaps forgotten what you previously said? You should be grateful for your forgetfulness which forces you to speak the truth. For you thought that in comparing opposites one should not put on the one side the necessity of the seed and on the other side the activity of the will. You would find this to be stupid if you saw that in that way those on the bad side who belong to the first man contracted the infection of sin by the bonds of generation without the activity of their will, just as those little ones who belong to the second man become partakers of righteousness through the peace of rebirth without any activity of their own will. (2) If, however, you insist upon seed on both sides, just as through Adam the carnal seed was corrupted, so the spiritual seed is healthy through Christ. The apostle John meant this seed where he says, *And they cannot sin because his seed remains in them* (1 Jn 3:9). This will be seen, rather, in the good world to come where those in that world will not be able to sin, not in this evil world where even these who belong to the world that will be without sins have reason daily to ask pardon for their sins from the Father.

217. JUL. In this way he destroys the idea of natural sin and teaches that the causes of the substance are other than the causes of the will. And so that this interpretation is not attributed to our mind rather than to the teaching of the apostle, let us listen to what he added to this passage: *The law entered in,* he says, *so that the sin might abound. But where sin abounded, grace was even more abundant so that, as sin reigned for death, grace might reign through righteousness for eternal life through Jesus Christ our Lord* (Rom 5:20-21). Show us, then, how your sin, that is, inherited sin, began to abound after the law; show us what increases that sin received after the ministry of Moses.

AUG. (1) Rather, show us how, as you put it above,[224] the reign of sin collapsed when the law was given, though the apostle says that sin abounded when the law was given. I, however, state what I said because it is obvious even if I do not state it. Original sin, of course, existed even before the law, because *through one man sin entered the world, and* with it *death was passed on to all human beings* (Rom 5:12); there was also voluntary sin, because *those who sinned without the law will perish without the law* (Rom 2:12). *But the law entered in so that sin might abound* (Rom 5:20), because to these kinds of sins which existed before the law there was added also that sin which is called transgression. *For where there is no law, there is also no transgression* (Rom 4:15). (2) Where because of all these kinds of sins *sin abounded, grace was even more abundant* (Rom 5:20). For in those who share in it grace wipes out the guilt of all these kinds and also grants to us that our delight in sin is conquered by our delight in righteousness and that we later come to that life where there will be no sin at all. Why, then, should things which are unlike not be brought together in comparison, as you said a little before, since this comparison is based on opposites? On one side there is birth, on the other rebirth; on one side the reign of death, on the other the reign of life; on the one side an abundance of sins, on the other the forgiveness of sins. On the one side there is delight in sin coming from a defect of nature and leading to habitual sin; on the other a battle against the concupiscence of the flesh through the help of the Holy Spirit that leads to the peace of victory which endures no enemy within or without. Hold on to these points if you want to be healthy, and do not rage against these ideas which are a part of sound doctrine.

218. JUL. You, of course, maintain that the apostle discussed natural sin in these passages. Above he had said that this[225] sin existed up to the law so that we would understand that it ceased to exist after the law. But now he says of that same sin that it began to increase and abound after the law. We have shown that both of these statements are compatible with the Catholic interpretation we follow. But with what impudence do you claim for your teaching that one and the same sin is said earlier to have ceased when the law was given, but is now said to have increased? How, then, did natural sin abound after the law? Did the genitals begin to be aroused more passionately so that power seemed to be added to your

sin by the new increase of their movements? Or was the law given to the new-born to warn those who were born from sexual desire that they should improve upon how they were made and correct the act which their parents performed when they begot them? After all, you say this desire is diabolical and the root and the fruit of sin. Did the law finally warn them that they should render undone what had been done so that, when they refused to obey, they would incur the serious sin of disobedience? No fool could give this command, not to mention the law which God gave.

AUG. (1) Did we say somewhere that original sin increased after the law? Or do we want you to understand this in the words of the apostle, *The law entered in so that sin might abound* (Rom 5:20)? For it abounded, not because that kind of sin increased which already existed previously, but because there was added to it another kind of sin which did not exist without the law, that is, transgression, as we showed a little before. But there is the concupiscence of the flesh and the passion of the sexual organs which the chastity of the saints fights against. This concupiscence pleases you much along with the fight it causes, though even marital chastity fights back against it, making good use of it only for procreating children, but opposing its other movements. When you try to admit or introduce it along with the fight it causes into the peace of paradise, you yourself arrange not to enter paradise. (2) No matter how much it is protected by your defense and adorned with your praise, it is either a defect, or it has been corrupted, and it is rightly hateful to the soldiers of Christ who subdue it in battle. You yourself play along with it so that you say that you fight against it and are not ashamed to praise it. Human flesh that is born through it is sinful flesh; on this account he willed not to be born through it who was born in the likeness of sinful flesh[226] and, for this reason, was not born in sinful flesh, though in true flesh. From this concupiscence, your darling, far too fair in your eyes, but ugly in the eyes of all the saints, the bond of original sin is contracted by birth to be removed only by rebirth. The former was the work of Adam; the latter is the work of Christ. The former is the work of him through whom sin entered the world; the latter is the work of him who takes away the sin of the world.[227] One who passes over from Adam to Christ has this understanding of Adam and Christ.

219. JUL. What, then, was added to natural sin after the law? In the law it is shown not only not to have been forbidden or condemned, but not even to have been mildly reproached or slightly revealed.

AUG. It is revealed even in the law, but only if the veil is removed for you.[228] After all, what else is revealed by the damnation of the soul of that infant who is not circumcised on the eighth day?[229] What else is revealed when the offering of a sacrifice for sin is prescribed when an infant is born,[230] as I already mentioned above?

God's Plan in Giving the Law

220. JUL. (1) Surely not even you are so foolish as to say that the inherited sin became greater after circumcision. How, then, did it abound after the law since it is neither blamed nor revealed in the law? But see how the following conforms to a sane interpretation which locates sin only in the will of the sinner. The apostle says that sin existed up to the law[231] so that we would understand that transgression existed after the law, that is, violating the commandments that were promulgated. Sin of this kind abounded when the law entered in, because transgression made its guilt more odious, and just as prior to the law the act of an evil will was a sin, so after the law it began to be a transgression. And yet, God did not give the law with the intention that mortals should become worse because of its sanction. (2) The law, after all, is neither sin nor the cause of sin; rather, *the commandment is holy and just and good* (Rom 7:12). But the wickedness of sinners wounded itself with the knife by which it ought to have been cured, and it opposed the plan of God so that it was endangered by that which ought to have healed it. And so, the apostle said that the idea behind God's plan in giving the law suffered injury from the way things turned out. Because there was not the result of human conversion which the lawgiver intended, but just the opposite came about in very many cases, he said that the actions of sinners had gone to the point that the law seemed to have been given for no other reason than that the evil might become more evil and that transgression might be added to sin.

AUG. (1) You say these things, because you do not understand the plan of God in giving the law, the plan which the apostle Paul revealed, and you plunge into blasphemies and say that the idea behind God's plan by which he gave the law suffered injury as if something else resulted than what God thought would happen and as if what the lawgiver intended did not come about once the law was given. God who foreknows all that will be was, according to your wisdom, deceived by his own intention. Do you not heed the words of scripture, *Many are the thoughts in the human heart, but the plan of God remains for eternity* (Prv 19:21)? If, then, you wish to know, to the extent that a human being is permitted, the plan with which almighty God, who has foreknowledge of all things, gave the law, look at what the apostle says: *For if a law was given that could give life, righteousness would, of course, come from the law* (Gal 3:21). (2) And as if we said, "Why, then, was it given?" he says, *But scripture enclosed all things under the power of sin so that the promise might be given to those who believe through faith in Jesus Christ* (Gal 3:22). There you see the plan of the law which God gave. Who, however, does not know that sin abounded when the law entered in, not because of a defect in the law, but because of a defect in human beings? But this defect, by which forbidden things cause more delight and the law becomes the power of sin,[232] is healed only by the Spirit that gives life, not by the letter that kills.[233] The letter, nonetheless, was useful to this extent that, when it killed through the transgression of the letter, as the desire to sin increased because of its prohibition, it made human beings seek for the Spirit that gives life and forced those who fatally placed their trust in their own virtue[234] to demand the help of God's grace. For under the law, though it was holy and just and good,[235] they, nonetheless, were failing and unable to help themselves to do what was holy and just and good by their own powers.

221. JUL. (1) Sin is rightly said to have abounded, the kind of sin which the will of each person committed both before the law and after the law. But before the law the will committed sins; after the law it committed transgressions. Something grows and abounds when it receives increases in its kind, as after Moses a heap of transgression was added to the sin of free will. It was, after all, of the same kind, though at a different time; that is, it came from an evil will which both before the law and after the law sinned, not because of insuperable coercion, but by blameworthy action. (2) Since this is the case, nothing from the words of the apostle can be in agreement with you, for he did not teach that, when the law entered in, inherited sin became either more abundant or more serious. Nor is it right to say that what is shown in no sense to pertain to the will of the newborn abounded because of sins of the will. After the law, then, there did not abound what the law could neither prevent nor punish. *But where sin abounded, there grace was even more abundant so that, as sin reigned for death, so grace might reign through righteousness for eternal life* (Rom 5:20-21).

AUG. (1) Original sin certainly did not increase after the law, but the law, nonetheless, found that sin, the removal of which the law symbolized by the circumcision of an infant. In the same way, the law found sins of ignorance which did not increase when the law was given, since ignorance was itself rather lessened because the knowledge of the law was added. But the sin without which no one is born increased with the acquisition of the will since the original concupiscence attracts the assent of the sinner. But sin abounded, that is, grew excessive, after the law produced knowledge of sin[236] and people also began to sin by transgression. (2) If you were willing to heed this and yield to the truth, you would not be compelled by any necessity openly to contradict the apostle who cries out, *Through one man sin entered the world, and through sin death, and in that way it was passed on to all human beings* (Rom 5:12). Since he says, *It was passed on to all*, what else do you do, when you say it was not passed on to all, but contradict the apostle? And if you contradict the apostle, you contradict Christ. Why, then, are you surprised that the Church of Christ detests you people who by your deadly views try to withdraw the sick little ones from the saving medicines of Christ?

Death to Sin through Baptism into Christ

222. JUL. (1) The apostle explains himself more clearly as he goes on. He teaches that at the loss of human health God was warned by the bounty of his mercy and brought forth for the desperate situation a remedy more efficacious than usual so that he obligated by his gifts those whom he had not corrected by his commandments. He demanded devotion in the future without imputing the sins which human beings already committed so that they would thereafter strive to preserve the righteousness which they had attained by the short cut of faith. The abundance of the preceding sins, then, demanded the help of such abundant mercy because, unless the generosity of God's pardon were that great, no other method would help such serious illnesses. (2) But in this praise for the divine gift the apostle saw that the way lay open for the objection of those who could say: "If we rightly judge the merits of different causes from their results, the multitude of sins has also caused God's mercy to abound; we must persist in sin so that the riches of grace do not fail." In meeting this sort of objection, then, he says, *What, then, shall we say? That we should remain in sin so that grace may abound? Heaven forbid! For how shall we who have died to sin still live in it? Or do you not know that whoever of us have been baptized in Christ Jesus have been baptized into his death? We have, then, been buried with him through baptism into death so that, as Christ rose in the glory of the Father, so we might also walk in the newness of life* (Rom 6:1-4).

AUG. (1) Do not these words of the apostle cause you to choke? For you yourselves call them to mind so that we do not forget how you are trying to undermine the firm foundations of the house of God. You madman, after the apostle said, *If we have died to sin, how shall we live in it?*, he added, *Or do you not know that whoever of us have been baptized in Christ Jesus have been baptized into his death?* in order to prove that those baptized in Christ have died to sin. Are you so deaf that you do not hear these words? So blind that you do not see them? Admit, then, that baptized little ones have died to sin; at long last admit original sin, for they had no other sin to which they might die. (2) Or state clearly that they need not be baptized or that, when they are baptized, they are not baptized in Christ Jesus or are not baptized into his death, and wipe out, if you can, the words of the apostle who says, *Whoever of us have been baptized in Christ Jesus have been baptized into his death.* But, if you cannot wipe out these words, as you cannot, then, when you hear, *whoever*, do not try to exclude the little ones; permit Christ to be Jesus also for the little ones, since he saves his people from their sins, not excluding the little ones, but including them. It was for this reason that the angel said, *You shall call his name Jesus* (Mt 1:21).

223. JUL. (1) He says that we already died to sin at that time when we professed to renounce the world and all sins in order that we might receive the gift of pardon and that we ought for this reason to live mindful of this gift so that we

may learn to be buried with Christ and to manifest his resurrection by evident holiness. And, as after he rose from the dead, he suffers no weaknesses of the body,
no scourges, so we too should strive to be invulnerable with regard to all sins and
vices. *For if we have been conformed to the likeness of his death, we shall also
share in his resurrection, knowing that our old self was nailed to the cross with
him so that the body of sin might be destroyed and so that we might no longer be
slaves to sin. For one who has died has been justified from sin* (Rom 6:5-7). (2)
The apostle binds the faithful by his clear argument. He says, If you will to become partakers of his resurrection, imitate also the power of his death in order
that you may live in virtue, having died to the vices. Then you will be sharers in
that happiness, if you have borne the image of his death by dying to sins. For our
old self has to learn to be nailed to his cross so that it may destroy the body of sin
by courage, for example, in suffering. In accord with his custom Paul called the
vices, not the substance of the flesh, the body of sin. For he continues as follows:
*So that the body of sin might be destroyed and so that we might no longer be
slaves to sin. For one who has died has been justified from sin.*

AUG. (1) However you interpret the body of sin, you will not deny that the little ones baptized in Christ Jesus have died to sin. Otherwise, you will clearly
deny that they were baptized into the death of Christ Jesus, and for this reason
you will deny that they were baptized in Christ Jesus. For *whoever of us have
been baptized in Christ Jesus have been baptized into his death* (Rom 6:3). Tell
me, then, to what sin do the little one die when they are baptized in Christ Jesus?
But you will have absolutely nothing to say unless you understand and reply
along with the whole Church of Christ: *Through one man sin entered the world,
and through sin death, and in that way it was passed on to all human beings in
whom all have sinned* (Rom 5:12). (2) There is the sin to which the little ones die
when they are baptized into the death of Christ Jesus. I beg you: *Do not be like
the horse and the mule which do not have understanding* (Ps 32:9). Listen to this:
*If we have died to sin, how shall we live in it? Or do you not know that whoever of
us have been baptized in Christ Jesus have been baptized into his death?* (Rom
6:3). Whoever of us, then, have been baptized in Christ Jesus have died to sin because we have been baptized into his death. (3) Listen to this: *Whoever of us have
been baptized,* for it is not the little ones without the grown-ups nor the
grown-ups without the little ones, but *whoever,* that is, whether little ones or
adults, *have been baptized in Christ Jesus have been baptized into his death,* and
for this reason we have died to sin. Either, then, state openly that the baptism of
Christ is not necessary for little ones, or tell me the sin of the little ones to which
they die when they are baptized in Christ, or at long last acknowledge original
sin since you can find no other.

224. JUL. The apostle was, of course, speaking with living people, and he
told them that righteousness was conferred through the sacraments. How, then,

can he say that someone who has died has been justified unless it is that he clearly shows that in this passage he calls death renunciation and that he is using the term "death" to show that believers ought to stop sinning, just as the dead stop doing anything.

AUG. You contentious fellow, if in this section of the apostle's words renunciation is called death in the sense that one who renounces sin dies to sin, recall how in the Church of Christ in which you were baptized the mysteries of baptism are celebrated, and you will find that the little ones also make a renunciation by the lips of their sponsors, just as they believe through the lips of their sponsors, though this is perhaps no longer practiced among you. For you have grown worse, yourselves going astray and leading others[237] into error so that they agree with you that a little one about to be baptized does not need to make a renunciation, because it did not contract original sin. Or if the little one must renounce sin, tell me which sin, and at last correct your error.

Christ's Death to Sin and Ours

225. JUL. *For if we have died with Christ, we believe that we shall live with Christ, knowing that Christ, having risen from the dead, dies no more; death will no longer have dominion over him. For in that he died to sin, he died once, but in that he lives, he lives for God. So too, consider yourselves dead to sin, but living for God in Christ Jesus* (Rom 6:8-11). He says: Just as Christ, who died once to sin, that is, died once on account of our sins, dies no more, but lives in the glory of God, so consider yourselves who have died to sin to live and to be dedicated only to the virtues.

AUG. (1) What an amazing explanation! The apostle says that Christ died to sin, and you say, "That is, on account of our sins." When he says, *So too, consider yourselves to have died to sin* (Rom 6:11), are we, therefore, to suppose that he is saying: Consider yourselves to have died on account of your sins? He certainly does not say this in this passage, nor do you understand it that way; rather, you admit that they died to sin so that they would not live for sin. Show me, then, that Christ too had died to sin so that the apostle did not say, *So too*, inappropriately. After all, he died for the sake of taking away our sins, but he also died to sin. But how did he do this, since he had absolutely no sin, neither original nor personal, if not because the likeness received the name of that of which it was a likeness? (2) For we know that Christ came in the likeness of sinful flesh[238] because he came in real flesh, but not like other human beings in sinful flesh. He died, then, to the likeness of sin which he bore in his mortal flesh, and he accomplished the mystery of our salvation so that we die to sin, the likeness of which he bore. We are baptized into his death because, just as true death was brought about in him, so a true forgiveness of sins is brought about in us. But the little ones are also included here: *Whoever of us*, after all, *have been baptized in Christ Jesus have been baptized into his death* (Rom 6:3). (3) For human beings are not baptized in Christ in such a way that some are baptized into his death and some are not baptized into his death. Rather, as the apostle said in whom Christ himself spoke: Whoever are baptized in Christ Jesus are baptized into his death, and for this reason whoever are baptized in Christ Jesus die to sin. If *whoever*, then the little ones are, of course, included too. But to what sin do the little ones die? At long last confess the condition of their birth so that you do not deny their rebirth. Confess the sinful flesh in the little ones so that you do not deny that the likeness of sinful flesh also died for the little ones.

226. JUL. (1) Where in this passage, then, does he accuse nature? Where does he blame the beginnings of the human substance? Where does he blame the man's arousal? It is clearer than daylight that the teacher of the nations challenges only the will to renounce its hidden and shameful ways[239] and to begin to live a better life by the correction of its actions. But let our explanation now be summed up and not continue to interpret the statements of the apostle in these passages. Let us listen to him as he discusses his thoughts. At the end of his discussion it will be clearly seen with whose teaching and faith he agrees. We, of course, say that the apostle spoke of the sin of the human will which is present in every sinner, but you say that he spoke of that sin which you believe, following Faustus, was transmitted by generation and acquired by everyone without the will. (2) Let our hostile debating, then, cease, if you will, and let us—to be gentle with you—set aside the dignity of the apostle. For, even if his words were in harmony with you on every point, that dignity could demand that, given the splendor of his office, he held nothing so shameful and that, though there is an ambiguity in his words, there is no depravity in his thoughts. Let us grant him this point alone in the present dispute, namely, that we believe that as a man of sound mind he understood his own writings better than you. He said, *Therefore, let sin not reign in your mortal body so that you obey it* (Rom 6:12). (3) Already at this point I could say that this testimony is an exhortation which proves that he was concerned with sins of the will because, if they were natural sins, justice could defend us against them, and pity could in the end weep over them, but we could in no sense be warned to avoid them. For this evil of insanity which gripped anyone who demanded devotion in avoiding elements of our nature would be a greater evil than any natural evil, if there could be any such. But the apostle approved nothing that one could correctly blame; he, therefore, pointed out the sin of the will which he taught we ought to avoid.

AUG. (1) Who does not know that the apostle did not speak to little ones, but to those who can understand the words of a speaker and obey the commandments by the help of God's grace? But people also work with their children so that, as they acquire the use of reason, they manifest the fruits of obedience so that they did not receive the grace of God in vain,[240] when they were reborn without knowing it. That fair favorite of yours is ugly in the eyes of all who subdue her, I mean, the concupiscence of the flesh through which a human being is born and with which a human being is born. The apostle, nonetheless, commands us to hold this concupiscence in check; he does not permit it to reign and gives it the name sin because it takes it origin from the first sin, and whoever consents to its desires for what is forbidden commits sin. It will not exist in us when we shall have an immortal body. And so, since he could have said, *Let not sin reign in your body*, why did he add a word and say, *In your mortal body* (Rom 6:12), if it were not that we should hope that this concupiscence which he calls sin will not exist when we will not have a mortal body? (2) Tell us, then, why he did not say: Let sin not exist *in your mortal body*, but said, *Let sin not reign*, if it was not that this concupiscence, which cannot fail to exist in mortal flesh, reigns in those who consent to its desires to commit sins. And if they are conquered by it, they are dragged off wherever it pulls them by a mightier force than they are held back by the law, if they are not helped by grace. But in those who by God's gift do what he has commanded, that is, who do not obey it when it is aroused and insistent, and do not offer their members to it as weapons,[241] it is indeed present, but it does not reign. Its existence is proved when they desire to commit sins, and it is proved not to reign when they do not commit them because the delight of righteousness wins out. How can we be commanded not to obey it, unless it gives orders and tries to persuade us? But how can it do this if it is not present in us?

227. JUL. *And do not offer your members to sin as weapons of iniquity, but offer yourselves to God, as having come back to life from the dead, and offer your members to God as weapons of righteousness. For sin does not have dominion over you; you are, after all, not under the law, but under grace* (Rom 6:13-14). You ought, he says, to serve God more faithfully to the extent that you do so more freely. Sin did, of course, have dominion over you when vengeance for your guilt hovered over you.[242] But having obtained the benefits of the grace of God and caught your breath, after laying aside the burdens of guilt, you ought, now that you have been warned by a natural sense of decency, to express your gratitude to your healer.

AUG. In your usual manner which stems from your error, you do not acknowledge grace except in the forgiveness of sins so that afterward human beings themselves make themselves righteous through free choice. But the Church does not say this; the whole Church cries out what she learned from the good teacher: *Bring us not into temptation* (Mt 6:13). The apostle does not say this; he says, *We pray to God that you do nothing evil* (2 Cor 13:7). Christ does not say this; he says, *I have prayed for you, Peter, that your faith may not fail* (Lk 22:32). In this sense, then, grace makes us not to sin and does not wipe away the sins we have committed. Grace helps us in both ways: both by forgiving what we have done wrong and by helping us to turn away from evil and to do good.

How We Were Once Children of Anger

228. JUL. But here there arose an occasion for the same question which he had explained before. That is, the objection might be raised that those who were set free from the law which led to anger could sin in security under the goodness of God's grace. And so, he added immediately, *What then? Shall we sin because we are not under the law, but under grace? Heaven forbid! Do you not know that, if you offer yourselves as slaves to anyone in obedience, you are slaves of that one whom you obeyed, either it is of sin or of the obedience leading to righteousness?* (Rom 6:15-16). Are we going to believe him now concerning the nature of sin about which he has spoken so far? He says, *If you offer yourselves as slaves to anyone in obedience, you are slaves of that one, whether it is of sin or of righteousness.* Where, then, does the apostle refer to that sin which you imagine hovered over the seeds before the will existed, before the actions of the obedient, before the age of knowledge and conscience? That certainly cannot be found except in the books of the Manichees.

AUG. They are not the books of the Manichees where we read, *For we too were by nature children of anger, just as the rest* (Eph 2:3), a text which you translate from the Greek in a new way and with impudent lips so that the apostle seems not to have said: *by nature,* but: "of course."[243] That is, "We were, of course, children of anger." And perhaps you will dare to make this correction in your manuscripts, for you do not want to accept that all the Latin manuscripts would not have this reading, if the reliability of this reading were not greater in proportion to its antiquity. Nor should the apostle not have admonished us to be obedient to righteousness and not to sin on the grounds that all of us human beings are born under the power of sin and our origin lies in guilt.[244] For when the guilt from our birth is removed by the pardon of our rebirth, we ought to obey the Spirit of righteousness to which we ought to assent, and we ought not to obey the concupiscence of the flesh against which we ought to fight. We ought to do this, of course, so that we bear in mind that this faithful obedience is itself the gift of God which he promised through the prophet when he said, *I will give them a heart for knowing me and ears that hear* (Jer 24:7). What else is this but ears that are obedient?[245]

229. JUL. But if the apostle, nonetheless, obtains from people some credence at this time, he shows that he calls only those people slaves of sin who have clearly been obedient to sin by their own will. And by a change of it, that is, of the will, they began to serve righteousness. He, therefore, put obedience in the middle and attributed to it the fact that they were eager to obey the vices formerly or to obey the virtues afterwards.

AUG. *Those who place their trust in their own virtue* (Ps 49:7) are vain just like you, and they will be destroyed just like you.

230. JUL. *Thanks be to God that you were slaves of sin, but have become obedient from the heart to that standard of teaching to which you were introduced. Having been set free from sin, you have become slaves to justice* (Rom 6:17-18).

AUG. Are you deaf? Listen to the apostle giving thanks to God because they obeyed his teaching from the heart. He did not say, *Thanks be to God*, because his teaching has been preached to you, but *because you have obeyed. For not all obey the gospel* (Rom 10:16), but only those to whom it has been given that they obey. In the same way, the Lord said, *To know the mysteries of the kingdom of God has been given to you, but it has not been given to those others* (Mt 13:11).[246] They would not, then, have obeyed from the heart, that is, from the will, if the will were not prepared by the Lord.[247] Otherwise, if the Lord did not do this, the apostle's giving thanks to him for this would be a lie.

231. JUL. A change in obedience, he says, that was made from the heart set you free from sin and made you cling to holiness.

AUG. But this change comes from the right hand of the Most High. Listen to the man of God confessing this grace in the psalm, and learn who changes the will of a human being for the better. He says, *And I said, Now I have begun; this change comes from the right hand of the Most High* (Ps 77:11).

The Humanity of the Apostle's Command

232. JUL. *What I say is quite human on account of the weakness of your flesh. For, just as you offered your members to serve uncleanness and iniquity for greater iniquity, so now offer your members to serve righteousness for sanctification* (Rom 6:19). O teacher filled with the Spirit of God, truly golden vessel and trumpet sounding not with shrill notes, but with pure sounds! He wins authority for his words by the humanity of his exhortation.

AUG. O deceiver filled with an heretical spirit, attributing everything to the will of a human being in opposition to the one who says, *What do you have that you have not received?* (1 Cor 4:7). You Pelagian, the apostle said these things as one who plants and waters. But he knew that *neither the one who plants nor the one who waters is anything important, but God who gives the increase* (1 Cor 3:7). He did not merely give commands, but he also prayed to God that those to whom he preached God's words would not do evil. Elsewhere he clearly says, *But we pray to God that you do nothing evil* (2 Cor 13:7).

233. JUL. So that he would not seem to command anything arduous or unattainable for human beings, he used an expression to evoke confidence, and said, *human*, that is, something that is easy, doable, and that becomes easier by a comparison of the two ways of acting. He says: I do not ask from you an effort that is equal to the highest aims of virtue. And in order that you might attain the virtues I do not give commandments that are as new to you as the power of the virtues is

great. I order nothing harsh; I enjoin nothing that can scarcely be borne for fear that, if I should command something of the sort on behalf of the splendor of righteousness, you would complain about the weakness of the flesh and claim that you cannot endure the constant struggle. Now, then, I confront you with this moderate demand that you show the same sort of eagerness for the virtues which you previously gave to your sins. And though it is an injury to moral goodness if it is sought with the same sort of devotion that was spent on moral evil, it is, nonetheless, sufficient for this discipline in which you find yourself, if you pursue righteousness with at least the same intensity with which you pursued iniquity and uncleanness.

AUG. They will not, nonetheless, do this unless they fight against that fair favorite of yours, the concupiscence of the flesh, with the strength of love. Every human being is born with that law of the members that resists the law of the mind,[248] and all are held guilty[249] by its bondage if they are not reborn. Mortals do not conquer it by their own spirit unless they are driven by the Spirit of God: *For whoever are driven by the Spirit of God are the children of God* (Rom 8:14). Go ahead now, and plunge headlong by extolling free choice in opposition to this Christian and apostolic truth, and put your trust in your own virtue,[250] not so that you rise up, but so that you fall down.

234. JUL. Let us, therefore, believe the teacher of the nations, and let us repay him with our testimony to his truth. For, as he said, what he commands is truly human, namely, that the correction of the will should remove the vices of the will.

AUG. But this human correction only takes place with the help of God. After all, who corrects the will of a human being but the one to whom we say, *God of virtues, convert us* (Ps 80:8) and *You, O God, will convert us and give us life* (Ps 85:7). *For the Lord directs the steps of human beings, and they will choose his ways* (Ps 37:23). But if he does not direct them, human beings will not choose the way of God, even if the law orders them to choose it.

235. JUL. But as this was human, so that other idea, if he had thought it, was not only inhuman, not only harsh, but also unjust, and not only unjust, but also insane. I mean the idea that, if he knew that sin was innate, he should blame human beings of his era for the defects of that ancient birth, that he should command that they should hold back from what he believed was inborn, and that he should with a threat prescribe that I must lay aside those things which I began to have before the soul entered my body and my body entered this world.

AUG. Is concupiscence of the flesh, then, not inborn, or does he not command that we hold back from it who says, *Hold yourself in check* (Sir 30:24) and *Flee the desires of youth* (2 Tm 2:22)?[251] Why did he not say: Flee the desires of the will? Youth is the name of an age, but ages belong to a nature, not to the will, and that concupiscence begins to burn especially from the age of youth. Its power is, of course, dormant in an infant, just like reason, just like the will. But the eye of a Christian, not of a Pelagian, distinguishes what nature takes from the work of the creator and what it contracts from the contamination of sin. Nature praises the creator for the good it has, and it needs that same one as savior on account of the evil by which it was corrupted. For with regard to the guilt with which human beings are born they receive no commandment except to be reborn.

Final Summations and the End of the Book

236. JUL. (1) The apostle would most correctly be admonished by those whom he wanted to correct that he should consider how much he commands and should know that the first step of a good counsel is to be moderate in commanding. A teaching, of course, loses all authority if justice cannot defend it, and that teaching has full authority which the scale of justice commends. For this reason it is clear that the apostle, the venerable instructor of the churches, when giving an account of his role as teacher with his reasonable counsel, justice, and humanity, had no idea of natural sin, but taught, as was really the case, that we were slaves to our vices only through our will and that we can by the same will serve the cause of righteousness, if our will is corrected. (2) In the explanation of this passage I was up to now concerned to show that the Manichees cannot be defended in any way by the words of the apostle Paul. And the truth is clearly seen from the tenor of his language which he maintains through the whole corpus of his writings. Let this, then, be the end of the second book. At this point we must warn that nothing is left for the traducianists except impudence. For, since they admitted that they have no defense in reason, they drew their whole comfort from the words of the apostle which we have explained. Since it has become clear that he prescribed in these words nothing morally offensive, nothing incompatible with holiness and reason, it is evident that their position has collapsed. For both reason along with many authorities of the scriptures and the religion of the Catholics which is rooted in God has knocked it down, and now the content of this passage offers it no defense.

AUG. (1) It is evident to all who read these words with a sound mind and understanding that, although you spoke many words of your own in opposition to words that were no more mine than those of the blessed apostle, you had found nothing to say, and that by the rambling roar of your ranting you made those who do not understand think that you said something. Whether you like it or not, *Through one man sin entered the world, and through sin death, and in that way it was passed on to all human beings* (Rom 5:12). What does *in that way* mean but: through sin, not without sin? For death would not be passed on if sin did not lead the way; after all, death follows after and does not precede sin. (2) From it stem all the miseries of mortals *from the day they emerge from their mother's womb* (Sir 40:1), as scripture says. When you say that these miseries happen to the little ones without any sin, you really make God unjust, but you also help the Manichees in a horrible fashion. To avoid making God unjust, the Manichees attribute these miseries which are present from the time mortals are born to the immutable nature of evil and to the substance of darkness that comes from the other principle. The Catholic faith defeats those wicked people along with you because it attributes all these miseries to that sin which entered the world because of the will of the first human being. This death which puts the soul to flight and kills the body also followed upon that sin, though you say that it would have naturally come upon human beings even if Adam did not sin. (3) From this it follows that you say that there would have existed in paradise not only this imperious sexual desire in which you find so much delight, but also the worst of fevers and countless other diseases by which we see that little ones are afflicted and die, even if no one had sinned. For you say that little ones suffer these evils without any guilt of sin. Restrain yourselves, I beg you, with your false and harmful praises; hold yourselves back from the infants and nurslings whom you praise by your cruel error, as if they had no sin. Allow the little ones to come to Christ the deliverer in order to be set free; once you have been defeated and corrected, allow the second man to heal the wretched nature which the first man corrupted.

Notes

1. Ambrose, *Penance* (*De paenitentia*) I, 3, 13: SC 179, 62-64.
2. See *Answer to Julian* I, 4, 14.
3. See Mt 1:21.
4. See Cicero, *Tusculan Disputations* (*Tusculanae*) IV, 3, 7.
5. See Ps 63:2.
6. See Jn 1:12.
7. See I, 7, where Augustine cites Pelagius' praise for Ambrose.
8. Ambrose, *The Sacrament of Rebirth, or Philosophy* (*De sacramento regenerationis, sive de philosophia*). See *Answer to Julian* II, 6, 15.
9. I have conjectured "*ratione*" in place of "*oratione*."
10. See I, 1, where Augustine says that Turbantius had been freed from the Pelagian error.
11. See Ps 68:27.
12. Augustine engages in multiple plays upon the Latin verbs: *cluere*: to be esteemed and *fluere* to flow. He goes on to explain that *cluere* means the same as *pollere*: to enjoy a good reputation, but that Julian does not enjoy such a reputation, but stains with filth (*polluere*) the Catholic teachings.
13. See Sir 40:1.
14. *Marriage and Desire* was dedicated to Valerius, an influential official at the imperial court.
15. See Ambrose, *Commentary on the Gospel of Luke* (*Expositio Euangelii secundum Lucam*) 7, 141: CCL 14, 263.

16. See above I, 113.

17. See above I, 3, where Julian begins his argument from justice.

18. See above I, 28, where Julian begins his argument that without justice God cannot be God.

19. See Sir 40:1.

20. See above I, 41, where Julian begins to discuss his definition of sin.

21. See Rom 8:3. Christ's flesh is the likeness of sinful flesh, while the flesh of the descendants of Adam is sinful flesh.

22. See I, 45-48, where Julian argues that the newborn cannot have sin because they lack the use of the will.

23. Julian uses "*Poenus*" as a derogatory term; see above I, 7, where he calls Augustine "the Punic commentator." As a noun, it means a Phoenician or Carthaginian, because Carthage was founded by the Phoenicians.

24. See above I, 94, where Julian begins the Pelagian interpretation of Jesus' words, *If the Son has set you free, then you will truly be free* (Jn 8:36).

25. See above I, 126, where Julian offers his interpretation of Romans 9:21.

26. See Rom 5:12.

27. *See Ambrose, The Sacrament of Rebirth or Philosophy (Ed sacramento regenerationis, sive de philosophia)*, cited above in II,8.

28. See I, 113, where Julian cites *Marriage and Desire* II, 5, 8; see also Rom 9:21.

29. See I, 113.

30. See *Marriage and Desire* I, 1, 1.

31. Julian cites his previous work, *To Turbantius*. See *Marriage and Desire* II, 27, 44, where Augustine cites Julian's ideas as they were reported by the author of the excerpts who omitted a good deal of Julian's argument.

32. *Marriage and Desire* I, 1, 1.

33. Julian is again quoting from his work, *To Turbantius*. See also *Marriage and Desire* II, 28, 47.

34. See *Answer to Julian* III, 24, 54 and 25, 57.

35. Following a number of manuscripts and the suggestion of Primmer, I have omitted "*debere.*"

36. *Marriage and Desire* II, 28, 47.

37. Following the reading in Migne and one manuscript, I have added "*si*," though it is not found in Migne or in the text of the CSEL edition.

38. Augustine refers to the practice of the African Church in accord with which infants received the eucharist.

39. The CSEL text has "*parvulum*," but I have followed a single manuscript which has "*parvulis*," since Julian did not deny that Christ came as a little one.

40. The CSEL text has "*collige*"—a conjecture by the editor; I have followed Migne and a number of manuscripts which have "*colligitur*," as Primmer has suggested.

41. I have followed Primmer's reading of "*rationi* " instead of "*rationis*."

42. See 1 Jn 2:16.

43. See Jn 12:31 and 14:30.

44. Instead of "*nam*" which is found in the CSEL text, I have conjectured "*quamvis.*"

45. See the quotation from Ambrose, *The Sacrament of Rebirth, or Philosophy (De sacramento regenerationis, sive de philosophia)*, above paragraph 8.

46. I have followed Migne and the majority of the manuscripts in reading "*iam*" in place of "*etiam*," as is found in the CSEL text.

47. *Marriage and Desire* II, 27, 45.

48. Ambrose, *Commentary on the Gospel of Luke (Expositio Euangelii secundum Lucam)* 4, 67: CCL 14, 131.

49. Ambrose, *Commentary on the Gospel of Luke (Expositio Euangelii secundum Lucam)* 7, 234: CCL 14, 295.

50. That is, in books one and two of *Answer to Julian*, which Augustine wrote in reply to Julian's *To Florus*.

51. *Marriage and Desire* II, 27, 45.

52. See *The Two Souls* 11, 15 for Augustine's definition of sin, a definition which Julian exploited repeatedly in the previous book of this work. See, for example, I, 44, 45, 47, 104.

53. I followed Primmer's conjecture of "*conceditis*" instead of "*contenditis*," which is found in the CSEL text.

54. *Marriage and Desire* II, 27, 45.

55. *Marriage and Desire* II, 27, 45.

56. I have followed Primmer's suggestion and Migne in adding "*et.*"

57. Augustine plays on the Latin verbs: Christ did not come to bring (*ferre*) his own sin, but to take away (*auferre*) our sins.

58. I have followed Primmer's conjecture of "*nationis*" instead of "*rationis.*"

59. *Marriage and Desire* II, 27, 45.

60. *Marriage and Desire* II, 27, 47.

61. I have followed Primmer's suggestion and read "*vitiosorum*," which is found in one manuscript, instead of "*vitiorum*," which is found in the CSEL edition.

62. I have followed Primmer's conjecture of "*indicaretur*" instead of "*iudicaretur*," which is found in the manuscripts.

63. I have followed "*calumniam*," a reading given in the critical apparatus of CSEL rather than the CSEL reading of "*caluminare*" or the reading of "*colligam*" which is found in Migne.

64. See Rom 5:17-19.

65. *Marriage and Desire* II, 27, 45.

66. The CSEL edition has "*uniuersitas*" where Migne has "*diuersitas.*" I have followed Migne.

67. *Marriage and Desire* II, 27, 45.

68. The manuscripts omit "*in mundum,*" though the CSEL edition adds it.

69. *The Proceedings against Pelagius* 23-24, 57.

70. The Latin "*in eo, in quo*" can mean: in him in whom—the sense in which Augustine takes it just below—but Julian must, I think, take it in a causal sense: insofar as or inasmuch as.

71. *Marriage and Desire* II, 27, 46.

72. See Rom 6:12.

73. *Marriage and Desire* II, 27, 46; Julian abbreviates what Augustine had said.

74. See Rom 5:20.

75. The CSEL text has "*operiatis*," though all the manuscripts have "*aperiatis*," which I have followed, as Primmer has also advised.

76. See Gn 17:12.

77. See Sir 40:1.

78. See Gn 17:14.

79. I have followed Primmer's conjecture and deleted one "*potuit esse*" as well as "*melius.*"

80. *The Two Souls* 11, 15.

81. See above I, 44, 47, 104 and II, 38.

82. See Rom 7:12.

83. *Marriage and Desire* II, 27, 46.

84. See Jn 3:8.

85. See Ambrose, *Commentary on the Gospel of Luke* (*Expositio Euangelii secundum Lucam*) 7, 27: CCL 14, 224.

86. See Wis 11:21.

87. See Rom 5:12.

88. I have read "*irritatio*" in place of "*imitatio*," following the suggestion of Primmer.

89. See *The Deeds of Pelagius* 11, 23-24 and 32-33, 57.

90. See above II, 85. Augustine gave the same response already in *The Punishment and Forgiveness of Sins* I, 11, 14.

91. *Marriage and Desire* II, 27, 46; see also above II, 85.

92. I have followed Primmer and one manuscript in reading "*si omne*" instead of "*sin*," which is found in the CSEL edition.

93. See 2 Pt 3:13.

94. *Marriage and Desire* II, 27, 46.
95. *Ibid.*
96. *Ibid.*
97. Caelestius' appeal was heard by Pope Zosimus before a Roman synod in September of 417, though he was not condemned until the summer of 418 when Zosimus issued his letter *Tratoria.*
98. Augustine refers to Pelagius' trial at the Synod of Diospolis in late December of 415.
99. Virgil, *Aeneid* 11, 396.
100. The citation from Virgil reads literally: "the head (*caput*) and cause of these evils." Augustine here plays upon the word "*caput*," saying that Julian does not have a sound head, because he had Pelagius as his head, while claiming that it is Adam—and not either Augustine or Julian—who is the head of these evils.
101. See *Marriage and Desire* II, 27, 46.
102. See *The Deeds of Pelagius* 11, 23 and 32, 57.
103. *Marriage and Desire* II, 27, 46. I have followed the CSEL edition which places the whole above text in quotation marks, though the first part of it is a paraphrase rather than an exact quotation.
104. Ambrose, *Penance* (*De paenitentia*) I, 3, 13: SC 179, 62.
105. I have followed Primmer's conjecture and added "*eius.*"
106. See Sir 40:1.
107. See Rom 9:21.
108. See Ps 25:10.
109. See Sir 40:1.
110. See Gn 17:14.
111. See Lv 12:6-7.
112. See 2 Cor 1:22.
113. See 1 Pt 4:10.
114. Following Primmer, I have read "*amovisti*" which is found in several manuscripts instead of "*ammovisti*," which the CSEL text has.
115. See Mt 1:21.
116. See Gn 17:14.
117. Augustine plays on the words: "*parce*: with restraint or sparingly," "*parsimonia*: restraint or parsimony," and "*parco*: spare or show mercy."
118. See Mt 1:21.
119. See Ps 8:3 and Mt 21:16.
120. See Jn 1:9.
121. See 2 Cor 5:5.
122. See Rom 5:5.
123. See Sir 40:1.
124. See above 93 to 106.
125. See Rom 9:22-23.
126. See 1 Pt 4:18.
127. See 1 Jn 4:7.
128. See *Marriage and Desire* II, 27, 46-47, with minor changes and some omissions.
129. See Rom 5:12.
130. See Rom 5:19.
131. See Dn 3:49-51.
132. The Latin has "*qua*," "*quam*," or "*quasi*," in various manuscripts. The CSEL editor expands that on the basis of II, 72: "by which (*qua*) knowledge of sin was brought about." I have followed the simpler conjecture: "*quamvis.*"
133. See Phil 1:19.
134. Gal 2:21.
135. See above 121, 129, 133, and 140.
136. See *Confessions* V, 3, 3, for Augustine's encounter with the Manichean bishop, Faustus.

137. See above 147.

138. See above 142.

139. See Jn 14:6.

140. See Rom 1:23.

141. See Gn 17:12.14.

142. See Rom 7:7.

143. Augustine puns on "you perish: *peritis*" and "the uneducated: *imperitis*."

144. See Rom 10:3.

145. I have followed the conjecture "*ablationibus*" instead of "*ablutionibus*," since there were no ritual ablutions prescribed in Genesis.

146. See 1 Cor 3:6.

147. I have followed Primmer's suggestion and read "*opera*," which is found in one manuscript, instead of "*opere*," which is found in the CSEL edition.

148. See Ps 49:7.

149. See Rom 12:3.

150. See Phil 2:13.

151. See Acts 16:14.

152. See above 117.

153. See Rom 4:15.

154. See Gal 3:17.

155. See Gn 17:14.

156. See Rom 9:11.

157. Ambrose, *Penance* (*De paenitentia*) I, 3, 13: Sc 179, 62.

158. Ambrose, *Commentary on the Gospel of Luke* (Expositio Euangelii secundum Lucam) 7, 234: CCL 14, 295.

159. Cyprian, Letter 64, 5: CSEL 3, 720.

160. See I, 52. The CSEL edition refers to Hilary, *Commentary on Psalm 118* (*Tractatus in Psalmum CXVIII*) XXII, 6: PL 9, 641, though that does not seem correct. See *Answer to Julian* I, 3, 7, for a series of citations from Hilary which Augustine most likely took from a collection of sayings ultimately derived from Hilary.

161. See Phil 1:19.

162. See *The Deeds of Pelagius* 14, 30.

163. See 1 Cor 1:31.

164. Migne has "*testamentis*" where the CSEL edition has "*temptamentis*."

165. See Rom 5:5.

166. See Ps 49:7.

167. That is, in *To Turbantius* I; see *Answer to Julian* III, 25, 58.

168. I have followed Primmer's suggestion and read "*operam*," which is found in one manuscript, instead of "*opera*," which is found in the CSEL edition.

169. See Mt 26:28.

170. In Julian's version "death" is repeated so that it is explicit that death was passed on. In this respect his text follows the Greek.

171. See above 56 and 57.

172. The Latin "*in quo*" is either masculine or neuter. Hence, "in whom" and "in which" are equally possible translations of the Latin. "*In quo*" can also have a causal meaning—either "in that" or "because." In a question it can mean: "in what way."

173. See also Mk 15:13, Jn 19:6, and Mt 27:23.

174. Julian is referring to Rom 5:19.

175. See above 134 and 135.

176. Ambrose, *Commentary on Luke* (*Expositio Euangelii secundum Lucam*) 7, 234: CCL 14, 295.

177. Augustine's Latin "*non actione hominum, sed ratione iam seminum*" contains assonance that cannot be reproduced in English.

178. Julian is replying to book two of *Marriage and Desire*; Augustine wrote for Marcellinus the three books of *The Punishment and Forgiveness of Sins and the Baptism of Little Ones*.

179. *The Punishment and Forgiveness of Sins* I, 11, 13.

180. The traducianist account of the origin of the soul was not, despite Julian's claim, condemned. Augustine himself never came to a definitive answer to the question of the soul's origin and even wrote the four books of *The Nature and Origin of the Soul* to justify his agnosticism on this question.

181. In 419 Julian wrote two letters, one to the Romans and another to Rufus, the bishop of Thessalonica. Augustine dedicated the four books of his *Answer to the Two Letters of the Pelagians* to Pope Boniface.

182. See *Answer to the Two Letters of the Pelagians* III, 10, 26. Despite the fact that Julian treats this sentence as a quotation, it is by no means that.

183. Ambrose, *Commentary on the Gospel of Luke* (*Expositio Euangelii secundum Lucam*) 7, 234: CCL 14, 295.

184. See Heb 7:5.9-10.

185. See Rom 7:23.

186. See Gal 5:17.

187. See Jn 12:31.

188. See above 54.

189. See above 56 and 57.

190. Julian's Latin has "*in eo in quo.*" Since he took the phrase as expressing a causal connection, I expressed that in the translation here.

191. Following Primmer's suggestion, I have read "*liberum non erat,*" which is found in one manuscript, instead of "*non licuit,*" which is found in the CSEL edition.

192. See Phil 1:23.

193. See 2 Cor 5:4.

194. See Rom 2:12.

195. See Rom 5:12.

196. See Is 9:6.

197. See Rom 7:23.

198. See Lk 19:10.

199. The Latin for "pattern" is "*forma,*" and Augustine admonishes Julian to recognize the form who is Christ and not to be deformed or out of form with Christ.

200. See Gal 3:27.

201. See Eph 4:24.

202. I have here translated "*in quo*" in the causal sense in which Julian understood it.

203. See *The Grace of Christ and Original Sin* I, 27, 28, where Augustine's cites Pelagius' claim that with grace we can more easily do what we are commanded to do.

204. See *Marriage and Desire* I, 23, 26.

205. See Gen 17:14.12.

206. See Lv 12:6.

207. Augustine plays upon "*infantem*: infant" and "*non fantem*: not speaking."

208. Ambrose, *Penance* (*De paenitentia*) I, 3, 13: SC 179, 62.

209. See *The Grace of Christ and Original Sin* I, 43, 47, for Pelagius' tribute to Ambrose.

210. See, for example, above 147.

211. Rv 7:9.

212. See Rv 7:9.

213. Ambrose, *Penance* (*De paenitentia*) I, 3, 13: SC 179, 62.

214. See Rv 7:9.

215. See *Marriage and Desire* II, 27, 46.

216. The Vulgate has Julian's version, and Augustine adds the word "sin" in Rom 5:16.

217. See Mt 18:22.

218. I have followed here the reading "*quos*" found in Migne rather than the "*quod*" in the CSEL edition.

219. Cyprian, Letter 64 5: CSEL 3, 720.

220. Julian uses the proverbial expression: *nodum in scirpo quaerere*: to look for a knot in a smooth stem of a bulrush, i.e., to give oneself unnecessary trouble.

221. See Phil 2:8.

222. See above 135.

223. The last clause of the Latin text, "*multiplicarique iustitiam*," seems to need help, since righteousness can hardly have been multiplied by disobedience. I have followed the conjecture of the translator of the BAC edition and have added "through obedience."

224. See above 198.

225. The manuscripts and editions begin the sentence with "*Ad hoc*," but I have followed A. Primmer's conjecture of "*Ac hoc*."

226. See Rom 8:3.

227. See Jn 1:29.

228. See 2 Cor 3:16.

229. See Gn 17:14.12.

230. See Lv 12:6.

231. See Rom 5:13.

232. See 1 Cor 15:56.

233. See 2 Cor 3:6.

234. See Ps 49:7.

235. See Rom 7:12.

236. See Rom 3:20.

237. See 2 Tm 3:13.

238. See Rom 8:3.

239. See 2 Cor 4:2.

240. See 2 Cor 6:1.

241. See Rom 6:13.

242. I followed "*reatuum*" found in one manuscript, as Primmer suggested, instead of "*reatum*," as in the CSEL edition.

243. There is no variant reading of the Greek text which would justify such a translation. Julian's version has perhaps taken the Greek φύσει (*natura*) in the sense in which "naturally" can mean "of course." For example, in his *Commentary on the Letter to the Ephesians* I, c. 498, Jerome mentions, "Certain people have for the passage just explained: *And we were by nature children of anger*, translated "of course" instead of "by nature," merely because the word "φύσει" is ambiguous, but though it sounds that way, it should be explained in accord with what we have said."

244. See Ambrose, *Penance (De paenitentia)* I, 3, 13: SC 179, 62.

245. The Latin word for obeying: *obaudire* is a compound of the Latin word for hearing: *audire*.

246. See also Mk 4:11 and Lk 8:10.

247. See Prv 8:35 LXX.

248. See Rom 7:23.

249. I have followed the reading "*reus est*," found in one manuscript, instead of "*usus*," which is found in CSEL.

250. See Ps 49:7.

251. I have interpreted the sentence as a question though the CSEL edition takes it as a statement.

BOOK THREE

Book Three

The Implications of Divine Justice

1. JUL. Reverence for all the virtues ought, of course, to have flourished in the human race. With a mind that was always wise, one ought to have resisted sins and to have earned the favor of the creator by good actions. Lastly, one ought at least to have rejected the vices that were long practiced and to have returned to the bulwarks of conversion and penance, since the earlier and happier level of continual devotion is seen to be both rare and far too difficult. Reverence for God surely ought to have remained inviolable at least to the extent that we would not have to defend the divine law with such a struggle. But because the fury of sinners has gone so far that we must teach with most strenuous efforts that God is just, let us count on the help of his justice whose cause is at stake, and let us fulfill what we promised in the preceding book.

AUG. (1) You seek the help of God to fill your empty books, and you do not seek his help to correct your perverse ideas. I wish, nonetheless, that you would say why you ask God's help for this work, since it is up to your free choice whether to produce it or not to produce it. Is it so that you might have available those resources which do not lie in your power and without which you cannot accomplish this, such as—to omit other things—food and time free to write? These things God almost always supplies to us through the wills of other people. (2) You see, then, that, when you ask his help to fill your empty books, you ask of almighty God that he produce in the wills of human beings what will help you and what will not hinder you. For if human beings refused to supply you with food and appropriate supplies, if they refused ultimately to stop bothering and hindering you, you could not write or dictate these works. You hope, then, that the wills of the human beings among whom you live will be moved by the help of God so that you lack nothing necessary. After all, though you do not believe it, *the will is prepared by the Lord* (Prv 8:35 LXX). Either, then, at last correct your teaching, or cease to demand God's help to defend it.

2. JUL. Since it was established in the first volume by clear definitions that God is so just that, if he could be proved not to be just, he would have been proved not to be God,[1] and since no doubt remained on this point, it was also evident that justice is nothing other than the virtue which never judges anything unjustly, never does anything unjust, but repays to each one what is owed without injustice and without grace, that is, without partiality.[2]

AUG. As for "without injustice," you speak the truth: no one is punished who does not deserve it. But if the justice of God were "without grace," Christ would never have died for sinners, that is, for those who merit nothing good and much evil; he would in fact never have adopted into his kingdom little ones who had no preceding good works or good will. And he would not have been unjust in depriving other little ones in the same situation of a share in his kingdom, for he never judges unjustly, never does anything unjust, and repays to each one what is owed without injustice. Recognize, then, the little ones who are vessels of honor by grace, namely, those who are adopted into the kingdom of God, and the other little ones who are not adopted into that honor, that is, those who are vessels of dishonor by judgment, and at long last admit original sin so that you do not make God out to be unjust.

3. JUL. The essence of that virtue, however, is preserved if he does not punish any of his subjects except for those sins which it is clear were committed by free will.

AUG. That sin was committed by the free will of the one in whom human nature was condemned,[3] and from that nature human beings are born subject to condemnation if they are not reborn in the one who was not born subject to it. You want to overthrow this Christian teaching, but you are overthrown while it remains standing.

4. JUL. God would neither give to human beings commandments which he knew could not be observed because of their nature, nor would he judge any guilty for what belongs to their nature.

AUG. But "Adam existed, and we all existed in him,"[4] when he sinned so that he destroyed in himself all except those whom that one would set free who came to seek what was lost.[5]

5. JUL. Nor would he attribute to anyone the sins of another, and for this reason he would not on account of the sins of their parents condemn innocent children to eternal punishments. For by themselves they did nothing either good or bad by which, as we are taught, they imitated the sins of their parents. From these premises it was established[6] that God both exists and is just, and it has been shown that, if he did something unjust, he would have undergone as great a loss in divinity as he suffered a loss in justice.

AUG. You speak the truth, and for this reason he does nothing unjust when he weighs down the children of Adam with a heavy yoke from the day they emerge from the womb of their mother,[7] and that would certainly be unjust if there were no original sin.

6. JUL. Oh the unhappiness of human error! In fact, when I consider this account of our conflict, I am stricken by great pain. Could this point enter into doubt, and could this issue need defense? Could it be doubted, I repeat, in churches which profess that they believe in Christ whether God would judge justly, that is, according to reason?

AUG. Because this point is not doubted, scripture says that there is a heavy yoke upon the children of Adam from the day they emerge from the womb of their mother,[8] and the Pelagian wisdom is not better than that of the Church!

7. JUL. But out of reverence for the facts I have been too forgetful of the argument we are dealing with. For I am amazed that there could be doubt about the justice of God, though it is clear that in the synagogues of the traducianists there is no doubt about his injustice.

AUG. Because there is no doubt about the justice of God, we believe that the heavy yoke upon a little one is just, and because we believe that this is just, we do not believe that a little one is free from original sin. Moreover, in the Catholic Church from which the Pelagians have gone forth from us, it is not, as you claim, that there is no doubt about his injustice; rather, there is no doubt about his justice. In that Church it is taught and learned[9] that not even an infant who has lived one day on earth is free from the filth of sin,[10] and for that reason we recognize in the evils which the infant suffers not an unjust, but a just God.

8. JUL. And this is surely worse to the extent that the pursuit of evils is worse than the neglect of what is good, to the extent that to be intentionally sacrilegious is more destructive than to doubt the truth, to the extent, finally, that to dare to bring accusations against God is more criminal than to refuse to show him reverence.

AUG. But you bring accusations against God when you deny that little ones have any sin, though you see that by his judgment they are weighed down by a heavy yoke.

Even a Fool Would Not Deny God's Justice

9. JUL. As David the prophet is witness, *The fool said in his heart that there is no God* (Ps 14:1 or 53:1). He did not, nonetheless, say that God exists, but is unjust. The voice of all of nature cries out in such agreement that justice belongs inseparably to God that it would be easier to find someone who denies his substance than someone who denies his justice. There could be someone who thinks that what he does not see does not exist, but there has never been found anyone who said that what he believed to be divine is unjust.

AUG. You yourself are found to be such a person. For to whom if not to such as you does scripture say, *You thought unjustly that I was like you* (Ps 50:21). But since Catholic Christians know both that God exists and that he is just, they cannot doubt that, if human beings who have been born die in infancy without being reborn, even though they are images of God, they are not taken into the kingdom of God, and this is not unjust, but a punishment of original sin.

10. JUL. That fool, then, seemed to stand at the very pinnacle of sins by deny-ing God. But we have found that the nation of the Manichees and traducianists has surpassed him with their sacrileges.

AUG. I know the renown and trustworthiness of the teachers of the Church of Christ who have believed what I believe, have taught what I teach, and have de-fended what I defend concerning original sin and the justice of God. Hence, I ought to listen to your abuse as if it were praise for me.

11. JUL. But to return to the point from which we digressed, it was clear that he whom we profess to be the true God can do nothing in judgment that is op-posed to justice, and for this reason none can be held guilty for the sins of others. And so the innocence of the newborn can by no means be condemned on account of the sinfulness of their parents, because it would be unjust that guilt is passed on in the seeds.

AUG. (1) Why, then, would scripture have said, *Their seed was cursed from the beginning* (Wis 12:11). For scripture did not say this as it said, *The seed of Canaan and not of Judah* (Dn 13:56), where it showed those to whom they be-came like and those in comparison to whom they became worse. Rather, it said that their seed was cursed, and it wanted us to understand that they were natu-rally evil, just like all the children of Adam, some of whom become children of God by grace. For where scripture says, *Not unaware that their nation is wicked and that their malice is natural and that their mind could not be changed forever, for their seed was cursed from the beginning* (Wis 12:10-11), I think that it blames nature, not imitation. (2) And how can it be nature unless it is nature as corrupted by sin, not nature as it was created in the first human being? From what beginning, then, was the seed cursed but from that in which sin entered the world through one man?[11] They could not be changed by themselves, but they could be changed by almighty God who did not, nonetheless, change them by his judg-ment which is certainly most just, although most hidden. The apostle, after all, knew that he was changed from that lump, not by his choice, but by the grace of God, when he said, *We were also by nature children of anger, just as the rest* (Eph 2:3).

Punishing Children for Parents' Sins

12. JUL. (1) Although this stands in such great light that nothing is found to be more unambiguous and more true, I had, nonetheless, promised to prove by the testimony of God's law this very point, namely, that it would be most unjust if the crimes of parents are attributed to their newborn children and that God is so opposed to this that he forbade even in his law that the wickedness of a judge should do anything of the sort. I had promised that I would do this, but since the second book was taken up with explaining the statements of the apostle Paul, it is

fitting that in the first parts of this volume I fulfill my promise. (2) We read, therefore, in Deuteronomy in the list of the commandments which structured the life and conduct of the people that God had most clearly commanded this. For he wanted us to understand this from the preceding and the following commandments between which it was placed. He said, *You shall not unjustly take the wages of the poor and the needy from among your own people or from among the sojourners who dwell in your cities. You shall pay them their daily wage before the sun sets, because they are poor and place their hope in it. Otherwise, they will cry out against you to the Lord, and the sin will be held against you. Parents will not die for their children, and children will not die for their parents. Each will die for his or her own sins* (Dt 24:14-16).

AUG. (1) God said this about children already born, not about children condemned in their first parent in whom all sinned and in whom all die. And he gave this commandment to human judges so that parents would not die for their children or children for their parents when only the parents or the children were found guilty. But God did not bind his own judgments by this law, either when he judges by himself or when he judges through human beings to whom he gives the prophetic spirit. For, when he destroyed all the rest except for Noah and his family, he did not separate out the infants who had not yet imitated their parents,[12] nor did that fire wipe out the people of Sodom without their children.[13] If he had wanted to do this, the almighty certainly could have. (2) And Achan alone was found to be the transgressor of the commandment, and yet he was killed along with his sons and daughters.[14] What about so many cities conquered under the same leader, the man of God, Joshua the son of Nun? Were they not all slain so that no one was left breathing? What evil, then, did the little ones do? Was it not on account of the sins of their parents, sins which they could neither know nor imitate, that they suffered the common punishment by divine judgment? God, then, judges in one way and commands human beings to judge in another, though God is undoubtedly more just than any human being. You ought to have thought of these examples earlier so that you did not delay over ones that are not relevant to the issue.

13. JUL. (1) *You shall not pervert the justice due to sojourners and orphans and widows. You shall not accept the cloak of a widow as a guarantee, for you were a slave in Egypt, and the Lord your God set you free from there. On this account I command you to carry this out* (Dt 24:17-18). When God set the norm for judging, he immediately took care to sanction this so parents would not be put to death for the crime of their children nor children for the crime of their parents. He showed, therefore, that this is the very beginning point of justice which he commanded to be preserved in judgment so that blood relationship would not weigh down the innocent and so that the hatred which a particular person deserved would not carry over to the family. (2) In the case of actions, then, justice

distinguishes those people whom kinship links together. And it would not do this if a volitional cause and a seminal cause were the same or if the act of choice were passed on to the children by propagation. We have, then, explained more than enough by this one testimony that the ancient authority of the law which God gave has crushed this most wicked depravity of judgment which the new error embraces. And this sentence was certainly pronounced on this case so that it has left no room for doubts.

AUG. God is opposed to you, for he said in the Book of Leviticus, *And whoever shall be left of you will perish on account of their own sin and on account of the sins of their parents* (Lv 26:39).

14. JUL. When establishing the norm to be observed in trials, he prescribed that the innocent should not be included in the accusations against their relatives and, as he excluded a parent from the punishment of a sinful child, so he excluded a child from the condemnation of a parent. He, of course, showed by the similar exclusion of each of these persons both that the sins of parents cannot be transferred to their children and that the sins of children cannot be transferred to their parents.

AUG. The little ones have you by the throat, for we read so many times that they are not killed on account also of their own sins, but only on account of those of their parents.

15. JUL. Let those, then, who contrary to this statement say that there is the inheritance of sin also say that the sin also is transmitted back to parents. Thus, if sins come down from parents to children, they would also mount up from children to parents, though the authority of God's law shows that the sins of parents do not harm their children, just as the sins of the children do not harm their parents.

AUG. The authority of God's law did not want children to pay the penalty for their parents in human judgments, not in God's judgments in which God says, *I shall punish children for the sins of their parents* (Ex 20:5).[15] You ought to read the words of the law which you like so that you bear in mind that you will hear those that you do not like.

16. JUL. (1) Striving, then, to go against this statement, let them claim that God treats equally cases that he commanded us not to treat equally. The law of God can, of course, be denied more easily than it can be corrected, and though to deny it is sacrilegious, to correct it is even more sacrilegious and more absurd. For if you respect one of his two decrees and reject the other, you are forced against your will by that part which you accept to obey also the other part which you reject. For the dignity of the decree which you like also defends that decree to which you are opposed, and it is utterly absurd for persons to believe that they show respect for the commandments when they dare to attack a part of them. (2) For this reason it is more logical to deny the whole law than to correct it, but only an unbeliever will try to correct it. Religious and wise people, therefore, accept

the whole law and praise the whole law. No one, of course, should be disturbed because the ceremonies of the old sacrifices are seen to have ceased in the era of the new testament. The case is not the same with the virtues as with the victims. The permanence of the commandments is one thing; the temporariness of the sacrifices is another. With the coming of Christ who was foreshadowed by the former victims, those sacrifices which had been instituted earlier were fulfilled, not condemned. Nor do we say that they were wrongly carried out in their own times, but, when the fulfillment came which had been promised to those ties, the sacrifices ceased.[16]

AUG. How is this relevant? God said that he would punish children for the sins of their parents, not that he would impose the sacrifices of parents upon their children. And though parents could also imitate their evil children, God still never said, "I will punish parents for the sins of their children." But whenever he spoke in this vein, for he did so often, he said that he would punish the children for the sins of their parents, and by this he showed that he punishes the sins contracted by birth, not by imitation.

The Commandments of the Old Law Remain

17. JUL. But the commandments which embody piety, fidelity, justice, and holiness have not only not ceased, but are even increased. And this law of justice to be observed in judgments which we quoted from Deuteronomy does not belong to the ceremonies which were intended only for their era, but to the commandments which are lasting. It did not cease along with circumcision, but has endured along with justice.

AUG. I have already told you that these judgments were given to human beings as commands and not imposed upon God as rules for his decisions. Hence, if a human judge says, "I shall punish the children for the sins of their parents," he says something most unjust and contradicts God's order, but God is neither a liar nor unjust when he says this.

18. JUL. If one believes Moses through whom God speaks rather than Augustine through whom Mani speaks, it is evident that children are not held guilty by their nature for the sins of their parents.

AUG. Even you yourself know that I am defending in opposition to you that faith which the holy and renowned Catholic teachers who came before us learned and taught in the Catholic Church. But because, if you dare to attack them, even your own followers do not tolerate you, you have singled me out, and you try to convince them to flee from me whom you have gone after with the insult of a false accusation. And in that way they will also flee from the faith which, when it is defended, condemns you. I have already told you this above: When in return for defending the Catholic faith I hear abuse from heretics, I regard it as praise.[17] Why do you work so hard to preach to us what we know? Moses spoke the truth, but you have nothing to say. It was not a human being, but God who said, *I will punish the children for the sins of their parents* (Ex 20:5), and God did not in this passage command that a human being should do this. Rather, he indicated what he himself does.

19. JUL. And so the sins of parents are not passed on to their descendants although they are born from them, just as the sins of children are not passed back to their parents who could in no way be begotten by their children. In that way, then, birth of children from their parents cannot be an obstacle to innocence, just as birth of parents from children cannot do harm since it does not occur.

AUG. You cannot, nonetheless, deny that parents can imitate their children or that God never said, "I shall punish parents for the sins of their children." When, therefore, he says, *I shall punish children for the sins of their parents* (Ex 20:5), he does not lay the blame on imitation, but on generation—not on generation from that one in whom nature itself was changed for the worse so that on its account human beings even had to die. But in some way, nonetheless, some sins of certain parents are passed on to their children, not by imitation, but by generation, and are punished in them. And for this reason he does not say: *To the third and fourth* imitation, but *generation* (Ex 34:7). You, of course, do not like this, but whether you like it or not, you hear it.

In Any Case There Is No Inherited Sin

20. JUL. (1) The issue is, of course, settled, but I still warn the reader to be attentive to what I say. Suppose that there emerged some people who proclaimed by taking liberty with words what the traducianist tries to bring about by argument. That is, suppose these persons declared war on the law of God and scorned fearlessly the statement we quoted; suppose they maintained in whatever ways they could that both of these rules which God wanted to be observed are false; suppose they undermined the statement about which we are speaking from both sides to the extent they could. Suppose that they even thought that the parents are often condemned for the sins of their children, and ought to be, and that children are often condemned for the sins of their parents, and ought to be. They could, nonetheless, not maintain a transmission of such sin even according to their own views. (2) Why? Because, even if it were agreed that the statement of the law is false which testifies that such relationships cannot be defiled by an exchanging of serious sins, it remained unshaken that there is no inheritance of sin. For it is agreed that the means by which the guilt of parents passed to their children and that of children to their parents was not generation. For the sins of parents affected their children, and the sins of the children also affected their parents, where generation could not be the cause. (3) Let what I have accomplished here

be clearly seen. The authority of the law of God is inviolable, and no arguments of unbelievers can overthrow it. By its sanction it has perfectly, clearly and unconditionally declared that it is a hateful opinion and a perversion of judgment, one which the law had commanded that we should resolutely avoid, namely, if children are declared guilty for sins of their parents. By that lightning bolt the whole structure of inherited sin collapses, but the faith which we defend is protected by such great bulwarks of the truth that it cannot be shaken even by that sacrilege which can deny the law of God.

AUG. You seek a place to stroll, rich with your wandering wordiness, but hateful to those who stick to the facts and despise needless words. You are, of course, defeated by the opponents whom you have, and you set up for yourselves opponents to defeat whom you do not have. After all, who says to you that it is false that God wanted this to be observed in human courts when parents and children have their own personal cases pertaining to the life which each of them individually leads so that children are not punished for their parents or parents for their children? No one is opposed to the law or to you when you say this. But do not be deaf toward God. He says, *I shall punish the children for the sins of their parents* (Ex 20:5), and, though he says this repeatedly,[18] he never says that he punishes the parents for the sins of the children. Hence, you should know that he looks not to who of them imitates whom, but to who are begotten by whom.

Julian Challenges Augustine Directly

21. JUL. Now, then, let me direct my words to the person with whom we are dealing. Do you yield to the law of God—at least in what you say publicly, for we know what you do when you argue—or do you resist it? If you yield, your argument is destroyed; if you resist, your agreement with the law is destroyed. If you yield, the treachery of the traducianists is slain; if you resist, that of the Manichees is revealed, since it is clear that it is impossible for your opinion and the law of God to agree.

AUG. I yield to the law of God, but you do not yield to it. I do not deny that a child ought not to be condemned in place of a parent or that a parent in place of a child when they have their own separate cases. But you do not want to hear the words in Leviticus, *They will perish on account of the sins of the parents* (Lv 26:39), and in the Book of Numbers, *Punishing the children for the sins of their parents to the third and fourth generation* (Num 14:18), and in Jeremiah, *Exacting punishment for the sins of their parents upon the heart of their children after them* (Jer 32:18). You do not heed these and other similar testimonies; you do not yield to these and similar testimonies of the law, and yet you do not cease to speak and to raise the Manichees as objections to the Catholics.

God Does the Opposite of What He Commands

22. JUL. Or are you going to say that God, of course, commanded this, but that he did not do what he commanded, but in fact did the opposite of what he commanded us to do?

AUG. Why do you not notice how foolish you are to think this? God, after all, sometimes does the opposite of what he commanded us to do. There is no need for me to mention many examples lest it take too long. See, I say what everyone knows. The divine scripture gave a commandment to human beings when it said, *Let not your lips praise you* (Prv 27:2), and yet we should not say that God is arrogant or proud when he does not stop praising himself countless times. And on the point at issue, I have already shown above how without any injustice God also killed the little ones along with their parents for the sins of their parents. And yet, he commanded human beings that, when they judge, they should not condemn children in place of their parents. If you would take note of this, you would not make such statements. Or if you do take note of this and still say these things, notice that what you say is pointless.

23. JUL. Though it is already most obvious how sacrilegious it is, after it has been scarcely pointed out, let us see how this looks after a little examination, with all due respect to the divinity whose justice we are defending. Is he compelled by the necessity of certain things which weigh upon him or by his feebleness to become a transgressor of his own law? Or, since neither of these is the case, is he compelled by the love of sinning alone? But not even Mani could say this, and for this reason he made up the story that your God endured a serious battle.[19]

AUG. You toss words around because you are pressed by the facts; God is not a transgressor of his own law when, as God, he does one thing and commands another to human beings as human beings.

24. JUL. If neither some disaster nor feebleness nor the love of transgression weighed upon him, how is it possible that he destroys by his judging the standard of justice which he entrusted to us in giving us commands? How is it possible that he in fact rages, not against this justice, but against the reverence due to himself? So great, indeed, is the power of justice that it convicts those who depart from it and is not lessened by the authority of those who abandon it. How is it possible, finally, that he wants us to do what is just, while he himself does what is unjust? Does he want that we seem more just than he—or rather, not that we seem more just than he, but that we seem just and he seems unjust?

AUG. What are you saying, you, a human being with such foolish ideas? To the extent that it is higher, divine justice is more inscrutable than human justice, and further removed from it. After all, does any just human being permit that a crime be committed which that person has the power to prevent? And yet God permits this, though he is incomparably more just than all just human beings, and his power is incomparably greater than all other powers. Bear these ideas in mind, and do not compare God as judge to human judges, for we must not doubt that he is just, even when he does what seems unjust to human beings and does what would be unjust if human beings did it.

25. JUL. Or is what he does just, that is, attributing to people the sins of others, while he commands us to do what is unjust, namely, that we declare each person guilty for the sins of that person's own will.

AUG. Read the answer we gave above, and learn if you can the sense in which original sins are understood as the sins of others and as our sins, but are not the sins of others for the same reason that they are ours. They are, after all, the sins of others because each of us does not commit them in our own life, but they are ours because "Adam existed, and we all existed in him."[20]

God's Justice and Our Justice

26. JUL. And where does he get such great envy or malice? It would be envy, after all, if in giving commands he deceived his creatures so that they did not try to imitate his virtues to the extent they could. But it is malice or even cruelty if he punishes mortals for unjust actions which they commit when they obey his law.

AUG. I have already shown above that God does some things justly which, if human beings do them, they act unjustly. For God justly takes vengeance for injuries to himself, but human beings are told, *Do not avenge yourselves, my friends; leave a place for God's anger, for scripture says, "Vengeance is mine; I shall exact payment, says the Lord"* (Rom 12:19).

27. JUL. Or does perhaps he not punish them because he acts prudently, but even rewards his servants when they have obeyed his commandments which, nonetheless, teach injustice? And how did it benefit him to show his disapproval if, by doing unjust acts, mortals also came to the point to which they would have come by observing justice? And though those whom he deceived lose nothing of happiness, he himself is deprived of the consciousness as well as the honor of goodness and justice. How much more tolerable it would be to withdraw your necks from the burden of religious profession than to wander through such dangerous and deadly paths!

AUG. You go in circles and say nothing. Distinguish divine justice from human justice, and you will see that God justly punishes children for the sins of their parents, but that, if human beings claim that for themselves in their judgment, they are unjust. Do not wander off from the just path so that, when you hear that the sins of parents are punished in their children, you either do not want God to act that way or you want human beings to act that way, because you resist God's testimonies or commandments.[21]

28. JUL. Because God does not permit his servants to do the sort of action which you claim that he himself does, it is evident that you have abandoned respect for him no less than for human reason, and on this account we are not led astray, as you say, by the Pelagian error, but we are guided by the law of God so that we maintain that it is unjust for the sins of parents to be attributed to the children.

AUG. Not once, but many times God said that he punishes children for the sins of their parents, but in these passages he did not say that he punishes parents for the sins of their children or punishes one child for the sins of another or friends for the sins of their friends or citizens for sins of fellow citizens or something of the sort. He wanted us to know that, when this is said, it is generation, not imitation that is blamed. And you too could understand this in the words of God if you were not prevented by the Pelagian error.

29. JUL. We mourn the fact that the inheritance of sin, the daughter of the Manichees, but your mother, has in these troubled times so prodigally spawned this idea.

AUG. You do not reason, but offer abuse and resort to slander. Read again the ancient commentators on the words of God, and see that it is not in these troubled times, but long before us, that they understood in the words of the apostle his perfectly clear statement that *through one man sin entered the world, and through sin death, and in that way it was passed on to all human beings* (Rom 5:12). They understood that this refers to the birth which is healed by rebirth, not to the imitation to which you, rather, have given birth in these troubled times. For this reason the storm of your new teaching has driven you forth from the face of the Catholic Church like dust which the wind drives from the face of the earth.[22]

King Amaziah's Observance of the Law

30. JUL. (1) It has become clear, then, that what we maintain has been commanded by God. And though the clear truth of this statement which is adapted to the intellect of all admits no mark of obscurity in itself, nonetheless, so that you do not appeal to the slowness of our wits and say that we do not understand what was commanded, let us explain how the law is understood by still another testimony no longer of a commandment, but of action carried out in accord with the commandment. (2) We read in the Fourth Book of Kings about Amaziah, the son of Joash, king of Judah. It says, *After the kingdom was solidly in his hands, he killed his servants who had killed his father. But he did not kill their children according to the testament of the law of the Lord by which it was commanded: Parents shall not die for their children, nor children for their parents* (2 Kgs 14:5-6). You see how this reliable history showed the justice of the king in his judging. He was a devout man, but since he is reported to have wavered in his mind on

several matters, the authority of the law of God that was cited added to the confirmation of his judgment. For lest this deed have little weight if one considers the doer, it is praised for having been carried out in accord with God's law and testament.

AUG. God wanted this to be the judgment of human beings, not his own. He said, *I shall punish the children for the sins of their parents* (Ex 20:5).[23] He did this even through a man, when through Joshua, the son of Nun, he killed not only Achan, but also his children[24] and when through the same leader of his people he condemned to death, by a not unjust severity, the children of the Canaanites along with their parents, even the little ones who had not yet imitated by their actions the sins of their parents.[25] Do not multiply your writings with many words and much folly, but pay careful attention to God's scripture so that you do not find what you think that what you have opened up in one place is closed off against you in another.

The Logic of Contradictory Propositions

31. JUL. (1) We usually believe two or three witnesses even against a person's life.[26] How much more ought we to believe for the honor of God two sacred witnesses, the law that is contained in Deuteronomy and the history that includes the actions of the kings! He himself has prescribed how he wants us to judge; the judgments pronounced in accord with his law testify to how we ought to interpret what he commanded. Is there still any doubt that the inheritance of sin cannot be proved by the authority of the scriptures? (2) These are certainly opposite views over which we struggle with such long conflicts, that is, the one which you defend and the other which we defend, and they are so contrary and opposed to each other that we fight—you by persecution, we by argument, you by rage, we by reason. Both sides, then, agree that these views are different from and opposed to each other, that is, that children are punished for the sins of their parents and that children are not punished for the sins of their parents; that there is a natural sin and that there is no natural sin; and that God's law prescribes that the sins of the parents be held against the children and that the law of God prescribes that the sins of the parents not be held against the children. (3) It is clear that these opinions and statements are in conflict with each other and cannot both be true. For it is shown by the rules of learned argumentation that, when two opinions arise about doubtful matters, both of them can be false, but both of them cannot be true. They can both be true in different kinds of things and in those which have a so-called intermediate state, but it cannot happen in contraries or in those things which do not have an intermediate state.[27] These points are known to logicians, but on account of the reader unacquainted with this discipline we shall illustrate it by an example.

AUG. You look for material with which to fill your most wordy books so that you even try to teach the readers of them logic when there is no need. You do not think of how the Church of Christ casts aside a logician whom she sees to be a heretic. After all, who does not understand that you are doing this in order to empty of meaning with your wordy wisdom the cross of Christ[28] who shed his blood for the forgiveness of sins for all for whom he died, including, as you admit, the little ones?

32. JUL. (1) Suppose there comes, for example, into question the color of Goliath's hair;[29] one might state that he was black-haired, the other white. Both of these different opinions can be false, but both of them cannot be true. For it cannot be true that he was black-haired if he was always white-haired or that he was white-haired if he remained black-haired at every age. These two opinions which cannot both be true can both be false in this way: if his hair color was neither white nor black, but yellow or a mixture of the contraries as the whiteness decreased, but without blackness being dominant. (2) Things that are different and contrary can, therefore, be more easily denied together than affirmed together. But those contraries which do not have an intermediate state, as for example good and bad, just and unjust, innocence and guilt, cannot at one time come together in one and the same thing. So it is necessary that, when one of them is admitted, the other is denied, that is, that a commandment or a counsel or a help cannot at one and the same time be both just and unjust. In the same way a human being cannot at one and the same time be both guilty and innocent, both good and bad.

AUG. No one is looking for what the color of Goliath's hair was, but in order to lie in ambush, you are looking for colors to wrap yourself in like a chameleon. If this logic which does not build you up, but puffs you up and makes you ridiculous because it makes you a braggart, if this logic, I repeat, which claims that one and the same person cannot be both good and bad at the same time is admitted to the laws of Christian argumentation, a single human being cannot be at the same time good by reason of nature and bad by reason of vice. Yet the truth cries out that this is possible, and you do not deny it. You yourself are even called as a witness against your logic when of these two, which you do not doubt to be contraries, as is correct, you attribute one to the creator of human beings and the other to their will. Let your logic, then, blush, and let it abandon this debate with the Catholics, as you have abandoned communion with them. But if you want to return, as we hope, let this logic remain outside.

33. JUL. (1) Let us, then, apply the examples to the issue. These two contradictory statements, namely, that the sins of parents should be held against the children and that the sins of parents should not be not held against the children, cannot both equally be admitted to be just. For if it is justice that the offspring are held guilty for the sins of their parents, it is necessarily injustice, if the offspring are said not to be guilty on account of the same sins. And as it is good to com-

mand justly, so it is evil to order anything unjustly. And although an obvious matter loses force by arguing for it, nonetheless, because it helps to strengthen by the support of the law of God a cause that stands on its own, let us stick to this topic. For it is one on which anyone of sound mind is not allowed to wander through the perils of the present questions. (2) You grant, then, you preacher of natural evil, that the law of God forbids that children be punished for the sins of their parents. You also recognize that this commandment was not understood by that people in any other way than the observance of it which we are now defending. And for this reason you recognize that, in obedience to the commandments of God, King Amaziah reined in by a praiseworthy moderation the anger he had felt because of the slaying of his father, and he spared, not out of cowardice, but out of justice, their children when he killed the murderers of his father. (3) Amaziah is, of course, praised, and he is reported to have done this in accord with God's law and is commended for having obeyed the will of the Lord.[30] But it is still not passed over in silence that he was contaminated by the remnants of idolatry, and he is shown not to have imitated the devotion of David his father. Though he had fallen from that holiness of his people, he upheld in judgment the justice that the law of God taught. Such was the power which reverence for clear justice had! Consider, then, the evil your faith embraces: you attribute to God whom we profess to be eternal and loving and just this injustice which neither the pride of a king nor the grief of an orphan carried out.

AUG. (1) Amaziah was a man who was not permitted to judge about hidden matters which he could not know. Hence, he observed in his judgment the commandment which was given to a human being that he should not kill the children for the sins of their parents. But how could a sin so great that it became our nature, a sin which entered the world through one man and without which no human being is born, be punished by human beings? For it was passed on to all human beings along with death so that its punishment accompanies it even to everlasting death except when God's grace heals our birth by rebirth? This sin, then, belongs to God's judgment, not to that of human beings, just like many other things about which human beings are completely unable to judge. (2) And for this reason he commanded that parents and their children already living their separate lives should be judged by a human being in one way, though he himself judged otherwise when in accord with his inscrutable justice he condemned the sinful nature, which he knew in its root, along with its stem, even though it had not yet sprouted into a plant. For he was going to set free from this condemnation those he wanted through his no less inscrutable grace. And yet, he punished children already living separate lives for the sins of their parents living separate lives; this was something God did not want a human judge to be permitted to do, because he himself knows why he does this justly when he does it, but human weakness does not know it.

34. JUL. (1) But let us press home this point. It is established that injustice cannot be an attribute of God; it is also established that he prescribed that the sins of parents should not harm the children. The very dignity of the one giving the command implies that what he forbids is unjust. But to deal with you more generously, I give you the opportunity to reply concerning these two opinions which I put together above, that is, that sins of parents are held against the children or that they are not. Which do you think ought to be taken as justice? If you say your opinion at least agrees with the judgment earliest, I ask whether you think that our opinion which remains is just or unjust. You will undoubtedly declare it unjust. But the authority of the law commands that it be observed. (2) You see, then, that there necessarily remains one of these three: Either you must admit that the law of God is unjust; in fact, you must by the law accuse God himself of injustice. Or you must have recourse to the words of your teachers and say that your God did not command the law given to Moses.[31] Or if you do not dare to affirm either of these, you must admit that the affirmation of the inheritance of sin is contrary to the teachings and commandments of the law. For one should not believe that you could be so foolish as to say that God upheld justice in his commandments, but injustice in his judgments or that, at least in accord with your teaching, he observed justice in his judgments, but in his commandments taught injustice. Though we dealt with this point above, we had, nonetheless, to repeat it now.

AUG. You repeat odiously what you say idly. For you are free to turn over and over with your wordiness the same ideas which you cannot maintain with truth, and to say without measure what you cannot defend by any measure.[32] For you want it to seem that these two ideas are contradictory to each other: that children are punished for the sins of their parents and that children ought not to be punished for the sins of their parents, as if I say one of them and God says the other. Are you deaf? God said them both! Therefore, both of them are just because it is the just one who said them. But in order that you may understand that God did not say things that are mutually contradictory, distinguish the persons of God and of the human judge in accord with the different cases. Then you will not make God out to be guilty, even though he punishes children for the sins of their parents, nor will you force a human judge to act that way. But you raise the objection against me that these two statements are mutually contradictory with such great wordiness and complication for no other reason than that you talk much and think too little.

Julian's Accusations of Bribery and Corruption

35. JUL. (1) But if you say that the two of them are just—both what we say and what you say, that is, both what the law of God says and what the Manichee

and traducianist have made up—we, of course, suppress the power of clear reason and confront you in a kinder and gentler fashion. Why, then, if you believe that this statement of ours is good and that statement of yours is good, have you upset the whole of Italy with such great divisions? Why have you hired people and stirred up rebellions at Rome? (2) Why have you fattened herds of horses throughout almost the whole of Africa at the expense of the poor and sent them under the care of Alypius to tribunes and centurions?[33] Why have you bribed the powers of the world with gifts from the inheritances of matrons so that the straw of public fury might be set blaze against us? Why have you dispelled the quiet of the churches? Why have you stained the days of a religious emperor[34] with the impiety of persecutions if we say nothing other than what you too are forced to admit is good?

AUG. (1) As the charges you bring against us are false, so are the teachings which you fashion for yourselves. But speak to the extent you can every evil against us with your lies;[35] we shall only defend against you the Christian and Catholic faith. And what need is there to repay you with similar reproaches and not rather believe the gospel and rejoice that because of these false accusations of yours our reward in heaven is increased?[36] (2) But in this matter now at issue between us how can we believe that both what you say and that what we say are good? For we say that God declared, *I shall punish the children for the sins of their parents* (Ex 20:5), while you praise his commandment to human judges, namely, that they should not punish the children for the sins of their parents, to the point that you refute, as if it were ours, his statement about what he himself would do. And you reject it as if it were false and unjust, and you do not perceive that on this issue you oppose and slander not us, but God.

36. JUL. But up to this point I may have used a gentler manner of speaking. Now, however, the brightness of reason's flame shows that there is no agreement between the evil and the good, between the profane and the sacred, between the pious and the impious, between the just and the unjust, and that there is, therefore, no conflict between God's commandments and his judgments. But it is contradictory to hold the sins of some people against others and to command that such sins not be held against others. For it is necessary that, if one of these two is granted, the other is denied, that is, if one of them is just, the other is shown to be unjust. But in the law of God it was forbidden that the sins of parents be held against their children, and for this reason the same authority completely destroyed its opposite, that is, the opinion of inherited sin along with the Manichees.

AUG. It annoys me to state the truth so many times, even though it does not embarrass you to utter nonsense so many times. God says that he punishes children for the sins of their parents; God says—but says to human beings—that they should not punish children for the sins of their parents. We should approve of both statements since God says both of them.

Manicheism and Inherited Sin

37. JUL. I have surely shown that we defend nothing else than this: first of all, that reason approves it as perfectly just, then, that God also upholds this by his law, and third, that what God commanded was carried out, just as we interpreted it,[37] and was praised. We have also taught that this is true justice and that God showed it was pleasing to him when he also commanded it. And in this way it is established that the Manichean inherited sin finds no support either in reason or in the testimonies of the law.

AUG. (1) The Manichees say that nature was always evil without any beginning, and they maintain that every evil comes from it. But the Catholics—which you refuse to be—claim that our nature was created good, but corrupted by sin, and from the infants to the elderly it needs Christ as a physician, *because he has died for all; all have, therefore, died* (2 Cor 5:14). Hence, the Manichees suppose that evil must be separated from the good so that it exists elsewhere. But though we separate evil from good with our mind and do not believe that what is called evil is a substance, we do not, nonetheless, think that evil must be separated from those who are set free in such a way that it exists somewhere else; rather, we know that it must be healed in them so that it does not exist at all. (2) The Manichees, after all, say that evil is an evil substance; we say that it is the defect of a good substance and is not a substance. Notice the great difference, and stop begrudging the little ones Christ as a physician so that the anger of God does not remain over them,[38] for God says, *I shall punish the children for the sins of their parents* (Ex 20:5). Look at the one who said this; it is God, not Mani! Look at the one who said, *Through a man death came, and through a man the resurrection of the dead, for just as in Adam all die, so too in Christ all will be brought to life* (1 Cor 15:21-22). It is Christ's apostle, not Mani's disciple! (3) Look at the one who said, "All of us human beings are born under the power of sin."[39] It is a Catholic bishop, not Mani or Pelagius or a Pelagian heretic! Hence, since human beings also punish sinful actions, though only God punishes the sin from our origin, God commands human beings that they should not also condemn the children for the sins of their parents, though he says that he punishes the children for the sins of their parents. Distinguish divine and human judgments, and you will find that these two are not self-contradictory.

Julian Appeals to the Prophet Ezekiel

38. JUL. But there may be someone so misguided as to want it to be proved by clear statements that God does not judge otherwise than he has commanded that we should judge. That is a sign of terrible stubbornness; nonetheless, since weapons are available to the truth to provide fully satisfying proofs, it is no trou-

ble for most eager witnesses to show this. Filled, therefore, with the Holy Spirit, the prophet Ezekiel said: (2) *The word of the Lord came to me and said: Son of man, what is the meaning of those who speak this proverb in the land of Israel: Our parents have eaten sour grapes, and the teeth of the children are set on edge? As I live, says the Lord God, this proverb will no longer be spoken in Israel because all souls are mine, the soul of the child, just as the soul of the parent. All souls are mine. The soul that sins will die. But human beings who will be just, who will act with judgment and justice and will not eat on the mountain tops and will not raise their eyes to the desires of the house of Israel and will not defile the wife of their neighbor and not approach a woman who is menstruating, who will not oppress another and will return a pledge to a debtor and will not commit robbery, who will give their bread to the hungry and cover the naked with a cloak, who will not lend their money for interest and will not accept increase and who turn their hands away from injustice and make a just judgment between two neighbors, and who walk in my commandments and keep my ordinances to carry them out, these are just persons; they will truly live, says the Lord God.*

And if parents beget evil children who shed blood and commit sins, who do not walk in the way of their parents, but eat on the mountain tops and defile the wife of their neighbor, who oppress the beggars and the poor, who commit robbery and do not return a pledge, who set their eyes on idols and commit iniquity, who lend with interest and accept increase, they truly will not live; they have committed all these iniquities; they will truly die, and their blood will be upon themselves. But suppose these parents beget children who see all the sins which their parents committed and are fearful and do not act that way. They have not eaten on the mountain tops and have not raised their eyes to the desires of the house of Israel and have not defiled the wife of their neighbor; they have not oppressed others and have not withheld pledges or committed robbery; they have shared their bread with the hungry and covered the naked with a cloak; they have turned their hands from iniquity and have not taken interest or increase; they have done justice and walked in my commandments. These children will not die for the sins of their parents; they will truly live. But since their parents have practiced extortion and committed robbery and have done evil in the midst of my people, they have died in their sinfulness.

And you said, Why is it that the children have not suffered for the iniquity of their parents? Because the children have acted with justice and judgment and mercy and have kept all my statutes and observed them, they will truly live, but the soul that sins will die. The child will not suffer for the injustice of its parent, nor will the parents suffer for the injustice of their child. The justice of the just will be upon themselves, and the sinfulness of the sinful will be upon themselves. But if the wicked turn away from the iniquities they have committed and keep all my commandments and act with justice and judgment and mercy, they will truly live and will not die. Whatever sins they shall have committed will not be remembered; they will truly live in the justice which they practiced. Do I really will the death of sinners, says the Lord God, and not rather that they should turn from their evil ways and live? But when the just turn away from their justice and commit injustices like all the injustices which the wicked commit, they shall not live if they do this. All the righteous actions which they performed will not be remembered; in their transgression by which they fell and in their sins by which they sinned, they will die.

And you have said: The way of the Lord is not right. Hear now, O house of Israel. Is it my way that is not right? It is your way that is not just. When the just turn away from their justice and commit a transgression, they will die in the transgression which they committed. And when the wicked turn away from the injustice which they have committed and have acted with judgment and justice, they will preserve their lives and live so that they may turn away from all their iniquities which they have committed. They will truly live and will not die. And the house of Israel says, The way of the Lord is not right. Is it my way that is not right, O house of Israel? Is it not your way that is not right? Therefore, I shall judge each one of you, O house of Israel, according to your own ways, says the Lord God (Ez 18:1-30).

AUG. (1) This passage is the promise of the new testament through the prophet Ezekiel, and you do not understand it. In it God distinguishes according to their own actions, if they are already adults, those who have been reborn from those who have been born. For those of whom he says, *The soul of the parent is mine, and the soul of the child is mine* (Ez 18:4), undoubtedly are leading their own lives. But if the child were still in the loins of its father, as scripture says that Levi was in the loins of Abraham when Abraham offered the tithe to Melchizedek,[40] it could not then be said, *The soul of the parent is mine, and the soul of the child is mine* (Ez 18:4), when the soul was, of course, one. (2) But veiling the mystery which was to be revealed in its own time, the prophet did not mention the rebirth by which each human being passes from Adam to Christ. But what he did not say at that time he wanted to be understood in this time in which the veil was going to be removed for those who pass over to Christ.[41] For since you profess that you are Christian, although you prove yourself an anti-Christ by trying to make Christ to have died in vain, I ask you: If human beings do all the acts of righteousness which the prophet Ezekiel mentioned with so many repetitions, are they truly living even if they have not been reborn? If you say that they are truly living, Christ contradicts the anti-Christ and says, *Unless you have eaten my flesh and drunk my blood, you will not have life in you* (Jn 6:54), for you are forced to admit that this food and drink belongs to the reborn, whether you like it or not. (3) But if you are worn down by so great a mass of authority and reply that they who have done all these good acts are not truly living if they have not been reborn, tell me what the reason is, and see that rebirth is opposed to birth, not imitation to imitation in the text in which the apostle put Adam on the side of sin and Christ on the side of righteousness.[42] But I shall show you more clearly that the passage you mention from the prophet Ezekiel pertains to the new testament in which is found the inheritance of the reborn. I shall not do this now, but when you have said all those things which you wanted to say about his words with your customary wordiness.

39. JUL. (1) Does God not seem to be a competent defender of his judgments since he not only passed judgment on this question in many chapters, but also offered arguments? Clearly, as one who foresaw the errors of our time, he justly and providently produced with such a great luminous abundance of his words two results: one, that no one would be disturbed by any ambiguity of language, the other, that no plank of an excuse would be left for those who willingly plunged themselves into the sea by shipwreck. He speaks to the Jews who, while spending their captivity in serious sins, claimed, in order to lessen the hatefulness of their own transgression, that it was not due to their own behavior, but to their parents, and he challenges them with the authority of a father. (2) *Why is it that you repeat this proverb: Our parents have eaten sour grapes, and the teeth of the children have been set on edge? As I live, says the Lord God, this proverb will no longer be spoken in Israel because all souls are mine, the soul of the child, just as the soul of the parent. All souls are mine. The soul that sins will die* (Ez 18:1-4).

AUG. When he says, *This proverb will no longer be spoken in Israel* he shows that it was customary to say: *Our parents have eaten sour grapes, and the teeth of the children have been set on edge* and he does not blame the fact that it was said, but promises a time when it will no longer be said. But why did they say this except because they knew that God said: *I shall punish the children for the sins of their parents* (Ex 20:5).

God Confirmed His Judgment with an Oath

40. JUL. To provide an example of the justice of his judgment and to confirm it, God uses an oath and adds authority to the decree by his swearing to it. The apostle understood this manner of speaking, for he explained it to the Hebrews as follows. He says, *Wanting to show to the heirs of the promise the immutability of his plan, God added an oath so that we might have the strongest consolation from two immutable things, because of which God cannot possibly lie* (Heb 6:17-18).

AUG. There too he promised the new testament.

41. JUL. He says, then, that it is shown by these two things that God cannot lie: because he made a promise and because he swore that he would fulfill what

he promised. It is not that without such an oath God's word tended to be weak and doubtful, but in order to add weight to his truth by mighty proofs, he used that kind of language which makes us believe even human beings who often deceive us. By this weight, then, God warns in the present case as well and forbids that anyone should infer with regard to God's people what the traducianists claim, but should know that God cannot judge in a way he detests. *As I live, says the Lord God, this proverb will no longer be spoken in Israel* (Ez 18:3).

AUG. You would be right in saying that it will no longer be spoken in Israel if you had in mind the true Israelites, those who have been reborn among whom this will no longer be spoken. For among these who are not reborn it is right to say it, since in accord with the apostle's words to the Romans they are not Israel: *For not all who are descended from Israel are Israel* (Rom 9:6), and here he surely wanted us to understand the children of the new testament, that is, the children of the promise. After this there follows, *But your descendants will be named after Isaac; that is, it is not those who are children of the flesh who are children of God, but the children of the promise are counted as descendants* (Rom 9:7-8).

42. JUL. What does this mean that it *will no longer be spoken* since even today it is asserted by such great efforts of the Manichees? But this is what God says: that no one who comes from the people of Israel and accepts the authority of this scripture will dare to believe something of this sort after my declaration. Moreover, everyone who persists in this opinion and does not obey these words will also not be counted in the true Israel.

AUG. If, then, after his declaration God wants us to understand that no one will believe this, we must ask why before this declaration it was not wrong to believe that children were to be punished for the sins of their parents. And if one asks correctly, one will find that he said, *I shall punish the children for the sins of their parents* (Ex 20:5), on account of their birth into subjection, and from that birth there came the proverb about the sour grapes. But the new testament was promised on account of the rebirth into freedom, and in it this proverb will no longer be said. For through the grace of Christ we renounce the inheritance that brings loss and comes from Adam, when we renounce this world in which it is necessary that the children of Adam be weighed down by a heavy yoke, and certainly not unjustly, *from the day they emerge from the womb of their mother until the day of their burial in the mother of all* (Sir 40:1). For this reason the sacred mysteries give sufficient evidence of what is done since even the little ones make these renunciations.

The Reason behind God's Judgment

43. JUL. After he had reproached the foolishness of this proverb and sanctioned his statement by his divine pronouncement and oath, he also chose to disclose the reason behind his justice as to why relatives are not burdened by one another's sins. He said, *All souls are mine, the soul of the child, just as the soul of the parent. All souls are mine. The soul that sins will die* (Ez 18:4). By the individual character of the souls, then, he showed why this limitation upon the sentence was most just.

AUG. This individual character of the souls pertains to their separate lives. For one cannot be reborn unless one has been born. But why did Levi pay the tithe when he was in the loins of Abraham, if it was not because in those loins there was not as yet the individual character of their souls?[43]

44. JUL. He says: The soul of the parent is mine and the soul of the child is mine; by that testimony, as by many others, we are taught that the soul which God claims as his own owes nothing to the seed. Hence, it is most wicked, he says, and stupid to say that my possession, my image, is weighed down by the actions of others.

AUG. (1) You separate the flesh, then, from God's property, since you think that he claims as his own only the soul, and you have forgotten that scripture said, *For just as the woman came from the man, so a man comes through the woman, but all things come from God* (1 Cor 11:12). Surely this was said in reference to the flesh or in reference to both, but not in reference to the soul alone. Since, however, it pleases you that God should say, "It is most wicked and stupid to say that my possession, my image, is weighed down by the actions of others," why do you not ask why it is just that the soul is weighed down by the flesh derived from the parents, that is, from the works of God himself. *For the corruptible body weighs down the soul* (Wis 9:15). And I think that you acknowledge that the corruptible body is a work of God. (2) Why, then, did the image of God deserve to be weighed down by the corruptible body as an impediment for coming to a knowledge of things, if there is no original sin? Why do you not make God say this as well: "It is most wicked and stupid to say that my possession, my image, should depart from the body without baptism through the unbelief or neglect of its parents—or of any people among whom it lives—or through any necessity and that it should not be admitted to my kingdom and truly live because it did not eat my holy flesh or drink my blood"?[44] Or will you also argue against this statement of Christ and cry out with the words: "Of course, even if it has not eaten the flesh of Christ and not drunk his blood, it will truly live"? That is the cry of no one but the anti-Christ! Go, express these ideas, teach these ideas! Let Christian men and women hear you; let those who are corrupt at heart hear you; let those who have fallen away from the faith[45] hear you, love you, and honor you. Let them feed, clothe, and adorn you, and by following you who are lost, let them be lost themselves as well. But *the Lord knows those who are his own* (2 Tm 2:19), and we should not despair even about you as long as he shows you his patience.

45. JUL. I gave to my image this status that against its will no one from outside would harm it, but that it would of its own accord choose either sin or righteousness, either reward or accusation of guilt.

AUG. This can be said of the original human nature, but not of this nature which has been corrupted and condemned. After all, in paradise before the sin the corruptible body did not weigh down the soul. Or are you so corrupt in mind that you would dare to say even this? But if you do not dare to say this, tell me, you who do not want to admit the origin of sin with the Catholic Church, why the image of God merited to be weighed down by a corruptible body.

46. JUL. (1) You are angry at me, then, because I believe God's oath rather than the dreams of a Manichee, a Manichee who does not produce the arguments of a mind that is awake, even if he is not able to produce any testimonies of sound faith. Though no testimonies can ever be found great enough to be able to undermine the foundations of truth, they will, nonetheless, at least for now bring him some consolation, if they are suitably expressed, for the feeling of shame over his stupidity. God continues to fortify by an oath what he made sacred by his commandment. (2) He continues to make clear by examples what he ratified,[46] and he says that, if a parent observes every kind of righteousness with untainted devotion and has a child who indulges in wicked behavior and turns aside from the ways of its parent, the moral stature acquired by the parent's concern for justice will be of no benefit to the child. So too, in contrast to this sinner, he portrayed a child who with better counsel fled from the ways of its parent, and he shows that the wickedness of the parent does the child no harm. He treats the state of righteousness and of sin the same, claiming that the sins of the parents are not passed on by the seeds, just as virtues cannot be passed on. But all souls come under his dominion, and in this way he shows that your claim is sacrilegious, namely, that the souls and bodies of the newborn fall under the dominion of the devil.

AUG. I have already answered you. You talk endlessly and foolishly. The whole human being, that is, soul and body, by its substance falls under the dominion of the creator. But by a defect, which is no substance, the human being was handed over to the devil, though under that same power of the creator under which the devil himself stands.

God's Arguments against Inherited Sin

47. JUL. Having defended the well-balanced scale of his judgment, he now accuses your view in the case of those who held similar ideas. *And you said, Why*

is it that children have not suffered for the iniquity of their parents? Because the soul that sins will die. The child will not suffer for the injustice of its parent, nor will the parents suffer for the injustice of their child. The justice of the just will be upon themselves, and the sinfulness of the sinful will be upon themselves (Ez 18:19-20). Who of us could ever argue with as much skill as God argued through the mouth of his prophet by making divisions, comparisons, and repetitions?

AUG. And yet, though God did this, you mix your verbosity with the clarity of his words, because you know that you do not have a good case.

48. JUL. He was not content to have explained only this, but also added another argument from the works of mercy in confirmation of this justice. He declares to those very persons who sinned voluntarily that, if they have recourse to penance and amend their lives, their past errors do not harm them. He says, *But if the wicked turn away from the iniquities they have committed and keep all my commandments, whatever sins they shall have committed will not be remembered; they will truly live in the justice which they practiced* (Ez 18:21-22). That is, since I have come to this degree of mercy that I pardon even personal sins of those who amended their lives, how is it possible that I hold the sins of others against the newborn? Or is it possible that, when it is created, innocence is guilty in my eyes, though it still has influence with me, if I seek it back, even after it has been lost?

AUG. The case of penitents is one thing; that of the newborn is another. For you do not, of course, find a way to show that God is just if even in the newborn he finds no sins and yet weighs them down with a corruptible body and with so many and such great troubles besides. The evils that infants suffer are past counting: fever, coughing, rashes, pains of various members, diarrhea, worms, and countless other woes stemming from the flesh, more torments from their cures than from their diseases, wounds externally inflicted, blows from beatings, and attacks of demons. But you wise heretics, you are ready to fill paradise with such flowers to avoid admitting original sin. For if you say that these evils were not going to exist there, I ask you why they exist in little ones who have, as you claim, absolutely no sin. But if you are not ashamed to say that they were going to exist there, what need is there for us to say what sort of Christians you are?

49. JUL. (1) This was displeasing to the worshipers of idols; our faith which you see is formed by this law is also displeasing to you. Those without religion, therefore, said, *The way of the Lord is not right.* God said, *Hear, then, O house of Israel. Is my way not right? Is it not your way that is not right? Therefore, I shall judge each one of you, O house of Israel, according to your own ways, says the Lord God* (Ez 18:29-30).[47] Do you see the testimonies by which we are protected? Do we follow an ambiguous teaching? Do we snatch at general terms? Do we defend the faith by either weak or obscure arguments? (2) We detest what God detests; we understand what God explains; we maintain what God argued

for; we believe that on account of which God has sworn an oath: *The child will not suffer for the injustice of its parent, nor will the parents suffer for the injustice of their child. The justice of the just will be upon themselves, and the sinfulness of the sinful will be upon themselves* (Ez 18:20). It is clear how God promises that he will judge, that is, he will not hold the sins of parents against their children nor the sins of children against their parents. And for this reason there is also established by the clear testimonies of the scriptures this principle about which reason does not allow any doubt, namely, that God maintains the same justice in his judgments that he had in his commandments.

AUG. (1) From this at least understand that God said these things about these parents and children who were already living their individual lives. For, when he said, *The child will not suffer for the injustice of its parent, nor will the parents suffer for the injustice of their child*, he immediately added, *The justice of the just will be upon themselves* (Ez 18:20). After all, in this world can we say of little ones that their justice is upon them since they cannot as yet live their own life either justly or unjustly? How, then, do they deserve to suffer whatever punishment they suffer at this age, if they contracted no sin from their parents? For the most just God does not impose undeserved punishments upon anyone, nor does he permit them to be imposed, and it cannot be said that the little ones suffer these evils to test their virtue, since they as yet have none. (2) Moreover, if you think of the world to come which belongs to the inheritance of the new testament, it is right to say even of little ones who die at this age: *The justice of the just will be upon themselves, and the wickedness of the wicked will be upon themselves* (Ez 18:20). For those who have been born will be distinguished from those who have been reborn so that the latter will truly live in that kingdom in which righteousness dwells, but the former will truly die in the punishment where injustice endures torment. But what is the righteousness of those who have been reborn but that which is transferred to them from Christ in whom all will be brought to life? And what is the injustice of the others but that which is transferred to them from Adam in whom all die?[48]

Was Ezekiel Speaking Only of Adults?

50. JUL. (1) But lest you should try to mock the ears of the simple with a quibble and say that God was speaking here of those who were adults, that is, that he said that the sins of parents did no harm to those children who had eliminated natural evil by the holiness of their actions, we shall prove that nothing supports this deceit. For God absolutely forbade that the injustice of parents should lead to accusations against their children, but that each of us should be held responsible for our own injustices, nor can the mind of a believer be in any doubt about this. And yet, let us take another look at the corpse of your view which has been

run through by so many lightning bolts of the law. How do you think that we should interpret these words of God? Is it in the sense that the sins of parents are no obstacle to newborn children, just as they are not to adult children? (2) Or are the sins of parents not allowed to harm only children of adult age who are acting righteously, while, before the little ones expel the natural poison by their own righteousness, they are weighed down by the crime of their parents? In that way what God said through the prophet would not happen does happen.

AUG. Indeed, in that way there does happen what God says in another passage: *I shall punish the children for the sins of their parents* (Ex 20:5). Though he says both of these, that is, that the sins of parents do not belong to their children and that he punishes the children for the sins of their parents, he surely cannot contradict himself. And so those who ask correctly how both of these are true understand that one pertains to birth and the other to rebirth. But you who lead astray your own heart, fear him, and you will not call the truth you hear a quibble.[49]

51. JUL. But we turn to this idea. Do you, then, profess that the alternative, which has equal weight, is true, namely, that the just acts of parents benefit their children and make them holy and are not said to benefit only those who at an older age have spoiled their natural righteousness by their own sins? Since God has denied both of these and has clearly explained one by the example of the other, you maintain that the denial, which you see is opposed to your arguments, is false in the case of little ones, and in this way you disprove both of its parts by the condition of the newborn. When you do this, you perpetrate two evils at the same time: the one, because you attack[50] the statement of God, the other because you claim that a righteous child is born from a righteous parent and a sinful child from a sinful parent.

AUG. (1) I do not claim that the prophet's denial was false, but that you did not understand it. He, of course, foretold the rebirth. The rebirth alone makes children to be free from their parents' sins, which fall under the judgment of God, not under the judgment of human beings. But when you deny that birth contracts from the parents the infection of the ancient death, you try to eliminate the very reason for rebirth. For though the bath of rebirth washes away whatever sins it finds, other sins could also be healed by doing penance, as they can be healed in those who are not permitted to be reborn a second time. But that sin which is contracted by birth is not removed except by rebirth. The righteous are born of God, not of human beings, since they become righteous by being reborn, not by being born, and for this reason they are also called children of God. (2) Read the gospel: *They are born not from blood, nor from the will of the flesh, nor from the will of a man, but from God* (Jn 1:13). Why do you seek to unite things of very different kinds? Human beings are born from the flesh of human beings; they are reborn from the Spirit of God. Why is it surprising, then, if, just as one receives righteousness from the Spirit of righteousness, so one contracts original sin from the sinful flesh? After all, the one man would not have come in the likeness of sinful flesh to set us free, if all of us did not have sinful flesh. Therefore, though your heresy is an enemy of this Christian grace, do you still dare to be surprised and to complain that the Church of Christ detests you?

52. JUL. But if you cannot bear the noise of the truth that cries out against you and try to escape another way, you will run into stronger opposition. For if you say, "The statement of the prophet is certainly true, but true in the case of adult persons; it says that relatives are not weighed down by one another's sins. But in little ones it is false in one of its parts in which it says that they are not guilty on account of the evil deeds of their parents, but it is not false in the other in which it says that they are not helped by any virtues of their parents." Then you will clearly reveal the foulest desire, not for argument, but for fictions, not to say something, but to speak, not, ultimately, the desire of a sane person, but of a Manichee gone crazy, if you suppose that you may reject what you wish and accept what you please contrary to clear reason, contrary to the honor of God, contrary to his examples, contrary to the testimonies of his commandments, and contrary to the explanation of his judgments.

AUG. (1) The statement of the prophet is not false in any part. But you do not understand what he foretold by it. I do not want to say that you lie, but you certainly do not know what you are saying—something I can say without injury to you. For it makes a big difference how and in what sense one interprets these words which you say the prophet spoke, namely, that children are not helped by any virtues of their parents. After all, do you deny that by the faith of their parents children are presented to the Church, our mother, to be reborn and to God's ministers to be baptized? How, then, are children not helped by any virtues of their parents? (2) Or will you dare to say that Christian faith is not a virtue? Or are they not helped when they are admitted into the kingdom of God by nothing else but that same rebirth? With reference also to temporal benefits, why is it said to Isaac: *I shall do this for you on account of your father, Abraham* (Gn 26:24)? Why was Lot, the son of Abraham's brother, helped by the merits of his uncle,[51] if children are not helped by any virtues of their relatives? Finally, why because of the sins of Solomon was the kingdom diminished for his son, though it was not completely destroyed on account of the good deeds of David, if children are not weighed down by any sins of their parents and not helped by any of their virtues?[52] (3) O you, a man with a tongue, but no intelligence! Distinguish these; see here, if you can, what was foretold through Ezekiel. It is, after all, evident that a parent who has not been reborn is no obstacle to a child who has been reborn for the attainment of eternal life, the life with which Ezekiel said that the child *will truly live* (Ez 18:21). It is also evident that a parent who has been reborn does not benefit a child who has not been reborn in this regard and, in turn, that a child who has been reborn is of no benefit to a parent who has not been reborn and that a child who has not been reborn is no obstacle to a parent who has been reborn so that the one truly lives and the other truly dies. If you cannot, however, see this, why can you not be quiet?

Charges of Marcionism and Manicheism

53. JUL. Who are you that you are aroused by the frenzy of Marcion and burst on the scene to slay justice? Who are you that you subject both the judgments and commandments of God to the censorship of your tongue still slimy with the mysteries of the Manichees? No one has ever tried to do this without first having denied those judgments and commandments. But with Mani as your leader, you will dare to tear open the testament of God to which reason, justice, piety, and truth, like a column of sacred witnesses, have attested by their seal, as the prophets faithfully wrote it down. You have long ago lost the holiness of intelligence and the beauty of religion, if you suppose that this statement found in Ezekiel either brings help to or does not entail destruction for your inherited sin.

AUG. Wordiness parades about in an abundant poverty, in which the truth is not seen, or, if it is seen, it is rejected, the truth in which is found, not a most empty abundance of words, but a most certain abundance of reality. A straightforward and truthful person is one thing; a learned slanderer is something else. The prophet speaks the truth to children and parents who are living their separate lives; you slander with the Pelagian madness the Catholics who correctly understand the prophet by branding them as Manichees.

54. JUL. *The injustice of the unjust,* he says, *will be upon their head; I shall judge each one of you according to your own ways. Parents will not die for their children, nor children for their parents. The soul,* he says, *that sins will die; because all souls are mine, I shall judge each of you in accord with your sinfulness* (Ez 18:20.30.20.4.30).

AUG. God who says this is the same God who says, *I shall punish the children for the sins of their parents* (Ex 20:5). Unless you understand how both of these are true, you should in no way believe that you have understood the truthful prophet, no matter how much wordiness I endure from you with your slanders.

55. JUL. Look at the clarity, at the crowd of the judgments, at the dignity of the judges which your inherited sin does not fear to treat with abuse and against which it tries to bring a summary judgment. Here there is no doubt that you should not be ashamed to make that reply which you see remains. That is, you should reply that the statement of the prophet, in fact, the statement of God through the prophet, is true and that the argument of the wise is invincible by which they teach that it is most unjust to hold the sins of parents against their children.

AUG. Shame on you! You are most unjust. For he who said, *I shall punish the children for the sins of their parents* (Ex 20:5), is not unjust.[53]

56. JUL. Nor are you ashamed to think that the seed of all human beings is defiled by guilt from the will and that this justice, nonetheless, does not hold for the sin of Adam alone. Rather, his is the one sin which is held against all. At this I do not know what I should do first. Am I to laugh, because that is what your singular foolishness demands? But the ruin of many whom you deceive calls for pity and tears. Shall I then be pierced with deep grief? But the monstrosities of your arguments draw from me a loud guffaw, though my heart is sad.

AUG. (1) Tell me what you are going to say, excellent judge that you are. Under your leadership we must believe that Ambrose was a deceiver, though your teacher, Pelagius, said of him that not even an enemy dared to find fault with his faith and his utterly flawless interpretation of the scriptures?[54] Go ahead, find fault with him, for you are stronger and more powerful as an enemy of the cross of Christ than if you were an enemy of Ambrose. You more brazenly show hatred for the grace of God than if you showed hatred for that man of God. Find fault with him, I repeat; mock him with your attacks; weep for him in grief. With the great power of your eloquence, after all, you can change your nonsense into elegance and your madness into mercy.[55] (2) Say, then, that he erred terribly and was miserably foolish when he maintained that the discord between concupiscence of the flesh and the spirit was turned into our nature as a result of the transgression of the first human being.[56] Who, after all, is born without it from the time that human beings began to be born, since they are, of course, born in sinful flesh? But you, you most clever fellow, do not believe that this sin was of such a kind and so great that it could then change nature itself into this evil and, in punishment for this indescribable apostasy, rightly bring nature under condemnation along with the whole human race. This situation which all sober persons experience as evil and judge to be evil, you who are drunk on the Pelagian doctrine declare to be good. (3) With an amazing eloquence you are able to heap praises upon that sexual desire which holy men and women accuse with groans. And with that same eloquence, you are able to locate it, like a fair and beautiful tree, amid the groves of paradise. Even if no one had sinned in paradise, you would put it there, just as it now exists, namely, as it thrusts itself upon those who do not want it and challenges the hearts of the chaste to combat. Shame on you, O blessedness of the Pelagians! And see where you may flee since the chaste flee from you.

57. JUL. (1) If anything from our age survives longer than this generation, who, after all, could believe from the written records that there existed a man who believed and swore that what is natural is not natural, that what belongs to generation does not belong to generation, that what pertained to some persons only because they were parents does not pertain to the condition of being parents? I suspect that the next generation will think that these statements were made up rather than defended by any mortals. (2) Your reason[57] and faith suffer from this drifting at sea and this nausea and vomiting, for you say: The sins of

parents cannot be passed on to their children by nature, because a matter of choice is not bound up with the seeds, but the sin of Adam, which was conceived by the will, was passed on to all human beings by nature because a matter of choice was bound up with the seeds. You also say: God does not condemn children for the sins of their parents, because it is the height of injustice, but he condemns the descendants of Adam on account of the sin of their parents, something that cannot be defended by any justice. (3) Finally, you say: What belonged to Adam only because he begot children by the law of marriage does not belong to the condition of begetting children by which[58] spouses become parents. Is this to steer a course or to drift at sea? Is this to digest food or to become nauseous? Is this to eat solid food or always to vomit it out? In the same words you affirm what you denied; in the same words you deny what you affirmed, and you are angry that we do not yield to a man who is broken by a grave illness and cannot hold down what he eats.

AUG. (1) Heaven forbid that we should say that God does not punish children for the sins of other parents since God's scripture so often and by name testifies as to which children have been punished for the sins of which fathers to the point that God delayed punishment for a particular grave sin of King Ahab, sparing him, but punishing his son.[59] But who is able to search out the limit or plan and standard of God's justice in the case of sins of some parents for which their children are punished? On this account God keeps to himself these judgments, but he forbade a human judge to exact such punishment. (2) The apostasy, however, of the first human being in whom the freedom of his own will was supreme and unimpeded by any defect was so great a sin that by his fall the whole of human nature was brought down. The great misery of the human race is a sign of this; that misery is so well known to all of us from the first cries of infants to the last gasps of the dying. As a result, those who deny it claim for themselves a greater part of human misery by such horrible and incredible blindness. You yourselves do this, for you are still not afraid to say that Adam was created mortal so that, whether he sinned or not, he was destined to die, even after the Palestinian trial in which Pelagius himself condemned you who say such things.[60] (3) But go on as you please, and even accuse so many Palestinian bishops of being Manichees. Shout out that Pelagius for a while yielded to the Manichees so that he would not be condemned by them. Fill paradise with the fruits of passion, and scatter through those happy fields the many and great evils we see infants suffer, as if they were not pains of punishment, but scents of springtime.[61] And mock me as if I were drifting at sea, while you are sunk in these depths and are perishing. (4) Mock me as if I were nauseated and vomiting, while you lie dead and stink from your restless chatter, as if from worm-filled garbage. Accuse me as if I affirm what I denied and deny what I affirmed, though, as I have shown with regard to your previous volume, it is rather you who did this. The readers will be able to see that I did not do this, and they will be able to discover how deceptively you said that I did. Say that I am broken by grave illness and cannot keep down what I eat, while you have completely lost the breath of life and cannot even take nourishment.

A Scriptural Basis for Augustine's View?

58. JUL. Even you see, of course, that the matter is not worthy of discussion. Nonetheless, to help careless souls who devour certain quite vulgar opinions that favor their bad morals as a comfort for their bad consciences, we ask whether you have found the occasion for such a stupid idea in any passage of scripture. If you say, *Through one man sin entered the world* (Rom 5:12), we admonish you to reread the previous book of the present work; if you keep it in mind, you will not be able to steal for yourself the statement of the apostle.

AUG. We, rather, admonish you to read the apostle and to see that these few words of his with which we are concerned are so clearly against you that you have tried in vain, not with a small book, but clearly with a very lengthy and long-winded book, not to turn them, but to twist them into your heretical view, not to explain them, but to make them obscure.

59. JUL. But if you say that there is one form of baptism[62] by which human beings of different ages are made holy, you will admit, even without my saying anything, that it contains no mention of a corrupt generation or of diabolical flesh or of Adam. We shall, nonetheless, fully reply to this in its proper place, though it has nothing to do with inherited sin.

AUG. When you begin to reply, what will you be seen to be but a heretic as usual?

60. JUL. Therefore, against the great authority of the witnesses we have produced, against plain justice, against clear reason, muster at least one statement of the law by which you may show that you were led astray. I added this point precisely because, even if there were such a statement which might be thought to prove something of the sort by the ambiguity of its language, it would have to be explained by lucid teaching of other statements in a way that was appropriate to justice.

AUG. We produce certain, not ambiguous testimonies of God against you, just as we have already produced many. But because they refute your darkness, they do not seem bright to you, and you close your heart against whatever troubles you by the brightness of its light so that the night of your error is not dispelled from it.

61. JUL. Now, however, since not even a slight basis for this opinion is found in the holy scriptures and, quite the contrary, the faith which we defend is protected no less by reasons for it than by examples and testimonies, you are completely filled with a deadly stubbornness when you suppose that we should

assent to the dreams of the Manichees to the detriment of the law, the detriment of reason, the detriment of prudence, and the detriment of justice.

AUG. To the detriment of the law you do not hear: *I shall punish the children for the sins of their parents* (Ex 20:5). To the detriment of reason you do not see that the evils which the little ones suffer, though they committed no personal sins in this life, have no just causes before God except for the sins of their origin. To the detriment of prudence you do not avoid bringing forth or defending a new-fangled doctrine which denies original sin in opposition to the most ancient foundation of the Catholic faith. To the detriment of justice you are so unjust that you are not afraid to raise under my name the infection of the Manichean plague as a charge against so many holy men, sons and fathers of the Church of Christ, disciples and teachers, who came before us, and against the mother of them all, the Catholic Church.

62. JUL. But pay attention to what we say against this opinion. Even if you could prove that the sin of Adam is held against his children, you would still agree that the crimes of other parents do not harm their offspring.

AUG. Who would agree to this error but someone who does not believe God when he says, *I shall punish children for the sins of their parents* (Ex 20:5).

63. JUL. It would be clear that it was not due to generation, but to some other cause that the children were seen to be held subject to the sin of one parent before an unjust judge.

AUG. You most clearly call God unjust for he most clearly says that he will punish children for the sins of their parents.

The Damage to All Procreation and Generation

64. JUL. The result would be that, as the estimate of the judge was sullied by the indictment of innocents, so the status of generation was defended by the examples of other parents. After all, if the cause of the inherited sin,[63] if the cause of the sin were found in the act of procreation, this condition would have defiled all procreation.

AUG. God cries out, *I shall punish the children for the sins of their parents* (Ex 20:5); hence, because he is truthful, you wander from the path of truth.

65. JUL. But since the status of a different generation was not seen to be different, it was surely evident that, even in that marriage in whose guilt its offspring shared, generation had not been corrupted.

AUG. (1) Even if generation is not different when children destined to die are born of parents destined to die, the words of the apostle, *The body is indeed dead on account of sin* (Rom 8:10), do not, nonetheless, concern other parents, but that one who sinned with such great wickedness that we are not able to measure and grasp it. But how great God judged it to be we have learned from quite suitable witnesses, namely, God's scripture and the misery of the human race. We see the greatness of that misery imposed upon his offspring due to his sin by the judgment of God which is certainly not unjust. Because we are Christians, we say that, if no one had sinned, there also would not have existed in paradise, not merely the eternal death of the soul and body, but not even the temporal death of the body and all these great evils which we see that little ones suffer. (2) But even if other parents commit many sins, because they sin with a weak soul and in a corruptible body which weighs down the soul,[64] nature does not become destined to die because of their sins, and by God's secret and just judgment the children receive for the sins of these parents a punishment that is far different and far less. For he arranges all things in measure and number and weight,[65] and he truthfully says, *I shall punish the children for the sins of their parents* (Ex 20:5).

Julian Sums Up What He Has Done So Far

66. JUL. What, then, have we accomplished? We have shown that it is so certain that there is no inheritance of sin that, even if you teach that children are punished on account of the sin of Adam, it is agreed that sins cannot be innate and that sin cannot be passed on with the seed, since you admit that this is not the case in all procreation. And for this reason, even if vices are passed on to other persons, they are not, nonetheless, mingled with fetuses. Now, however, you and I have agreed that the sins of parents could only be passed on to children by a defective and guilty generation, but it has been established by reason, by examples, and by the law that the status of generation could in no way be corrupted. And this is confirmed by your concession, for you say that the sins of no parents apart from those two are passed on to their children. Hence, it has been irrefutably established that the fertility of the first human beings was not destroyed by the devil and that no sin could come from birth.

AUG. We do not say this to you; rather, you say to yourself what we do not say. By divine, not human justice children are also punished for the sins of other parents. God, after all, knows when and how to do this with perfect justice, but human beings do not know this and must pass judgment in accord with their knowledge. For, when they judge, they can know what each person has done, though they do not always know even this. But how do human beings know the sort of bonds by which a nature is linked to the nature from which it was born? That one sin, however, by which human nature was changed so that it had to die, even if there were no other sins, is sufficient for condemnation unless the bonds of birth are untied by rebirth; this is what we say, even if you do not want to hear it. You do not conquer this with the truth, even though you persist in attacking it with your wordiness.

The Question of Natural Sin

67. JUL. We are, then, asked why we do not agree that sin is natural. We reply: Because it has not a shadow of probability, not to mention of truth,[66] not a shadow of justice, nor of piety; because it makes the devil appear to be the creator of human beings.

AUG. It clearly makes him appear to be so, but to you, not to those who know how to distinguish a defect from a nature, although a defect exists in a nature. Read the Letter to the Hebrews and see that they have solid food who have their minds trained to separate good from evil,[67] something that you do not have. Therefore, when we say: Human beings are born with a defect, you think that we are saying that the devil is their creator. You are so blind or stubborn that you cannot or will not notice even the bodily defects with which some are born. If we ask you how they merited such defects, you will find nowhere to flee except over the cliff, as long as you do not want to return to the solid rock of the Catholic Church.

68. JUL. For it brings a charge of injustice against God the judge.

AUG. It is you who do this because the heavy yoke upon the little ones is unjust if there is no original sin.

69. JUL. For it attacks and destroys free choice, though by its defenses the Church of Christ is most of all protected against various errors.

AUG. It is you who destroy free choice when you deny it the grace of God to restore and assist it.

70. JUL. You say that all human beings are so incapable of any virtue that in the wombs of their mothers they are filled with sins from long ago.

AUG. How could we say that they are justified by grace, that is, made righteous, if we said that human beings were incapable of virtue?

71. JUL. You write that the force of those sins not only drives out natural innocence, but also forces people thereafter into all the vices through their whole lives.

AUG. This necessity of ours is lessened by the grace of God and ended by the grace of God. Here too your wordiness does not achieve anything.

72. JUL. You swear that this law of sin also remained and thrived in the prophets and apostles, men outstanding for the great brilliance of their morals and miracles, even after they received the grace of Christ's sacraments, the grace which you think you help out with all these infamies of your teaching.

AUG. Because they did not praise it, the prophets and the apostles faithfully fought against your darling, sexual desire, that is, the concupiscence of the flesh that resists the concupiscence of the spirit.

73. JUL. It extinguishes attempts at every sort of goodness; it condones the moral foulness of God's works, that is, of human nature; and it increases it in in-

famy because it brings against all the commandments of the law the charge that
they are impossible to observe, that is, that they are unjust.

AUG. The apostle who says, *I do not do what I will, but I do what I hate* (Rom
7:15), locates the possibility of his becoming perfect in the grace of God in opposition to you. He does not place his trust in his own virtue[68] so that he does not become vain in contrast with you.

74. JUL. It was no less disgraceful than sacrilegious to cling to the shame over
the sex organs as the highest testimony for his position.

AUG. We do not cling to the shame over the sex organs, but we rather recognize the source of this shame, something which you refuse to do. For we listen to
the perfectly clear testimony of scripture to which you are deaf, though you
ought to be silent. After all, when people hear that the first human beings were
naked and were not ashamed,[69] who would fail to see the reason why they were
ashamed to be naked after their sin and why they hastened to cover with some
sort of loincloths those members they were ashamed of?[70] But we have found a
man who would locate in paradise, even if no one had sinned, the sort of sexual
desire which we must resist in order not to sin, the sort of sexual desire of which
even the impudent are ashamed. And in saying such things, he is not ashamed of
this great and sacrilegious monstrosity. I ask you, if this desire imposes on you,
as we believe, only the difficulty of resisting it, but does not manifest your will,
why do you think that you should reward it so greatly with praise, even if it is
false praise?

75. JUL. And he[71] is swollen with accusations against God instead with the
sacred authorities.

AUG. Is this not a sacred authority: *The body is dead on account of sin* (Rom
8:10)? And is this an accusation against God and not praise for God: *He will
bring to life even your mortal bodies* (Rom 8:11)? In my opinion, it was not
God's accuser, but God's preacher, a man filled with God, who said this, and he
showed by it that Adam was not created so that, whether he sinned or did not sin,
he was destined to die.[72]

76. JUL. And he claims that there is a tyrannical excess in God's commandments.

AUG. God's commandment is not tyrannical, but we must ask his help in order to carry it out. You reject this because you place your trust in your own virtue.[73]

77. JUL. And he claims that there is a barbaric injustice in God's judgments.

AUG. Because God's judgment is not unjust, we must recognize original sin
in the misery of the human race which begins with the wailing of the little ones.

78. JUL. And he proves that there is a Punic dishonesty in God's oaths.

AUG. Does God speak in Punic when he says, *I shall punish the children for
the sins of their parents* (Ex 20:5)?

79. JUL. Instead of all the arguments and syllogisms he relies on the dreams and madness of Mani.

AUG. Neither the one who said, *We were also children of anger, just as the rest* (Eph 2:3), nor the one who said, "All of us human beings are born under the power of sin, and our very origin lies in guilt,"[74] was either a Manichee or dreaming and mad.

80. JUL. These are the reasons, then, which set us afire to attack any natural sin and which make us disdain and despise the fellowship of those who are depraved.

AUG. If you were not yourself depraved, you would not call the Catholic and pious assembly of so many great teachers the company of those who are depraved.

81. JUL. They cause us to be no more terrified by the rumblings of the whole world than if we saw a rustling grove of gruesome lupine stirred either by unclean pigs or by rushing winds.[75]

AUG. The Catholic Church spread through the whole world, which wisely shuns your mouths, is not a grove of lupine, but has willed to be safe from your cunning bites.[76]

82. JUL. We believe, therefore, that God is just and pious and truthful, and for this reason we hold that his law commanded nothing that is impossible, that his testimonies endorse nothing that is false, that his judgments utter nothing that is unjust, but that he is the creator of human beings whom he creates not subject to any sin, but full of natural innocence and capable of the virtues of the will.

AUG. Why, then, does he not admit into his own life his own image, if it has not undergone the rites of exsufflation, exorcism, and baptism? Is that the way he rewards innocence? Or is the guilt contracted by birth, if not forgiven by rebirth, justly punished by the denial of life and by the death that ensues? The apostle would not have testified that they were separated from life if it were no punishment.[77]

Either a Manichean God or an Enemy of God

83. JUL. On the basis of these premises, it is necessary to hold one of these two conclusions. That is, either God is believed to be the sort of God the Manichean traducianist imagines, or along with all those who yield to the doctrines of inherited sin, you are understood to be the sort of person the God who deserves our honor battles against. But God cannot be the sort of God Mani had dreamed up; he is, rather, the faithful and just and true God, the sort of God which all the holy scripture, every law, and our faith venerates. And for this reason it is your teaching whose destruction offers honor to God, just as its acceptance does injury to him.

AUG. If you think that God is faithful, why do you faithlessly keep the savior, that is, Jesus, from the little ones? If you think he is just, why do you believe that there is a heavy yoke over the little ones without any sin that merits it? If you believe he is truthful, why do you not believe him when he says, *I shall punish the children for the sins of their parents* (Ex 20:5)?

Jeremiah Is Used to Interpret Ezekiel

84. JUL. It is time to turn to other topics, but the importance of the case demands of us that we also take up those points which we think were passed over in the previous book. A wise reader will perhaps judge this unnecessary; nonetheless, because we have found that a case that has not been decided is exposed to risks from the plaintiffs,[78] even if they are slight ones, one must remove from those whom you have already deprived of defense any hope of consolation.

AUG. (1) Since you have begun to turn to other topics, we ought now to show what we promised above,[79] namely, that the prophecy of Ezekiel in which he said that children are not punished for the sins of their parents, just as parents are not punished for the sins of their children, has to do with the prediction of the revelation of the new testament. After all, the prophet Jeremiah also says something of the sort and shows there that about which this is said. Among other things he said, *Return, virgin of Israel, return to your cities in grief. How long will you be turned away, my daughter without honor? For the Lord has created a salvation for the new planting, and in that salvation human beings will walk about. Thus spoke the Lord: They will still speak this word in the land of Judah and in its cities when I shall bring back its captivity: Blessed be the Lord upon his righteous and holy mountain and those who dwell in Judea and in every city of it. Along with the farmer one shall also be raised up for the flock. For I have given drink to every thirsty soul and given food to every hungry soul. On this account I rose up, and I saw, and my sleep became pleasant for me. For this reason, look, the days are coming, says the Lord, and I shall plant Israel and Judah with the seed of human beings and the seed of cattle. And it will be that, as I watched over them to bring them down and to afflict them, so I shall watch over them to build them up and to plant them, says the Lord. In those days they will not say: Parents have eaten sour grapes, and the teeth of the children have been set on edge. Rather, each will die for one's own sin, and the teeth of the one who has eaten the sour grapes will be set on edge* (Jer 31:21-30). It is, of course, clear that this pertains to the day of the new planting about which he was speaking when he said this.

(2) In that passage, when the seed of human beings and the seed of cattle, which God promised that he would sow, are spiritually understood, they bring us to understand those who preside and those who are governed. But it had long

been impressed upon the hearts of the people that it was written in the old testament, *I shall punish the children for the sins of their parents* (Ex 20:5). And so that no one would think that God's scripture contradicted itself, in order to show more clearly that the former statement belongs to the old and the latter to the new testament, he immediately added, *Look, the days are coming, says the Lord, and I will establish a new testament for the house of Israel and for the house of Judah, not in accord with the testament which I established with their fathers in the day I took their hand to lead them out of the land of Egypt* (Jer 31:31-32), and so on. (3) Birth belongs to that former testament, but rebirth to this latter. Hence, in the former children are punished for the sins of their parents, but in the latter, in which the bonds of birth are broken by rebirth, it is not said: *Parents have eaten sour grapes, and the teeth of the children have been set on edge* (Ez 18:2), but *the teeth of the one who has eaten sour grapes will be set on edge* (Jer 31:29), because each person will not die for the sin of a parent, but for one's own sin, if one has committed sin. But you have not shown how the words of scripture, *I shall punish children for the sins of their parents* (Ex 20:5), are in harmony with the prophecy which says, *Children will not inherit the sin of their parent* (Jer 31:30). These will, of course, remain mutually contradictory unless each of these two is referred to one of the testaments, as the prophet Jeremiah showed with perfect clarity.

A Return to Julian's Exegesis of Romans

85. JUL. (1) Therefore, when we came to the statement of the apostle Paul which the traducianist had been accustomed to peddle to those unfamiliar with scripture, that is, *Through one man sin entered the world* (Rom 5:12), I showed first of all that the traducianists had been removed from the sanctuary of that passage by the testimony of that statement itself. For, when the teacher of the nations pondered the antiquity of sin, he set forth a definite number as the strongest of bodyguards to protect generation. Hence, by saying that through one man sin entered the world, he showed at the start that he did not have in mind generation which cannot come about except with two persons. And I showed that he distinguished between intercourse and the sin of the parents when he said that sin entered the world, but entered through that number which could not lead to conception. I showed quite sufficiently through the whole book that the apostle did not point out there the nature of sin, but its form, because it was established that the transgressors who came later received it by imitation, not by generation. (2) But we read that the Letter to the Hebrews says concerning the Jews, *Descendants were born from the one man, and him as good as dead* (Heb 11:12), that is, from Abraham, and earlier in the same letter we also read concerning Christ, *He who sanctifies and those who are sanctified are all from the one* (Heb 2:11). And

so, I do not want the traducianist to take up one of these passages or similar ones, if he can find any, and argue that some weight has been removed from our response. For we stated in our response that the apostle mentioned one person through whom sin was passed on so that we would be kept from thinking of generation. And since we have found in this letter that generation was referred to by naming one person, I thought, I say, that I should go back over this point. I warn the reader, then, to be attentive, for this contradiction will be destroyed in many ways.

(3) In that passage, then, in which Abraham is mentioned, Sarah, his wife, is included; the order of the words runs as follows: *By faith he who is called Abraham obeyed to go off to that place which he was going to receive as an inheritance, and he went off without knowing where he was going. By faith he stayed in the land of promise as in a foreign land, dwelling in tents with Isaac and Jacob, heirs with him of the same promise. For he looked forward to the city which has foundations, of which God is the builder and maker. By faith Sarah, who was sterile, also received the power to conceive, even past the age for that, because she believed that he who had made the promise was trustworthy. On this account descendants were born from the one man, and him as good as dead, descendants like the stars of heaven in number and like the countless grains of sand along the shore of the sea* (Heb 11:8-12).

(4) Since he mentioned both of them, that is, Abraham and Sarah, and said that she was worn out in accord with the law of old age, but received by faith the power to conceive, he added without danger of being misunderstood that so many peoples were born from the one man that they were comparable to multitude of the stars. Both the praise for those people of faith and the truth of what happened demanded that the union of the parents be explained. The art of offering praise warned him that, in order to emphasize the great number of offspring, he should mention, not both, but one of the two parents. He, of course, wanted to show the great things which unwavering faith merited; when he said that by the power of God a countless multitude were propagated, he considered it to be more conducive to the praise of that work if he said that they were procreated from one rather than from two, especially since, in the increase of the praise which the last words topped off, there was no loss to the history which he developed before with the mention of both persons.

AUG. (1) I have no idea what someone understands who does not understand that you have nothing to say. You had said that the apostle said, *Through one man sin entered the world* (Rom 5:12), because that man offered an example of sinning to the rest. You said, "For if he wanted us to understand generation in that passage, he would have said: Through two, not: *Through one man.*"[80] And yet, if he wanted us to understand an example, he would rather have said: Through one woman, not: *Through one man*, since it is clear that she offered the example of sinning to her husband. But because sin which is to be healed only by regeneration entered the world through generation, he said, *Through the one man* because, as the example of human sin began with the woman, so generation began with the man. Sowing the seed, which is the man's task, undoubtedly precedes conception, which is the woman's part. (2) But, look, a perfectly clear testimony has been found by you or by someone else who perhaps offered this to you as an objection. It says without any ambiguity that countless persons were born from one, though they, of course, had two parents in order to be born, a man and a woman, but it says this most correctly on account of the beginning of generation which comes from the man's seed. Therefore, when the apostle wanted to set forth praiseworthy examples of faith, he began with Abel himself and, after having mentioned Abraham, came to Sarah. He had, of course, already passed from him and was speaking about his wife, and yet, when he came to mention the generation of so immense a people, he returned to him because he fathered the child she bore.

(3) If you had borne this in mind, as you ought to have, you would not speak so blasphemously against the faithful preacher of the faith who wrote the letter and you would not say that he was warned by "the art of offering praise." I ask you: What was he warned to do? Was it that he should lie by stating that they who were born from two parents were born from one? Was it perhaps, as you think, that "he considered it more conducive to the praise of God's work"? You are much mistaken; God is not pleased by false praise. You often quite gladly offer such praise to sexual desire,[81] but falsity is very displeasing to the Truth. For I do not know why you present yourself, not as one who praises, but as one who fawns upon sexual desire. Will it, therefore, love you more? You are, of course, mistaken; it does not love human beings, but clearly arouses them to love what they should not love. (4) But if in some manner of speaking one can say, not falsely, but truly, that those who have been born from two parents have been born from one, then, where the apostle said, *Through one man sin entered the world*, why do you think that he could not have meant generation on the grounds that generation requires two parents, not one? For everyone knows that the parent who sows the seed is the one who most of all or first of all generates a child and that the woman either does not generate, but bears a child—or, if bearing a child is correctly called generation, she first conceived from the man who generates the child and afterwards generates the child she has conceived. (5) And so, since the apostle wanted us to understand that the sin which Christ removes by regeneration entered the world by generation, he said, *Through one man*. Hence, the man either is the parent who then most of all or first of all generated the child, especially because, as we have already said and as we must emphasize, he would have said: Through one woman, if he said this on account of the first example. For from her the example of sinning took its beginning in the human race, and he

would have rather passed over the man who he knew followed the woman's example so that he sinned by imitating her.

86. JUL. In the Letter to the Hebrews, then, where there is discussion of generation, many are said to have come *from the one man* but in the Letter to the Romans where the apostle was speaking about sin, he said that sin entered *through one man* and by that number he clearly taught that he had in mind absolutely nothing to do with generation.

AUG. To speak in that way against matters that are clear is not, as you suppose, praiseworthy eloquence, but incredible impudence.

87. JUL. (1) But where it says of Christ, *He who sanctifies and those who are sanctified are all from the one* (Heb 2:11), we can take this as referring, not to Adam, but to God. For by God's power Christ was created according to the flesh, as well as all the human race, and in this way the similarity to the other passages could add nothing of weight to destroy our interpretation of the apostle where he said that sin entered the world through one man. Let that which follows, nonetheless, be especially fixed in the mind of wise readers so that they realize that I have up to this point acted with far more indulgence than the situation demanded. (2) For even if we agree that in very many testimonies we are taught that generation, which can only be accomplished by two persons, is, nonetheless, often said to be done by one, the doctrine of hereditary sin will derive no advantage. Why? Because there are some words which we use in an extended sense and others which we use in a proper sense. Those words, then, which are used in their proper sense are applied without any loss of meaning, but those which are said in a metaphorical sense are not allowed to impose on their principal objects, that is, on their proper objects a meaning prejudicial to their definitions. All this is done without any fault when we use other terms in an extended sense for things about which there can be no doubt.

AUG. But you are going to introduce doubt even into clear matters which are against you.

88. JUL. But when an idea contrary to the opinion of everyone is introduced by that sort of expression and has its entire support in the literal sense of the expression, one is seriously mistaken if, when its proper term is readily available, it is falsely designated by a borrowed name of an improper term. When the statement, then, concerns children, since no one doubts that everyone who is born has two parents, and this does not need to be explicitly stated, it will not pose a problem for the mind if I say that a certain person was born from one. My statement will surely lead no one to think that this person was born either without a father or without a mother.

AUG. (1) Whoever is born, of course, has two parents, but in order to be born, one parent begets the child by sowing the seed, the other brings it forth by giving birth. From this it is quite clear to which of them we should most of all and first of all attribute the act of generation so that you may stop pouring clouds of wordiness over matters that are set forth in the light of day. But who speaks in such a way as to say that anyone was born of one parent? Everyone, after all, who hears this thinks only of the father, and only one father begets a child by sowing the seed. But two or more children are often correctly said to have been born of one father when they could be thought not to have one father. But where we are to think of the father and the mother, who is said to be born of one parent except as a lie? (2) After all, if it is evident that two people were walking together or did something together, you cannot say without a lie, can you, that there was one person who was walking or one person who did this, because it is evident that there were two? Will not your lie be more brazen, the more obvious it is that there were two? The singular number is used instead of the plural in a figure of speech, for example, in the plagues which struck Egypt. There scripture speaks of the frog or the locust in the singular, though they were many. But if it said one frog or one locust, who would have any doubt that this lie was more foolish to the extent that the truth was more obvious? (3) Stop peddling this fog to people un-trained in these matters, and understand that sin entered the world through one man, not as you say, but as the apostle says. *Through one man*, not because he set an example, for that would be said of the woman, but because he was first in the process of generation. Because he first sowed what she conceived, and he begot what she bore, *sin entered the world* (Rom 5:12). In the same way scripture said, *Abraham begot Isaac; Isaac begot Jacob* (Mt 1:2), and this manner of speaking continued through all the subsequent generations. It did not say: Abraham and Sarah begot Isaac, or Isaac and Rebecca begot Jacob. (4) And where it was nec-essary to mention the mothers, the evangelist did not say: Judah and Thamar be-got Phares and Zaram, but said: *Judah begot by Thamar* (Mt 1:3), and wherever he added the mothers, he ascribed the act of generation to the fathers. He did not say: The father and the mother begot the child, but the father begot the child by her. From this you may understand that scripture said in that way that countless children were born from the one Abraham, because he, one man, begot them by Sarah. And so it said, *Through one man sin entered the world* (Rom 5:12), so that we would understand in those words the beginning of generation which comes from the man, not an example to imitate which in the human race entered the world through one woman rather than through one man.

Proper Sense and Figurative Expression

89. JUL. But when sin is dealt with, and contrary to the opinion of everyone and contrary to all reason it is falsely claimed to be innate. . . .[82]

AUG. It is not falsely claimed to be such contrary to the opinion of everyone and contrary to all reason; rather, contrary to your error this sin is shown to be original by the testimony of scripture and by the misery of the human race.

90. JUL. And this sin is said to have been passed on by one in a proper sense if it set an example of transgression, but it is said most improperly to have been passed on by one if this sin made that innate which could not be passed on to descendants except through two persons. . . .

AUG. In fact, it entered through one man who sowed what she bore, but an example came first in her, and he followed it.

91. JUL. And since the apostle taught that sin was passed on, but passed on through one man, and since the truth showed that this properly has to do with setting an example, the traducianist acts with intolerable impudence when he says that this number distorted by a figure of speech also favors his side.

AUG. (1) What do you think that you are doing in repeating so often that new name, as if it were an insult, so that people take flight from the truth of the ancient Catholic doctrine, while they fear the newness of that name? What can one not mock in this fashion? But by vanity, not by common decency.[83] After all, the apostle says, *Through one man sin entered the world, and through sin death, and in that way it was passed on to all human beings* (Rom 5:12). Both of us accept these words. If we are traducianists on account of the sin which was transmitted by generation so that it was passed on to all human beings, you are traducianists on account of the sin which you imagine was transmitted by imitation so that it was passed on to all human beings.[84] (2) And the apostle was seen first as a traducianist, for whether he had in mind this sin which he clearly had in mind or that one which you erroneously say he had in mind, he, nonetheless, opened himself up to receive that name by saying that sin entered the world through one man and was passed on to all human beings. But if the word "transmission" does not fit this statement in which he said that sin entered the world through one man and was passed on to all human beings, then this name does not fit us or you or the apostle, but to say this, to make this objection, and to repeat this constantly and odiously quite clearly fits your stupidity.

92. JUL. For it is an unheard-of monstrosity if someone tries to create a new doctrine, even a tolerable one, by using words in a loose or ambiguous sense, while abandoning the proper sense of words. But it is infinitely more loathsome that with equivocal statements Augustine tries to support obscene doctrines that even attack the justice of God, admitting that the statements are against him in their proper sense, but supportive of him in their borrowed sense. What learned person would rely on such an argument which, when it comes to the test, its enemy regards as a kinsman, but that man regards as a fugitive and as someone he has kidnaped?

AUG. You say those things about figurative and proper senses. You do this with contempt for the few people who understand you and find you raving mad, and you choose to seem to say something to the many people who do not understand you, though you are saying nothing. It is better that I leave you to the learned few who easily understand, even if I do not point it out, that you have nothing to say rather than that I say in refutation of you things which, though they are true, many do not understand. Nonetheless, where the apostle said, *Through one man sin entered the world* on account of the source of generation and, for that reason, the symbol of the one to come,[85] on account of regeneration, the words are not used figuratively, but properly.

93. JUL. The words, then, in the Letter to the Hebrews, *All from the one*, called for the praise of God, though after mentioning the parents, but the statement about Christ, *He who sanctifies and those who are sanctified are all from the one* (Heb 2:11), is referring to God.

AUG. Rather, after mentioning the parents, the mother should not have been omitted, especially because he had moved on from the father and was speaking about the mother. It should have said: The descendants who had been born, not from one parent, but from two, were born from two, so that the praise of God might be true, not false. It should have been said that way, unless it was also true that they were born from one, and this was not said as a figure of speech, but in the proper sense, on account of the father, the source of the seed, not in order to increase God's praise by a lie, as you suppose. Surely, to say: A person did what two or more persons did could be a figure of speech. But whoever says that one person did what two did, unless the one of those two is the source of the action, is either lying or mistaken, as we said a little before regarding the locust and the frog.[86]

94. JUL. The apostle spoke this way to the Corinthians, *For as the woman came from the man, so the man comes through the woman, but all things come from God* (1 Cor 11:12). But in the third place reason shows that, even if neither of these ideas which we support were the case, the statement, nonetheless, by which Paul argues that sin entered this world through one man, did not form an alliance with the Manichees.

AUG. It is you rather who are shown to be loathsome[87] when you say these things. For what alliance does the apostle have with Mani, since the apostle says, *The body is, of course, dead on account of sin* (Rom 8:10), a point which destroys your heresy? But Mani says: The body is unchangeably evil on account of the evil nature that is coeternal with the good. Likewise, in the same passage where he said, *The body is dead on account of sin*, the apostle says, *He who raised Christ from the dead will also bring to life your mortal bodies* (Rom 8:11). But Mani says that bodies of flesh do not belong to the creation of the good God, but to the evil nature, and that Christ was not raised from the dead, but did not die. You, then, who are not Manichees, but are unwell with another disease, tell me how the body is dead on account of sin, if you say that the death of the body did not enter the world through the sin of that one man, but by the law of nature.

95. JUL. And in this way our response remains unshaken; it shows that the apostle did not claim that nature was damaged and destroyed by one man through generation, but that only the will of sinners was damaged, while nature remains whole and entire.

AUG. (1) Are you so blind or do you so blind people by your murky discourses that you dare to deny that bodies are born with defects? Do bodies not belong to the nature of human beings? Or, as the Manichees say, is the good soul held captive in the bodies of the nation of darkness? You refuse to notice and bear in mind how much help you give, though unwittingly, to their madness. State the merits of those defective bodies, you who deny that little ones contract any sin from their parents. Look, the Manichees say: This mortal flesh is not a part of God's creation, but a product of the nation of darkness, so that even the bodies of human beings who you say were made to the image of God are born, not only corruptible and subject to the condition of death, but also are often born defective. (2) What will your heresy reply to them except that, even though God is our creator and maker, this is human nature and that, even if no one had sinned, such bodies of human beings would be born even in paradise? Oh dreadful and damnable words! We, on the other hand, say not only that, if these parents had not first sinned, the bodies of human beings would not be born in paradise corruptible and subject to the necessity of death, but also that many of them would not be born ailing and twisted and deformed with countless defects. And so, we judge those who say that they would be born such to be most deserving of condemnation, for we attribute these defects not to nature created that way from the beginning, but to nature later damaged as a punishment for sin. In that way we destroy both you and the Manichees by the unshaken and ancient solidity of the Catholic faith.

A Return to Book Two of Marriage and Desire

96. JUL. But let us return to that book which he dedicated to Valerius and in which he set forth only those statements excerpted from one book of mine which he was going to discuss and refute. And in the first book of the present work I had got as far as those statements of Augustine in which his impudence was disclosed by which he tried to escape the hatred for that opinion. For he did not want to be thought to say that the devil was the creator of human beings, and for that reason he stated that God is the source of evil persons and that he creates their substance with such merit that it receives guilt before the use of reason and is placed by the hands of its creator in the kingdom of the devil.

AUG. Anyone who distinguishes nature from its defect does not say what you say; anyone who intelligently reads what I say does not think that I say what I do not say.

97. JUL. He said that God is a potter who makes vessels of anger and of destruction.[88]

AUG. However much you may fail to understand how God makes from the same lump one vessel for an honorable purpose and another for a dishonorable purpose,[89] he does this, nonetheless, without producing a third kind of vessel for neither an honorable nor a dishonorable purpose. You want the little ones to be such vessels, and you suppose that it is no mistreatment for the image of God not to enter the kingdom of God. For you love that kingdom so little that you believe that not to be in it is not even a slight punishment for human beings, but none at all.

98. JUL. But they are forced into destruction, not by the act of free will, but by the power of their maker.

AUG. You can say that God forces into destruction, not just any human beings, but his own children who have been reborn, in making those live who he foresees will abandon the faith, though he could take them from this life before they are corrupted by evil.[90]

99. JUL. He has tried to support this great outrage of his unnatural doctrine by statements from the apostle Paul which I explained in the context of the whole passage, and I showed that the prophet Isaiah, from whom it is clear that he took the comparison with the potter, fully defended the cause of divine justice.

AUG. What have you shown[91] to those who read with understanding, but that you tried to distort the words of the apostle with all your talk, but could not?

100. JUL. With all the strength that the truth provided me, I devoted the second book to the explanation of the apostle with the arguments of Augustine set opposite to them, and I now, therefore, return to the order of his book.

AUG. You devoted the second book, not to an explanation of the apostle, but to a foolish attack under the guise of an explanation of him, and it is vanity, not the truth that provided what you said.

101. JUL. (1) And so, after he cited for himself one chapter from the short preface of my first work as if to attack it and added that chapter about his God as a potter who makes sinners, he accused me. How consistently and fairly he did this may, of course, be revealed by his words: "It is not true, then, as you put it, deceiving yourself and others, that 'if any say that there is free choice in human beings or that God is the creator of the newborn, they are called Pelagians or Caelestians.'[92] For those are also statements of the Catholic faith. (2) But if any say that human beings have free choice to worship God in the right way without his help or if any say that God is the creator of the newborn in such a way that they deny to the little ones a redeemer from the power of the devil, they are called Pelagians or Caelestians. We both, therefore, say that human beings have free choice and that God is the creator of the newborn; this is not the reason you are Caelestians or Pelagians. But you say that anyone is free to do good without the help of God and that little ones are not rescued from the power of darkness and in

that way transferred into the kingdom of God;[93] this is the reason that you are Caelestians or Pelagians."[94] I have often shown that you are swimming in the swamp of your impiety and fear, and it is clear that a wise reader will have no doubt about this.

AUG. Others have known that you cannot swim, but are drowning; they recognize that you are a heretic, for you have lost your good sense as well in that same drowning.

102. JUL. And so a wise reader will not doubt that I did not lie in the first book when I wrote that all who flee from the odium of our society rush over the cliffs of the Manichees who deny free will and God the creator of human beings, and I showed by including a passage from the writings you sent to Boniface that you immediately took up in plain words what you tried to fend off from yourself.[95] Nonetheless, your answer which I just quoted, also admits the same thing, for you said, after all, that it is the Catholic faith which believes that there is free will and that God is the creator of the newborn, both of which points it is certain that the Manichees deny along with you.

AUG. You do not want to see this, but you rather help the Manichees who attribute so many great evils which we see little ones suffer, not to the merits of sins, but to the nation of darkness. For you have nowhere to flee when you are asked about the source of these evils. But since we refer all these evils to the free choice of the man in whom human nature was corrupted, though it was created good, they are defeated along with you by the Catholic truth.

103. JUL. (1) But because you take up only the name of the Catholic faith as a tenuous cloak, while you are stripped of its solid substance, you want us to believe that you too hold what the Catholics profess, that is, that human beings have free choice and that God is the creator of the newborn. But if you stated this with sincerity and faith, put an end to the controversy by silence; let the reputation of accusers revert to us for raising as objections to you what you shall have wiped out by your safe denial. (2) Add only this to that statement, that, if any sect or if any argument should be found which tries to destroy this twofold confession which you profess to be Catholic, either it is not yours, or you no longer defend it. But if you want to defend with bountiful arguments those points which you are going to say that you have denied, explain the definitions of free choice, and mark off its limits with clear distinctions as if by certain boundaries.

AUG. As its hostile defenders, you destroy free choice by defending it, because you do not want it to be recalled to its own limits by the goodness of its almighty and true defender.

Works Befitting for the Just Hands of God

104. JUL. State also that God is the creator of the sort of human beings as are fitting for his just hands.

AUG. O you foolish new heretics! If defective works are not fitting for the hands of God, will you dare to remove from the hands of God any bodies of human beings, since you see that at times some of them are born defective? Why not, then, admit with the Catholic truth that the first choice by which the human being sinned damaged the nature from which God makes what is fitting not only for a good maker, but also for a just judge? Otherwise, the Manichees will force you to attribute human bodies to an evil and unjust maker.

105. JUL. You certainly have done none of these things. Rather, after you answered that Catholics, among whose number you pretend to be, admit free choice, you immediately added a definition which snatched back what you seemed to have granted. For you said, "But if any say that human beings have free choice to worship God in the right way without his help, they are called Pelagians," and also, "We say that human beings have free choice, but you say that a person is free to do good."[96]

AUG. "A person is free to do good without the help of God." If you had added here, "The heretics say," even though I did not say those words, you would not have deviated from my thought. It is, after all, true that the heretics, that is, you yourselves, say that a person is free to do good without the help of God. But the reason why I did not read there: "without the help of God," my own words in this sentence which you yourself quoted a little earlier,[97] I ascribe, as long as I can, to a defective manuscript rather than to you. And so, continue with the rest.

Freedom to Worship God Properly

106. JUL. (1) You are a complete liar when you say that we claim that free choice suffices for each person to worship God in the right way without the help of God. After all, the worship of God means many things: the observance of the commandments, the eradication of vices, the simplicity of one's manner of living, the celebration of the mysteries, and the profound doctrines which the Christian faith holds regarding the Trinity or the resurrection and many others of this sort. And so, how is it possible that we should say without qualification that without the help of God free choice is sufficient for his worship? For we read in the gospel that the Lord says, *I confess to you, Father, Lord of heaven and earth, for you have hidden these things from the wise and prudent and revealed them to little ones: Yes, Father, for that was pleasing in your sight* (Mt 11:25-26). (2) Freedom of choice by itself could not, of course, discover all these things which are contained in the doctrines and mysteries, though natural reason could, as the teacher of the nations testifies, teach us that idols should not be worshiped and

that the God who makes himself known as the creator of the world should not be spurned.[98] Neither we nor any of the wise, therefore, say what you invent; rather, we state that God makes human beings with free choice and helps them by countless forms of divine grace so that it is possible for them to keep the commandments of God or to break them. And this is why we maintain that there is free choice: Since God shows his goodness in so many ways, that is, by commanding, blessing, sanctifying, restraining, challenging, and enlightening, all those who already have the use of reason have the freedom either to observe or to reject the will of God.

AUG. (1) You mention so many ways in which God helps us, that is, "by commanding, blessing, sanctifying, restraining, challenging, and enlightening," but you do not mention: by giving his love, though the apostle John says, *Love comes from God* (1 Jn 4:7). About this love he also says, *See what sort of love the Father has given us that we are called and are the children of God* (1 Jn 3:1). In this love which is given to the human heart by the Spirit, not by the letter, we also understand that power about which the same apostle said in his gospel, *He gave them the power to become children of God* (Jn 1:12). (2) You say that human beings give themselves this power by free choice, because you have the spirit of this world, not the Spirit which is from God,[99] and on this account you do not know the gifts God has given us. For this reason you do not have peace with the Church from which you have departed, nor do you have the love which you deny is a gift of God, nor the faith, because you are heretics. For *peace to the sisters and brothers and love along with faith* do not come from human free choice, but *from God the Father and the Lord Jesus Christ* (Eph 6:23). If you recognize the teaching of the apostle in these words, then recognize in your own words that you are a heretic.

107. JUL. (1) We do not, therefore, believe that without the help of God free choice is capable of that worship of him which those initiated into the mysteries offer him, but we confess that freedom of choice is an ample witness to the justice of God. We are taught that, at the time when each of us must appear before the judgment seat of Christ to receive recompense for what we did in the body, whether good or evil,[100] God never judges unjustly; he never holds a sin against one unless the person who is punished for it could also have avoided it.

AUG. (1) You remind me well of what I should say against you. Certainly *we all must appear*, as the apostle says, *before the judgment seat of Christ that each of us might receive recompense for what we did in the body, whether good or evil* (2 Cor 5:10). Will you separate the little ones from the totality of us? Tell me, then, what good they did in the body by their own free choice in order that they might receive the great good of the kingdom of God or what evil those little ones did by their own will that they will be kept from this life of God. But if, as[101] is necessary, you admit that without any acts of free will which each performs in the body, the former are brought to life in Christ, why do you not admit that the latter die in Adam, since you know that, as the symbol of the one to come,[102] Adam was contrasted with Christ? (2) Or will you open your mouth with your eyes closed and say that the spirit of righteousness in whom they were reborn benefitted the former, but that the sinful flesh in which they were born was no obstacle to the latter? Who but you people would dare to say that? But when human beings of adult age hear or read that each of us will receive recompense in accord with what we did in the body, they should not put their confidence in the virtue[103] of their own will, but rather pray that the Lord may prepare for them such a will that they may not enter into temptation. After all, *the will is prepared by the Lord* (Prv 8:35 LXX), and the Lord himself says, *Pray that you may not enter into temptation* (Mt 26:41), and the apostle says, *We pray to God that you do nothing evil* (2 Cor 13:7).

108. JUL. Your first statement, then, will achieve nothing by its obscurity, but the second in which you repeat that you admit free choice, but not so that you believe a person is free to do good, strips naked your deepest feelings.

AUG. You force me to attribute to you what I just before attributed to the manuscript.[104] See, you repeat, after all, my sentence so that you do not complete it with my words which are quite necessary and against you. For I said, "No one is free to do good without the help of God," but you say that I said: "I admit free choice, but not so that I believe a person is free to do good," and you do not add what I added: "Without the help of God." I am not charging you with theft; I am asking in civil court for the restoration of what was taken. Restore my words, and yours will be completely ineffective.

The Denial of Free Choice

109. JUL. (1) Look, we are now pressing you closely, as we did in the first book, to show how you do not deny free choice. But let this fact sink into our reader, namely, that you have admitted that Catholics preach[105] that there is free choice and that God is the creator of the newborn, two points which only Mani has denied. But since both of us have in common granted these points, and since freedom of choice is compatible neither with you nor with your teaching, the conclusion is that you and your teaching hold absolutely nothing of the Catholic faith. I ask you, therefore, what the power or what the definition of free choice is. (2) Certainly no change in natural things lies in its power. For none have ever changed in themselves the functions of the senses so that, for example, sounds are received by the nose or odors by the ears; none have changed the character of their sex; none have ever been able to change into the form of another animal. None have been able to exchange by free choice the hairs of their body for a natural fur; none have by their native talent obtained for themselves either the quality

or quantity of their bodies. By these examples one can run through everything which pertains to this condition. (3) Let us, then, turn from natural things to a consideration of external things. Who hold in the power of the will the fertility of the fields, success in navigation, fame, and wealth, and the secure possession of fame, so that they may claim that they were endowed by God with a will free to acquire these or like things? Natural things proceed in their unchanging order, but external things are carried along by the uncertainties of chance. In which, then, is there found the free choice on account of which human beings surpass the other animals, on account of which they were made to the image of God, and which alone preserves the justice of God's judgment? In what, I ask, does this free choice consist? As the Manichees certainly deny it, so even you admit that the Catholics defend it. Undoubtedly it consists in the fact that it is possible for human beings either to turn their will to a serious sin or to hold it back from a serious sin without any of the unavoidable compulsion found in natural things.

AUG. (1) To hold back the will from a serious sin is nothing else than not to enter into temptation. But if we had this in the power of our own will, we would not be warned to ask it from the Lord in prayer. When the psalmist says, *Turn away from evil* (Ps 37:27), he, of course, says this in order that one may hold back his will from serious sin. And yet, though the apostle could have correctly said: We command you not to do anything evil, he said, *We pray to God that you do nothing evil* (2 Cor 13:7). There you see why I said that no one is free to do good without the help of God, and not what you say that I said. The apostle prayed for this help for the faithful, but he did not remove from human nature free choice. (2) You proud and boastful people, do not place your trust in your own virtue;[106] make yourselves subject to God, and pray that you may hold back your will from serious sin and not enter into temptation. Do not suppose that you do not enter into temptation when you restrain by a strong will your concupiscence of the flesh from some evil action. You do not know the wiles of the tempter; you enter into greater temptation when you ascribe this to your will without the help of God. I wish you would teach us the sense in which you said that those things which are called external among human goods and evils, such as riches and poverty and so on, "are carried along by the uncertainties of chance." For the Catholic faith also removes these from the power of human beings, but attributes them to God's power. (3) I say this, however, because I fear for you that you may also add this idea to your error, namely, that you may deny that whatever human beings suffer or acquire whether in their bodies or in external possessions falls under divine providence and, for this reason, also attribute whatever evils little ones suffer to the uncertainties of chance. In that way you would try to remove them from the judgment of God, though, as the Lord himself says, not even a sparrow falls to the earth apart his will.[107] For you see that your heresy faces shipwreck over this misery of little ones, since under a just

God there would be no such misery, unless human nature merited to be damaged and condemned by the magnitude of the first sin.

110. JUL. A few examples may throw light on an unambiguous question. A human being is as free to will as not to will to commit a sacrilege, as free to will as not to will to kill a parent, as free to will as not to will to commit adultery; it is just as possible to give true as to give false testimony and just as possible to obey God's commands as to obey the persuasions of the devil.

AUG. (1) You speak the truth; this is the sort of free choice which Adam received, but what the creator gave and the deceiver corrupted must, of course, be healed by the savior. You do not want to admit this along with the Church; for this reason you are heretics. You, though a human being, do not consider in what condition you are, and you are as blindly proud in evil days as if these were the good days when there existed the sort of free choice which you describe; then human beings had not yet become like a vanity so that their days passed like a shadow.[108] For God is no vanity, and human beings were made to his likeness, the likeness which is renewed day by day through his grace.[109] (2) One did not yet say, *I was conceived in iniquities* (Ps 51:7); one did not yet say, *For who is clean from filth? Not even an infant who has lived a single day on earth* (Jb 14:4 LXX). Finally, one did not as yet say, *I do not do what I will, but I do what I hate* (Rom 7:15) and, *I know that the good does not dwell in me, that is, in my flesh, for I can will the good, but I find that I cannot bring it to completion* (Rom 7:18) and, *I see another law in my members that resists the law of my mind* (Rom 7:23).

(3) This evil was not present in Adam when he was created upright, because human nature was not yet corrupted; he had a ruler whom he abandoned by free choice and did not as yet look for a deliverer by whom he might become free from sin. For, if those words, *I do not do what I will* (Rom 7:19), and others of the sort, were the words of someone, as you claim, not yet under the grace of Christ, then you are refuted on this point too, for Christ has found human beings with wills so weak for doing good, and human nature can repair that weakness of free choice for doing good only through the grace of Christ. (4) And for this reason what I said is true: No one is free to do good without the help of God, and you removed "without the help of God," precisely so that you might have an open field in which to ramble on about many points with more wordiness than eloquence. In these points you do not delight the reader, but rather hinder as much as possible someone who wants to understand. Make yourselves subject to God so that you may be corrected. No one is free to do good without the help of God. Why do you extol the human will in order to cause its downfall? Pray rather that you may not enter into temptation.

111. JUL. In the above example, however, I spoke of the perfect will rather than the actual achievement, for it is easier to avoid parricide, sacrilege, adultery, and other such sins than to commit them. After all, an evil will does not al-

ways have the opportunity to carry out what it wants, but refraining from these, on the contrary, consists in doing absolutely nothing, unless perhaps you call it an effort not to want to make an effort. I pass over those things which the holy scriptures, which the prophets, the evangelists, and the apostles produced, have taught, as well as those which the teachers renowned for Catholic soundness, such as John, Basil, Theodore,[110] and others of the sort have taught, namely, that it is a much greater effort to commit serious offenses than to avoid them.

AUG. I wish you possessed the faith of these people and would not deny original sin in the little ones.

The Will Is Captive Neither to Justice Nor to Injustice

112. JUL. Meanwhile, with regard to the present task, I teach that free choice was given for no other reason and cannot be understood in any other way than that a person is not carried off by a captive will either to justice or to injustice.

AUG. (1) The apostle cries out, *I do not do the good that I will, but I do the evil that I hate* (Rom 7:15). You must, of course, explain how he is not carried off by a captive will through the law which he sees in his members that resists the law of his mind and holds him captive under the law of sin.[111] For, to speak for a moment in accord with your view, if this man groans under the weight of a bad habit, because he has not yet been brought under the grace of Christ, as you claim, does he have or not have free choice of the will? (2) If he does, why does he not do the good that he wills, but does the evil that he hates? If he does not have free choice because he is not yet under the grace of Christ, look, I say to you again what I have already said, and I see that I must say it to you often: No one can have free choice of the will to do the good which one wills or not to do the evil which one hates except by the grace of Christ. This does not mean that the will is carried off as a captive to good in the same way as to evil, but that, once set free from captivity, it may be drawn to its deliverer by the sweet freedom of love, not by the bitter servitude of fear.

113. JUL. The enticements to the vices are, of course, sweet, and the torments of punishments which persecutors stir up are frequently bitter. But the censure of moral goodness repels the former, and the greatness of patience removes the latter.

AUG. You speak out among those *who place their trust in their own virtue* (Ps 49:7); watch out that you do not cry out among those who will be tormented for their pride.

The Various Helps of God's Grace

114. JUL. The possession of the virtues is, nonetheless, not difficult, for, apart from the reign of a good conscience, it enjoys the promised height of eternal blessedness. There are also present the helps of God's grace which never abandon the will in the cause of virtue, and although there are many kinds of grace, they are always applied with moderation so that they never drive free choice from its position, but offer helps, as long as it wills to rely on them, without, nonetheless, overwhelming a reluctant mind. For this reason, as some rise up to the virtues from the vices, so others fall back to the vices from the virtues.

AUG. (1) How is it possible that the helps of God's grace should drive free choice from its position? They, rather, set it free, after it had been driven from its position by the vices and made subject to wickedness, so that it may return to its proper position. But when we ask you what those helps of God's grace are, you mention those which you listed above, namely, that God helps "by commanding, blessing, sanctifying, restraining, challenging, and enlightening," all of which are also done by human beings according to the scriptures. (2) For human beings give commands and bless; they sanctify through the divine sacraments, restrain by rebuking, challenge by exhorting, and enlighten by teaching; *and yet neither the one who plants nor who waters is anything, but only God who gives the increase* (1 Cor 3:7). But the increase is that each person obeys the commandments of God, and one does this, when one really does this, only with love. For this reason the Church *produces the increase of the body for building itself up with love* (Eph 4:16). Only God gives this love, for love comes from God.[112] (3) You do not want to mention this love among the helps of grace which you list so that you do not grant that the very fact that we obey God is due to his grace. You, of course, suppose that the choice of the will is removed in this way, though a person can only obey God by the will. But—and here is what you do not want–*the will is prepared by the Lord* (Prv 8:35 LXX), not by words that sound in the ears, but as, when the queen prayed and was heard, God changed and transformed the anger of the king into gentleness.[113] For, as God acted in the heart of that man in this divine and hidden manner, so *he produces in us both the willing and the action in accord with good will* (Phil 2:13).

115. JUL. How, then, can you admit free choice when you say that only one option is possible for it, that is, to do evil, but that it is not possible to turn away from evil and to do good?[114]

AUG. I do say that it is possible for the human will to turn away from evil and to do good, but it is possible for the will which God helps by his grace, not the will which Julian ungratefully puffs up with pride.

116. JUL. I am silent for the moment about the madness with which you rage against the whole law which you believe imposed commands upon mortals which it saw they had no ability to carry out.

AUG. What you say is not true. God commands these things which can be done, and he himself gives to those who can and do carry them out the fact that they do carry them out, and by commanding he warns those who cannot to ask him so that they can. And because not all of them are carried out by each of the saints, God knows how to help them toward humility, and he helps those who say daily, *Forgive us our debts* (Mt 6:12), to have obedience in such a way that there is also reason for him to grant pardon.

117. JUL. But I ask with which poets you plunge into the Hippocrene[115] so that, not as a poet, but as a blasphemer, you imagine a bipartite beast, for you fashion its body out of the necessity for evil and cover only its face with the word for freedom.

AUG. You picture for yourself what you want; your empty heart is free to toy with empty images. After all, why do you prop up a good will with the support of grace, while an evil will leans on no support in order to be evil or to continue to be evil? Or does your scale, which you try to balance with equal weights on both sides so that the will is just as free for good as it is for evil, prove here that you are out of your mind by its tipping to one side?

118. JUL. For you argue in this manner in that book which you sent to Rome: "The will which is free for evil actions is not free for good actions."[116]

AUG. Why do you not add what you read there: "if it has not been set free"? Or why is it that the Lord said, when he was speaking about the fruits of the branches, that is, of good actions: *Without me you can do nothing* (Jn 15:5), except because no one whom he does not set free is free to do good?

119. JUL. (1) And here you call someone a Caelestian who thinks that anyone is free to do good; you, therefore, call that free which you claim can only do evil. Find, if you can, another definition of something not free, and defend this as free. If you have not lost your mind to the point that you fail to see the definition of "free" in its reality, you, at least, ought to have understood from its opposite what is the essence of freedom.[117] (2) Suppose, after all, that you could be likewise in doubt about what is meant by eyesight and that you defined it in this way: sight is either to have the eyes destroyed or to be unable to see anything because of some impediments when one opens them. Suppose that you think this definition corresponds to sight, but you turned to express the definition of its opposite, that is, of blindness. You would find no other definition than this: In a living being to whose nature eyesight belongs, there is either a destruction of the eyes or an barrier of denser fluid that removes the ability to see. You would undoubtedly come to your senses and see that one definition cannot fit opposite realities. (3) And so it would turn out that, if blindness could not be said to be anything but the privation of sight in the eye of a living being at the time when it ought to see, we are also given the definition of sight by the denial of those things by which you defined blindness. That is, sight would be nothing else than the appropriate capacity to see at a suitable time, when the eyes are not destroyed or closed. Once these

facts have been pointed out, if you fought back with stubbornness, you would achieve nothing but that your hearers would either believe that you are struggling with shameful obstinacy against your own conscience or, if you convinced them that you really think so, they would judge that you have the eyes of your mind destroyed no less than the one who according to your definition had sight.

AUG. I do not want you to define, but to put an end[118] to blindness and see that Christ could not have correctly said, *Without me you can do nothing* (Jn 15:5), if they were able to be free to do good without the grace of Christ.

Definitions of "Free" and "Not Free"

120. JUL. And so, to apply the example to the present issue, you could have grasped at least from the definition of "not free" what you ought to call "free." For, even if your mind was clouded regarding the definition of free choice so that you thought one should call "free" that which we have learned is determined to one of two contraries, you ought to have seen that "captive," that is, "not free," cannot be defined otherwise than as that which is shown to be determined to one of two contraries. And so, one should define freedom by a denial of captivity. Then, because what is not free must be determined to one of the two contraries, its opposite, that is, "free," is not allowed to be determined to either of them.

AUG. (1) Why do you wrap obvious matters in complicated language? One is free for evil who by the will does evil either in action or in speech or just in thought alone. But who among human beings of a more mature age cannot do this? One is free, however, for good who by a good will does good either in action or in speech or just in thought alone, but no one can do this without the grace of God. If you say that someone can, you contradict him who said, *Without me you can do nothing* (Jn 15:5); you also contradict him who said, *Not that we are capable of having some thought as if by ourselves, but our ability comes from God* (2 Cor 3:5). (2) I think he meant that he was not capable of having some good thought, not a bad thought, by himself, but was capable by God; a good word and a good deed, however, come from a good thought. And so, those who are not capable of having some good thought by themselves certainly are not capable of saying something good or doing something good by themselves, but if they are under the power of grace, their ability comes from God. For this reason he said, *For it is not you who speak, but the Spirit of your Father who speaks in you* (Mt 10:20), and *Whoever are driven by the Spirit of God are the children of God* (Rom 8:14). (3) With my eyes on these words, I said that no one is free to do good without the help of God; out of fear of these words you said that I had said that no one is free to do good, and you removed "without the help of God," which I added. Hence, I have no doubt that you already know that you are defeated, but you carry on with endless and empty words so that you are not seen to be defeated, when you define free will so that it could not be free if it could not do both, that is, both do good and do evil. And for this reason you must remove freedom from God who can have only a good will, but cannot have a bad will.

121. JUL. Since this is so and since you struggle wretchedly against this argument, it is uncertain what it is more suitable to think of you: whether you defend what is false contrary to your conscience or you think what is false is true. And in this case it is uncertain whether you have lost the eyes of reason, though it is certain that you have destroyed the eyes of faith.

AUG. Do you comfort yourself in your defeat by hurling insults?

122. JUL. Let us briefly repeat what has been accomplished: Free choice, which is helped toward evil by the pleasures of the vices and the persuasions of the devil, but toward good by the teachings of the virtues and various kinds of divine grace, can only exist if there is kept from it the necessity of both righteousness and of sin.

AUG. If you included among the various kinds of divine grace the love which, as you read most clearly in scripture, does not come from us, but from God[119] and which God gives to his children,[120] that love without which no one lives a life of piety and with which no one lives anything but a life of piety, that love without which no one has good will and with which no one has anything but good will, you would be defending a truly free choice and not inflating it with pride. If, however, you call that a necessity by which any are compelled against their will, there is no necessity of righteousness because none are righteous unwillingly. Rather, the grace of God makes them willing from unwilling. But if no one sins unwillingly, scripture would not say, *You have sealed my sins in a sack, and you have noted if I have done anything unwillingly* (Jb 14:17).

123. JUL. The Catholics confess the truth of this claim, but the traducianists deny it along with the Manichees, their teachers.

AUG. These are insults, not judgments. I wish that you could exercise judgment. What lout is not able to hurl insults?

124. JUL. We have, therefore, stated the truth, for those whom you deceive become Manichees for fear of being called heretics and, while they are afraid of a false ignominy, they commit a true crime, like animals that are surrounded by feathers so that they are forced into nets and are driven to true destruction out of an empty fear. But we say that God is the creator of the newborn, and because of the dignity of their maker, we believe that the human beings he makes do not come from his hands wicked and guilty in any sense, before they have use of their will, for it is certain that the God of the Catholics, who is the true God, can make nothing that is evil. When you deny one of these, you destroy both of them. You say, of course, that you believe that God is the creator, but the creator of evil human beings, and in this way you disown your own teaching, since you deny that you hold that the devil is the creator of human beings.

AUG. Whatever is due to God in human beings who are born with a defect is good, because what is just is also good, but God is the author of natures, not of defects. Come to the point now. Let us see what you are going to say about this. How are the little ones not rescued from the power of darkness when they are transferred into the kingdom of Christ by the sacraments of the Church?[121] For however heavy are the coverings of great wordiness with which you wrap yourself, when you come to this point, you will be revealed stark naked as a heretic.

125. JUL. For when you attribute to the work of God the sort of beings he cannot make, you show that what you had said that he makes is not due to him.

AUG. Only God can make human beings. Tell me, rather, how little ones are not rescued from the power of darkness when they are reborn through the divine sacraments.

Crimes and Blasphemy against God's Justice

126. JUL. Though this has been done quite extensively in the first book,[122] let us, nonetheless, also state here at least briefly what you hold. You are afraid to attribute a substance to the work of the devil, but you are not afraid to ascribe to God, not just any crime, but a great crime. The nature of human flesh holds more respect in your eyes than the justice of God. For you were afraid to attribute to the devil the substance of a human being, as if it were something great, and you attributed the deformity of an outrage to the justice and holiness of God, as if it were nothing great.[123] But of the two opinions, though both are false, it is more tolerable to attribute the flesh to the work of the devil than to attribute injustice to the works of God.

AUG. You rather blaspheme against the justice of God, for you say that under his omnipotence little ones suffer such great evils without any sins that merited this. But tell me now how you separate them from those whom God rescues *from the power of darkness* to transfer them *into the kingdom of his beloved Son* (Col 1:13).

127. JUL. For as you said in this passage that the little ones are created guilty by God in[124] the power of the devil, so in the later parts of your book you vomited forth something more horrid than the sacraments of the Manichees, when you said of God, "He creates the evil,[125] just as he feeds and nourishes the evil."[126]

AUG. When you come to those same parts of my book, the sense of that which you here raise as an objection will there become evident. But now tell me how, when little ones are reborn and transferred to the kingdom of Christ, they are not rescued from the power of darkness.

128. JUL. God, therefore, creates evil.

AUG. You do not understand the sense in which he says in the prophet, *I create evils* (Is 45:7).

129. JUL. And innocents are punished on account of what God did.

AUG. They are neither innocent from their origin, nor are they punished for what God did.

130. JUL. And they are owned by the devil because God did this.

AUG. The apostle handed a man over to Satan,[127] but with justice, not with malice, and God *handed over some to an evil frame of mind* (Rom 1:28), and I wish you were not also among them.

131. JUL. And God holds against human beings the crime committed by his own hands.

AUG. It is not a crime committed by God's hands that the little ones contract from their damaged origin.

132. JUL. And what the devil gently suggested God skillfully and continually creates and propagates and guards and fashions.

AUG. God does not fashion what the devil suggests, but from the nature which the devil damaged God fashions well what he fashions.

133. JUL. And he demands of human beings in whom he implanted evil the fruit of goodness.

AUG. God did not implant evil, but God purifies by rebirth the evil which our damaged birth implanted.

134. JUL. And afterward he tells the lie throughout the whole law that God is just.

AUG. You are the liar, but in denying[128] that the children of Adam have a sin that deserves their heavy yoke,[129] what do you try to show but that God is unjust?

135. JUL. And is one who is capable of so many crimes still called God?

AUG. Because God commits no crimes, he is not capable of this crime either which you attribute to him, namely, that without any guilt of original sin little ones suffer so many great evils which he either produces or permits.

136. JUL. *The memory* of the Manichees *will perish with an outcry*, because *the Lord will remain forever. He has prepared his seat for judgment, and he will judge the world in justice* (Ps 9:7-9). There is no crime in God. He does not, therefore, create evil persons because, if they were evil by nature, God could not create them, and for this reason, as it is a mark of Catholics to confess that God is the creator of the good, so it is properly a mark of the Manichees to believe that God is the creator of the evil.

AUG. If you were not deaf to the words of God where it says, *He will judge the world in justice* (Ps 9:9), you would also recognize God's justice in the punishments of infants. For by reason of their nature they are good because God creates them, but they are evil by reason of the defect on account of which God heals them. In that Catholic statement there perishes not only the memory of the Manichees, but also that of the Pelagians with the noise of their endless talk.

137. JUL. But let us look at the rest.

AUG. See, you already move to other words of my book, and you say nothing against what you had quoted from my previous words as if you were going to refute them. For in order to press you with the authority of the apostle, I stated that you say that little ones are not rescued from the power of darkness and in that way transferred to the kingdom of God.[130] In saying nothing against this, you were revealed, as I said above,[131] stark naked as a heretic. But I did not have to work at stripping you because you did not dare to cover yourself with any foolish covering of your words in opposition to the apostolic faith of our ancient mother, the Church.

Julian Turns the Discussion to Another Topic

138. JUL.[132] "Listen, then, for a few moments to what is at stake in this question. Catholics say that human nature was created good by the good God, the creator, but that, having been wounded by sin, it needs Christ the physician. The Manichees say that human nature was not created good by God and wounded by sin, but that human beings were created by the prince of eternal darkness out of the mixture of the two natures which always existed, the one good and the other evil. The Caelestians and Pelagians say that human nature was created good by the good God, but that in newborn little ones it is so healthy that they have no need at that age of any medicine from Christ. Acknowledge, then, in your doctrine the name that belongs to you, and stop raising as an objection to Catholics who refute you a doctrine and a name that does not belong to them. For the Truth refutes both groups: the Manichees and you. After all, he says to the Manichees, *Have you not read that he who made human beings in the beginning made them male and female? And he said, For this reason a man will leave father and mother and will cling to his wife, and they will be two in one flesh. And so, they are now not two, but one flesh. Therefore, what God has joined together, let no one separate* (Mt 19:4-6). In that way, of course, he indicated against the Manichees who deny both these points that God is the creator of human beings and the one who unites spouses. But to you the Truth says, *The Son of Man came to seek and to save what was lost* (Lk 19:10). Now you exemplary Christians reply[133] to Christ, 'If you came to seek and to save what was lost,' you did not come for little ones. They were not lost, but were born safe and sound. Turn to the adults; from your own words we give you directions: *It is not the healthy, but those who are ill who need a physician* (Mt 9:12). And so it happens that the Manichee, who says that the evil nature is mixed into a human being, at least wants the good soul to be saved by Christ. But you maintain that there is nothing to be saved by Christ in little ones, when they are safe and sound in body.[134] And so, the Manichee hatefully finds fault with human nature, but you praise it cruelly. After all, those who believe your praises will not present their infants to the

savior."[135] I have emphasized in my first work that you do nothing more than make yourself barely intelligible.

AUG. I am quite intelligible, whether you like it or not. But you are going to say nothing against them and only want that people do not understand my perfectly true and solid statements. Finally, the facts themselves show that you could not refute them.

139. JUL. And I showed that more than half of your statements take more effort to understand than to refute.

AUG. You make an effort—which is more difficult for you—and you are refuted. But you do not make the effort to understand me—which you can very easily do. Rather, you struggle to refute me—which you cannot do.

140. JUL. If I wanted to do that point by point, I would seem to be doing something superfluous in repeating the same things and something tedious in going after all of them.

AUG. See how you carry on so that the readers move away from what I said and think that you answered, while they forget what you set out to refute.

Julian Sums Up Augustine's Arguments

141. JUL. For this reason all your writings which you have published against us aim at one goal, namely, that you convince us that there are natural evils and that either the devil is the creator of human beings or God is the creator of sins. I think, nonetheless, that it will contribute to the pursuit of brevity if I gather into one spot from their various locations especially those arguments by which, when you are in the dark, you suppose that you defend your opinion. And I shall first back them up by adding an explanation so that it is evident what they are aiming at, but then I shall refute them, not scattered about, but gathered together, not under cover, but unwrapped.

AUG. With an amazing pursuit of brevity you produce eight books to my one, which you do not undermine with all your long-winded wordiness. Tell me now, if you can, how you are not forced to say to Christ, even if not in words, at least in these perverse thoughts of yours, "If you came to seek and to save what was lost, you did not come for little ones. They were not lost, but were born safe and sound. Turn to the adults; from your own words we give you directions: *It is not the healthy, but those who are ill who need a physician*" (Mt 9:12).[136] Reply to that. Why do you try to cover up and hide the truth with empty words?

142. JUL. (1) In the latter parts of your book, then, after you said, "God creates the evil, just as he feeds and nourishes the evil," you add, "Because what he gave them in creating them pertains to the goodness of nature and the increase that he gives by feeding and nourishing them he certainly did not give to their malice, but as a good help to the same good nature that he created in his good-

ness. After all, insofar as they are human beings, there is in them the good of nature of which God is the author, but insofar as they are born with sin, destined to perish, if they are not reborn, they belong to the seed cursed from the beginning[137] because of the defect from that early disobedience. He who also makes the vessels of anger, nonetheless, makes good use of this defect, *in order to make known the riches of his glory toward the vessels of mercy* (Rom 9:23), so that, if any who pertain to that same lump are set free by grace, they do not attribute it to their own merits. Rather, *the one who boasts should boast in the Lord* (2 Cor 10:17). This fellow abandons this faith. For he does not want the newborn to be under the power of the devil so that little ones are not brought to Christ to be rescued from the power of darkness and transferred into his kingdom.[138] And so, he accuses the Church spread throughout the whole world, because everywhere in the Church all the little infants to be baptized undergo the rite of exsufflation[139] only so that the prince of this world might be driven out of them."[140]

(2) Likewise, further on, you speak of sexual desire without which there cannot be the union of spouses; we defend it as natural and as belonging to God's work, not as if it were some great good, but like the senses of bodies which God made. But in many writings you try to maintain that it is implanted in the human inner organs by the devil, and you rest your doctrine upon a sense of shame over it. You speak of this sexual desire in the latter part of your book, as you do frequently, and you say, "For the same reason we do not blame the proper union of spouses because of the shameful passion of bodies. For that union of spouses could have existed, even if no sin had first been committed, and the couple would not have been ashamed over it. But this passion came to be after the sin, and in their shame they were forced to conceal it. As a result of this, though their married descendants make a good and licit use of this evil, they avoid being seen by other human beings when engaged in this act, and in that way they admit that it is a source of shame, since no one ought to be ashamed over what is good. Hence, one who in shameful passion has licit intercourse makes good use of an evil, but one who has illicit intercourse makes bad use of an evil."[141]

AUG. (1) Why did you break up my statement? And after the omission of a few lines, why did you add, as if it followed: "Hence, one who in shameful passion," and so on? My words were omitted, however, where I said, "In this way we are taught two points: the goodness of the praiseworthy union from which children are born and the evil of the shameful lust as a result of which those who are born must be reborn in order to avoid condemnation."[142] (2) Why do you remove these words of mine from the middle of my statement, and after having removed them add other words of mine as if they followed? What is it that you are doing? Why do you do this? It is not enough that you set aside those statements which you had quoted out of order from my book for the purpose of refutation and move on to other topics so that the order is disturbed and the passage you had quoted slips from the memory of the reader? Besides that, you do not faithfully quote those words whole and entire, which you interject out of order as you please. Rather, you break them up as you wish, take away what you wish, and join them as you wish. But do whatever you wish; you will be seen to be refuted and defeated, as you do not wish.

143. JUL. "After all, that over which both bad and good people blush is more correctly called evil than good, and we do better to believe the man who said, *I know that the good does not dwell in my flesh* (Rom 7:18), than to believe this man who declares it a good."[143]

AUG. It would not have been a big chore to complete this sentence too from my book. For I said, "Than to believe this man who declares it a good, for, if he is ashamed of it, he admits that it is evil, but if he is not ashamed of it, he adds impudence—a worse evil."[144] But I do not know why you did not quote this since you were unable to reply to these words, just as to the others which you quoted as if to refute and refused to touch.

Accusations of Unintelligibility

144. JUL. (1) And after a bit you add, "For human nature, whether it is born from a marriage or from adultery, is the work of God. If it were evil, it ought not to be born; if it did not have evil, it would not need to be reborn. And to sum up both points in a single statement, if human nature were something evil, it ought not to be saved, and if there were nothing evil in it, it would not need to be saved. Hence, one who says that it is not something good denies a good creator for the nature that has been created, but one who denies that there is evil in it begrudges a merciful savior to the nature that has been corrupted. For this reason, in the case of human beings who are born, we should not excuse adulteries because of the good which the good creator produces from them, and we should not accuse marriages because of the evil which the merciful savior must heal in them."[145] (2) I have quoted so many words from your writing because you expended a great effort of thought upon them in order to appear to say something clever. And in accord with our own practice of doing nothing out of cunning, but from the vantage point of the truth, since these points can scarcely be understood from your words, they must be divided up by our repetition. You said, then, that the Manichees blame the nature of the flesh and maintain that human beings were made from the mixture of two natures, the one good and the other bad, but that we whom you call heretics say that human nature created good by the good God, as its author testifies, is so healthy in infants that they have no need of the medicine of Christ. But you said that you yourselves hold that Adam's nature was once created good by the good God, but was, nonetheless, damaged by sin and, therefore, needs the medicine of Christ. (3) In the first book of the present work I proved by juxtaposing the views of both of you how your faith differs in no re-

spect from the profanity of the Manichees, from which it is clear that it originated; there it became evident that you are mated with Jovinian out of fear, but
with Mani purely out of love. In the present book, then, we must also debate in
this manner, but I shall first set forth our views and then yours. You spoke the
truth, then, in saying that we hold that human nature was created good by the
good God, but only up to this point is this our teaching. For you either did not see
or suppressed one clause by which our sentence was completed, but you set forth
another of your own, for it is not ours. For we not only say that the nature of a human being was created good by God in Adam, but that it is created good in all the
little ones by the same God who was the author of that first human being. For that
reason we maintain that he is the creator of all human beings.

AUG. What else, after all, do we too say about the Lord God, the creator of all
human beings? But—and God keep us from this!—you deny that God the savior
is necessary for little ones, when you maintain that their nature is so good that
you claim there is no evil in it on account of which it needs Christ the physician.
Reply to this; first refute what you set forth for yourself to refute. Show why little
ones about to be baptized undergo the rite of exsufflation, or maintain that they
ought not to undergo exsufflation by declaring war on the whole of the Church
back to its beginning. Do this; take a stand here; strike, if you can, this foundation with something to shake it. Why do you take refuge under the skins of your
wordiness? Why do you spread empty smoke so that the readers forget these
points once they are covered and obscured by it so that they think that you are
saying something, though you are not able to reply at all.

145. JUL. (1) You not only removed, then, this clause from our statement, but
you also injected your own, which might at first sight involve something objectionable, but on examination it vanishes. For you stated that we say that nature is
created good by the good God, but is so healthy that it does not have any need of
the medicine of Christ.[146] See, then, the great poverty of truth under which you
struggle, for even in these terms which are called ἀντίΘετα[147] you are not afraid
to carry out so obvious a deception. For, though above you had said: "good nature," you added: "is so healthy." Is "healthy" the ἀντίΘετον of "good"? (2)
Surely, when we say "good," we set nothing opposite to this in the proper sense
but "evil." But if the situation demands that we say "healthy," we set opposite to
it "frail" or "sick," so that, if something is healthy, it is certainly not said to be
frail; if it is frail, it is not said to be healthy. But when we say: "This is good," we
do not set as its opposite the term "healthy," but the word "evil." You should,
then, have said that we stated that the nature of human beings was created good
by God, but that it is so good in little ones that it looks for no improvement of its
creation, or if you preferred to indicate those things which were good by a different term, that is, one of health, you should have written the whole with an harmonious expression. (3) But now you slip like a little eel between the rocks of your
definitions; for, when the truth forced you to admit that we say that the nature of

human beings was created good by the good God and that you see in that part of the sentence much reason and nothing objectionable, you immediately moved to other words and added: But we defend it as healthy so that we do not believe the medicine of Christ is necessary for it.[148] If you do all this through ignorance, you are found to be extremely dull-witted, but if you do it with cunning, you are found to be most shrewd.

AUG. Under what circumstances would you say these things except when you have nothing to say? For we ought not, as you suppose, to have called "healthy" what we called "good" in order to avoid contraries that are not truly such. If I wanted to point out the great ignorance with which you say this, I would delay like you over matters that are not necessary. Get rid of those things which are superfluous and which, even if they were true, would not help you in the least, and state, if you can, how you do not deny to little ones Christ the physician. For when you begin to speak, it will be immediately apparent why you thought you should introduce these vain and irrelevant ideas.

The Little Ones' Need for Christ the Physician

146. JUL. Look, for I shall briefly reply that we do not deny the medicine of Christ to little ones whom we know are innocent; we even admit that they especially need that medicine in greater abundance. For they are born tiny and frail; they not only cannot get food by their own effort, but cannot even implore the help of their parents; they are subject to so many mishaps that even a thicker milk or the sleep of their nurses at times spells their death.

AUG. (1) See how you hinder the memory of the reader by introducing superfluous ideas. You do not deny that Christ the physician is necessary for little ones on account of the evils of the body, by the frailty of which the weak are injured or killed, and you do deny that Christ the physician is necessary for them because they are under the power of the devil and that in order to be set free from his power those about to be baptized undergo the rite of exsufflation. In this way it is understood that you proposed this objection raised against you, as if to resolve it, only so that you would not be discovered to have been afraid of it. But you did not attempt to refute it because your spears would bounce back from that most solid and adamantine foundation to slay you instead. And for this reason you introduced the needless discussion about contraries so that the readers would forget that the objection was not refuted and would leave you to catch your breath in whatever nonsense you might introduce, as if you were making a response, though saying nothing. (2) You have introduced the idea that the frailty of the infant body is subject to many mishaps, as if infants would either be tormented in it or be weighed down by its great weakness or as if anything evil could happen to them at that age, if human nature remained as it had been created. Show me, if you can, why the Church of Christ subjects little ones about to be baptized to the rite of exsufflation, or maintain, if you can, that they should not undergo the rite of exsufflation, or shut up, if you cannot. In fact, shut up because you cannot.

147. JUL. In accord with the condition of a mortal body they meet with the trials of illnesses and the penalties of pains and the risks of diseases. We confess, therefore, that the medicine of Christ, who is also their maker, is necessary not only for little ones, but also for the nature of all mortals.

AUG. And so, you believe that all these evils would have existed in paradise, if no one had sinned, and you imagine there the deaths of human beings as well as of animals, because you believe that the mortality of bodies was common to all beings there. O you wretches, if you considered the blessedness of that place with a Christian heart, you would not believe that even the other animals were going to die there, just as they were not going to be wild, but subject to human beings with an amazing gentleness. Nor would they seek their food by killing one another, but would take their nourishment in common with human beings, as scripture says.[149] Or if extreme old age brought their dissolution so that only human nature would possess eternal life there, why should we not believe that they would be taken from paradise when they were about to die or that they would leave when they felt that death was imminent so that no living being met with death in that place of life? For even those human beings who sinned could not have died, if they had not left as a punishment for their sinfulness that place of such great happiness.

148. JUL. As its weaknesses are relieved in the present life by various kinds of remedies, so they will be completely done away with in the bodies of the righteous at the coming of the resurrection.

AUG. Do you include among these righteous the little ones who have done nothing either good or bad by their own will? Or do you separate them from the righteous, though you do not separate them from the joyous resurrection of the flesh? Why, then, have you singled out the bodies of the righteous in which these evils will be done away with at the coming of the resurrection? But if the little ones are counted as righteous on account of the righteousness of the second man, who is the source of their rebirth, why are they not counted as not righteous on account of the sin of the first man who is the source of their birth?

Different Views of Christ's Medicine

149. JUL. You see, then, in how many important respects we confess that the medicine of Christ is necessary for human nature. But I know that you will cry out that we are mocking you, for by the term "medicine" you did not mean this medicine which helps bodies, but the grace of Christ, which you claim we deny. To this we can reply that you should be blamed for this, for you refused to speak

in proper terms about the issue you want us to understand. But because we only recently understood the medicine which you meant and which you falsely stated that we denied without making any distinctions, let us reply also to this point which you introduced in your second book, just as we also publicly testified by our first work that we confess that, from the time Christ instituted its rite, the grace of Christ, that is, baptism, is so necessary for all ages in common that we strike with an eternal anathema anyone who denies that it is also useful for little ones.

AUG. We are dealing with medicine. Christ wanted his grace to be called by that name where he said of himself, *It is not the healthy who need a physician, but those who are ill* (Mt 9:12). But you say that the grace of Christ is not necessary to heal little ones, but only to adopt them into the kingdom of God. Do not, then, pretend that you are replying when you see that you cannot reply.

150. JUL. Since we teach this with a clear declaration, you are proved guilty of a public lie, for you write that we defend the good nature of human beings to the point that we deny that the medicine of Christ is necessary for the healthy nature in infants.

AUG. (1) I spoke the truth; you certainly deny to little ones the medicine of Christian grace which is given only to Christians, but not to all human beings, including unbelievers, just as it is not given to puppies and piglets, baby fishes and worms, and every kind of any living thing. For you, of course, maintain that little ones are born without any guilt from their origin which is healed by rebirth. (2) For this reason, when you were caught in great difficulties, you recently removed the term "medicine" and substituted "grace," because you can say that grace is necessary for little ones on account of adoption, but you cannot say that they need medicine from the sacraments of Christ, when you dare to promise them eternal salvation, even if they are not Christian. You do not want Christ to be Jesus for them. He is called that, as the angel testifies, as the gospel testifies,[150] precisely because he saves his people, not from diseases and wounds of the flesh, from which he saves some people and some birds and reptiles, but from their sins.

151. JUL. Since this grace is, nonetheless, also called medicine, without harm to the law of justice, it makes other bad people good, but makes the little ones, whom it makes good by creation, better by renewal and adoption.

AUG. (1) Then Jesus' words, *It is not the healthy who need a physician, but those who are ill* (Mt 9:12), are false with regard to little ones, insofar as they refer to the medicine which Christ offers only to Christians, since you say that they are in good health, but, in order to escape hostility, you say that they need the medicine of Christ. But how does Christ renew those whom he finds new, most recently born, if they contract nothing of the oldness of sin? (2) Or are you also going to say that it is not something old that is renewed, though you read in the Letter to the Hebrews, *When he calls this one new, he declares the first one old*

(Heb 8:13)? State, then, why the newly born are old, since you say that they are in good health with respect to the oldness of sin, though in order to avoid the indignation of true Christians you pretend that they are renewed by Christ. Finally, it is one thing to be healed and another to be renewed. For healing them, medical care is needed; for renewing them, restoration is needed. It is evident, then, that your heresy indeed denies to the little ones the Christian medicine.

152. JUL. See, then, it is clear that we do not deny that the grace of Christ is useful for little ones. What controversy, then, remains on account of which the traducianist accuses us of error? Is it because we do not agree that Adam's nature was created good, but that the nature of all other human beings was created evil? I admit, of course, that we not only do not agree to this, but even attack it with all our strength. Having, then, removed those childishly woven nets and vulgar manias[151] of your imagination, because of which you were whispering that we deny the grace of Christ to cradles, let us engage in battle on this issue in which is found the whole point of the conflict. In that order which I promised, since I have already defended our teachings, let us weigh the views of Mani, to whom you pretend to be opposed, and your own views.

AUG. You have not defended your teachings; rather, you showed that they were indefensible.

Augustine and Mani Compared

153. JUL. Mani, therefore, says that human beings were created by the prince of darkness, that is, by the author of evil, out of the mixture of two natures, one good and the other evil. What do you say? That human beings are created by the good God, but are all created evil.

AUG. In a newborn human being there is both the nature which you do not deny is a good, for which we praise God the creator, and a defect, which you do not deny is an evil if, at least when under pressure, you admit that Christ the physician is necessary for little ones. For you cannot deny that the same Christ said of himself: *Those in good health do not need a physician* (Mt 9:12).

154. JUL. (1) Between you and Mani there is no disagreement about the character of our nature, but only about its author. For you attribute this evil to God who you admit is the creator of little ones, while Mani attributes it to the prince of darkness who he thought is the creator of human nature. No big obstacle has been left for your establishing an alliance. Soon I shall, nonetheless, prove that, although no traces of the truth are found with either of you, his statements are more self-consistent than yours. But what do we say? (2) We undoubtedly profess something which is opposed to both of you, namely, that the good God did not create an evil nature and that the prince of darkness did not make or mix into it another nature. Rather, God, the author of all things, not only made the good

nature of human beings at first, but also makes that nature in each individual who is born, for whom the help of the creator is, nonetheless, both useful and necessary in many ways. Though the meaning of "creation" is different from "gift," the assessment of the work is in this case not more important than that of the worker. Both of you, therefore, you and Mani, equally defend natural evil; that is, both of you equally say that the nature of human beings is evil, but he does so more truthfully, while you do so more deceitfully.

(3) For you both equally think that this evil was poured out into the human organs by the devil. He introduces a beginning with no one, but you—in order that you might seem to distance yourself from him by something, which is really nothing—try to exempt from it only those two human beings. But you do not set these persons free from sin; rather, with the development of a more learned mind, you say that it was not something natural in them, though you argue that it became something natural through them. And so, in order that your deceit might not go unpunished here, the addition of stupidity has made amends for the theft which you committed against your teacher. For to believe that something which you admit was derived from the will is natural is the mark—I will not say: of an uneducated, but—of a drunken mind. (4) But more on this elsewhere; let us now follow up this issue. Mani, therefore, states that evil is natural; you agree. He says that sins are there at birth; you agree that it is so. He says that the nature of human beings is evil; you support this as well. He, of course, says this of all human beings; here you resist and ask that the first union of two human beings be set apart, not, of course, to defend them from guilt. On the contrary, you claim that they are the authors of natural evil. Even if we could grant you this, your teacher, nonetheless, will not grant this, but will correct your slow mind even by the rod so that it will be necessary for you either to yield to his authority or to leave his school entirely. He concludes at the end and says there cannot be a good author for an evil nature and, for this reason, human beings are the work of the prince of darkness, that is, of the devil, who you both admit is naturally evil.

AUG. (1) The Catholic faith states in opposition to you and to the Manichees that human nature that was created good by the good God was injured by the great sin of disobedience so that even their descendants contracted from it the merit and punishment of death, but that the good God does not deny to those descendants his good workmanship. But, please, you who deny this, think of paradise for a moment. (2) Do you want us to locate there chaste men and women struggling against sexual desire, pregnant women who are nauseated, without appetite, and pale, some others who suffer miscarriages, still others groaning and screaming in childbirth, all the babies themselves who wail, smile later, and still later speak, but only in baby talk, and are afterward led off to school? There they learn letters, crying under the lash, the rod, and the cane, the different punishments allotted for their different talents; there are, moreover, countless diseases and attacks of demons and animal bites, by which some are tormented and some are even slain. But those who are healthy are reared under the uncertainty of these mishaps by their parents who are wretched with worry over them. There would also be in paradise bereavements and grief and longing with heartache for lost loved ones. (3) It would take too long to run through all the evils with which this life abounds, though these are not sins. If, then, these were going to exist in paradise without any sin coming first, as the punishment for which they would exist, look for some people to whom you might preach this—certainly not believers, but mockers. Surely, if such a paradise were painted as a picture, no one would call it paradise, even if this name were inscribed above it, and no one would say that the painter had made a mistake, but one would recognize a mocker.

(4) But none of those who know you would be surprised if your name were added to the title and it said: The Paradise of the Pelagians. If, however, you are embarrassed over this—for no trace of shame should really be thought to have been left in you, if you are not embarrassed over this—change, I beg you, your perverse ideas and believe that human nature was changed into these miseries by that great sin. Believe that these evils could not have existed in paradise and that, for this reason, that couple went forth from it, whose descendants also deserved to endure such things, because the infection of sin was passed on to all along with the state of punishment. (5) This Catholic teaching both defends the justice of God, because he willed, not without justification, that the life of mortals involve punishment, and it overthrows you and the Manichees—you because you ascribe to paradise an unhappiness that is horrible because of such evils, but the Manichees because they claim that the nature of their god and, hence, nothing other than their god himself is unhappy because of such evils. For that reason it should not bother me that you set before me Mani as my teacher to punish with rods my slow intellect, but I pray that it may bother you that in accord with the unspeakable and horrendous monstrosity of your error you would be taught by rods, even if you were born among the people of paradise. (6) If you shrink from that ugliest of absurdities along with us, as you ought, what, I ask you, is the source of this misery of children? It certainly does not come from the nature of evil, which the Manichees foolishly imagine. Where does it come from, unless, by that great sin which is beyond our estimation, human nature was so wounded and subjected to completely just punishments that from it there arose not only the corruptibility of bodies subject to so many painful misfortunes, but also the slowness of minds deserving of rods and other beatings. And so this wicked world runs through its evil days to its end in such a way that even the saints who have been rescued from eternal punishment by God's pardon and have received the pledge of imperishable salvation are commanded to endure the penalties of this life by the good use of them with a reward for their patience rather than that they merit to be without them after the forgiveness of sins.

155. JUL. But against this last point you completely rebel and, though you boarded one ship with Mani and the same spirit has directed your course, once the straits had been crossed, you thought you would land on another shore. But perhaps the choice of the nearest help makes your hesitation, though late, more tolerable. Into what harbor are you directing your voyage? You state, "I say that God is good and that God is, nonetheless, the creator of evils." Oh the flight from danger driven to shipwreck on the rocks, which had wanted to pour all the filth of Mani over him whom you take to be God!

AUG. (1) You do not deny, do you, that even in evil human beings the nature of both their mind and body is good? God is the creator of this good, which Mani calls an evil, and he assigns for this good, which he calls evil, an evil author. He does not, after all, spare even the soul, for as he says that his own is a soul of the flesh, so he says that it is an evil nature coeternal with the good God so that it cannot be good at all. But he says that there is another good soul in the same human being not made by God, but the very substance and nature of God stuffed into the miseries of this mixture, not because of any sinfulness of its own, but by an evil necessity for God. But he says that this whole product, which is the human being, is both evil and has an evil author. Do you see how different his views are and how they are, for this reason, insanely and wickedly foolish? (2) But you do not think that human beings can be born evil because the good God creates them. Maintain, if you can, that bodies cannot be born defective because the perfect God also creates them, and maintain finally that, just as human beings cannot be born evil, because the good God creates them, so they cannot be born slow-witted or feebleminded, because the wise God creates them. Or is feeble-mindedness not an evil, though scripture says that one should mourn incomparably more for one who is feebleminded than for one who is dead?[152] Just as, then, along with us you do not say that God is the author of feeblemindedness, though you admit that human beings are born feebleminded with God as their creator, so we do not say that God is the author of evil, and yet we can correctly say that human beings are born evil as a result of the bond of original sin with God alone as their creator, because he alone creates human beings.

156. JUL. It is absolutely clear that Mani's opinion is more logical: If some evil were created as part of their nature, it would be a sign of a creator like it.

AUG. Who but the Pelagian heretics think that way? Then, because human beings are created mortal, as you see it, not as a punishment, but naturally, they point to a creator who is mortal like them. And in order that your feeblemindedness might blush at least over the feebleminded, because human beings are naturally created feebleminded, they point to a feebleminded creator like them.

157. JUL. But the truth, first of all, demands that one cannot call evil, that is, a sin, something that is such as its nature has compelled it to be, and that sin is nothing but a free will that departs from the path of justice.

AUG. This original sin, however, also takes its origin from the will of the sinner, and so there is no sin without the will.

158. JUL. The innocent nature of all things is defended by these garrisons, and since it remains as it was created, it is proved to be subject to no sin.

AUG. But nature has not remained as it was created. Therefore, it is proved to be subject to sin, and it has made the rest of the human race subject to this sin as if it were its heritage. Insofar as it is created by God, this nature is, nonetheless, good.

The Non-Existence of Natural Evil

159. JUL. Natural evil, therefore, cannot exist, and for this reason no creature is naturally guilty, nor is an evil creator found for an evil nature which, of course, does not exist. Rather, as every creature, insofar as it is a creature, is good, so God, the author of all good natures, unsullied by any crime in his work, is proved to be good in every respect. This whole line of reasoning which Mani presented is overthrown by this one argument of the Catholics.

AUG. What you say is true. Of course, "every creature, insofar as it is a creature, is good," and so we both say this as well as what follows, namely, that "God, the author of good natures, unsullied by any crime in his work, is proved to be good in every respect." This whole line of argument, after all, is tied to the fact that "every creature, insofar as it is a creature, is good." And for this reason human beings, insofar as they are creatures, are good, but insofar as they are born from a damaged origin, they are not good and, for this reason, need to be reborn.

160. JUL. Mani who was wiped out by a lightning bolt of clear truth seems, nonetheless, to be breathing somewhat in comparison with you, for the whole structure of his teaching collapses when only its foundation totters, but you have three pillars that are teetering as much as his one. And for this reason see whether any part of your building can stand. Mani, then, in thinking that sin, which can only be voluntary, is natural laid his foundations on empty air, but set the rest upon it in a logical manner, as he saw it. He said that, because sin is natural, nature is evil, and that the author of something evil cannot be good, and that, for this reason, one should attribute the whole human race to the prince of darkness. This whole edifice could, of course, stand if that first point of his had not been undermined by the truth, namely, that it cannot be taught that sin, an act of a free will, is natural, and it is impossible that whatever was natural be a sin.

AUG. (1) This same line of argument can likewise be drawn up against you, for you are not so feebleminded that you would deny that feeble minds are born, that is, feebleminded human beings. Listen, then, to how much your feeblemindedness helps the madness of Mani. For, taught by you that feeblemindedness is natural, he says that the nature itself is feebleminded, just as you said, "Because

sin is natural, the nature is evil." Then he adds that the author of something feebleminded cannot be wise, just as you said that "the author of something evil
cannot be good." Finally, he concludes: And for this reason one should attribute
the race of feebleminded human beings to the prince of darkness, for you concluded in that way, when you said, "And for this reason one should attribute the
whole human race to the prince of darkness." (2) See, Mani defeats you by your
own words and slays you with your own sword. What are you going to do? For
nothing can help you against him and not crush you even more and run you
through, when you go on to say, "This whole edifice could, of course, stand if
that first point of his had not been undermined by the truth, namely, that it cannot
be taught that sin, an act of a free will, is natural, and it is impossible that whatever was natural be a sin." How does this help you, and how does it not choke
you more and more? Can you, after all, say that feeblemindedness cannot be natural? (3) There stands against you the point which Mani put first in the similar argument, namely, that feeblemindedness is natural. You thought that his other
ideas were logically constructed on this point as on a foundation right up to the
top, where he says that one should ascribe such a race of human beings to the
prince of darkness. But we destroy that first foundation of his, for we say that
feeblemindedness is natural, because human beings are born feebleminded as
the result of something that happens to them, that is, a defect, from which such an
origin is deservedly derived, not because human nature was first created evil, as
Mani foolishly supposes. And for this reason, we grant that what he logically
adds, namely, that the same nature is feebleminded, is true on account of the defect with which human beings are born feebleminded, not on account of what is
the work of the good creator in them. For they are born as feebleminded because
of a defect that befalls them, but they are created as human beings by the work of
God. (4) Finally, when he adds that the author of something feebleminded is not
wise, where we are supposed to understand that this something is a human being,
we say that this does not follow. We say that God is, of course, the author of human beings who are born feebleminded, although we do not say that he is the author of feeblemindedness itself. This feeblemindedness is not a nature and
substance which is only born because God creates it, but a defect of the nature
which befalls it because God permits it. But we certainly do not doubt that God
permits these things by his just judgment. In that way we destroy both the
Manichees, the evil architects of their own ruin, and the Pelagians, their feebleminded helpers.

Augustine's Three Points of Weakness

161. JUL. (1) By overthrowing the first definition, then, the wedge of reason
topples its rooftops to the ground. What hope do you have for yourself, since

three of your principles are as precarious as his one? For you say, first of all, that sin is natural; second, that God is good who creates, implants, and spreads evils, that is, sins; and third, that something voluntary is mixed in with the seeds. These three principal statements of yours are each tottering by itself; they are tottering, I say; or rather, like ropes of sand,[153] they slip away before they become solid. (2) One of them, that is, natural sin, lies there, already directly destroyed in Mani, but the other two, which are proper to your view, have collapsed, since they are linked together,[154] so that Mani is destroyed each time. For if he was unable to defend the claim that human beings are born guilty either because of an evil nature or because of the prince of darkness, how much more are you stupid people unable, who added an accusation against God in order to reveal the sins of the newborn? And for this reason, as nature cannot be a sin—by which bolt of lightning the doctrine of Mani collapsed—so it follows that what is sin cannot be natural, for something voluntary cannot pass into the status of a substance, as you suppose has happened. But it is much more certain that the good God never creates evil persons, and so it has been shown that there cannot be a sin in the newborn whom God creates.

AUG. (1) It is certain that the good God does not create evil persons, just as it is certain that the wise God does not create feebleminded persons. For if you say: The wise God creates the feebleminded, you will receive the answer: Why then does the good God not create evil persons? Having been alerted by this, when you are asked why they are born feebleminded, though God creates these human beings, you who do not want to admit original sin will perhaps find the defect from their origin. Or are you ready to say that, without the sin of anyone having first occurred, they could have been born even in that happiness of paradise so feebleminded that they could not be taught—I will not say: by rods, but—by clubs? (2) If you do not say this so that this absurdity does not surpass all feeblemindedness, tell me by what merit the image of God is born with such great mental deformity that it cannot without the punishment of beatings attain by any strength of maturity, by any length of time, by any work at studies, by any efforts of teachers—I will not say: wisdom, but—any useful learning. Tell me this, you who do not want to believe that the just God dismissed from paradise, that is, from the place of happiness, the damaged and condemned human nature. He dismissed that nature from paradise so that no death would occur there, that is, neither the temporal death of the body nor the everlasting death of the whole human being, and so that there would not arise in the region of blessedness the many and great evils of minds and bodies which we see in the human race and which had to arise from the root which became evil and was punished and from the mass which was condemned. He dismissed that nature so that these evils would arise rather in these lands assigned to the misery of mortals which was imposed on them with full justice, where guilt follows upon those who are born and where bitter toil does not withdraw from the reborn until the death of the body.

162. JUL. The issue is clear and has already been sufficiently dealt with in the first work. But since you chose to be so glib as to try to draw some distinction between yourself and Mani, it is necessary for me now to press my case so that it may be seen that the way is blocked not only for your past statements, but also if you should try to introduce any hereafter. We say, therefore, that the work of God is so good in the newborn that the natural features of its substance have no need of someone to correct them. For whoever think that what they admit God made he ought to have made otherwise undoubtedly find fault with him, since they admit that he is the maker of a creature that needs to be corrected to some other form.

AUG. (1) Be silent, please! You do not know what you are saying. Some children have been born with their mouths sealed, and doctors opened them. There lived in our area a certain Acatius, a member of a respected family among his people. He said that he was born with his eyelids sealed. Because his eyes, though healthy, could not open with the lids sealed together, the doctor wanted to open them with a knife. His pious mother did not permit this, but opened his eyes by placing on them a plaster made from the eucharist when he was already a boy of almost five or more years. For this reason he reported that he remembered this well. (2) I pass over that man born blind in the gospel whose eyes their maker himself restored, the eyes which he made defective in order to reveal his marvelous works. For in that case the reason why he was born blind was not passed over; it was not on account of his sin or that of his parents, but in order that the works of God might be revealed in him.[155] Ask the doctors, nonetheless, and let them tell you how many they help, when they can, so that bodily defects from birth do not remain or even kill the children. For, as some are born with the mouths sealed, so others are born with blockages in internal passages, and if these defects remain, they do not, of course, permit them to live. After all, when these human beings are helped by medical expertise, the works of God are not blamed when they are corrected. For what true worshiper of God does not know that they ought to be born in the condition in which they were born? (3) But even this pertains to the woes of the human race in which we live out these evil days filled, under the just judgment of God, with labors, sorrows, fears, and dangers. Heaven forbid that all these evils should be present in that happiness of paradise! And for this reason they have sprung up only from that root of sin. What about minds? If they are left as they are born and not developed by careful teaching by the great labor of teachers and of students, is it not clear what they will remain? But you, go ahead, fill your paradise with human beings born with defective minds and bodies in order that you may to your own misfortune deny original sin with your eyes closed and your mouth impudently open.

God's Gifts in Relation to Virtues and Vices

163. JUL. Having preserved the well-proved and moderate praise which is owed to natures, even in any newborn infants, we say that increases of the divine gifts are useful and necessary for all ages in common, but in such a way that neither virtue nor sin is ascribed to anyone except by one's own will.

AUG. Virtue is not ascribed to anyone except by one's own will, but *the will is prepared by the Lord* (Prv 8:35 LXX), as was the will of that king for which Esther prayed.[156]

164. JUL. And yet, the clemency of God is also shown to be more bounteous insofar as he sanctifies little ones without their knowledge; it pertains to the praise of mercy, since guilt does not dirty them without their knowledge, for that belongs to the laws of justice.

AUG. If no sin dirties them, why are not all sanctified? And why are all who are sanctified subjected to the rite of exsufflation?

165. JUL. But I am speaking of those virtues which are acquired by the full use of reason. And on this account I warn the reader to pay attention to what we are going to say, for we must emphasize that here, as we had to do frequently. The reader will see that the traducianists differ in no way from the Manichees since they raise no other objections against us as arguments than those which are found in the books of the Manichees. I, of course, did that also in the fourth book of my first work.

AUG. And I replied to you with my sixth book.

The Discovery of a Letter by Mani

166. JUL. But after the publication of those books, blessed father Florus, because of your prayers a letter of Mani was found at Constantinople and sent to these parts. It is worthwhile to include some statements from it so that all may understand the source of these arguments for inherited sin.

AUG. (1) How can you say that a letter was found and sent because of the prayers of anyone, if God does not produce acts of will in the hearts of human beings? The person who found it, of course, willed to look for it or willed to look for something in that place where it could be found. Or, since people will to talk about such things, those who had it willed to indicate that they had it so that they could show it and hand it over to someone willing who in turn willed to send it to these parts, (2) or however else it was brought about, surely, by the will of one or more persons, that this letter was found and sent. And yet, you say that this happened because of someone's prayers. Why, then, do you not admit that without any externally spoken command God prepares and arouses by a hidden impulse the wills of human beings to carry out most effectively what he wills, for you do not defend free choice in order to make it understood, but you praise it to destroy it?

167. JUL. In that first book I already argued in defense of concupiscence or the pleasure of the flesh, which is also called sexual desire and was given to the sexes on account of the male role in propagation, to teach that it is nothing but one of the functions of the body bestowed upon rational and non-rational animals in common and that it pertains to the work of God who equipped our flesh with the senses. Nonetheless, because Augustine fiercely attacks it and says that it is evil, that is, that it is natural sin and the mother of all sins, something of which he tries to persuade us especially by the shame it causes, and he mocks me because I blush to name it directly, ...

AUG. I do say that concupiscence of the flesh by which the flesh has desires opposed to the spirit[157] and which is also called sexual desire is evil. I say that now in this flesh it must be reined in and diminished by good habits, but that in eternal life it will be completely healed. It will not be separated from us like some evil substance that was added to or mixed into us, as the Manichees so foolishly think. But whatever you hold regarding it, I would not believe that you could locate in paradise such concupiscence as now exists, if I had not found it in these books of yours filled with vain and insane wordiness; for that concupiscence entices to what is forbidden and, unless it is resisted with a more vigorous will, it seduces the hearts even of the chaste, whether married or celibate, to commit sinful acts.

168. JUL. And, though in my previous writings I defended it from the lips of Mani by drawing a distinction, I shall again briefly rescue the quality of this desire from the betrayal of its accusers who, nonetheless, profess that they obey it unwillingly.

AUG. You can appropriately serve the sexual desire you praise, but we fight against it with the help of the Lord and defeat it as something we blame.

169. JUL. These words, then, old Augustine, are contained in your books, "Passion came to be after the sin, and in their shame they were forced to conceal it."[158]

AUG. From what is contained in your books it is apparent, young Julian, that you find nothing to say against my books and look for slanders which you bring against us with many words and little sense.

170. JUL. (1) So too, you said, "One who in shameful passion has licit intercourse makes good use of an evil, but one who has illicit intercourse makes bad use of an evil. After all, that over which both bad and good people blush is more correctly called evil than good, and we do better to believe the apostle who said, *The good does not dwell in my flesh*" (Rom 7:18).[159] Elsewhere you said, "Sexual desire is not the good of marriage; it is, rather, indecency for sinners, a necessity for those who have children, passion for the dissolute, and a source of shame for marriage."[160] (2) You also said, "What they afterward produced by procreation

is the good of marriage, but what they first covered over out of shame is the evil of concupiscence that everywhere avoids being seen and seeks privacy out of a sense of shame."[161] These and other claims which you are accustomed to use for this argument are more products of your memory than of your mind. Mani, therefore, was sick to the extent that he composed some ideas which he thought clever, but you were deluded when you thought you could hide what you read and kept in mind.

AUG. (1) Who is there, after all, who has even a slight knowledge of the Manichean teaching and does not know that the Manichees say that the concupiscence of the flesh is evil? But that is not a distinguishing mark of their teaching. For what else does he say who says, *The flesh has desires opposed to the spirit, and the spirit has desires opposed to the flesh. For these are opposed to each other so that you do not do what you will* (Gal 5:17)? (2) What else does he also say who says, *Whoever loves the world, the love of the Father is not in him, because everything that is in the world is the concupiscence of the flesh, the concupiscence of the eyes, and the pride of life, and that does not come from the Father, but from the world* (1 Jn 2:15-16)? The Manichees do not, therefore, hold as a teaching that is theirs alone that the concupiscence of the flesh is evil, and those who are not blind see that the apostles also say this. But your error gives aid to the distinctive and poisonous view of the Manichees, for you deny that concupiscence of the flesh comes from the sin of the nature which God created good, even though, whether you like it or not, chastity fights against this concupiscence which entices one to commit sinful acts. (3) And you do this so that the Manichees conclude that this concupiscence, which they prove to be evil by the struggle of the chaste and by the testimony of the apostles, came from the nation of darkness and the evil substance coeternal with God, and they hold that it is not an evil quality that needs to be healed, but an evil substance that needs to be separated and that it was not added to a good nature, but was mixed into a good nature. But go on and devise slanders against us out of the plague of the Manichees, though you give them such help that you make them invincible, unless you are also defeated with them by the Catholic truth which is truly invincible.

171. JUL. Now listen, therefore, and recognize what your father writes to a daughter of his, your sister.[162]

AUG. These attacks are not urbane, but vain.

Quotations from Mani's Letter to Menoch

172. JUL. "Mani, the apostle of Jesus Christ, to daughter Menoch. May grace and salvation be given to you by our God who is really the true God, and may he enlighten your mind and reveal his righteousness to you, because you are the fruit of the divine tree." And after a bit he says, "Through whom you were also

made resplendent by acknowledging both how you had been before and the kind
of souls from which you emanated, the kind of souls which has been mixed into
all bodies and clings to various savors and forms. For as souls are born from
souls, so the shape of the body is produced by the nature of the body. *What is
born of the flesh*, then, *is flesh, and what is born of the spirit is spirit* (Jn 3:6). But
understand by spirit the soul; soul is born of soul, and flesh of flesh."

AUG. (1) If I said to you that I absolutely do not know this letter of Mani,
though I would be speaking the truth, you would not believe me at all, and you
would argue with me, as usual, with all your empty talk. But if Mani said this,
why is it surprising that he destroyed himself? For, if the soul of a human being,
like the flesh of a human being, is born either evil or good—for they say in their
madness that there are two souls in one human being at the same time, one good,
the other evil, emanating from their diverse principles—if, then, the soul is born,
when the flesh is born, the evil soul is certainly not coeternal with God, nor is the
good soul brought into being by the eternal Father in opposition to the princes of
darkness, as his sect foolishly thinks. (2) But what difference does it make to us
however Mani says that souls are born, since we know and maintain that those
words of the Lord, *What is born of the flesh is flesh, and what is born of the spirit
is spirit* (Jn 3:6), are realized, not when a human being is born of another human
being, but when one is reborn of the Spirit of God? For this whole gospel passage
does not admit any other interpretation. Search, then, there for the words by
which you can peddle these myths of Mani, and show us, rather, how you are not
a supporter of the Manichees, on account of what I said above.

173. JUL. You know, of course, how Mani explicitly endorses the transmission of souls and the testimony he uses to cast blame upon the flesh, that testimony which is ever on your lips, namely, *What is born of the flesh is flesh, and
what is born of the spirit is spirit* (Jn 3:6).

AUG. I already stated how we interpret these words of the gospel for they
teach, not about birth, but about rebirth. Tell me, if you can, how you do not offer
support to Mani's sacrilegious words about the concupiscence of the flesh? For
you deny that it came down by subsequent propagation into our nature from the
nature which was damaged by transgression of the first human being, and as a result Mani is thought to have attributed it with perfect correctness to the nation of
darkness coeternal with God. You most foolishly and most impudently deny that
it is an evil by which the flesh has desires opposed to the spirit[163] and against
which the chaste wage war within themselves.

174. JUL. And so he teaches not merely by stating it, but by repeating it, that it
is a distinctive mark of his teaching to hold the transmission of souls—a point
which he tries to prove even by the likeness of bodies generating bodies. He
says, "As souls are born from souls, so the shape of the body is derived from the
nature of the body, and as flesh comes from flesh, so the soul comes from the
soul." But let us go on to the rest: "As, then, God is the author of souls, so through

concupiscence the devil is the author of bodies, through the concupiscence of the woman, as in the trap of the devil, by which the devil traps not souls, but bodies."

AUG. Mani could have said that the devil traps not bodies, but souls, for he says that bodies belong to the nation of darkness from which the devil also comes. Hence, according to Mani, the devil is said to trap not bodies which are his, but good souls which are not his. But our faith knows that the good God is the creator of both souls and bodies.

175. JUL. "He traps them by sight or by touch or by hearing or by smell or by taste. Take away at last the root of this evil tree, and you will immediately see yourself as spiritual. *For the root*, scripture says, *of all evils is concupiscence*" (1 Tm 6:10). You see with what spirit and for what reason Mani attacks the concupiscence of the flesh, saying that it is the law of sin which, if it were taken from bodies, his daughter to whom he is writing would see herself as having become spiritual. Let us listen to the statements of the apostle by which he tries to support this idea. "For *the flesh is opposed to the spirit*, because it is the child of concupiscence, *and the spirit is opposed to the flesh* (Gal 5:17), because it is the child of the soul."

AUG. Mani finds two substances in the words of the apostle, one good, the other evil, not one a good substance and the other a defect of a good substance contracted by birth from the sin of the first man that is to be healed by the rebirth through the righteousness of the second man. The Catholic faith mightily hurls this like an invincible spear against both the Manichees and you, and it lays both of you low.

176. JUL. You understand that the marrow of the Manichean teaching has been uncovered upon which your faith thrives. But he now continues to reproach us, that is, the Catholics: "Hence, see how stupid they are who say that this body was created by the good God, since they are certain that it was born of the spirit of concupiscence."

AUG. On this point the Manichees reproach both you and us, because we both say that the body of the flesh was created by the good God, while the Manichees say that the spirit of concupiscence is an evil substance, not the defect of a good substance, because of which the flesh has desires opposed to the spirit.[164] We say this in order to refute them, and you deny it in order to help them. After all, because they find that the concupiscence by which the flesh has desires opposed to the spirit is something evil, since even you resist it, it will be regarded as an evil substance, if it is not a defect, as you suppose, of a good substance. That is the teaching of the Manichees hostile to the Catholic faith, but with your help.

177. JUL. (1) "They have intercourse though their mind is unwilling, and they do it with secret shame at a time when they abhor the light so that their works may not be revealed. On account of this the apostle said, *It is not because one wills* (Rom 9:16), where there is understood: this act. For if we beget some-

thing good, it does not come from the flesh, because *the works of the flesh are evident; they are fornication* (Gal 5:19), and so on, or if we beget something evil, it does not come from the soul, because *the fruit of the spirit is peace and joy* (Gal 5:22). Finally the apostle cries out to the Romans, *I do not do the good that I will, but I do the evil that I abhor* (Rom 7:19). (2) You see the cry of an unyielding soul defending the freedom of the soul against concupiscence. After all, he grieves because sin, that is, the devil, produces in him every desire.[165] The authority of the law points out its evil when it blames all the uses of it which the flesh admires and praises. Everything concupiscence finds bitter is sweet to the soul, and by this bitterness the soul is nourished and grows strong. Finally, the mind of those who refrain from all use of concupiscence is awake, is enriched, and grows, but it becomes used to diminishment through the use of concupiscence." (3) Do you realize even this late that we have discovered the source, not only of your ideas, but of your language? For you embrace your teacher with such great affection that you not merely follow his paths, but walk in his footsteps, since in all your writings you maintain, just as those books which you dedicated to Marcellinus and these books which you sent to Valerius bear witness,[166] that it, namely, concupiscence of the flesh, which you call shameful, was mixed into human bodies by the devil.

AUG. (1) With what impudence you deny that it is shameful! Since you gladly praise it, I wonder now whether you faithfully fight against it. But when you had relations with your wife, even if you eagerly longed for the enjoyment of licit pleasure without any fear, you sought privacy, nonetheless, out of embarrassment. Hence, if the happiness of human beings in paradise had lasted, this darling of yours would not have been there at all, or she would not have produced against the least sign from the will any of her motions which it would be necessary to resist so that the due goodness would match that happiness. (2) But because you have gone so far in its praises that you maintain that such sexual desire as we now experience it to be would have existed in paradise, enticing the hearts of the chaste who struggle against it, who can fail to see that you oppose me not with wisdom, not with eloquence, but with impudence, since you are prevented by a perverse sense of shame from admitting that you have been defeated? We, then, do not say that concupiscence of the flesh is the substance of the evil nature, as the Manichees say, nor do we forbid all use of it, as the Manichees do, and we do not say that it is good, as the Pelagians do, nor do we praise its movements in opposition to the spirit, as the Pelagians do. (3) Rather, we say that it is a defect of the good substance which was changed into our nature by the transgression of the first human being,[167] as the Catholic Christians say, and we approve the licit and good use of that evil for the sake of procreating children, as Catholic Christians do. In that way we conquer and avoid both the Manichees and the Pelagians. The errors of each of them differ in such a way that the error which seems smaller is shown to be the helper of the one which seems greater. For when the Pelagians deny that what quite evidently is seen as evil is a defect of a good substance, they help the Manichees who say that the defect itself is an evil substance coeternal with the substance of the good God.

Concupiscence as Disparagement of Nature

178. JUL. You say that this concupiscence is the child of sin and the mother of other sins and that the apostle Paul complains about it when he says, *I know that the good does not dwell in my flesh* (Rom 7:18) and, *I do not do the good that I will, but I do that which I hate* (Rom 7:15). This is always explained by the Catholics so that it does not refer to a disparagement of nature, but to an odious way of life.

AUG. (1) And so are you a Catholic and Ambrose is not a Catholic? People have not become so foolish through infection from your foolishness—whomever you have been able to deceive—that they dare to have such a thought. Hence, pay attention for a bit. Neither we nor you nor the Manichees have any doubt about the discord between the flesh and the spirit about which scripture says, *I know that the good does not dwell in me, that is, in my flesh. For I am able to will the good, but I cannot bring it to completion* (Rom 7:18), and other passages of this sort. And this one is even more clear, *The flesh has desires opposed to the spirit, and the spirit has desires opposed to the flesh. For these are opposed to each other so that you do not do what you will* (Gal 5:17). (2) But with regard to the source of this discord in one human being there is disagreement, and three views are put forward in this disagreement, one ours, another yours, and the third that of the Manichees. But so that we do not seem to you to claim with arrogance or with falsehood that ours is Catholic, let Ambrose state this position. Not even an enemy has dared to find fault with his faith and his utterly flawless interpretation of the scriptures, as your own Pelagius has praised him.[168] Ambrose, then, says that this discord between the flesh and the spirit has befallen our nature through the transgression of the first human being.[169] But you say that it came from the force of habit, and the Manichees say that it came from the mixture of the two coeternal natures, namely, good and evil. (3) I could have said that persons who want to remain Catholic may choose whichever of these three they wish, and I ought not to fear that anyone would prefer you to Ambrose, while fleeing from the Manichees. But one who sees that no one is born without this evil judges that your view is most foolish, since you say that this evil becomes inveterate through the force of habit. (4) For, as soon as any persons begin to have the use of reason, if they desire chastity, they already experience the concupiscence of the flesh, which had been asleep because of their age, as if waking up and fighting back. And either they are led off conquered, or, if they are pious, they fight against it with the Lord's help so that they do not slip into consent to it.

If you do not want to accept this, why are you raging at me? Put the Manichees and Ambrose into the ring, and choose which side you favor, if you want to be Catholic, in the spectacle of this fight. I think that you will judge Ambrose the victor, but because you are not Catholics, we watch in safety even in that case, for Ambrose undoubtedly defeats both you and the Manichees.

Concupiscence and the Saints

179. JUL. By argumentation and the misuse of testimonies from scripture you, nonetheless, maintain that the apostle and all the saints were both polluted by and complained about this concupiscence which you call the law of sin.

AUG. The saints were not polluted by this evil, since it is clear that they are or were the strongest warriors against this evil. But so that they might not be indelibly polluted by this evil, let those, rather, fear it who most impudently praise it.

180. JUL. (1) What does Mani say? "Through concupiscence the devil is the author of bodies; through it the devil entraps bodies, not souls. Remove," he says, "the root of the evil tree, and you will become spiritual." About this the apostle cries out to the Romans, *I do not do the good that I will, but the evil I abhor* (Rom 7:19). He also calls us stupid because we say that this shape of the body belongs to God, though we admit that it was begotten through concupiscence. (2) You see, then, the great agreement that exists between you and Mani in your attack on us. You fight with his words; you rely on his arguments, and you call us liars when we say that you not only were, as you yourself write,[170] but are even now his disciple. And in this respect he was the wiser, for, since he believed that this concupiscence of the flesh was introduced by the devil, he concluded that whatever is clearly brought forth by diabolical concupiscence does not belong to the work of God.

AUG. Our previous answer holds good against all of this, and along with it the others above, which those who want to can read.

181. JUL. But you are the more dim-witted; while claiming that a human being is the fruit of diabolical concupiscence, you, nonetheless, attribute it to the works of God, not as a good produced out of an evil, but as an evil and one generated from an evil root, and yet having a good author, though the devil claims it as the fruit of his root.

AUG. A human being is something good, even one who at an adult age is an evil person. For the fact that a person is evil does not deny the fact that one is something good because of being a human being, and God is the author of this nature, that is, of this good, whatever evils it contracts from its origin or adds by its will. For defects are not substances and natures, but the nature damaged by the same defects needs to be healed by the savior who is the creator by whom it was created. This is what overthrows both the Manichees and you who are not fighting with me, but with Ambrose whom I set against the Manichees in this battle in which he defeats both them and you.

182. JUL. By these words the devil rightfully plucks all those born of concupiscence like fruit from his own tree; and so, you blaspheme, like Mani, at how we defend concupiscence of the flesh as created by God.

AUG. (1) If you had wanted to come to the reason why infants about to be baptized are both subjected to exsufflation and purified by exorcism, you would on that point most clearly be seen not only by the learned, but even by ordinary Catholic Christians to be a new heretic. But because you quoted that passage from my book as if you were going to refute it,[171] but you were so afraid to deal with it that you avoided it with your deceptive wordiness and covered over by many words what you passed over, I set before you again the apostle, whether you like it or not. And I stress that he says of God the Father: *He rescued us from the power of darkness and transferred us into the kingdom of his beloved Son* (Col 1:13). (2) Make the little ones an exception to this, if you can, and dare to say that they are transferred into the kingdom of Christ by rebirth, but are not rescued from the power of darkness. Prepare yourselves, nonetheless, to receive, as you fully deserve, those same breaths of exsufflation into your faces which are used for both adults and little ones in the Church. You need to have the devil blown out of you by the very rite of exsufflation which proves true what you deny.

183. JUL. I discussed in my first book[172] that statement of yours where you say, "Sometimes sexual desire does not move them, though the mind wills it, and at other times it does, when the mind is against it,"[173] and you accuse its pride by which it arises even when the mind is unwilling. This was explained not only with Manichean ideas, but even with their words. For when Mani blamed us because we said that human beings are created by God, though we admit that they were conceived by the pleasure of the couple having intercourse, he said, "The foolish say that God created what they are certain is born of concupiscence when they have intercourse though the mind is unwilling."[174]

AUG. But Mani does not understand that God can produce something good even from an evil of a human being and that human beings themselves can through marital chastity make good use of the evil against which they fight back when it entices them to immorality that deserves damnation. But since you deny that this evil is evil, why do you fight against it to avoid an immoral life, and why do you necessarily live an immoral life if you do consent to it?

184. JUL. Your statement, "It is the evil of concupiscence that everywhere avoids being seen and seeks privacy out of a sense of shame," was phrased by Mani in this way, "They do it with secret shame at a time when they abhor the light so that their works may not be revealed."

AUG. Just as Mani does not know what good is produced by the evil of carnal concupiscence, so you also do not know the evil for which a sense of shame seeks privacy, even in case of the good act of marriage.

185. JUL. You said that one who has licit intercourse makes good use of an evil,[175] in order to remind us that one should rather believe the apostle who said that the good does not dwell in his flesh,[176] and you want this which is not a good, but an evil dwelling in the flesh of the apostle to be seen as concupiscence of the flesh. Mani did not state this otherwise than you did. For after he said, "So that their works may not be revealed," he said, "On this account the apostle cries out to the Romans, *I do not do the good that I will, but I do the evil that I abhor* (Rom 7:19). For he was grieving," he said, "because sin, that is, the devil, was producing in him every desire.[177] The authority of the law proves the evil of concupiscence, when it blames all the uses of it which the flesh admires and praises."[178]

AUG. Does the apostle blame all use of carnal concupiscence? After all, he says, *And if you take a wife, you have not sinned, and if a virgin marries, she does not sin* (1 Cor 7:28). Mani, therefore, does not know what he is saying. But neither do you understand what you are saying, for you think the apostle meant something other than the concupiscence of the flesh which another apostle said does not come from the Father, but from the world.[179] And the learned Catholic teacher has both learned and taught in the Catholic Church that by it the flesh has desires opposed to the spirit[180] because of the transgression of the first human being.[181]

A Difference between Mani and Augustine

186. JUL. (1) The point which you thought was quite valuable for maintaining a distinction between yourself and Mani, namely, that you said that nature was created good, but only the nature of the first human beings, while all nature thereafter was ruined by concupiscence, Mani also discussed as follows. He said, "It is worth noting that the first soul which flows from the God of light received this structure of the body to rule it by its rein. The commandment came along; sin which seemed a captive came back to life; the devil found his opportune moments; he introduced into the structure of the body the matter of concupiscence and killed it by it. The law is, of course, holy, but holy for the holy soul, and the commandment is both righteous and good, but for the righteous and good soul." (2) So too, in that letter to Patricius,[182] he says, "The one formed as if from the flower of the first substance was better than those that followed." It is, then, nothing great, nor does it contribute anything to your defense that you thought that you should exempt from your accusation of human nature Adam, whose state we shall soon discuss more fully. Here let it suffice to have shown

that nothing is found so fresh in your ideas that it has not already become trite by Mani's tossing it about.

AUG. (1) Mani says that not only human beings, but the whole world and everything that belongs to it are composed of the mixture of two coeternal natures, namely, of good and of evil, and he attributes to the good God as its maker the very structure of the world, though made out of a mixture of good and evil. But he says that the animals and everything that springs from the earth and human beings themselves are the works of the evil mind which he ascribes to the nation of darkness. This is the reason why he says that the first soul flowed from the god of light and received this structure of the body in order to rule it by its rein. For he says this, not about a human being, but about the good soul, which he supposes to be a part of and the nature of God mixed into the whole world and everything in it, but deceived in human beings by concupiscence. (2) As must be often emphasized, he wants this concupiscence not to be the defect of a good substance, but to be an evil substance. He says that Adam was not free from the evil substance, but had less of it and much more of the light. Do you see how much the Catholic faith is opposed to this madness which says that the nature of God is corruptible and even corrupts it by mixing it with the evil nature? The Catholic faith holds that all the evils of the human race, no small part of which we see even little ones suffer, and the concupiscence itself by which the flesh has desires opposed to the spirit,[183] come only from the good nature that was also well made by the good God, but was damaged by the personal will and transgression of the first human being. You, on the other hand, would fill paradise with all these evils, but your paradise! (3) When you deny that these evils come from a good nature, what do you do but make all these evils which you do not want to come upon little ones from the sin of the good nature to be attributed to the mixture with the evil nature which the raving error of the Manichees introduces? You see, then, even though you do not want to see, that the insane and perverse Manichees must be defeated along with you so that they do not win out through your help; in fact, you see that by the help of the Lord they have already been defeated along with you.

187. JUL. (1) Mani persists, of course, in attacking us and adds, "But these people have dared to say, contrary to the books of the gospels and the apostles which they read often, but in vain, that this concupiscence is something good; you should see that their holy men have slept at times with their daughters and have at times had intercourse with many concubines and wives. Nor do they see these words of the apostle, *What fellowship has light with darkness, a believer with an unbeliever, Christ with Belial?* (2 Cor 6:14-15). They go astray, enclosed in a cloud of concupiscence, and they enjoy its poison so that they are seized by madness and, when they do this act, they think that God has permitted it, as if they do not know that the apostle said, *It is shameful even to mention what they do in darkness* (Eph 5:12)." (2) You see, of course, how he blames the shameful act and thinks that it counts heavily against us who do not call evil what

we nonetheless admit ought to be concealed out of shame. You have, then, fashioned for yourself no garment to cover the ugliness of your doctrine except for the rags in which you grew up and received as an inheritance from your father and teacher. He, therefore, persists in standing up to us, and in addressing us, he says, "Come on, you defender of concupiscence, tell us of its fruits and works in plain language. See, contrary to it I am not afraid of that light which it fears and which it hates. *For all who do evil hate the light and do not come to the light so that their works may not be revealed* (Jn 3:20). Do you see that concupiscence is the origin of the evil because of which wretched souls are subject to sexual desire like slaves, not like free persons, because this is the only thing we do, even though our mind is unwilling?"

(3) This is the reason that you also say, "Why is it that we have it in our power to move our lips, tongue, and hands and to turn our back, neck, and hips to their appropriate tasks, but when it comes to conceiving children, members that were created for this function do not obey us?[184] Rather, one waits for sexual desire to move them as if they were independent, and sometimes it does not move them,[185] though the mind wills it, and at other times it does, when the mind is against it."[186] You, of course, listed all the functions of the members and while declaring that they obey the command of the will, you mention the acts of sexual desire which are the only acts we do even though the mind is unwilling. (4) What does Mani say? He says, "Do you see that concupiscence is the origin of the evil because of which wretched souls are subject to sexual desire like slaves, not like free persons, because this is the only thing we do, even though the mind is unwilling?" But let us see what else he adds. "Finally, every sin is outside the body because it is an action. But those who commit fornication sin against their own bodies. For no sin exists before it is committed, and after it is committed only the memory of the action remains, not the reality itself. But because the evil of concupiscence is natural, it exists before the sin is committed; it is increased when it is committed, and it both is real and lasts after it is committed."

(5) Why, then, do you quarrel with us because we call you a Manichee, since nothing other than what you say is contained in his writings, nor is anything else contained in yours than that of which he wants to convince us. That question which flows from the lips of the people, but was put there by you, is already found in that letter of Mani, that is: "If sin is not natural, why are infants baptized, since it is established that they have by themselves done nothing evil?" I, however, said that it flies about on the lips of the masses, because it is a rather ordinary argument grasped even by any slower people. (6) But in your books you rest your complete hope in it, and your master follows it up in this way, "I must question these people with these words: If every sin is an action, why do any people receive the purification of water before they commit sin, since they have committed no sin by themselves? Or if they have not yet committed sin and need to be purified, it is possible to show that they are the sprouting of the naturally

evil tree, the same people whose madness does not allow them to understand either what they say or what they claim." (7) Do you hear how he abuses us? He says that we are out of our minds and do not understand either what we say or what we claim, when we deny the sprouting of the evil tree, though we baptize with purifying water those who have committed no sin, that is, little ones. Many of his statements have, of course, been set forth, but if the title did not indicate Mani who calls himself the apostle of Christ and his daughter Menoch, they would surely lead us to think that you are their author. Since, therefore, you say nothing other than what you learned from the teaching of Mani, do you think that in the estimation of Catholics you should be regarded otherwise than he is through whom you have imbibed the mysteries of such teachings?

AUG. (1) At last you have finished those passages which you thought you should state in opposition to us from the letter of Mani, which you rejoice to have found by the help of the prayers of your colleague, Florus. In it Mani certainly brings accusations against the concupiscence of the flesh by which the flesh has desires opposed to the spirit.[187] But he thought that he should raise it as an objection for Catholics, as if they say that concupiscence is good because they praise the good of marriage in accord with the sound teaching of the Lord and the apostles. After all, how could Mani distinguish the evil of carnal concupiscence from the good of marriage, since the Letter to the Hebrews says that only those who have minds trained to separate good from evil have solid food?[188] (2) But clearly you have fallen in a way you could not avoid into the jaws of this Mani, for you praise concupiscence of the flesh so much that you would locate it even in paradise, that is, in a place of great blessedness, not the sort of concupiscence that would have existed there if it ought to have existed there, but precisely the sort of concupiscence that now exists. That is, the inhabitants of that place would enjoy its blessed peace in such a way that they would fight within themselves against the stirrings of concupiscence in an internal war so that they would not fall into consent to forbidden and immoral relations. This evil could not exist in paradise, except perhaps on that painting about which we spoke above which would have as its title written above it: The Paradise of the Pelagians.[189]

(3) Though this concupiscence tempting chaste hearts with its hidden stirrings could not be pictured by any skill of a painter, one could paint pregnant women refusing the food they need out of disgust and wanting harmful foods out of twisted delight, nauseated, vomiting, pallid, at times suffering miscarriages, and witnessing in childbirth by their misery to the punishment which mother Eve received. Though the painting is without sounds, it would reproduce, nonetheless, the faces of the sorrowful, the groaning, and the weeping, as best it could, and all those newborns weeping because of the common lot of those who are born and because of the wide range of different punishments, and many children later weeping under the blows from their teachers. (4) If any persons unfamiliar with it saw this painting, read the title, and asked for the reason, this amazing ex-

planation would be offered them, though by you, of course. You would say: The condition of the human race even in paradise would be precisely such, because it is that way here where the offspring of human beings likewise contract no sin from their origin. If they accepted that, they would become Pelagians, but if they refused to yield to this laughable nonsense, they would be charged by you with being Manichees.

(5) But reply to this argument, holy bishop of God, Ambrose, a man taught by the Church and a teacher of the Church. Tell them that the concupiscence by which the flesh has desires opposed to the spirit and from which Mani, who does not know what he is saying, sets his traps for the unlearned, does not come to our nature as the result of a mixture with some other nature, as he so foolishly supposes, but comes to our good nature that was created good by the good God as the result of the transgression of the first human being.[190] Out of your impudent bullheadedness you might perhaps choose to offer assistance to the great impurity of Mani rather than yield to the holiness of Ambrose. Do as you please, but Mani will not be happy even with you as his helpers, since by the Catholic faith Ambrose defeats you both in Christ's name and power. (6) For, if this concupiscence were such that by its carnal stirring it neither preceded nor exceeded the will of human beings, but always followed their choice, Mani would surely find nothing in it that he might correctly blame, nor would any of us maintain that married couples in paradise could not have had it. Nor would Ambrose say that we contracted it from the transgression of the first human being, because he would see that it does not have desires opposed to the spirit. But now it is such that it has desires opposed to the spirit, even if it does not win out when the spirit fights back, and those enjoying that blessed peace in paradise could not, therefore, have it, nor may we believe that God is corruptible by being mixed with the evil nature. It remains, then, that the faith of Ambrose about the infection of the first sin defeats both you and the Manichees.

Augustine's Summary Statement under Attack

188. JUL. (1) There remains that we examine that idea of yours which you promised to reduce to one statement and which you briefly, as cannot be denied, and cleverly inferred, "If human nature were an evil, it ought not to be born; if it did not have an evil, it would not need to be reborn. And to sum up both points in a single statement, if human nature were an evil, it ought not to be saved, and if there were no evil in it, it would not need to be saved."[191] (2) In this passage you must not be denied the praise due to your talent; in defense of your case, after all, it could not be stated better. The nature of reality, nonetheless does not permit that your clever precision establish anything. *It is*, indeed, *difficult for you to kick against the goad* (Acts 26:14), for whatever you firmly state is melted away like

ice by the fire of approaching truth. Finally, pay attention now to what we reply. You concluded in this way: "Certainly, if human nature were an evil, it ought not to be saved." We agree; you have, of course, spoken the truth: "If it were an evil, it ought not to be saved," because something evil, that is, naturally evil, neither merits nor is capable of salvation. (3) Why would it not be capable of it? Because it could not become something other than it was made to be. But it would not merit it because there was nothing in it which God's clemency might choose to set free. But when we say, "If it were," of what certainly cannot be, we do not win for it some hope for the conclusion that is denied; rather, we usually speak about impossible states of affairs in order to destroy an alternative opinion which results. For example, if this or that were the case, something else[192] would certainly follow so that, when the former is impossible, the latter for whose destruction it was introduced is also denied for even better reason. (4) We have, then, already frequently shown that nothing can be evil by nature, but now without prejudice to your established conclusion we approve the part of your statement where you said, "If human nature were an evil, it ought not to be saved." You have located salvation in baptism, and you have argued logically that, if the Manichees spoke the truth when they said that nature is evil, the Christians would be foolish to believe that the remedy of baptism should be applied to the evil nature. And, therefore, those who uphold the evil nature of human beings are forced to deny grace, and this is converted so that those who uphold grace praise the nature of human beings for the salvation of which they understand that it was provided.

AUG. (1) What you say is not true; you are a deceiver or you are deceived. It is not one who maintains that the nature of human beings is evil, but one who maintains that it is an evil, that is, it is not one who maintains that it is evil, but who maintains that it is something evil, who is forced to deny grace. For, when it is evil, it then needs grace the more. An evil man is, of course, an evil nature because a man is without a doubt a nature; so too, an evil woman is an evil nature because a woman is surely a nature. How, then, is one who says this forced to deny grace since grace helps evil natures, that is, evil human beings, so that they cease to be evil? (2) But we say one thing when we say: This human being is evil, and we say something else when we say: This human being is an evil. The former can be true; the latter cannot. So too, if we say: This human being is defective, this can be true, but if we say: This human being is a defect, this cannot be true. Hence, do not be in error or lead others into error, and understand that I spoke in this way, "If human nature were an evil, it ought not to be born; if it did not have an evil, it would not need to be reborn," as if I had said: "If human nature were a defect, it ought not to be born; if it did not have a defect, it would not need to be reborn." (3) Similarly, there follow the words where I said that I summed up both of them in a single sentence; I said: "If human nature were an evil, it ought not to be saved; if there were no evil in it, it would not need to be saved," as if I said: If human nature were a defect, it ought not to be saved; if there were no defect in it, it would not need to be saved. See, I have made my words simpler, not so that you might find something to contradict, but so that you would understand that you could not find anything to say.

189. JUL. Notice, then, what is accomplished by this: The denial of grace is not tied to the praise of human nature. On the contrary, these four are so linked together that one cannot be maintained without the other, but the disparagement of nature produces the denial of grace, and the praise of grace leads to the approval of nature, for these are fully reciprocal in either part. You, therefore, put it well: "If human nature were an evil, it ought not to be saved." The Manichees say both of these, namely, that the nature of the flesh neither can be saved nor ought to be saved by grace.

AUG. But they say that the nature of the flesh is evil in the sense that they mean that it is an evil, not that it has an evil, because they suppose that the defect itself is not added to a substance, but is the substance.

190. JUL. After this you introduce a statement dear to you and say, "But if there were no evil in human nature, it ought not to be saved. Hence, one who says that it is not something good denies a good creator for the nature that has been created, but one who denies that there is evil in it begrudges a merciful savior to the nature that has been corrupted."[193] Let the readers, then, be attentive, and they will see that you said nothing else than what you said one should not say, for you declared that an evil is naturally present in that being which you said is not naturally evil.

AUG. I did not say that it is not evil, but that it is not an evil; that is, to speak more plainly, I said that it was defective, but not a defect. Read it again and understand!

191. JUL. But it is impossible to understand that an evil nature as anything else than to have inborn that which is evil.

AUG. Whether the evil is inborn, like feeblemindedness, or contracted by the will, like murder, an evil human being can be called an evil nature because a human being is also a nature, just as a bad horse can also be called a bad animal because a horse is also an animal.

192. JUL. To make the conclusion short and simple, if an evil is in a nature so that the evil is born from it along with the very seeds, the nature is proved to be evil beyond any doubt.

AUG. Even if it is proved to be evil, it is, nonetheless, not an evil because, even if it proved to be defective, it is, nonetheless, not a defect.

193. JUL. But if it is preserved from evils and defended as good, evil cannot arise from it, nor can evil be in it by nature. Your conclusion, therefore, is destroyed because the statement which you introduced in the second place did not amend the first statement, but repeated it.

AUG. If it is defended as good, it is not thereby preserved from evil. The same nature is good insofar as it is a nature and evil if it is damaged. But no nature whatsoever is an evil. My conclusion, then, is not destroyed where I said, "If human nature were an evil, it ought not to be saved; if there were no evil in it, it would not need to be saved."[194] But if you wish to speak the truth, say rather that your argument is destroyed by which you wanted to refute my conclusion.

194. JUL. You say, "If human nature were an evil, it ought not to be saved; if there were no evil in it, it would not need to be saved."[195] What else have you shown than that one and the same reality ought to be saved for the very reason on account of which you have said that it ought not to be saved?

AUG. It ought to be saved because it is evil, not because it is an evil; if it were an evil, it ought not to be saved. It is evil, after all, not because it is an evil, but because it has an evil, just as it is defective, not because it is a defect, but because it has a defect. Because it is defective, then, it ought to be saved, but if the nature itself, that is, the very substance, were a defect, it ought not to be saved. How, then, did I say that one and the same reality ought to be saved for the very reason on account of which I said that it ought not to be saved, since it is one thing to have a defect and another to be a defect? It ought, therefore, to be saved because it has a defect, not because it is a defect. But if it were a defect, it ought not to be saved. You see that to reply is not the same thing as not to be silent, since you see that you have not replied and yet you refused to be silent.

Augustine as Mani's Faithful Soldier

195. JUL. And in this way you have come around to the point that by your argument you rehabilitate Mani whom you have scorned with your statement. For, by saying, "If it were evil, it ought not to be saved," you have donned the guise of his attacker, but by adding, "If there were no evil in it, it would not need to be saved," you have shown that you are his faithful soldier. Since, then, it has been shown that your statement has the same content as Mani's, namely, that the nature of human beings is evil, for both you and he equally maintain that an evil is present in it, and you have declared that an evil nature ought not to be saved, we have absolutely established that your faith attacks both nature and grace with your armed forces united.

AUG. (1) When you change my words in order that you may seem to make a reply, do you make it difficult or impossible for the readers either to recall to mind or at least to reread and see a little earlier in this book of yours my words where you yourself quoted them as I said them? For I did not say: If it were evil, it ought not to be saved, since it ought to be saved precisely in order that it might not be evil. Rather, I said: "If it were an evil, it ought not to be saved."[196] (2) By having an evil, it is, of course, evil, and when that evil is destroyed, it is beyond any doubt saved. The nature is not a defect; otherwise, it would be destroyed when the defect is destroyed. But when salvation destroys the defect, what is saved in this way but the nature? When the defect is said to be healed, it is not the defect itself, but that nature in which the defect existed that is saved, and if the nature were a defect, salvation would not save it, but would rather terminate it. (3) Moreover, good health could never be produced in this way because, if it were, the healed nature would remain once the defect which made it unhealthy was destroyed. But if the nature were a defect, it would not be healed when the defect is destroyed, but would itself be destroyed. And in this way, if human nature were not evil, but were an evil, that is, if it were a defect, it ought not to be saved; if there were no evil in it, that is, if it were not evil by reason of a defect, it would not need to be saved. See what I said; do not try by changing my words to make room, not for your replies, but for your bickering.

196. JUL. It follows that no one can praise the grace of Christ without praising the good work of the creator in nature.

AUG. What you said is true, and for this reason the work of the creator is praiseworthy even in an evil nature, because even an evil nature is something good insofar as it is a nature, and grace is necessary for this good to be set free from evil.

197. JUL. Surely there is no question here about the desires of adults, but only about the character of the newborn in whom we are examining the state of nature. Along with Mani, therefore, you maintain that this nature is guilty without any involvement of their own will, condemned, and full of evils, that is, of serious sins, while we defend it as free from crime and from the evil of sin, as innocent and capable of virtue.

AUG. We recognize you; we recognize the great defender of little ones who does not permit the savior to come to the help of the little ones whom you defend. But if you do permit him, tell me, please, when they are baptized in good bodily health, from what evil, from what defect, from what disease are they saved? What are you going to say, you who fashion for yourself a paradise which you are not embarrassed to fill with the unmerited punishments of little ones?

The Little Ones Are Blameless in Nature and Will

198. JUL. Do you, then, blame this criminal, defective, and condemned nature in little ones because of their own will or because of the condition of their birth? If because of their own will, that is, so that the little ones are said to have sinned by their own actions, a monstrous idea arises, but the transmission of sin is denied, for their nature does not receive from another what it could have itself committed. But if it obtains so many evils, not by its own action, but by the condition of its birth, it is proved to be naturally wicked.

AUG. I do not blame the nature of little ones because of their own will, for no child is born because it wills to be, and I only blame their nature because of the condition of their birth because they are born in misery, not because they are born. For, even if no one had sinned, because God's blessing made it fertile, human nature would also have been born in paradise until the number of the saints which God foreknew was complete. But those little ones in paradise would not weep, nor would they be speechless or unable to use reason for a time; they would not lie weak and unable to act without the use of their members, and they would not be afflicted with diseases or be injured by animals, killed by poison, or wounded by any accident. (2) They would not lose any sense or part of the body, nor would they troubled by demons. When they grow into childhood, they would not be controlled by beatings or educated with labor, nor would any of them be born with so foolish and dull a mind that they would be corrected neither by labor nor by pain. Except for the size of their bodies on account of the capacity of their mothers' wombs, they would be born just as Adam was created. They would not now be such children as we see, nor would they endure such sufferings if that great sin did not change human nature and condemn it to these miseries. They are, therefore, not this way because of the condition of birth, but because of the infection of sin and the condition of its punishment.

199. JUL. How do you and Mani differ in your judgment upon nature? You say: Because he admits that it is evil. If, then, you reject this, declare that it is good, and the dispute is ended. You will be immediately captured in the nets of truth for your salvation. But you protest. Let us, then, listen to what you produce, you Aristotle of the Phoenicians.[197] You say, "So great an evil is present in it that it is owned by the devil and merits eternal fire."[198]

AUG. (1) But when you deny that human nature is owned by the devil, you undoubtedly deny that it is rescued from the power of darkness when it is transferred into the kingdom of Christ by rebirth,[199] and you accuse the whole Catholic Church of the great crime of lèse majesté.[200] For by the laws of this world a person who hisses at[201] the image, though a lifeless image, of the emperor is held guilty of no other crime. But little ones undergo exsufflation in the rite of exorcism before they are baptized; living images, then, not of some ruler, but of God, are subjected to exsufflation. Or rather, in exsufflation the devil is blown out who holds the little one guilty by the infection of sin so that, when he is driven out, the little one is transferred to Christ. (3) Let the madness of Julian, then, be blown out so that the Church is not declared guilty of lèse majesté in the purification and exsufflation of little ones. But if a little one is not rescued from the power of darkness and remains in it, why are you surprised that it will be with the devil in eternal fire since it is not permitted to enter the kingdom of God? Or since the Pelagians devise some place of rest and eternal life for non-baptized little ones apart from the kingdom of God, are Christ's words, therefore, false: *Those who believe and are baptized will be saved, but those who do not believe will be condemned* (Mk 16:16)? Whoever deny that little ones believe by the lips of those who bring them for baptism also deny that they receive baptism because they fight back in the hands of those who bring them.

200. JUL. But their nature is not so evil that anyone but a Manichee could bring accusations against it.

AUG. Did Mani, therefore, say, "We are all born under the power of sin, and our very origin lies in guilt"?[202] But because a learned Catholic teacher said this, what are you but a deceived and deceiving heretic?

201. JUL. He says, "I who verbally acquit nature, but condemn it in my judgments, am not a Manichee."

AUG. You condemn it by your judgment and by an unjust judgment, since you want it to suffer such great evils without having merited anything evil.

202. JUL. What, then, should I accuse first? The impudence of the liar, the passion of the debater, or the profanity of the man who believes such wicked ideas? I understand, nonetheless, that we should use the words of the prophet: *We are the blessed ones of Israel because what is pleasing to God has been made known to us* (Bar 4:4).

AUG. But is it true that what is pleasing to God has been made known to you? Stupid fellow, it does not please God that little ones are weighed down by a heavy yoke without any infection of sin. They contract, therefore, an infection from that first and great sin. When you refuse to admit it, what do you do but ascribe to God an unjust judgment?

There Is No Other Evil except Sin

203. JUL. But the disapproval of the readers will take the place of the duty to attack you; let us pass on to the rest. Certainly there is in the world no other evil which is truly evil except what we call sin.

AUG. If the punishments of sins are not also evil, how will you defend the truth of what God said, for he said that he creates evils.[203] He must not, after all, be said to create sins.

204. JUL. And from this sin there arises, according to you, the natural evil in each person; nothing else, therefore, is a true evil but evil merit.

AUG. It is not merely evil merit, but also the punishment which evil merit receives that is an evil, for it is not true that sin is a true evil and that the punishment of sin is not a true evil. If, then, there were no evil merit in little ones from their origin, whatever evil they suffer would be unjust. And these evils could not have existed in paradise precisely because there would have been no evil merit there if the happy obedience of the two had lasted. And, for this reason, since little ones here have evils which would not have existed there, they also have evil merit which they would not have except on account of their origin.

205. JUL. Mani says that nature is evil for no other reason than that he thinks it has evil merit for which he supposes that punishments must be imposed, and you also affirm that there is evil in human nature and no other evil than what Mani maintains, that is, the concupiscence of the flesh which you preach was introduced by the devil, and you say that nature has evil merit so that you persist in condemning it to eternal torments. You, therefore, undoubtedly declare it most evil and condemned, just as Mani does.

AUG. Shame on you! Concupiscence of the flesh is not from the Father, but from the world,[204] that is, from human beings whose offspring fill the world. The Manichees, however, attribute this to the nation of darkness, and you help them when you do not want this evil to have turned into our nature by the transgression of the first human being in accord with the faith of Ambrose,[205] that is, in accord with the Catholic faith.

206. JUL. Let us, then, see how the second part of your statement also amounts to this. After all, you said, "One who says that human nature is not something good denies a good creator for the nature that has been created, but one who denies that there is evil in it begrudges a merciful savior to the nature that has been corrupted."[206] If, then, as you have been forced to admit, one who denies that it is something good also denies its good creator, that is, God, and if for nature to be evil means only that it naturally has evil merit, your admission also props up the truth we state, namely, that you deny that God is the good creator of human beings, since you swear that their nature is evil both by reason of its defects and by reason of its punishments.

AUG. Even if human nature is evil because it is damaged, it is not, nonetheless, an evil because it is a nature. For no nature insofar as it is a nature is an evil, but a good, and without that good there could be no evil, since a defect can only exist in some nature, though a nature that was either never damaged or has been healed can exist without a defect. If the Manichees understood this, they would not be Manichees at all with their introduction of the two natures of good and evil opposed to each other. If, then, you see the difference between the Manichees and us, be quiet; if you do not see it, be quiet.

207. JUL. We do not, then, begrudge a savior to that nature which we defend by the dignity of its creator, but we deny that it is an evil so that we do not become Manichees, and we deny that there is an evil in it so that we do not once again become Manichees under a different name.

AUG. You are certainly opposed to the Manichees when you say that nature is not evil, but you are Pelagians when you say that there is no evil in it, and without knowing it you offer help to the Manichees when you say that the evil which is clearly present in it does not come from the transgression of the first human being so that they come to the conclusion that there is another substance and nature of evil.

208. JUL. We, however, say that nature's being damaged is the merit of a person, not of nature, in each individual by one's own choice doing either good or evil. And for this reason we claim that what can be damaged is healed by the grace of Christ because nothing else is shown to have been injured than what we teach is healed.

AUG. Of course, you begrudge a savior to the little ones; if one can believe that it would help you, you ought to undergo exsufflation, just as they do, in order that you may be rescued from the power of darkness and transferred into the kingdom of Christ.[207]

209. JUL. In the baptized what is removed is not the guilt of concupiscence of the flesh,[208] which is natural, but the guilt of evil concupiscence.

AUG. The apostle John said that concupiscence of the flesh does not come from the Father, but from the world,[209] in that way bringing us to understand that it is evil. But you say that concupiscence of the flesh, which is natural, does not involve guilt, but evil concupiscence does. For you, of course, concupiscence of the flesh is not evil, even when one desires fornication because, as you say, one who makes use of it in that way makes a bad use of a good. Concupiscence itself, then, is always a good, as you would have it, whether by it one desires marriage or adultery. For, if one desires marriage, one makes good use of a good and, if one desires adultery, one makes bad use of a good. Carry on your fight with the apostle John, not with me. After all, you disagree with him when he says that the evil concupiscence, which he calls concupiscence of the flesh, does not come from the Father, but from the world,[210] as long as you say that concupiscence of the flesh is good, even when one desires an evil by it, and that for this reason it is never evil. But, believe me, there is no Christian who does not prefer to agree with the apostle John than with you.

210. JUL. And in this way it is proved that concupiscence is not a sin by the testimony of both the creator and the redeemer of the human race.

AUG. Why is it that you say so inconsiderately that there is no sin in our nature? As if sin could exist anywhere at all but in a nature, even if it were not contracted from our origin, but committed by the will. Whether it is the sin of an angel or of a human being, it is clear that it exists either in an angel or in a human being. But who has strayed from reality to the point of denying that a human being or an angel is a nature? Why is it likewise that you speak with your eyes closed? Why is it, I ask, that you say that concupiscence is not a sin? Do you not see that in that way you argue against the apostle? For he showed quite clearly that concupiscence is a sin when he said, *I did not know sin except through the law. For I would not have known desire if the law had not said: Do not desire* (Rom 7:7). What could be said more clear than this testimony? What could be said more foolish than your statement?

Julian Sums Up His Arguments

211. JUL. To repeat what has been accomplished, I have shown by the testimony of God's commandments and his judgments that your view of inherited sin is opposed to the justice of God.

AUG. It is, rather, you who are opposed to the justice of God, since you would have it that he unjustly laid a heavy yoke upon the children of Adam from the day they leave the womb of their mother[211] when you deny original sin, and this has been proved by the testimony of the scriptures and by the misfortunes of the little ones which could not exist in any paradise but yours.

212. JUL. I have demonstrated that concupiscence of the flesh was given to bodies by God, their creator, to attract the sexes to the work of procreation and by the citation of his writings I showed that only Mani brings accusations against it.

AUG. But this is the concupiscence of the flesh, which God's scripture teaches is evil, for through it, *The flesh has desires opposed to the spirit* (Gal 5:17). But you help the Manichees and attribute it to the nation of darkness coeternal with God when you do not want it to belong to original sin and dare, moreover, to locate it in God's paradise.

213. JUL. And I showed that you have no other arguments for the transmission of sin than those which Mani gave.

AUG. Ambrose was not a Manichee, but an invincible defender of the Catholic faith who laid low both you and the Manichees; he said that the discord between the flesh and the spirit, in which through your darling, the flesh, has desires opposed to the sprit, was turned into our nature by the transgression of the first human being.[212] You were forced to admit this, convinced and compelled by the testimony of your leader praising the same bishop.[213]

214. JUL. By an examination of your statement I revealed that you deny free choice and God as the creator of the newborn.

AUG. I do not deny free choice which you destroy with your praises, but I am, rather, its defender by confessing the grace of God. By trusting in your own virtue you mislead this choice, as countless sacred testimonies proclaim. We do not deny that God is the creator of the newborn, but you deny that God is the savior of the newborn, as those statements which both of us have made reveal to the readers.

215. JUL. I have proved that you declare that nature is evil by an explanation of that idea which you promised to reduce to a single sentence.[214]

AUG. I have shown that human nature is not an evil, but that there is an evil in it, establishing the first of these points by the substance of that same nature and by God as the creator of that substance and the other by the misery of that substance and by God as its savior from that misery. But the careful and intelligent reader could have discovered that you were unable to invalidate my argument, even if I had not replied to you.

216. JUL. And so I trust that it is clear even to those who are very slow to understand and are deceived by your authority that you recoil in disgust only at the name of Mani, but that along with all the supporters of inherited sin you adhere with full faith to his teachings which are no less disgusting than stupid.

AUG. (1) What is clear even to the slower folks is other than and quite contrary to what you think. For it is, rather, clear even to the very slow, if they are not too tired to devote careful attention to reading the writings of us both, that I proved not only that I am an enemy of the error of the Manichees and overthrow their wicked doctrines with the help of God who is the Truth, but also that you provide help to the madness of the Manichees. And as a result, they boast of being absolutely undefeated, unless the Catholic faith, which by God's mercy we defend, defeats them, not through you or by you, but rather along with you. (2) But you chose me alone to abuse with the label and charge of Manicheism, the more hatefully the more often you did it. You supposed that in that way you could without incurring hatred destroy, by the horror of that unspeakable name, but not by the truth of the charges brought, the most well-founded Catholic faith which refutes you and the renowned multitude of its holy defenders who learned and taught the same things we learned and teach. *But God's firm foundation remains, for the Lord knows those who are his* (2 Tm 2:19). But you cited the words of my book as if you were going to refute them, and I leave to the readers to notice and discover for themselves how, after you tested a very few of them for the semblance of some sort of fight, you avoided the many more that remained by spreading here and there the clouds of your wordiness, for this would take too long to point out here.

Notes

1. See I, 28 where Julian begins his argument on the basis of God's justice.

2. See Rom 2:6. Here, in the context of justice, the term "*gratia*" connotes for Julian favoritism and partiality, a corruption of justice, while for Augustine it means God's gift or grace, something that is unmerited.

3. The Latin of Migne and the CSEL has "damnatam." I have conjectured "*damnata.*"

4. Ambrose, *Commentary on the Gospel of Luke* (*Expositio Euangelii secundum Lucam*) 7, 234: CCL 14, 295.

5. See Lk 19:10.

6. I have followed Primmer's conjecture of "*constabat*" instead of "*constat.*"

7. See Sir 40:1.

8. See Sir 40:1.

9. In accord with Primmer's suggestion I have followed one manuscript which has "*discitur*" instead of "*dicitur*" which is found in the CSEL edition.

10. See Job 14:4 LXX.

11. See Rom 5:12.

12. See Gn 7:19-24.

13. See Gn 19:24-28.

14. See Jos 7:22-26.

15. See Num 14:18; Dt 5:9; Jer 32:18.

16. I have followed Primmer's conjectures of *"prave dicuntur"* in place of *"praedicuntur"* and of *"fuerat"* in place of *"fuerant."*

17. See above 10.

18. See Ex 34:7, Nm 14:18, and Dt 5:9.

19. The Manichean explanation for the presence of evil in the world involved a primordial conflict between the good principle and the evil principle as a result of which parts of the good principle were captured by the evil principle so that in the present time the world and each human being is a mixture of good and evil.

20. Ambrose, *Commentary on the Gospel of Luke* (*Expositio Euangelii secundum Lucam*) 7, 234: CCL 14, 295.

21. See Ex 20:5 and Dt 24:16.

22. See Ps 1:4.

23. See also Num 14:8, Dt 5:9, and Jer 32:18.

24. See Jos 7:24-25.

25. See Jos 6:21 and 10:40.

26. See Dt 17:6 and 19:15.

27. Nothing can be both living and dead at the same time, but some things admit an intermediate state or states, for example, between wealthy and poor there are many degrees so a person could be both wealthy and poor at the same time in relation to different standards, or one could be wealthy in terms of earthly goods, but poor in judgment.

28. See 1 Cor 1:17.

29. See 1 Sam 17:4.

30. See 2 Kgs 14:6.

31. The Manichees rejected the Mosaic law along with all of the scriptures of the old testament.

32. Augustine begins his reply with a flourish of multiple rhymes: *"odiose* hatefully" and *"otiose,* idly," *"loquacitate,* wordiness" and *"veritate,* truth" and then uses *"modo,* measure or manner" in a double meaning.

33. Julian made a similar charge of bribery in I, 42 and 74; again, Augustine treats it as a pure slander.

34. The referent of *"princeps"* is not clear. Julian may refer to the emperor Honorius, who reigned from 395 to 423 and exiled Pelagius and Caelestius from Rome in 418.

35. See Mt 5:11.

36. See Mt 5:12.

37. See above 33.

38. See Jn 3:36.

39. Ambrose, *Penance* (*De poenitentia*) I, 3, 13: SC 179, 62.

40. See Heb 7:9-10.

41. See 2 Cor 3:14-16.

42. See Rom 5:18.

43. See Heb 7:9.

44. See Jn 6:54-55.

45. See 2 Tm 3:8.

46. I have followed Primmer's suggestion based on two manuscripts and read *"sanxit"* in place of *"sancit."*

47. The Latin version of Ezekiel which Julian cites here is quite different from that which he cites above in III, 38. Perhaps it is a paraphrase rather than a citation, though the CSEL edition treats it as a citation.

48. See 1 Cor 15:22.

49. Augustine has an untranslatable pun: *"cave illum,* fear him" and *"cavillum,* quibble."

50. I have followed Primmer's conjecture of *"oppugas"* instead of the CSEL reading of *"oppugnat."*

51. See Gn 14:14-16.

52. See 1 Kgs 11:11-13.

53. See above 15.

54. See *The Grace of Christ and Original Sin* I, 43, 47, where Augustine cites a fragment from Pelagius' *In Defense of Free Choice* (*Pro libero arbitrio*).

55. Augustine plays upon the contrast between *uanitas* and *urbanitas* as well as between *vecordia* and *misericordia*.

56. Ambrose, *Commentary on the Gospel of Luke* (*Expositio Euangelii secundum Lucam*) 7, 141: CCL 14, 263.

57. I have followed the reading of *"ratio"* instead of the CSEL text which has *"natio"*

58. I have conjectured *"qua"* in place of *"quia."*

59. See 1 Kgs 21:29.

60. See *The Deeds of Pelagius* 23-24, 57.

61. Again Augustine employs an untranslatable set of rhymes: not *"poenales dolores"* but *"vernales odores."*

62. It is not clear whether Julian is referring to the liturgical formula for the conferral of baptism or to a verse of Paul, such as Rom 6:3. See 2, 112 where Julian argues that there is not a single grace of baptism, but various graces for various ages.

63. I have followed Primmer's conjecture of *"transmissi"* instead of *"tramitis"* found in the CSEL edition.

64. See Wis 9:15.

65. See Wis 11:21.

66. I have followed Primmer's conjecture of *"nedum"* instead of *"necdum."*

67. See Heb 5:14.

68. See Ps 49:7.

69. See Gn 2:25.

70. See Gn 3:7.

71. It is not clear whether the subject continues to be the law of sin or has at this point become Augustine. I have opted for the latter.

72. See *The Grace of Christ and Original Sin* II, 11, 12, where there is listed among the charges brought against Caelestius at the Council of Carthage in 411 or 412 the proposition: "That Adam was created mortal and would die whether he sinned or did not sin."

73. See Ps 49:7.

74. Ambrose, *Penance* (*De poenitentia*) I, 3, 13: SC 179, 62.

75. See Vergil, *Georgics* I, 75.

76. Augustine plays with the noun, *lupinum* a name for a plant used for fodder and manure, and *lupinus*, the adjective for fox-like or cunning.

77. See Eph 4:18.

78. I conjecture *"reorum"* instead of *"rerum."*

79. See above 39-42.

80. See II, 56 and 183, where Julian expressed this idea, though not in these precise words.

81. Augustine plays on *"libenter*, gladly or lustily" and *"libidini*, sexual desire or lust."

82. Augustine's reply divides Julian's sentence over this and the next two paragraphs.

83. Again Augustine has a practically untranslatable rhyme: *"vanitate, non urbanitate"*

84. The Latin for "transmitted: *traductum"* is from the same root as "traducianist."

85. See Rom 5:14.

86. See above 88.

87. Augustine puns on *"foedus"* which as a noun means an alliance and as an adjective means ugly or loathsome.

88. See Rom 9:22.

89. See Rom 9:21.

90. See Wis 4:11.

91. I have followed Migne and Primmer in reading *"ostendisti"* instead of *"ostendis te."*

92. This quotation within the quotation is taken from the document containing the excerpts from Julian's *To Turbantius.*

93. See Col 1:13.

94. *Marriage and Desire* II, 3, 8.

95. See I, 14 or I, 85.

96. *Marriage and Desire* II, 3, 8. The CSEL editor added the clause in brackets on the basis of paragraph 108 below.

97. See above 101.

98. See Rom 1:20.

99. See 1 Cor 2:12.

100. See 2 Cor 5:10.

101. I have followed Primmer's suggestion based on two manuscripts and have added "*ut.*"

102. See Rom 5:14.

103. See Ps 49:7.

104. See above 105.

105. I have followed Primmer's suggestion of "*catholicos praedicare*" instead of "*catholicis praedicari.*"

106. See Ps 49:7.

107. See Mt 10:29.

108. See Ps 144:4.

109. See 2 Cor 4:16.

110. Julian undoubtedly refers to John Chrysostom, Basil the Great, and Theodore of Mopsuetia. Julian appealed to the words of Chrysostom in *Answer to Julian* I, 6, 21, and during his exile Julian lived with Theodore.

111. See Rom 7:23.

112. See 1 Jn 4:7.

113. See Est 15:11.

114. See Ps 34:15.

115. The stream of Hippocrene on Mount Helicon was, according to mythology, created by the hoof of Pegasus and was consecrated to the muses. By drinking from the Hippocrene one became a poet.

116. *Answer to Two Letters of the Pelagians* I, 3, 7. Julian has shortened the sentence he quotes significantly.

117. I have, along with Primmer, followed one manuscript which omitted "*non*" and have also followed his punctuation of the sentence.

118. Augustine plays about the two verbs: "*definias*, to define" and "*finias*, to end."

119. See 1 Jn 4:7.

120. See 1 Jn 3:1.

121. See Col 1:13.

122. See I, 52.

123. I have followed Primmer's suggestion and dropped "*ita*" and "*id est*" from the text of the CSEL edition.

124. I have followed three manuscripts which have "*in*" instead of "*de*" which would require a further conjecture.

125. See Is 45:7.

126. See *Marriage and Desire* II, 17, 32.

127. See 1 Cor 5:5.

128. I have adopted Primmer's conjecture of "*negans*" instead of "*negas*" along with the change in punctuation.

129. See Sir 40:1.

130. See Col 1:13.

131. See above 124.

132. The manuscripts omit: JUL. here, most likely because the passage is a long quotation from *Marriage and Desire* I, 3,9.

133. I have followed Primmer's conjecture of "*respondetis*" instead of "*respondete*" which is found in the CSEL edition.

134. Following Primmer's suggestion I have restored "*in corpore*" which the CSEL edition omitted, and changed "*sint*" to "*sunt.*"

135. *Marriage and Desire* II, 3, 9.

136. *Marriage and Desire* II, 3, 9.

137. See Wis 12:11.

138. See Col 1:13.

139. The rite of exsufflation, or "blowing out," was formerly a part of the ritual of baptism in the Catholic Church. The priest administering the sacrament would blow in the face of the person being baptized to symbolize the expulsion of the devil.

140. *Marriage and Desire* II, 17, 32-18, 33.

141. *Marriage and Desire* II, 21, 36.

142. *Ibid.*

143. *Ibid.* Julian omits a few words of the citation from Romans as well as truncates the end of the sentence, as Augustine points out.

144. *Ibid.*

145. *Ibid.*

146. See above 138, where Julian cites *Marriage and Desire* II, 3, 9.

147. Julian uses the Greek words for "contraries" and "contrary."

148. See above 138. Julian all but quotes from *Marriage and Desire* II, 3, 9.

149. See Gn 1:29-30.

150. See Mt 1:21.

151. The "*maniae*" were images of ugly faces hung up as charms. Julian plays upon the similarity with Mani's name, which was changed by his Latin followers to "*Manichaeus*" to avoid the connotation of madness. See Augustine's *Heresies* 46.

152. See Sir 22:10.

153. To make ropes of sand was a proverbial expression for a futile activity.

154. Primmer suspects a lacuna in the text at this point, which he would fill in as follows: "The other two, which are proper to your view, have collapsed, before they were constructed, while Mani is destroyed each time, but retains the logic, nonetheless, of his teaching."

155. See Jn 9:1-3.

156. See Est 15:11.

157. See Gal 5:17.

158. *Marriage and Desire* II, 21, 36.

159. *Marriage and Desire* II, 21, 36, with slight changes.

160. *Marriage and Desire* I, 11, 13.

161. *Marriage and Desire* I, 7, 8.

162. Though there are three letters addressed to Menoch in Mani's writings, the letter which Julian presents here is not considered genuine. See G. J. D. Aalders, "L'épitre à Menoch attribué à Mani," *Vigiliae Christianae* 14 (1960): 245-249.

163. See Gal 5:17.

164. See Gal 5:17.

165. See Rom 7:8.

166. Augustine dedicated to Marcellinus *The Punishment and Forgiveness of Sins and the Baptism of Little Ones* and he wrote for Valerius *Marriage and Desire*.

167. See Ambrose, *Commentary on the Gospel of Luke* (*Expositio Euangelii secundum Lucam*) 7, 141: CCL 14, 263.

168. See *The Grace of Christ and Original Sin* I, 43, 47, where Augustine cites from book three of Pelagius' *Defense of Free Choice* (*Pro libero arbitrio*).

169. See Ambrose, *Commentary on the Gospel of Luke* (*Expositio Evangelii secundum Lucam*) 7, 141: CCL 14, 263.

170. Julian refers to Augustine's *Confessions* IV, 1, 1, where he admits that he was a member of the Manichean sect for nine years.

171. See above 101.

172. That is, Julian's *To Turbantius*.

173. *Marriage and Desire* I, 6, 7.

174. See above 176 and 177 where Julian cites similar words from the Letter to Menoch.

175. See *Marriage and Desire* II, 21, 36.

176. See Rom 7:18.

177. See Rom 7:8.

178. See above 177, 1 and 2.

179. See 1 Jn 2:16.

180. See Gal 5:17.

181. See Ambrose, *Commentary on the Gospel of Luke* (*Exposition Euangelii secundum Lucam*) 7, 141: CCL 14, 263.

182. Julian means *The Letter of Mani known as "The Foundation"* which was addressed to Patticus and is one of the most important of the Manichean writings, against which Augustine wrote *Answer to the Letter of Mani known as "The Foundation."*

183. See Gal 5:17.

184. Julian omits *"ad nutum uoluntatis"* from *Marriage and Desire* .

185. I have followed Primmer and one manuscript in reading *"facit"* instead of *"faciat."*

186. *Marriage and Desire* I, 6, 7 with some omissions.

187. See Gal 5:17.

188. See Heb 5:14.

189. See above 154.

190. See Ambrose, *Commentary on the Gospel of Luke* (*Expositio Euangelii secundum Lucam*) 7, 141: CCL 41, 263.

191. *Marriage and Desire* II, 21, 36.

192. I have conjectured *"aliud "* here in place of *"illud."*

193. *Marriage and Desire* II, 21, 36.

194. *Marriage and Desire* II, 21, 36.

195. *Ibid* .

196. *Ibid* .

197. Carthage was a colony of the Phoenicians; hence, "Phoenicians" was often used for Carthaginians. The treachery of the Phoenicians (*perfidia Poenorum*) was legendary among Romans. Julian uses the term in contempt and referred to Augustine previously as "the Punic debater."

198. Despite appearances this is not a quotation from any of Augustine's works. Augustine replies to a similar charge in *Answer to Julian* III, 2, 7.

199. See Col 1:13.

200. The crime of *"maiestas imminuta"* or *"laesa"* was an affront against the dignity or sovereignty of the state.

201. The verb for "hisses at" is the same as that for the act of exsufflation.

202. Ambrose, *Penance* (*De poenitentia*) I, 3, 13: SC 179, 62.

203. See Is 45:7.

204. 1 Jn 2:16.

205. See Ambrose, *Commentary on the Gospel of Luke* (*Expositio Euangelii secundum Lucam*) 7, 141: CCL 14, 263.

206. *Marriage and Desire* II, 21, 36.

207. See Col 1:13.

208. I have followed Primmer's conjecture of *"concupiscentiae"* instead of *"concupiscentia."*

209. See 1 Jn 2:16.

210. See 1 Jn 2:16.

211. See Sir 40:1.

212. See Ambrose, *Commentary on the Gospel of Luke* (*Expositio Euangelii secundum Lucam*) 7, 141: CCL 14, 263.

213. See *The Grace of Christ and Original Sin* I, 43, 47, where Augustine cites from book three of Pelagius' *Defense of Free Choice* (*Pro libero arbitrio*).

214. See above 188.

BOOK FOUR

Book Four

Julian Enters into Battle with the Manichees

1. JUL. (1) I think that a serious reader could wonder why, though I divided my little work into a certain number of books in accord with the custom of writers, I am resolving the questions of one book in another. Among these there is the issue which I discussed in the third book, namely, that the statement that the people of the Jews were descended from the one man, Abraham,[1] brought little or no damage to the meaning[2] of the apostle who said that sin entered the world through one man[3]—and by that number he eliminated the idea of an original evil. (2) This reader, however, whom I am now setting out to satisfy, might suppose that the former point should have been placed in the second volume.[4] The reader should, then, recognize that the reliability of my answer, which supplies at least in the following book those points which are thought omitted, does not cause any inconvenience to the debate and results, not from any upset due to haste, but both from the necessity of the issues and from the rationality of our plan. There is, in fact, an abundance of great minds available whose examples justify my following such a way of writing, but it is a foolish boast to invoke for the defense of a simple matter the impressive support of names from antiquity and to render suspect the solid grounds of the case.

(3) I, therefore, ended the second book, which I had devoted to defending the views of the apostle, with the discussion that was strictly necessary, so that the addition of trivial questions would not extend it to an excessive length. But since, once the duty of serious discussion was fulfilled, I was happy to face the silly questions as well and wanted to have regard even for certain very slow people who can be troubled even by feeble objections, I showed in my third book how many people could be said to have been born from one.[5] It is, nonetheless, also most fitting if the following volume pays the debt of the previous one so that there is seen to be a great harmony between the books and the readers are invited to come to a knowledge of the whole work, when, if they thought that some points were postponed in the first books, they understand that they were not overlooked.

(4) Having, then, shown that what we have done is appropriate to the trustworthiness and seriousness of the work, let us do battle with the Manichees on behalf of the works and laws of God, driving off from the former the deformity of natural evil and from the latter the injustice of cruel judgments, teaching that justice lost nothing of its goodness in the precepts of God's laws and that the devil mingled nothing of his evil in the seeds of God's works, and, finally, that

God's laws are worthy of his rule and that God's works are most worthy of his creation.

AUG. (1) The Manichees would welcome your entering the battle as a great help so that they might not be overcome in battle against us, if it were not that the Catholic faith overcomes you also along with them. For they are not allowed to attribute the discord between the desires of the flesh and of the spirit and the miseries of the human race with which the nature of mortals is rife, beginning from the wailing and woes of the little ones, to the mixture of the two natures which they introduce, because all of these are by divine authority and by the most true reason attributed to nature damaged by sin, a nature which God created good and which he does not deprive of the gift of fecundity and of his good activity of creating, once it has been damaged. (2) In denying this, you try to smash the weapons by which the Manichees are defeated, but they are so strong and invincible that they lay low both of you, whether they reach you through piercing and slaying them or reach them through piercing and slaying you.

Two Truths Which Exclude Inherited Sin

2. JUL. Once these two truths are thus believed,[6] namely, that the works of God are not evil and that his judgments are not unjust, the whole doctrine of inherited sin is crushed, just as, on the contrary, if the impiety of inherited sin is accepted, these two are destroyed, namely, God's creation and his judgment, actions by which alone he can be understood as God.[7]

AUG. God's works are not evil, since he even produces good from any evils whatsoever, and in his goodness he also helps to heal the little ones whom he has made well from the lump which was destroyed through the transgression of the first human being. Nor are his judgments unjust when, by a heavy yoke upon the children of Adam from the day they emerge from the womb of their mother,[8] he imposes punishment only upon the merits of sins. When these truths are believed and understood, the error of both the Manichees and of the Pelagians is extinguished—the error of the Manichees because they want to attribute these evils of the human race to some principle or other of evil, a principle coeternal to the eternity of God, but the error of the Pelagians because they do not want to attribute them to sin.

A Warning about the Nature of Augustine's Attack

3. JUL. Now, then, let us consider those ideas which the destroyer of natural goods has put together. But in order to urge our readers toward both understanding and discernment of points which have been complicated by the exchange of answers, I warn them of the nature of his attacks. He professes to respond to our

writings which he says were forwarded to him in a brief document, and he quotes some small pieces of my sentences and censures ones that are not contained in my work.

AUG. Thank God that I replied to every point in those four books of yours by my six books.[9] From your four books that person excerpted what he chose as he chose, and his document was sent to me and reached me.[10] I think that you are not going to say that I wanted to refute in that document some points which are not contained in your work. But even if you say this and prove it, I ought to be glad that you did not say what you ought not to have said. And I wish that you had not said at all whatever words of yours are most correctly blamed.

Augustine Is Accused of Misrepresentation

4. JUL. (1) He, therefore, speaks to Valerius: "Notice the other points on which he supposes that he is in harmony with this title just mentioned in opposition to us. He says, God who formed Adam from the earth made Eve from his rib and said, She will be called *Life, because she is the mother of all the living* (Gn 3:20). That is not the way scripture has it, but what difference does it make to us? After all, it often happens that memory is mistaken about the precise words, while it still preserves the thought. It was not God, but her husband who gave Eve her name so that she was called Life. The passage reads as follows: *And Adam called his wife by the name, Life, because she is the mother of all the living*" (Gn 3:20).[11]

(2) The astounding erudition of the teacher who does not permit even a slight deviation from the scriptures! He blames our ignorance, but deigns to pardon our forgetfulness because of which it happened that I said that the woman was given the name, Life, by God. In that way he tried through this brief opportunity to appear both erudite and kind. But just as his diligence in having discovered the one who named the woman is not to be admired, so his impudence in wanting to pardon what you cannot blame is not to be tolerated. For one does not read it in my work as it is contained in the report of this man.

(3) Indeed, after citing the testimony of the law by which the creator is shown to have said, *It is not good for man to be alone. Let us make for him a helper like him* (Gn 2:18), I said: "What does this mean: *It is not good for man to be alone?* Had God made something that could not correctly be said to be good, especially since he had made all things not merely good, but also very good? How, then, did he say: *It is not good for man to be alone?* By those words he did not find fault with the status of the creature, but showed that sexual union could be harmful for the human race unless succeeding generations were produced by means of the two sexes. For, even if Adam hoped that he could have become immortal if he did not sin, it is, nonetheless, evident that he could never have become a father

unless he found a wife. She was taken from his side while he slept, and she heard the work for which she was prepared at the first imposition of her name: *She will be called Life, because she is the mother of all the living* (Gn 3:20). By these words it was shown that no human being would thereafter be able to exist or to live who had not come to be by means of conception."[12]

(4) Since, then, it is clear that, though the issue was a minor one, I had, nonetheless, not said something such that anyone could blame it apart from singular impudence, the brand of public fraud is imposed upon the most needy man of all who, when he wishes to give what he does not have, at one and the same time sins equally both by the lack of ownership and by the boast of his generosity.

AUG. If you did not quote the words of God's book as I found them in that document, I have pardoned, not you, but the one who wrote it that way. Both of us ought to pardon him. But if you think that I did not find this in the document, but that I quoted those words as a lie, as if I found them there, so that there might be something for me to attribute to your error, as it were, I now certainly pardon you for having thought so badly and incorrectly of me.

Julian's Failure to Mention Concupiscence

5. JUL. (1) After he blamed this with such seriousness, he goes on to the rest and warns his patron to pay attention to what follows: "God," he says, "formed the members of the male and the female suited for generation."[13] But inserting only this from the same chapter of my statements, with very many lines entirely omitted, in which I emphasized especially the newness of souls which owe nothing to either the flesh or the seed, he added my words, "He ordained that bodies be born from bodies, though he intervenes in their production by the power of his action, governing everything that exists by the same power by which he created it. If, then, the child only comes through sex, and sex only comes through the body, and the body only comes through God, who can have any doubt that fecundity is correctly attributed to God?"[14]

(2) And so, after he cited these words from my book, he emphasizes that he himself admits that they were Catholic in their meaning. Who, then, would not think that the man had changed? Yet he does not become forgetful of himself, but judges similar the condition of his evil teaching and the condition of his shame in the sense that the former too is restored to life after its obvious demise, just as the latter grows hard with constant rubbing. He, therefore, approves my statement and with his spontaneous embracing of it drives the sword of his hasty judgment into his own belief. But, then, after this, as if his strength were unimpaired, he declares that there remains something with which to fight. For he continues as follows: "These points are true and Catholic statements. In fact, they were written with truth in the books of God, but they were not stated in a Catholic

sense by this man, because the intention with which he stated them is foreign to a Catholic heart. Now he begins to introduce the reason why he said them, namely, the Pelagian and Caelestian heresy. Notice, in fact, what follows."[15] (3) Here he again adds our statements, "What does the devil recognize as his own in the sexes as a result of which, as you say, he rightfully owns their fruit. Is it the difference of the sexes? But this is found in the bodies which God made. Is it their union? But this is defended by the special right of both its blessing and of its institution. These are, after all, God's words: *A man will leave father and mother and will cling to his wife, and they will be two in one flesh* (Gn 2:24); these are God's words: *Increase and multiply and fill the earth* (Gn 1:28). Or is it perhaps fecundity? But that is the reason for the institution of marriage."[16]

(4) To this he replied that the devil does not recognize either the difference of the sexes or their union or the fecundity of the sexes as that by which he rightly owns their fruit. But with all these acquitted, he finds that which he attributes to the devil, and he attacks our moral integrity which he calls fear, on the grounds that amid so many gifts of bodies and of the sexes we were afraid to mention concupiscence. He, therefore, speaks to his patron against me in this fashion: "But among all these he refuses to mention the concupiscence of the flesh which does not come from the Father, but from the world.[17] The devil is called the prince of the world, and he found none of this concupiscence in the Lord, because the Lord did not come as man to us human beings by means of it. (5) For this reason he himself also said, *Behold, the prince of this world comes, and he will find nothing in me* (Jn 14:30)—that is, no sin, neither the sin which we contract by being born, nor the sin which we add as we continue to live. Among all these natural goods which he listed he refused to mention this concupiscence over which even marriage which boasts of all these goods is ashamed. Why, in fact, do married people withdraw and hide that act even from the eyes of their children, if it is not that they cannot accomplish that praiseworthy union without shameful lust? This was the reason that those first human beings were ashamed when they covered their sexual organs which were previously not sources of shame, but objects of praise and pride as works of God."[18]

(6) In the four books of the first work, blessed father Florus, I dealt with the topic of marriage, the topic of intercourse, the topic of bodies, the topic of the sexes, the topic of God's work, and finally the topic of our esteem for God, which is necessarily harmed by the degradation of his works, just as it is praised by their goodness. And through the whole work of my writings the truth which cannot be overshadowed at all has proved that the devil has not added something to the formation of the body or to the senses, and in that way it has been made perfectly clear that the opinion of inherited sin was drawn from the slime of Mani.

AUG. (1) Those who read both my books and yours understand without difficulty how you behaved in those four books of yours and how you were refuted by our reply. And yet, even when they do not read your books, but only mine, it is evident in them that your heretical teaching has been destroyed. But though you replied to my one book with those four books of yours so that you touched upon scarcely a third of it and refuted none of it, you had such confidence in them that you wrote these eight books of yours against my one second book on the same issue, as if you thought that I was not to be defeated by the strength of your arguments, but to be terrified by the number of your volumes. You, of course, realized that you accomplished nothing by that former fourfold reply so that you thought this eightfold reply was necessary. (2) If your wordiness advances by such increments, who would not be terrified, not by the truth, but the numerousness of your books, which it annoys me to count? You are a man eloquent with a stupendous wealth of words, who thought that you should first write your four books in reply to my one and your eight books in reply to my second. Who would not fear that you might perhaps consider writing in reply to my six books more than a thousand of yours, if you now reply with sixteen to the one of them which is first[19] and go after each of those which follow with double the preceding number, while showing us how much you speak because you do not understand what you say?

Nothing Remains to Be Attributed to the Devil

6. JUL. (1) Though it is agreed that this has been done there more than enough, let it be repeated in the present discussion, at least briefly. Let us, then, turn to the man with whose erudition we are doing battle. You agree, of course, that we have correctly inferred that, if the baby came only through sex, if sex came only through the body, and if the body came only through God, there can be no doubt that fecundity pertains to God's works and that the prince of darkness recognizes nothing as his own in the sexes because of which he might hold onto their fruit by asserting his right. For the difference also pertained to sex, and the union pertained to the difference of the members, and the fruit of fecundity pertained to God, who had been the creator even of the parents. And for this reason nothing had remained on account of which the fecundity of the union should have been attributed to the devil.

(2) What comfort or defense do you suppose that you derive from the decency of my words, because I was unwilling in this passage to mention concupiscence of the flesh? Even if I had passed it over in silence in the whole work, that reality would not have received any disparagement or injury, for it was defended by having been designated by more decent terms and by words perfectly clear for the understanding. Suppose, then, that I chose more prudently than the topic of our debate demanded to cover over by silence the name of that reality which we cover with clothing. (3) Should we on that account jettison all reason, all truth?

Will the intellect, the arbiter of these debates, surrender because there is something which out of decency cannot always be brought before the ears, as it cannot always be brought before the eyes? What wrong, nonetheless, is involved in calling it concupiscence of the flesh, which I too have called it where the context demanded, and though you affirm that you find it uncontrollable, why do you mention it so often?

AUG. I say that it can be controlled, I mean, the flesh, but by those who fight against it, not by those who praise it.

Augustine Accepts All the Premises

7. JUL. But on this topic I said after a bit, "Why, then, are God's creatures under the power of the devil,[20] since they are born from the bodies God made, from the union of the sexes which he distinguished by forming them, but united by blessing them? And God multiplied them by giving them fecundity, and he made the little ones from the matter of the seed. If you admit that the matter of bodies comes through God, that the sexual organs of bodies come through God, that the union of the sexual organs comes through God, that the power of the seed also comes through God, and that the form and life of the newborn also comes through God, what do you think remains on account of which you ascribe so many works of God to the devil?"[21] You, therefore, call the whole of another person's argument a heresy, though you admit all its members are correct and Catholic.

AUG. Do we not call heretics the Novatians, the Arians, the Eunomians,[22] and some others, even though they professed the whole creed along with us? To leave unmentioned other points pertaining to your heresy, how can you want us not to call you heretics, since you deny that little ones are rescued from the power of darkness when they are transferred to Christ?[23] For in these little ones about to receive the Holy Spirit, the whole Church from the beginning, which praises the name of the Lord from the rising of the sun to its setting,[24] drives out by exsufflation and exorcism the unclean spirit.

And He, Nonetheless, Rejects the Conclusion

8. JUL. For after, under compulsion from God, you praised our inference which is defended by so great a truth that it as a whole was brought to bear against you, an inference which you could not harm even by insults, you bring accusations against its consequence.

AUG. (1) You do not understand that what you call its consequence is your mistake. For from these true statements which you make, as if you were Catholics, there does not result the claim which makes you heretics. After all, as Catholics, you say that the baby comes through sex, that sex comes through the body, that the body comes through God, so that fecundity is rightly attributed to God. But it does not follow, then, does it, that human beings are born from this fecundity so that they are free from the filth of sin, even if their lives have lasted only a single day on earth?[25] You, then, are heretics, not for making those true statements, but for denying this one which is equally true. For God is certainly not the author of simple-mindedness, though he is the author of the baby, even when it is born simple-minded. (2) Understand in this way, if you can, that there is inborn in human beings a defect from their origin of which God is not the author, though God alone is the creator of human beings. Bear in mind, of course, that you have deviated from your own teaching by which you deny that God produces the will in the minds of human beings. For I have willingly praised your words which I admit that Catholics also say, though you say that I praised them under compulsion from God. See how God produces in us the will as well,[26] a point which you are accustomed to deny even in opposition to the apostle.

And Yet He Claims Heresy Is Introduced

9. JUL. "If, then," I said, "the baby comes only through sex, and sex comes only through the body, and the body comes only through God, who has any doubt that fecundity is rightly attributed to God?"[27] This is so certain that it forced even your lips to praise it.[28] But after the praise which you gave to this passage, you warn that heresy is being introduced, though the words I added only repeated by way of explanation what was contained in the premises.

AUG. You had not said, had you, "What, then, does the devil recognize as his own in the sexes?" in those statements which I had admitted that you spoke the truth? For here you began to introduce the idea of your heresy. You imply that the devil could not recognize something as his own in the sexes, because the body and sex came through God as their creator. And yet, the devil recognizes in himself both the good that comes from God and the evil that comes from himself, the former in his nature, the latter in his sin. So too, he recognizes in the sexes what belongs to God, such as sex itself, and the body, and the spirit, but he also recognizes what is his own, because of which the flesh has desires opposed to the spirit.[29] For the former come from the creator whose punishment the devil could not escape; this latter comes from the wound which the devil inflicted.

Augustine's Horrible Intention and Feeble Reason

10. JUL. I said, in fact: "What, then, does the devil recognize in the sexes that, as you say, he rightfully owns their fruit? Is it the difference of the sexes? But this is found in the bodies which God made. Is it their union? But this is defended

by the special right both of its blessing and of its institution. Or is it perhaps fecundity? But that is the reason for the institution of marriage."[30] What, then, was new here? What disagrees with the previous conclusion you approved which you thought you should blame after such praise? Certainly nothing! And for this reason what is inferred with such ugly inconsistency? Since I introduced nothing new into the discussion, while your judgment on my statements changed, what we infer is that your intention was most horrible, and your reason feeble.

AUG. (1) You are surprised that after the praise of God's works I blame your insidious question. For you, of course, raised the question and asked, "What, then, did the devil recognize as his own in the sexes?"[31] And wanting to persuade us that he recognized nothing of his own in the sexes, you mentioned those things which really do not pertain to the devil, namely, the difference by which the female sex is distinguished from the male, and the union by which the two sexes are united so that children might be born, and the fecundity by which the children themselves are born. We admit that all these would have existed in paradise, even if no one had sinned. But there would not have existed there what they experienced when those two covered their genitals who, before they sinned, were naked and not ashamed.[32] (2) With regard to this concupiscence of the flesh by which the flesh has desires opposed to the spirit,[33] this concupiscence without which no human being is born, and with regard to this discord between the flesh and the spirit which the Catholic teacher who was so excellently praised by the lips of your Pelagius says[34] was turned into our nature by the transgression of the first human being,[35] why have you said nothing about this? When you asked what the devil recognizes as his own in the sexes, you mentioned other things which do not belong to the devil, and you refused to mention in answer to your own question that which belongs to him. I blamed this question of yours as deceitful, not the works of God which I rightly praised.

11. JUL. And we infer that your praise for Catholic truths comes from your fear, not from your faith.

AUG. He recognizes our faith in our Catholic praise who through it points out and drives out your error.

12. JUL. But the fact, then, that you blame what you praised comes not from judgment, but from madness.

AUG. I do not blame what I praised, but I praised the truth which you spoke. I, however, blamed your insidious question since you saw the answer which ought to have been given you and were silent about it as if there were no answer which could be given. You will see whether this is due to judgment or to madness if you would quiet down from your madness.

13. JUL. You will, of course, never be free of this madness, unless you first reject your foul teaching. For, faced with the perilous Symplegades[36] between the shame of repentance, which is never scorned by Christians, and the lack of

argument, you must either accept the good statements by which you are being overwhelmed or smash them.

AUG. They are not good statements, Julian, which deny that Christ is Jesus for the little ones or which confess that he is Jesus, that is, the savior, for little ones only in the same way that he is for every mortal creature, as scripture said: *You will save human beings and cattle, Lord* (Ps 36:7). It was not for that reason that he took such a name when he came in the likeness of sinful flesh.[37] Rather, the angel said, *You shall call his name Jesus, for he will save his people from their sins* (Mt 1:21). They are not good statements which separate the little ones from this people and, for this reason, say that Christ is also Jesus for them because he saved them, not from their sins, but from their rashes. Come to your senses, I beg you; I think that you were not born of parents who held such beliefs, and you were certainly not reborn in a church which held such beliefs.

Augustine Focuses on the Omission of Concupiscence

14. JUL. Let us, nonetheless, see which of my statements you took up to attack with the charge of error. You say, "But among all these he refused to mention the concupiscence of the flesh which does not come from the Father, but from the world.[38] The devil is called the prince of the world, and he found none of this concupiscence in the Lord, because the Lord did not come as man to us human beings by means of it."[39] You certainly said that I was introducing heresy, though you add none of my statements to prove this.

AUG. I add those sentences of yours in which you asked what the devil recognizes as his own in the sexes.[40] You were, of course, saying them deceitfully, since you saw concupiscence of the flesh, whose motions even chaste spouses must generally resist, and you were silent, and you pressed me with a question filled with deceit, as if there was nothing that one could answer. Or, if you did not see it, you were certainly introducing your heresy with this blindness.

15. JUL. But you say that I refused to mention concupiscence of the flesh. I who refused to mention it kept silent, and if I kept silent, I said nothing for you to find fault with. Who, then, promotes an error by keeping silent? Oh the novel monstrosities of crimes as yet unheard of ! He says that by my silence I put together a perverse teaching!

AUG. Not by your silence, but by your deceitful questioning, as I showed above. And yet, it is correct to find fault even with silence, when one does not say what one ought to say in order that it would seem impossible to give an answer.

16. JUL. Let every wise person consider this and laugh at hatefulness of speech accused under the charge of silence. You admit, then, that I said nothing that you could accuse.

AUG. Quite the contrary, what you said with your questions is quite rightly blamed. For, in order that people would think that there was nothing that one could say in reply to you, you refused to mention that which could be said. Or why do I not at least blame the blindness by which you could not even see that?

17. JUL. In picking on our silence, you brought forth that point which could not, of course, be defended earlier. But now after the letter of Mani,[41] whose sentences I quoted in the third book, became public, it cannot even be hidden.

AUG. Mani does not correctly blame concupiscence of the flesh, nor do you correctly praise it. He does not correctly blame it, because he does not know where this evil comes from; you do not correctly praise it, because you deny that it is evil. He does not correctly blame it, because he attributes it to an alien nature mixed into ours; you do not correctly praise it, because you do not want it to be due to our damaged nature. He does not correctly blame it, because he believes that a part of God is corrupted by it; you do not correctly praise it, because you try to bring dishonor even on the happiness of paradise through it.

Augustine Agrees with the Words of Mani Himself

18. JUL. Augustine said, "He refused to mention the concupiscence of the flesh which does not come from the Father, but from the world.[42] The devil is called the prince of the world, and he found none of this concupiscence in the Lord, because the Lord did not come as man to us human beings by means of it."[43] In the words of Mani himself you profess that concupiscence of the flesh was not made by God, but created by the world, the world of which you say the devil is the prince.

AUG. (1) Is it I who say that the devil is the prince of the world? Does not the Lord himself say this? Would I have said this, if I had not read in scripture that he said it? And since you yourself also read it there, why did you think it should be raised as an objection against me? The devil, nonetheless, is not the prince of heaven and earth and of every heavenly and earthly creature in the sense in which scripture said, *The world was made through him* (Jn 1:10), but because the earth with the human beings who fill it is called the world in the sense in which scripture said, *And the world did not know him* (Jn 1:10), in the sense in which it said that the devil is *the prince of this world* (Jn 12:31), in the sense in which it said, *The world was placed under the evil one* (1 Jn 5:19), in the sense in which it said, *But because you are not of the world, the world has, therefore, hated you* (Jn 15:19), and countless passages of the sort.

(2) And for this reason, as the holy scriptures teach us, we understand "the world" in accord with the difference in the sentences, now in a good sense and now in a bad sense. The heaven and the earth and every creature of God in them belong to the good things of the world, but *the concupiscence of the flesh and the*

concupiscence of the eyes and the ambition of the world, or as you yourself cited it, *the pride of life* (1 Jn 2:16), belong to its bad things. Just as, then, we read "the world" in scripture, now in a good sense, and now in a bad sense, so read there, if you can, at some time the concupiscence of the flesh or concupiscence of the eyes used in a good sense. But you will not find them in that sense, just as you will not find in that sense the pride of life, which is added to those two evils as a third.

Mani and John Used the Same Words with Different Intent

19. JUL. But I said that you certainly did use the words of Mani, because, even if some of these words are contained in the letter of the apostle John, it is certain, nonetheless, that this teacher of the Church did not there hold with regard to the flesh or with regard to the sense of the flesh or with regard to marital concupiscence anything like what Mani made up by borrowing his words. It was not an injustice that I said the words belonged to the one whose meaning they served so that the words are judged by the merit of their intention. And just as in Saint John the words should be respected due to their apostolic dignity because they teach the truth, so in Mani they should be seen as veiled, not explicit signs of those people.

AUG. Why do you add, "marital," and speak of "marital concupiscence," in order to cloth your shameful darling with the honorable name of marriage? John spoke of concupiscence of the flesh, not of marital concupiscence. The latter could have existed in paradise, even if no one had sinned, in the desire for fecundity, not in the itch of pleasure. Or at least it would always be subject to the spirit so that it would not be aroused unless the spirit willed it. It would never have desires opposed to the spirit so that the spirit would also be forced to have desires opposed to it.[44] Heaven forbid, after all, that in a place of such great happiness and in human beings happy there with such great peace there should be any discord between the flesh and the spirit.

The Intention of the Apostle John

20. JUL. The apostle John was, of course, challenging the faithful to the pinnacle of all the virtues and extended the pursuit of sanctity to the heights of a life like the Lord's. For brevity, he included under the term "the whole world" all the stimuli of all present goods and pleasures. He said, *Do not love the world or the things which are in it. If any love the world, the love of the Father is not in them, because everything which is in the world is the concupiscence of the flesh, the concupiscence of the eyes, and the pride of life. These do not come from the Father, but from the world. And the world is passing away along with its concupis-*

cence, but those who do the will of God remain for eternity (1 Jn 2:15-17). In terms of the surface meaning of the words, he declares his hatred for all the elements, and he proclaims that the world and everything in it do not come from the Father and ought not to be loved.

AUG. (1) You are speaking nonsense. No one, not even an ordinary Catholic, understands the world in this passage so that he thinks of one of the elements. Nor, when the apostle says of Christ the Lord, *He is the propitiation of our sins, not only of ours, but of the whole world as well* (1 Jn 2:2), is anyone so foolish as to think that we ought to understand here the sins of even the elements? This totality, then, which is called the world in this way is understood to be only in the human beings who are throughout the whole world, that is, on the whole earth wherever it is inhabited. (2) The apostle, then, in this passage called human life itself the world, not the life by which one lives in a godly way, but that by which one lives in a merely human way. For this reason he forbids us to love it and says, *Everything which is in the world is the concupiscence of the flesh, the concupiscence of the eyes, and the pride of life. These do not come from the Father, but from the world* (1 Jn 2:16). If you can do anything, show me that the concupiscence of the flesh was ever mentioned in a good sense in any passage of the scriptures, and do not pour clouds of wordiness over clear words.

The Apostle Defended Himself in His Gospel

21. JUL. (1) He is certainly an apostle and one loved by the Lord Jesus with a special love. Nonetheless, even if the Gospel he wrote or the gravity of his Letters had not indicated his intention, these words which we quoted could have brought no prejudice to the issues, but these words would have been forced to yield to all the scriptures which assert that the world was made by God. But in the venerable prologue of the Gospel which he wrote, John himself defended himself. He said, *The Word was God; through him all things were made, and without him nothing was made* (Jn 1:1.3). And then later, he said, *He was the true light that enlightens every human being who comes into this world; he was in this world, and the world was made through him* (Jn 1:9-10). And he says again, *The Word was made flesh in order that he might dwell among us* (Jn 1:14).

(2) In these words he left no obscurity in his meaning, but showed that he knew and affirmed that God is the creator of the whole world and of everything in the world. And he made it clear that his views were not open to attack from the Manichees. For one who states that God is the creator of all natures uses in an improper sense without any damage to the faith the names of substances in order to signify immoderate desire.

AUG. (1) But you want us to understand that, even when it is immoderate, concupiscence of the flesh is not an evil, but a good, and that those who make immoderate use of it make bad use of a good rather than of an evil. And for this reason, if concupiscence of the flesh is a good, moderate concupiscence is a moderate good, and immoderate concupiscence is certainly an immoderate good. But to use moderate concupiscence is, as you say, to make a good use of a good. While to use immoderate concupiscence is, as you say, to make bad use of a good. Wine is undoubtedly a good, for every creature of God is good,[45] and one who uses wine moderately makes good use of a good. But one who uses wine immoderately makes bad use of a good. But John would never have said that wine does not come from the Father, as he said that concupiscence of the flesh does not come from the Father.[46] (2) You do not, therefore, find the concupiscence of the flesh which does not come from the Father, because concupiscence, even when it is immoderate, is, according to you, a good, and that person, rather, is not good who makes immoderate use of a good, that is, who makes bad use of a good. Why, then, do you hesitate to say briefly and openly what you say obscurely and in long ramblings, namely, that what John said is false and that you speak the truth? After all, what he said is false: *Concupiscence of the flesh does not come from the Father* (1 Jn 2:16), from whom come all natural goods, if, as you say, concupiscence of the flesh is good even when someone makes immoderate use of it, but the person is bad who makes bad use of the good.

Why We Are Not to Love the World

22. JUL. The apostle John, therefore, commands us not to love the world or those things which are in the world, and he says that the love of God cannot exist in those who love the world.[47] But he does this, not so that under the pretext of removing love of the world he makes us understand that someone other than the true God is its creator, but so that the faithful may recognize that no desires of the present life should be preferred to the virtues. Otherwise, their mind busy in amassing wealth or in attaining pleasures would be pulled away from the vigor of the Christian philosophy, which is the true philosophy. *For everything which is in the world is the concupiscence of the flesh, the concupiscence of the eyes, the pride of life. These do not come from the Father, but from the world, and the world is passing away, but those who do the will of God remain for eternity* (1 Jn 2:16-17). By the term "world," then, he indicated the conduct of human beings who have no idea that there is anything after this life as well as the various displays and sexual misconduct of mortals.

AUG. (1) If, then, "by the term 'world,' he indicated the conduct of human beings who have no idea that there is anything after this life as well as the various displays and sexual misconduct of mortals," these include those things which he said are in the world and do not come from the Father. Among them that fair darling of yours, namely, concupiscence of the flesh, holds first place. But you seem to have wanted us to understand that the concupiscence of the eyes is found in the conduct of human beings who have no idea that there is anything after this life, because by clinging to these things which they see, they refuse to believe in those things which they do not see. And you seem to have wanted us to understand worldly ambition, or the pride of life, in the displays of mortals, and concupiscence of the flesh in sexual misconduct. In that way you seem to have included all three which John mentioned. You say this as if there could be the sexual misconduct, which you blame, if one does not consent to the concupiscence of the flesh, which you do not think should be blamed, but which you even praise by calling it a good.

(2) But what is more insane than to call sexual misconduct an evil and the desire for sexual misconduct a good? What is more insane than to think that by the term "concupiscence of the flesh" the apostle of Christ brought accusations, not against concupiscence of the flesh, but against sexual misconduct, which would not exist at all, if a person were not enticed, pulled, and possessed by concupiscence of the flesh? You say this as if this great teacher had not found a reason to blame concupiscence of the flesh, but to blame under its name a person who sins sexually, though a person who sins sexually ought not to be blamed except for obeying its desires. Stop speaking so much and being wise so little. You will never succeed, no matter how great is the river of your wordiness by which you are carried off into the depths; you certainly will never succeed in making sexual misconduct an evil and the desire for what pertains to sexual misconduct not an evil, even if one does not consent to such concupiscence in order not to commit the sin.

Mani and Augustine Have Misinterpreted John

23. JUL. (1) So too, he said in his Gospel, *The world was made through him, and the world did not recognize him* (Jn 1:10), not, of course, so that the elements lacking reason might seem to have been able either to recognize or to deny Christ, but to indicate by the term "world" the crowds of unbelievers. In the same manner, then, in the present case as well, he says that everything which is in the world, that is, all kinds of human beings who cling to pleasures so that all the goods of a rational animal are measured by the senses, either in the signs of power or in the masses of wealth, have become swollen with hateful pride, which does not come from God, that is, is not pleasing to God, but comes from the world, that is, is conceived by the depravity of the human will. And, therefore, he says, pride ought not to corrupt you with its rivalry, because those who do the will of God become possessors of eternal happiness and do not flit away with the frailty of present realities.

(2) The apostle John, therefore, commands us to hate the world, just as the Lord showed in the gospel that we should hate, not only our body, but also our soul. He said, *Those who do not hate their parents or brothers and sisters, even their own souls, are not worthy of me* (Lk 14:26), though the soul of the faithful certainly cannot hate itself, since by the most well-advised love it earns its own happiness by pains and even dangers. What, then, have we achieved? That in accord with the custom of the scriptures the apostle John did not attack the nature of reality by the term "world," but the vices of wills, and that he said that concupiscence of the flesh does not come from God, just as everything which is in the world. Mani takes this up, as if he were being logical, not in accord with the meaning of the apostle, but in accord with his own unbelief, and he states that the concupiscence of the flesh, the flesh itself, and ultimately the whole world were not created by God. Having followed him, you believe that concupiscence of the flesh was created, not by God, but by the devil.

AUG. I say that this concupiscence of the flesh is an evil, the concupiscence of the flesh which John says does not come from the Father and which Ambrose says was turned into our nature as the result of the transgression of the first human being.[48] For this reason, John says that it comes from the world, for he wants us to understand it comes from human beings. Mani too calls this concupiscence of the flesh an evil, but he does not know where it comes from. But you call it something good, because you too do not know where it comes from. And by denying that it comes from the source from which Ambrose says it comes, you make Mani think that he correctly attributes it to the nature of evil, which he foolishly thinks is coeternal with God. Therefore, Bishop Ambrose explains what the apostle John says so that you are refuted along with Mani. For that which is turned into our nature through the transgression of the first human being is certainly not an evil coeternal with God. Let Mani, therefore, be silent. And it is, nonetheless, an evil. And so, let Julian also be silent.

Saint John Blames Only the Excess of Concupiscence

24. JUL. It is clear, then, that blessed John gave you no occasion for error, but that you drank in what Mani offered. And, now that the reputation of the apostle has been defended, let us briefly join battle[49] on this question. What do you think Saint John is teaching here, when he declares that concupiscence of the flesh and concupiscence of the eyes do not come from God? Does he blame the genus of concupiscence, which becomes a vice, not because of a licit moderation, but because of a forbidden excess? Or does he blame only the excess which is not natural, but voluntary?

AUG. If it becomes a vice, at least at that point concede that it is an evil. But why do you contend that it is something good even then and say that one who exceeds its permitted amount makes bad use of a good? For in that way it is not concupiscence itself, but the person who makes bad use of it who becomes vicious. Do you see how you do not know what you are saying when you are not consistent even in your definition?

The Genus and Species of Concupiscence Are Good

25. JUL. (1) If you say that by the term "concupiscence" he blames even that very limit by which one enjoys the licit pleasure of natural acts so that concupiscence of the flesh is seen to have been rejected as a whole, then admit openly that the sense of sight and the world itself and whatever is in the world were created by the devil, because they are all equally said not to come from God. And if you agree to this, you certainly will not become a Manichee, for you are one even now! But you will show that you are a Manichee by your open admission, just as you already did by your arguments. (2) But if you are frightened over the exposure of your error and say that, by mentioning concupiscence of the flesh and concupiscence of the eyes and by mentioning the world, the apostle referred, not to the realities themselves which, when they are held within their licit bounds, are harmless, but become blameworthy when they run on to actions that are forbidden, it will be clear, as we showed in the first work, that it is not the genus of natural concupiscence, not its species, not its limit, but only its excess that falls under blame. And so, be wise, and avoid this testimony of the apostle in the future lest, if you defile it by even a slight mention, you may be proved to be defended in no way, but openly revealed.

AUG. But, you quarrelsome fellow, the limit of concupiscence, which you say is licit, is not observed when one consents or yields to its impulses and moves to its excess; in order that one may not go to this excess, one resists an evil. Who, after all, would doubt that it is an evil which, if you obey it, you do evil and, if you fight against it, you do good? A person, then, who wants to live temperately, should not consent to the evil which you praise, and one who wants to live as a believer should not agree with you when you praise an evil. Therefore, in order that people may avoid you, they must know that concupiscence of the flesh is an evil; in order, however, that they may avoid both you and the Manichees, they must know where it comes from.

Adam Had Concupiscence of the Flesh before the Sin

26. JUL. I expounded this passage in the second book of my first work,[50] and I showed that concupiscence of the flesh, the concupiscence which stimulates the expectation[51] of taste and of the eyes, existed in Adam before sin.

AUG. I amply replied to this second book of yours in my fourth book.[52] For, as you blabber nonsense here, so you did there. You, after all, did not in any sense show that concupiscence of the flesh by which the flesh has desires opposed to the spirit began to be present in the human being before sin. Whatever that new factor is which those two human beings experienced in their members after the sin as a result of which their sense of shame covered their genitals,[53] it was undoubtedly contracted by sin.

27. JUL. Here I must, nonetheless, ask in what dreams it was revealed to you that you should think that the term "concupiscence" indicated the passion of a couple having intercourse. For, without harm to the wealth of the truth which our long discussion has opened up, let us suppose that it had not yet become clear that the senses of the flesh are due to the same author as its form.

AUG. The senses of the flesh by which the flesh somehow reports to the spirit present bodily things are distinct from movements of carnal concupiscence by which the flesh has desires opposed to the spirit and rushes into whatever is forbidden and immoral, unless the spirit itself also has desires opposed to it.[54] This discord between the flesh and the spirit is ascribed, not to the creator of the flesh or of the senses, but to the evil tempter and to the human transgressor, by those whose sane faith condemns the insane error of the Pelagians and the Manichees.

Concupiscence of the Flesh Has No Relation to Sex

28. JUL. But if we pretend that this is unclear, the thickest cloud of doubt will immediately enfold you. This concupiscence of the flesh, of course, contains absolutely no reference to the sex organs. I shall say, then, that by this term the apostle John strikes at ears thirsting for various songs; I shall say that by this term he chastises the palate of gluttons; I shall say that he blames the noses who die amid[55] scents, and ultimately everything except what you think. Choice is free where we have no pressure from a word that expresses something particular. Either, then, deny that those things we mentioned are desired, and reject, as is your custom, common sense, or, if your impudence has not been aroused to the point that it tries to resist these words, admit that the condemnation of sexual pleasure is not found in this passage either.

AUG. You say this, as if we say that concupiscence of the flesh surges up only into the pleasure of the sex organs. This concupiscence is, of course, recognized in whichever sense of the body the flesh has desires opposed to the spirit. And because, if the spirit does not have stronger desires opposed to it, it drags one off to evil actions, it is proved to be an evil. On its account scripture says: *Was anything created more wicked than the eye?* (Sir 31:15). And God, the creator of all bodies and senses, surely, created the eye, not its wickedness. See how you may understand—if you do not fight against the truth—that an evil is present in our nature, even when it is created, though it is a good created in a good way by the good God. But learn from Ambrose where this evil comes from so that you do not offer support to Mani for introducing another, that is, an evil nature coeternal with God.

29. JUL. How can it help you, then, that, when dealing with the union of the sexes, I refused to attack with the term "concupiscence" the fecundity of the couple having intercourse? For you yourself along with Mani could not prove it diabolical, and it had already become clear from the logic of the previous discussion that the sensation by which the body of those united sexually is affected belongs to the work of the same one to whose creation the bodies, marriage, and the seeds are attributed.

AUG. The power of sensation is one thing; the defect of concupiscence is another. Distinguish these two carefully; do not be mistaken egregiously. The power of sensation, I repeat, is one thing; the defect of concupiscence is another. Read the gospel; it says, *He who sees a woman in order to desire her has already committed adultery in his heart* (Mt 5:28). It did not say: "He who sees," which is to perceive by that sense of the body which is called sight, but it says: *He who sees in order to desire*, which is to see for the purpose of sin. Sight, then, is a good sense of the flesh, but concupiscence of the flesh is an evil movement. If spouses makes good use of this evil, they do not make it good, but they force it to serve their good action. For they do an action that is only good, even if they do it by means of this evil, provided that they do not do anything on account of it. If a husband, however, should do something on account of it, but with his wife, the apostle would not grant him pardon on account of marriage,[56] unless he recognized that it was a sin.

30. JUL. After the first work which I dedicated to the holy Turbantius, there would, of course, have been no need to discuss the necessary sense of shame over natural acts, since it was so fully treated there that, unless people entirely abandon their minds, no ambiguity could arise over this issue.

AUG. Perhaps, after the holy Turbantius read your work, which you mention that you wrote for him, he came back to life in the Catholic faith, precisely because he recognized that you failed on this issue.

Intercourse and a Sense of Modesty

31. JUL. (1) Since, nonetheless, the defender of inherited sin cannot be turned away from this topic by even a half inch and wearies with his rhetorical elegance my modesty by using different words,[57] I want to define the act of intercourse itself with that brevity which is appropriate to matters which have been decided. Both in this passage, then, and in the following ones I said with regard to the words, *For this reason a man will leave father and mother and will cling to his*

wife, and they will be two in one flesh (Gn 2:24): "In order to describe God's works with accuracy, the prophet came close to endangering modesty."[58] As if he found prey, he triumphs, exults, and cries out, "There you have at last an honest admission pulled from him by the force of the truth! Let him state the reason why in describing the works of God the prophet came close to endangering modesty. Is it that we need not be ashamed of human works, but should boast of them, though we ought to be ashamed of God's works? In proclaiming and expressing the works of God is the prophet's love or labor not a source of honor, but a danger to modesty? (2) After all, what could God do that his prophet should be ashamed to say? And what is worse, should a human being be ashamed of some work that was produced in the human being, not by a human being, but by God, especially since all artists strive with as much labor and toil as they can to have nothing to be ashamed of in their works? But we are surely ashamed of the very same thing that those first human beings were ashamed of, when they covered their sexual organs. It is the punishment of sin; it is the wound and vestige of sin; it is the allurement and enticement to sin; it is the law in the members that resists the law of the mind.[59] We are ashamed of it, and we are right to be ashamed. For, if it were not present, what would be more ungrateful on our part, what would be more impious, if in our members we were ashamed, not over our defect or our punishment, but over the works of God?"[60]

(3) It has certainly become clear how he triumphs; he is unable to apply the reins to his joy. He has in hand my sentence by which he can show that natural desire is evil and consign it to the works of the devil. He says that this sentence was pulled from my lips by the force of the truth, and he declares that it is most criminal and sacrilegious if we admit that those parts which we say were made by God should be covered out of a sense of modesty. But too carried off by his glee, he was not able to weigh what he said. For he claims that there is nothing to be ashamed of in the works of God, but that the activity of the sexual organs is something to be ashamed of, and that it cannot, therefore, be ascribed to the works of the creator. Hence, he has unexpectedly admitted that this activity is not only morally good, but righteous, since it was given to our bodies not only by God the creator, but by God the judge. I showed in the third book of my first work that sin could not be the same thing as punishment.

AUG. You did not show what you foolishly boast that you showed. In fact, in a certain passage having forgotten what you said before, you yourself admitted that sin is also the punishment of the sinner. When I previously answered you, I had shown this clearly enough, even proving from the apostle that sins are punished by sins.[61] For when he said of some people that they exchanged the glory of the incorruptible God for the likeness of an image of a corruptible human being and of birds and animals and reptiles, he immediately showed that this sin was punished by other sins. He said, *For this reason God handed them over to the desires of their heart, to uncleanness, so that they treated their bodies shamefully among themselves* (Rom 1:23.24), and the other things which he wrote there. Nor would it say in the psalm, *Add sinfulness upon their sinfulness, and let them not enter into your righteousness* (Ps 69:29), if the just judgment of God did not punish their preceding sins by additional sins.

Further Evidence of Augustine's Inconsistency

32. JUL. And so, we need not belabor this point, but I call attention to the cleverness of the debater. He does not want God to have created the punishment which he says God imposes, declaring that what he wants to fit with God's judgments does not fit with his works.

AUG. It is clear that you do not understand the sense in which scripture said, *God did not create death* (Wis 1:13), though by his judgment the sinner dies. It fits, therefore, with his judgment that the sinner should die, and yet death does not fit with his work because *God did not create death*. His judgment, of course, is just, namely, that each should die for one's own sin, though God does not create sin, just as he did not create death, and yet he killed the one whom he judged worthy of death. Where we read, *God did not create death*, we also read, *Death and life come from the Lord God* (Sir 11:14). Whoever distinguishes God's works from God's judgments certainly sees that these two are not contrary to each other. And if you had been able to see this, you certainly would not have spoken this nonsense.

33. JUL. In God's works, therefore, there is no cause for shame; in his judgments, however, there is the greatest deformity. It is certain, of course, that guilt merits punishment. But does the confusion owed to the sin, therefore, return as punishment so that one can name without shame what the guilty person did, but one cannot say without disgrace what God did in his judgment?

AUG. (1) Why do you complicate what has been explained and make involved what was simple so that you might seem to say something to slower minds, of which there are many in human beings, though you say nothing? For you are a man who would rather convince people by shamelessness than by eloquence that it is little or no deformity that, though the flesh ought to be subject to the spirit, it has desires opposed to the spirit, or that it is not the just judgment of God to abandon sinners so that those for whom God would have been their true happiness are punishment for themselves, or that anyone should be ashamed over one's sin, but not over one's punishment. For people generally would not be embarrassed over their sins, if there followed no punishment which they felt, and the punishment makes them ashamed, as impunity would not have.

(2) But what eloquent person would want to be opposed to matters that are perfectly clear, unless he has been abandoned by the truth?[62] We, however, freely speak of both of these: both what a person did willingly and what he suf-

fered unwillingly, that is, the disobedience of the spirit and the concupiscence of the flesh in opposition to the spirit. But you should be embarrassed to speak of one of these for fear of reminding us of how we should refute your error. And now when you mention concupiscence of the flesh and passion, lest you be said to be embarrassed at the name of your darling, you are more afraid to be embarrassed, and you are not afraid to be in error.

Augustine Restores to God's Work the Shame He Banished

34. JUL. It is clear, nonetheless, that our opponent is rolling in the same mud which he is trying to avoid. For, since he invented the idea that the punishment that is sexual desire was justly imposed and teaches that this justice is in accord with the divine sentence, but does not deny that God's action is found in pronouncing the sentence from which he says sexual desire has arisen, a desire over which he admits one should be embarrassed, he, of course, has restored to the work of God the shame which he had banished.

AUG. (1) I have already told you: *God did not create death* (Wis 1:13), but in pronouncing the sentence, these are God's words: *You shall die the death* (Gn 2:17). See, God causes the sinner to receive in recompense what God himself did not create. And because he is, nonetheless, the God of vengeance,[63] he also says that he creates evils.[64] And certain things are said in the Book of Ecclesiasticus to have been created as vengeance.[65] But when sin is also the punishment of sin, God does not commit sin by a wicked action, but by a just action he makes the sin to be the punishment of the sinner.

(2) Who, after all, would deny that it is a sin to believe lying prophets? And yet, this was the punishment of King Ahab inflicted by divine judgment, as the history of the kings testifies.[66] And no one is so foolish as to think that the lies of the false prophets should be praised and as to say that God is the author of a lie, when by his just judgment he causes someone to be deceived by a lie, when he sees the person is worthy of such a punishment. Read the scripture, and understand; do not assault your ears by the roar of your wordiness so that you do not understand.

God's Punishment Becomes an Incentive to Sin

35. JUL. To this, nonetheless, he added as a corollary of particular impiety his statement that God inflicted a punishment of the sort which would be an enticement and incentive toward sin, a punishment which as the unconquerable law in the members would resist the law of our mind.[67] With that sort of vengeance God would multiply, not punish sins, and he who was angry over the evil will by which sin was committed would for the future produce the necessity of sinning.

Let the madness of the Manichee see what sort of judgment this is, since it is clear that this judge whom Augustine dreamed up pretends that he is horrified at sin, but clings to sins with such great affection that they could not find a more diligent guardian.

AUG. Read what scripture says: because *they did not want to keep God in mind, God handed them over to an evil frame of mind so that they did what was not right* (Rom 1:28), and see that certain sins are also the punishment of sins. In order to understand how God does this, reread what I about warned you about in connection with King Ahab. His sin was, of course, to believe the false prophets, and yet this sin was also, under the vengeance of God, the punishment of the sinner. Consider this, and do not bark at the truth lest people come to recognize this punishment in your case as well.

Saint Paul on Covering Our Shameful Members

36. JUL. What, then, do you want, you most subtle of debaters? Do you want that there should be in the works of God a sacrilegious sense of shame, because everything which God has made ought to be done anywhere so that our timidity does not seem to cast blame on our maker? The apostle Paul, then, was in error; in describing the works of God, he said, *Our more shameful members have greater honor, and God balanced the body by having given greater honor to that member which lacked it so that there would not be a division in the body* (1 Cor 12:23-25).

AUG. Read carefully, and inspect the Greek manuscript. You will find the apostle called *less honorable* what you call *more shameful.* And if you ask why they are less honorable, though they were formerly so honorable that the couple was naked and not ashamed,[68] you will find, if the heat of argument has not blinded you, that sin came first in order that this might follow, and that God did not produce anything *less honorable* in the first human beings. In the same way God did not create death,[69] though only God makes the body, and yet, *the body is dead on account of sin* (Rom 8:10), as the truthful apostle says.

Actions Which Are Not Done in Public

37. JUL. (1) The precaution of decent people is also mistaken which extends veils of modesty over natural acts. You yourself, then, go and evacuate before the eyes of people the remains of food, an act which you surely admit does not have to do with sexual desire. In fact, to win authority for your teaching by example, do in the church all those acts which you say are performed at a sign from the will, and content to hide the activity of intercourse alone, which you formerly gave up by your decision and now perhaps give up also due to old age, state that it

involves a great sacrilege if something which has God as its creator avoids the public gaze.

(2) Eat, then, in the forum or in meeting places in which your debates are heard, and when clothes are a burden under the blistering sun, covering only that part of your body which the devil aroused, walk about naked in your other parts. For you declare it ungrateful and irreligious if anything which is attributed to the works of God is covered. Since you do none of these things—if you have not gone so far as to do them—you confirm by these actions one of two things: Either that all these things which you will not carry out in the public eye pertain to the devil, or that your teaching has collapsed, as at least your belly, if not your heart, bears witness.

AUG. (1) Of those members which modesty conceals, some are causes of disgust; others are causes of desire. The former are concealed so that they do not cause disgust, such as the evacuation of the remains of food, but these latter are concealed so that they do not cause desire, that is, either in order that they may not remind us to desire that which is usually done by them, such as those members which are properly called "pudenda" from "*pudor*" (shame), or when they are used to carry out the very act to which concupiscence leads. For, when it causes shame to leave naked or to strip the other parts of the body more distant from these, it has to do with the fact that concupiscence of the flesh draws its nourishment over a wider range through sight. For this reason those unchaste men wanted to strip the chaste Susanna, as much as possible.[70] (2) We can, therefore, well understand that God also commended the care for the same sense of modesty when he also clothed with tunics those who made loincloths for themselves, when they were ashamed of their nakedness, and precisely with tunics made of skin,[71] in order to signify the death which was linked to these bodies which were now corruptible.

(3) But it is custom which forbids whomever it forbids to eat in public, and to act contrary to the custom is rightly a cause of shame. For the ancient Romans, as you have also read, ate dinner and supper in the view of all. Why, then, do you stroll about in empty space, not by arguing, but by hurling insults? Look at those first parents who were naked and not ashamed.[72] Notice what they covered, and admit what they felt. They moved from loincloths to tunics.[73] The covering of the human body began and increased from the area where the name "pudenda" was imposed upon human members. There is a greater concern for modesty in the area where modesty resists concupiscence. (4) For it is a cause of shame for a rational nature to have something in its flesh where, if one does not want to be dishonored by immodesty, it is necessary to fight back, both for married couples so that they are not defiled by illicit intercourse and for those living in continence so that they are not defiled by any intercourse. Heaven forbid that this discord between the flesh and the spirit could have existed in paradise, if no one had sinned. But it does not take hold of us as a result of a mixture with an alien nature.

From where, then, does it come down to us, if not from the transgression of the first human being?

Concupiscence Is Defended by Its Presence in Animals

38. JUL. (1) These are silly matters, and ones which produce more disapproval than labor for our pen, but they necessarily follow upon your faith. I, nonetheless, still warn the reader to be alert. You have, of course, tried to maintain that one should not be ashamed of what is shown to be a work of God, but you were, of course, unable to accomplish this, though you promised most emphatically that you would remove shame from sexual desire if it is proved to be the work of God. In the first work I proved this so that I think that even you would have no doubt on this point when you read it, but since this argument of yours means that those books have not yet come into your hands, I will not refuse to point this out in the present book as well.[74]

(2) By whom do you think the irrational animals were created, animals which are aroused at certain times by a most ardent desire so that it even provokes great ferocity in some of them? At that time the wild boar is savage; at that time the tiger is worst. Above all the frenzy of mares is remarkable.[75] In the spring the plants swell; in the spring the abundance of fresh sap flows. And the farm animals seek to mate on certain days.[76] It would take a long time to mention each of them. All the kinds which flying holds up, which swimming plunges down, which wandering scatters, through the air, through the waters, through the groves, but which neither reason has raised up nor sin pressed down, are inflamed with the well-known pleasure of bodies joined in intercourse.

(3) Have they, then, received that ardor of the sexes from which they suffer by the work of God or the devil? You will undoubtedly shout: By the work of God. God, then, kindles the fire of sex with natural pleasure, something that Mani certainly denies with more logic than you. For that man, from whom you learned to condemn concupiscence of the flesh, weighing what he ought to say, attacks the reality which he had declared diabolical and had excluded from the works of God, wherever he could find it. And as a result, just as he consigned to the devil as their author the bodies of human beings because of concupiscence, so he consigned to him all living things because of human beings. (4) But though you remain in the camp of Mani to this point and carry about his largest snake[77] from which you breathe forth a lethal venom for unfortunate minds by means of natural evil and accusations against marriage, you do not, nonetheless, want the spears handed you by your teacher to be hurled at all natures. And being more familiar with the brute animals—which you, nonetheless, spare in order that you may blame the condition of rational animals with greater authority—you agree that God made in their bodies what the devil made in ours, though you still admit

that the same thing exists in human beings as in animals, though it is more gentle in human beings.

(5) In order, then, that the wise reader may grasp what has been accomplished: You do not deny that bodily desire in the animals was made by God. That passion is, therefore, not unworthy of the works of God which is found to be more violent in these substances which have drawn nothing from the evil of the devil, even by the least will. Concupiscence, then, has been defended by the example of the animals; defended as well by the dignity of its author, it is neither evil nor diabolical. God, the fashioner of bodies, made it, and that nature which is exempt from sin has it. Since this, then, has become clear, I ask whether you agree that God made this desire which human bodies feel. If you agree, our discussion has ended; you will remain corrected, and Mani will remain crushed. (6) But if you say: In the bodies of human beings it could not have been made by God, I reply that you think that that pleasure and the concupiscence of the flesh are unworthy of the works of a human being, but not of God. There can, of course, be no doubt that, if you say that what you admit was everywhere else made by God could not be made in a human being,[78] you do not remove the testimonies owed to concupiscence, but seek testimonies not owed to the human body. See, then, the sacrilege which is the goal of your sect. You say that something is unworthy of the flesh of a mortal which was not unworthy of the work of the creator. In this sense, then, you have not reproached sexual desire, but exalted the human being whom you had wanted to accuse.

(1) Those who declare war on the truth have such a constant reward that they are always faced with results opposed to their effort. I, therefore, now confront your words more logically, as all wisdom recognizes. In assessing and describing the works of God is reason not heard, are the examples of all creatures not considered; has, instead, the insanity of one man been raised up to such a degree that he thinks it something unsuitable to his own organs which he sees thrives in companions of his nature through the work of God? After all, neither the origin nor the design of our bodies is different from those of speechless animals.

AUG. (1) State, then, that resurrection and everlasting incorruptibility is not owed to human bodies because they are earthly, like the bodies of the animals. State that the end cannot be different when the origin is not different. Say these things, if you like, and by the impulse of your empty wordiness show us how much progress you have made by secular literature against the words of the gospel. But if you will not dare to say this, admit in accord with the Christian faith that this too is the penalty of human beings, namely, that they are compared to mindless cattle and have become like them.[79] This, then, is misery for them; the animals, on the other hand, cannot be in misery. So too, concupiscence of the flesh is a punishment for human beings, but not for the other animals, in which the flesh never has desires opposed to the spirit.

(2) Or do you want to make mortal natures equal so that you claim that the flesh has desires opposed to the spirit in the other animals as well? But if you do not do this so that you do not lack understanding like the horse and the mule, acknowledge that sexual desire of the sort we describe would not have existed in paradise if no one had sinned, namely, the desire by which the flesh has desires opposed to the spirit.[80] Such desire, of course, does not exist in animals from whom you have provided such protection for your darling that among them you could be verbose while they are speechless. For, if in human sexual desire the flesh did not have desires opposed to the spirit, but sexual desire was found in human beings such that it arose at a sign from the will when there was need, but when there was no need, it would offer no enticements for our will to fight by checking and reining them in, we would not reprimand you, because you wanted so unhappily to locate it in paradise, that is, in a dwelling of such great happiness.

The Flesh Marks Our Affinity with the Animals

39. JUL. For, as we received the image of God by the reason of the mind, so we experience our unity with the animals by the affinity of the flesh. Though its form is different, it is, nonetheless, the same substance with regard to the material of the elements, destined, of course, in accord with the merits of the rational mind to see eternity, either wretched with pains or glorious with rewards.

AUG. (1) If, as you say, "in accord with the merits of the rational mind," the flesh, earthly and corruptible like an animal's, is, nonetheless, destined to see eternity with a very different end, why do you not accept that, in accord with the merits of God's image which had been deformed by no sin, the flesh was originally created so that, though it was made out of earthly material, it would, if no one had sinned, have remained in eternity and incorruptibility? Nor would the corruptible body have weighed down the soul, that is, the image of God; rather, the body would have been subject to the soul so that, for the sake of begetting children, even the genital organs would have been aroused at a sign from the will, just as the other members by which we do something. Or concupiscence of the flesh would have been such that it would not have arisen unless the soul, that is, the image of God, willed it, and it would not have drowned the mind's thought by the intensity of its pleasure.

(2) For, if it were at present that sort of desire, scripture would not say of it that it did not come from the Father, but from the world,[81] that is, from human beings who are born for the world through it and with it and who will undoubtedly perish unless they are reborn for God. It is appropriate to believe that for the bodily material common to us and the other animals there would have been a different beginning due to the merit of the image of God, before sin began to be, just as there is a different end, now that sin has been committed.

40. JUL. For what reason, then, would that which had not been unworthy of creation by God himself be unworthy, not of the image of God, since the substance of the soul is different from that of the flesh, but of the perishable servant of the image of God? God, therefore, made bodies; God distinguished the sex of the bodies; God made the genital organs; God implanted the longing in order that these bodies would be united; God also gave power to the seeds; God works upon the material of the seed in the secrets of nature; but God makes nothing evil, makes no one guilty.

AUG. "God makes nothing evil, makes no one guilty," but insofar as God makes them, not insofar as the lump of clay out of which he makes them is damaged and corrupted.

God Set a Limit for Sexual Desire in Human Beings

41. JUL. God made the sexual desire of human beings, just as he made that of animals. But God put irrepressible instincts in the animals, while setting a limit for rational human beings. The prudence and decency which God gave them provide clothing for them. God, therefore, blames, not the limit, not the genus, but its excess, which arises from the insolence of free will and brings accusations, not against the state of nature, but against the merit of the agent.

AUG. (1) Why, then, does sexual desire resist the spirit in human beings, something it does not do in animals, if not because it pertains to the nature of an animal, but to the punishment of a human being, either that there exists what would not have existed, or that what would have been obedient, if it were not produced or damaged by sin, offers resistance? For, if "God puts irresistible instincts in animals," you certainly admit that sexual desires—since they are what you call instincts—are held in check by human beings, but they would in no sense be held in check if they were not aroused wrongly. For, look, you say that God set a limit for sexual desire in human beings. Why does it not remain within the limit which God set for it, but goes beyond it unless it is held in check? How is it, then, called something good when it urges and compels human beings to sin if they do not resist it? Do you see that your special darling either came to be from sin or was damaged by sin in the nature of a human being? And do you see that, on this account, the first human beings covered their genitals after the sin, though before the sin they were naked and not ashamed.[82]

(2) Why, after all, do you say: "The prudence and decency which God gave them provide clothing for them"? Were human beings, then, stupid and indecent, lacking in wisdom and impudent, before the sin, when they were not ashamed of their nakedness? Thanks be to sin! For they would otherwise have remained such. If this is most absurd to say, natural wisdom and decency, of course, covered their genitals, but before the sin they were nothing to be

ashamed of.[83] An excess of desire, then, is sinful, but its impulse is also a defect. And they were embarrassed over its impulse, when they refused to leave naked those members which your darling was enticing against their will.

42. JUL. Note well now the conclusion which is drawn from your teaching, namely, that one should not cover out of modesty whatever is believed to be good. We, however, have proved that this pleasure[84] naturally implanted in the sexes is not evil and pertains to the work of God. And, for this reason, you will abandon either your impiety or your modesty. But why should we suppose[85] this? *If the Ethiopians will change their skin, or the leopard its spots* (Jer 13:23), you will also succeed in purifying yourself from the mysteries of the Manichees.

AUG. You, on the contrary, will not cease to help the Manichees unless you say along with Ambrose and with all the Catholics that your darling, which even the Manichees blame as evil, was turned into our nature as a result of the transgression of the first human being.[86] Otherwise, in agreement with those unspeakable heretics whom you unwittingly help, so evident a defect of human beings will be thought to have a principle coeternal with God.

Lessons in Morality from the Animals

43. JUL. (1) It follows, therefore, that you should lay aside all shame, and while friendship with your teacher lasts, you should enter into alliance with the Cynics. As Cicero recounts in his *Duties* the arguments even of some Stoics go along with some of them. "They, of course, blame the common morality because we treat as improper on account of the word we use for them those things which in fact are not shameful, while we call by their own names those things which are in fact shameful. To perpetrate a robbery, to practice deceit, to commit adultery are in fact shameful, but using these words is not indecent. To go about having children is in fact something decent, but to speak of it is indecent." He goes on to say, "Many arguments are made in the same vein by the same people against modesty: Let us, however, follow nature, and let us flee from everything that does not receive approval from the eyes and ears."[87] (2) You, who are displeased by this natural, genuine account of modesty, either state that to go about having a child, which demands the practice of modesty, is more abominable and awful than robbery, sacrilege, and parricide, all of which in fact have the greatest turpitude, but have no indecency in their names, or if you are ashamed to accuse marriage to the point that, even compared to crimes, marriage outweighs them, encourage married couples to speak of that union as confidently and as freely as we are accustomed to mention parricide and robbery.

(3) In fact, if in order to mock Christian ears, as is your custom, you add that the union of bodies aimed at having babies is unstained by any sinfulness, but can be regarded as good within its limit, give your approval to the famous action

of Theban Crates, a wealthy and noble man. He was so devoted to the sect of the Cynics that he gave up his father's wealth and moved to Athens with his wife, Hyparcis, as dedicated a follower of this philosophy as he was. As Cornelius Nepos reports, when he wanted to have intercourse with her in public and she pulled up his coat as a cloak in order to cover herself, she was beaten by her husband. He said, "You are still too undisciplined in your feelings, for you do not dare to carry out with others present what you know you are doing correctly."[88] Such an attitude is really what you owe to your flocks, namely, that natural members should be used without any objection from modesty because they are proved to be good by the fact that they were created by God for the multiplication of bodies.

(4) Be grateful, then, to the four-footed animals. Since they defend by their examples the senses of your bodies from ownership by the devil or from the lips of the Manichees, follow their freedom in having intercourse to attest to the goodness of the act. It is, of course, fitting that the animals offer instruction in morals to those to whose members they have offered their protection. And to seal what we have done by repetition, you said that, if God created sexual desire, it should not be covered up out of shame; though we have dealt fully with that point in the four books of the first work, we have, nonetheless, shown in the present work as well, by the testimony of all the animals, which by the way you admit were created by God, that the desire of the sexes was created by God, though in the case of human beings we still admit that it should be hidden out of modesty.

(5) It is a consequence, then, of your teaching that after their long absence you present us again with the fine spectacle of the Cynics and make use of the natural members, because they were made by God, before the eyes of the city. Do you perceive how you were blindfolded when you attacked my statement in which I said: "In order to describe God's works with accuracy, the prophet came close to endangering modesty"?[89] After all, as your teacher, whose lies I quoted in the previous book, criticizes these ideas in accord with his myths in a logical manner, for he flatly denies with regard to all bodies that they were made by God, so you, who admit—albeit fearfully—that God is the creator of bodies, though you ascribe their senses to the prince of darkness, dared to treat this in an impudent manner. This has been crushed by the power of the truth as great as the reliability with which the evangelist said that by God *all things have been made, and without him nothing has been made* (Jn 1:3).

AUG. (1) Could you have made the animals equal to human beings in regard to concupiscence of the flesh or sexual desire, if you did not believe that those first parents of the human race, as if they had corruptible bodies, were destined to die, even if they had not sinned? And the Catholic Church condemns this in the newfangled error of your heresy so that Pelagius, your leader, out of fear of his own condemnation, condemned among others this point raised as an objection to him in the presence of the fourteen Eastern bishops who heard his case as judges.[90] In that court you yourself were certainly condemned, who say that Adam was created so that he was going to die whether he sinned or did not sin. You contradict the apostle who says, *The body is dead on account of sin* (Rom 8:10). (2) Moreover, if those bodies were not destined to die unless sin came first, they were, of course, not corruptible either so that they would not weigh down those blessed souls. *For the corruptible body*, as scripture says, *weighs down the soul* (Wis 9:15). And, for this reason, just as death and corruption could not have been common to animal and human bodies, though they had in common the same earthly material, so they could not have in common the same desire for propagating offspring. Rather, there was either no desire in human beings so that they also used their sexual organs which were moved by the will to the task of begetting children, just as they used their other members for their appropriate tasks, or there was not the sort of desire that is found in the animals, but a desire obedient to the least sign from the will and never pulling down the mind from the watchfulness of thought, not even, ultimately,[91] amid the pleasure. (3) But now the preceding sin by which human nature was changed for the worse has made those things which were appropriate for the nature of an animal punishments for human nature. In this evil, however, by which the flesh has desires opposed to the spirit, there is greater reason for shame because between the two components, each of which belongs to our nature and of which the one ought to rule and the other obey, there has arisen a discord over which we should not only feel pain, but over which we should also be very ashamed. What good, then, did the help of the Cynics which you summoned, but which was not relevant to the issue, offer you, since even the animals which you made equal to human beings could not help you who were losing your way on this way of your error.

Various Different Reasons for Nakedness

44. JUL. (1) Time warns us to pass on to other issues, but because it is certain that you have nothing to peddle to uneducated ears aside from the shame over the natural members, I shall touch upon what might be thought to remain, as briefly as I can. Who, then, would deny that this decency by which we cover our genitals varies according to persons, places, duties, and customs? Thus nakedness which is quite indecent in public gatherings involves no shamefulness in the baths. Bedroom attire which is sparse and not careful is one thing; attire for the forum which is more careful and more extensive is quite another. Why is it that a lack of care tends to be evidence of close familiarity and that people take greater care about their attire to the extent that there is present a person less well known or of greater dignity? Why is it that no one finds fault with sparse clothing in sailors or most workers? (2) And lest this simplicity of attire be attributed to persons rather

than their work, in accord with the custom of all, the apostle Peter was stripped down, even after the resurrection of the Lord, while fishing on the boat.[92]

From this turn your eyes to procedures of doctors; in the pursuit of health they bring their art into parts over which we feel shame. The nakedness of athletes is even beautiful. In fact, among certain peoples, not merely the young folk and those joined in sexual liaisons, but all people of both sexes are unclothed, and they have intercourse without looking for privacy. Why is it surprising that the Scots and the barbarity of their neighboring peoples do this, when even the philosophy which we mentioned above approved the same practice and the teaching of the traducianists has gone to such lengths?

(3) What amount, then, of modesty will be maintained, or among so many differences of it and among undertakings in part necessary, in part sanctioned by society, what limit will be maintained by which it can be taught that the devil mingled natural ardor into the sexes? And, for this reason, as it is clear that the defense of your opinion has been destroyed by duties, places, customs, arts, and whole peoples at once, so there remains undefeated what we defend under the tutelage of reason itself and the apostle Paul, namely, that God, the author of the universe, created all bodies, all members of bodies, and all the senses of bodies, but arranged that modesty would clothe certain of our members in accord with the circumstances of the times, while natural goodness displays certain others for which it would be as improper to use a covering, as it would be inappropriate to expose their private genital parts.

AUG. (1) You, rather, inappropriately spatter with the fault of inappropriateness those of whom scripture says, *They were naked and not ashamed* (Gn 2:25). And they were certainly then just as upright as they had been upright when created. For, as we read in scripture, *God made human beings upright* (Eccl 7:30). At that time of such great uprightness were they so depraved as to expose their private genital parts imprudently, impudently, indecently, and inappropriately? Recognize, then, that there was as yet no reason for being ashamed when those members, which are now rightly called "pudenda," were not yet causes for shame. For there did not dwell in the members the law that resists the law of the mind,[93] though now no one is born without it. (2) Disobedient human beings had not yet received by the just judgment of God, who rightly abandoned those who abandoned him, the disobedience of their own flesh. For to have desires opposed to the spirit is certainly the disobedience of the flesh, even though it is not allowed to carry out what it tries to carry out, because the spirit has desires opposed to it.[94] This, then, did not exist when they were naked and not ashamed.[95] They did not, therefore, inappropriately expose their private genital parts in shameful[96] nakedness; rather, they did not feel anything inappropriate in their genitals.

Why do you gather foolish words, like light leaves,[97] in order to cover with them your carnal argument against spiritual authority, like the flesh which has desires opposed to the spirit? Why do you ask about the amount of modesty or its limit which should be maintained among so many differences of it which are caused by different necessities, arts, opinions, and customs, whether correct or misguided? (3) Look, you have human beings, not of some nation, such as the Scots, but the parents of all the nations; you have, not people made evil by some evil opinion, like the Cynics, and any others disfigured by the deformity of a similar lack of reverence, but human beings created upright by God. You have, not human beings constrained by the necessity of some work, as was Peter's nakedness, by which you thought you should cover yourself, but human beings free in the paradise of delights. See them, before the sin revealing their freedom, but after the sin teaching modesty. Before the sin they were naked and not ashamed; after the sin they were ashamed of their nakedness. Before the sin their genitals, which were not yet sources of shame, were left uncovered; after the sin they covered their genitals which were now a source of shame.[98] These, therefore, are good enough witnesses, and by their nakedness which was first not a source of shame, and afterwards was a source of shame, they refute the stubbornness of the Pelagians and the impudence of certain nations and of the Cynics.

The Presence of Natural Concupiscence in Christ

45. JUL. Since this point has been dealt with in the present work to the extent that its previous treatment allowed, I come to that statement of yours where you said that this natural concupiscence was not found in Christ. For you spoke against me: "But among all these he refused to mention the concupiscence of the flesh which does not come from the Father, but from the world.[99] The devil is called the prince of the world, and he found none of this concupiscence in the Lord, because the Lord did not come as man to us human beings by means of it."[100] You have publicly declared, then, that Christ, whom the Catholic faith confesses to be a true man in all respects, did not have in his flesh this concupiscence of which the apostle John speaks. But as his words taught, John declared that concupiscence of the flesh and concupiscence of the eyes along with the whole world do not come from the Father,[101] and we have shown how this ought to be understood.

AUG. You have shown, in fact, how you understood it or rather how you failed to understand it, not how it ought to be understood. On this point, in fighting for the truth, I replied to you regarding your argument which is not true, but wordy.

46. JUL. You have grabbed the term "concupiscence," and you want Christ's body to be without senses of both the eyes and of inner organs.

AUG. You would not say this if you had good sense, not in the body, but in the mind.

Julian Accuses Augustine of Apollinarism

47. JUL. (1) I warn the reader, then, to be fully alert at this point, for he will see that you revive the heresy of the Apollinarists with an addition from Mani.[102] Apollinaris, of course, is said to have first introduced such an incarnation of Christ that he said that he assumed from the human substance only the body, while the deity itself took the place of the soul, and that Christ was thought to have assumed, not a human being, but a cadaver. Afterwards this view began to be destroyed by the evidence of reason and of the gospel, evidently because this would have made it necessary to charge with falsity that whole claim of Christ that he was a human being, a human being whom the Jews persecuted for having spoken the truth, if he had assumed only flesh, since a human being has to be both a soul and a body together. Or it would have made it necessary to charge with falsity his statement in the gospel, *I have it in my power to lay down my soul and to take it up again* (Jn 10:18).[103] (2) After all, what soul would he lay down if he had not assumed one? Since, therefore, Apollinaris was overthrown by the authority of such testimonies and of clear reason, he thought up something else which might give birth to his heresy, which lasts up to the present, and he said that there was indeed a human soul in Christ, but that he did not have the senses of the body, and he declared that he was unable to be suffer any sins.

AUG. (1) The Cypriot bishop of holy memory, Epiphanius, in the little book he published on heresies,[104] wrote that some of the Apollinarists said that in the Lord Jesus Christ the body was consubstantial with the divinity, but that others denied that he assumed a soul, while others maintained, on account of the statement, *The Word was made flesh* (Jn 1:14), that he did not assume flesh from created flesh, that is, of Mary, but that the Word became flesh. But afterwards, thinking of something or other, they said that he did not assume a mind. I have never read, except in your book, your claim that the Apollinarists maintained that Christ did not have the senses of the body and was incapable of suffering, nor have I ever heard it from anyone. (2) But since I see that you are seeking how to extend your empty chatter so that, though you are only wordy, you might seem rich in words, I shall immediately reply. Let whoever believes either of those statements of the Apollinarists which I mentioned above or that Christ did not have the senses of the body or was incapable of suffering be anathema. But in order that you may recognize yourself: Let whoever believes that the flesh of Christ had desires opposed to the spirit be anathema.

The Apollinarists Remove from Christ Our Senses

48. JUL. And they held that Christ did not avoid sins by the virtue of his judgment, but that by the blessedness of a flesh which was deprived of our senses, he could not experience the desire for sins.

AUG. (1) We do not say: "By the blessedness of a flesh which was deprived of our senses Christ could not experience the desire for sins." Rather, we say that because of the perfection of virtue and a flesh which was not begotten through the concupiscence of the flesh he did not have a desire for sins. It is one thing not to have had an evil desire; it is something else not to have been able to feel it. He would have felt it, after all, if he had had it. For he did not lack the sense by which he would have felt it, but he had a will by which he did not have it.

Do not be surprised that Christ, though a true human being, yet good in every respect, refused to have an evil desire. For who apart from you denies that the desire by which we desire evils is evil? Who, I repeat, apart from you tries to persuade us that the desire which is admittedly a desire for sins is not a sin and is not something evil, though one does an evil action if one consents to its persuasion? (2) Christ could have felt this desire, if he had it, and he could have had it, if he had willed to. But heaven forbid that he should have willed to!

If, nonetheless, he had evil desire and, to use your word, "a desire for sins," it would have begun to exist in him from his will, because he was not born with it, as we are. And for this reason, his virtue meant that he did not have it; our virtue means that we do not consent to it and that we imitate him so that, as he did not commit sin because he did not have this desire, so we do not commit sin because we do not consent to it. And as he willed not to have this desire and was able not to have it, so let us too will to be without it because we will be able to be without it. His grace will, of course, set us free from the body of this death,[105] that is, from sinful flesh, the grace of him who came to us in the likeness of sinful flesh, not in sinful flesh.[106]

The Heretical Implications of Such Apollinarism

49. JUL. (1) With such heavy flattery he speaks against the Catholic faith, as the facts reveal, not merely no necessary ideas, but even sacrilegious ones. For, when he wants to show that there was something more in the body of Christ so that he would not lose dignity by his sharing in our flesh, he deprived him of the fullness of our natural senses. He did not see the extent of the destruction to which the loss of the truth would lead, even when the truth was destroyed out of flattery.

The opposition against this stirred up by Catholics was fierce because in accord with such a faith the mysteries of Christ would suffer a greater loss than the members of Christ. For, if Christ was, for this reason, they say, born of the family of David,[107] born of a woman, born under the law,[108] to give us an example to follow in the footsteps of him who committed no sin and on whose lips no deceit was found,[109] but did not, nonetheless, put on the characteristics of our substance in every respect, if he possessed either flesh without a soul or a human nature without the senses which nature gave us, we are not taught that he could have fulfilled the role of an example and of the law.

(2) After all, why would it have been worthy of praise to scorn the enticements of the senses if by a gift of nature he was incapable of them? What is admirable in his controlling his eyes, if by the help of his flesh they do not wander? What is great about withdrawing the nose from tempting odors, when it is not able to perceive them? What is admirable about the daily maintenance of a strict frugality at meals, if he could not feel their enticements? What difficulty, finally, would there have been in the fast extended to the fortieth day, if hunger could not bother him? What respect would the discipline of the ears deserve for only listening to decent words, if he suffered a natural deafness for indecent ones? But what is the glory of chastity if he lacked virility rather than will power, and if what he was thought to accomplish by the strength of his mind came from the weakness of his members?

AUG. (1) These points are correctly stated, not against Apollinaris or one of the Apollinarists, for I do not think that they said that Christ's flesh did not have the senses of the human body, but against anyone whoever it is who says this. We, however, say that he perceived beautiful and ugly sights by his eyes and smelled fragrant and foul odors by his nose and heard harmonious and discordant sounds by his sense of hearing and distinguished bitter from sweet things by taste and rough and smooth, hard and soft, cold and hot things by touch. And he was able to sense and perceive whatever else can be sensed and perceived by a sense of the body, nor did he lack the ability to father children, if he had willed, and yet his flesh never had desires opposed to the spirit.

(2) But if it is, as you suppose, a great good to hold back from sins because there are desires to be conquered, but it would not be something great if those desires were lacking, then anyone would be more praiseworthy for virtue to the extent that one was more filled with desires in the flesh. And for this reason, according to your horrible and hateful depravity, Christ ought to have been most filled with desires in his flesh, just as he was the greatest of all human beings in his virtue. If you sense the great impiety in the sense of this idea, do not delay to change the sense of what you say, and to distinguish desires from the senses, for desires are what are sensed by certain persons rather than what senses anything. Otherwise, a person would be thought to have more lively senses to the extent that one is more ardent in desire, and Christ would be believed to have burned with fiercer desires to the extent that he had purer senses.

If Not an Apollinarist, Surely a Manichee at Least

50. JUL. (1) What reward, finally, is there for endurance if the pain of wounds and blows could not reach the mind, because the path of the senses is blocked?

What, then, did this flattery of Apollinaris accomplish? That all the beauty of the virtues which Christ revealed in himself wilts, once it has been emptied of meaning by inappropriate praises of his nature, and stripped of all the splendor of its truth it exposes the teaching of the mediator to mockery.

To this there is added the fact that, as someone more fortunate by birth, not by virtue, he would have lost not only trophies won by his actions, but would have also been pressed with charges of fraud if he said to mortals: Strive for the patience of him who feels nothing, and come through true crosses to the virtues of a false body that suffers nothing, or: By conquering the real impulses of your nature, imitate the chastity of him whose impotence made him appear chaste. Certainly nothing more irreligious, nothing more wicked can be thought up than these lies.

(2) Even if[10] Apollinaris had not said all these, by that one statement he did make, namely, that Christ the man lacked those senses which are given by nature and fall into sins, not by use, but by excess, he silently accepted all these points which are reported by the Catholics to the detriment of his view. The Catholic faith is, of course, built up by the affirmation of all these points, while by the denial or implicit denial of them the heresy of Apollinaris is crushed and condemned.

(3) Imagine, then, what one ought to judge about you. You condemn the union of the sexes, like a Manichee. You separate the nature of Christ from the community of human beings, in accord with the Manichees. You bring accusations against the concupiscence of the flesh, in accord with the statements of your teacher, Mani. You say that the concupiscence of the senses was not present in the body of Christ, either in accord with the Manichees or in accord with the Apollinarists. And, nonetheless, you do not want to be called by us either an Apollinarist or a Manichee. And yet, I surrender; I offer you this gift, nor do we regret this generosity. As far as I am concerned, it will be all right that you are not thought to be a follower of Apollinaris. He is, of course, the inventor of a lesser impiety. But as far as you are concerned, it is not permitted that you should be called anything other than a Manichee.

AUG. Ambrose was neither an Apollinarist nor a Manichee, but an attacker of heretics. He said that any human born by means of your darling cannot be without sin, since he both understood and explained the apostle Paul, as he ought to have. But, as I have often shown, you help the Manichees more to the extent that you think that you are more free from them. You are, however, a new Pelagian heretic, a man most loquacious in your arguments, most slanderous in your claims, most deceptive in your public statements. Finding nothing to say, you say many silly things; you bring a false accusation against the Catholics, while you lie about being a Catholic.

51. JUL. I showed in the third book of my first work that beyond all refutation Christ too must be said to have contracted guilt from the flesh of Mary, if one be-

lieves in natural sin, and that you place him under that power of the devil because you claim that the whole substance of human beings belongs to the possession of the devil.

AUG. What you mention that you showed in your third book I proved that you did not show in my fifth.[111]

Augustine Makes Christ a Eunuch

52. JUL. And having for this reason left this topic aside for the present, I demand that passage where you read that Christ was naturally a eunuch.

AUG. (1) Where, after all, did you read that I said this? You must be making up lies, as usual. The possibility of fathering children, which we say the flesh of Christ did not lack, as we know the flesh of eunuchs does lack it, is one thing; the desire for sins, which you try to persuade us that Christ had, though you boast to be a Christian, is something else.

For, a little before you said, "Christ would also have been pressed with charges of fraud, if he said to mortals: Strive for the patience of him who feels nothing," as if it follows that one will not feel pains that have been inflicted if one wills not to have and is able not to have evil desires. Or he would have been pressed with such charges if he said, as you yourself put your words together, "By conquering the real impulses of your nature, imitate the chastity of him whose impotence made him appear chaste." (2) For you are so outstanding a lover of chastity that a man who desires illicit intercourse, but resists his desire so that he does not carry it out, seems more chaste to you than one who does not even desire such evils, not on account of the inability of the flesh, but on account of the peak and perfection of virtue.

In fact, on your view, the former is chaste, but the latter is not chaste at all, but only seems to be, because, according to you, if the latter were chaste, he would desire these evils by nature, but would hold in check the same natural desire by the virtue of the mind. (3) And so, as a result, there follows, as I already showed above, that horrible absurdity, namely, that one is more chaste by the will to the extent that one conquers a greater desire of his nature and does not permit that desire, no matter how great it is, to run off into some excesses of sexual license. But one who holds in check a lesser desire for sexual sins is less chaste, because, according to your wisdom or rather madness, one who does not desire what is forbidden is not chaste at all. See what you insanely try to impose upon Christ, namely, that he should be by nature the most filled with desires of all, because he could in that way be the most chaste of all by the virtue of his will. As you argue, the spirit of continence would, of course, be greater in him to the extent that he held in check greater concupiscence of the flesh. Your darling, whom you love too much, has led you to this destruction.

Julian Defends the Full Masculinity of Christ

53. JUL. (1) Even if he was born of a virgin as a sign,[112] he did not, nonetheless, shun the male sex, but assumed its reality, in every respect whole in his organs, whole in his body, a true human, a complete man, if one believes the sermon of the apostle Peter in Acts.[113] Outstanding for his perfect chastity, he guarded both his mind and his eyes, never relaxing the strength of his mental powers, but since he did all this because of the strength of the mind, not because of the feebleness of the flesh, his sleep, food, beard, sweat, toil, and the cross and lance testify that concupiscence of the flesh was present in the senses of the whole body and that he had the reality and healthy condition of his members. He really had, therefore, the senses of the body, but he ruled them.

(2) This is why the faith of the Catholics triumphs over the pagans, why it triumphs over the Manichees, for as the word of the cross, so the word of his flesh is foolishness to those who are perishing, but the power of God to those who are being saved.[114] This is how he showed his love for us, for the piety of the mediator assumed all those members which the impiety of the Manichees attacks. I am, therefore, ashamed of nothing in my Lord. I cling to the reality of the members into which he entered on account of my salvation in order that I might receive the solid support of his example.

AUG. (1) The reality of the members, which every Christian acknowledges, is one thing; the desire for sins, which you want to introduce into Christ, is something else. For you say that concupiscence of the flesh, that is, sexual desire, which you prefer to call natural concupiscence, is good, and you blame only its excess so that whoever allows it to go beyond the permissible bounds incurs guilt, as one who makes bad use of a good. But whoever permits it to go as far as what is licit and permissible and does not permit it to go further is worthy of praise, as one who makes good use of a good. (2) Consequently, since we see that some are naturally such that they are driven by a great sexual desire and others by a lesser desire, if through resisting it both sorts are chaste, you are forced to say that the former make good use of a greater good and that the latter make good use of a lesser good. By your teaching, then, persons will have a greater abundance of this good of yours to the extent that they are more filled with lust, and they will have a greater struggle in fighting for chastity against their desire to the extent that they have a greater abundance of this natural good. And for this reason they will also be more praiseworthy in their virtue to the extent that they resist more strongly a greater good than if they fought against a lesser one.

(3) Because, then, Christ undoubtedly lived in mortal flesh as the most chaste of all, you will ascribe to him greater natural desire to the extent that you will not be able to find someone more strong in holding desire in check. After all, in that way he will say to his followers without the charge of deceit: "By conquering the real impulses of your nature, imitate my chastity. These impulses are, of course,

good, and yet they must be held in check and conquered, just as I had greater desires, but held them in check and conquered them. Otherwise, you might say to me: You conquered them; you lived most chastely in your mortal flesh, because you had by the blessedness of your nature the least desires which you might conquer most easily. Be chaste, then, because, in order to take from you any obstacles which might excuse you from imitating me, I willed to be born more filled with desire than you, and yet I never permitted the greatest desire to go beyond the limits permitted to it." These are the horrible monsters your heresy has spawned.

Without Sexual Organs Christ Cannot Be Our Model

54. JUL. (1) I proclaim that all holiness remained in him because of the goodness of his mind, not because of a defect of his flesh. In that way his nature is defended both by its creation and by its assumption, and the life of a human being is guided by the imitation of his virtues. One of these two cannot be praised without the reality of the other. His sacred work will have as much dignity as the reality of his human body has, and the defense of his flesh will have as much dignity as the sanctity of his way of life demands. (2) And, on the contrary, the disparagement of one is shared by both, because he loses as much from his virtues as he loses from his members, and if something is clipped from the fullness of his substance, all the beauties of his moral conduct perish, and what he lacks at birth undermines his suffering. Finally, if the substance of his flesh is reduced by the removal of his natural parts, all the display of the virtues disappears. I shall, therefore, deny nothing that is clearly natural in the members of the mediator who was born of a woman. And see how different are the limits of reason and of shame; the faith of Christians is not embarrassed to say that Christ had sexual organs, even though we conceal these in our own case as modestly as possible.

AUG. The faith of Christians is not embarrassed to say that Christ has sexual organs, but you ought to have been embarrassed or, rather, to have trembled in fear to have said that Christ's sexual organs were at times aroused by sexual desire, even against his will—for he who lived a celibate life ought to have never willed this—and to have said that that part of his holy body became erect for some forbidden uses against his holy choice. Every kind of holy person also suffers under the sort of desire which you try to attribute to the Holy of holies.[115] But if you do not dare to say that the sexual organs of Christ were often aroused against his will and became erect because of desire, why do you dare to believe, you wretch, why do you dare to say that the nature of Christ had such desire that you compel people to think what you do not dare to say?

Saint Paul Foresaw the Rise of the Manichees

55. JUL. (1) In that way nature has prescribed that there are certain parts which both reason and faith speak of with respect, and yet modesty and decent living do not permit that they be exposed to sight. In this way the teacher of the nations also attributes reality to Christ's flesh and holiness to his spirit. He says, *It is a great sacrament of piety which has been revealed in the flesh and has been made righteous in the spirit; it has been seen by the angels, preached to the nations, believed in in this world, and assumed into glory* (1 Tm 3:16).

(2) As he taught that this must be believed with truth, so he foretold that attackers of it would be born at the end of the world. For there immediately follows: *But in the last times some will withdraw from the faith, giving their attention to deceiving spirits and to the teachings of demons speaking lies with hypocrisy. They will have their conscience seared and will forbid marriage; they will abstain from foods which God created for believers and those who have come to know the truth to eat with gratitude. For every creature of God is good* (1 Tm 4:1-4).

The apostle foresaw and punished this defilement of the churches which you have vomited forth as a result of your following Mani and this apostasy of those withdrawing from the faith which consists in the preaching of natural sin and in the condemnation of marital intercourse. He pointed out not only what would be said, but what would follow from it.

AUG. And you, nonetheless, who can only spit out slanders and vomit forth insults, have not dared to contradict the words of the Catholic man of God whom you cannot say is a Manichee. He chokes you and says that no one can be born from the union of a man and a woman free from sin.[116] For I mentioned these words of his in the first book for Valerius,[117] which you tried to refute by four books, but you were afraid to touch any of his words. And in this book to which you are now replying, I did not leave these words unmentioned,[118] and you are still speechless before them, although you do not fear to accuse this man in me, while you do not mention the name of him whom you do not dare to attack openly.

Augustine Is Less Logical than Mani

56. JUL. (1) For his statement that they would teach people to abstain from foods does not, of course, blame in the eyes of a wise person the moderation of Christians, nor does it denounce the possibility of there being human beings who demand a commitment to a life of abstinence. But it shows that he expressed what would logically follow, when those people arose who said that all animals which were created by God as food for mortals were defiled by a diabolical evil,

because these animals were born from concupiscence and sexual union. It shows that it would follow that people should give up certain foods, if their propagation is thought to be diabolical. For this reason, you also remove from animals this infamy stemming from the union of bodies so that a basis for your deception might remain.

You say, nonetheless, that human beings, who were made to the image of God, belong to the dominion of the devil on account of this concupiscence of their parents. (2) Both you and Mani, then, have one reason for disparaging substances and transferring them to the devil. But he condemns all living beings on account of this desire which is experienced in the sex act, while you do not condemn all living beings, but—what is worse—only the better ones. For you acquit pigs, dogs, and asses so that you seem to escape the Manichees, but you condemn, for the very same reason that Mani did, all human beings who were made to the image of God. And though you locate natural evil only in the image of God, you preach against us, you prosecutor of the saints and patron of asses!

AUG. (1) What is it that you are saying, you slanderer of Catholics and helper of the Manichees? What is it that you are saying? You ought to have been ashamed of such stupidity, even if you had the mind of an ass! Could not someone who said that human beings could become wretched because of their ignorance of the truth, but that asses could not become wretched because they do not know the truth, be called an accuser of the saints and a patron of asses by someone with a mind like yours? And yet, that person would have spoken the truth.

Why, then, do you not understand, you ass, that it is likewise the truth that from the union of a male and a female human beings cannot be born free from sin, while asses can? Or do you suppose that you escape the subsequent blows from authority and reason because you hitch human beings and asses in their companionship in desire to the chariot of your error? (2) Ambrose was not speaking of animals, but of human beings, when he said, "The principle, then, was preserved that no one born of a man and a woman, that is, through that union of bodies, is seen to be immune from transgression."[119]

Was this man, was this teacher of the Church, therefore, an accuser of the saints and a patron of asses? A corruptible body, of course, belongs to both asses and human beings, but it does not, nonetheless, weigh down the soul of an ass, but the soul of a human being. Scripture surely says of a human being, *The corruptible body weighs down the soul* (Wis 9:15). Recognize, then, in sexual desire both the nature of an animal and the punishment of a human being if you do not have the soul of an ass.

Christ's Chastity Is Imitable and Admirable

57. JUL. Christ, therefore, no less true man than true God, lacked nothing belonging to nature, but it was right that the one who was giving an example of perfection should excel in the pursuit of all the virtues. And it was right that his chastity lofty in its constant integrity, aroused by no longing of desire, because it was the virgin spouse of his holy mind, and his greatness of soul, which subdued all his senses and conquered all sufferings, should be for all the faithful both imitable because of their humanness and admirable because of their loftiness.

AUG. (1) You say that the chastity of Christ was lofty in its constant integrity, but you are a man to whom chastity does not seem to have integrity where by the greatness and perfection of good will forbidden acts are not only not committed, but are also not desired. For those who desire sins, even if they resist their desire and do not commit them, fulfill the words of scripture, *Do not go after your desires* (Sir 18:30), but they do not fulfill what the law says, *You shall not desire* (Ex 20:17).

Christ, then, who most perfectly fulfilled the law, desired nothing that was forbidden, because he certainly did not have the discord between the flesh and the spirit which was turned into the nature of human beings by the transgression of the first human being,[120] for he was born of the Spirit and the Virgin, not through the concupiscence of the flesh. (2) In us, however, the flesh desires forbidden things in opposition to the spirit so that it carries them out, unless the spirit also has desires in opposition to the flesh so that the spirit wins out. You say that the mind of Christ subdued all his senses, but it is something that resists which needs to be subdued. The flesh of Christ, however, had nothing that was unsubdued, nor did it in any way resist the spirit so that the spirit had to subdue it. With this example of perfection set before us, each imitator ought to aim at this: to strive and to long not to have at all the desires of the flesh which the apostle forbids us to carry out.[121] For in that way we can by daily progress lessen those desires which we will not have at all when salvation is complete.

Christ's Choice of Chastity Does Not Condemn Sex

58. JUL. As with everything, you have, then, in a most impious manner declared that something that belongs to human nature was not present in the flesh of Christ. Deceived as you are, you have drawn this from no stream of the reasonable scripture, but only from the muck of the Manichees. But in order that the means of defending the truth may be seen as greater, let us concede that you imagined that in Christ the concupiscence, as you say, of the flesh was not present. This was certainly condemned, first in the madness of Mani and afterwards in that of Apollinaris. What help, nonetheless, could it offer your doctrine? For it would not immediately follow that it is an evil, if he had not chosen to assume it.

For he would be said to have arrived by the gradually increasing merits of his good actions at the very best, but not, nonetheless, to have condemned goods beneath him by the choice of the higher ones. As he did not condemn marriage by the pursuit of chastity, so he would not have condemned the sense of the genital flesh, even if he had chosen not to have the capacity for it in his substance.

AUG. (1) I said already above that Christ not only did not commit, but did not even desire forbidden acts in order to fulfill the law which says, *You shall not desire* (Ex 20:17). These words, which extinguish your heretical teaching, certainly flow into the hearts of the faithful from the stream of holy scripture, not from the muck of the Manichees. You say that I imagined that in the flesh of Christ there did not exist the concupiscence which resists the spirit, while you did not even spare his dreams. We know that Christ did, of course, sleep, and if your darling was present in him, she at times surely deluded his sleeping senses by such dreams that it seemed to him that he was even having intercourse, and so his flesh aroused by the stimulus of this good of yours would make his genitals uselessly erect and pour forth useless seeds.

(2) If, however, you are afraid to believe this of the flesh of Christ—for you are not so hardhearted as not to tremble at those words which I spoke with a tremor in my heart, though it was to refute you—you surely ought to say that the nature of Christ lacked such concupiscence of the flesh as we know the flesh of other human beings and even of the saints did not lack, not only without any loss to them, but even with praise for his perfect virtues.

You said, however, that it does not follow that this is an evil, even if you concede that Christ chose not to assume it, just as he did not condemn marriage because he chose not to have a wife. This can be said about the sexual desire of animals for which it is not an evil, because they do not have the good of reason, and as a result their flesh does not have desires opposed to the spirit. But that which resists the spirit of a human being who wills to do good is not something good, no matter with how much wordiness you would defend it. (3) Christ, then, refrained from sin in such a way that he also refrained from all desire for sin, not so that he resisted that desire which existed, but so that it never existed at all, not because he could not have had it if he had willed to, but he would not have rightly willed to have what the sinful flesh, which he did not have, would not have forced him to have even against his will.

Hence, for that perfect man, who was not born through concupiscence, which indiscriminately desires both forbidden and permitted acts, but was born of the Holy Spirit and the Virgin Mary, whatever he desired was permissible, and whatever was not permissible, he did not desire. For heaven forbid that he who was born of the flesh which was conceived through the Holy Spirit should have had in himself a discord between the flesh and the spirit.

The Body of the Savior Lacked Nothing Natural

59. JUL. And to confirm a clear issue by an example: It is better to have reason than not to have it. But human beings were created with reason, while animals were created without reason. But the four-footed creatures should not be called either something evil or the work of the devil just because human nature is superior to them. Suppose, then, that, when Christ formed his own members, he chose not to introduce into them the sense of the sexual organs which he was not going to use. Did he, therefore, make something evil when he formed the members of Isaac, Jacob, and all others and gave them sex and its sense? Or, when he came to these members, did he summon the devil for help so that the devil would mingle into the members which God himself formed the requisite pleasures? You were, therefore, unable to win even a small point through the person of Christ against the works of God, as we have shown by the help of God both in this and in the previous work. For it has become clear that the body of the savior had nothing less of the nature of human beings.

AUG. It has, rather, become clear that the nature of human beings, in comparison to that integrity, rectitude, and good health in which it was originally created, now has all these things in a lesser degree. Christ came to restore this nature to integrity, to correct it, and to heal it, for he had integrity without any corruption, rectitude without any depravity, good health without any desire for sin.

60. JUL. And, for this reason, in that nature of ours there can be no sin, because in him in whom that nature was whole, no iniquity was found.

AUG. Julian, you blaspheme enormously when you make the flesh of Christ equal to the flesh of other human beings. You do not see that he came, not in sinful flesh, but in the likeness of sinful flesh.[122] That would have in no way been true, unless the rest had sinful flesh.

61. JUL. We are not taught, then, that the sexual concupiscence is evil and diabolical, whether it was present in the flesh of Christ or not.

AUG. Concupiscence of the flesh is evil, even when one does not consent to it to do evil, for it is that by which the flesh has desires opposed to the spirit, even if, because the spirit has desires opposed to it, it does not carry out what it attempts to carry out, namely, an evil action.

62. JUL. I hurry on to other points, but I am much held back here by amazement over the situation. Why is there such a great rage against another person that, if you do not understand the scriptures, you do not at least weigh your own words? Instead, you constantly argue in such a way that whatever you hurl at me is turned back against you with greater force. You said, of course, that there is no cause for shame apart from the concupiscence of the flesh which is seen in sexual arousal.

AUG. I did not say this. There are, after all, other causes of shame, either so that something improper does not occur or because it has occurred. But when one asks the cause of this shame with which we are now dealing, that cause is found to be most true by which it came about that these members are properly called "pudenda," though they were not before a cause of shame when those righteous and perfect human beings were naked and not ashamed.[123] If you had chosen to consider this prudently, you yourself would not impudently have resisted the perfectly clear truth.

Without Concupiscence Christ Needed No Clothing

63. JUL. You said, however, that apart from this concupiscence of the flesh, it is a sacrilege to judge anything to be shameful which we believe God has made, but that Christ did not have this concupiscence of the flesh which produces the cause of shame in mortals. You have not seen, then, what happens to these statements, namely, that he, that is, Christ, ought to have presented himself in public naked and to have had no regard for shame, so that he would not incur the sacrilege you speak of, that is, by being embarrassed over his own flesh which did not have concupiscence and over his own works and those of the Father. But if he did not have concupiscence and, nonetheless, observed the duty of modesty, it is irrefutably shown, according to your view, that a sense of shame was due to the human body, not to human passion.

AUG. (1) By this argument of yours, so clever and elegant, you ought to deny that John's baptism was administered for the forgiveness of sins, because Christ who had absolutely no sin was baptized by it. But if he could have been baptized for another reason, not for the reason that the others were, that is, not on account of sinful flesh which he did not have, but on account of the likeness of sinful flesh which he assumed in order to set free sinful flesh, he could also cover his members, not for the reason that the others do, but to conform to those who do cover their genitals, though he had nothing to be ashamed of. In the same way, when Christ was baptized, he conformed to those who were repentant, though he was washing away nothing that needed repentance.

(2) Those things which sinful flesh needed were, of course, fitting for the likeness of sinful flesh. For even the sight of the naked human body, wherever it is unusual, offends the human gaze. For this reason even angels who appeared to human beings like human beings chose to appear clothed, as human custom demanded. But if we recall where this custom took its origin, there comes to mind the case of the first sin in those human beings who, before they sinned, were decently and respectably naked in that place of such great beatitude. That is, they were not yet ashamed of their own flesh, which became disobedient to them with desires opposed to the spirit, when they were disobedient. Christ's clothing, then, offers you no help to avoid being an impudent defender of concupiscence of the flesh.

The Need for Bold Language about the Flesh of Christ

64. JUL. You see, therefore, that you called it sin to no purpose, if we admit that a covering should be used for these works which God made, since our Lord and the maker of the human being instituted this custom and, when he became man, he followed it. May the majesty of the redeemer, of course, grant us pardon, because we have spoken boldly about his flesh in order to defend the truth of the mystery and to destroy the outrages of the Manichees. For, if the faith did not demand it, reverence would not have touched upon Christ's modesty.

AUG. You do not boldly say true things about the flesh of Christ; rather, you unfortunately say false things, not in order to destroy the outrages of the Manichees, as you delude yourself, but rather in order to help them. If you think of conquering Mani, do not say that what is evil is good, but state where the evil comes from, the evil which you cannot show is good. For when you refuse to say with Ambrose that this comes from the transgression of the first human being,[124] you surely bring it about that the Manichee boasts that he speaks the truth about the alien nature.

65. JUL. You say, "But this fellow refused to mention concupiscence of the flesh. He is silent, because he feels ashamed, and with the amazing impudence of shame—if one can say this—he is not ashamed to praise what he is ashamed to mention."[125] It displeases you, therefore, that we know that our less decent parts should, according to the apostle, be clothed with the requisite decency.[126] For in this he follows the counsel of the creator so that what he established in the private area of the body we too cover with decent clothing.

AUG. You say amazing things, namely, that Adam and Eve followed the counsel of the creator at that point when they abandoned his commandment by following the counsel of the deceiver. For before they committed this sin when they were still righteous and perfect, did they not follow the counsel of the creator so that they left naked that which he established in the private area of the body and did not take care to cover it with decent clothing? You impudent fellow, it is worse to praise than to expose what they felt when they were embarrassed.

Natural Languages Use Plain Language for the Members

66. JUL. These differences in expression, nonetheless, which you not only do not imitate, but even accuse, differences whose services we make use of, have been discovered by the stylistic elegance, not of all languages, but of Greek and Latin. The other languages, which are called natural because further studies contributed nothing to them of richness or elegance, use the perfectly simple names for the members. For this reason, among the Hebrews, whose language contains the purity of the scriptures, all things are indicated by their proper terms.

AUG. You are greatly deceived. You speak as if in the Hebrew language there were no figurative expressions in which the words are, of course, not proper, but metaphorical. But whatever may be the case, how does this help you? In the Hebrew sacred writings we read both of the time when those first human beings were naked and were not ashamed and of the time when they were ashamed of their nakedness and what members they covered.[127] Hence, we are able to know what they experienced and of what they were ashamed. If you want to cover yourself on this issue over which you are ashamed, be silent at last.

67. JUL. The sexual organs of both sexes are mentioned with the same carefreeness with which the feet and knees are mentioned. Even though this authority is on our side, we did not neglect the helps of a more modest mode of speech, for the neglect of decorum without any constraint from the circumstances is open to a perfectly just reproach. For decorum should be preserved no less in words than in actions to the extent that the nature of the case permits. Natural concupiscence, then, has not been able to be charged with the reproach of shame and has been defended by the dignity of its creator, only in order that it might be removed from the dominion of the devil and might be located among the works of the one who made the world and bodies. It has been defended, not as a great good since it is, of course, common to human beings and to animals, but as a means necessary for the sexes. It is accused only by Mani and the traducianist, his heir. Hence, it is evident that the whole fiction of natural sin, whose whole defense lay in the accusations of nature, has vanished.

AUG. (1) See, you still say, "Natural concupiscence"; see, you still clothe your darling, as much as you can with the ambiguous vesture of verbiage so that her character cannot be understood. Why, after all, do you not say: Concupiscence of the flesh, but say: Natural concupiscence? Is not the desire for beatitude a natural concupiscence? Why do you speak ambiguously? Call your darling whose protection you have undertaken by her own name. What are you afraid of? Or have you perhaps become upset at her desperate case and forgotten what she is called? On the contrary, though your memory is alert, you do not want to call her concupiscence of the flesh, for you know that those who read this name in the holy scripture as only signifying something evil are offended by praise for her. (2) But using this term and calling it natural concupiscence you try to locate it among the works of the one who, as you say—and it is true—made the world and bodies, though John says that it does not come from the Father.[128] God, of course, made the world and all the bodies too. But that the corruptible body weighs down the soul[129] and that the flesh has desires opposed to the spirit[130] is not the previous nature of human beings as they were created, but the consequent punishment of them as they have been condemned.

You say, "It is accused only by Mani and the traducianist, his heir." I rejoice that I am receiving your insults along with these men whom you dare to blame in me, but do not dare to name. (3) Does not he in that way accuse your darling who says that concupiscence of the flesh opposed to the spirit was turned into our nature by the transgression of the first human being?[131] And who is this? That man with whose "faith and utterly flawless interpretation of the scriptures," as Pelagius, your founder, praises him, "not even an enemy has dared to find fault."[132] Defend you darling against this accuser. In defense of her, insult as much as you can this teacher of mine and that teacher of yours who praised him. Show in that way that your protection is sufficiently free and loyal so that sexual desire does not abandon you, her defender, as if you were bashful, though she will not find another who blushes less in her defense.

The Devil's Claim upon the Fruit of the Sexes

68. JUL. And for this reason I had to ask what the devil recognized as his own in the sexes on account of which he rightfully plucks their fruit. For he had neither framed their flesh, nor formed their members, nor given them genitals. He had not differentiated the sexes and had not instituted marriage or its union without which marriage cannot exist. Nor had he dignified it with fecundity nor endowed it with pleasure.

AUG. The devil, of course, made none of these, but he persuaded the human mind to the disobedience upon which the disobedience of the flesh followed as a punishment and as a source of shame. As a result original sin is contracted by which the newborn is subject to the devil and destined to perish with the same devil unless it is reborn.

69. JUL. You have tried to counter all these arguments with the timidity of a deer and the cunning of a fox, and you have deceived your patron for whom you write, so that you say that on account of a natural sense of the body, that is, concupiscence of the flesh, the prince of darkness has dominion over the works and the image of God, though it was necessary that the senses of the flesh have the same author as the nature of the flesh had.

AUG. (1) You do not know what you are saying. The senses of the flesh are one thing; concupiscence of the flesh is another. The latter is experienced by the senses of both the mind and the flesh, just as a pain is not itself a sense of the flesh, but unless the sense were present, it could not be felt. By the sense of the flesh which is called touch, we sense differently rough and smooth things, and so on, but by concupiscence of the flesh we desire indifferently illicit and licit things, which are differentiated, not by desire, but by intellect. Nor does one refrain from illicit things unless one resists concupiscence. Evil acts, then, are not avoided, unless evil concupiscence is reined in, that concupiscence which in your horrid impudence or rather madness you call good. You are neither embarrassed, nor are you horrified that you have come to such a disgrace that none are set free from their own evil unless they do not consent to your good.

(2) Concupiscence of the flesh, therefore, by which we desire things which are forbidden, does not come from the Father.[133] In vain do you think, or rather you wish us to think, that, where John the apostle said this, he used concupiscence of the flesh for sexual misconduct. Of course, if sexual misconduct does not come from the Father, that does not come from the Father which conceives and brings forth sexual misconduct if one consents to it. For, by its urges which we are commanded to resist, what, I ask you, does it attempt to come to but sexual misconduct? How, then, is it something good which tries to come to something evil? How is it a good of ours which tries to come to something evil? How is it a good of ours which compels us toward something evil? This evil, Julian, must be healed by the divine goodness, not praised by human vanity, iniquity, and impiety.

The Mockery of Attacking and Praising the Same Things

70. JUL. It is evident, then, that you did not strive to refute the objections, but to mock in a wretched fashion your patron for whom you were writing so that he would think that you had brought to him something raw which you might rightly chew on, though you had praised it by your concession of the previous statements and by the formation of bodies.

AUG. I praised the formation of bodies which is good even in a bad human being, not the evil without which no one is born. Unwilling to say along with Ambrose where it comes from, you help Mani who says that it comes from an alien nature.

71. JUL. I admit, nonetheless, that you have thought very much about what you said, and your intelligence and zeal are evident. You have, of course, weighed most carefully what you should say in defense of the inheritance of sin. No one else could have written more cleverly in defense of natural evil. Not even you yourself, in fact, could have carried this out with such finesse if the lies of your old teacher had not helped your intelligence.

AUG. I am proud that my teacher against both you and Mani is clearly Jesus whom I confess, though you deny, to be Jesus also for the little ones, because "Adam perished and they all perished in him,"[134] and they are saved from perdition only by the one who came to seek what had been lost.[135]

72. JUL. You have understood, of course, that a serious sin could by no means be attached to the little ones who merit nothing on their own unless you condemned their bodies and that, for this reason, you needed the help of Mani who excluded concupiscence of the flesh from the works of God and attributed both marriage and bodies themselves to the devil as their author.

AUG. (1) I do not need the help of Mani; rather, fighting against him, I destroy by the help of God the help which you offer him. And God offers me this help even through his most distinguished followers, not only through the prophets and the apostles whose statements you try to twist in your perversity, but also through later teachers of his Church: Irenaeus, Cyprian, Hilary, Ambrose, Gregory, Basil, John, and very many others.[136]

These are men of the soundest faith, with the sharpest minds, most rich in learning, and most renowned in reputation. Without detriment to the praise of bodies and marriage, they have all taught original sin, knowing that Christ is Jesus even for the little ones, something which you impiously deny. (2) For he himself saves his people in which the little ones are also included, not from fevers and other such diseases and misfortunes, something which in his abundant goodness toward all flesh he bestows even upon those who are not Christians, but saves them as Christians from their sins.[137] You do not fear to call Manichees these sons and fathers of the Catholic Church, who are so many and so great, men who taught her, when they were placed in her highest position, what they learned at her breast. And when you openly pursue me as if I were alone, you accuse them more insidiously to the extent you do so more indirectly and more wickedly to the extent you do so more insidiously. In this great crime your own words completely condemn you. For you slander me with so unspeakable a name for no other reason than that I say about original sin what they say.

Julian Invites Augustine to Cross over to the Catholics

73. JUL. The deformity, therefore, of the cause which you defend has brought it about that you are thrown into confusion by the truth and put to flight. But if you would want to cross over to the Catholics, how much more elegantly and fully would you yourself follow what we maintain!

AUG. Oh what a brash mouth for such a blind mind! Are they, then, not Catholics to whom I cling in the communion of this faith which I defend against your vain words and calumnies? Are these not Catholics—not to mention others, but to repeat the same ones—Irenaeus, Cyprian, Hilary, Ambrose, Gregory, Basil, John of Constantinople? And are Pelagius, Caelestius, and Julian Catholics? Dare to say this, if you can. But if you do not dare, why do you not return to these men from whom I do not depart? Why do you admonish me to cross over to the Catholics? Look at these Catholic lights; open your eyes. Cross over to these men whom you slander in me, and you will immediately restrain yourself and stop slandering me.

74. JUL. And yet I do not dare to affirm that you are endowed with a sharp and alert mind, since in the choice of the task to take up I see your judgment to be so slow and distorted.

AUG. State the reason why some are born slow-minded, for Adam was not created like that. You reject the idea that human nature was changed for the worse through his sin and that this sin is harmful for the newborn in relation to all the defects they suffer.

An Impious, Stupid, and Indefensible Teaching

75. JUL. For if, without any harm at all to the faith, in the manner of the schools you tried to knock down those points which are invincible, merely in order to show the strength of your learning, but once the mock debate was over, you would concede the victory to those against whom you debated, we would approve your love of learning, but we would blame your example as irreligious. But with shameful stubbornness you maintain a teaching that is not tinged with even a faded color of verisimilitude, a teaching which you cannot defend by any testimonies of the law—which are, of course, never opposed to reason. And this is a teaching crazy[138] in its impiety, horrifying in its stupidity, lying only in the groins of desires, and run through by goodness, by argument, and by the sacred law. One of these three follows: You are judged to suffer either the chains of a mind like lead for understanding or of that crime which, as we have heard, is contained in the mysteries of the Manichees, or both at the same time.

AUG. (1) No matter how much you seem to yourself to fight in the name of reason against the divine testimonies which we offer, you do not overthrow them; rather, they cause you trouble since you kick against the goad.[139] Say as much as you can that he lies "in the groins of desire" who says to you that one conceived by the union of the two sexes is not free from sin.[140] This is Ambrose, Julian. He defeats you, a man whom you do not dare to deny is Catholic defeats you and whom you are certainly not going to call a Manichee.

Moreover, you state that I either have a mind like lead for understanding or am bound by the crime of Mani or suffer from both of these at the same time. Regarding the crime of Mani or your abuse we have already answered you often, and we shall perhaps still respond more opportunely where it seems necessary. (2) Now, you wordy heretic, respond concerning a mind like lead for understanding. There is certainly no one who would not choose, if it were in the power of a human being, to be born with a mind lively and very keen for understanding, and who does not know how rare such persons are? All these few, nonetheless, if they are compared to the mind of the human being who was created first, are judged to be like lead. For then the corruptible body did not weigh down the soul,[141] as it does now. After all, it either was not corruptible, because Adam was not going to die if he had not sinned, or if he was going to die, as you new heretics say, even if he had not sinned, he whom God created first and who had as yet done nothing evil was, nonetheless, not created so that his soul was weighed down by his body.

(3) Who, after all, would deny that this is a punishment except someone who is weighed down more than the rest? Suppose, then, that a Manichee asks where this evil of slowness comes from, not in bodies, but in the human minds themselves where God's image is found. This slowness gradually comes to a feeble-mindedness which is to be laughed at or, rather, as scripture advises, to be mourned.[142] We reply that these and all other evils with which we cannot deny or doubt children are born are to be attributed to the sins of the first two parents and of others after them, because they cannot be attributed to the will of the newborn.

(4) Since of the other animals some are, of course, born with their specific defects, why is it surprising that the evil spirits take them into their power, just as they took the swine,[143] as we know? As human beings can damage the members of irrational animals, so those evil spirits can damage even the seeds. Our question concerns human beings in whom the image of God would never have suffered the punishments of the diverse defects with which we see that they are born and which they could suffer justly only if the sins of their parents came first. In denying this, you both abandon the Catholic faith and help the wicked teaching of Mani more than he dared to hope, so that he thinks that he is certain and secure in saying that the true God is not the maker of human beings and in introducing the nation of darkness.

Justice Demands That Merits Be Ascribed to Actions

76. JUL. (1) For our part we have nothing which we believe worthy of admiration in our mind, for we understand that sin cannot exist without the will, that bodies cannot exist without God, that the senses of the body cannot exist without bodies, that marriages cannot exist without intercourse, and that the newborn cannot exist without God's activity. And we hold it as indubitable that what is known to be unjust is not divine and that what is known to be divine cannot be unjust. No less, however, than those things we have said, it is evident that it is unjust if the sins of some people are imputed to others who were not there and did not even consent.

(2) Hence, enlightened by these rays of sunlight we despise with perfect right the caverns of the Manichees who think that there can be sin without the will, that human beings are not made by God, that the senses of the body belong to one author and the bodies to another, that God exists but is overwhelmed with charges of injustices, that he who is regarded as the eternal creator of all things is weighed down by the crime of injustice, or that he retains any shadow of justice if the willful acts of some persons are attributed to the beginnings of others. And for this reason we attribute merits to the actions of their parts, not to their natural gifts.

AUG. I have already replied to you about all these points, and they do not become stronger against me because they are repeated so often and with such hate by you. State, rather, if you can, why human minds are often born with such defectiveness, since we are agreed that the just God is the maker of the whole human being, but you deny that there is any original sin. You would not, however, say that we impute the sins of some persons to others who were not there when they were committed, if you would recall that scripture says that Levi was in the loins of Abraham when Abraham paid the tithe to Melchizedek, the priest of the high God.[144] For in that case you would see, if stubbornness has not blinded you, that the human race was in the loins of Adam, when he committed that great sin.

The Devil Is the Prince of This World

77. JUL. But to return to the issue, you said that I "refused to mention concupiscence," because "it does not come from the Father, but from the world.[145] The devil is called the prince of this world, and he found none of this concupiscence in the Lord, because the Lord did not come as man to us human beings by means of it."[146] Here one must note that, when you spoke of something natural and said that it came from the world, you added that we must believe that the devil is the prince of the whole world with the result that you claim that he is the source, not of voluntary acts, but of natural things, namely, of natures.

AUG. (1) In the passage where I wrote, "concupiscence of the flesh," you removed from it my words, "of the flesh," and where I said, "The devil is the prince of this world," you added, "whole," and said, "of the whole world," which I did not say. Do as you please; say what pleases you or those whom you please as well. I said, "the concupiscence of the flesh," which John says does not come from the Father, but from the world,[147] that is, from human beings who are born in the world, destined to perish unless they are reborn in Christ. This concupiscence of the flesh is not sexual misconduct when it is resisted, but when it is carried out, that is, when it arrives at that to which it impels one. For this reason the apostle Paul says, *Walk by the Spirit, and do not carry out the desires of the flesh* (Gal 5:16). He does not say: Do not have such desires. He knew, of course, that this gift would indeed be ours, but not in the present life.

(2) I called the devil the prince of the world, just as God's scripture calls him that,[148] not as your folly suspects or slanders us. I did not, therefore, say that the devil is the author of natures, but the prince of the world, that is, of human beings with whom the world is full on this earth, human beings who are born in the world and are not reborn in Christ. From those, of course, who are reborn in Christ, the prince of the world is cast out; the sacraments signify this when even little ones about to be baptized undergo the rites of exorcism and exsufflation.

Reply to this, if you can. Do not will that your reader become foolish as a result of your wordy folly and be turned aside from the issue and be misled. (3) Say, if you dare, that it is good to desire something evil. Say that evil actions are not from the Father, but that the desire for evil actions is from the Father. Say that the devil is not called the prince of the world. Say that human beings situated in the world are not called the world. Say that unbelieving human beings with whom the world on this earth is full cannot be understood as the world in the bad sense. Again, say that believing human beings, with whom, though they are fewer, the world on this earth is also full, are likewise called the world in a good sense, just as it is not absurd that a tree full of apples is also said to be full of leaves. Say that, when the little ones are baptized, they are not rescued from the power of darkness[149] and that the images of God are throughout the whole Catholic Church subjected to the rites of exorcism and exsufflation with great insult to God, or say that they are owned by the devil without any guilt from sin. If you will dare to say these things, you will immediately be exposed; if you will not dare to say them, you will even so not remain hidden.

The Devil Found No Sin in Christ

78. JUL. After you said this, you added, "For this reason the Lord himself also said, *Behold, the prince of this world comes, and he finds nothing in me* (Jn 14:30), and you add on your own: "That is, no sin, neither the sin which we contract by being born, nor the sin which we add as we continue to live."[150] Show, then, that the Lord said in the gospel that he did not have any sin which is contracted by being born.

AUG. Show that the Lord said that he did not have the filth without which Job says that there is no infant who has lived a single day on earth.[151] And yet, where he says, *Behold, the prince of this world comes, and he will find nothing in me* (Jn 14:30),[152] we understand that he did not find this filth either, if we understand correctly. For, if from what he said we are not to understand what he did not say, he did not name the devil, but the prince of the world. He said: *And he will find nothing in me*; he did not say: He finds no sin in me. And yet, we say what he did not say, but what is understood from what he said.

He Would Have Found in Christ Sin Contracted by Birth

79. JUL. Why do you deceive unhappy souls by lying that something has been shown which has not been shown? The Lord says in the gospel, *Behold, the prince of this world comes, and he finds nothing in me* (Jn 14:30). It is certain that the devil came upon no sin in him, because the devil was defeated in every temptation which the devil brought against him, whether when he was fasting,[153] or

later, in the form of his persecutors, when he was preaching.[154] The savior, then, declares that the devil found no sin in him. He would certainly have found sin in him, if any sin were contracted from the condition of the flesh, because he too was born of a woman, from the offspring of David,[155] of the race sprung from Adam.

AUG. (1) But the Virgin had not conceived him through the concupiscence of the flesh, and for that reason the propagation of the flesh was passed on to him without the propagation of sin so that he had, not sinful flesh, but the likeness of sinful flesh which was going to save sinful flesh. Moreover, before Adam sinned, he had neither sinful flesh nor the likeness of sinful flesh, for he was not going to die, unless he sinned. But after he had sinned, sinful flesh now begot sinful flesh, because it begot sinful flesh through that concupiscence of the flesh, which before the sin either did not exist in him or did not resist the spirit. And on this account he was not ashamed to be naked.

(2) Christ, however, who was not born through that concupiscence of the flesh, was born without the sin which all sinful flesh contracts. He undoubtedly did not have the sinful flesh on account of which all die, but he died, nonetheless, on account of the likeness of sinful flesh. For, if he did not die, he would not only not have had sinful flesh, as he in fact did not, but he would not have revealed the likeness of it which he had assumed for our salvation.

(3) You, therefore, who cannot deny that Christ came not in sinful flesh, but in true flesh, though in the likeness of sinful flesh, must show us sinful flesh because, if there is none, there is certainly no likeness of it either. But, because Christ alone had the likeness of sinful flesh which was not sinful flesh because it was not born from the union of the sexes, what remains but that sinful flesh belongs to all who are born from such a union, since they pertain to the world of which the devil is the prince, and they are set free from this evil only if they are reborn in Christ?

Christ Would Have Been Either Guilty or Not Human

80. JUL. The devil, then, would have found natural sin in him if there were any natural sin; he would hold Christ's body subject if he had poisoned the body either in the first father or in his mother. And it would not have mattered to the conditions of his substance whether there arose an intention of his will since it would be too late and ineffective; in struggling against his nature, he would not wipe away the sin from his birth, but would only annoy his tyrannical jailer, since it remains true that the will could not have been free if the nature had remained captive. If, then, sin existed in the senses and condition of the flesh itself, if the very nature of human beings belonged to the dominion of the devil, Christ was either going to be guilty, or he was not going to be human. If, then, a curse is

attributed to the nature of humanity, either a sin will also be given to, or humanity will also be taken away from, that one who became flesh in order to dwell among us.[156]

AUG. No sin will be ascribed to him in whom the prince of the world could find no sin, nor will humanity be taken from him in whom there was both a human soul and flesh, though there was not sinful flesh, but the likeness of sinful flesh.

81. JUL. And Mani did both of these. He imagined that evil naturally exists in the flesh and said that there was no flesh in Christ to avoid admitting that there was sinfulness in him.

AUG. The Manichean heretic denies the flesh of Christ; the Pelagian heretic wants to make sinful flesh equal to the flesh of Christ. The Catholic Christian distinguishes the likeness of sinful flesh from sinful flesh to avoid blaspheming against the flesh of Christ.

But Christ Lacked Nothing Human and Had No Sin

82. JUL. But the Catholic faith has crushed Mani on both counts, namely, by declaring that evil does not naturally exist in the flesh and that, for this reason, Christ lacked nothing of humanity and had no sinfulness. He cries out, then, aware of his stewardship, *Behold, the prince of this world comes, and he finds nothing in me* (Jn 14:30), that is, nothing that he could blame, because he could not disparage the nature whose will he had not bent toward sins.

AUG. On the contrary, he found no sin, neither the sin that is contracted by one who is born because he was conceived in no iniquity, nor the sin which is added as one lives because he was led astray by no temptation. Of these two sins the one is that on account of which we read, *I was conceived in iniquities* (Ps 51:7); the other is that on account of which we say, *Lead us not into temptation* (Mt 6:13).

The Devil's Reasons for Tempting Christ

83. JUL. The will was even his reason for tempting Christ, for in accord with his trickery he wanted to take him captive by persuasion, since he could damage no one by creation.

AUG. He does not damage anyone by creation since he creates no one, but he damaged by his evil persuasion what he found created good. After all, he is not the source of the nature which is created by God's goodness in a human being, but of the guilt with which human beings are born of their own parents as a result of propagation from the damaged first parents. But why is it surprising if he tempted Christ in whom there was no sinful flesh? For there was also no sinful flesh in those human beings whom he first cast down by tempting them. And through their concupiscence of the flesh of which they were ashamed, sinful flesh has been propagated, which the likeness of sinful flesh which has no evil would heal from this evil.

Christ's Righteousness Came from His Voluntary Actions

84. JUL. Hence, the incarnation of Christ defends the work of his divinity. In bringing to me my nature and his will of which he offered to me a mirror and a standard and in declaring that the devil had found no sin in him, he showed that guilt is not derived by the creation of flesh, but only from the will. Finally, as we read nowhere in the scriptures that Christ fled from a sin that he knew is contracted by the newborn, we are emphatically taught by that clear testimony that the righteousness of the man he assumed came, not from the difference of his nature, but from his voluntary action.

AUG. (1) You say that the scriptures nowhere say "that Christ fled from a sin which he knew is contracted by the newborn." Why would he have fled, since he himself had not contracted it, but came to save those who contracted it? Why, I ask, would he have fled what no one flees from except when one takes flight to him? You say that "we are emphatically taught by that clear testimony that the righteousness of the man he assumed came, not from the difference of his nature, but from his voluntary action." But did Christ, then, not have even this difference in his nature, namely, that he was born of a virgin so that he was now not only the Son of Man, but also the Son of God? Did, therefore, that assumption of a human nature which made God and man one person contribute nothing to that man toward the excellence of the righteousness which you say he had from voluntary action? (2) Does the defense of free choice so drive you headlong against the grace of God that you say that even the mediator himself merited by his will to be the only Son of God and that what the whole Church confesses is false, namely, that she believes in Jesus Christ, the only Son of God the Father almighty, our Lord, who was born of the Holy Spirit and the Virgin Mary?

For, according to you, the man was not assumed by the Word of God so that he was born of the Virgin, but having been born of the Virgin, he afterward made progress by the power of his own will and brought it about that he was assumed by the Word of God. That is, he did not have a will of such goodness and greatness because of that union, but arrived at that union by a will of such goodness and greatness. And the Word was not made flesh in the womb of the Virgin, but afterward by the merit of the man and his human and voluntary virtue. (3) From this it also follows for you that, as you believe that he was assumed by the Word of God because he willed to be, so you believe that many could have been assumed in that way, if they too had likewise willed it, or could be assumed if they would will it. And for this reason you believe that he turns out to be the only one because of the laziness of the human will, though there could have been more, if human beings had willed it. If you say this, where is your shame? If you do not say it, where is your heresy?

Saint Peter's Testimony against Original Sin

85. JUL. For the apostle Peter says, *Christ died for us, leaving you an example to follow in his footsteps; he did not commit sin, nor was deceit found on his lips* (1 Pt 2:21-22). Certainly the statement of the apostle agrees with the words of the Lord. The Lord says in the gospel, *The prince of this world comes, and he finds nothing in me* (Jn 14:30). The teacher of the Church commends to us this same point and says that there was no sin in Christ, but he teaches by his truthful testimony why he had no sin. He says, *He committed no sin* (1 Pt 2:22); he did not say: He assumed no sin, but: *He committed no sin.*

AUG. Certainly, he who contracted no original sin had no sin, because he did not commit any, just as Adam would have had no sin, if he had not committed any, because he did not have original sin.

86. JUL. But if there was a sin in nature, Peter's statement would be misguided. For he had, of course, thought that it could suffice as testimony to his spotless holiness, if he defended his actions from sin, though it would have been believed that sin dwelled in him through a natural venom. Therefore, if he had any thought of natural evil, he would have more carefully and precisely mentioned this point and would have written: Christ left us an example; he neither committed sin, nor did he inherit the sin which we contract by being born. And in that way it would correctly follow that deceit was not found on Christ's lips.[157] But if the apostle had this in mind, he would never have made mention of his example. After all, whom would he have presented to human beings for their imitation, if the nature of a strange flesh set him apart and if the difference of his substance undermined the severity of his teaching?

AUG. Others surely understand how you are saying nothing, even if you do not understand it. When he was, of course, proposing to human beings an example in Christ for their imitation, what need was there for the apostle Peter to say anything about original sin, as if any in imitating Christ could bring it about that they would be born without it, as he was? In the same way, by imitating Christ they could not bring it about that they were born as he was born of the Holy Spirit and the Virgin Mary. Hence, in order to imitate Christ, our will is reformed,[158] but in order to be free from original sin, our nature is reborn.

Natural Sin Undermines the Example of Christ

87. JUL. (1) To this is added the fact that the idea of natural sin would not only remove all zeal for discipleship, but would accuse[159] of fraud the praise which was offered him. After all, with what seriousness, with what honesty would it be said that deceit was not on his lips, when, if he had come in another condition of the flesh than what is ours, he would be found guilty of having perpetrated an evil deceit, not only by his teaching—which is less serious—but also by being born—which is more serious?

How monstrous it would have been! Though human beings were established in natural evil and in the kingdom of the devil and were sinning under the deadly necessity of their inborn disease or were naturally serving the law of sin which reigned in their members, he would have forced them under the threat of punishment to strive to equal him, and he would have imposed his righteousness upon human beings of that flesh by the evil of which he had been so frightened that, though he chose to express under its appearance the model of virtue, he himself avoided the reality of that nature. (2) How much more correctly would the illness of sinners and the carefreeness of the coerced say to him: We all offer good advice to the sick when we are in good health.[160] If you were in this condition, you would think far, far differently.

To what point, then, has your impiety gone? It necessarily follows that, if one believes that sin is naturally present in our flesh, Christ too either assumed this flesh and is held subject to this evil, or he did not assume it and is bound with the unforgivable sinfulness, not of birth, which is seen to be false in his case, but of deliberate deception. (3) Since all this is foul with such great filth of blasphemies that it can hardly be explained without horror, even when it is torn to pieces, may the dignity of the mediator be present by example to his work and to our faith.

In claiming truth for his words and those of the apostle, our faith never ceases to preach that Christ, a true man, took flesh of the same nature as we have from the womb of Mary and that, a true man in every respect, he had no sin. To prove this it was enough for the apostle Peter to say that he committed no sin! He taught that he who committed no sin could not have any sin. There was no deceit found on his lips;[161] to those who share his nature which he himself created in all, he offered a holy example. And so it is established that there is no innate sin, since Christ had none, who without loss to the honor of his deity became incarnate in order that he might be imitable by us.

AUG. (1) O you man of many words and little wisdom, what if human beings said to Christ: Why are we commanded to imitate you? Were we born of the Holy Spirit and of the Virgin Mary? Finally, can we have as great a virtue as you have, for you are a man, but you are also God and for this reason coeternal with the Father and omnipotent, equal to the omnipotent Father? Ought he, therefore, not to have been born in that way, or ought he not to have been assumed into the unity of the person by the Word of God in order that he would not give such an excuse to human beings who do not want to imitate him? (2) But he himself proposed to us the Father for imitation, though the Father was certainly never a man, and whoever by his grace both will to imitate him and can imitate him do imitate him without loss or diminishment to his divinity so that they love their enemies and do good to those who hate them. And they do not say to him: You can do this because you are God and because your enemies can harm you in no way, but we are weak human beings and we are commanded to love those who inflict upon us so many and such great evils by their persecutions.

In the same way Christ's imitators do not say to him: We cannot do those things which you exhort us to do by your example because your excellence is far more powerful than our weakness. (3) And for this reason he who was born of the Holy Spirit and the Virgin Mary ought not to have lacked concupiscence by which he would desire sins, even though by resisting it he would not have committed them; otherwise, human beings would say to him: First have bad desires, and conquer them if you can so that we can imitate you by conquering ours.

Moreover, what do you say, Julian, about that man who said, *I do not do what I will, but I do what I hate* (Rom 7:15)? You claim that he is not driven to this necessity by the concupiscence with which he was born, but by bad habits. Did Christ not offer an example to such human beings in order that they might imitate him? Did he scorn them and will that they should be excluded from imitating his virtues? If they, then, said to him: You do not know what we suffer from the burden of habit by which we are weighed down. You are not weighed down; for that reason you can talk that way. "We all readily give good advice to the sick when we are well."[162] Do you want that Christ should also be weighed down (4) by such a habit and that he should conquer it so that, with their excuse removed, he would be imitable by such persons? Or will you at last laugh at your foolish talk and be silent for us?

A Challenge to Augustine's Praise for Jerome

88. JUL. (1) But with these matters taken care of, as the topic demanded, I want to challenge you at least somewhat concerning the confidence with which you say, though you praise the writings of Jerome, that there was no sin in Christ, though in that dialogue which he composed under the name of Atticus and Critobolus with a marvelous elegance as was fitting such faith, he tried to show by the testimony of a fifth gospel, which he says he translated, that Christ had not only natural, but also voluntary sin, on account of which he knew that he must be cleansed by John's baptism.[163] From another testimony of John the evangelist he accused Christ of being a liar.[164] (2) In that letter which you sent to Alexandria you boast about that work to the point that you say that Pelagius, overwhelmed

by the masses of the scriptures in it, cannot defend free choice.[165] But the Catholic man who was attacked replied to that work.[166] I now made mention of it only so that you would recognize that you not only are not in agreement with the holy scriptures, but not even with the supporters of your teaching.

AUG. (1) If you had quoted the words of Jerome, I would perhaps show how they are to be accepted without the blasphemy which you try to attribute to him. And if I could not, I would not, nonetheless, think that his faith which he held in common with other most illustrious teachers of the Catholic Church should be rejected because he is found, if he has indeed been found, to have said something on which he did not agree with them.

But this fact from the life of this man is enough for me against you, namely, that, although he holds concerning original sin what you reject to the point that because of it[167] you call me a Manichean, you do not, however, dare to call him that. Here it is clear that you are deceived by your imprudence, but slander me contrary to your prudence. (2) I, in fact, set before you the statement, not of Jerome, but of Ambrose, and not rephrased in my own words, but expressed in his words.[168] In that statement he says that Christ could not have been free from sin in any other way than if he were free from that conception which the union of a man and a woman produces.[169] There you see that it follows that, if I am a Manichee on account of that statement, so is Ambrose. But because he is not, this statement makes or proves no one to be a Manichee. Though you see this—for it is not the sort of thing that you are unable to see or that you can fail to see—you are, nonetheless, so abandoned by the validity of your case that you slander me with the name of Mani, not out of imprudent ignorance, but out of shameful deceit.

Augustine Praised the Blasphemies of Jerome

89. JUL. (1) For with regard to the blaming of pigs and goats you abandon the Manichees whom you follow with regard to accusing human nature. Along with them you destroy in Christ, not the appearance of his flesh, but the basis of his example. You also at times remove natural sin from Christ by your words so that you do not seem to place him under the power of the devil, something that not even Mani did. But you praise Jerome who was not afraid to blaspheme Christ to the point that he said that he became familiar even with voluntary sin. (2) Constantly wallowing among the various filth and lies of your friends, you cause injuries only to the Catholics, because they say that God is not the author of evil, that human beings who are made by him are not naturally evil, that the laws of God are just, that his image can turn away from evil and do good, and that Christ committed no sin in his members or in his commandments or in his judgments. And so, if you become aggravated at the assertion of the truth, we believe that the

wise can, nonetheless, be instructed and that some of the people whom your lies have wounded can be healed.

AUG. (1) I answered you above concerning the example of Christ: We ought neither to deny its excellence by which, though a whole man in every respect, yet born of the Spirit and not conceived by the concupiscence of the flesh, he lived here a life of perfect righteousness beyond all human beings. Nor ought we to excuse ourselves on account of this excellence from striving to imitate him in accord with our state. For married believers do not imitate his celibacy, and they do, nonetheless, imitate him in not engaging in adulteries and other illicit forms of intercourse. And if those who lead a celibate life in a holy manner imitate him more fully, they cannot also imitate him insofar as he not only did not do forbidden acts, but did not even desire them. For a celibate living a holy life all intercourse is forbidden, since all marital intercourse is illicit for such a person. Why, then, is it surprising if, as one born of the Spirit and the Virgin, he had no evil in himself?

(2) Who, on the other hand, except someone weighed down by more serious evils would deny that it is something evil against which even the saints daily petition the Father in accord with the teaching of the Lord himself? For when we say, *Lead us not into temptation* (Mt 6:13), we ask God's help against our concupiscence. *For each is tempted*, as scripture says, *pulled and enticed by one's own concupiscence* (Jas 1:13). May this Father, then, whom we petition keep us from being so bold as to say that the sin to which concupiscence of the flesh draws us does not, of course, come from the Father, but that the concupiscence which draws us to this sin does come from the Father. May he keep us from being so bold as to say that it is something evil to which it draws us, but that it is not something evil which draws us to it.

(3) But if the truth cries out that it is evil, surely he who was born without any evil did not have it, and for this reason, just as he did not commit sin, so he did not desire sin either. We, therefore, imitate him when we do not commit sin, not by not having the desire to sin, but by not consenting to it. And yet, we imitate the Holy of holies[170] when we live well in such a way that we, nonetheless, do not lack a reason to say in our prayer, *Forgive us our debts* (Mt 6:12).

I did not, however, praise Jerome, as Pelagius praised Ambrose, saying that not even an enemy dared to find fault with his faith and utterly flawless interpretation of the scriptures.[171] And for this reason, if I am displeased by anything, I find fault with it in the writings of a friend, just as in my own. But it is one thing for a Catholic to be in error on some point; it is quite another to found or to hold a heresy involving a great error.

There Can Be No Sin without the Will

90. JUL. (1) But let this suffice on this topic. Let us now come to that question on which a great part of the dispute is centered; tried and exhausted by its power, the ambassador of the Manichees has produced proofs of his loyal response and of his fine mind. For, after he praised and approved my statements which I cited above, with nothing new intervening, he approached that section in which the argument which we promised was presented. And when I asked why those whom God made were under the power of the devil, I replied to this in his name: "Because of sin, not nature,"[172] and I answered on my own behalf, "But, as you yourself agree, just as there cannot be a child without the sexes, so there cannot be a sin without the will. Little ones, then, have at the time of their conception a will, though they do not have a soul, or they have at the time of their birth a will, though they do not as yet have the use of reason."[173]

(2) When, therefore, he came to this passage, he set forth only this portion of our objections, that is, "But, just as there cannot be a child without the sexes, so there cannot be a sin without the will," and he replied, "Yes, that is quite right. For so it was that *through one man sin entered the world, and through sin death, and in that way it was passed on to all human beings, in whom all have sinned* (Rom 5:12). Through the bad will of that one man all sinned in him, when all were that one man, and on that account each individual contracted from him original sin."[174]

I urge the reader to pay careful attention to our dispute. What good did it do you, O most learned of bipeds, not to complete my sentence since, even though the explanation of the previous statement was contained in that part which you suppressed, the whole force of it is, nonetheless, equally found also in that part which you decided to deal with? (3) I, of course, set forth faithfully, as your agreement has also revealed, what you are accustomed to say, and in asking how the little ones whom God had made were under the power of the devil, I replied in your place: "Because of sin, not nature."

Surely you see that I perpetrated no fraud because of this. I said what is on the lips of the traducianist, even if this is not in his teaching. And to this I replied, "But, just as there cannot be a child without the sexes, so there cannot be a sin without the will." By an impudent deceit you split this into two parts. For, in mentioning what we said, namely, that, just as there would have been no child without the sexes, so there would have been no sin without the will, you omitted that which followed concerning the will of little ones, and you reply: "Yes, that is quite right. For so it was that *through one man sin entered the world* (Rom 5:12). Through the bad will of that one man all sinned in him."[175]

(4) Is this an answer? Is this an argument? Is this, finally, even to show respect for good sense? The wise surely laugh at the cleverness of sophisms in which the simplicity of the respondent is mocked through sameness of the words used.

Though those sophisms are themselves not solid with the truth, they give such an appearance by their charming veneer. But what a monstrosity of an argument this is which is neither solid with the truth nor made charming by a sophism! I certainly said that sin could not exist without free will; if that is granted, your teaching is destroyed, for you think that a sin can exist in the nature of human beings who are guilty without any will.

AUG. (1) I had only read from your work what the document which was sent to me contained. For, after I discovered your books from which someone or other excepted that passage, I replied to all points.[176] We, however, also say that sin cannot exist without free will, and our teaching, nonetheless, is not destroyed on this account, as you say, when we say that there is original sin. For this kind of sin also came about as a result of free will, not as a result of the personal free will of the one who is born, but as a result of the will of Adam in whom we all originally existed when he damaged our common nature by his evil will.

(2) The little ones, then, do not have at the time of their conception or birth a will for sinning, but that man at the time of his transgression committed that great sin by his free will, from which human nature contracted the infection of original sin so that the holy psalmist might say with complete truth, *I was conceived in iniquities* (Ps 51:7). And another holy man could also say, *For who is clean from filth? Not even an infant who has lived one day on earth* (Jb 14:4 LXX). These words of truth scorn the vanity of your wordiness.

Lessons in the Logic of Contrary Propositions

91. JUL. With what impudence, then, do you approve my statement without abandoning your teaching, though the statements of the two sides cannot be joined together in any alliance, as contrary propositions cannot both equally partake of the truth? Just as, if I agreed that there is natural sin, it would be necessary that I lose the right to the statement which claims that sin can only exist in the free will, so, on the contrary, since you agreed that I spoke well in declaring that there is no sin without the will, you ought to have immediately cast aside that opinion by which you believed in natural sin.

AUG. (1) That sin cannot exist without free will is one thing, and we too say this, because even original sin could not have existed without the free will of the first human being. That "sin," as you yourself said, "can only exist in the free will" is something else, and we do not grant this. For original sin does not exist in the will of the newborn, but it does not exist in the will of the first man either, though it could not exist without it. That sin cannot exist without the will is one thing, and that sin can only exist in the will is another.

For, if we are correct to say: Birth cannot exist without conception, it is not, therefore, also correct to say: Birth can only exist in conception. But this case is so different that birth cannot be in conception and conception cannot be in birth. (2) Sin, however, can be in the will, as it was in the will of the first human being; it can also not be in the will, as the original sin of each newborn is not. It is absolutely not in the will of anyone, but is not without the will of that first human being.

That holy man who said to God, *You have sealed my sins in a sack and have noticed if I did anything without willing it* (Jb 14:17), did not, of course, have a sin in his will which he committed without willing it. What about that man who says, *I do not do the good that I will*, and immediately adds, *but I do the evil that I do not will* (Rom 7:15)? Is he to be said to have sin in his will, according to you people, who want us to understand that he is being driven to sin, though he does not will to, by the force of habit?

(3) Stop, then, sneaking up from nearby and gradually crossing the border so that, because we say that sin cannot exist without free will, you claim that we say that it can exist only in a free will. It is as if we said that charcoal cannot exist without fire and you claimed that we said that charcoal can only exist in fire. If you did not know this, admit that you were not an intelligent debater, but if you knew it, admit that you hoped that you would not have an intelligent reader.

Whatever Is Natural Is Not Voluntary

92. JUL. For it is evident that whatever is natural is not voluntary.

AUG. If it is evident that whatever is natural is not voluntary, it is, then, not natural that we will to be alive and well, that we will to be happy. Who would dare to say this but you? And once admonished, perhaps not even you.

93. JUL. If sin, then, is natural, it is not voluntary; if it is voluntary, it is not inborn. These two definitions are as contrary to each other as necessity and will are contrary, where the affirmation of the one is produced by the denial of the other. For, as "voluntary" is nothing but "not coerced," so "coerced" is nothing but "not voluntary." These two, then, cannot exist or live together, so to speak, because their nature is such that the one is alive when the other is dead.

AUG. Why do you not notice that there is also a non-voluntary sin, at least in the one who says, for whatever reason he says this, *But if I do what I do not will, it is no longer I who do it, but the sin that dwells in me* (Rom 7:19)? Why do you not notice that there is also a necessity by which it is necessary that we will to live happily? And why do you with your eyes closed set these opposite to each other, as if there could not be the will of a necessity and a necessity of the will?

Julian Pleads That Augustine Be Consistent

94. JUL. Since, therefore, this is so irrefutable that it can be destroyed by no argument, choose which you prefer, and consistently uphold either your view or ours so that you ascribe guilt either to necessity or to the will. But when I say, "which you prefer," I do not give this advice, as if your opinion were still concealed, for you have learned from Mani to attribute to nature serious sins, but I give this advice in order that the true character of your argument may be noted.

AUG. Whether you like it or not, because you say this often, it is necessary that you often hear that he was not a Manichee who said that the discord between the flesh and the spirit was turned into our nature as a result of the transgression of the first human being.[177] When you deny the cause of this evil, an evil with which you are not permitted to deny that every human being is born, you bring it about that the Manichee says that there is in us a mixture with another nature and that he wins out unless he is conquered and slain along with you.

Why Are God's Creatures under the Power of the Devil?

95. JUL. Let the wise and cautious reader, then, weigh what you have answered me. We are certainly dealing with little ones who have no will in their own mind, and the question about them is why those whom God made are under the power of the devil, since you agree that they themselves did nothing evil.

You have proclaimed that they belong to the dominion of the devil because of sin, not nature. To this our response arose, "But as there cannot be a child without the sexes, so there cannot be a sin without the will."[178] To this you replied: "Yes, that is quite right," that is, sin cannot exist without the will. But, once you had affirmed this, with what impudence did you add, "But *through one man sin entered the world* (Rom 5:12), through the will of that one."[179]

AUG. (1) Ought I, because we were dealing with little ones, not to have shown that the true statement you made does not interfere with my statement, that is, that sin cannot exist without the will? For even original sin has as its cause only the will of that one from whom it takes its origin. Though you made that statement with a hostile intention, I answered that it was not against me, and I granted that it was true. And I showed how it was not opposed to me—something that you had not seen.

(2) You could, after all, have said in accord with your intention that sin cannot exist without the personal will of the one who has the sin. And if you had said that, I would never have granted it; for original sin is contracted without the personal will of the newborn. But you said what is true, namely, that sin cannot exist without the will, because even original sin was produced by the will of that one who sinned first by that will which damaged human nature so that any human being born through the concupiscence of the flesh, which was covered because the

guilty were ashamed, would not become free from guilt except by being reborn through the grace of the Spirit.

Sin Is Said Even to Reign without the Will

96. JUL. Did anyone ask you about Adam's deeds, or did anyone ask whether he sinned by the will? This question will soon be raised against you. Granted, you like to mock others. But what sort of monstrosity is it that you do this to yourself? I can, of course, hardly persuade myself that you suffer so great a monstrosity, not because you are deceived, but because you believe it. In one and the same line you agree that sin cannot exist without the will, and you immediately add that sin, which you had said does not remain without the free act of the mind, reigns in all human beings without the will.

AUG. (1) Why do you substitute your words for mine so that you remove my meaning, unnoticed by those who hear or read this? I did not say that sin cannot remain, but that it cannot exist without the will. But from your own words I will disclose how big a difference there is. For where you said, "A child cannot exist without the sexes," who would not agree that you spoke the truth? For a child does not exist without the sexes of the man and the woman. But if you had said: A child cannot remain without the sexes, who would grant that you had in this case spoken the truth? The child, after all, remains without the sexes of the parents without which it could not, nonetheless, come to be. Nor do they who caused the child to be cause it to remain.

In the same way sin, which cannot exist without the will, can remain without the will. So too, the sin of Adam is what remains from their origin in his descendants, except in those for whom it has been forgiven in Christ. (2) When it is not said to exist in them even without the will, we, of course, refer to Adam's will which caused a sin to exist which, by remaining, is also in his descendants. We are not referring to a will which caused to remain a sin which could already have existed even without the will.

But if you say that "to be" is the same as "to remain," I do not argue about words, but I state clearly: With reference to its remaining, every sin can be without the will. What sinner, after all, would also will the sin to remain which he did not commit without the will? And the sin, nonetheless, which was committed by the will, remains when the sinner does not will it. It remains, then, until it is forgiven, and if it is never forgiven, it will remain for eternity. After all, it was not said as a lie in the gospel: *They will be guilty of an eternal sin* (Mk 3:29).

Julian Points Out the Difference in the Prepositions

97. JUL. Morever, a big difference is found in these statements, for you had said, "Sin does not exist without the will," and you answered, "But sin exists through the will of the one." Does, then, the following response introduced by a preposition with the accusative case agree with the previous declaration formulated with a preposition with the ablative case?[180] The question was whether a serious sin exists without the will, and it was determined that it cannot. You added that sin entered through one man, though the question concerned, not that through which it began, but that without which it could not exist.

AUG. (1) I said that sin cannot exist without the will in the same way that we say fruit or grains cannot exist without roots. Here we can say even without offending the grammarians that fruit or grain can only exist through the root. Since both, then, may be said correctly, though the one is expressed by a preposition with the ablative case and the other by one with the accusative case, why is it that you lay snares for us with the cases of the nouns, like webs of spiders,[181] that are weaker to the degree they are more subtle? Search for dying flies to trap by these nets.

(2) Not such were those men whom we follow in order to scatter your snares. Not such was the apostle who said, *The body is dead on account of sin* (Rom 8:10). Not such was Hilary who said, "All flesh comes from sin, that is, is derived from the sin of our father Adam."[182] Not such was Ambrose who said, "We are all born under the power of sin, and our very origin lies in guilt."[183] I wish that you would be firmly and salutarily caught by the nets of these fishermen of Christ. Then, once having been corrected, you will better decline the accusative case by which you have accused yourself and the ablative case by which you were removed by the Catholic Church.[184] But if you follow prepositions correctly and entirely, why do you not lay aside your pride and set before you these teachers of the Church?[185]

Julian Admits That Adam Committed Some Sin

98. JUL. Surely the deception is seen as hateful which was immediately punished by that penalty which clings to sins, namely, that it entraps its own author before it proceeds to the destruction of its hearers. Look, we do not, after all, deny that the first human being fell into some sin, but the question is how this sin could be found in the newborn. Define what you think was the condition of the first sin; you say: "The will was free, for sin cannot exist without the will." We approve this. But you add: "But this sin which cannot exist without the will clings to those who are born without a will."[186]

AUG. It clings to them through infection, not through choice.

99. JUL. What you had granted, then, is false, namely, that sin does not exist without the will if, though it is committed by the will, it could, nonetheless, be passed on to others without the will.

AUG. What I granted is not false, because original sin was not committed without the will of that man from whom the newborn take their origin, but the sin which was not able to be committed by him without the will was able to be passed on to others through infection without the will. And for this reason the sin could not have existed without the will so that there would be that sin which is passed on to others without the will, just as grain could not have existed without roots so that there would be that grain which could be passed on to other places without roots.

100. JUL. Sin, then, now exists without the will when it is found in these from whom you remove bad will.

AUG. (1) Sin exists, that is, remains absolutely without the will. It would not, after all, remain unless there were something which might remain, but only the will brought it about that there was the sin which would remain without the will, at least if sin is only sin and not also punishment, for because of this latter everyone sins unwillingly. In that way both statements are true, namely, that sin cannot exist without the will and that sin can exist without the will, just as these two statements are true, namely, that a child cannot exist without the sexes of the parents and that a child can exist without the sexes of the parents. For the former meant that it cannot come to be without them, but the latter that it can remain without them.

(2) In one passage you yourself spoke correctly both about sin and about a child when you said, "As a child cannot exist without the sexes, so sin cannot exist without the will." Just as we understand that a child cannot exist without the sexes of the parents, because it cannot come to be without them, and that it can be without the sexes of its parents, because it can remain without them, once it already exists, why do we not understand in the same way that sin too cannot exist without the will, because it cannot come to be without it, and that it can be without the will, because it can remain without it, once it already exists?

The Results of Augustine's Cleverness Revealed

101. JUL. See, then, where your cleverness has got you: You are trying to convince us that something does not exist because of that because of which it can exist.

AUG. What about you, O great defender of free choice even against the grace of God? Will you deny that some sin which can exist because of free choice does not exist because of free choice? After all, it does happen because of free choice that sin exists when a person sins by willing to, and it happens because of free choice that sin does not exist when a person does not sin by willing not to. Look, we have found that something, and the very thing about which we are arguing, that is, sin, does not exist because of that because of which it can exist, that is, because of free choice. What about that, you quarrelsome fellow? Will my cleverness bring me to this point? Or have your eyes lost their keenness on this point?[187] Do not be hasty; it is better to pay attention to what you say than to strive to contradict.[188]

102. JUL. That is, sin exists without the will for the same reason that it cannot exist without the will.

AUG. Sin certainly does not exist without the will for the same reason that it cannot exist without the will, but for different reasons; both statements can, nonetheless, be true. For it cannot exist without the will because without the will it cannot come to be so that it exists, but it can exist without the will because what came to be can remain without the will.

An Impossible Alliance and Monstrous Combination

103. JUL. (1) So that sin loses its condition for existing by its condition for existing, and it is without that without which, by definition, it cannot exist. This is to deny the facts! Did Anaxagoras do anything of the sort when he said that snow is black?[189] You tell us that the nature of something is denied by its fruits. Though necessity and will are opposed so that, as we have shown above, they destroy each other by their attack upon each other, you subject one to the effect of the other in a new and impossible alliance and monstrous combination, and you say that necessity has arisen from the fruits of the will so that the will has destroyed itself by its reproduction and has changed its proper status by having acted. And, to express the matter itself in its own terms, as soon as the will began to exist, it ceased to be a will.

(2) What can be said—I will not say: more stupid, but: more crazy than that? Since these two, then, cannot exist together, that is, necessity and will, and since you affirm what we said, namely, that sin cannot exist without the will, and since you also agree that there is no will in little ones, you are forced, because you are caught in a stranglehold, to agree that there is no sin in these little ones, because you have declared that it cannot exist without the will.

AUG. (1) You would not say that necessity and will cannot exist together, if you were given knowledge of what you are saying. For, though there is a necessity to die, who would deny that there can also be a will to die? For this reason the apostle says that he has the desire to be dissolved and to be with Christ.[190] When, therefore, one for whom it is necessary to die wills to die, necessity and will exist together, something that you had denied could occur with your vain will, but with no necessity.

But the fact that a necessity—and often a necessity contrary to the will—is also produced as a result of the will is, of course, foolish to deny. For a man who willingly strikes himself a lethal blow dies even if he does not will to. Likewise, those who willingly commit a sin have the sin unwillingly; such persons are willingly unchaste and unwillingly guilty. Against their will the sin remains, though it would not have come about against their will.

(2) And for this reason, sin both cannot exist without the will because it comes to be only by the will, and it can exist without the will because it remains even without the will, though it was committed by the will. And now there is without the will even a necessity which the will produced without necessity. For the one who says, *I do not do what I will* (Rom 7:16), is surely weighed down, according to you, by the necessity of a habit, but you maintain that he produced this necessity for himself by his will so that you do not do away with free choice. And you do not believe that something like that came about in human nature so that, as the result of the will of the first human being from whom the human race took its origin, there has come about the necessity of original sin in his descendants. Look, those things which you proposed as impossible have been made possible by the force of habit, which is not without point called by some a second nature.

(3) You had said that we say something more absurd than the one who said that snow is black, namely, that sin "loses its condition for existing by its condition for existing, and it is without that without which, by definition, it cannot exist." Does sin not lose its condition for existing by its condition for existing so that by the force of habit sin is brought about without the will, though the habit is produced only by the will? Is the nature of this reality not denied by its fruits? For the habit is the fruit of the will because it arises from the will, and the habit denies that it does by the will what it does.

(4) You say that "necessity and will are opposed so that they destroy each other by their attack upon each other." For this reason you accuse us because "we subject one to the effect of the other," saying that "necessity has arisen from the fruits of the will," though you see that the necessity of a habit is the most obvious fruit of the will. Has not what you thought impossible, namely, that "will has destroyed itself by its reproduction and changed its proper status by having acted," produced the force of habit through its reproduction, if necessity has, according to you, destroyed the will? But if it has not destroyed it, in a human being weighed down by the burden of a habit there can certainly exist together both the will for righteousness and the necessity of sin. For *I am able to will the good* is a profession of will; *but I find that I cannot bring it to completion* (Rom 7:15.18) is a confession of necessity.

(5) You, however, said that will and necessity cannot exist together, though you see that they exist together when they are in harmony and that they exist together when they are in conflict. But what you claimed was impossible is ridiculous, for you said that nothing more stupid, nothing in fact more crazy can be

thought than that, "as soon as the will began to exist, it ceased to be a will," as if this does not happen when a person who has begun to will something wrong immediately repents and ceases to will it. Nonetheless, in saying such things, you say that you force me, caught in a stranglehold, to agree that no sin exists in the little ones, though you do not, even by your stranglehold, break the bond of the Catholic truth by which you are being most wretchedly strangled unless you assent to it.

The Claim That We All Were That One Man

104. JUL. (1) But the text which you added, *Through one man sin entered the world* (Rom 5:12), as we have shown here that it was cited most inappropriately, so in the second book we explained how it should be interpreted. But now, with the present argument completed, I would like to reexamine that most shrewd statement, for you spoke as follows: "*Through one man sin entered the world, and through sin death, and in that way it was passed on to all human beings, in whom all have sinned* (Rom 5:12). Through the bad will of that one man all sinned in him, when all were that one man, and on that account each individual contracted from him original sin."[191]

You say that they all sinned at the time "when all were that one man." (2) I have, however, already noted that you wrote this to Marcellinus,[192] and that testimony proves that you believe and embrace the transmission of souls, having received[193] it from the bowels of Mani in particular, whose statements I included in the third book.[194] This is, of course, so ugly that, though you mean it, you do not, nonetheless, by any means dare to say it openly. But in the present case let us postpone for the time being this point which is slain both by the foulness of its first defender and by the cowardice of his follower, namely, you.

At the present I want to examine this, namely, the great disturbance by which you are tossed about in arguing. You say, in fact: "Through the evil will of that one man all have sinned in him, when all were that one man." If all were that one man, how did all sin through the evil will of that one man, since all these who you say were in that one could have sinned by their own will? In fact, to turn the argument around, that man was more unfortunate than all, for he alone bears the hatred, though all sinned in him, according to your teaching.

The little ones, then, had a will, not only before they were born, but before their great grandparents were born, and they made use of the judgment of choice before the seeds of their substance were created. Why, then, do you fear to say that at the time of their conceptions they had free will by which they do not contract sin naturally, but commit sin freely, if you believe that those who are conceived today had so many centuries ago awareness, judgment, and the ability to will? In those books which you dedicated to Marcellinus you did not hesitate to say this, obviously to show the madness by which the enemies of God are bound. (3) For there you speak as follows: "These little ones sinned in Adam so that they are created like him."[195] What could be said more falsely, more insanely, more foully than that they sinned first so that they were created? That is, by their actions they merited that they could exist so that they did something, and their action is prior to their substance. Let it suffice to have pointed out these statements which are more appropriate to the rites and symbols of Bacchus[196] than to writing.

From this statement, then, there flowed the response in which you said, "All sinned in him when they were all that one man, from whom each individual contracted original sin."[197] (4) For here there is no need to labor to show that, since will is the act of a person, will cannot exist before the person whose will it is. But I want this point to be understood most of all: Even according to this view there is no original sin. For, if all who sinned were in him, they contracted no original sin because they all committed it by their own acts. The inheritance of sin, then, is destroyed not only by the Catholic truth, but even by all the arguments of its patron. The nature of lying, of course, has this peculiarity: that it does not maintain consistency in its deception, but unrestrained in shame and covetous of what is another's, it is uncovered in everything which it has stolen.

AUG. (1) The apostle said that sin entered the world through the one man in whom all have sinned, and Ambrose understood him. But Julian tries to twist the same words of the apostle into his own perverted meaning. Why does Ambrose himself not reply to him instead? Listen, then, Julian; he says, "All die in Adam, because *through one man sin entered the world, and through sin death, and in that way it was passed on to all human beings, in whom all have sinned* (Rom 5:12); that man's sin is the death of all."[198] Listen to still another passage. He says, "Adam existed, and we all existed in him; Adam perished, and all perished in him."[199]

Say to him, if you dare, that, because one soul sinned by its own will, so many souls which did not as yet have their own wills could not have perished. (2) Attack my hesitation about the origin of souls because I do not dare to teach or state what I do not know; state what you please about the deep obscurity of this topic, provided, nonetheless, that this teaching remains firm and unshaken, namely, that the sin of that one is the death of all, and all perished in that one, for which reason the new Adam came to seek and to save what had been lost.[200]

Say to Ambrose: And those, therefore, who you say perished in that one who sinned by his own will also sinned by their own will. But Ambrose had been able to understand this idea which you cannot, namely, that this was not said on account of the choice of each individual, but on account of the origin of the seed from which all were going to come. (3) In accord with this origin all were in that one man, and all these who were still nothing in themselves were that one man. In accord with this origin of the seed, Levi is also said to have been in the loins of his forefather Abraham, when Abraham paid the tithe to Melchizedek, and because of that Levi himself is shown to have paid the tithe, not in himself, but in that one in whose loins he was. He neither willed nor refused to pay the tithe, because he had no will when in terms of his own substance he did not yet exist, and yet in accord with the nature of the seed scripture said neither falsely nor foolishly that he was there and paid the tithe. For this reason the only exception from this paying of the tithe by the sons of Abraham who were in his loins when he paid the tithe to the priest Melchizedek was that priest to whom it was said: *You are a priest forever according to the order of Melchizedek* (Ps 110:4).

(4) Though even he was according to the flesh the seed of Abraham because the Virgin Mary from whom he took his flesh was descended from that seed, he was himself not held subject to that same seed, since he was not conceived as a result of a man's seed, but was free from the bond of concupiscence which causes the seed to be sown. Say, not to Ambrose, then, as I said, but to that man who wrote to the Hebrews and said, *And, as one must say, on account of Abraham, Levi, who receives tithes, also paid the tithe, for he was still in the loins of his forefather when Melchizedek met him* (Heb 7:9-10). Slander this man with your blind wordiness, and say if you dare: When Father Abraham paid the tithe by his own will, how could Levi have paid the tithe, that is, have given the tithe, since he had no will because he did not yet exist at all?

(5) By that argument or, rather, by that error you also say to us: When the first man sinned by his will, how could those who did not as yet have a will of their own, since in terms of their own substance they were still nothing, sin at the same time in him through his will? On the contrary, stop chattering foolishly, and understand that all those who, since they were not yet born, could do nothing either good or bad by their own wills could have sinned in that one man in whom they existed by means of seed, when by his own will he committed that great sin and damaged, changed, and subjugated in himself human nature, with the exception of that one man who, though his descendant, was not procreated by means of seed. And if you cannot understand this, believe it.

Augustine's Reason for Attributing Marriage to the Devil

105. JUL. But after this reply he tries to wash away another point on which he was beaten by me. After I had inquired about the will of the little ones, I, of course, continued: "But you deny this, namely, that a sinful will is present in the newborn, and you say, nonetheless, that little ones are under the power of the devil, nor do you hide the reason why you think they live under his power. You, of course, say: Because they are born from the union of the two sexes, they are under the enemy power."[201] It is evident from the testimony of his statements that he claims the little ones for the demon on the grounds that they were born

from the union of the two sexes. On this account I showed that he attributes to the devil marriage which was instituted by God and which cannot exist without this union.

AUG. You could not by any means show this, though you tried with much effort. Those who read both your slanders and my refutations can see this.

Children Belong to the Devil because of Sexual Union

106. JUL. He, therefore, now poses this objection for himself, putting my interrogation first. "You say, then," he says, "that they are under the power of the devil, because they are born from the union of the two sexes."[202] Let us listen to how adequate a reply he makes to this. "Clearly I say," he says, "that they are under the power of the devil on account of sin, but that they are not free from sin because they were born from that union, which cannot produce even what is good without shameful desire. Ambrose of blessed memory also said this."[203] O the disastrous depravity of the man! Oh the unspeakable intention! Oh the shameful falsity!

AUG. (1) Exclaim, exclaim as much as you can; add to your exclamations: O the violence! A man, an innocent man, of course, you suffer violence so that you are forced to call Ambrose a Manichee. Heaven forbid, you say, that I should call him that. Why? I ask. Or do you here show how great is the strength of free choice, when you suffer such great violence to say it, and yet you do not say it? Why, then, do you say that I am what you do not say that he is, since he said so long ago what I am now saying and since on that view on account of which you call me a Manichee he and I are in full agreement? Or, because you do not find a way of escape, do you feign anger, and exclaim, though you are not in fact angry, but upset?

But in these exclamations of yours I hear: "Oh the disastrous depravity of the man!" Because I, of course, am disastrous and depraved in choosing to agree with Ambrose, but I would be blessed and righteous if I chose to agree with Julian. (2) I hear: "Oh the unspeakable intention!" Our intention is, of course, unspeakable because we set Ambrose over against Julian, but it would have been speakable if we preferred Julian to Ambrose.

But what about the third exclamation of yours that I hear? "Oh the shameful falsity!" Do you say that Ambrose's view is false, that is, that he himself held what is false? Or do you say that we falsely attribute it to him, though he did not himself hold it and that he did not at all say what we say that he said? Or do you say that, because we do not understand it, we have a mistaken opinion about it, though it is itself true? But you would not speak so contemptuously of Ambrose that you would attribute shameful falsity to that man. You, however, have not dared to say that we made it up and pretended that he said it, for the writings of that teacher are known to so many that you were afraid to throw yourself over that cliff. (3) But this statement is so straightforward that one who understood it could hardly seem clever, but one who thought it needed explanation could easily seem superfluous.

Finally, in order that what I am saying can be seen, I shall quote here again the very words of the most blessed Catholic bishop. He, therefore, that one with whose faith and utterly flawless interpretation of the scriptures your Pelagius says not even an enemy has dared to find fault,[204] said, when he was speaking of the birth of the Lord, "And so, as a man he was tempted in every way, and in the likeness of human beings he endured all things. But as born of the Spirit he held back from sin. For every human being is a liar,[205] and no one is without sin but the one God. The principle, then, has been preserved," he says, "that no one born of a man and a woman, that is, through that union of bodies, is found to be free of sin; he, however, who is free of sin was also free of that mode of conception."[206]

(4) Since you do not deny that Ambrose said this and since you see that it is clear and straightforward, why do you cry out: "Oh the shameful falsity!" For whom is it shameful? For him or for me? If for him, see who it is toward whom you are being contemptuous. If for me, see how slanderous you are. But, you say, you too say this. I clearly do say it because it is true; if you do not think that it is true, why because of one and the same statement which he says and I say is he not a Manichee, but I am? How much more justly do we exclaim: "Oh the shameful partiality!" which would undoubtedly force you to be ashamed if in your own person your sense of shame were like your mouth.

Augustine Has Falsely Claimed to Have Left the Manichees

107. JUL. Does this man dare to say that he does not condemn marriage and to mock the ears of the uneducated with such an outrage that he says that he has left the company of Mani who has by his frequent declarations located in the kingdom of the devil the union of the sexes, the marital act, and the love and feeling of the parents? And adding the help of his keen mind to these lies of Mani, he, of course, declares that sexual union is diabolical and that it belongs to the spouses both because of their act and because of the flesh, and on account of it he assigns innocents to the kingdom of the devil, while the parents are absolved. And so, ever, of course, an enemy of God, he defends those who serve the devil, as he says, through sexual desire.

AUG. You are mistaken, and you lead others who agree with you into error; they do not serve the devil through sexual desire who use the body of their spouses for the sake of procreating children so that children are born in order to be reborn. Nor is the evil of sexual desire, nonetheless, defended in that way; rather, they are defended who make good use of the evil. After all, there is a good use even of an evil. For in the holy scriptures there are found benefits from even Satan himself, while the blame for him remains, as well as the praise for one who makes good use of that evil.

Augustine Wrongly Appeals to Ambrose's Authority

108. JUL. But he consigns the little ones who he says are made by God to the dominion of the enemy, and in that way he does not blame the work of the demon, whose ministers he absolves from guilt, but the work of God which the pleasure conscious of being a gift of the devil could not reach. He brings, therefore, accusations against the marital act, but excuses the passions; he attacks innocence, but defames divine justice. He was not afraid to write: "I clearly state that they are under the power of the devil, because they are born from that union."[207] When he saw the outrage of that view exposed, he tried to defend it by some authority which he could not draw from the scriptures. He added that Bishop Ambrose held the same view. It is not surprising, of course, that he brings accusations even against the dead, when he brings accusations against the innocent.

AUG. (1) What does whoever hears this suppose that you raise as an objection against us but that this statement of the most blessed Ambrose which we cited is not his and that we have made it up as if it were his? For, when I read this, I too thought that you were doing nothing else,[208] but after I came to those words which you add, where you do not deny that Ambrose said this, I found that you are, rather, a horrible accuser of that great teacher. For whatever you say against me because I say that no one conceived by the union of man and woman is free from sin, you certainly say against him as well who said and wrote this before I did.

(2) But when, in refuting and resisting you, I claim that little ones are under the power of the devil on account of original sin unless they are reborn in Christ, I certainly defend from your wicked accusations not myself alone, but also Ambrose and his other companions who hold and teach this faith, and the whole Church of Christ. That Church testifies by the exorcism and exsufflation of little ones at baptism that she has received this, holds this, and faithfully believes this.

No Defense, But at Least Some Consolation

109. JUL. How much more correctly you would say: Mani also said this same thing in the letter to Patricius;[209] he also said the same thing in the letter he wrote to his daughter Menoch,[210] and he said in many other writings those ideas which you totally absorbed. But you try to bring into your company the bishop of Milan, and because you cannot have a defense, you want to find some consolation.

AUG. (1) What Ambrose said is solidly against Mani. For Mani said that an alien nature of evil has been mixed into us, but Ambrose says that our nature was damaged by the transgression of the first human being.[211] But in this statement with which we are now dealing, Ambrose defended the birth of the flesh of Christ, distinguishing it from the sinful flesh of the others,[212] but Mani completely denied his flesh. What Ambrose believes, therefore, I too believe, but what Mani believed neither Ambrose nor I believe.

Why is it that you try to separate me from Ambrose and link me to Mani? For, if to say that original sin is not contracted by the newborn from a mixture with an alien nature, but from the corruption of our own is the teaching of the Manichees, Ambrose says this along with me. Why do you not try to link both of us to the Manichees? (2) But if this is not the teaching of the Manichees, as it certainly is not, and I say this along with Ambrose, why do you not agree to separate both of us from Mani? Why, then, as you say, do I try to bring into my company the bishop of Milan, when you try in vain to separate me from his company?

What do you mean when you say that, because I could not have a defense, I want to find some consolation. For me as well as for Ambrose, whether you like it or not, Christ is our common defense in the Catholic faith. Ambrose is clearly my consolation because along with him I receive your insults, nor does he alone console me greatly on this issue, but also Cyprian, and Hilary, and others like them, whose Catholic faith you attack with abuse in me. (3) Do not be envious, then, that Ambrose, Cyprian, and Hilary are consolations for the injuries I suffer, for you are compelled against your will to see how great a difference it is that Pelagius and Caelestius and perhaps someone else are the consolations for the condemnation you suffer.

What about the fact that I show that Ambrose combats the Manichees in defense of the Catholic faith and that in this conflict you offer to the Manichees in opposition to Ambrose either consolation in their defeat or, what is worse, help in their resistance? For the Manichees say that evil has its own substance and nature coeternal with the good substance and the nature of God. It is impossible, they say, that evils can arise from goods. (4) Ambrose contradicts them and says: "Evil things arise from good ones, for evil things are only those which are deprived of goods. Evil things, nonetheless, cause the good ones to stand out. The privation of good, then, is the root of evil."[213]

What do you say when confronted with these positions? "The order of reality does not permit," you say, "that something evil comes from something good or that something unjust comes from something just."[214] We quoted these words of yours which you said in defense of the Manichees and against Ambrose in that famous work in which you chose to reply to my one book with your four. If you were the judge in this controversy, your verdict would certainly declare that Ambrose is defeated by the Manichees. And you are not embarrassed, though you are the slanderer of those whom you openly accuse, the flatterer of those whom you likewise accuse, but indirectly, and the helper of those by whose name you accuse others.

Without Prejudice to God's Law or Work

110. JUL. Are the writings of disputants ever prejudicial to the law of God or the work of God?

AUG. Here you now begin to admit that we did not make up this statement as if it were a statement of Ambrose, but that it was really his, for you try to free yourself from him so that you say, "Are the writings of disputants ever prejudicial to the law of God or the work of God?" But go on, state the other things by which you will be judged to be an even more impudent enemy of the Catholic faith.

111. JUL. For the time being it is amply sufficient for me to prove by this statement that you never read in the sacred writings what you believe, since in such a case you have produced nothing but a few, short words of a bishop which you state. If you had been able to stumble upon something with greater authority, you would have undoubtedly held yourself back from these.

AUG. Let the readers see whether I have failed to produce divine testimonies or whether you have tried in vain to destroy those which I produced.

The Authority of Ambrose and Cyprian

112. JUL. But it is good that you earlier relieved us of the burden of such persons. For in the book which you composed for Timasius against free choice,[215] when the saintly Pelagius recalled those venerable men, both Ambrose and Cyprian, who taught free choice in their books, you answered that you were not bound by the authority of such persons. You even said that, if they held some incorrect view, they wiped it out by progress toward the better life.[216] Your words are reported only that you may be embarrassed at having stirred up hatred over names alone. But the statements either of Ambrose or of others, whose reputation you try to stain by association with yours, are defensible by a clear and benevolent argument.

AUG. (1) Who but someone who reads this can believe that such a great blindness of heart could have befallen you? You say that, if I had been able to stumble upon, that is, to find something with greater authority, I would have held myself back from the statements or, as you put it, a few, short words of disputants. And you yourself immediately say that Pelagius, whom you call saintly, used as witnesses in defense of free choice the venerable men, Cyprian and Ambrose. Nor do you notice how, by saying this, you refute your teacher and your heresy itself. For, according to your statement, if Pelagius had found in the canonical writings something with greater authority in favor of that which he was defending, he would have held back from the testimonies of disputants. Under what circumstances would you have said this, if Ambrose had not so upset you that Pelagius suddenly found you an opponent?

(2) But I earlier relieved you, as you put it, of the burden of such persons, namely, Ambrose and his companions. Clearly you are weighed down by this burden so that you are not only overwhelmed, but even crushed and are turning into the dust which the wind blows from the face of the earth.[217] For those many, great, holy, and illustrious bishops of God, sons of the Catholic Church as learners, but her fathers as teachers, have not spoken of the sin of the first human being and of succeeding generations of mortals subject to it so that they disagreed with one another or so that anyone of them disagreed with himself. Rather, they certainly spoke so that whoever reads them without an heretical mind cannot doubt that holy scripture must be interpreted in no other way on this topic or that the Catholic faith must not be thought to be anything else. By their weight you are already being crushed so that you have accepted their statements to which you are opposed as "defensible by a clear and benevolent argument."

(3) Let us, then, hear a clear and benevolent argument. If these statements are defended by some clear argument of yours, why are your curses hurled against me because of them? For those statements which you detest and blame in me are precisely those which you defend in their disputes. But if they are not defended, but more cleverly refuted in the guise of a defense, heaven forbid that this argument should be clear and benevolent. It is, rather, a mocking flattery which is called a defense precisely so that no offense of the Catholic peoples who venerate the same men need be tolerated.

Ambrose and Others Said Some Things Incautiously

113. JUL. (1) After all, they obviously said some things in a rather simple fashion and, while they were thinking about something else, they had no need to confront questions arising on their flanks. For, since they frequently praised marriage and did not think that any longing was implanted in bodies by the devil, and since they did not subject to the kingdom of the devil God's works, that is, the members of our nature, but explained, as the opportunity presented itself, that marriage was instituted by God and given as a blessing and that choice is free, it is only fair not to judge them to stand in the company of your crime, if you find any words either unclearly or carelessly placed in their writings.

(2) After all, just as it does not count against the holy scriptures that all heresies hide and try to defend themselves by some testimonies from them, so, too, we shall not allow the reputation of Catholic men to be condemned on account of certain words which they uttered incautiously. For they had no intention either

of condemning marriage or of denying free choice or of wounding innocence, and if they had had this intention, they would not have supported your teaching, but would have lost the dignity of their office.

AUG. (1) Oh clear and benevolent argument of defense! Ambrose, that is, said in a rather simple fashion that no one born from the union of a man and a woman is free from sin, and while he was thinking about something else and had no need to confront questions arising on his flank, he negligently and carelessly spilled into his writings and discourses the Manichean venom, as you call it. You most loquacious fellow, because you are afraid of human beings, you spare a human being, but you do not defend his statements. For, if these statements are defended by a true argument, they are undoubtedly truthfully defended, and they are true. And if this is the case, original sin is correctly defended, and your teaching is destroyed. If, however, these statements are defended by a false argument, that clear and benevolent argument of yours, as you call it, is not an argument, but a deception.

(2) But Ambrose, after all, "frequently praised marriage"; we too do this. You say that he "did not think that any longing was implanted in bodies by the devil"; if you mean a good longing, we do not think that either. But if you mean a bad longing, we think that it was, just as Ambrose did. Nor, you say, did he "subject to the kingdom of the devil God's works, namely, the members of our nature," as if the members of adulterers are not works of God and members of our nature which are, nonetheless, clearly subject to a defect and, for this reason, to the devil. "They explained," you say, "as the opportunity presented itself, that marriage was instituted by God and given as a blessing and that choice is free." We do that too. "It is only fair," you say, "not to judge them to stand in the company of your crime." On the contrary, it is insane to judge because of your crime that we do not stand in their company.

(3) You say that "it does not count against the holy scriptures that all heresies hide and try to defend themselves by some testimonies from them." And in that way you want that some words which we use as objections against you, words which Catholic commentators "uttered," as you suppose, "incautiously," should not count against them. What does this amount to but saying that even in the holy scriptures those words which the heretics take as their own were uttered there incautiously and, therefore, are not true? What could be said that is more criminal? Or if those words are true, but not understood by the heretics in their true sense, this comparison has no basis. For, if you concede that the statements of either Ambrose or Cyprian or of other Catholics which we set against you are true, you will uphold original sin.

(4) Hence, just as we along with them praise marriage as well as admit free choice and defend innocence, so you should say along with them that little ones are not free from sin. Otherwise, we are with them, and you are against them. You do not defend their statements as you had promised, but find fault with

them. Since you, of course, are forced by your teaching to blame their statements and to maintain that they are false, you will in no way be allowed to present for these authorities that defense of them which you had promised. For even in accusing them you are found to fawn upon them, and in your fawning upon them you are found to accuse them.

If Alive Today, Ambrose Would Defend the Catholic Faith

114. JUL. I conjecture and declare freely that, if one of them were still alive in these days and saw that the glory of Christian doctrine has been extinguished and that free will was taking its leisure in all things, while pretending to attribute to necessity whatever it freely commits, if one of them saw that the disparagement of God's works and the overthrow of his law is being presented to the hearing of peoples under the name of a grace that is ineffective, he would be aroused with complete bitterness against you. He would realize that natural sin cannot be separated from the impiety of Mani, and he would clearly and carefully defend the Catholic faith, after you had been either corrected or condemned.

AUG. (1) Why, then, do you say: after we had been corrected, and not after they themselves had been corrected as well? Where is that which you promised freely to conjecture and declare? Look, your vanity is not free, and your freedom is false, for you were afraid to say that, if Ambrose were still alive in these days, he would, after hearing you, first correct himself and then us. But though you were afraid to mutter this like a free man, you, nonetheless, wanted it to be understood. See what we have come to in these days, namely, that if Ambrose were living here in these days, he would learn that he had been a Manichee and that, after hearing Julian or Caelestius or Pelagius himself, he ought not to be one anymore, but ought to be healed of that wicked plague under your directives and care.

(2) What a picture comes to the mind of one who ponders this! What a sight it would be to see Ambrose standing before Pelagius or, if the latter would permit, sitting and learning about the new paradise full of the disasters of this world which we see little ones suffer, where it would be necessary, even if no one had sinned, that the flesh have desires opposed to the spirit.[218] And so that it would not pull the spirit to forbidden and sinful actions, it would also be necessary that the spirit have desires opposed to the flesh. Ambrose used to say that this dissension had been changed into our nature by the transgression of the first human being,[219] but now under instructors like you he would not dare to say this.

(3) It would also be necessary in such a paradise that pregnant women be pale, suffer long losses of appetite, and groan and wail in giving birth; it would be necessary that children be born with diverse defects of minds and bodies, that a few clever ones learn to read and write with less labor, but still not without labor,

while the rest who are a little slow or quite slow are either struck by the rods of their teachers, the more to the extent each is slower, or remain untutored and un-educated. The feebleminded would not even be given to teachers, but would be raised, destined to be mourned or mocked. Before infants could will anything evil, they would be troubled by diseases, tortured by pains, cared for by excruci-ating treatments, tormented by demons, and expire as devastation conquers them.

(4) But suppose that Ambrose, in horror, refused to believe this and replied that, if no one had sinned, all these evils would absolutely not have existed in that place of such great blessedness where they could not exist even after the sin, since those two from whose transgression these evils followed were ejected from it. Suppose that he had replied that for this reason those evils come from the wretchedness of mortals which would not have existed if human nature, which was damaged and changed by the most grave sin of the first human being, had not merited to propagate this world full of so many and such great woes in which even the redeemed, though they have already received the pledge of everlasting salvation, do not lack such evils, but when they leave this world, they will then be without them. If Ambrose, then, gave such answers, he would be forbidden by your illustrious syllogisms to say these things for fear that, when concupiscence of the flesh is blamed and original sin is believed, marriage would be con-demned, free choice taken away, the works of God disparaged, and the over-throw of the law ensue in the name of grace.

(5) It is clearly not so, not so! Be ashamed! Or, rather, be afraid to think such thoughts! On the contrary, if that man were still alive, he would resist you even more forcefully and more authoritatively than we do in defense of the Catholic faith and of the grace or justice of God, showing how those conclusions do not follow which you think follow. For one can live rightly, not if concupiscence is either denied or praised, but if it is reined in. Nor is the creator of nature dispar-aged when the nature, which could be damaged, but not created by the enemy, is shown to need healing by the creator. Nor is marriage condemned which makes good use of shameful concupiscence. Nor is free choice taken away, but we are shown by whose help it may be free for what is good. Nor is the law overthrown by grace, but fulfilled. That exemplary teacher would exemplarily defend all these ideas, and he would hurl into your impudent faces those statements we made above about your paradise, statements which really follow from your error and are either laughed at or abhorred by all human beings as sick and crazy.

The Inexorable Demands of Logic

115. JUL. After all, it is within the rights of no one to accept the premises and reject what follows from them. A person, then, who says that little ones belong to

the dominion of the devil because they are begotten from sexual union undoubtedly condemns this union in which the work of nature consists and at the same time the creation of this nature.

AUG. This seems so to you, but Ambrose saw that it is not true, something that you do not see. He said that children born of a man and a woman, that is, through that union of bodies, are not free from sin,[220] and yet he does not condemn this union and at the same time the creation of this nature. The union of the spouses for the sake of procreation is, of course, a good of marriage, but some good actions are done only with the evil of defects, just as bad actions are not done without the good of our members. No matter how great the defects by which any nature is spoiled, its creation is always good. For, just as the creation of the body is good, even when one is born diseased, and the creation of the mind is good, even when one is born feeble, so the creation of a human being is also good, when one is born subject to the infection of original sin.

Augustine Cannot Create New Rules of Logic

116. JUL. (1) For either both are denied together, or both are accepted together, and though the rejection of both is in one's power, the selection of only one of them does not fall within a person's choice, apart from the fact that it is easier to blame illicit intercourse on a defect of the will, while the fruitfulness of the seeds is defended, than to defend the sex act, while its fruits are accused. The wavering between fear and impiety from which you suffer will not, therefore, be able to create new rules of argumentation so that you may accept one of two propositions that are linked together and exclude the other one to which it is united. "Agile deer will graze in the air"[221] before the conclusion will be denied after the acceptance of its premise.

(2) The apostle Paul uses this form of argument when he says, *If the dead do not rise, Christ has not risen either. If Christ has not risen, your faith is empty* (1 Cor 15:16). *But Christ has now risen* (1 Cor 15:20); it is established, then, that the resurrection of the dead will take place. And to emphasize this by a brief example for the sake of the reader: Let the question be raised whether what is just is good. I ask whether you admit that everything just is right. When this is granted, I add another question: whether you declare that everything right is also good. When this too is granted, I conclude, whether you like it or not: If everything just is right, and everything right is good, then everything just is good. Those who want to resist this conclusion after accepting the premises do not shake the edifice of reason, but expose themselves to ridicule.

(3) Let the comparison, then, be applied to the present case. The question is whether there is sin in a nature. I asked whether you granted that there is no sin without the will. You agreed, as your statements testify. I further asked whether

you thought there was a will in a little one. You said here too that there was not. What follows in the third place, if there is no sin without the will? [222] This is so certain that it cannot be called into doubt even by the Academic skeptics,[223] whose riches amount to holding nothing as certain. When, therefore, after accepting the first two propositions, you deny the third in which the conclusion of the two is found, you do not destroy the foundations of reason, but you reveal your own madness.

AUG. (1) Are you so foolish as to think that sin does not exist in a nature, though sin could not exist at all except in a nature? For it is either in an angel or in a human being which are undoubtedly natures. If, then, sin did not exist in any of these natures, it would, of course, exist nowhere. And for this reason, when the question was posed whether sin exists in a nature, you had intended to show that sin does not exist in a nature. You understand, then, that your intention was foolish and that you raised this question foolishly if you are not extremely foolish.

See, I destroy the foundations of your reason because it is not true reason. And yet I do not, as your insults claim, reveal my madness, but your error. (2) After having granted the two propositions which you accept, I deny the third precisely because it does not contain the conclusion of those two, as you think it does. I, of course, grant that there is no sin without the will because without the will sin cannot be committed. But for another reason it can again be correctly said that sin can exist without the will, because it remains as long as it is not forgiven, even when the will by which it was committed has ceased. So too, I grant that sin cannot exist without the will because even original sin was not committed without the will of the one from whom it took its origin. (3) Hence, when I also grant the proposition that the will to sin does not exist in a little one, from these two the third is not inferred, namely, that there is no sin in a little one. But it would be inferred, if, just as I grant that there is no sin without the will, I would also grant that no one has a sin without a will of one's own. Hence, a little one does not have a will for sinning, but a little one would not have sin if that man had not sinned by the will from whom the little one contracted it.

For something of the sort can also be said about the very birth of a human being. If, after all, you said: No one is born except because of the will, I would not without reason grant this. But if you said: No one is born except because of one's own will, I would not grant it. In this way, then, since we are dealing with the sin of a little one, its original sin, just as its birth, could not exist without the will, but could exist without its own will.

Intercourse Like Babies Has Its Source in God

117. JUL. If those priests, then, whose statements we are explaining heard that there was a doubt whether marital intercourse was good and if I asked them

whether bodies are created by God, they would admit it. And after they granted this, I would ask in addition whether they agreed that marriage was established by God. After they had likewise agreed to that, I would finally ask whether child-bearing would exist without intercourse. After they said that it would not, what would follow? Evidently that, if the body comes only from God, if intercourse takes place only with the body, if the baby only comes from intercourse, both the baby and intercourse have the same source as bodies have.

AUG. Is this question at issue between us, namely, whether marital intercourse is good? For we both say that it is good. Why is it, then, that you think so ill of those priests whose statements you do not explain, as you falsely claim, but pollute,[224] that you want to persuade them, as if they were in doubt, about something that you prove that neither they nor we doubt? Marital intercourse which takes place for the sake of procreation is good. But Ambrose who said that no one born from the union of the two sexes is free from sin did not repudiate marital intercourse; rather, he saw the evil by the good use of which one does what no Catholic doubts is a good act.

You are speaking nonsense; you waste time on needless points. You abandon the question at issue, and you undertake to prove a point not in doubt as if it were in doubt or even denied. Why, then, is it surprising that you produce so many books and such empty ones?

The Manichees and Traducianists Are Struck by Lightning

118. JUL. These wise men and Catholic priests would undoubtedly accept this conclusion. And seeing that no one other than the true God produced anything in the senses of the flesh or anything in the baby conceived by the sexes and seeing that God had made nothing which was evil and that an evil is nothing other than an evil will which sins without any coercion from natural elements, they would surely declare that the Manichees and the traducianists have been struck down by bright lightning bolts of Catholic reason.

AUG. (1) Why, then, do you falsely and shamelessly claim that you defend and explain the statements of those whom you call wise men and Catholic priests, if even their statements are struck down by your bolts of lightning? But if they are defended and explained and, for this reason, remain whole and entire, you are, rather, struck by their lightning bolts. For Ambrose's statement that no one born from the union of a man and a woman is free from sin is either false or true. If you say it is false, you, therefore, attack the statements of wise men and Catholic priests, as you admit they are; you do not defend and explain them. But if, in order that their statements may be defended and explained as they deserve, you grant that this statement of Ambrose is true, you are, rather, struck by the lightning bolts of the statements of Catholic bishops.

(2) Why is it that you boast and say that, if those most blessed and most learned men had heard your syllogisms, they would have declared that we, whom you call Manichees and traducianists, "have been struck down by the lightning bolts of Catholic reason"? Would they make this declaration against themselves and say that they themselves have been struck down along with us by your lightning bolts? Why do you not dare to say directly what you are shown to say indirectly?

We admit original sin along with Ambrose, and you hurl lightning bolts with such power that, on account of these statements common to him and to us, we are struck down by them, while he is explained! (3) You are foolish; you do not distinguish him from us, and you, of course, accuse both him and us. You do not, nonetheless, strike with your lightning bolts either him or us, if you do not want to destroy the testimony of Pelagius, your teacher. For he said that not even an enemy has dared to find fault with his faith and utterly flawless interpretation of the scriptures.[225] As a result, though you are clearly understood to be an enemy of his faith and utterly flawless interpretation of the scriptures, you do not, nonetheless, dare to find fault with him. But by finding fault with me, you think you show what evil he speaks.

O you, a man run through, but not admitting it,[226] you are compelled by a great force to gasp out murky fallacies; in vain do you dream up the attacks of one who casts bolts of lightning since you rather breathe out the smoke of one struck by lightning. These are surely the arguments by which you try to teach Ambrose and the other teachers, his companions, that there is no original sin, namely, that God formed bodies and instituted marriage and that without intercourse there would not be child-bearing. (4) These arguments we grant; we also grant those which you add, namely, that the child and intercourse have the same source as bodies have, at least if you wanted us to understand marital intercourse when you said this. And yet this is known to be true by itself and does not follow from your argument; otherwise, when you say, "If the body comes only from God, and intercourse is carried out only through the body," and you want to conclude from this that "intercourse has the same source as bodies have," someone else can say: If the body comes only from God, and adultery is carried out only through the body, adultery has the same source as the body has. You see the great injury to God with which this is said and the great evils which your syllogisms teach.

(5) Just as, then, it does not follow that adultery should be attributed to God because it is carried out only through the body of which God is the source, so it does not follow that intercourse should be attributed to God because it is carried out only through the body of which God is the source. But we, nonetheless, grant that intercourse, at least marital intercourse, which is carried out for the sake of procreation, should be attributed to God as the source, not because this follows

from your premises, but because it is seen to be true, when it is considered in another light.

But the conclusion you seek to draw from this does not follow from those previous statements, nor is it true. For it does not follow that, because God made the body, because God instituted marriage from whose union a child comes, and because God creates the offspring of living beings, your addition is true, namely, that "no one other than the true God has produced anything in the senses of the flesh or anything in the baby conceived by the sexes." (6) Where, after all, did the devil produce the evil he brought about with the first human beings if not in the senses of their flesh? For their senses were, of course, corrupted by his evil persuasion, when their assent to sinning was brought about. And where did he produce whatever evil he afterward produced for the human race if not in the babies conceived by the sexes, that is, in the children of human beings?

But how can you say that "God made nothing which is evil"? Is not hell evil for the damned? Indeed, is there anyone who believes you when you say that "there is no evil other than the evil will which sins without some coercion of natural elements"? To pass over countless evils which the bad angels and human beings suffer against their will, shall eternal punishment itself which is the greatest evil not be feared? And yet it is not an evil will, but the punishment of an evil will. There are your arguments by which you think that your word is a lightning bolt, though your heart is a cinder.

The Need to Pardon Ambrose's Careless Remarks

119. JUL. Stop, then, bringing charges against men of sound mind and bishops of the churches. Do not subject their somewhat careless remarks to judgment, for it is not a brief hesitation, but stubborn persistence that merits anger. Let us, of course, imitate that zeal by which they built up peoples by exhorting, entreating, and correcting them. Would they have done any of this if they had believed in your fashion that sins are not voluntary, but natural?

AUG. (1) We too build up peoples in accord with our modest ability by exhorting, entreating, and correcting them, as Ambrose did, and we, nonetheless, hold and state concerning original sin the same thing that Ambrose held and stated—not Ambrose alone, but Ambrose along with all his other great companions. Since you call them "bishops of the churches" and "men of sound minds," with what sort of mind do you bitterly reprehend and falsely defend those truths which they learned and taught with their well-known agreement? And you blame me, saying that I bring charges against them, though you see that I am their defender against your charges which you hurl at them indirectly. You say, "Do not subject their somewhat careless remarks to judgment." Is that the way you defend and explain them? (2) Do you not, rather, reproach and accuse them by the mention of carelessness and condemn, as no one can doubt, those statements which you say were uttered carelessly and are, therefore, false?

We beg you: If you say that those statements which you defend are false, state that those with which you find fault are true. You say, "It is not a brief hesitation, but a stubborn persistence that merits anger," as if you were producing something by which you could show that they changed their view about original sin—I do not say: after a brief time, but: at least after a long persistence, or even at the end of their life. You are saying foolish things; you are saying crazy things; you are saying perverse things and things opposed to your own salvation. Be silent, I beg you. Why do you say so much?

Augustine Ascribes Human Bodies to the Devil

120. JUL. (1) But let us go on to the other points. What you say has, of course, no validity, namely, that you ascribe to the devil, not bodies, but sins. As we have frequently shown, you utterly deny this with no other aim than to avoid the hatefulness of Mani whose poison you breathe forth. For you ascribe to the prince of darkness bodies, yes, bodies, since you declare their union diabolical and accuse the genitals, their movement, and their fruits. As a result of your first instruction,[227] you openly blame the members, not the defects. You call diabolical the same act about which Mani too is angry that it thrives in the sexes, as I showed in his writings.[228] And so that our readers may receive from a repetition something they can retain: Either show that there is will in little ones, or remove from them serious sin.

(2) When you do not do this, but claim that they are owned by the devil on account of the fact that they were born from the union of bodies, you show that you ascribe to the hostile power, not sins which cannot exist without the will, but bodies themselves. Just as, then, that desire which is found both in human beings and in animals is natural and established by God, so this desire, from which you suffer in the fluctuations of your arguments so that you find yourself in the midst of various and contrary teachings has been conceived as much from stupidity as from impiety. It is not unjustly that we distinguish Ambrose from your gang, nor do we call him a Manichee, as you want.

AUG. (1) You have labored entirely in vain to come to this false and ridiculous conclusion by long and twisted, false and fleeting turns. In it you said that it is not unjustly that you distinguish Ambrose from our gang, and that you do not call him a Manichee. If you do not call him one, you should certainly not call me one either, but if you think that I should be called a Manichee, you are forced to call him one as well along with all those great and famous teachers of the Church. About original sin, on account of which you call me a Manichee, they say without any obscurity or ambiguity the same things that I say, as I quite clearly showed in the first and second of my six books which I published against your four.[229]

(2) But if Ambrose were still alive in these days, he would, of course, be terrified by your logic. For, once he found from false inferences that what he had held is false, he would no longer dare to say that little ones born from the union of the sexes are not free from sin for fear that he would on this account place them under the power of the devil. He would, then, cease to be a Manichee because of your instruction. Oh what a loss he suffered in not having been able to hear you!

Moreover, because you call me a Manichee on account of this view, Ambrose, of course, who persevered in this view, left this life as a Manichee, as you claim. (3) You ought, then, not to defend him, something that you can in no way do, but to mourn for him, because you cannot teach him anymore. But if you had been able to do so, once rebuked and corrected by your instruction, he would certainly forbid in the church he ruled that little ones about to be baptized should be subjected to exorcism and exsufflation lest in so many innocent images of God who were in no sense, as you claim, placed under the power of the devil, God himself would receive so grave and so clear an injury. But if Ambrose would forbid that this practice be carried out, he would be driven from the Catholic Church along with you.

Heaven forbid, after all, that this should be called correction rather than deception. Heaven forbid, then, that this man should stand with you in opposition to our Catholic mother; rather, he must invincibly oppose you in defense of her. (4) Why is it, then, that you think that I must be separated from him on this issue? I say, just as he did, that no one born from the union of the bodies of a man and a woman is born free from sin, and yet I do not attribute bodies to the devil as their creator, because he did not either. Just as we both blame the defect of nature, so we both reverence the author of nature. If, because I say that the concupiscence of the flesh by which the flesh has desires opposed to the spirit has turned into our nature because of the transgression of the first human being, I, therefore, blame the members, not the defects, he did this too. But if the defects have one origin and the members another, neither he nor I blamed the members.

(5) Neither Ambrose nor I said that the newborn have a will of their own, but both Ambrose and I say that through the sinful will of the first human being there was produced the defect of concupiscence from which the newborn contract original sin through the union of the sexes. Both of us, therefore, ascribe to the hostile power newborn human beings before they are reborn, not on account of their substance of which God is the creator, but on account of the sin which entered through the one and was passed on to all human beings,[230] of which sin the devil is the author.

Why is it that you falsely and most impudently claim that you defend and explain the statements of Ambrose and other people like him? (6) Who is so blind as not to see that you find fault with them, while I defend them, that you pollute them, while I explain them? Ambrose made these statements in speaking of Christ. He said, "And so he was tempted as a man in every respect, and he endured everything in the likeness of human beings, but as born of the Holy Spirit, he refrained from sin, for every human being is a liar,[231] and no one is without sin except the one God. The principle, then, has been preserved that no one born of a man and a woman, that is, through that union of bodies, is free from sin. But he who is free from sin is also free from that manner of conception."[232]

(7) You claim that these statements are completely false and that they contain the impious Manichean teaching, and on this account you find fault with and defile the statements of Ambrose. But I declare that they are perfectly true, and I show that they are not only not favorable to Mani, but are even opposed to him, as I have already done. I, then, rather defend them, and defend them from your impious charges. Even you, then, see whether he is on our side or yours, but because you fear those people who love him, you, of course, try with hypocrisy to excuse him whom you are found guilty of savagely accusing.

Jovinian's Alleged Attack on Ambrose

121. JUL. (1) You say that Jovinian attacked Ambrose with insults,[233] a point on which I, nonetheless, believe you lie. But let us grant that your accusation against Jovinian at least is true and that he called Ambrose a Manichee. But it is clear that Jovinian was crazy. For no one in his right mind could call a Manichee a man who preached that nature is good, that sins come from the will, that marriage was instituted by God, and that little ones are made by God. If Jovinian thought that the preference Ambrose showed to virginity was an accusation of marriage, he did not know what he was saying at all. To be opposed to is one thing; to be ranked above is another. The praising of a good is, of course, a step toward what is better, but the denigration of nature is the road to Mani.

(2) Since Ambrose, then, did not condemn marriage and did not call the union of spouses either the work of the devil or the necessity of sin, Jovinian acted wrongly in comparing him to Mani and in thinking that there is no difference between one who condemns marriage and one who praises virginity.[234] For, if Ambrose said that children, who were born from the lawful union of bodies which was instituted by God, lied of their own will in imitation of the ancestors[235] after they began to have the use of reason, he did not, nonetheless, want this union to be seen as the necessity of lying, but as an indication of its universality.

(3) After all, his statement that those born of parents lie[236] is the same as if he had said: Every human being, provided one has control of one's choice, has at some time lied. He knew, of course, that no one has come to be without the union of parents, except Christ. The wise man, therefore, wanted the marital act to be a

sign, not of sinfulness, but of universality. But he declared that Christ, as he showed by the miracle of his mother, avoided every lie, and this statement is strongly opposed by Jerome, whose disciple you are, for he with full deliberation tried to attribute to Christ a lie.[237] Ambrose, then, was not correctly called a Manichee, if indeed he was so called, for in opposition to your error he frequently praised creatures.

AUG. (1) We too frequently praise creatures. Why is it, then, that you say that Ambrose does this in opposition to our error, since he does this in accord with our faith? Ambrose, however, showed by other passages of his writings as well the sense with which he set forth those words which I raised as an objection to you and which you were afraid to mention for fear that your darkness would be refuted by their brilliant light. Hence, Ambrose, we see, did not once stumble upon that statement rather carelessly or incautiously, as you say, but explained with a quite clear exposition that his teaching on original sin is Catholic teaching.

(2) Why and in what sense did he say, "The principle has been preserved, namely, that no one born of a man and a woman, that is, through that union of bodies, is free from sin, but he who is free from sin is also free from this manner of conception"?[238] He said this, because he wanted us to understand here, not the sins of human beings after they began to have the use of reason, as you imagine, but original sin. Pay attention to what he says elsewhere, "That the Jordan turned back[239] signified the future mysteries of the saving bath by which the little ones who have been baptized are restored from evil to the original state of their nature."[240] Tell me, Julian, from what evil they are restored if they do not contract original sin.

(3) Listen again to another passage; he says: "For intercourse with a man did not open the gates of the Virgin's womb; rather, the Holy Spirit poured spotless seed into that inviolable womb. For among those born of a woman the holy Lord Jesus was absolutely the only one who did not experience the contagion of earthly corruption because of the new manner of his immaculate birth; rather, he shrugged it off by his celestial majesty."[241] Answer me, Julian, what is this contagion of earthly corruption which the Lord Jesus alone of those born of a woman did not experience because of the new manner of his immaculate birth. Listen again; he says, "Before we are born, we are stained with infection." And a little later: "And if even a child one day old is not without sin, then those days of the mother's pregnancy are for even better reason not without sin."[242] (4) I can mention many statements of this man whom you have admitted is a man of sound mind. But what is enough to one for whom these statements are not enough? From these statements, then, understand that you are also not permitted to twist and distort, as you have tried to do, those words into another sense than that in which Ambrose spoke them about those who are born from the union of bodies, where he did not lay the blame on God's creation, but on original sin.

Why do you hold before me Jerome, whose disciple you accuse me of being, when there is at present no question about his words? If you had, nonetheless, quoted his words, I would show that they do not contain what ought to cause displeasure, or I would leave them to be explained by those who understand them better. Or if they were undoubtedly opposed to the truth, I would reject them with the freedom which is fitting.

(5) Look at Ambrose again whom you do not dare to call a Manichee, though you call me one because I say about original sin what he says. For, if you did not call Ambrose a Manichee because he preached that nature is good, that sins come from the will, that marriage was instituted by God, and that little ones were made by God, you should not call me one either because I faithfully preach the same truths. But if you think that I should be called a Manichee because I admit original sin, Ambrose too admits this. Why do you not think that we are both Manichees? But you insolently call me a Manichee, but secretly think that he is one, not because of the distinctness of the truth, but because of the extinction of your freedom. (6) For you do not dare to say of him what you dare to believe. Or if you do not believe this of him, you certainly do not believe this of me, because, even if you think that we are in error, it is easy to see that we are not Manichees, since we do not maintain that there is a distinct substance of the sinner which God did not create; rather, we maintain that original sin was propagated by a voluntary failing of the nature which God created good. It is, then, easy for you to see this, and at the same time easy for you to see that we are both opposed to the Manichees. But you fend off that name from Ambrose with hypocrisy, while you hurl it at me in slander.

Augustine Is Worse than Jovianian

122. JUL. (1) But as Jovinian is proved to be his enemy, so in comparison to you he receives pardon. After all, when will the judgment of the wise grant you so much pardon that they compare you to Jovinian in merit? He said that there was a necessity of good; you say that there is a necessity of evil. He said that human beings are held back from error by the mysteries, but you say that they are not even set free by grace. He destroyed the virginity of Mary by the condition of her giving birth; you hand over Mary herself to the devil by the condition of her being born. He sets better things on a par with the good, that is, virginity with marriage, but you call the marital union diseased and devalue chastity by comparing it to this utterly ugly union, and you do not put a level between these, but you use different categories, not, of course, preferring virginity to something good, but to something evil. (2) It is, however, a mark of the lowest value if something cannot be found pleasing except when compared with what is absolutely the worst. What, after all, did he hold that was as injurious to God as what

you hold? He wanted to modify the strength of God's judgment in the direction of kindness; you want to do this in the direction of malice. He says that before God the good and the best will enjoy equal honor; you say that the good and the impious, that is, the innocents and the devil, will be tormented by one punishment. He, then, wants God to appear most merciful; you want him to appear most unjust. He says that human beings who have received the sacraments cannot sin, but you claim that God himself sins by lack of power in his sacraments and by lack of moderation in his commandments and by cruelty in his judgments. Since there is as great a disparity between you and Jovinian as there is likeness between you and Mani, Jovinian is shown to be more tolerable than you to the extent that Mani is more horrible than Jovinian.

AUG. (1) How smart you think you are when you compare me with Jovinian and try to show that I am worse. But I rejoice to receive along with Ambrose this utterly false insult from you, though I am sad that you are so insane. You, of course, say that I am worse than Jovinian for the same reason that you say that I am a Manichee. And what is this reason? That original sin, of course, which you deny along with Pelagius, but we admit along with Ambrose. Along with him, according to you, we are both Manichees and worse than Jovinian, and whatever else you say with impudent lips, not lips, of course, that speak the truth, but that speak evil, the Lord taught us to rejoice and be glad when we hear any sort of evil spoken of us, not because it is the truth, but because we fight for the truth.[243]

(2) Look, I do not say that there is a necessity to sin, because Ambrose did not say that either, and yet I do say that little ones are renewed from evil, something that Ambrose said too. And there is, therefore, no necessity to sin, because what birth contracts can be healed by God. How much more can what the will adds be healed by God! I do not say that human beings are not set free even by grace; heaven forbid that Ambrose should say that! But we say what you reject, namely, that they are set free only by grace, not only so that their debts are forgiven, but also so that they are not brought into temptation.[244] We do not hand Mary over to the devil because of the condition of her birth, but we do not do this precisely because that condition is removed by the grace of rebirth. We set virginity above marriage, not as something good above something evil, but as something better above something good. (3) We do not say, as your slanders have it, that the good and the impious will be tormented by one punishment, but that the good will have none, while the impious will be tormented, not by one, but by different punishments in accord with the difference of their impiety. We do not say that God sins by lack of power in his sacraments, by lack of moderation in his commandments, and by cruelty in his judgments, for his sacraments are useful for those reborn by his grace, his commandments are salutary for those he has set free, and his judgments are justly apportioned to the good and the evil.

Look, we repel from ourselves those points on which you say that we are worse than Jovinian; try to repel from yourselves, if you can, these points on which I shall show that you are worse than this same Jovinian. (4) He said there was a necessity of doing good; you say that the desire for evil is good. He said that human beings are kept from error by the sacraments; you say that the desire to walk the right path is not inspired by God, but acquired by free choice. He destroyed the virginity of Mary by the condition of her giving birth; you make the holy flesh born of the Virgin equal to the flesh of the rest of human beings, not distinguishing the likeness of sinful flesh from sinful flesh. He makes the better equal to the good, that is, virginity to marriage; you make evil equal to good. For you say that the discord between the flesh and the spirit is just as good as the harmony of marriage. (5) He says that before God the good and the best will have equal honor, but you say that certain good people will not only have no honor in the kingdom of God, but will not even see that kingdom. He says that human beings who have received the sacraments cannot sin; you say that human beings can avoid sin more easily by the grace of God, but that without that grace human beings can avoid sin by free choice. With the audacity of the giants[245] you resist God who said, when he was speaking of the good fruits, *Without me you can do nothing* (Jn 15:5). Though you, therefore, stand apart from the error of Jovinian only in the direction of what is worse, you, nonetheless, subordinate us to him and make us, rather, equal to Mani. You are protected by a great defense; it is as if you founded a new heresy precisely in order that, when we refuted you, we could not make you the equals of any heretics. (6) On this issue, nonetheless, on which you find me to be worthy of hatred because of original sin and someone to be set, rather, on a par with Mani, I stand, whether you like it or not, with Ambrose whom Jovinian called a Manichee, as you do. But he did so openly, while you do it deceitfully. Finally, he is defeated on one count when Ambrose is proved not to be a Manichee, but because you wanted to have a twofold heart,[246] you are defeated on two counts. You accuse Ambrose of being a Manichee; I show that he is not. You deny that you accuse him; I show that you do accuse him. Both of these points, however, will be obvious to one who has read what Ambrose said above.

Augustine's Appeal to the Book of Wisdom

123. JUL. (1) But let us look at the rest too. On these points which we have treated, I think the reader has been informed more than enough concerning the validity with which Augustine attacks any of my words or defends his own opinion. And for this reason it will not be necessary to prove this point by a repetition of everything we have written. For, though he scarcely quotes for himself individual and scattered lines from my book and often enough praises them, he also

at times brushes against them with a very brief insult, and yet what he thinks he should attack was not spoken by me in the way he suspects. Hence, I direct the readers to that work of mine; they will see that this claim corresponds to the truth. This man, of course, who complains that the objection was raised against him that he brings charges against nature and the seeds could not maintain the continuous patience of pretending, but after he calmed the hearing of his patron with his tricks, he put forth his head like a turtle.

(2) For, after he had said that, if Adam had not sinned, human beings could beget children as we are accustomed either to move our limbs or to trim our nails,[247] he added: "If the seed itself had no curse, what is the meaning of the statement in the Book of Wisdom: *They were not unaware that their nation was wicked and that their malice was natural and that their thought could never change, for their seed was cursed from the beginning*" (Wis 12:10-11).[248] And he follows up this testimony which he cited with the following argumentation: "Of whomever wisdom is speaking, she is, of course, speaking of human beings."[249]

There is the man who declares that he has abandoned the beliefs of the Manichees. On the occasion of the statement which he does not understand, he declares the seed accursed, malice natural, and the thought of the wicked unchangeable. (3) Rumor has it that those living near the falls of the Nile have lost their hearing because of the roar of the falling waters.[250] Opinion might have made this up which spreads about greater stories on the basis of great ones. The example is, nonetheless, valid for chastising the deafness of the foolish who because of the noise of their borrowed terror resist, like deaf asps, the cries of reality.[251]

Augustine shouts: The race of human beings is wicked; their malice is natural; their thought is forever unchangeable; their seed is cursed from the beginning. And are people still found who suppose that he has not yet been branded all over with the mark of Mani? Let whoever are public followers of this filth be questioned today; if they say anything else, we should be thought to have lied. (4) If, then, malice is natural, how do you pretend not to declare nature evil? If the seed is cursed from the beginning, how do you say that you accuse the defects of wills, not of seeds? If the thought of the wicked is unchangeable, how do you perjure yourself in confessing free choice? There only remains that you call Manichees those Jews, Sirach or Philo, who are believed by an uncertain opinion to be the authors of the book called Wisdom.

AUG. (1) Whoever may have been the author of this book, it is well that you do not reject its authority. It is a suitable book, then, from which we may produce against you the testimonies which we can find. For even your teacher, Pelagius, in the Book of Testimonies or of Chapters which he published,[252] quoted from this book passages which he believed suited his aim. Especially because the author of this book was not a Manichee, he proves sufficiently and clearly that even those who are not Manichees and who have merited to be read and accepted in the Church of Christ could say that malice was natural without in any way finding fault with what God, the most wise and most good creator of all natures, has established and created.

(2) For this reason the apostle is understood to have said in the same sense: *For we too were once by nature children of anger, just as the rest* (Eph 2:3). Certain writers translated this, not word for word, but in terms of the sense, when they said: For we too were once naturally children of anger. But when he says, *Just as the rest*, he shows that all are by nature children of anger unless the grace of God separates some of them from the mass of perdition. In speaking of those who have no share in this grace the apostle Peter, therefore, said, *But these were begotten naturally, like dumb animals, for captivity and death* (1 Pt 2:12). They did not, of course, strip themselves of their old selves.[253] Unless every human being was born old, no little one would be renewed by being reborn.

(3) Heaven forbid, then, that human beings should be said to be naturally children of anger to the injury of the creator; in the same way one is said to be naturally deaf or naturally blind or naturally sick without injury to him. Likewise, another is naturally feebleminded, another naturally forgetful, and still another naturally irascible, and there are countless other defects either of bodies or, what is worse, of minds which were created by God's work and were damaged by the same God's hidden, but just judgment. For the same God is the creator of the whole human being, and though one is a human being by nature to the praise of God, the same person is, nonetheless, a defective human being by nature, but by no means to the reproach of God.

(4) We know, therefore, that we should attribute to the creator, not defects, but natures, but one who wants to resist Mani must say where the defects come from. And it is quite easy to reply concerning the defects of other things which we say are created by God, but are by his most wise providence subject to his angels, whether good ones or even bad ones, that their seeds can also be damaged by those to whom they are subject, not only so that they become defective, but also so that they are conceived and born defective. The question concerns the human being, the rational animal, the image of God, whose nature would in no way become the plaything of the devil, whom we correctly believe to be the source of defects, if it was not by the just judgment of God on account of original sin.

(5) Finally, not even you yourselves, as far as I know, dare to say, though your teaching entails this terrible absurdity, that so many and such great natural defects would have come to be in paradise if, because no one sinned, that happiness of human nature in which our nature was created had lasted. But, when you deny original sin, you immediately cause the introduction of a nature which God did not create, and from the mixture with it there come the defects with which human beings are born. O you perverse heretics, you are the helpers of the Manichees and the slanderers of others with the name of the Manichees, and as for Catholics

who harmoniously speak against you the same truths, you contentiously accuse some, while you deceitfully fawn upon others.

Julian's Defense of the Book of Wisdom

124. JUL. (1) Perhaps the reader may now wonder how this testimony ought to be interpreted; this man who appropriated it for himself showed that it certainly does not have to do with inherited sin or with the view of the Manichees. After all, he said, "Of whomever wisdom is speaking, she is, of course, speaking of human beings,"[254] for if wisdom were speaking of natural sin, it would not have said this about certain beings, but about all of them. The position of the Manichees universally disparages the nature of all mortal beings, but the statement about which we are asking receives even from its kidnapper the testimony that it was uttered, not against all, but against some mortal beings.

(2) From this it is clear that the statement which by no means condemns all, but many, had nothing to do with inherited sin. Since, therefore, it has been shown that nothing from it points to that sacrilegious idea, let the soundness of this book be defended by the support of its author. He speaks to God: *You are merciful to all because you can do everything, and you overlook the sins of human beings on account of their repentance, for you love everything which exists, and you hate none of these things which you have made. For how could something last unless you willed it to? You, however, spare all because they are yours, Lord, who love souls. For your good spirit is in all; on this account you correct in part those who go astray and of those who sin you admonish and appeal to them that, having left aside their evil ways, they may believe in you, Lord* (Wis 11:24–12:2).

AUG. (1) How does God have mercy on all since another passage of scripture says: *Do not show mercy to all who work injustice* (Ps 59:6), unless because all human beings are also among those to whom he does not show mercy in the sense that all kinds of human beings are meant, just as scripture said, *You pay tithes for every vegetable* (Lk 11:42), that is, for every kind of vegetable. But how does it help you that the words of the Book of Wisdom did not speak about all human beings where it said that their malice was natural? After all, because it spoke of certain human beings, not of all of them, it did not compel us to think that no others were such, since the apostle says, *We too were once by nature children of anger, just as the rest* (Eph 2:3).

(2) It was not, however, nature, but grace that separated Israelites of that time, not, of course, all of them, but the devout, from these of whom scripture said, *Their malice was natural* (Wis 12:10), and on this account the devout were also called children of God. One must also examine how scripture said, *You love everything which exists* (Wis 11:25), since the wicked also exist, and elsewhere

scripture said, *You hate all who work injustice* (Ps 5:7). He loves them, then, insofar as they are human beings, but he hates them insofar as they are unjust. And he both condemns those who are unjust and makes them exist because they are human beings. For it said, *You hate none of those things which you made* (Wis 11:25). God, then, loves human beings so much that, even when they are unjust, he loves them insofar as they are human beings, though he hates them because they are unjust. And for this reason the unjust whom God hates are both human beings, because God loves his own work, and they are wretched because God loves justice.

Augustine's View Is Opposed to the Words from Wisdom

125. JUL. Do you see how inimical to your view is the gracious language of this author's praise for God? He says that God creates and loves souls, something which you deny when you swear that the souls of the innocents are under the power of the devil and are hateful to God, though they have nothing other than what they have received from their maker.

AUG. (1) According to you, then, whoever are born feebleminded receive even their feeblemindedness from God their maker, though scripture says that we should mourn for them more than for the dead.[255] But God, of course, loves even the souls of these in a certain manner, that is, so that they exist, so that they have sensory awareness, so that, though the keenness of their minds is dulled, they, nonetheless, surpass the animals. But that love of which scripture says, *God loves no one who does not dwell with wisdom* (Wis 7:28), is a different love. Tell us why God loves more the souls of the little ones to whom he provides the bath of rebirth in order to send them into his kingdom and why he does not offer this benefit to others, since no merits of their wills differentiate them, nor is there before God any favoritism,[256] as you often stupidly object to us.

(2) And yet, where scripture said, *You love souls* (Wis 11:27) and did not say: all souls, let there be no problem. Perhaps it was said that way in the sense that God creates all souls, but does not, nonetheless, love them all, but only those which he separates from the rest, not by their merits, but by the bountifulness of his grace, so that they dwell with wisdom. For *God loves no one who does not dwell with wisdom* (Wis 7:28). *The Lord, however, is the giver of wisdom* (Prv 2:6).

126. JUL. Your teaching which contains natural evil and wickedness which cannot[257] be changed also rejects the repentance which the Book of Wisdom says that God gives.

AUG. On the contrary, we say in opposition to you that God gives repentance too, because, though each person does penance by the will, the will is prepared by the Lord,[258] *and this change comes from the right hand of the Most High* (Ps

77:11), as the sacred psalm sings forth, and because the Lord looked at Peter in order that Peter might weep.[259] For this reason his fellow apostle said of some people, *Perhaps God will grant them repentance* (2 Tm 2:25). And when malice is said to be unchangeable, it is unchangeable for a human being who cannot change it, but not for God who can do all things.

127. JUL. But the fact that Wisdom taught that God admonishes sinners to abandon their malice and believe in him completely overthrows the theory of natural evil because it is certain that congenital characteristics cannot be left aside.

AUG. Congenital characteristics can be left aside, but only when the Almighty causes this in a human being. For corruption is also congenital to the body, though the body will, nonetheless, be incorruptible.

The Canaanites Were Not Punished for Original Sin

128. JUL. (1) Having on this basis explained God's patience and his most gentle providence by which he does not will the death of those who die but that they return and live,[260] the Book of Wisdom continues to prove what it had said by examples and makes mention of those who, by living very bad lives in the land of Canaan, had kindled the anger of the Almighty so that it threatened them with a most just punishment with the triumphs of the Israelites who were already living under the law of God. *For you hated those former inhabitants of your holy land because they did actions hateful to you through potions and unjust sacrifices and killed their children without mercy; you willed to destroy them by the hands of our parents in order that the latter might receive a dwelling place worthy of the children of God, which is the land more dear to you than all others* (Wis 12:3-7).

The author testifies to why God willed the seven nations to be destroyed, for after they were for the most part destroyed, the land of the promise was given to the Israelites. (2) In order that there might not seem to be in the one nature of human beings a distinction based on a favoritism in the eyes of God,[261] he teaches why the Canaanites deserved to be killed. *You*, therefore, *hated the former inhabitants of your holy land* (Wis 12:3), he said. Why? Surely according to you he ought to have added: Because they were begotten of a diabolical union, because they were owned by the prince of darkness, because Adam defiled all who would come from his line. But he says none of these.

But what reason does he give for his hatred? Only the actions they carried out by free will. *You hated them*, he says, *because they did actions hateful to you* (Wis 12:3). (3) But in order that we might know what these actions were and in order that you would not call these actions of the nations sexual desire, he continues with the kinds of action themselves: *Through potions and unjust sacrifices, and they killed their children without mercy* (Wis 4:5). That is, they performed magic rites and sacrifices which were unjust, when they were offered to idols, after the worship of the creator was abandoned. And to those sacrilegious rites they consigned their own kin; that is, they placated the demons by the monstrosity of killing their children. See, then, how the author does not speak of that sin which Mani made up, that is, the sin that clings to all mortals by their nature, for the author mentions that the Canaanites offended most of all in that they did not hold back from killing even their own little ones. The death of the children surely would not redound to the hatefulness of their killer, if on account of the one sin both the murderer and the child were displeasing to God.

AUG. (1) You say these things as if all human beings are punished on account of some one kind of sin or as if we say that those who are already living adult lives are children of anger[262] on account of original sin alone. *Those who do not believe in the Son*, as the Son himself says, *will not have life, but the anger of God will remain over them* (Jn 3:56). But some over whom the anger of God will indeed remain are worse than others, and yet not all are struck down and destroyed like these people we are dealing with, who owned the land which was given to the Israelites.

Why is it that you say: "See, then, how he does not speak of that sin which Mani made up"? (2) Here you want people to understand original sin, a sin which Mani did not make up; rather, like the other Catholics, Ambrose defended it both against you and against Mani. For original sin is not the mixture with an alien nature which Mani introduces; rather, it is the worsening of our nature because of the sin which entered the world through one man and which was passed on to all human beings,[263] the sin which you deny in opposition to the Catholic faith.

Are you so blind that you do not see that, if original sin does not exist because it is not mentioned here, the other sins which are not mentioned here will not exist either, whether smaller or greater than these? Did the Sodomites escape destruction because scripture did not say of them that they practiced magic and offered sacrifices of their own children? (3) Or did these Canaanites escape destruction because scripture did not say of them that their men did not commit shameful acts with other men? Scripture is not, nonetheless, silent about their malice being natural; this malice is found in all human beings, but is less in some and greater in others, just as the bodies of all are corruptible, but weigh down some souls less and others more[264] in accord with the different judgments of God, which are, of course, hidden, but undoubtedly just.

Why, then, is it surprising if, when scripture explains the reason why such punishment came upon them, it mentions not only their voluntary malice, but also their natural malice? Besides the common infection of the human race, something more had been added to this natural malice as a result of the prophet's curse. For the saintly Noah cursed his nephew, Canaan, their ancestor,[265] not unjustly, of course, but so that the people were subject to it in his offspring in the succeeding generations. (4) This is also clear in their little ones who were destroyed along with their parents—and this by God's order—without exempting any age,[266] because the adults displeased God especially through their custom of offering the blood of their little ones to demons. Nor did God command that the same little ones be spared; on the contrary, he commanded that they not be spared at all. From this understand the words: *the seed accursed from the beginning* (Wis 12:11), for you will not dare to call him unjust who commanded this.

(5) If this had come to your mind, you would not have separated the innocence of the children from their impious parents on the grounds that their parents "offended God most of all in that they did not hold back from killing even their own little ones. The death of the children surely," you say, "would not redound to the hatefulness of their killer, if on account of the one sin both the murderer and the child were displeasing to God." Nor do you see that the killers of their children were displeasing God so that he commanded that those same children also be killed along with them. Nor is it the case that, because those parents most wickedly sacrificed even their children to demons, those same children ought not to have likewise perished, like the cursed seed, as did happen, not by a human outrage, but by God's judgment which is, of course, just, though hidden. You do not pay attention to this, when you are carried off by eloquence without wisdom, and you wish to be eloquent with a river of nonsense, while you are abandoned by the light of the truth.[267]

The Canaanites Sinned by Imitating Ham

129. JUL. (1) *But you have*, the Book of Wisdom says, *spared even these as human beings, and sent wasps preceding your army, not because you were unable to subject the impious to the righteous in battle, but because by judging them gradually you gave them time to repent* (Wis 12:8-9). By the stings of insects, it says, you goaded on even those sacrilegious persons so that they might take notice of the power of him who punishes them from the playfulness of his penalty. But after the sins, whose rejection was hoped for and sought, were shown to be voluntary through God's plan and the kind of punishment, then the invective of the writer turns against the stubborn profanity of those who were punished, and he says that they became so familiar with grave sins that they seemed as though they were somehow inborn. (2) He says, *Not unaware that their nation was most wicked and that their malice was natural, and that their knowledge could never change, for their seed was cursed from the beginning. Though you did not fear anyone, you gave pardon to their sins* (Wis 12:10-11).

When, he says, you so kindly and so patiently granted them a time for repentance and offered them a ray of hope in the warning so that you defended your justice and mercy from all disparagement and from every suspicion of cruelty, they, nonetheless, spurned your admonitions, just as they scorned the blessing you previously sent them, as if they wanted to prove that they were descendants of that Ham against whom blessed Noah had hurled curses by his paternal judgment, after his nakedness was mocked. (3) Why, then, is it surprising if the writer called to mind their ancestor who[268] was punished by the severity of this sentence because of the merit of his wickedness in order to mark his descendants who continue to emulate him, for in the law imitation is also frequently blamed in terms for the relationship of descendants?

In that way, of course, the Lord said to the Jews in the gospel: *You are from your father, the devil* (Jn 8:44). And Daniel, we read, attacked in that manner the immoral elders, though they stemmed from the tribe of Israel; he said, *Seed of Canaan, not of Judah* (Dn 13:56). Ezekiel, the prophet, also upbraided the people of Jerusalem; he said, *Your mother was a Hittite, and your father an Amorite* (Ez 16:45).[269] This usage, then, means that the disgrace of their family is added to the hatefulness of their will, and the will is shown to cling too much to the sin by the merit of which even the seeds suffer reproaches. (4) But this same custom is also observed with respect to good things, as when a person who is seen to be good in every respect is said to blossom with natural virtues. For this reason blessed Job stated that he drew from the breasts of his mother the inclination toward mercy by which he helped the needy. (1) In fact he stated that it came with him out of his mother's womb.[270] A likeness or an exaggeration or an ambiguous expression cannot, then, be prejudicial to clear issues. For, since it is certain that mortals are never asked to correct natural elements, but that God commands that human beings cease doing evil, it is shown to be truer than true that there cannot be any natural sin.

AUG. (1) You thought, of course, that you had explained the words of the Book of Wisdom, but you are not permitted to escape from them by words of folly. For it is obvious enough, and it is clear in what sense that nation was called most wicked and its malice natural and in what sense it was also called the seed cursed from the beginning. For if, as you think, it was said on account of the emulation, that is, the imitation by which they imitated their ancestor, Ham, whom his father, Noah, cursed as a punishment for his sin, then, when God brought a perfectly just penalty upon this nation, he would certainly have commanded that its little ones be spared, since you cannot say that they merited punishment by imitation of their ancestors. (2) Since, then, he not only did not command that they should be shown mercy, but he himself even commanded that they should receive the same punishment as their parents, though he could not, of course, command anything unjust, it is clear enough that their malice was said to be natural and that they were even called the seed cursed from the beginning, not on account of an exaggeration, not on account of imitation, but on account of generation.

For the prophet's authority was on guard against your error in the case of this very seed which is under discussion so that the righteous Noah cursed his sinful son, Ham, in Ham's son, that is, in Canaan.[271] He did this so that we would understand from it that children are bound by the sins of their parents unless this bond contracted by birth is removed by rebirth. (3) From this Canaan, then, the Canaanites took their origin who were called the seed cursed from the beginning, and God commanded that their little ones be killed along with their parents, since the little ones were themselves this same seed, not by imitation, but by line of descent.

Daniel, the prophet, wanted us to understand that the shameless elders were like these Canaanites, when he said to them, *Seed of Canaan, not of Judah* (Dn 13:56), as if he said: You are like the children of Canaan, not like the children of Israel. In the same way it was said, *Generation of vipers!* (Mt 3:7), on account of a certain likeness to the malice of vipers. But where the Lord said, *You are from your father, the devil* (Jn 8:44), he really wanted us to understand imitation, not the seed, nor did he say: You are the seed of the devil. And where scripture says, *Your father is an Amorite, and your mother a Hittite* (Ez 16:3), it is clear that scripture said this, because those to whom this was said imitated those people. Nor, finally, did scripture say there: Seed of the Amorites or Hittites. (4) It is not, therefore, as you said: On account of the merit of a will that clings too much to sins "even the seeds suffer reproaches." Heaven forbid, after all, that scripture should blame offspring which do not deserve it, as you blame human beings who do not deserve it.

But where the saintly Job says, as you mention, that the inclination toward mercy "came with him out from his mother's womb" and you think that he said this in order to praise this inclination much, not because this was the case, why, I ask you, do we not agree that some people are merciful by nature, if we do not deny that some others are cruel by nature? For there are some natural factors which begin to appear at the age when there the use of reason begins, as is the case with reason itself. (5) Accordingly, human beings who are by nature children of anger are given commandments about how to live, because grace is also given so that the one who commands also helps us, and in that way we conquer not only evils which are added by the will, but also those which are born with us. For what is impossible for human beings is easy for God.[272] But when the law comes, those become transgressors, not righteous, to whom the grace of God is not given. On this account scripture says, *For who sets you apart? What do you have that you have not received?* (1 Cor 4:7). But these also live for the benefit of the children of mercy so that, when they see those others and understand what has been given to themselves by grace, not by merit, they may not be filled with pride, but those who boast may boast in the Lord.[273]

The Book of Wisdom Upholds God's Justice

130. JUL. The Book of Wisdom continues: *Who will blame you if the nations which you have made perish, since there is no God other than you who has care for all? But since you are just, you arrange all things justly. Also, to condemn a person who ought not to be punished you consider foreign to your power, for your power is the beginning of justice* (Wis 12:12.13.15). It certainly supports the argument of the wise that the greatest attribute in God is justice, which Mani and the traducianist absolutely deny with every effort of their myths.

AUG. To whom shall I compare you in offering insults except to yourself? But if you understood that God was just, you would never attribute congenital defects either of the human body or of the mind, defects which you cannot deny, to the work of God, but to his judgment, and for this reason you would understand original sin or sins, not deny them.

131. JUL. Finally, after a little it continues: *For by chastising them, you have made your children to be of good hope, because in judging you give room for repentance over their sins. For if you have set free the enemies of your servants, even those deserving death, with so great a torment by way of warning, allowing time and place for their malice to change, with what great care do you judge your children, to whose parents you gave both the oaths and covenants containing your good promises? When, therefore, you administer discipline to us, you scourge our enemies many times so that we may bear in mind your goodness when you judge* (Wis 12:19-21).

AUG. Why God, though he has foreknowledge of all that will be, gave time and place for their malice to change, even to those of whom scripture said that their thought could never change, is revealed clearly enough where it says, *You have made your children to be of good hope, because in judging you give room for repentance over their sins* (Wis 12:19). A time and a place for repentance, then, is given even to the children of anger who are destined for death and who will not do penance, for there are among them or there will come to be from them children of mercy who will benefit from that from which those others did not benefit. And so, the patience of God is not pointless and fruitless, even toward the children of perdition. For it necessarily benefits those who are set apart from the mass of perdition not by human merits, but by the grace of God, when they either give thanks that by God's mercy they are set apart from them or are born from parents destined to perish, though by God's providence they themselves are not destined to perish

The Cursed Seed and the Children of God

132. JUL. You see, then, the great distinction that the surface meaning of the words made concerning the natures of the two peoples. It calls the Israelites the children of God and the Canaanites the cursed seed. If this literal meaning referred to generations and births, one would have to say that religious people are generated in one way and the irreligious in another.

AUG. Because we understand grace when we hear "children of God," are we supposed not to understand and to acknowledge nature when we hear "children of human beings"? What is it, then, that you are saying, you contentious fellow, for you do not find anything to say? Recognize what is true; pay attention to what is clear. The Canaanites are called the cursed seed because they were offspring so bad that, under God who is most just in punishing and giving commands, not even their little ones were spared who had not followed after their parents by any voluntary imitation. But the Israelites are called the children of God, not because they were offspring by nature, but because they were adopted by grace. Whether, then, they are both called children or both called seed, how does this sameness of the names help you where there is so great a difference in the realities?

There Is No Transmission of the First Sin

133. JUL. It would, nonetheless, be established that, even according to this foolish idea, there is no transmission of the first sin, for the seeds of the many nations at the same time clearly teach that it was interrupted.

AUG. The seed of that one man, the seed which is all human beings, is one thing; something quite different is the different seeds of the different nations which do not interrupt the former seed, because they are all descended from him. Nor by their variety do they bring it about that the sin of the first man by which human nature deserved to be changed is injurious to any of his descendants born long afterwards, but that it is more or less harmless. For, just as certain parents made original sin worse, so others lessen it, but no one takes it away except that one of whom it was said, *There is the lamb of God; there is the one who takes away the sins of the world* (Jn 1:29), for whom no good of a human being is impossible and no evil is incurable.

Natural Malice Does Not Point to Defective Seeds

134. JUL. But, just as that which is said concerning the praise of the Jews does not mean that any of them should be believed to be resplendent with inborn holiness, so too that which is called natural malice does not mean to teach that

the seeds are defective, but without prejudice to the nature whose essence is unchangeable, which obtains whatever it has from God its author, this variation in
the choice of words marks either an intent to attack or a duty to praise.

AUG. (1) If no one of them has inborn holiness, how did God say to Jeremiah: *Before you came forth from the womb, I made you holy* (Jer 1:5)? How was it said of John
the Baptist, *He will already be filled with the Holy Spirit from the womb of his mother*
(Lk 1:15)? This was also shown by his rejoicing when Mary, pregnant and virgin,
greeted Elizabeth, pregnant and married.[274] Or were these words also spoken, not to
proclaim the facts, but out of a duty to praise? Go ahead; be so foolish; it remains for
your madness to say this. After all, why do we set Jeremiah or John before your face
swollen as it is with pride, when you do not distinguish Christ himself from sinful
flesh? For, when you say that no flesh is sinful from its origin, you make him equal to
the rest so that you are forced to deny that even he had inborn holiness, though he was
born of the Holy Spirit and the Virgin Mary, utterly free from any sin, because he was
free from that conception which results from sexual union.[275]

(2) Even[276] Jeremiah and John, though they were made holy in the wombs of
their mothers, still contracted original sin. After all, by what other merit would
their souls have perished from their people if they were not circumcised on the
eighth day,[277] that is, if they did not come to the grace of Christ? For that circumcision of the flesh symbolized that he would rise on the eighth day, that is, after
the seventh day of the Sabbath, on account of our justification. They were, then,
both by nature children of anger from the wombs of their mothers and children of
grace from the wombs of their mothers. For they did not as yet have that holiness
which would remove the bond of the succession of guilty generations which had
to be removed in its own time, and yet they had that holiness which marked them
as heralds of Christ from their mothers' wombs.

(3) But you, a new heretic, want to be considered a religious professor of
physics when you say that malice is said to be natural and that the seed is said to
be cursed without prejudice to the nature whose unchangeable essence has obtained whatever it has from God its author. Do not those at least who are born
feebleminded warn you to be reasonable? Still, not even the feebleminded themselves dare to say that God is the author of their feeblemindedness. Nor, of
course, has a mingling with a foreign nature, as Mani foolishly and insanely
thought, introduced this defect, but the worsening of our own nature. Those
whose faith is healthy, therefore, find nothing that merits this defect and any
other natural defects except original sin.

Elsewhere the Seed Is Said to Be Blessed by God

135. JUL. Just as the seed is said here to be cursed, so elsewhere the seed is indeed said to be blessed, where the authority of the passage is greater. The

prophet Isaiah speaking about the Israelites said, *They will build houses, and they themselves will dwell in them. They will cultivate vineyards, and they themselves will eat their fruits. They will not build, and others dwell there. They will not cultivate, and others eat. For the days of my people shall be according to the days of the tree of life; the works of their labors*[278] *will last; my chosen ones will not labor in vain, nor will they beget children in a curse, because their seed is blessed by God* (Is 65:21-23).

AUG. (1) If you understood this prophecy of Isaiah, you would not set it before us so that you might escape, but set it, rather, before yourself so that you might be corrected. For you would see another seed, not mortal, but immortal, and not carnal, but spiritual, the seed which John the Evangelist saw when he said, *All those who are born of God do not sin because his seed remains in them* (1 Jn 3:9). According to this seed no one sins, because, even if one sins as a human being, one has, nonetheless, another seed according to which one cannot sin, because one is born of God. According to this seed children are not begotten in a curse. At these words of the prophet you ought to have been alert and noticed that this would not have been promised to the people of God as a great gift unless children were begotten in a curse according to the other seed which comes from Adam. But they are not begotten in a curse according to Christ because he is the seed blessed from the beginning. (2) For he is the Wisdom of God of which it was said, *It is the tree of life for all who embrace it* (Prv 3:18). For this reason this prophet, or rather God through the prophet, also said: *The days of my people will be according to the days of the tree of life* (Is 65:22). These words promise eternal and immortal life, not to the carnal, but to the spiritual Israelites. Since in that life the cultivators and builders will not die at some time, spiritual vineyards and houses will not be owned by others, but by their cultivators and their builders themselves who will live forever. Recognize, then, the two kinds of seeds, one for birth, the other for rebirth, and do not be unbelieving, but believing.[279]

The Consistency and Rationality of the Catholic Faith

136. JUL. Let the little boys face the problem of the differences between these words so that, as capable of nothing greater than their sounds, they quarrel over little words[280] which really refer to each other. But the Catholic faith believes that the law of God does not argue against itself, nor does it admit any authority destructive of reason. It does not listen to any opinion or flattery that would sully divine justice. But as it not only believes, but also knows that God is the creator of all natures, it at the same time ascribes sin to nothing but the free will. For all these reasons it has no doubt that the inheritance of sin is false.

AUG. (1) The Catholic faith, rather, does not doubt that there is original sin, and not little boys, but serious and solid men, who were taught in the Church and have taught the Church, defended this faith up to the day of their death. You people, however, do not believe that the law of God argues, as you say, against itself, and you argue against it with blind impiety or impious blindness. For you boast that you admit no authority destructive of reason so that by your reasons, which are not reasons, but deceptions, the authority of God might be destroyed rather than explained. And yet no one ought to be so dense at heart as to be deceived by the reason of Pelagius which he produced, as if he were explaining the apostle. He said, "*The body is dead on account of sin* (Rom 8:10), was said because the body dies to sins when it turns away from sins."[281]

(2) Against this nonsense one should not argue, but listen to the apostle himself who says, *But if Christ is in you, the body is indeed dead on account of sin, but the spirit is life on account of righteousness. But if the Spirit of him who raised up Jesus from the dead dwells in you, he will bring to life even your mortal bodies by his Spirit dwelling in you* (Rom 8:10-11). What could be more obvious? What could be more clear? Who, I ask, would deny original sin in the face of this clear statement but a mad heretic? On account of this sin the body is, of course, even now dead, though the spirit is life on account of righteousness. But God *will bring to life*, he says, *even your mortal bodies* (Rom 8:11). Who would bark against this truth except a rabid fool who boasts that he "does not listen to any opinion or flattery that would sully divine justice," though whoever has been deceived by you is, rather, forced to deny divine justice? Since there are so many defects either of bodies or of minds with which human beings are born, if they are said not to contract any merit of sin, the justice of God's judgment is undoubtedly denied. And so, when you ascribe sins to the will in such a way that you refuse to ascribe original sin to the will of the first human being, you force those who believe you to ascribe all the evils which infants contract or suffer to the unjust judgment of God.

Notes

1. See Heb 11:12.
2. I have followed the conjecture in the NBA edition of "*sensui*" instead of "*sensus.*"
3. See Rom 5:12.
4. Julian dealt with the interpretation of Romans 5:12 in the second book, but dealt with Hebrews 11:12 only in the third book.
5. See III, 84-95.
6. I have followed the suggestion in the NBA edition in reading "*sic*" instead of "*si.*"
7. See I, 122, for Julian's claim that without omnipotence and absolute justice God would not be God.
8. See Sir 40:1.
9. Augustine replied to the four books of Julian's *To Turbantius* in the six books of his *Answer to Julian*, a work which Julian seems never to have seen.
10. Augustine wrote the first book of *Marriage and Desire* on the basis of complaints he received from Valerius about Julian's teaching; he wrote the second book of that work after having received excerpts from it which were made by someone other than Julian.
11. *Marriage and Desire* II, 4, 12.
12. Julian, *To Turbantius.*

13. Julian, *To Turbantius*; see *Marriage and Desire* II, 4, 12, where Augustine cites these words from the excerpts from Julian's work.

14. Julian, *To Turbantius*; see *Marriage and Desire* II, 4, 12, where Augustine again cites from the excerpts made from Julian's work.

15. *Marriage and Desire* II, 4, 13.

16. *Marriage and Desire* II, 4, 13.

17. See 1 Jn 2:16.

18. *Marriage and Desire* II, 5, 14.

19. Since Julian replied to the first book of *Marriage and Desire* with the four books of *To Turbantius* and replied to the second book of *Marriage and Desire* with eight books, Augustine suggests that Julian may reply to the first book of the six books of his *Answer to Julian* with sixteen books.

20. Augustine cites this sentence from the excerpts from Julian's *To Turbantius* in *Marriage and Desire* II, 5, 15.

21. Julian, *To Turbantius*.

22. See Augustine, *Heresies* XXXVIII, XLIX, and LIV. The Novatians followed the Roman priest, Novatus, in denying reconciliation to those who had fallen away during the persecution. The Arians were followers of the Alexandrian priest, Arius, and the Eunomians, also called Aetians, were followers of Eunomius of Cappadocia, Aetius' disciple. Both heresies denied the equality of the Son and Holy Spirit with the Father. Augustine obviously means by "the whole creed" a pre-Nicean form of the creed, that is, the Apostles' Creed.

23. See Col 1:13.

24. See Ps 113:3.

25. See Jb 14:4 LXX.

26. See Phil 2:13.

27. Julian, *To Turbantius*; the passage is cited from the excerpts from Julian's work in *Marriage and Desire* II, 4, 12.

28. The PL, BAC, and NBA editions treat this sentence as part of the previous quotation, but Julian is referring to Augustine's praise in *Marriage and Desire* II, 4, 13.

29. See Gal 5:17.

30. Julian, *To Turbantius*; see *Marriage and Desire* II, 4, 13, where Augustine cites this passage as he had it from the excerpts.

31. Julian, *To Turbantius*; also cited in *Marriage and Desire* II, 4, 13

32. See Gn 2:25 and 3:7.

33. See Gal 5:17.

34. I have followed the reading "*dicit*" found in one manuscript instead of "*didicit*" which is found in Migne.

35. See Ambrose, *Commentary on the Gospel of Luke* (*Expositio Euangelii secundum Lucam*) 7, 141: CCL 14, 263.

36. The Symplegades were the rocks at the mouth of the Black Sea which were said to close upon and crush any ship sailing between them.

37. See Rom 8:3.

38. See 1 Jn 2:16.

39. *Marriage and Desire* II, 5, 14.

40. See *Marriage and Desire* II, 4, 13.

41. See III, 162-187.

42. See 1 Jn 2:16.

43. *Marriage and Desire* II, 5, 14.

44. See Gal 5:17.

45. See 1 Tm 4:4.

46. See 1 Jn 2:16.

47. See 1 Jn 2:15.

48. See Ambrose, *Commentary on the Gospel of Luke* (*Expositio Euangelii secundum Lucam*) 7, 141: CCL 14, 263.

49. I have conjectured "*manum conseramus*" instead of "*manum construamus.*"

50. Julian refers to his *To Turbantius*.

51. I have conjectured *"spem"* which is found in the manuscripts, instead of *"speciem."*

52. Augustine refers to his *Answer to Julian*.

53. See Gn 3:7.

54. See Gal 5:17.

55. The NBA edition suggests *"immorantes*, those who dally" instead of *"immorientes* , those who die."

56. See 1 Cor 7:6.

57. I have followed the conjecture in the NBA edition of *"nominibus"* instead of *"hominibus"* and have also conjectured *"cum"* in place of *"cur."*

58. Julian, *To Turbantius*, as cited in *Marriage and Desire* II, 9, 22.

59. See Rom 7:23.

60. *Marriage and Desire* II, 9, 22.

61. See *Answer to Julian* V, 3, 10.

62. Augustine puns on *"disertum*, eloquent" and *"desertum*, abandoned" as well as on *"liberet*, would want" and, in the next sentence, *"libere*, freely."

63. See Ps 94:1.

64. See Is 45:7.

65. See Sir 34:33.

66. See 1 Kgs 22.

67. See Rom 7:23.

68. See Gn 2:5.

69. See Wis 1:13.

70. See Dn 13:32.

71. See Gn 3:21.

72. See Gn 2:25.

73. See Gn 3:7 and 21.

74. Julian's first work is his *To Turbantius* which Augustine refuted in the six books of his *Answer to Julian*, Augustine did not cite Julian's work extensively as he does in the present work; hence, one has to infer what Julian said from what Augustine cited in book four of *Answer to Julian*.

75. See Vergil, *Georgics* III, 248 and 266.

76. See Vergil, *Georgics* II, 324-331. Julian's text of Vergil has *"herbae"* where modern editions have *"terrae."*

77. Julian alludes to the standard of Roman troops from the time of Trajan, namely, a lance with a leather snake attached.

78. I have followed the conjecture of the NBA edition of *"homine"* instead of *"homines."*

79. See Ps 49:13.

80. See Gal 5:17.

81. See 1 Jn 2:16.

82. See Gn 2:25 and 3:7.

83. The Latin for "genitals" is *"pudenda"* which is literally "shameful parts." Hence, Augustine is saying that the pudenda were not pudenda before the sin.

84. I have followed the conjecture of *"voluptatem"* suggested in the NBA edition instead of *"voluntatem."*

85. I have conjectured *"autumemus"* instead of *"autem."*

86. See Ambrose, *Commentary on the Gospel of Luke* (*Expositio Euangelii secundum Lucam*) 7, 141: CCL 14, 263.

87. Cicero, *Duties* (*De officiis*) I, 128.

88. The works of Cornelius Nepos (100-25 B.C.) have for the most part perished. Crates, the Greek philosopher mentioned, held a doctrine that combined Stoicism and Cynicism. See Diogenes Laertius, *The Lives and Sayings of the Philosophers* (*Vita et placita philosophorum*), VI, 85.

89. Julian, *To Turbantius*, as cited in *Marriage and Desire* II, 9, 22.

90. See *The Deeds of Pelagius* 11, 23-24.

91. I have followed the conjecture in the NBA edition of *"postremo"* instead of *"postrema."*

92. See Jn 21:7.

93. See Rom 7:23.

94. See Gal 5:17.

95. See Gn 2:25.

96. I have conjectured *"uerenda"* instead of *"uera."*

97. See Gn 3:7.

98. See Gn 2:25 and 3:7.

99. See 1 Jn 2:16.

100. *Marriage and Desire* II, 5, 14.

101. See 1 Jn 2:16.

102. See *Heresies* LV. Apollinaris of Laodicea, a theologian of the fourth century, denied that in the incarnation the Word assumed a human soul.

103. Though we normally translate the expression as "to lay down my life," the Latin says quite literally "my soul."

104. Augustine refers to the *Anacephalaiosis*, a little work attributed to Epiphanius of Salamis (315-403), which Augustine used as a source for his *Heresies*. Augustine did not know Epiphanius' large work on heresies, *Panarion* See *Heresies* LV, where Augustine provided much the same information as here on the Apollinarists.

105. See Rom 7:24.

106. See Rom 8:3.

107. See Rom 1:3.

108. See Gal 4:4.

109. See 1 Pt 2:12.22.

110. I have conjectured *"et si"* instead of *"et."*

111. Julian claims to have shown in the third book of *To Turbantius* that, given Augustine's teaching on original sin, Christ too must have contracted it; Augustine replied in the fifth book of his *Answer to Julian*. For Julian's accusations and Augustine's reply, see *Answer to Julian* V, 15, 52.

112. See Is 7:14.

113. See Acts 2:22.

114. See 1 Cor 1:18.

115. See Dan 9:24.

116. Ambrose, *Commentary on Isaiah The Prophet* (*Expositio in Isaiam prophetam*) . Only a few fragments of this work remain in passages cited by Augustine; see *Fragmenta in Isaiam* CCL 14, 405.

117. See *Marriage and Desire* I, 35, 40.

118. See *Marriage and Desire* II, 5, 14-15.

119. Ambrose, *Commentary on Isaiah the Prophet* (*Expositio in Isaiam prophetam*). This passage is also cited in *Marriage and Concupiscence* I, 35, 40 and II, 5, 15.

120. See Ambrose, *Commentary on the Gospel of Luke* (*Expositio Euangelii secundum Lucam*) 7, 141: CCL 14, 263.

121. See Gal 5:16.

122. See Rom 8:3.

123. See Gn 2:25.

124. See Ambrose, *Commentary on the Gospel of Luke* (*Expositio Euangelii secundum Lucam*) 7, 141: CCL 14, 263.

125. *Marriage and Desire* II, 7, 17, with slight changes.

126. See 1 Cor 12:23.

127. See Gn 2:25-3:7.

128. 1 Jn 2:16.

129. See Wis 9:15.

130. See Gal 5:17.

131. See Ambrose, *Commentary on the Gospel of Luke* (*Expositio Euangelii secundum Lucam*) 7, 141: CCL 14, 263.

132. See Pelagius, *In Defense of Free Choice* (*Pro libero arbitrio, 3*; see *The Grace of Christ and Original Sin* I, 43, 47, where Augustine cites Pelagius' words for the first time.

133. See 1 Jn 2:16.

134. Ambrose, *Commentary on the Gospel of Luke* (*Expositio Euangelii secundum Lucam*) 7, 234: CCL 14, 295.

135. See Lk 19:10.

136. See *Answer to Julian* I, 3, 5-6, 28, where Augustine musters texts from these and other Fathers of the Church; also see above, I, 52, where Augustine presents an abbreviated set of texts from these authors.

137. See Mt 1:21.

138. I have conjectured "*amens*" in place of "*tamen*" and changed the punctuation of the rest of the sentence.

139. See Acts 26:14.

140. See Ambrose, *Commentary on Isaiah The Prophet* (*Expositio in Isaiam prophetam*) 1: CCL 14, 405.

141. See Wis 9:15.

142. See Sir 22:10.

143. See Mt 8:32.

144. See Heb 7:9-10.

145. See 1 Jn 2:16.

146. *Marriage and Desire* II, 5, 14.

147. See 1 Jn 2:16.

148. See Jn 12:31, 14:30, and 16:11.

149. See Col 1:13.

150. *Marriage and Desire* II, 5, 14, with slight changes.

151. See Job 14:4 LXX.

152. Augustine's text has the future "*inveniet*" while Julian's has the present "*invenit.*"

153. See Mt 4:1-11.

154. See Mt 22:15-22.

155. See Rom 1:3.

156. See Jn 1:14.

157. See 1 Pt 2:22.

158. I have conjectured "*reformatur*" in place of "*formatur.*"

159. I have followed the conjecture in the NBA edition of "*argueret*" in place of "*urgeret.*"

160. See Terence, *The Girl from Andros* (*Andria*) 309; in his reply Augustine quotes the verse exactly.

161. See 1 Pt 2:22.

162. Terence, *The Girl from Andros* (*Andria*) 309.

163. See Jerome, *Dialogue in Answer to the Pelagians* (*Dialogus contra Pelagianos*) III, 2: CCL 80, 99, where Jerome says, "In the Gospel according to the Hebrews, which is written in the Chaldaic and Syriac language, but in Hebrew letters, which the Nazarenes use up to the present day . . . the narrative recounts: And, behold, the mother of the Lord and his brothers said to him: John the Baptist is baptizing for the forgiveness of sins; let us go and be baptized by him." The text, however, has Jesus answer: "How have I sinned that I should go and be baptized by him?"

164. See Jerome, *Dialogue in Answer to the Pelagians* (*Dialogus contra Pelagianos*) II, 17: CCL 80, 75-76, where Jerome says that Jesus denied that he was going to Jerusalem and then went, though, as Augustine points out, Julian did not provide Jerome's words.

165. Augustine's letter to Alexandria, perhaps to Cyril of Alexandria, from whom he received in 417 a copy of the Acts of the Synod of Diospolis, is not extant.

166. Pelagius wrote his *In Defense of Free Choice* (*Pro libero arbitrio*) in reply to Jerome's work.

167. I have followed the conjecture in the NBA edition of "*inde me*" in place of "*idem.*"

168. See *Marriage and Desire* I, 35, 40 and II, 5, 15.

169. See Ambrose, *Commentary on Isaiah The Prophet (Expositio in Isaiam prophetam)*: CLL 14, 40, 405.

170. See Dan 9:24.

171. See *The Grace of Christ and Original Sin* I, 46, 47.

172. *Marriage and Desire* II, 5, 15. Julian goes on to complain that Augustine has omitted part of his argument as the text itself makes clear.

173. Julian, *To Turbantius.*

174. *Marriage and Desire* II, 5, 15.

175. *Marriage and Desire* II, 5, 15, with the quotation from Romans abbreviated.

176. After receiving Julian's *To Turbantius*, Augustine wrote his reply in the six books of his *Answer to Julian.*

177. Ambrose, *Commentary on the Gospel of Luke (Expositio Euangelii secundum Lucam)* 7, 141: CCL 14, 263.

178. Julian, *To Turbantius.*

179. *Marriage and Desire* II, 5, 15; see above 90, where Julian cites more fully from this paragraph.

180. The preposition *"sine,* without" takes the ablative case, while the preposition *"per* through" takes the accusative case.

181. Augustine puns on *"casibus,* cases" and *"cassibus,* spider webs."

182. This passage attributed to Hilary of Poitiers is cited in *Answer to Julian* I, 5, 10 and below in VI, 33. See Jean Doignon, " 'Testimonia' d'Hilaire de Poitiers dans le 'Contra Iulianum' d'Augustin: Les testes, leur groupement, leur 'lecture,' " *Revue Bénédictine* 91 (1981) 7-19, where the author argues that the passage is a composite from Hilary's *Trinity (De trinitate)* 10, 24-25 and his *Commentary on Matthew (Commentarium in Matthaeum)* 10, 23-24.

183. Ambrose, *Penance (De poenitentia)* I, 3, 13: SC 179, 64.

184. The sentence involves multiple plays on words; for example, "decline" means both to run through the cases of a noun and to avoid. The word for "removed," namely, *"ablatus,"* is tied to the ablative case.

185. Augustine continues the play on the words: *"praepositiones,* prepositions" and *"praeponis,* set before," and *"deposita,* set aside," as well as *"elatione,* pride" and *"ablatus* removed" and *"ablativum,* the case."

186. Julian attributes to Augustine statements which he did not make, at least in these precise words.

187. Augustine plays upon *"acumina,* cleverness" and *"lumina,* eyes" as well as on *"acumina"* and *"aciem,* keeness."

188. Again Augustine plays on the words: *"attendere quid dicas"* and *"contendere ut contradicas."*

189. See Lactantius, *The Divine Institutes (Divinae Institutiones)* 3, 23; Anaxagoras of Clazomene was a pre-Socratic philosopher.

190. See Phil 1:23.

191. *Marriage and Desire* II, 5, 15.

192. See above II, 178; for Augustine's words to Marcellinus, see *The Punishment and Forgiveness of Sins* I, 10, 11 and III, 7, 14.

193. I have followed the conjecture in the NBA edition of *"acceptam"* instead of *"acceptum."*

194. See III, 172, where Julian cites the letter of Mani to his daughter Menoch.

195. See *The Punishment and Forgiveness of Sins* I, 11, 13.

196. Bacchus was the god of wine. Julian speaks of "orgies" and *"thyrsi"* which were wands carried by worshipers of Bacchus.

197. *Marriage and Desire* II, 5, 15, with minor changes.

198. Ambrose, *Commentary on the Gospel of Luke (Expositio Euangelii secundum Lucam)* 4, 67: CCL 14, 131.

199. Ambrose, *Commentary on the Gospel of Luke* (*Expositio Euangelii secundum Lucam*) 7, 234: CCL 14, 295.

200. See Lk 19:10.

201. Julian, *To Turbantius.*

202. *Marriage and Desire* II, 5, 15.

203. Ibid.

204. See Pelagius, *In Defense of Free Choice* (*Pro libero arbitrio*) 3; see *The Grace of Christ and Original Sin* I, 43, 47.

205. See Ps 116:11.

206. Ambrose, *Commentary on Isaiah The Prophet* (*Expositio in Isaiam prophetam*) 1: CCL 14, 405.

207. *Marriage and Desire* II, 5, 15, though with an omission.

208. I have followed the reading of one manuscript of "*aliud agere*" instead of "*agere.*"

209. Julian means *The Letter of Mani known as "The Foundation"* which was addressed to Patticus and against which Augustine wrote *Answer to the Letter of Mani; known as "The Foundation."* See III, 186.

210. See III, 172, where Julian cites the letter of Mani to Menoch.

211. See Ambrose, *Commentary on the Gospel of Luke* (*Expositio Euangelii secundum Lucam*) 7, 141: CCL 14, 263.

212. See above 106.

213. Ambrose, *Isaac and the Soul* (*De Isaac et anima*) 7, 60:CSEL 32/1, 685.

214. Julian, *To Turbantius*; see *Answer to Julian* I, 9, 43-44 and VI, 21, 66, where Augustine cites the same sentence.

215. Augustine wrote *Nature and Grace* for Timasius and James, two former disciples of Pelagius who were first won over to Augustine's teaching. They supplied Augustine with a copy of Pelagius' work, *Nature.*

216. See *Nature and Grace* 61, 71.

217. See Ps 1:4.

218. See Gal 5:17.

219. See Ambrose, *Commentary on the Gospel of Luke* (*Expositio Euangelii secundum Lucam*) 7, 141: CCL 14, 263.

220. See Ambrose, *Commentary on Isaiah The Prophet* (*Expositio in Isaiam prophetam*) 1: CCL 14, 405.

221. Virgil, *Eclogues* 1, 59.

222. There seems to be an omission; perhaps one should add: "and if there is no will in a little one, but that there is no sin in a nature."

223. The Academic skeptics were Plato's successors in the Academy; in his early work, *Answer to the Skeptics*, Augustine refuted their claims and suggested that they in fact were concealing their true teaching.

224. Again Augustine uses an untranslatable rhyme: "*deluis*, explain" and "*polluis*, pollute."

225. See *The Grace of Christ and Original Sin* I, 43, 47.

226. Augustine's Latin has the untranslatable pun: "*Homo confosse, et non confesse.*"

227. Julian refers to Augustine's nine years as a follower of Manicheism.

228. See III, 172-187, where Julian quotes from Mani's Letter to Menoch.

229. Augustine refers to his *Answer to Julian*, a work which Julian, it seems, never saw.

230. See Rom 5:12.

231. See Ps 116:11.

232. Ambrose, *Commentary on Isaiah The Prophet* (*Expositio in Isaiam prophetam*) 1: CCL 14, 405.

233. See *Marriage and Desire* II, 5, 15.

234. I have followed the NBA edition's conjecture of adding "*virginitatis.*"

235. I have conjectured "*proavorum*" instead "*proborum*" found in Migne or the NBA edition's conjecture of "*pravorum.*"

236. This is not a direct quotation from Ambrose, but a paraphrase of Ambrose's *Commentary on Isaiah*.

237. See above, 88 where Julian makes this accusation against Jerome.

238. Ambrose, *Commentary on Isaiah The Prophet* (*Expositio in Isaiam prophetam*) 1: CCL 14, 405.

239. See Ps 114:5.

240. Ambrose, *Commentary on the Gospel of Luke* (*Expositio Euangelii secundum Lucam*) I, 37: CCL 14, 25.

241. Ambrose, *Commentary on the Gospel of Luke* (*Expositio Euangelii secundum Lucam*) 2, 56: CCL 14, 55.

242. Ambrose, *Defense of David* (*De apologia David*) 11, 56: CSEL 32/2, 337; see also Job 14:4 LXX.

243. See Mt 5:11.

244. See Mt 6:12-13.

245. Augustine alludes to the myth of the rebellion of the giants against Zeus, a parallel to which enters Christian literature on the basis of Gn 6:4-5. Jerome, for example, compares all heretics because of their rebellion against God to the giants in his *Commentary on Isaiah* (*Commentarium in Isaiam*) VI, 13, 3: CCL 73, 226.

246. See Sir 2:14; also see Augustine's *Lying* 3, 3, where he explains that a liar has a two-fold heart or mind.

247. See *Marriage and Desire* II, 8, 20 where Augustine said, "But, if sin had not first occurred, this seed would have come forth from the man in the tranquil obedience of his members to a sign from his will."

248. *Marriage and Desire* II, 8, 20; Julian's version substitutes "curse" for "defect."

249. *Ibid.*

250. See Pliny the Elder, *Natural History* (*Historiae naturalis libri*) VI, 181, or Ammianus Marcellinus, *History* (*Rerum gestarum libri*) 22, 25, 9.

251. See Ps 57:7. Wasps were supposed to have no venom of their own, but to borrow it from vipers; see Tertullian, *Answer to Marcion* (*Adverus Marcionem*) III, 8, 1: CCL 1, 518.

252. Pelagius wrote a *Book of Selections from the Divine Scriptures* (*Eclogarum ex divinis scripturis liber*), also known as *The Book of Testimonies* or *Book of Chapters*. Some fragments remain in Jerome's *Dialogue in Answer to the Pelagians* (*Dialogus contra Pelagianos*) and in Augustine's *The Deeds of Pelagius*. In *The Deeds of Pelagius* 3, 7, Augustine cites a passage from Pelagius' work in which he quotes Wisdom 7:7.

253. See Col 3:9.

254. *Ibid.*

255. See Sir 22:13.

256. See Rom 2:11.

257. I have conjectured "*nescia*" in place of "*nesciat.*"

258. See Prv 35:8 LXX.

259. See Lk 22:61-62.

260. See Ez 18:32.

261. See Rom 2:11.

262. See Eph 2:3.

263. See Rom 5:12.

264. See Wis 9:15.

265. See Gn 9:25.

266. See Dt 2:34.

267. Augustine again has an untranslatable multiple rhyme: "*flumine vanitatis . . . disertus, desertus lumine veritatis.*"

268. I have followed the conjecture in the NBA edition of adding "*qui.*"

269. Below Augustine cites Ez 16:3 which reverses the order of the parents.

270. See Jb 31:16-18.

271. See Gn 9:25.

272. See Mt 19:26.

273. See 2 Cor 10:17.

274. See Lk 1:41.44.

275. See Ambrose, *Commentary on Isaiah The Prophet* (*Expositio in Isaiam prophetam*) 1: CCL 14, 405.

276. I have conjectured "*quin et*" instead of "*quia.*"

277. See Gn 17:14.

278. The Latin of PL has "*labiorum*, lips," but the Septuagint has πόνων and Jerome's *Commentary on Isaiah* (*Commentarii in Isaiam*) XVIII, 65, 23: CCL73A, 765-769 has "*laborum*" which is what I have conjectured is the correct reading.

279. See Jn 20:27.

280. I have conjectured "*voculis*" instead of "*poculis.*"

281. Pelagius; perhaps from his *Commentaries on the Letters of St. Paul* (*Expositiones XIII epistularum Pauli Apostoli*), fragments of which survive; see PLS 1, 1110-1374.

BOOK FIVE

Book Five

Only a Few Are Found to Be Wise and Virtuous

1. JUL. (1) It has been discovered from the dangers of every age that respect for judgment which is not corrupt flourishes in a few persons. Devoted to the pursuits of knowledge and desirous of the virtues, they either can discover the truth or dare to defend it, once it is found. As the apostle says, *They have minds trained for distinguishing good and evil* (Heb 5:14), and they are not broken by any storms of adversity. For they hear from the same teacher that they must resist sins even to the point of shedding their blood.[1]

These wise people, then, who seem few in comparison with the large number of the stupid, devote themselves at the same time to knowledge and to courage. For neither of these attains results or honor without the other. For unless courage is applied to the finest works through knowledge, it bursts forth in despicable madness. And, on the other hand, unless a wall of magnanimity encloses them, the laws of a tested justice immediately are open to plunder and are led off enslaved to crimes. (2) In different ages only rare individuals have emerged who have groomed, harnessed, and ruled this pair of horses without which one cannot triumph over the errors of the world. For both the aversion to labor and the diversity of worldly concerns impedes the pursuit of knowledge, and fear of the afflictions which are aroused by the wicked overwhelms their constancy. Faithful and wise souls, of course, overcome these kinds of attacks, but they are so few and far between that they seem to be insane among the masses of the insane because they are not insane.

AUG. (1) Does not this scarcity of people, which you mention, in whom there is both knowledge and courage, warn you of what you ought to think of the human race and of this whole mass of rational and mortal animals? For why does the race of mortals, either the whole race or at least a majority, not rise up in the pursuit of knowledge and the exercise of courage out of a natural desire so that we are rather amazed that a very small number turn away from and abandon that which the teaching of nature desires? Why does this race of mortals fall into the depths of ignorance and softness of cowardice, as if some burden or other were pushing it downhill?

(2) You, of course, say that an aversion to labor is the cause that makes human beings not to know what they ought to know. But I wish you would say why a person who is so well equipped by nature needs such great labor to learn things useful and salutary for one's nature, and so, while avoiding labor, one more comfortably and gladly reposes in the darkness of ignorance. Such a scarcity of

intelligent and studious persons, two qualities which lead to the knowledge of things human and divine,[2] and such a multitude of slow and lazy persons indicates well enough the direction toward which nature, which you deny is damaged, is pulled as if by its own weight.

(3) Nor do you consider in accord with the Christian faith what sort of man Adam was when created, for he gave names to all the kinds of living beings.[3] We read even in worldly literature that this was a sign of outstanding wisdom. For Pythagoras himself, with whom the name of philosophy originated, is reported to have said that the person who first gave names to things was the wisest of all.[4] But even if we had learned nothing of the sort about Adam, it would have been our task to conjecture with true reason as to the sort of nature which was created in that man in whom there was no defect at all. Who, however, would be so slow-minded as to deny that dull and sharp minds pertain to nature or as to think that slowness of either memory or intelligence is not a defect of the mind? (4) And what Christian would deny that those who appear most intelligent in this world so full of errors and sufferings, those whose corruptible bodies, nonetheless, weigh down their souls,[5] if they are compared to the intelligence of that man, differ from him far more than tortoises differ from birds in speed? If no one had sinned, the happiness of paradise would have been filled with such outstanding minds. God would, of course, have created from their parents children of the same sort as that man whom he created without parents, certainly children in his own image.

(5) For human beings had not yet become like a vanity so that their days passed like a shadow in this world of suffering.[6] If things were that way, would this complaint of yours have any place? Would the attainment of knowledge be filled with labor so that human beings would prefer to be ignorant because of their aversion to labor? Would we need this strength which, as you truthfully say, is scarcely found in a very few persons where there would be no affliction which we would have to endure bravely for the sake of the truth? Though all these factors, then, have been changed to their opposites, you deny that our nature has been damaged to the point that, with your help, Mani introduces an alien nature mixed into us, and in that way, while you leap forth as his inexperienced attacker, you become his unwitting helper.

Our God Is Trustworthy, Just, and Holy

2. JUL. (1) That book which is called Wisdom also shows this. When it sets forth the words of the wicked as they gaze upon the rewards of the blessed which have been revealed after the shadow of the present world, it says, *We judged their life madness, and see how were they counted among the children of God* (Wis 5:4.5). This is the reason, then, that the perseverance of the faithful which

scorns the wickedness of the times and chooses to be afflicted with the people of God rather than to have for a time the pleasure of sin[7] is branded with the name of stubborn contentiousness by those who say, *Let us eat and drink, for tomorrow we shall die* (1 Cor 15:32). And they think nothing is more suited to cautious counsels than to purchase the enslavement of a degenerate mind or the unreliable repose of the moment. (2) The result of this baseness of cowardly hearts is mainly that the disgusting teaching of the Manichees has unfurled its sails through the shipwrecks of the churches.

For, if authority had taken a free and manly stand in these who serve in the office of priesthood, public opinion would have crushed the schemes of the traducianists, just as unconquerable reason has vanquished them. But since nothing is judged of less value than religion by those who love the present world, they have come to the point of accusations against God so that the necessity lies before us to prove by such long discourses that our God who is the true God is trustworthy in his words, just in his judgments, and holy in his works.[8]

AUG. (1) If God is trustworthy in his words, why do you contradict him when he says: *I shall punish children for the sins of their parents* (Dt 5:9), and claim that this is not true? If he is just in his judgments, why do you refuse to admit that his punishing children for the sins of their parents is just? And why are you not afraid to say that, without any original sin to merit it, the children of Adam are weighed down by a heavy yoke from the day they leave the womb of their mother?[9] If he is holy in his works, why do you refuse to distinguish the uncleanness of the newborn from God's holy work by which he forms their nature, though it is polluted by an infection from its origin? That uncleanness forced the man of God to say that no one is clean from the filth of sin, not even an infant whose life lasts a single day on earth?[10] And as a result, you attribute to God's holy work the defects of minds and of bodies which are very many and at times very great. (2) When you refuse to attribute these evils to the merits of our origin which come from our nature damaged by sin, you immediately open a very wide doorway for the detestable Manichees to introduce the alien nature of evil. In horror you apparently level accusations against their wicked teaching, while you help them by your error.

The Ploys of the Defender of Natural Evil

3. JUL. The defender of natural evil attacks in this way the work of my books dedicated to these concerns. I have explained more than enough by the argumentation of the preceding volumes the force and the logic with which he does so. I have no doubt that from a reading of them it is clear to any wise person—I have testified in my preface that such are few and far between—that the enemy of the

truth is aiming at nothing else than to mock the ears of the simple and to seem to have escaped if he made some sort of serious reply.[11]

AUG. In your preface you testify that the wise are few and far between, but you neither say nor let anyone tell you what is the cause of this scarcity or why even those who attain wisdom by the rare capacity of their minds cannot attain beneficial knowledge without great labor. For you do not want to admit that human nature was damaged by the transgression of the first man. And you, nonetheless, send to read your books only the same wise persons whom you testify are most few and far between. You have so good an opinion of their intelligence that you try to refute for them one book of mine by eight books of yours, multiplying for them the labor of the children of Adam. By that labor they would learn that, even if no one had sinned, they would have had to labor in paradise itself in order to learn the books of the learned and, before that, to learn to read. This, after all, is your brilliant knowledge which no human beings can grasp save for the few who are wise, and these only when they labor in misery.

The Spread of Error Calls for a Longer Defense

4. JUL. (1) It is, therefore, clear that we have amply achieved our goal. Because, nonetheless, our work has become long, the wise reader should understand that we desired brevity, but that the requisites of the case demanded that the error which was more widespread because of the favor of the world[12] should be defeated by a broader battle line of the truth. It is, therefore, for good reason that our discourse is extended. For by the help of Christ I trust that it will turn out that no part of the impiety against which we are struggling will be judged to have been carelessly examined, insufficiently uncovered, or only somewhat stamped out. We neither can nor ought to abandon hope that in the course of time the storm that has been stirred up will subside and that the slothful mob which now is in an uproar will be corrected by the authority of the wise.

(2) But that desire is less important than our decision. For whatever outcome the state of the dispute will attain, the cause of goodness and faith will stand on our side. Nor are we inclined toward an outcome of popular success. For we know that story of the three young men in Babylon. When they were forced to adore the statue by the most arrogant king, they resisted with great fidelity, and they were not frightened by the blast of the furnace which was blazing to devour those pious boys. They replied in a way which was suited to their faith and constancy. They said, *God is powerful, O king, to set us free from this furnace, but even if he does not set us free, know that we do not worship your gods nor do we adore the statue you have erected* (Dn 3:17-18). See how they combined their holy desire with their decision, and yet they did not lessen the seriousness of their resolve because of their desire! They neither lower the courage of faith out

of desperation, nor do they hold it up out of longing. They, of course, temper their prayers, but they do not abandon their priorities. They diminish the things they endure, but subordinate what is less difficult to what is just.

(3) It is certain, they say, that our God can set us free, but it is uncertain whether he wills to do so. And so in the face of the doubtful outcome of the events the decision of the pious young men remains certain: to reject the idols and to endure the punishment. Let God worry about the good which our deliverance may bring also to others; for us in the meanwhile, they say, our unconquerable faith preserves true happiness. Such faith does not, then, have great need of gratifying those who are rather soft, since its glory is earned in adversity.

From this teaching which these illustrious masters left us, we too understand that we must maintain a moderation in our prayers regarding matters of prosperity, but we must hold to a steadfastness of decision regarding the teachings of the faith. We desire to help the people as well, once the swelling of persecutions has subsided. But if this does not happen, we stand ready to suffer whatever painfulness there is in insults and dangers rather than not to turn away from foul filth of the Manichees.

AUG. (1) We have often warned you, and we shall not cease to warn you where it seems opportune, about how much you help the Manichees when you do not attribute the heavy yoke upon the children of Adam from the day they leave the womb of their mother[13] to the just judgment of God on account of original sin. For in that way you make room for the alien nature of evil which their insane error teaches. Now since you boast that you are so strong that you offer your own, though "moderate prayers," for the many whom, as you say, "you desire to help once the swelling of persecutions has subsided," I ask you whether you desire this from God. If you do not, these are not Christian prayers, but if you do, how do you hope that, after your prayers have been heard, the Lord will grant this? That is, how do you hope that he will turn the hearts of human beings which are opposed to you to support and love for you?

(2) If you believe this, you have made progress; he has already begun to convert you, to change you for the better. Consider this, I beg you, and keep it in mind, and at long last admit that almighty God produces in the hearts of human beings their acts of willing and turns back to him those who were turned away. In that way you will experience his mercy and grace, and where he does not do this, you will experience his hidden, but just judgments. Perhaps he will hear our prayers so that, as he converted Turbantius,[14] a little before one of yours, but now one of ours, he will by a similar act of his mercy convert you to the Catholic faith.

Natural Sin Implies That Intercourse Is Blameworthy

5. JUL. But let us now come to the question at issue. It was clearly shown in my previous work and in the present work[15] that natural concupiscence without which the union of the sexes cannot occur was instituted by God who is the creator of both human beings and of the other animals. This is so important, even by the admission of my opponent, that natural sin cannot be defended at all without finding fault with it, that is, with carnal concupiscence and without discrediting intercourse.

AUG. (1) Though it may please you to call concupiscence natural or carnal, we find fault with that concupiscence by which the flesh has desires opposed to the spirit and draws it to what is forbidden unless the spirit has stronger desires opposed to it.[16] We say that this dissension did not exist in paradise when its occupants were naked and were not ashamed.[17] The facts themselves proclaim that this concupiscence began after the sin, since after the sin they covered their sexual organs which previously had not been sources of shame.[18] Nor were they first naked because of impudence, but because of innocence, for impudence is also a defect. But when they were not ashamed to be naked, they did not, of course, have the defect.

(2) Julian the heretic says that this evil by which the flesh has desires opposed to the spirit is something good; Mani, another heretic, says that this evil has been mixed into us from the alien nature of evil. Ambrose the Catholic defeats them both, when he says that this evil was changed into our nature by the transgression of the first human being.[19]

Natural Sin Points to the Shame of Its Author

6. JUL. Because we have shown this by the ability which the truth has conferred upon us, the wise reader ought to have no further doubt on this point. Wherever this natural sin is found in the writings of the traducianist, who cannot nonetheless open his mouth without it, it should not disturb those who hear it; it should, rather, testify to the shame of its author. But hereafter we shall touch upon it with requisite brevity, if the matter demands.

The traducianist, therefore, found fault with my words: "This union of bodies which involves heat, pleasure, and seed was established by God, and in its proper moderation it is recognized as praiseworthy."[20] But he passed over what I added, "But the devil does not dare with your audacity to claim for himself something from that which was naturally established and which also becomes at times a great gift for a pious couple."[21]

AUG. (1) That man omitted this who sent that document to which I was replying. Perhaps he understood what you do not understand who spoke so carelessly as to say that "the devil does not dare to claim for himself something from that which was naturally established and which also becomes at times a great gift for a pious couple." For we see that the devil does claim for himself those human beings who have, of course, been naturally established. Or are they perhaps not human beings who are rescued from the power of darkness[22] over which the devil holds sway? Are you really so foolish as to state that the devil does not claim for himself those whom he owns and holds subject to his power?

(2) But I shall not mention those who you can say are owned by the devil through their own evil will. What will you say to that young man about whom his father answered when the Lord questioned him that he was tormented from his infancy by an unclean spirit?[23] Did not the devil claim for himself the right to afflict his members and senses, which were all naturally established by God, their author, and are gifts common to both unbelievers and believers? Though he could not do this unless he received power from the good and just God, the man's creator, he, nonetheless, does this and proves that your words are utter nonsense. For you say that "the devil does not dare to claim for himself something from that which was naturally established and which also becomes at times a great gift for a pious couple." After all, you ought to have said, not that the devil does not claim for himself any of those goods which were naturally established, but that he does not create any of them.

(3) Perhaps that man who made some excerpts from your books to send to his friend saw this, and he spared you in omitting these words of yours. But I am grateful because you alert me to what I ought to say against your error. Search out, then, the merits of the little ones whom the devil claims for himself to torment them; since you will not find merits of their own, admit those from their origin. For if you persist in denying these as well, you will certainly be found guilty of bringing accusations against the judgment of God who allows his image to suffer these torments from the devil without deserving them.

Children Are Said to Be God's Work, but Born Guilty

7. JUL. (1) After having passed over these words, he accuses me for not having said, "With passion," and adds as was fitting the subtlety of his teaching, "The reward of a pious couple is the procreation of many children, not the shameful union of their members which a healthy nature would not experience in begetting children, though our damaged nature now does experience it. For this reason one who is born from it needs to be reborn."[24] How logical it all is! He says that the reward of the pious couple is the existence of children, but he sets that reward which he states that God gives, namely, children, under the power of the devil. But he calls diabolical the passion which exists in the shameful union of the members, and he does not deny that it is found in the parents whom he, nonetheless, absolves from guilt.

(2) Would you say that this man was born from a human being? What the parents do, he says, is diabolical, but they are not guilty. The fact that children are born is the work of God, but they are guilty. Does he still think that he is fighting, not against God, but against the demon? They surely deserve to suffer this madness who believe that there is natural sin.

AUG. (1) It is you rather who rage against God whom you undoubtedly accuse of being unjust if he weighs down with a heavy yoke the children of Adam from the day they leave the womb of their mother[25]—something you cannot deny—though they contract from Adam, as you maintain, no sinful merits. Believing that those who will read your words and mine are dull-witted, you say that I said what I did not say. When, after all, did I say, "What the parents do is diabolical"? For I declare that the union of chaste spouses for the sake of having children is a good act. But this union would not have been something to be ashamed of, if the sin of the man by which nature was damaged had not preceded it. As a result concupiscence of the flesh has become such that no one makes good use of that evil unless, because the spirit has desires opposed to it, one fights back against its urges that try to draw one to what is forbidden.

We do not, therefore, say: "What the parents do is diabolical." To make good use of an evil is so far from being diabolical that God makes good use even of the devil himself. But we do not deny that we make that other statement: "That children are born is the work of God, but they are guilty," not because of the work of God by which they are created in order to be born, but because of their sinful origin by which they are held bound if they are not reborn.

Evidence That Intercourse Has Not Changed

8. JUL. Both the form of the members and God's blessing, which was pronounced in almost the same way upon the animals as upon human beings, and the story itself bear witness that Adam would not have had intercourse with his wife in any other way than what has become usual. Just as the story shows that the nature of bodies was formed, so it does not say that it was changed. Nothing in opposition to this testimony of the whole world is found in the law of God, but only in the books of Mani who makes up the story that this concupiscence was poured into them by the prince of darkness.

AUG. (1) The fact that the form of the members was not changed by the sin of the first man does not prove that the same sort of concupiscence of the flesh existed before the sin as emerged when they covered their genitals and were ashamed at that over which you are not ashamed. For they also showed that, since the form remained the same, something else was changed within them. And yet, when the members themselves are deformed and monstrous at birth, a sense of shame forces you to admit that members would not be like that at birth in paradise, if no one had sinned.

But why is it surprising that even a nature damaged by sin did not lose the blessing of God which said, *Increase and multiply* (Gn 1:22.28)? For it did not follow that, because our nature lost immortality and happiness, it also lost the fertility which was given even to irrational animals in which, even if the flesh has desires, it does not have desires opposed to the spirit.[26] You try to introduce into the place of that most blessed peace and freedom this most wretched war with or the most shameful reign of your darling, since you maintain that, even if no one had sinned, the human race would have been such that we would either fight against sexual desire or would be slaves of sexual desire if we refused to fight it.

Julian's View of the Effects of Infant Baptism

9. JUL. We testify both by our action and by our word that all must be reborn by baptism. We do this, however, not so that by the conferral of this benefit they are thought to have been kidnaped from the dominion of the devil, but so that those who are the works God made become pledges God has given. As a result, those who are born in a lowly but not in a guilty state are reborn in a precious way, but without casting aspersions on their birth. And those who emerge from God's works of creation are improved by his sacraments, and those who bear the works of nature attain the gifts of grace. And their Lord who made them good by creating them makes them better by renewing and adopting them. It is, then, you must admit, right to say that we have destroyed the natural sin which Mani invented, but which you call original by changing its name. Nor has this sin been believed from antiquity by that Catholic faith which does not doubt that little ones are made by God and that nothing evil is made by him. And for this reason, before the use of free will, it does not, to the discredit of nature, make the works of God either guilty or under the dominion of the devil.

AUG. (1) We speak quite deliberately of original sin rather than of natural sin precisely so that it is understood to be a sin, not of God's work, but from our human origin, especially to signify that sin which entered the world though one man. That sin is not destroyed by the Pelagian argumentation, but by Christian regeneration.[27] We know well enough, however, why you say that all little ones must be reborn by baptism. That is the reason you are heretics and argue against the ancient teaching of the Catholic Church with your newfangled plague. You say that little ones are not rescued from the power of darkness[28] by the grace of the redeemer, though the Catholic Church subjects to the rites of exorcism and exsufflation the power of the devil, not the image of God.

(2) Why, then, do you say, "So that those who are born in a lowly but not in a guilty state are reborn in a precious way, but without casting aspersions on their

birth," and yet you do not notice the price which is paid so that they may be reborn at such a cost? What is that price, after all, but the blood of the immaculate Lamb? The Lamb himself cries out why this blood was shed. Does he not himself say: *This is my blood which will be shed for many for the forgiveness of sins* (Mt 26:28)?

You, great magician that you are, both say that this blood is also shed for the little ones and you deny that any sins are forgiven them by it. You say that they need to be bathed, and you deny that they need to be cleansed; you say that they need to be renewed, and you deny that they need to be purified from their old condition. You say that they need to be adopted by the savior, and you deny that they need to be saved.

(3) But we, of course, disparage them because we say that they are dead in their sins and in the uncircumcision of their flesh and are, therefore, baptized in the death of Christ so that those who had been dead in sin may die to sin.[29] And you defend them, you who, by denying that they are dead, bring it about that the one who has the power of death is not cast out of them and that they do not derive any benefit from the death of Christ, *the one* who *has died for all.* After the apostle said this, he immediately drew the conclusion and said, *All, therefore, have died, and he has died for all* (2 Cor 5:14-15). As a result, one who defends the little ones so that he denies that they have died does not defend them from death, but forces into the second death those whom he excludes from the benefit of the one who is proclaimed to have died only for the dead.

Concupiscence and the Birth of Isaac

10. JUL. After these points, he passed over that whole passage about Abraham and Sarah who received a son as a gift when their bodies were already beyond the age of having children.[30] He says that it does not have much weight against him, though not only the wise reader, but even the average one understands how much their example supports the truth. He should have been recalled from that impudence at least by that sentence which is formulated as follows: "And briefly to sum up," I said, "the point of this discussion, if the son God promised is given them through concupiscence, concupiscence is undoubtedly good since it fulfills God's promise; if the son is given them without concupiscence, it cannot be harmful for the offspring, since it was present neither when the child was conceived nor when it was born."[31]

AUG. Who says that Abraham's son was conceived without concupiscence of the flesh? For this act would not be carried out any other way in the body of this death, of which the apostle says, *The body is indeed dead on account of sin* (Rom 8:10). But Abraham made good use of this evil in marital intercourse; this evil was not present in the body of that life which existed in paradise before the sin. But if concupiscence of the flesh seems good to you precisely because the offspring which God promised was given through it, the devil should also seem good to you because through him was shed the blood of Christ which God had promised so that we might be redeemed. Or admit that something good can also be given through something evil.

Julian's View of the Force of Pleasure

11. JUL. (1) Having passed over these issues, this new naturalist declares that our statement is false, namely: "Just as clay which God then used was the matter, not the author of the human being, so this force of pleasure which forms and mingles the seeds does not now take the place of God's action, but offers to God from the resources of nature the matter from which he chooses to produce a human being."[32] He states that I correctly stated these points, except that I said that the seeds were formed by the force of the pleasure. He philosophizes in this way: "The pleasure of carnal concupiscence does not form the seeds. Rather, those seeds were already created in bodies by the true God. They are not produced by pleasure, but are aroused and spilled forth with pleasure."[33]

(2) It is surely clear that he produced this idea, not out of deceit, but out of a failure of intelligence. I, of course, called "the force of pleasure" the very structure of the male body upon which I held it necessary to impose the name "virility." This virility, then—for we have already used this word repeatedly—which consists in the structure and healthiness of the genitals and inner organs, gives strength both to desire and to potency. I called it the force of pleasure and of desire. For I preferred to call it, not simply pleasure, but the force of pleasure, in order to point out all the ardor which is felt both before the act and in the act.

(3) Those deprived of the genital organs, that is, eunuchs, do not, after all, have seed, though they surely feel some coals of the fire that has been put out. But since because of their particular disability they lost the power of the parts whose function produces the seeds from the inner humors, they are incapable of begetting children. God, then, established that there existed in bodies a power which, once developed at the proper times, would attain the power of fecundity if good health was present. Seeds are, therefore, produced in the body with the arrival[34] of mature manhood. For this reason a premature pleasure, of course, stimulates youngsters prior to puberty, but their ardor remains sterile without the requisite years. But the fact that the seeds are mingled with pleasure, though there is one pleasure which remains in the senses and another that is interior to the organs and closer to the action, is widely discussed among the medical authors.

(4) For this reason, that poet of Mantua, more knowledgeable on natural topics than the phony philosopher of the Phoenicians, also notes that the herds are

thinned down with hunger so that the herdsmen keep them from leafy branches and streams, "when the well-known pleasure draws them to their first mating. They also often hurry them along with running and wear them out under the sun, when the threshing-floor groans heavily with the pounded grain and the light chaff is carried off by the breezes. They do this so that excessive use may not dull the powers of the fertile soil and render its furrows lifeless, but so that it may inwardly suffer a certain dryness, eagerly seize the ardor of love, and hide it away within."[35] But on these points too which are not very pertinent to the issue, let it suffice to note the intelligence of this man.

AUG. (1) I have shown above quite sufficiently how foolish your words are which you say I passed over. Perhaps the person who sent the document saw that and omitted these words to spare you. But with regard to the point which, given the chance, you argue endlessly, you endlessly wordy man, about the force of pleasure which you said forms the seeds, I have no need to oppose you. For even you mention that these points are not very relevant to the question.

I had, of course, taken you to have wanted us to understand the force of pleasure as the force by which pleasure could produce something, not as the force by which pleasure itself is produced. After all, we are accustomed to speak so that we call the force of anything the force by which it has the capacity to produce something, not that by which the thing itself is produced. But as you have now explained your words, you claim that you said that the force of pleasure was the force by which pleasure can be produced, not the force by which pleasure produces what it can. It is as if you called the force of fire the force by which it is kindled so that it exists, though all human beings call the force of fire the force by which it burns or heats whatever it can.

(2) You have, therefore, spoken in an unusual fashion. But what difference does that make to us? In any case, we have learned not to fight over words when there is agreement about the facts. For we agree that not only human beings who come from seeds, but the seeds themselves are also works of God, however they may be produced. Let us not use as authorities naturalists or doctors or even poets where there is no need, and let us not argue about how one ought to speak, when we both know that what we are speaking about is true, namely, that the seeds of all natures are the works of God.

(3) But what you try to show from that is false, namely, that there are no defects in the seeds because the supremely good God is the creator of seeds. You would not say that if you knew the nature of the seeds as he knew it who said, *Human beings have become like a vanity.* And to teach that this nature which fell into mortality merited this, he added, *Their days pass like a shadow* (Ps 144:4). For the psalmist knew that Adam was made to the likeness of God, and yet he distinguished the defect of the damaged human origin from the divine creation. You should have also seen this idea in those words of yours by which you snapped at me. After all, you said, "But on these points too which are not very

pertinent to the issue, let it suffice to note the intelligence of this man," indicating, of course, that I am dull because I could not understand your words on points which were not very pertinent to the issue, as you admitted.

(4) But I ask you why human beings are born dull, for you yourself are not so dull that you would deny that dull and sharp minds pertain to nature, though even sharp minds, as we have already said in the previous sections, are dull, if they are compared to the mind of the first man, on account of this corruptible body which weighs down the soul.[36] That man certainly did not receive such a body that his soul was weighed down by it. And I too would distinguish in human nature as it now exists the difference between the defect of a mind and the work of so great an artist, to whom it is undoubtedly not correct to attribute the defects of human minds, however great they may be, so that you might learn by this rule to distinguish original sin, though it is in human beings at birth, from God's creation. (5) And in that way you would not deny its existence, because God who does not cause sin is the cause of human beings, just as one should not deny the defects of human intellects present from birth, because God from whose divine artistry all defectiveness is absent is the cause of human beings. But God knows how to make good human beings out of the substance damaged by sin, just as he knows how to produce good from the very sins of human beings whose defects are voluntary. For we see how much good he produced from the sin of those brothers who sold their brother out of envy,[37] and the sacred books are filled with many other examples.

Augustine Is Again Accused of Incoherence

12. JUL. But I am everywhere surprised at the consistency of this debater who declares that "seeds were created by the true God who also created bodies, though they are spilled forth with pleasure." He admits, then, that seeds are made by God, though he says that diabolical evil is present in them, and he is not embarrassed to believe that God produces the evil which is imputed to the innocent.

AUG. God does not produce evil when he produces good from evil. The defect of our origin which comes from sin and with which human beings are born is evil; God's work is good, though not without evil. The guilt of that evil is not imputed to the innocent, as you claim, but to the guilty so that, because it was contracted by being born, it may be removed by being reborn. For in that way all were present by reason of the seed in the loins of Adam when he was condemned, and he was, therefore, not condemned without them. In the same way the people of Israel were in the loins of Abraham when he paid the tithe, and he did not, therefore, pay the tithe without them.[38] Those authors who said that, after all, knew the nature of seed better than you, and they carefully committed to writing what we read in the Church of Christ in which those who have been born of Adam are reborn so that they do not remain condemned as children of Adam.

Augustine Claims That Sexual Desire Is the Devil's Work

13. JUL. Sexual desire has nothing to do, Augustine says, with the seeds, because it was produced by the devil. Married couples are enslaved to this desire, but God makes the seeds and makes the little ones from the seeds. But the parents, he says, who do the work of the devil, are neither guilty, nor are they punished. The little ones, however, whom God created are destined for serious sin and punishment. What the devil produced, that is, sexual desire, goes unpunished; by this we are taught that it is good since it does not also merit punishment. But what God produced is accused and condemned; by this we are taught that it is criminal since it cannot be defended from punishment even by a sense of shame on the part of its author.

And it comes to be believed that the divinity produces what even the worst sort of captivity could not tolerate. Those who wage war against the truth come up with this result: They say nothing that is not impious, nothing that is not insane so that it is clear that the state of the innocents is defended by no words as well as it is defended by the wickedness of their accusers.

AUG. (1) Do you make what I say false because you say what I do not say? I do not say that sexual desire has nothing to do with the seeds, since those who have their origin from seed are, of course, not born without sexual desire. But I say that God produces them without any defect on his part, even though he produces them out of the defective seed. Nor do I say that the parents who do the work of the devil are not guilty and go unpunished, but I say that they do not do the work of the devil when they make use of sexual desire, not for the sake of that desire, but for the sake of procreation. Thus it is surely a good work to make good use of the evil of sexual desire, as married couples do, just as, on the contrary, it is an evil work to make bad use of the good of the body, as the unchaste do.

(2) Nor do I say that sexual desire goes unpunished, for it will be destroyed along with death when this mortal body is clothed with immortality.[39] For it only exists in the body of this death from which the apostle desired to be set free.[40] It did not exist or did not exist as such desire in the body of that life which the man who was created upright[41] lost by sinning. Nor will sexual desire, like some substance, move to some other place, once we have been set free from and removed from it, but it will perish, like an illness, when our salvation reaches perfection, though it already ceases to exist now after the death of the body. For that desire which can only exist in the body of death cannot still exist in a dead body, but that desire which is destined to perish in the death of the body will not rise when the body is resurrected without death. How, then, will it be punished or unpunished,

since it will not exist because it has perished? (3) But they will go unpunished who by reason of rebirth have been freed from its guilt with which they are born and do not yield to its urges which arise and pull them to do what is forbidden. And if married couples do something, not for the sake of having children from it, but for the sake of sexual desire itself, they are healed by subsequent pardon.

But as for God's creating little ones from an origin that was rightfully and justly condemned, what he himself creates is good, because he creates human beings, and even bad human beings are something good insofar as they are human beings. Nor does he hold back the goodness of his creating them from those whom he foreknows will be condemned; in fact he knows from the beginning that they have already been condemned. Hence, we ought to be grateful that he sets free so many from their due punishment by grace that is not due them.

(4) If you think it cruel that little ones are condemned who you do not think contract original sin, it should seem cruel to you that little ones are not taken from this life who, according to you, have no sin at all, when God, of course, knows that they will die in many great sins without any change for the better. For, in terms of human reasoning, it seems more cruel not to set free someone stained by no sins, neither great ones nor small ones, though God could, than to condemn the offspring of the sinner. But since you cry out as loud as you can that the former is just, with what impudence do you claim that this latter is unjust?

Julian's Use of the Words of Saint Paul

14. JUL. (1) After this he tries to attack the point that we proved by the testimony of the apostle Paul, namely, that God produces human beings from seeds.[42] He argues that I acted deceitfully because I wanted to adapt to this case those statements which it is agreed were spoken with regard to grain, as if I cut off the statement of the apostle, as this fellow thinks, or recalled his testimony for any other reason than to show his intention, namely, that God should be believed to be the fashioner of all seeds.

For after blessed Paul had won faith in the resurrection by examples of the sort of reproduction encountered every day, he brought out a point which could apply to the whole of nature. He said, *But God gives to it a body as he wills and to each of the seeds its own body* (1 Cor 15:38); that is, he gives to every seed a body which its particular character demands. (2) I did not, then, intend that his statement about the grain should be understand about a human being, but for your destruction I seized upon the statement that a body is given to each of the seeds by God their author, since your teaching denies this. By no means, then, did I uselessly, as you suppose, make mention of that statement, nor did I deceitfully, as you falsely claim, misuse it. Nor do you believe, as you falsely swear, that a hu-

man being is made by God from human seeds, a point which I confirm not by
making a conjecture about your faith, but by understanding it.

AUG. (1) One who reads your words intelligently should notice how you
cited the apostolic testimony which the apostle used concerning the seeds which
are sown in the earth, namely, that they do not come to life unless they die. After
all, the discussion of the resurrection of the dead with which he was dealing required this. And the reader should also notice what we replied to your words in
that same book which you are now trying to refute.[43] The reader will find that
you said nothing there and say nothing here pertinent to the topic. For you are
trying to show with a great effort that God produces human beings from seeds, as
if we denied this, and you use the apostle as a witness when no necessity demands a proof of the point from you. And what is more stupid, you want us to understand with regard to the seeds of human beings what he said about the seeds of
grain because that was what the issue demanded. You cite his words, *What you
sow is not brought to life*, but you pass over what he adds to them: *unless it dies* (1
Cor 15:36). (2) You also pass over what he goes on to add: *And what you sow is
not the body that will be, but you sow the mere seed, whether of wheat or of something else* (1 Cor 15:37). Here it is clear enough what he was speaking about.
Having passed over these verses, you add what follows: *But God gives to it a
body as he wills and to each of the seeds its own body* (1 Cor 15:38). You do not
want us to understand here which seeds these are, that is, *whether of wheat or
something else*, but they are surely those seeds which, when they are sown, are
not brought to life unless they die. You try to transfer this statement even to human seeds. Though it can truthfully be said about them that God gives them a
body as he wills and to each of them its own body, it cannot, nonetheless, be said
that, when the seed of a human being is poured into the womb of a woman, it is
not brought to life unless it dies. But it clearly can be said about the body of a human being, for it will not rise unless it dies, and on account of this the apostle said
everything he said about the seeds of grain.

It was not, therefore, without reason that I thought that you passed over in this
testimony those words which made it clear which seeds the apostle was speaking
about. For you used him as a witness for fear—if you could have foreseen
this—that a reader with an alert mind might be warned that human beings could
in paradise be sown in the fertile fields of women by the male genital organs, just
as grain is sown in the earth by the hands of farmers. Then, just as there would
have been no urge of sexual desire for sowing the human seed, so there would
have been no pain involved in childbirth. (4) What, I ask, do those to whom this
tranquility is displeasing find pleasing in the flesh except what is shameful? Nor
would carnal concupiscence be shameful if the flesh wanted only what the mind
commanded and wanted it only when the mind commanded[44] and as much as it
commanded. Because, then, concupiscence is not now such, why do you give it

your support in opposition to us and not rather admit with us that it was born from sin or damaged by sin?

Julian Mocks Augustine's View of Sex in Paradise

15. JUL. (1) But now who among the wise could contain their laughter when they come to the examples you added to these points? For you say that the very words of the apostle would refute "this man who is ashamed to name, but praises without shame, not a devout will, but lustful pleasure. This fellow can, of course, be refuted from those seeds which farmers sow in fields. After all, why should we not believe that in paradise God could have granted to the man in his blessed state with regard to his seed what we see is granted to farmers with regard to seeds of grain? Then man's seed would be sown, as the seed of grain is sown, without any shameful lust."[45]

(2) How charmingly this fellow who modestly names and impudently praises them performs the dance of a farmer and recites the ritual songs of charlatans![46] But the next point cannot be read without laughter, namely that if Adam had not sinned, the woman could have been prepared for child-bearing, just like fields, perhaps so that in all her limbs and through tiny openings of her body, which doctors call "pores," shoots of children might burst forth, and thus fruitful in all her parts she might exude offspring like lice.[47] But if some burst forth even through her eyes, they would deprive her of sight when she gave birth, and if helmeted swarms went forth from the globes of her pupils, in her blindness she would undoubtedly curse her loss of sight. And offspring, not born, but exuded, would surely be killed without difficulty,[48] and as in the stories of the Myrmidons,[49] so in the teaching of the Manichee, there would be a people like lice or fleas.[50]

(3) But this would be a woman's way of bearing children. What would the man be able to do? He would undoubtedly not use his members, but garden tools, and deprived of genital organs he would thrust in plowshares and hoes. We, therefore, owe most abundant thanksgiving to the error of the first human beings by which the torments of so blessed a nature have been avoided. Childbirth deals more gently with women, and so does a husband, than if women felt the plowshares or burgeoned all over their bodies with undesirable fecundity. Let the faces of the Manichees be filled with ignominy, and let them seek your name, O Lord.[51] Oh the monstrosity of those who bring as charges against the innocents and against God the support of arguments and testimonies!

(4) Why, he asks, should we not believe that nature could have been made otherwise than we see that it has been made? As if one should seek what God could have created and not what he did create! Out of that desire to have an opinion he wants to find fault with what has been made so that we say that, because

things could have been made otherwise, the things which have been created do not bear witness to a good nature. Shall we, then, declare that, because God could have made mortals with two heads, those who have one head and who stand on their feet are, therefore, badly made? After all, they could have been made with a head on top and at the bottom. That form is often found in certain worms whose belly is enclosed by a head coming forth at each end so that beginning from each shoulder they are understood to have an end in the middle. Admit these frivolous ideas, and where will there be a end to this madness?

(5) God could, therefore, have made it so that human beings sprouted from the earth along with the flowers. With respect to his power, I do not deny that he could have done this. But he willed that they be born only from the sexes. Our present question is what he did, not what he could have done. In this place it is a crazy response to say: What exists is evil because God could have made things otherwise; this is to praise God with the intention of blaming him and to proclaim his omnipotence to the discredit of his intelligence.

It is not only no praise, but it is also a great insult to ascribe to his power what you subtract from his wisdom and to say that God had the strength, but lacked the intelligence. (6) Your blame for his foresight goes so far as completely to deny his power; he is not omnipotent if he cannot arrange things well. In fact, if he is lacking in the loftiness of wisdom, he retains nothing of the respect due to his divinity. Since even to hold this suspicion is utterly sacrilegious, there reappears that point on which your doctrine of inherited sin is strangled. God who made everything very good[52] established no creature such that in that kind which has been made it is shown that it could have been made either more suitably or more in accord with reason. Endowed equally with wisdom and omnipotence, he would, of course, not have created anything that a mere human being could have rightly criticized.

(7) All elements in absolutely all creatures which are found to be natural were made in the very best way so that any supposed improvement in them is found to be stupid and sacrilegious. The form of a horse and the form of a cow are, then, different in comparison to each other, but they have, nonetheless, received a harmony suitable in every respect in their own kinds so that a horse or a cow neither ought to have been nor could have been made otherwise than we see each has been formed. By this rule one could run through all the living things that swim or creep or walk or fly and finally through everything in the air and the heavens; we are surely shown that the form of no creature could have been created better for the kind for which it was made.

So too, human beings which were included above in the genus of walking animals were formed in every respect so that no one can imagine them made better. From God's wisdom they received in their bodies beautiful parts and shameful parts so that they might learn in themselves both modesty and confidence lest they should be thought ugly if they were completely clothed or become lazy and negligent if they were always completely unclothed.

(8) And for this reason human fecundity ought to have received no other members of the two sexes than it has, no other arrangement of the inner organs, no other sensations, and no other pleasure. Let us, then, warn the Manichees to stop finding fault with the works of divine wisdom and to correct the wickedness of their opinions. For it is not relevant to the issue if it is said that human beings would have begotten children otherwise than the whole world testifies that they do, and both reason and scripture, when it cries out that God made all things not merely good, but also very good,[53] bear witness that they could not have been made better than they were made. And for this reason, the teaching of the Manichees has been destroyed here as it has been through the whole work.

(9) In the future era, however, we admit that the bodies of the blessed will be more glorious and will not need help. But even this has been arranged in the best way by the most just and most wise God, namely, that our nature should by no means surpass[54] the state of our reward, but should be the first step in which there is found natural goodness and from which by the law of free choice our nature either would descend to the depths of punishment or strive for the height of glory through the paths which God has established.

AUG. (1) You, Julian, of course, did not think that people would read both my writings and yours. Rather, you wrote only for those who would be concerned to read and know your writings alone, while they were ignorant of or neglected mine and did not carefully inspect them both. You wrote only for people who would believe that I said only what they found in your writings cited by you as if they were from my writings. I said, "After all, why should we not believe that in paradise God could have granted to the man in his blessed state with regard to his seed what we see is granted to farmers with regard to seeds of grain? Then man's seed would be sown in that way without any shameful lust."[55]

(2) I see that because of this you have spread about your foolish words, as if you were replying to these words of mine, and you went so far and strayed so wide that you claimed that I said that, "if Adam had not sinned, the woman could have been prepared for child-bearing, perhaps so that in all her limbs and through tiny openings of her body, which doctors call 'pores,' shoots of children might burst forth, and thus fruitful in all her parts she might exude offspring like lice," and all the other things which it bores me to mention, though it did not shame you to heap them up. Among these you also said of the man that "he would undoubtedly not use his members, but garden tools, and deprived of genital organs he would thrust in plowshares and hoes."

(3) When not just any readers, but your fans, read this, they are embarrassed for you if they have any common sense. Would my words allow you to blabber these statements and others of the sort? But you passed over and failed to cite my words only so that you might prepare for yourself more ample room for raving. I

said that human beings could be sown "by the genital organs in obedience to a sign from the will."[56] You did not mention the genital organs so that you could run on about the limbs and tiniest openings of a woman exuding children through the pores of her body like lice and giving birth through the pupils of her eyes with blindness as a result.

(4) You did not, I repeat, mention the genital organs, as if we would say that, if Adam had not sinned, human beings would not have them, so that you could say with ridiculous—not charm, but —silliness that the man deprived of genital organs would thrust plowshares and hoes into his wife to impregnate her. Is there any question about the function[57] and shape of the members? Created whole and entire in their proper place, they would not need the stimulus of sexual desire and could obey the command of the will for producing children.

When you quoted my words, you did not want to mention these points which I mentioned so that you did not impose silence upon yourself. For then you would have been unable to open your mouth for those ideas which you thought were uttered with highly amusing raillery, though they were spoken with most stupid foolishness. I mean, concerning the children bursting forth through the whole body like lice and about using the tools of farmers for impregnating women. (5) For that reason you did not think that you should touch upon that other statement of mine, which I put in the same passage which you took up as if to refute, about the pains of women in childbirth. For, if women gave birth without the pains of childbirth, I think that they would have lacked, not the genital organs, but the penal sufferings. Moreover, the divine scripture, as all who read it know, testifies that this kind of suffering was passed on to all womenkind from the sin of Eve.[58]

You preferred to pass over this point in my words rather than to discuss it for fear that you would be told that in that blessed state of paradise, with the genital organs of both sexes whole and entire, couples could have intercourse without shameful sexual desire, just as with the female genitals whole and entire, women could bear children without groaning in pain. (6) But you prefer to locate in that place of such great blessedness not only the agony and groans of mothers in travail, but also the other labors and afflictions of mortals, not from the time they have free choice, but from the day they leave the womb of their mother,[59] rather than not to locate there your darling of whom you should be ashamed at least out of a sense of shame.

And you who deny that our nature was changed after the sin into this mortality admit, nonetheless, that it will be changed after the merit of a good will into the glory of blessed immortality. To the height of that glory little ones, as you cannot deny, ascend, not by the merits of their own will, but by those of another's will, though you do not want to believe that they have been hurled down by the merits of the will of another, the one in whose loins they, nonetheless, existed by reason of the seed, to the depths of the miseries with which we are familiar.

Lessons from the Healing of Abimelech's Wives

16. JUL. But let us go on to the other points. After he avoided the example of Abraham which I had used, he tried to maintain that Abimelech too, who along with his wives was reported to have been healed at Abraham's prayers, was able to return to the act of procreation from which he was prevented as a punishment. He also tried to maintain that one could understand that the womb of his wives had been closed, not by the withdrawal of sexual desire, but by some painful condition,[60] as if we emphatically stated that natural desire was seen to have been restored to them, though I was content to prove by those testimonies only that intercourse which could not have taken place without sexual desire was prevented by God's anger and was restored through God's pardon, whether through the removal of obstacles or through the restoration of the usual stimuli. We are, nonetheless, not taught that intercourse is diabolical, but that for this reason it too belongs to God's work, and among the humble, but not harmful functions of the body it is sinful not by its kind, not in its moderate use, but only in its excess.

AUG. (1) Who would not understand that if, because God was angry, something happened to the bodies of the women so that intercourse was prevented and, for this reason, children were also prevented which could not, of course, be conceived except by the couple having intercourse, then, when that impediment was removed, the same sort of intercourse was restored which exists in the body of this death, that is, with sexual desire? When bodies are healed, they are, of course, restored to the sort of condition which the nature of mortals, which forces them to die, has now obtained after the sin.

But in the body of that life in which, if the man had not sinned, he was not going to die, there was undoubtedly another condition; hence, there was either no sexual desire there or it was not the sort of desire which now exists by which the flesh has desires opposed to the spirit[61] so that one must either be subjected to it or fight against it. Of these the one is incompatible with moral goodness, and the other is incompatible with the peace of that blessed state.

(2) Do not, then, confuse those two lives because of your heretical wrong-headedness. We live in one way in the corruptible body which weighs down the soul;[62] we would live in another way in paradise if the uprightness of Adam in which he was created had lasted. Spouses would, therefore, also have intercourse in paradise for the sake of having children, but either with the genital organs obeying the mind without any sexual desire or with the urges of desire, if there was any desire, never resisting the will. If desire were such, it would not be a cause for shame, nor would it make us call shameful in the proper sense the members of the body which it entices or arouses by its urging, and it would not compel us to cover them. The words of God bear witness that these things happened after the sin and could only have happened as a punishment of sin. God said, *Who told you that you are naked unless you ate from the tree from which*

alone I had commanded that you should not eat from it? (Gn 3:11). Your nakedness, he says, would not have been called to your attention, if you had not violated my law.

(3) What, however, does it mean that his nakedness was called to his attention, for he certainly was not unaware of it, unless that urge aroused him so that
his nakedness forced itself to be noticed by its unaccustomed appearance and
caused him shame? For sin caused man's lower part to have desires opposed to
his higher part, that is, his flesh opposed to his spirit. But you close your eyes
against all this, and though God reveals that the man would not have been
ashamed of his nakedness if he had not sinned, you claim that he was created so
that, even if he had not sinned, he would have been ashamed of his nakedness.

God, after all, says: Who told you of your nakedness unless it is because you
have sinned? And you say—to quote your very words which you uttered just before: "And so human beings were formed in every respect so that no one can
imagine them made better. From God's wisdom they received in their bodies
beautiful parts and shameful parts so that they might learn in themselves both
modesty and confidence lest they should be thought ugly if they were completely clothed or become lazy and negligent if they were always completely unclothed." And for this reason, as you see it, human beings became far better by
sinning. For, unless Adam whom God made upright[63] sinned, he would have
lived unwisely in not distinguishing in his own body beautiful parts and shameful parts and would have lived impudently in covering no parts and negligently
in exposing all of them. For he would not have avoided these defects unless his
nakedness was called to his attention because he had sinned.

Saint Paul on the Natural Goodness of Intercourse

17. JUL. (1) Since we have treated this point sufficiently, let us hurry on to
those points which the Manichee once cleverly raised as objections concerning
natural evil, but, as I shall prove, he was misled by the complexity of the issues.
Briefly let us, nonetheless, first examine what Augustine replied against the testimony of the apostle. I said, therefore, that even the testimony of blessed Paul
proves with complete clarity that the familiar activity of the sexes was instituted
by God, the creator of bodies, for he attacked the indecent acts of those men
whom insanity had driven even to homosexual intercourse. He said, *Having
abandoned natural relations with a woman, they burned in their desires* (Rom
1:27). Then I inferred with the apostle as witness that God approved intercourse
with a woman as naturally instituted.

(2) In reply to this, then, he said, "The apostle did not speak of marital, but
natural relations. He meant for us to understand those relations which are
brought about by the members created for this purpose so that both sexes can be

joined by them in order to beget children. For this reason, when anyone is united by these same members even to a prostitute, the relations are natural, though they are not worthy of praise, but of blame. Hence, this expression, namely, natural relations, is not used to praise marital intercourse, but to denounce those indecent acts that are more unclean and more wicked than if one had sinful relations with women that were at least natural."[64] That is, these relations with a woman which the apostle declared natural are not taken to be marital relations so that we might be taught that they are good and licit. Rather, they were, he says, called natural because this expression indicates the differences of the sexes which were instituted for that purpose in order that they would be equipped for intercourse and childbirth.

(3) Since he is helped in no way by these contrivances, why did he delay so long? Obviously it is only for this reason, namely, that his followers might think that he solved the problem which they see he touched upon, but a brief discussion will make it clear that he said nothing. The apostle, of course, said that relations with a woman were instituted as part of nature, and he did not mention that another form of union was established in the beginning. Rather, while discussing those relations in which he knew that sexual desire was at all times a powerful force, he called that desire natural.

AUG. (1) Relations with a female are natural when the male partner uses that member of hers by which the nature of the same kind of living beings is propagated. On this account that member itself is often called "nature" in the proper sense. For this reason Cicero said that a woman saw in her dreams that she had a nature marked beforehand.[65]

Natural relations, then, are both licit, as in marriage, and illicit, as in adultery. But relations against nature are always illicit and are undoubtedly more indecent and more shameful—the sort that the holy apostle blamed in both women and men. He wanted us to understand that such people were more deserving of condemnation than if they sinned in natural relations either by committing adultery or by committing fornication. The natural and blameless relations of those who have intercourse could, then, also have existed in paradise, even if no one had sinned, for children would not be born for the human race in any other way in accord with God's blessing.

(2) But what but your heresy told you that the apostle called those relations natural in which he knew that sexual desire was at all times a powerful force? Heaven forbid, after all, that the apostle believed that this shameful sexual desire of human beings was a powerful force even at that time when they were naked and were not ashamed.[66] Nonetheless, even if the apostle said what you said, namely, "in natural relations with a woman sexual desire was at all times a powerful force," I would have a correct way of interpreting even these words so that I would not locate your shameful darling in the bodies of that blessed life. For they

were not yet bodies of this death, as you make them to be with your stupid ideas, loquacious tongue, and impudent effrontery.

(3) At all times, of course, since the two sexes began to be united, natural relations with a woman undoubtedly could not exist without this shameful sexual desire. They already had a body, not of that life, but of this death, when, having left paradise after the sin, for the first time the man and the woman had natural sexual intercourse. But if they had done so before, either there would have been no sexual desire, or it would not have been shameful. For it would not have tempted one who was unwilling, and it would not have forced a chaste person to fight against it. Either the sexual organs would carry out their function without it at the command of the mind, or if that desire existed, it would arise when there was need, following upon a perfectly peaceful sign from the will and not eliminating thought by its turbulent attack.

(4) By its many untimely impulses which need to be held in check, it admits that it is not now such desire; hence, it bears witness that it is either a defect or has been damaged. See why the apostle said, *I know that the good does not dwell in me, that is, in my flesh* (Rom 7:18). See the source from which the newborn contract original sin. Marital chastity makes good use of this evil; the religious abstinence of widows and widowers or the sacred integrity of virgins does better in not making use of this evil.

Marital Intercourse Is Good and Licit

18. JUL. We understood this, and since we were speaking about the creation of nature, we brought forth the views which the apostle clearly held. What, then, did you achieve when you reported that he called them, not marital, but natural relations? Or with what audacity do you add, "When anyone is united by these same members to a prostitute, the relations are natural, though they are not worthy of praise, but of blame."[67] For to point out here too what we have often shown, you have not produced even one sentence which does not have very much force against you. If relations in fornication are said to be natural, though not worthy of praise, but of blame, because they are relations with a prostitute, you will undoubtedly admit that marital relations are not worthy of blame, but of praise, because they are morally good and licit.

AUG. Marital intercourse is correctly said to be blameless, not because it is free from evil, but because it makes good use of an evil. For it is something good to make good use of an evil, just as it is something evil to make bad use of a good. Married couples, then, make good use of the evil of sexual desire, just as adulterers make bad use of the good of the body. I have already said this more than once, and I do not hesitate to say it still more often, as long as you are not ashamed to contradict the truth.

Sexual Desire Is Blameworthy Only in Its Excess

19. JUL. And where is that diabolical sin of yours which you try to attach to intercourse by the argument from shame? For sexual desire which is experienced in both its forbidden and its permitted use as a result of the condition of nature itself is not blameworthy, but[68] its depravity alone is blamed when it runs off to what was not permitted.

AUG. (1) It is not the depravity of sexual desire alone that is blamed when it runs off to what was not permitted, but yours is a great depravity when you do not blame it when it impels one toward what was not permitted. For when it impels one toward what is not licit, one immediately runs off to do it unless one fights against its evilness. And this is the concupiscence of the flesh by which the flesh has desires opposed to the spirit, against which the spirit also has desires,[69] precisely so that the spirit does not run off to what the desire impels it. Even that which impels one toward evil is, therefore, something evil. But if one does not run off after it because the spirit fights against it, one is not conquered by the evil. One will, however, be free from all evil only when there will be nothing against which to fight. (2) Nor, when this comes about, will an alien nature be separated from us, as Mani thinks in his madness; rather, our own nature will be healed. If, just as our nature is healed from guilt by rebirth and the forgiveness of sins, it were also now in good health without any illness, the spirit would not have desires opposed to the flesh in order that we might do only what is permitted. Rather, the flesh would agree with the spirit so that it would desire nothing forbidden in opposition to the spirit.

Natural Relations with a Woman and Moral Goodness

20. JUL. (1) To put the question precisely and briefly, do you think that, when the apostle Paul called relations with a woman natural, he indicated the possibility and the moral goodness of the act or only the possibility? That is, by this term "natural," did he want us to understand the relations which could have and ought to have existed or those which could have, but ought not to have existed? If you say, "Those which could have, though they ought not to have existed, such as take place in adulteries," then that other indecent act will also not be against nature because it uses natural members. (2) But if in horror you reply, as the truth also has it, that the apostle called those relations natural which, intended for procreation, are carried out morally, that is, naturally, as they could have been and ought to have been, upon the bodies of one woman or of many, as was permitted by reason of the times, you will undoubtedly admit that you argued foolishly and that by the expression "natural relations" blessed Paul did not indicate, as you had thought, fornication, but the morally good and legitimate union of bodies which is suited for begetting children.

(3) We, therefore, rightly defend in its whole genus what the Manichee attacks in its whole genus. For you say that this union of the sexes which was established by the devil is, along with pleasure, the cause of original sin and is the necessity behind all sins, and for this reason you bring accusations against nature. What could we have done that was more logical than, with the teacher of the nations as our witness, to have defended in the whole genus of nature and to have attributed to the work of God what you called naturally evil? The result is that in order to refute you we prove that what you call diabolical was established as part of nature. This is, of course, a legitimate and learned reply, namely, to defend in its species what is accused in its species and to defend in its genus what is blamed in its genus.

(4) This point was understood by Mani whom you equal in wrongdoing, but do not equal in intelligence. For he consigned all the substance of bodies to the devil, but you do not consign to him the entire substance, but the better substance, as we said in the previous book.[70] Surrounded, then, by its sacred guardians, the truth has triumphed; the truth which proves through the apostle that the activity of married couples is natural and, for this reason, pertains to God who is the author of nature has burst your fantasies, since you swear that it is the result of transgression and not natural.

AUG. (1) We have above already explained quite enough which relations with a woman the apostle called natural and why he called them natural, that is, when they are carried out by those members of the two sexes which were established for the propagation of their nature. It makes no difference whether they were the sort of relations which could have existed in paradise, that is, which did not make use of an evil, either because no sexual desire existed or because it only existed after a sign from the will, or whether they were the sort of relations which now exist once such relations began to exist. They could be either licit relations as in marriage which make good use of the good of the body and the evil of sexual desire, or they could be illicit relations as in adultery which make bad use of that good and of that evil, though adulterous relations do not, nonetheless, abandon those members which we call "nature" in the proper sense.

(2) There is no reason, then, why you should put the question precisely and briefly, as you say, whether the apostle wanted us to understand by what he called "natural relations" those which both could have and ought to have existed or those which could have, but ought not to have existed. For when he said this, the apostle did not have in mind either of these, but only the natural genital members of both sexes, that is, those created for generating the nature. For who does not know that licit relations with a woman both can exist and ought to exist, but illicit relations can exist and yet ought not to exist? Both of these sorts of relations, however, are natural, because both are carried out by the members of the two sexes created for propagating our nature.

(3) Take away your evasive digressions; take away the wordy and deceiving smoke of your vanity. The sexual desire of animals, then, is not a defect since that flesh does not have desires opposed to the spirit. If Mani had been able to make this distinction, he would not have separated the nature of animals from the work of the true God, nor would he have thought that human defects are substances. But unless you agree with and hold the teachings of Ambrose and the other Catholics that the discord between the flesh and the spirit was turned into our nature by the transgression of the first human being,[71] however much you seem to detest the Manichees, you will remain their detestable helper. For you maintain that what the truth cries out is an evil is good and deny that this evil comes from the worsening of our nature damaged by sin so that Mani, with your help, introduces into us the mixture with an alien nature.

A Tree Is Known from Its Fruit

21. JUL. (1) With similar cleverness you also try to undermine my statement that we ought to know a tree from its fruit in accord with the testimony of the gospel. I said this to show what is evident, namely, that one cannot teach that marriage is good, nor can one defend as the work of God even nature itself, which is brought to fulfillment by the action of marriage, if serious sins are said to sprout from it. To this, then, you replied, "Was the Lord speaking of marriage? Was he not rather speaking of the two wills in human beings, namely, the good and the bad, calling this one a good tree and the other one a bad tree, because good works spring from a good will and bad works from a bad will? But if we take marriage as the good tree, we are certainly going to have to take its opposite, fornication, as the bad tree. On the other hand, if he says that in the parable we should not put adultery in the place of the tree, but rather human nature from which a human being is born, in this case too the tree will not be marriage, but human nature from which a human being is born."[72]

(2) You are mistaken; the Lord is not speaking there of two wills, but of his own person. For, though he offered the Jews countless benefits, they did not at all cease from accusations against him. But since they were not able to attack his works, which they in fact highly praised, they excused themselves by mocking him as a Samaritan and as one possessed by a demon and by the spirit of Beelzebub. Then the Lord said, *Either make the tree good and its fruit good, or make the tree bad and its fruit bad, for from its fruit a tree is known* (Mt 12:33). That is, either blame my works which are good, as banished illnesses and recovered health declare. In that way you might prove me bad by the evidence of my bad works. Or, if you do not dare to attack these great benefits, pay to the good tree, that is, to me, the testimony my fruits deserve, and love the benefactor, you who praise the good works. (3) In that passage, then, Christ demanded that his person

be recognized from his works. And that has rightly supported us in teaching that nature and marriage should also be judged by the character of their fruitfulness so that, if the poison of sins flowed from them, the root should also be judged sinful.

Recognize, then, how blind you are in terms of understanding, when you thought that you removed the weight of my objection, by setting fornication over against marriage so that, as the good tree was marriage, so the bad tree would be seen as fornication. From the latter, that is, from fornication no fruitfulness ought to come lest its fruit should be proved evil, if marriage is proved good by its good offspring. For a human being, whether born from marriage or from adultery, comes not from the sinful action, but from the nature of the seeds.

(4) The sinful act which is committed by the will of adulterers does not upset the laws of the substance. But nature works with its own resources, and while the sin remains within the author of the evil will, the innocent child springs forth from the work of the creator. You, of course, saw that you had to reply in this way, but let the wise reader note how you tried to escape. For you say, "If we should not put adultery in the place of the tree, but rather the human nature from which a human being is born, in this case too the tree is not marriage, but human nature from which a human being is born."[73]

(5) This, then, is what you tried to say: Just as a human being is not attributed to fornication, but to nature, so the sin which is contracted from lawfully wedded parents is not to be attributed to marriage, but to the human nature which the devil infected by the ancient sin. In adulterers, then, you blamed the will of those making love, but you praised the human nature from which a human being was born even through illicit intercourse. In lawfully wedded parents, however, you praised marriage from which you say sin does not come. But you found fault with the nature which you say infuses a horrible sin.

(6) Let my reader, then, be alert at this point. If in fornication you judged human nature praiseworthy because it made the state of the newborn undefiled by the sins of those making love, how do you find fault with this same nature in the case of marriage which you say produced the state of natural sin? And so, you have declared not marriage, but human nature both a great good and a great evil. For what is more wicked than it if it begets sin? What is more hateful than it if it is owned by the devil? Let nature itself, then, see to the art which it has in the seed; meanwhile, with regard to its quality, in which all good and evil is found, it is proved to be most evil if, as being guilty itself and producing guilty offspring, it is shown to be a henchman of the devil's tyranny. It is right, then, that a tree should be known from its fruit so that what is the cause of evil is with full right called evil.

AUG. (1) The facts themselves declare well enough that the cause of original sin is neither marriage nor adultery. For that which is good in the nature of a human being is born of a human being as a creature of God, and the evil which it has on account of which it must be reborn is contracted from a human being. But the cause of this evil is the fact that *through one man sin entered the world, and through sin death, and in that way it was passed on to all human beings, in whom all sinned* (Rom 5:12). Those who intelligently read your words and mine see the great wordiness with which you have foolishly labored to twist these words of the apostle to another meaning.

(2) How, then, does it help you? Why, I ask you, did you cite the testimony from the gospel that *a good tree produces good fruit* (Mt 7:17)? You were talking about the good of marriage, and you wanted its good fruit to be human beings, as if to show that they were born without evil because marriage is something good, and *a good tree cannot produce bad fruit* (Mt 7:18). But, whether with the original damage, because of which the apostle says, *The body is dead on account of sin* (Rom 8:10), or without that damage, as you maintain in opposition to the apostle, human beings are born of human beings, not merely through marital intercourse, but also through sinful intercourse. And at times marriages are barren, while adulteries are fruitful.

(3) But as to whether the Lord wanted to convey two wills by the two trees, as we say, the one good by which a human being is good and which cannot produce bad works, that is, bad fruit, and the other bad by which a human being is bad and which cannot produce good works, that is, good fruit, or whether, as you say, he said these words about himself to the Jews, those who want to know this read the gospel; they do not read you.[74]

After all, when the Lord pointed out that those were to be avoided who came in sheep's clothing, but were inwardly rapacious wolves, he said, *From their fruit you will know them. Do people gather grapes from thorns or figs from thistles? In that way every good tree produces good fruit, but a bad tree produces bad fruit. A good tree cannot produce bad fruit, nor can a bad tree produce good fruit* (Mt 7:16-18). (4) And when the hypocrites were blamed in the Gospel according to Luke, these two trees were mentioned and were soon afterward clearly explained, when the Lord went on to say, *Good persons bring forth good from the good treasure of their heart, and bad persons bring forth evil from their evil treasure. For the mouth speaks from the abundance of the heart* (Lk 6:45). But where he said, *Either make the tree good and its fruit good, or make the tree bad and its fruit bad*—which you suppose he said with regard to himself—he immediately showed what he was speaking about; he said: *For from its fruit the tree is known. Brood of vipers, how can you speak good things since you are evil? For the mouth speaks from the abundance of the heart. Good persons bring forth good from their good treasure, and bad persons bring forth evil from their evil treasure* (Mt 12:33-35).

Do you see that you are mistaken, not I? Go back, then, to the cause of the evil work, and you will find the evil will; go back to the cause of the original evil, and you will find the evil will of the first human being and the good nature damaged by it.

What Is Natural Cannot Be Evil

22. JUL. But we say these things in order to show what is the result of your faith. In any case that truth which was established by the previous discussions remains unshaken, namely, that there is nothing evil apart from the work of the will which carries out what justice forbids and that what is natural cannot be shown to be evil. There remains, then, this unshaken tower from whose high point the banditry of different errors is repelled.

AUG. (1) What are you saying? Or what are your preceding discussions but the most wordy nonsense? What do you mean when you say, "there is nothing evil apart from the work of the will which carries out what justice forbids"? Is the bad will itself, then, not an evil, if there is nothing evil but its work? After all, it does not follow that the bad will has the ability to carry out the work. And for this reason, on your authority, a person's bad will is not something evil, when one cannot carry out the work. Who would tolerate this foolishness or rather this madness?

(2) If there is nothing evil apart from the work of the will which carries out what justice forbids, what are we to do with the conclusion that whatever human beings either do or suffer unwillingly are not evils? That will not be an evil about which the apostle cries out: *For I do not do the good that I will, but I do the evil that I do not will* (Rom 7:19). The punishment of eternal fire where there will be weeping and gnashing of teeth[75] will not be an evil, because no one will suffer that willingly, and it is not the work of a will that carries out what justice forbids, but is the punishment of one who is unwilling. Would you ever have such ideas, if you were not incredibly foolish or rather mad?

What do you mean when you say, "And that which is natural cannot be shown to be evil"? I pass over the countless natural defects of the body. But is natural deafness really not an evil? After all, it even hinders the faith from which the righteous live,[76] since faith comes from hearing.[77] (3) But if you were not deaf interiorly when the apostle says, *For we were also by nature children of anger, just as the rest* (Eph 2:3), you would hear with the ears of the heart. But go on further, and cry out with hearts that are blind and deaf: It is not an evil to be naturally forgetful, to be naturally dull-witted, to be naturally prone to anger, to be naturally lustful. Why, after all, do you not banter about these silly words without a worry, since in your judgment natural folly itself is not an evil?

In denying all original evil merit, you are forced to praise all natural defects to the point that you say that not only physically deformed, sick, and monstrous babies, but even feeble-minded ones would have come into existence in paradise, even if no one had sinned. And at the same time you would locate among the delights of that most blessed place your shameful darling by which the flesh has desires opposed to the spirit.[78]

Augustine's Attacks upon Marriage

23. JUL. (1) But let us follow up what the context demands. It is evident that you, the most subtle of debaters, extolled with great praises and blackened with even greater accusations one and the same thing, namely, human nature. Just as one cannot simultaneously do both at one time, by one action, and with one aim, so natural reason does not accept these contraries even under different circumstances, but is always full of the one, that is, of appreciation for the good, never on account of the evil, which its laws do not admit by reason of the dignity of their author, unless it is bitten by the most foul fang of the Manichee.

But with this out of the way, I ask what imaginary clouds of marriage you think that you should pursue. For if you say that it is not marriage, but nature which is the cause of a human being, and that marriage is also not the cause of sin, this marriage to which you offered praise has completely disappeared. (2) For what, then, is marriage intended if it is the cause neither of your evil nor of my good? You remove human beings from the morality of marriage so that you are not forced to ascribe them to fornication, and you remove sin from its connection with marriage so that you do not seem to condemn marriage.

What, then, worthy of praise is left for marriage to possess? Why are you afraid to attack in words what you have completely destroyed by the use of your argument? What will marriage be said to cause if it has no share in either natural evil or natural good? Do the name and morality of marriage, then, do nothing in human affairs? But you are trapped and trapped badly too. We must help out a breathless old man. There is left something that you could give it, and apart from it nothing else is found. That is, you could say that this marriage stands guard at the doors to prevent any rumor of indecency from breaking in upon the pleasure of those having intercourse, but that by its title it claims for that act morality and decency. (3) Without reason, therefore, you wanted to destroy the dignity of marriage by your deceitful praise; marriage is angrier at no one than at yourself.

Marriage completely drives you off and does not permit the tongues of the Manichees to enter to attack the union entrusted to its protection. They have, marriage says, brothels worthy of their teaching in which they may find satisfaction during the hours of the night. The sentinels of marriage defend that pleasure of those who act with modesty; sins are warded off, and the honor of morality is admitted. The privileges of marriage granted to it by the apostle defend honorable marriage and the sinless marriage bed. God, however, will judge fornicators and adulterers. Where, then, is the sinful union if the dignity of marriage, which you praised, is obedient to its function and to its secrecy?

AUG. (1) When you said that a tree is known from its fruit, you did not want this testimony from the gospel to help nature, but marriage. For these are your words: "If then the original evil is contracted from marriage, the cause of the evil is the marital union, and that is necessarily evil through which and from which the evil fruit appears, since the Lord says in the gospel, *From its fruit a tree is known* (Mt 12:33). How," you ask, "do you think we should listen to you when you say that marriage is good, though you declare that nothing but evil comes from it? It is clear, therefore," you say, "that marriage is guilty if original sin is derived from it and that it cannot be defended unless its fruit is shown to be innocent. But marriage is defended and declared to be good; its fruit, therefore, is proved to be innocent."[79]

From these words of yours it is, of course, clear that you wanted the tree to be understood as marriage and the fruits of the tree as those infants which are born as a result of the union of the spouses. (2) But since you were prevented from this by a perfectly clear argument, for such infants also come to be from adultery, you thought that you should flee to nature in order to hide in its depths. But you were not dealing with nature when you blindly used the gospel parable of the tree on account of the good of marriage and its good fruit.

Defend nature, then, against original sin; leave marriage aside. Call nature the good tree since it brings to birth human beings, whether from marriages or from adulteries. You, then, are saying that these human beings are the good fruit of the good tree so that they are not believed to have contracted by birth from their corrupted origin any guilt that must be removed by rebirth, so that they do not need the savior, so that they are not redeemed by his blood shed for the forgiveness of sins.[80] (3) Go ahead, do this, as a hateful heretic; fill God's paradise, even if no one had sinned, with the desires of the lustful, with the struggles of those fighting against desires, with the pains of mothers in travail, with the cries of bawling babies, with the diseases of the ill, with the deaths of the dying, and with the grief of the mourners. Go ahead, do that; that is just your line. For, according to you, such punishments follow upon the good fruit of the good tree and make their way into the paradise of delights, but of the delights of the Pelagians.

Moreover, as a clever dialectician, you mock my arguments; you say that I extolled with great praises and blackened with greater accusations one and the same thing, namely, human nature. But I am happy to have as my teacher, not Aristotle or Chrysippus,[81] much less Julian, a fool despite all his banter, but Christ. Unless human nature were a great good, he would certainly not have become man for the sake of that nature, for he was God. If that nature had not died by the great evil of sin, he would not have died for it, for he himself would have come and remained without sin.

(4) Again, as if human nature were not enough for you, since it is born of the same sort from adulterers as from married couples, you suppose that we need to be pressured about the goodness of marriage. You ask what marriage does in human affairs, if one should neither attribute evil to it, since evil is not contracted from marriage, but from the origin damaged by sin, nor attribute good to it, since a human being is also born from adulterers. And since we found that the moral goodness of marriage is distinct from the turpitude of immoral intercourse, you think that you can conclude from this that no original evil is contracted from marital intercourse. You do not see that, if the good of marriage were the reason why those born of married couples do not contract any evil, the evil of adultery would, of course, be the reason why those born of adulterers contract evil.

(5) Marriage, therefore, has its honorable role in human affairs. Its purpose is not that human beings might be born, since they would, of course, be born even if the two sexes were united under no law of marriage, but randomly in natural relations. Rather, its purposes are that they might be born in an ordered manner of propagation, that, just as the mothers are known with certitude by birth, so the fathers also might be held as certain because of the fidelity of marriage,[82] and that your shameful darling might not wander from woman to woman more disgracefully in proportion to her greater freedom.

But the fact that human beings are born with the identity of the father certain does not mean that they do not need a savior through whom they may be reborn so that they are set free from the evil with which they are born. Intercourse is not, therefore, sinful in marriage, as you falsely accuse us of saying, but the chastity of the spouses should be praised precisely because it alone can make good use of the evil which you monstrously praise.

Julian Offers Lessons in Logic

24. JUL. (1) Now that these points have been taken care of, I will at least briefly show how you, who up to now have been considered very subtle and intelligent, lie in the depth of ignorance. You say that you attribute the sin which is passed on to the offspring to nature, but not, nonetheless, to marriage,[83] just as, on the other hand, you attribute the sin to the nature of human beings, not to their sinful behavior. And you pretend that you praise marriage so that you are not clearly caught out as a Manichee, but you blame nature in which you claim that evil is present and from which you say that evil is propagated.

Is it possible, then, that you never heard the rules of argumentation and the laws of most sound reason? In all the categories, after all, the genera are more inclusive than the species, but from these there also arise subordinate genera. The species include more than the individuals, and there are genera which contain the species, but there are derivative species which contain the individuals.[84] To knock down the lower does not knock down the higher, but in their collapse the higher include all which they embrace.

(2) For example, animal is a genus, but in the breadth of its meaning it includes different species, namely, human, horse, cow, and so on. If, then, one species perishes, that genus does not suffer destruction. After all, imagine that the nature of cows vanishes from the world; the genus is, of course, not destroyed, since the nature of other animals remains. But, on the contrary, if the genus "animal" is taken from the world, all the species which are included in this genus undoubtedly perish, for no species of animal will remain if the genus "animal" is completely destroyed. Those genera which are higher, therefore, communicate to the species which they include their modifications and their merits. But the reverse is not true, namely, that the higher are changed by the different fates of their species as if the species were certain bonds of relationship.

(3) To apply the example to the present issue, the generality of human nature is a kind of genus for those systems located under it; this generality has these as its species: bodily position, the members, their order, their acts, and other things of this sort. It, therefore, bestows its own character upon all the subordinate species, but it is not held subject[85] to its species so that it is involved in the perils of things lower than itself. If, then, nature were blamed and believed to be subject to the devil and to be guilty, then marriage too which is subordinate to it and fecundity and the whole substance will be condemned. (4) It is impossible, then, to praise marriage which takes place in accord with nature if nature itself is blamed. It is necessary that the beauty of flowers which are cut down should die with their root. And to state the issue more clearly, the marital act cannot be called good if natural union is blamed, because what is scorned in the genus to which it inseparably clings cannot be honored in the species.

Moreover, when a bad will uses natural instruments for indecent acts, that power of pleasure and the seed, which never changes in accord with the will of those having intercourse, tolerates no alliance with sin, but offers the material to God who works upon it. It only blames the indecent act and the merit of the adulterer, not of the nature. (5) When, therefore, we were discussing natural factors, you were extremely dumb to blame nature while praising marriage, since it has been irrefutably established that a genus shares with its species whatever it has received.

And for that reason either the relations which the apostle calls natural will be judged good and lawful, and marriage will be honorable, and there will be no natural sin, or if nature is believed to be diabolical so that there is original sin, marital relations will also be declared damnable. And the Manichean doctrine is adopted not, of course, with a clear head, but nonetheless clearly. And because it is deadly, because there is no trace among them of truth or morality or faith, and because the idea of original sin can be found among no other people, it is evident that, just as we are Catholics, so you are Manichees.

AUG. (1) You certainly spoke of the tree and the fruit from which a tree is known when you thought that one should understand marriage and children in this parable; having been kept from that interpretation, because such fruit can also come to be from adulterous intercourse, you took flight to nature. And the act of your flight could not escape our notice. For in your own words which I shall now reproduce, it was seen quite evidently. While addressing me, you said, "With similar cleverness you also try to undermine my statement that we ought to know a tree from its fruit in accord with the testimony of the gospel." You said this "to show what is evident, namely, that one cannot teach that marriage is good, nor can one defend as the work of God even nature itself, which is brought to fulfillment by the action of marriage, if serious sins are said to sprout from it."[86]

(2) By these statements of yours you disclosed the act of your flight, when, after mentioning marriage, you added and said, "even nature itself, which is brought to fulfillment by the action of marriage." You, therefore, distinguished these two, and you showed well enough that nature is distinct from marriage by the act of which nature is brought to fulfillment. Why is it, then, that afterwards you want nature to be the genus and marriage its species? Is any genus brought to fulfillment by the action of any of its species? Not at all! After all, animal, which is the genus, is not brought to fulfillment by the action of a man or horse or cow or any other critter which is a species of that genus, for even if some species is lacking or is removed from the world, the genus still remains because it includes the other species, as you yourself have also argued. (3) That genus would, of course, not have remained whole if it were brought to fulfillment by the operation of the species which was removed. It is not more a genus if it has more species and less a genus if it has fewer, although, if all the species are removed, there will not be a genus either, just as if the genus is removed, there will be no species.

Marriage, therefore, is not a species, and nature is not a genus, if nature is brought to fulfillment by the act of marriage, just as agriculture is not a species of the harvest because the harvest is brought to fulfillment by the work of agriculture. Furthermore, if you say that nature is the genus and marriage is its species, you are undoubtedly forced to say that every marriage is a nature. For every horse is an animal, even though not every animal is a horse, precisely because the species is horse and the genus animal.

No nature, then, is made by a human being; for, though, as scripture says, a woman is joined to a man by the Lord[87] since this is done only with the Lord's help when it is done rightly, who does not know that marriages are works of human beings? (4) But if a human being does not make a nature, marriage is not a nature, because human beings make marriages. And for this reason, because marriage is not a nature, it certainly can by no means be a species of nature, as if nature were its genus.

Marriages, then, pertain to human morality, but the human beings themselves pertain to nature. It is permissible for us, then, to blame the evils of our damaged nature and praise the moral conduct that makes good use of the goods and evils of nature. I, therefore, praise marriages. But heaven forbid that I should praise the evil by which the flesh has desires opposed to the spirit.[88] Without that evil no human being can be born; the guilt of that evil can be removed only by being re-born. The good use of that evil is praised in marital intercourse. Hence, it is not the Manichees, but the Catholics who say that original sin is not contracted from being mixed up with an alien nature, but from the corruption of our own nature. Because you deny this, you are heretics.

Augustine in Comparison with the Manichees

25. JUL.(1) In order to avoid the odium attached to this name, you make mention of different heresies utterly to no purpose. For you say: The Arians call the Catholics Sabellians, though the Catholics make a definite distinction of the persons, while preserving the shared oneness of the nature. In the same way you say that we impose upon you the name of the Manichees, though you do not say that marriage is an evil, as the Manichees do, but you say that evil was passed to all human beings by the condition of nature.[89] I have no doubt that these arguments of yours will be mocked by the wise. For the Arians falsely say that the Catholics are Sabellians, though we make a distinction of the persons of the Father and of the Son and of the Holy Spirit without any confusion of them and without any change of their substance, and they most stupidly make the slanderous claim that there is no distinction between the unity and the trinity. In the same way, the Catholics rightly and correctly declare you Manichees, because your faith forces us to say this.

(2) The Manichees, of course, say that sin is natural; you say that it is natural. The Manichees say that the lust of bodies was implanted by the devil; you confirm that with many arguments. They claim that evil cannot be avoided by free choice because, of course, it is natural; with the same words you speak of free choice by which one can do evil, but cannot stop doing evil. Mani says that the seed is cursed; you try to prove this by the authority of scripture. Mani says that evil is incorrigible; you shout that this is true. But you say that only Adam had a better nature; Mani also says in the letter to Patticius[90] that one must believe that Adam was better than his descendants inasmuch as he was formed from the flower of the first substance. (3) You say that intercourse is diabolical on account of its natural motions and that the devil rightfully plucks human beings like the fruit of the tree he planted; Mani says this too, for you learned to believe and defend this from him. Mani says that both nature and marriage are evil,

while you say that marriage is good, but that nature is guilty. On this point you are not more religious; rather, he is wiser.

As, therefore, the Arian statement that the Catholics are Sabellians is false, so the Catholic statement is perfectly true that the traducianists are the same as the Manichees and that the distinction between you, an illusory one, of course, is not based on your faith, but on your ignorance. You and Mani, therefore, have one and the same faith, but he is less impudent than you with your seriousness are found to be. For one cannot easily stumble upon another Mani, or rather another Melitides,[91] who says that he condemns the nature of human beings, but does not disparage marriage.

AUG. (1) Any intelligent person who reads that book of mine soon discovers why I mentioned the Arians and the Sabellians and clearly sees that you acted deceitfully when you were unwilling to mention this issue in its entirety. For I said to you, "In fleeing from the Sabellians, the Arians fell into something worse, because they were so bold as to assert not a difference of persons, but of natures in the Trinity. In the same way, in trying to avoid the plague of the Manichees by moving in the wrong direction, the Pelagians are shown to hold with regard to the fruit of marriage more destructive views than the Manichees, since they believe that the little ones do not need the help of Christ the physician."[92] You would have mentioned these words of mine or at least this idea of mine, if you wanted to reply to me in any way, but after having passed these over, you say to yourself what you want so that you might seem to have replied to me, not by refuting what I said, but by not keeping silence.

(2) But now, with regard to your claim that I hold what the Manichees hold, you are greatly deceived, or rather you are deceiving those whom you can. For the Manichees say that evil is coeternal with God, that the same evil is a substance, and that it is a certain alien nature which absolutely cannot be changed into good either by itself or by the good God. They state that by being mixed with the immutable evil the good soul, which they are so bold as to believe is the nature of God, was defiled and corrupted and, for this reason, at every age a human being has need of a savior by whom the soul may be set free after being purified, restored, and rescued from such captivity. (3) But when you fled from the Manichees by moving in the wrong direction, you fell into this darkness of impiety, namely that, because you claim that the little ones are safe from all evil, you do not think that the savior is necessary for the poor children, and somehow or other through the circuitous path of your error you run to help the very Manichees whom you are fleeing because you deny the evil of our damaged nature. As a result, whatever evil one correctly believes or clearly finds in little ones is attributed to the mixture with the alien nature, and that is precisely what they want it.

In order to avoid the Manichees and the Pelagians, the Catholic Church says that evil is no nature or substance, but does not deny that the voluntary evil, which through one man was passed on to all human beings, damaged our nature and substance, which is mutable because it is not the nature of God. And it confesses that the savior is necessary for persons of every age in order that that evil may be removed which is not incurable for God. (4) Hence, we cannot say the same things as the Manichees about natural sin, about the lust of bodies, about free choice, about the cursed seed, about the incorrigible evil, about the nature of the first human being, about union of the sexes, or about the power of the devil over human beings. For we do not say that there were two natures or substances, one of the good, the other of the evil, everlasting without any temporal beginning and that from some temporal beginning they were mingled. Otherwise, we would say among many other absurd and crazy things that even the nature of God can be defiled and corrupted.

(5) But with regard to your claim that I alone say that marriage is good and nature is guilty, to pass over others, I give you the apostle Paul, whom you also declare to have praised marriage. But he says regarding the guilt of our nature from its origin that the body is dead on account of sin.[93] I give you another man who understood this, my teacher, the Catholic Ambrose; though he praises marital chastity, he still says, "We are all born under the power of sin, and our very origin lies in guilt."[94] You slanderer, you contentious rascal, you wordy fellow, what more do you ask?

Julian Returns to the Definition of Sin

26. JUL. (1) But enough has been said against these frivolous ideas. Let us come to that most complicated question which, as I said above, deceived your teacher by its subtlety.[95] You tried to meet our objection, not by explaining it, but by posing something else more difficult. For I explained that in the case of human beings of an adult age who do evil by their own will, we both praise the innocent beginnings of their nature, and we rightly reprehend the deviations in their actions. And I said that there are two elements which can be put to contrary uses. But in little ones there is only the one element, that is, nature, because the will does not exist. That one element must be attributed to either the demon or God.[96] I concluded that, if nature existed because of God, original evil could not exist in it, but if it were consigned to the devil because of the inborn evil, there would be nothing by which a human being might be claimed for God's work.

(2) When you came to those passages, you answered with your usual reliability that my inference was correct, but that in the little ones there are two elements: nature and sin.[97] But this sin—to recall the previous definitions—is nothing but the will to keep or to do that which justice forbids and from which we are free to hold back.[98] After, then, it was established that sin is nothing but the choice of an evil will, you replied, you Epicurus of our age,[99] that there is sin in

little ones, but there is no will. The fourth book has shown what a disgrace this involves. After I had said in these passages, "If sin comes from the will, the will which commits sin is evil; if sin comes from nature, the nature which commits sin is evil,"[100] you tried to confront me with the question which you clearly did not think up on your own. (3) For when we were in Carthage a few years ago, it was proposed by a certain man named Honoratus, your friend and fellow Manichee, as your correspondence shows.[101]

I have made mention of this fact only so that it might be clear that this is the question which deceived Mani and Marcion so many ages ago. Against my words: "If sin has become a nature, the nature which commits sin is evil," you, therefore, speak as follows, "I ask him to reply, if he can, to this: Just as it is clear that all evil actions come from an evil will, like the fruit from a bad tree, so let him state where the evil will itself, that is, the tree whose fruit is bad, has come from. If it comes from an angel, what was the angel itself but a good work of God? If it comes from a human being, what was the human being but a good work of God? (4) In fact, since an angel's evil will comes from the angel and a human being's from a human being, what were these two before these evils came to be in them but God's good work and a good and praiseworthy nature? You see, then, evil arises from good, and there was absolutely nothing else but good from which it could arise. I mean: the evil will which was preceded by no evil, not evil deeds which come only from an evil will, as from a bad tree. But an evil will could arise from something good, not because it was made good by the good God, but because it was made out of nothing, not out of God. What then do his words mean, 'If nature is a work of God, one cannot permit that the work of the devil be passed on through the work of God'? Did not the work of the devil, when it first arose in the angel who became the devil, not arise in the work of God? (5) Hence, if an evil which existed nowhere at all could come to be in the work of God, why could not an evil which already existed somewhere not be passed on through the work of God? Are not human beings the work of God? Sin, then, was passed on through human beings, that is, the work of the devil through the work of God.[102] And to state this in other words, the work of a work of God was passed on through a work of God.' "[103]

These very many words which I have cited from your discourse have completely revealed the chief source of the ancient error. You have produced nothing more clever in your statements, nothing more convoluted in your argumentation. Pursued on the whole field of the debate and driven by the hostile weapons of the truth from every place where you had tried to take a stand, you came at last to that pit which Mani had dug amid the darkness of questions. (6) You testified to the difficulty of this issue when you said, "I ask him to reply, if he can, to this,"[104] and since it is agreed between the two of us that this passage is difficult, I warn the reader to be fully alert. One who is first attentive will safely follow the fine distinctions appropriate to the topic which I hope to fatten up with the help of Christ.

You have, then, asked: From where does evil come? I ask what evil you mean. This name is common to sin and to punishment. Besides, punishment is called evil in an improper sense, though this is justified by the gravity of that sentence by which it is imposed. You will reply that you are talking about sin, not about punishment.

AUG. (1) You have completely revealed your stupidity as much as possible, when you admit that sin is an evil and say that it is not evil, but it is called evil in an improper sense to burn in the punishment of eternal fire. But you give an amazing explanation of this absurdity. You say, "Punishment is called evil in an improper sense, though this is justified by the gravity of that sentence by which it is imposed." If, then, in order to say this, you weigh the punishment of the condemned person not from the misery of the one who suffers it, but from the justice of the one who condemns, state more openly that the punishment, which you say is called evil in an improper sense, is good. Punishment is, after all, the penalty for sin, and the penalty for sin is, of course, just. Punishment, therefore, is just. And everything which is just is good. Therefore, punishment is good.

(2) Do you not see that, unless you distinguish the one condemned from the one who condemns so that you say that the condemnation itself, which is the punishment and penalty for sin, is a good work on the part of the one who condemns, but that the death of the one condemned is evil—do you not see, I repeat, that unless you distinguish these two in that way, you are brought to the point that you say that by their evil actions human beings do not come to graver evils which they suffer—and this is true—but they come to greater goods? And this is so false and said with such folly that to think such a thought is as great an evil as is the punishment of having a blind heart. Therefore, it is not called evil in an improper sense. Rather, it is evil for the one who suffers it, but it is good for one who imposes it, because it is just to impose punishment upon the sinner. If you do not want to mouth madness, distinguish these two.

The Question of the Existence of Evil

27. JUL. You ask, therefore, where evil comes from, the evil which is rightly called evil, that is, sin. I answer that it is quite stupid to ask about the origin of something whose definition is still not settled. Let us see, then, first, whether it exists, then, what it is, and lastly, from where it comes. I did this in the first book of the present work, but I was careless there to some extent. It is still in doubt whether evil exists.

AUG. If you were to say that evil exists and I were to say that it does not, then the question at issue between us would be whether evil exists. On that question you would undertake to show that evil exists, because that would have been denied by me. But since neither of us denies it, neither of us should have any doubt about it, why do ask that a doubt should be raised about that over which there is no doubt unless it is out of a desire to talk, so that you might boast, not over the refutation of my words, but over the multitude of your books?

From Where Does the Evil of Sin Come?

28. JUL. (1) But frequent sins and severe judgments testify to the existence of evil; it is, therefore, proved that sin exists. We ask what it is: whether it is a body which is seen to be composed of many components, or whether it is a single something, such as one particular element purified from mixture with the others at least by thought. But it is none of these. What is it then? An inclination of the free will which justice forbids or, to use the previous definition: the will to do that which justice forbids and from which one is free to hold back. Consider, then, whether sin cannot be found beyond the bounds of this definition lest what we think has been captured may wander off elsewhere.

(2) Let us, then, consult the justice of the judge so that it may be clear from his testimony whether every kind of sin has been well confined within these limits. Does God impute that which he knows cannot be avoided? But that would be no justice, but the highest deformity; rather, if this happens, sins are not punished, but are increased. For wrongdoing is normally punished by a just judge; if by a corruption of justice wrongdoing enters into the judge himself, wrongdoing is avenged, not punished by the judge. Justice, therefore, does not impute something as a sin unless one is free to hold back from it. But something can be said to be free only if it was placed in the possession of an emancipated will without any unavoidable coercion from natural factors. Its definition, then, is excellent and complete: Sin is the will to do that which justice forbids and from which one is free to hold back. With these aspects taken care of, let us ask where it comes from, for this question had been asked in a most disorderly fashion prior to these definitions. Where, then, does sin come from? I reply: From the free will of the one who commits it.

AUG. Is it really up to the free will of the one who commits it where it is said, *But if I do what I do not will, it is no longer I who do it, but the sin that dwells in me* (Rom 7:20)? Do you see that, when you ask where sin comes from, and you reply, "From the free will of the one who commits it," you are thinking only of that sin which is not also the punishment of sin? Do you see that, when human beings do what they do not will, and the apostle, nonetheless, cries out that it is sin, this does not at all fit your reply? Do you see that it does not fit that definition which you mentioned when you said that sin is the will to do that which justice forbids and from which one is free to hold back? How is one free to hold back when one cries out, *I do what I do not will* (Rom 7:20)? Human nature, then, sinned in one way when it was free to hold back from sin; it now sins in another way after freedom has been lost when it needs the help of the deliverer. And that former sin was only sin, but this present sin is also the punishment of sin.

Justice Imputes Only Sin Freely Committed

29. JUL. But let us see whether what the previous definition established is supported by the agreement of all. Surely no wise person and no Catholic can have a doubt about this, namely, that it is not sin unless it can be avoided and that it is justice only if it imputes to those it punishes what they by themselves committed by their own free will, when they could have avoided it.

AUG. To the first man was imputed the kind of sin which he was able to avoid if he willed to, but the whole nature damaged by his sin, even in his descendants, needs the savior to be able to avoid sins even once the age has also been reached at which one can make use of reason. Before this age, however, there is present the guilt from our origin which was contracted by birth and which must be removed by rebirth. By denying this, you state with perfect clarity that Christ Jesus is not Jesus for the little ones, though he is called by this name, as the angel testified, precisely because *he will save his people from their sins* (Mt 1:21), while you do not want to include the little ones in his people.

Points on Which Mani and the Traducianist Agree

30. JUL. (1) But, while we hold firmly to these points, Mani and the traducianist reject them with like minds. Let us, then, see what they say. Mani writes that sin is natural; Augustine agrees that sin is natural. Both of them, therefore, disagree with the definition we previously set forth and are united in calling sin natural. Let us see what they say about the kind of sin as well, that is, what they think that the sin is which they both affirm is natural; for they perhaps disagree at least in the next step.

What does Mani write to his daughter? He writes that the concupiscence of the flesh and that pleasure intended for the act of propagation are shown to be diabolical by the fact that this act avoids the eyes of the public.[105] (2) What does Augustine say? Exactly the same thing: That concupiscence of the flesh is the fruit tree of the devil;[106] the law of sin is the cause that it "everywhere avoids being seen and seeks privacy out of a sense of shame."[107] They are not, therefore, in disagreement about either the first or the second question about sin.

What about the third? When he is asked where evil comes from, Mani says, From the eternal nature of darkness. What does Augustine say? My teacher, he says, who thought that evil never had a beginning exaggerated on this point; it began through the will of the first human being. In fact, it had already begun through the will of a higher, that is, of an angelic nature. But from that time it became natural. His teacher undoubtedly beats him and with his full authority hauls him into court.

What judgment is a Catholic going to make between them? Mani is, of course, most stupid for thinking that there is natural sin, but compared with the mind of Augustine he seems quite intelligent. (3) For they agree that sin is natural, and they admit that this sin by which they think that the whole human race is possessed is of one sort. But after this the disciple dares to say that in one man alone that is not natural which he admits is innate in all. The Catholics will undoubtedly disgrace him by schoolboy beatings and rank him below his teacher who blasphemes more logically. But they will exclude both of them together, the teacher and the disciple, from the company of believers. See, then, how patiently we deal with you. You do not like what Mani says, namely, that evil is natural. State, then, that no one is born guilty, and you have escaped by, of course, denying original sin. But you do not say that; you admit, then, that you wish neither to leave your teacher nor to join the Catholics.

AUG. (1) Are we not to say that the good God made the world because Mani also says this? But when the question is asked from what he made it, we differ on this point. For we say: From those things which did not exist, because he spoke and they were made.[108] But he says: From two natures, namely, good and evil, which not only already existed, but always existed. These statements on which we do not agree do not, then, prevent us from being their allies on the basis of those statements on which we agree. So too, if we were asked whether God exists, both we and the Manichees reply: God exists, and in this both of us are separated from that fool who *said in his heart: There is no God* (Ps 14:1), but when we are asked what sort of a God he is, we differ greatly from the unspeakable myth of the Manichees. For we say and defend that God is incorruptible, but they present the myth of a corruptible god.

(2) When we are asked about the Trinity itself, we both say that the Father and the Son and the Holy Spirit are of one and the same nature. But we are not for this reason Manichees, nor are they for this reason Catholics. For they say other things about the Father and the Son and the Holy Spirit, and on these points we differ completely from them and are utterly opposed to them. Hence, we confidently maintain those points upon which we agree with them against the errors of others who deny them, and we are not afraid that they will call us Manichees and, for that reason, place themselves ahead of us, because we say along with the Manichees what they refuse to say and are, therefore, rejected by us.

(3) As, then, Arians are heretics because they do not say along with us that the essence of the Trinity is one, a point on which the Manichees agree with us, so you are heretics for not saying along with us that sin is natural, a point on which the Manichees agree with us. But we are not for that reason Manichees. For we

do not say in the same sense as the Manichees what they also say. After all, we say that our good nature was damaged by the voluntary sin of that one from whom we are descended as a result of which we are all born under the power of sin, and our very origin lies in guilt, as Ambrose says.[109] Mani brings into us an alien evil nature and claims that we sin because of our mixture with it. Finally, we offer to the savior even little ones in order that our nature may be healed. But he does not think that Christ is needed to heal our nature in us, but to separate the alien nature from us. You see, then, the great difference between us, even in our common statement that sin is natural.

(4) So too, in our common statement that concupiscence of the flesh is evil because of which the flesh has desires opposed to the spirit,[110] we are found to be worlds apart when we are asked where this evil comes from. For we say with Ambrose that this foul discord between the flesh and the spirit was turned into our nature by the transgression of the first human being.[111] But Mani says along with his followers that an alien nature, which always existed, became attached to us so that the flesh and the spirit are opposed to each other. For this reason we ask the savior that this defect might be healed in us. But he asks that the alien nature which cannot in any way be healed might be taken away from us.

Why do you not notice here too the great difference by which we are separated on our common statement that concupiscence of the flesh which fights against the spirit is evil? (5) Why do you not notice that we are not Manichees just because we say some things along with them and that you are heretics because you do not say those things along with them? For if you would say with them that evils are natural and would say along with us in opposition to them where they come from, namely, that they are not from an alien nature coeternal with God, you would not be Pelagian heretics. But now by denying that concupiscence is evil because of which the flesh has desires opposed to the spirit and by denying that it comes from our damaged nature, you make the Manichees conclude that it comes from an alien nature. And so, you are new heretics, and you help the old heretics from whom you flee in the wrong way.

Stop confronting me with Mani as my teacher; rather, be a follower of Ambrose along with me. And look at the Arians and imitate them at least on the points on which they were wiser than you. For they do not call us Manichees, although we say along with the Manichees that the Father and the Son and the Holy Spirit have one nature, a point on which they contradict us with great vigor.

Nothing as the Cause of the Evil Will

31. JUL. (1) You considered it a strong objection when you stated the source from which the evil will came to be in the first man himself or in the devil who was created as an angel.[112] You say, nonetheless, that the evil will arose in the

work of God, that is, either in the angel or in the human being, not because it was the work of God, but because it was made out of nothing. Watch out, then, that you too do not by other paths say that the necessity of evil is eternal. For, if this was the cause of the emergence of evil in God's work, namely, that it has been shown to have been made out of nothing, this nothing always existed before there was made that which would exist; that is, before there was made that which would exist, something never existed, and this something which never existed is said to have been nothing.

(2) From eternity, then, there never existed that which did not exist before it was made by God, whose substance alone is without beginning. This void, that is, nothing, before it was brought to an end by the existence of things, always existed. This nothing, then, was not made, but creatures were made, and that nothing ceased to be. In that creature, then, which was made out of nothing, you say that evil arose because the creature was made out of nothing. You, therefore, attributed the evil that arose in the man to his origin, and you say that his origin, that is, nothing, was the cause of sin. For, you say, evil arose in man, not because he had been made by God, but because he had been made out of nothing.

(3) If, then, evil arose because the state of the preceding nothing demanded it, and this nothing was eternal, you have by different paths fallen into and are completely trapped in the snare of your teacher so that you both say that evil existed from eternity. But on this point too he is the wiser, for, in introducing natural sin, he said that the substance of darkness was eternal which compelled this evil to be present without the will of the sinner. He, therefore, named an author of the reality whose necessity he devised so that the evil which pervades substances is seen to have a cause that necessitates this. But with an intolerably leaden mind, you affirm the necessity of evil, while you deny an author of the necessity. You leave the effect both in little ones and in the first one who committed sin, and you say that one can understand that it is something great that this nothing is able to do very much, though it is nothing.

AUG. (1) You are not able to do anything, but in claiming that nothing, though it is nothing, is able to do something, you do not understand that, when God is said to have made what he made from nothing, nothing else is said but that he did not make it out of himself, for before he made something, making something was not coeternal to him. "Out of nothing" then means: "Not out of something," because, though God made some things out of other things, he did not make out of any things these latter from which he made the others.

(2) But if it were made out of the nature of God, no being could have sinned, nor would it have been made. Rather, whatever it would have been, it would have been from God, and it would have been what he is, just as the Son is and the Holy Spirit. Because they are from him, they are what he is, the one by being born, the other by proceeding. And they are from him in such a way that he was never before them. And this nature absolutely cannot sin, because it cannot

abandon itself, nor does it have a better to which it ought to cling and by abandoning which it could sin. The rational creature, nonetheless, was not created so that it was under the necessity of sinning, but, if it were the nature of God, it would not have the possibility of sinning either, because the nature of God neither wills to be able nor is able to will to sin.

The Destructive Power of Nothingness

32. JUL. (1) For you maintain that this nothing from which all things were made was the cause of sin. According to your view, then, the power of this nothing does as much as the power of the prince of darkness does according to Mani's view. Both of you, then, say that the first evil was necessary. He gives something solid, though evil, as its cause; you give something empty, though equally evil. He says it is a destructive substance; you say that it is equally destructive, but nothing. See, then, where your syllogism leads. When there was not yet anything created, nothing was the sign of an eternal void. But this very nothing, that is, the void, was brought to an end when creatures began to be. (2) For the nothing ceased to be when something began to be. Therefore, even when that nothing was, it was not, because it is understood to have been when there was not yet something. But afterwards when things were made, this sign of the void, that is, nothing, lost its name, as it never has a substance. It has come about that what never existed in reality has also lost its name. By its destructive power, then, you think that evil arose both in the angel and in the human being. What can be said more crazy than that?

AUG. You are seen to be crazy with the desire to speak ill. I did not say that nothing is destructive, for it is not something which could be destructive. Neither an angel nor a human being can be compelled to sin by some force. And they would not have sinned if they had not willed to sin, for they could also have not willed to sin. But they would not even have been able to sin, if they were the nature of God.

Nothing's Great Dominion

33. JUL. You say, a thing which did not exist had great power for the sole reason that it never had been, but it began to have very much power after it lost even its name. And this nothing attained its great dominion after even its name perished.

AUG. If that which is nothing were something, it would be said to have attained great dominion in your thought, since vanity or falsity has dominion over you so that it compels you to chatter this inanity for so long a time.

A Move from the Sins of the Innocent to Nothing

34. JUL. Congratulations on your wisdom! By the rules of a new system of logic invented by you, you adopt the conclusions after denying the premises, and you put together bodies deprived of their heads. We do not begrudge you your subtle arguments; rather, we feel sorry for you with Christian pity, because you have found an outcome worthy of your teaching. That is, having begun with the grave sins of the innocent, you have come to nothing.

AUG. It is you rather who have come to nothing, and it so delights you that you are still unwilling to withdraw or return from it. You claim that I said that which is nothing is something in order that you might say nothing so much.

Even the First Sin Did Not Come from the Will

35. JUL. Oh the soundness, Oh the elegance of the debater! He says, Evil did not arise in the human being because he was made by God, but because he was made out of nothing.[113] We have already pointed out the cleverness by which the greatest power has been substituted for this nothing. Now I give warning about that point which even the previous discussion made us understand, namely, that not even the first evil was initiated by the will of the sinner, if the condition of a race that comes from nothing requires that evil to arise.

AUG. No condition of a race that comes from nothing requires that sin arise, since that is required which is compelled to be given or done. But the angel or the human being from which and in which sins first arose were not compelled to sin by anything; rather, they sinned by free will. And they could have willed not to, because they were not compelled to will to sin, and yet they could not have willed to sin if they had the nature of God and were not made out of nothing.

A Clear Pact between Augustine and Mani

36. JUL. You have, then, ascribed a nature to even the first evil, but an emptier one than Mani had, though equally eternal. We should not fight over this; it is perfectly clear that there is between the two of you a pact which the chain of natural evil and of eternal evil joins together.

AUG. You idiot, that which is nothing cannot be eternal; what is not anything cannot be something eternal; what, finally, does not exist cannot be eternal.

The First Sin Was Begotten by Eternal Darkness

37. JUL. I certainly acted as was appropriate to the good faith of the discussion. The point which you had produced in your argumentation, namely, that an

evil will came to be in God's work because the human being was made out of nothing, has been examined and crushed by reason. For it shows that you said in different words the same thing as Mani made up and believed, namely, that the first sin was also begotten by the destructive power of eternal darkness.

AUG. We already warned you above that what does not exist cannot be eternal. Why is it, then, that you say that I should be compared to Mani on the grounds that Mani said that the first sin was begotten by the destructive power of eternal darkness? He ascribed a substance to that darkness, but I could not ascribe a substance to nothing so that on this account I too established a sort of eternal darkness, that is, an eternal nothing. But as I could not ascribe to nothing a substance, so I could not ascribe to it destructive power or eternity. In no way, as we already said, can what is nothing be destructive or eternal. In vain, therefore, have you wanted to argue against me about nothing.

The Origin of the Evil Will in Adam

38. JUL. (1) But lest, when you see yourself exposed, you try to escape by saying that you did not say: Evil arose in the work of God because it was made out of nothing, but: It could arise because it was made out of nothing, we must show that you are bound by much more damaging snares. For, if you say that you attributed the possibility of evil, not its necessity, to the powers of that eternal nothing, we reply that the fact that an evil will could arise in a human being is surely nothing other than free choice. For an evil will could arise, just as a good will could also arise. This is the freedom in which reason is employed, and on this account a human being is said to have been made to the image of God; this is the freedom by which he is superior to the other creatures. (2) If, then, the fact that an evil will could arise in the human being is nothing but freedom of choice, and if this is so great that by its marks of honor a human being takes precedence over other living beings, you, who claim that this possibility existed in the human being, not because he was made by God, but because he was made out of nothing, declare by a new trick of your teaching that that nothing, that is, the ancient void, is the cause of so great a good, namely, of free choice.

Finally, to make things clear by a brief question, with regard to your words, "But an evil will could arise, not because a human being was made by God, but because he was made out of nothing,"[114] do you believe, I ask, that the fact that a will could arise is something good or something bad? (3) I mean: Do you think that the very capacity for the will to arise, which you attributed to nothing, is good or very bad? If you say that it is good, then it is not God, but nothing which is the cause of the good. But if, seeing that this is utterly insane, you declare that it is evil, which you, of course, say should not be attributed to God, but to nothing, you will publicly declare that we have brought nothing to bear against you deceitfully, but that the bad faith of your teaching has collapsed because of the good faith of our arguments. What we have accomplished, then, stands unshaken, namely, that you and Mani have attributed the evil will of even the first human being to the eternal necessity at its origin.

AUG.(1) Somehow or other you saw the reply that could be made to you, but you have in vain tried to resist the truth, when you pretended to reply to my words, but were in fact not replying to my words. For you argued as if I had said, "But an evil will did not arise from something good," which I did not say. Rather, I said: "But an evil will could arise from something good, not because the good was made by the good God, but because it was made out of nothing, not out of God,"[115] as you yourself also quoted those same words of mine.[116] Why is it, then, that you thought you should reply as if I said: "But it did not arise," though I said, "But it could not arise"? And why did you speak at such length against the one who said that the fact that the necessity of evil arose from good came from the fact that the good thing was made by God out of nothing, not out of God, though I attributed to such an origin, not the necessity of evil, but its possibility? For I did not say that for that reason evil arose from the good, but that it could arise. (2) And you brought accusations for so long against nothing, and you made nothing destructive, as if nothing compelled the angel and the human being to sin with inevitable necessity.

Now then at last return to my words, as you began to return. For you pose for yourself the question, as if it suddenly entered your mind what I might reply, though I stated this long before in that book against which you are struggling. For you say that I could reply that I did not say: "Evil arose in the work of God, because it was made out of nothing, but: It could arise, because it was made out of nothing." This, of course, is what I said: I said it could arise for this reason; I did not say that it arose for this reason. I attributed the possibility of evil, not its necessity, to this origin. (3) When the rational creature was first created, it was created so that, if it did not will to sin, it would be pressed by no necessity to will to sin or to sin, even though it did not will to, that is, unwillingly, so that it would not do the good that it willed, but would do the evil that it did not will.[117] Here there is already found not that sin which is said to be merely sin, but that which is also the punishment of sin.

It could, nonetheless, absolutely not will something evil or do some evil, even unwillingly, if it were not made out of nothing, that is, if it were the nature of God. For only the nature of God was not made out of nothing, because it was not made, and for that reason it can change in absolutely no way. When we say this, we do not ascribe power to nothing, as if it could produce something or has produced something, though it is nothing. But we say that the nature of God is not a nature which was able to sin. (4) It follows, however, that a nature which is not the nature of God was made and is, for that reason, not coeternal with God. And if it was made, it was made out of nothing, because those natures which are made from other natures also trace their lineage back to nothing. For the natures from which they were made were nothing before they were made, that is, they did not exist at all.

But you say, "An evil will could arise, just as a good will also could arise." You say this as if either the angel or the human being were made without a good will. Man was made upright, as scripture said.[118] The question, then, is not how the good will with which he was made, but how the evil will with which he was not made, could have come to be in him. (5) And you say, not paying attention to what you say: "An evil will could arise, just as a good will also could arise." And you suppose that this belongs to the nature of free choice, namely, that it can will both, that is, both to sin and not to sin. And you think that man was made to the image of God in this respect, though God himself cannot will both. For no one, not even a madman, would say that God can sin, or do you dare to say that God does not have free choice?

(6) Free choice, then, is a gift from God, not from nothing, but in God himself who cannot sin in any way, there is the highest form of free choice. For, if he could be unjust, he could, of course, not also be God. If, after all, he is God, it follows absolutely that he is just. And for that reason, though he has free choice in its highest and greatest degree, he cannot, nonetheless, sin. The angel or the human being, then, was able to sin precisely for this reason, that is, each of them was able to make bad use of this gift of God, namely, free choice, precisely because neither of them is God, that is, each is made by God, not out of God. Understand this, and be quiet. Or say what you understand, not what you do not understand.

Things Made out of Nothing Which Cannot Sin

39. JUL. But not content to have conquered in one way, I shall now prove the falsity of your argument, whose impiety I have revealed. When you wrote, "An evil will could come to be in the work of God, not because it was made by God, but because it was made out of nothing,"[119] you ought to have seen how strong an objection to this is raised by the examples of other creatures which, though equally made out of nothing, are still not capable of an evil will. Finally, the very elements, which truly are made out of nothing, cannot have any awareness of a will so that by evil acts they reveal a necessity at their origin. The living things and other things which fill the world do not, however, come out of nothing, but from something already there. Where, then, is the power of the ancient void which forced the evil will to exist, since it is clear that none can sin except for the rational animal?

AUG. (1) You could think that I was proved guilty of falsity if, after I said that our bodies can be wounded because they are earthly, you showed that there are many earthly bodies which cannot be wounded. For a wound cannot exist except in the body of a living being which is called flesh. Here I would have to admonish you about what you could not see, namely, that this sentence cannot be turned around. For it is not the case that, as it is true that everything that can be wounded is an earthly body, so it is also true that every earthly body can be wounded. Why did your boastful quickness in matters of logic doze off so that you did not notice that, where I said that the rational creature was able to sin because it was made out of nothing, I meant it to be understood that every being that can sin was made out of nothing, but not that everything which was made out of nothing can sin?

(2) As if I had said this latter, you have raised as objections against me other things and the very elements of the world which, though they were made out of nothing, cannot sin, for only the rational animal can sin. Now, then, wake up and see that every being which can sin was made out of nothing, and it does not also follow from this that everything which was made out of nothing can sin. Do not, therefore, parade before me other things which were made out of nothing and cannot sin. For I do not say that every being which is made out of nothing can sin, but I do say that every being which can sin is made out of nothing.

It is the same as if I had said: Every cow is an animal; in that case there would certainly have been no reason to mention in opposition to me many animals which are not cows. For I did not say that every animal is a cow, but that every cow is an animal. (3) Once again, then, I say: Every being which can sin is made out of nothing; I do not say: Everything, therefore, which is made out of nothing can sin. As if I said that, you mention many beings which, though they are made out of nothing, still cannot sin.

Get rid of your cleverness with which you mock slow minds, or get rid of the blindness because of which you do not see the obvious. But when I say: The nature which was created rational could sin because it was made out of nothing, not out of God, pay attention to what I say so that you do not again with your empty wordiness spew forth nothing at me and claim that I said that what is nothing has the power of producing something. (4) This is what I say: The nature which was created rational could sin because it was made out of nothing. What else does this mean but that it could sin precisely because it is not the nature of God? For if it were not made out of nothing, whatever it might be, it would naturally come out of God. If it naturally came out of God, it would be the nature of God. If it were the nature of God, it could not sin. Hence, it could sin, although it was made by God, because it was made out of nothing, not out of God. If you understand this and refuse to resist the truth, you will on this question stop your arguing.

Will Is Nothing But an Uncoerced Act of the Mind

40. JUL. Since, then, this major point has been revealed, what was it that persuaded you to believe that the destructiveness of the ancient nothing was the
cause of an evil will? Certainly it was to make us understand that you believe that
everything which was created out of nothing is guilty and that the whole world is
enslaved to the devil. Because, then, it became clear to me that there has been a
long-standing agreement in doctrine between you, I reply to you and to Mani
equally from now on. You, of course, ask that I who deny that there is a nature of
evil should reply if I can to the question: From where could the evil will in the
first human being come to be? But I reply that you do not understand what you
are saying. For the will is nothing but the act of the mind without anything forcing it.

AUG. (1) What is an act of the mind but an act of a nature? For the mind is undoubtedly a nature; hence, will is an act of a nature, since it is an act of the mind.
When, however, you above set down nature as the genus and placed its species
under that genus, you certainly spoke as follows: "The generality of human nature is a kind of genus for those systems located under it; this generality has these
as its species: bodily position, the members, their ranking, their acts, and other
things of this sort."[120] In this argument of yours, then, you said that the acts of nature were a species of nature. From this there follows for you what you do not
want, namely, that every act of nature is a nature, if nature is the genus and its
species are acts of nature, just as every horse is an animal, because animal is the
genus, while horse is a species of this genus. (2) And for this reason, since will is
an act of the mind and since will is, therefore, shown to be an act of a nature, will
is, by your line of argument, a nature, because you added such species to nature
as to their genus.

Why, then, do you find fault with the fact that a sin which the evil will commits is called natural, since you are shown to say that the will itself is a nature?
But suppose the will is not a nature; it surely cannot, nonetheless, exist except in
a nature. For, insofar as it belongs to a human being, it is an act of the rational
soul, and the rational soul is a nature. Permit now, I beg you, that sin be called
natural, because, when a human being sins, a nature surely sins; a human being
is, of course, a nature. In the same way a sin can correctly be called spiritual,
when a spirit sins. For the apostle was not mistaken when he said, *Spirits of wickedness* (Eph 6:12), for these spiritual beings are undoubtedly natural, since a
spirit is clearly a nature, whether it is the creator or a creature. (3) A sin which is
committed by the will of either an angel or a human being, we do not, nonetheless, call natural in the sense that the sin which was committed by free will was
committed out of necessity, even though a nature sinned, for both an angel and a
human being are natures.

For Adam who sinned because he willed to sin could also have willed not to sin, and he was created so that he could both have willed and have not willed and so that he had either of these in his power. But original sin is something else; though the newborn contract it without any will of their own, their very origin was still damaged by the will of the first human being. So too, in an adult human being that sin is something else on account of which the apostle says, *For I do not do the good I will, but I do the evil which I do not will* (Rom 7:15). And yet even this necessity is not incurable for him to whom we pray, *Rescue me from my necessities* (Ps 25:17).

The Will Can Have No Preceding Cause

41. JUL. (1) You ask, therefore, about the necessity of that reality which cannot exist if it is subject to necessity. If this free act of the mind which is active without coercion from its origin has a cause assigned that is prior to the act, it does not in any sense come to be, but is destroyed. For the very name "will" has no other meaning than not to owe its action to some matter. When you ask from where the will has come to be, you ask for something prior to the will itself; you are not seeking its beginning, but its destruction. For will is understood to be absolutely non-existent if it is attributed either to darkness or to nothing. Nor can it any longer be called will, for will can only exist in the act of the mind with nothing forcing it. If, then, someone forces it, there is an act, but it is not will, for the second part of the definition, that is, "with nothing forcing it," completed its meaning.

(2) If, then, will is nothing but the act of the mind with nothing forcing it, it is, of course, a bad question to ask about the origin of the reality whose mode of being is destroyed if something precedes it. Consider, then, what it is that you are asking, when you ask: "From where could the bad will, like a bad tree, come to be in the first human being?"[121] since you admit that will came about from an origin. For will is the act of the mind with nothing forcing it. All natural things force what follows to exist, but if the will is forced by preceding causes, it immediately ceases to be will and loses its mode of being if it admits an origin.

AUG. (1) If the will does not have an origin because it is not forced, then human beings also do not have an origin so that they are human beings, since they were not forced to exist. For how could one who did not exist have been forced? And a human being is certainly a nature, and you said, "Natural things force what follows to exist." I beg you, pay attention to what you say; do not wag your tongue with your eyes closed, like someone who talks while dreaming. No being which does not exist can be forced. Also see how crazy it is to deny that things which have come to be have an origin, since origin (*origo*) is derived from coming to be (*oriundo*).

After all, what is and does not have an origin always was, but if it was not and now is, it came to be; if it came to be, it has an origin. And the will to sin, then, which was not and now is, has certainly come to be. For, if it is and has not come to be, it always was, but it did not always exist. Therefore, it came to be. (2) Now shout against the perfectly evident truth, for that is appropriate to your empty wordiness, and say: "It has, of course, come to be, but it does not have an origin"—or what is even more crazy: "It both was not and now is, and it, nonetheless, has not come to be."

But if you do not say this so that you are not judged to be most stupid and utterly foolish, ask from where the evil will of the human being has come to be. For you cannot deny that it has come to be, because you cannot deny that it was not and began to be. Ask, I repeat, from where it came to be, and you will find Adam himself; from him there has come to be the evil will which was not previously in him. Ask also what sort of man he was before the evil will came to be from him, and you will find that he was good. For he became evil by that will, and before it came to be from him, he was just as he was created by the good God, that is, good.

(3) This, then, is what my teacher and your nemesis, Ambrose, said, "Evils have come to be from good things."[122] You deny this, and you say, "The order of reality does not permit that evil comes from the good and something unjust from what is just."[123] You offer so much help to the Manichees for introducing the nature of evil, from which they say evils come to be, that they would be grateful for you as a supporter of their error, if you were not also defeated along with them. After all, it is you who with an amazing eloquence or rather madness defend the little ones so that you keep them from the savior. You fight against the Manichees in such a way that you help them in opposition to the savior.

Again Augustine and Mani Are in Agreement

42. JUL. (1) Since will, then, has been well defined as an act of the mind with nothing forcing it, why do you look further for causes which were excluded by the definition of will? Consider, then, what will is, and you will stop asking where will comes from. For will is the act of the mind with no one forcing it. If you try to go a half an inch further, you immediately tear down what has been established. What, then, does Mani say? That this act has come to be because the human being was made out of the nature of darkness. What do you say? You say: Because the human being was made out of nothing. Hence, the one says: An evil will exists because the human being was made out of nothing. The other says: An evil will exists in the human being because the human being was made out of darkness. Both of you, therefore, deny that necessary addition to the definition of the will, that is, "with nothing forcing it."

(2) For, if there was as much power in nothing as in something, this power which forced the will to exist excluded from it its mode of being expressed by the words: "with nothing forcing it." But it removes no less the disgrace of evil; for that is not a sin which does not come from the free act of the mind. And the result is that with the loss of the truth there has perished the odiousness of all evil, and the nature of evil has disappeared when the sin of the will has disappeared. But the sin of the will disappeared when the definition of the will was curtailed. It has, therefore, become clear that the mode of being of sin and of the will is such that, if it is attributed to preceding causes, it loses its responsibility and its wrongness. Where, then, is the nature of evil, when it has been established that evil does not exist?

AUG. (1) I cannot say how much I am astonished at your effrontery, at how you speak of the nature of evil, though you do not speak of natural evil, or at how you do not speak of natural evil, though you speak of the nature of evil. What is more foolish than your definitions, for you think that one should not ask where the will comes from, since it is the act of the mind with nothing forcing it? For, as you suppose, if someone says from where it comes, your words, namely, "with nothing forcing it," will not be true, because that from which it comes forces it to exist, and for this reason it does not come from anything so that it is not forced to exist.

Oh what strange stupidity! Human beings, then, do not come from anything, since they are not forced to exist, because there was nobody to be forced before they existed. The will, of course, comes from something, and it is not forced to exist. And if we should not ask for its origin, we ought not to ask for its origin, not because the will does not come from something, but because it is obvious where it comes from. (2) For the will comes from the one whose will it is; the will of the angel, for example, comes from the angel; the will of a human being from the human being; the will of God from God. Even if God produces in a human being a good will, he, of course, does this so that the good will comes to be from the one whose will it is. In the same way he acts so that a human being comes to be from a human being. For it is not true that, because God creates a human being, a human being is, therefore, not born of a human being.

Each person, however, is the author of his or her own evil will, because one wills evil. But when the question is why a human being can have an evil will, though it is not necessary to have such a will, one is not asking for the origin of the will, but for the origin of the possibility. And the cause is found to be that, though the rational creature is a great good, it is, nonetheless, not what God is, for his nature alone is unchangeable and immutable. (3) And when one asks for the cause of this fact, one finds this, namely, that God did not beget rational creatures out of himself, that is, out of his own nature and substance, but made them out of nothing, that is, out of no thing. It is not that nothing has some power, for if it had some, it would not be nothing, but something. Rather, it is that for each nature to have been made out of nothing is the same as for it not to be the nature of God which alone is immutable.

Nor are those things which are made out of other things exempted from this origin, for the things which were made so that other things were made out of them were not made out of existing things, that is, they were out of absolutely nothing. Any other things can, however, change in their own different qualities, but only the rational creature which has the use of reason is changeable in its will. Whoever carefully and intelligently considers these points will recognize that you said at length about nothing nothing that pertains to the issue.

It Is Sin Only If It Is Voluntary

43. JUL. What, after all, is evil, that is, sin? The will to do that which justice forbids and from which one is free to hold back.[124] What is the will? The act of the mind with nothing forcing it. If, then, sin comes from the will and if the will comes from the act of the mind with nothing forcing it, neither the condition of nothing nor that of darkness brought it about that there existed this act which is forced by nothing so that it can exist without anything forcing it. And for this reason there is no natural sin, no original sin, for these two expressions indicate one thing, namely, that the sin is not voluntary, but the truth demands that it cannot be sin unless it is voluntary. And so, one who says that there is an evil which is clearly inborn does not prove that there is sin in nature, but reveals that he is himself criminal because of the depravity of his judgment. Look, I have replied to that point to which you thought no reply could be made. The question which you thought invincible was, of course, merely nonsense.

AUG. (1) You exult foolishly and say, "Look, I have replied," where anyone intelligent who reads your words or anyone not very slow who also reads mine will immediately find that you were not able to reply. For, no matter with how much complexity you try to explain the uncomplicated and complicate the obvious, sane persons cannot deny that one's own will comes to be from each person, and that the will of a human being can only arise from a human being. And for this reason, the evils of human beings began to exist because of their evil will, and we know that prior to their evil will the nature of human beings was good; evils, therefore, have come to be from goods.

(2) Ambrose says this; Mani is destroyed because of this; Julian denies this in favor of Mani and against Ambrose. Julian says, "If nature is the work of God, the work of the devil is not allowed to pass through the work of God."[125] As a result, Mani says that human beings are not the work of God, since the apostle says that sin and death, that is, the work of the devil, are passed on through them.[126] For according to Julian, "the work of the devil is not allowed to pass through the work of God," and the apostle says the work of the devil was passed on through

human beings. Therefore, human beings are not the work of God. This is Mani's conclusion, coming to him, Julian, with your help. But the apostle who fights for the truth says that human beings are the work of God in order to knock Mani down and that the work of the devil was passed on through the work of God, that is, through human beings, in order to knock you down along with him.

Another Point of Agreement between Mani and Augustine

44. JUL. I remind you of this: Even you often said in your writings that darkness is not a creature, but that, when the light is absent, the darkness remains, so that to grow dark is the same as to exclude the light. What is excluded you call a creature; what remains is darkness. This is a common opinion among philosophers, and I do not now ask whether it should be thought to be true or false. But I insist on this point: You say that darkness is the same as nothing, but you argue that in a human being, that is, in God's work, evil came to be because the human being was made out of nothing. Hence, you affirm that the cause of evil was that nothing, the nothing which you also declare to be darkness. And so, you say that the necessity of evil stems from the condition of darkness. You, therefore, do not disagree with your teacher on this point either, since you both equally attribute the evil will to eternal darkness.

AUG. (1) A little before I already answered you as clearly and briefly as I could, when you were saying nothing about nothing, and now you have in vain chosen to take refuge in darkness. You will not be hidden; the light of truth, after all, pursues you, and says that creatures which are not what their maker is were made from nothing in such a way that this nothing is not thought or understood to be something or to have some power to do something. For, if it did, it would not be nothing. And for this reason nothing is neither any body nor a spirit, nor something that pertains to these substances, nor any unformed matter, nor an empty place, nor darkness itself, but absolutely nothing. For where darkness is found, there is some body that lacks light, either air or water or something else. Only a body can either be illumined by corporeal light so that it is bright or be deprived of light so that it becomes dark. (2) And for this reason there is no creator of this corporeal darkness but the creator of bodies, and for this reason in the hymn of the three young men light and darkness praise him.[127]

God, therefore, made all things out of nothing; that is, if we look to their first origin, he made all the things which he made to exist out of these things which were not, as the Greeks say: ἐξ οὐκ ὄντων.[128] The Catholic Church strongly resists the Arians so that this would not be believed concerning the Only-Begotten, who is God from God, light from light, and for this reason: not out of nothing. Therefore, when we say that the evil will could have come to be from the good, not because the good was made by the good God, but because it was made out of nothing, not out of God, we do not attribute a nature to nothing, but we distinguish the nature of the maker from the nature of those things which were made. And so, these latter can change, either because of the will, as the rational creature could, or because of their own qualities, as the other things, precisely because they were made out of nothing, not out of God, though only God made them, that is, because they are not the same thing as that nature which was not made and which, for this reason, is alone immutable. If, then, you want either to avoid or to defeat the Manichees, hold onto this idea; grasp it by understanding it, if you can, or by believing it, if you cannot, namely, that evils have come to be from good things, nor is evil anything but the lack of a good.

Definitions of the Necessary and the Possible

45. JUL. (1) But, as the truth exposed and destroyed you both, so a consideration of our duty demands from us that we explain what it is that produced the obscurity of this question which has already been disarmed. All things which come to be are said to arise either as necessary or as possible. But I call necessary in this context, not that which we often call useful, but that which was compelled by greater causes. Hence, we call necessary, not that which is in the domain of the will, but that which is forced to exist. But we call possible that which does not have any necessity either to exist or, on the other hand, not to exist, but is both able to exist and able not to exist under certain conditions.

(2) Let the reader, then, hold onto what in this context we call necessary and what we call possible. And to begin with grand examples, that God made the world came to him as something possible, not as something necessary. That is, it was possible for his omnipotence to create what he created, but it was, nonetheless, not necessary; that is, he was not forced by something to create, but created because he willed what he would, of course, not have created if he had not willed to. But that which was present as possible for the creator became necessary in his work; that is, it was not possible for the world which was ordered to exist by the Almighty to exist or not to exist; rather, it was forced to exist, since the Almighty ordered that it exist.

AUG. How was the world forced to exist, since it was not before it existed? How is anyone forced if one does not exist? Would it not be enough for you to say: The world was made by the will of God, not by its own will? But go on, let us see what you are trying to show from this distinction between the possible and the necessary, a distinction which we could have understood better if you had chosen only to mention it and not it explain it as well. After all, who could fail to see that everything which comes to be of necessity also can come to be, but not everything which can come to be also comes to be of necessity? If, then, you want to call that possible which can come to be so that it is not necessary and wanted to call that necessary which not only can come to be, but also comes to be of necessity, speak as you wish; where the facts are evident, we should not quarrel over words. It is enough to know that everything necessary is possible, but not everything possible is necessary.

Whatever Is Natural in Creatures Is Necessary

46. JUL. What, therefore, came from the possibility of the creator was changed into the necessity of the creature. He also made different natures and different species in the natures, while preserving that order which stemmed from the beginning of things so that some are necessary and others possible. Whatever, then, creatures have as part of their nature, they have obtained as something necessary.

AUG. (1) If whatever creatures have as part of their nature, they have obtained as something necessary, then human beings do not have as part of their nature the fact that they have sexual intercourse, but that they can have sexual intercourse. Nor are those relations with a woman which the apostle mentioned natural,[129] but their possibility is natural. For, if one does not will to have them, these relations do not exist, though they can exist, if one wills that they do. The possibility of those relations is natural, not the relations themselves. For those relations which do not exist if we do not want them are not necessary, and the apostle was mistaken when he said that relations with a woman are natural.

Also what has happened to your previous statement that nature is the genus and marriage its species, since spouses are united, not by necessity, but by will? Or when you said this, had the distinction of those two, that is, the necessary and the possible, perhaps not yet entered your mind? (2) And is the fact that a human child is born after the union of the sexes not natural, because it is not necessary? For it is not necessary that conception and birth follow when a man and a woman have intercourse. But you defined that which can come to be, but is not necessary, as possible, not as necessary. And do we not eat naturally? And since we do not eat if we do not will to, this too is, for that reason, possible, not necessary. But to deny that these things are natural is nothing but to want to remove a large part of nature. What you said, then, is false: "Whatever creatures have as part of their nature, they have obtained as something necessary," since they have as part of their nature these things which I mentioned and others which it would take too long to mention, but they have not obtained them as something necessary.

Free Choice Is Necessary, But Willing Is Possible

47. JUL. (1) But those creatures[130] which have sensation as they develop do not always receive everything as necessary, but receive many things as possible.

One can see this in all bodies, but a discussion of this issue would get rather long. Let us at least give a few examples. It is the nature of bodies that they grow by addition and are destroyed by division. Those which suffer death can, therefore, be wounded. That they can be wounded, then, they have as necessary, but that they are wounded they have as possible. Thus the condition of having things as possible is necessary, though the realization of the possibility is not necessary. For example, a horse, a cow, and similar animals have a vulnerable nature, and for this reason they are necessarily capable of being harmed. But that they are wounded is not always necessary. (2) For, if they are protected from injury by the diligence of those watching over them, they can escape being wounded, but if they are not protected, they can also be wounded.

There is, then, a great difference between what is possible and what is necessary, and unless this distinction is preserved, one falls into countless errors. To make this clear by an analogy, certain enemies of medicine erred when they argued that this art has no benefit. They argue this way: Does medicine try to help those who are going to die or those who are going to live? If those who are going to die, it cannot help them. If those who are going to live, it does so to no point. For those who were going to die will die, even despite the effort of medicine, and those who were going to live could have been saved, even without the benefit of it.

(3) What an elegant, what a clever conclusion! But it is destroyed by the defenders of medicine in this way: This art, they say, benefits neither those who are going to live nor those who are going to die, at least if they are going to do so necessarily, but it benefits those who are possibly going to experience either of them. Medicine, then, does not help one who is undoubtedly going to die, because it cannot make the person immortal. But it also does not help one who is undoubtedly going to be healthy. Rather, it helps one who, if not cared for, can be in danger, but who can be rescued if cared for. As the learned art can help neither one who is going to live nor one who is going to die as a necessity, so it can help those who are going to die or going to live as a possibility.

Those first people who malign the efforts of physicians bring a proposition that starts off as possible to a conclusion that is necessary. (4) This kind of argument can be extended to countless topics. For example, the law forbids the commission of murder; it also forbids giving an occasion through negligence by which one falls into danger, as with the goring bull[131] and with the parapet of a house.[132] But one can say: Does this carefulness help one who is going to live or one who is going to die? If one who is going to die, it cannot help; if one who is going to live, it offers needless care, if each of these contraries will necessarily ensue with these precautions and without these precautions. But this is false; with perfect right one takes care of mortals so that they escape by the help of carefulness what they could have suffered without such carefulness. A possible result is one thing, a necessary one another.

(5) Let us now show how we are helped by these preliminary remarks. God made human beings with free choice and a good nature, but a nature which is capable of the virtues so that they might acquire the virtues by themselves by their own mind. This free choice could not exist unless it had the possibility of sinning. They have freedom, then, as a necessity, but willing as a possibility. They cannot not be free, but they cannot be forced into either act of the will, and the effect produced by something necessary is possible. It is possible, then, that they sin, but it is not necessary, because it is not the agent, but the creator who is judged guilty of what is necessary. And what human beings can do is entirely from God, but they are considered to be agents as a possibility.

AUG. (1) What do you say about the devil of whom scripture says, *The devil sins from the beginning* (1 Jn 3:8)? Does he have the possibility or the necessity of sinning? If he has the necessity, you must explain how he is excused from grave sin in accord with your line of argument. But if he has the possibility, he can, then, also not sin; he can have a good will; he can do penance and obtain God's mercy, because God will not despise a contrite and humble heart.[133] Certain people have held this view on the authority, it is said, of Origen.[134] But, as I think you know, sound Catholic faith did not accept this. For this reason some either try to prove or wish that Origen too was free from this error.

(2) It remains, then, that[135] prior to the punishment of eternal fire, this necessity of sinning is for the devil a great punishment for his great sin, and he is not excused thereby from serious sin, for his punishment is equal to his very great sin, namely, that he finds delight only in evil and cannot also find delight in righteousness. But he would, of course, not have already come to this penal necessity of sinning unless he had first sinned by free will with no necessity. That definition, then, of sin, when one does that which justice forbids and from which one is free to hold back, pertains to that sin which is only to sin, not the sin which is also the punishment of sin.

God Provides Help for Doing Good

48. JUL. They, therefore, do both evil and good by their own will, but they also owe their goodness to God who provides on this side, not a predetermination, but a help.

AUG. Human beings certainly do both good and evil by their own wills, as you say, and the possibility of each of these in them has an equal weight, and God offers his help for good actions. Why, then, is the nature of mortals more inclined toward sinning, if original sin had no effect? And yet, with regard to the help which you are forced to admit God provides, let it be noted what sort of help you say it is. You, of course, say that it is the law, not the Spirit, though the apostle Paul teaches that we are assisted by help of the Holy Spirit.[136] I thought that I should mention this lest those who hear or read your statement about the help God provides might perhaps forget about your heresy.

Without This Distinction Sins Are Ascribed to God

49. JUL. The distinction, then, has such force that, if in ignorance of it we draw a necessary conclusion from what begins as possible, all sins are attributed to God. Seeing this, Mani imagined that the darkness was the source of sin, for he was not able to distinguish between the possible and the necessary. Everything, then, which human beings have as a part of their nature they have obtained as necessary, because they could not be other than they were made to be.

AUG. I have already shown a short time before how foolish this statement is, for it is really stupid to say that human beings have as part of their nature, the possibility of eating, but do not naturally eat foods suited to their nature and that human beings have as a part of their nature the possibility of intercourse, but do not naturally have intercourse with the sexual organs of the two sexes. Who would say this if one considered at all what one says? For both of these are natural, namely, that these things can be done and that these things are done, but the former is present even when we do not will it, while the latter is present only when we will it.

An Evil Act is Something Possible

50. JUL. The evil they do they do as something possible.

AUG. (1) Pay attention to the apostle who says, *I do the evil that I do not will* (Rom 7:19), and answer whether he does not have a necessity to do evil, who does not do the good that he wills, but does the evil that he does not will. But if you do not dare to oppose the apostle, look, the man who does evil out of necessity destroys and does away with your definitions. He, of course, does evil out of necessity who does not will it and does it. But if what he does unwillingly is only to desire carnally without any assent of the mind or action of the members, such concupiscence of the flesh is also evil, even if one does not consent to it to do evil. And yet, it delights you to praise it.

But if the one who cries out, *I do the evil that I do not will* (Rom 7:19), is compelled so much that he offers his members as weapons to sin, then evils are not merely desired, but also committed of necessity. Where are your definitions which you draw up with so much wordiness? Like smoke, they have, of course, faded and perished. (2) You teach that the necessary and the possible must be distinguished with great care. You say that the necessary is that which is done necessarily, but the possible is that which can be done, but is not done necessarily. Hence, you attribute necessity to the necessary, but you constrain the possible by no necessity. You do not ascribe evil actions to the necessary, but to the possible, and you say of human beings: "The evil they do they do as something possible," lest anyone be said to do evil by necessity, not by will.

But he who contradicts you most vigorously steps forth and says: What are you saying? Look, *I do not do the good that I will, but I do the evil I do not will* (Rom 7:19). It is well known that the first human being did evil by will, not by necessity. But this one who says, *I do the evil that I do not will* (Rom 7:19), shows that he does evil by necessity, not by will, and weeping over his wretchedness, he mocks your definitions.

Sin Arises from Possibility, Not from Necessity

51. JUL. If possibility had not been necessary, the effect would not have been possible. It is necessary, then, that they could do evil and good, but that they do evil they owe, not to what is necessary, but to what is possible for them. Where, then, there is the possibility of both alternatives, there is the necessity of neither. Thus it turns out that sin is nothing but the will to do that which justice forbids and from which one is free to hold back. But if will is nothing but the act of the mind with nothing forcing it, then, just as for God to create the world was something possible, but for the world itself it was necessary to come to be, so something like this is understood to be the case in the image of God. That is, human beings are not forced to have the will they choose, but they have it as something possible. The evil they do, however, entails the necessity of guilt. So too, serious sin necessarily provokes horror, though the sin arises, not from necessity, but from the possibility of the one who commits it. The work, then, of possibility is proof of a free being.

AUG. (1) One who has read our answer to you above has already ceased to pay any attention to you. For the apostle who says, *I do not do the good that I will, but I do the evil that I do not will* (Rom 7:19), indicates clearly enough that he is driven by necessity to do evil and shows that what you say is false: "That they do evil they owe, not to what is necessary, but to what is possible for them," along with the other silly things you foolishly spout. So it turns out that the definition which says that sin is the will to do that which justice forbids and from which one is free to hold back pertains only to that sin, as I have already warned above, which is only sin, not the sin which is also the punishment of sin. (2) For because of that punishment this man was doing the evil that he did not will. If he were free to hold back from it, he would by no means have said, *I do not do the good that I will, but I do the evil that I do not will* (Rom 7:19).

Just as, then, we acknowledge that human beings were blessed in the body of that life where they were free to do what they willed, either good or evil, so acknowledge that human beings are wretched in the body of this death where you hear them say after the loss of freedom, *I do not do what I will, but I do what I hate* (Rom 7:15) and, *I do not do the good that I will, but I do the evil that I do not will* (Rom 7:19) and, *Wretched man that I am, who will set me free from the body of this death?* (Rom 7:24).

Sin Attributed to Necessity Is Attributed to God

52. JUL. The blaming of this man does not have to do with what is necessary, because whatever is attributed to what is necessary strikes at the creator himself.

AUG. Does this evil of the man where he says, *I do the evil that I do not will* (Rom 7:19), strike at the very creator of the man? And yet, it is quite clear that the one who does evil in this way attributes it to necessity. He, of course, does by necessity what he does not do by will.

Sin Cannot Be Attributed to Nature

53. JUL. Just as, then, what comes from necessity cannot be attributed to what is possible for me, so what comes from possibility cannot be attributed to what is necessary. That is, just as the nature of my body and mind cannot be attributed to my will so that I seem to be that way because I willed it, since I could not will before I existed, so the evil of the will cannot be ascribed to a nature so that the works of possibility are mingled with necessity.

AUG. (1) That which can be done in such a way that it is not necessarily done is, of course, quite obviously and clearly distinguished from necessity. You call this the possible as if that were impossible which not only can be done, but also is necessarily done. But since you chose to impose such names on these two, let us understand, as best we can, and put up with it. But what do you mean when you say, "The evil of the will cannot be attributed to a nature"? When an angel or a human being wills something, does not a nature will something? And are an angel and a human being not natures? Who would say this? If an angel and a human being, then, are natures, a nature certainly wills whatever an angel wills, and a nature wills whatever a human being wills. How, then, can the evil of the will not be attributed to a nature, since only a nature can will something? (2) Should the sin of one's will not be imputed to a human being, because a human being is a nature and the evil of the will, as you claim, cannot be attributed to a nature? Or has your folly advanced so far that you say that what cannot be attributed to nature ought to be imputed to nature? For who would say that what is imputed to a human being is not imputed to a nature, unless there is someone so foolish as to deny that a human being is a nature? Do you see how much you say without knowing what you are saying?

If, then, you say that the will cannot be attributed to necessity, even this is not universally true. For at times we will something which is necessary, as it is necessary that those who persevere in living good lives become blessed. At times it is also necessary that we will something, as it is necessary that we will happiness. Hence, there is even a certain blessed necessity, because it is necessary that God always lives both immutably and most happily. But since there are also certain necessities so foreign to the will that there is necessity where there is no will and that there is will where there is no necessity, the statement is at least partially true that the will cannot be attributed to necessity. But let the one who says that the evil will cannot be attributed to a nature, show us, if he can, a will, whether evil or good, where there is no nature, or let him show us that there could be a will if there were not a nature which wills something. Notice, then, how you are cut off from the truth. You say: An evil will cannot be attributed to nature, but the truth says: As long as there is any will, it cannot be cut off from a nature.

Mani Led Forth the Traducianist Armies

54. JUL. (1) Not grasping the subtlety of these distinctions, Mani has, therefore, led forth the armies of the traducianists against us. For he argues in this way: Where does evil come from? From the will, of course. Where does the evil will come from? He answers: From a human being. Where does a human being come from? From God. And he concludes: If evil comes from a human being, and the human being comes from God, evil, therefore, comes from God. And after this, as if he were being religious, to avoid making God sinful, he offers the nature of darkness to which we are supposed to attribute the evil.

On this issue Augustine too says: Where does evil come from? From the will. Where, he asks, does the will itself come from? From the human being who is the work of God. And he infers: If evil comes from the will, and the will comes from the human being, and the human being is the work of God, evil, therefore, comes from God. (2) As if trying to free himself from seeming to call God sinful—something which his doctrine of inherited sin shows he does—he offered us in place of God a nothing which is equally destructive, that is, darkness to which we are supposed to attribute this evil. He says, "For evil arose in the human being, not because he was the work of God, but because he was made out of nothing."[137] As if the truth could not respond: And with what impudence does your God first tell the lie that there is a will in a human being and then condemn the will, though he knows that this evil, that is, sin, came from the necessity of darkness, that is, of the nothing at the beginning? We have declined "nothing" in its different cases so that the power of the traducianist who puts his hope in nothing may be clearly seen.[138] (3) But see the feebleness of the God whom the traducianist introduces. He is not able to overcome nothing itself, and though he made human beings out of nothing, he could not rescue them from the condition of evil which came from nothing. But having become more bitter because of the difficulty of the task, he charged human beings with his own sins, and he condemns the sins of nothing to the destruction of his own image. The old Manichee deals more kindly with him; he says that God was not utterly devastated by the nation of darkness, while the traducianist introduces so great a feebleness on the part of God that he imagines that he was overcome by nothing.

AUG. (1) No one is overcome by nothing, but you are overcome by saying nothing. Nor have I placed my hope in nothing,[139] but you have brought all your wordiness to nothing. Of course, if you correctly understand what you say incorrectly, God is overcome by nothing in the sense that no reality overcomes God. For what is nothing but no reality? God also cannot overcome nothing in the sense that there is no reality which he who overcomes all things does not overcome, for he is over everything. But Mani did not grasp, as you say, the subtleties of your distinctions, and for this reason he says: "If evil comes from a human being, and the human being comes from God, evil, therefore, comes from God." And terrified by this conclusion, we are supposed to deny that a human being comes from God or that evil comes from a human being or to say that both of them are false, as Mani does. And in that way he would introduce for us some sort of substance of darkness which makes human beings and which is the primordial evil from which all evil is thought to arise.

(2) You, then, with your most subtle distinctions, with what wisdom do you suppose one should resist this cleverness? You say: I shall say that evil comes from human beings as something possible, not as something necessary. As if he could not reply to you: If evil comes as something possible, and the possibility comes from nature, and nature from God, evil, therefore, comes from God. If you are not afraid of this conclusion, neither am I afraid of that one, since both of us admit that the first human being did not sin as a necessity, but as a possibility. For, when we say that the human being was able to sin because his nature was not made out of God, although he could not be at all unless God created him, we do not say this in the sense that the necessity of sinning was imposed upon him as a result of this, as you falsely accuse us. He was, of course, able to sin and not to sin, but if he had not been made out of nothing, that is, if his nature were made out of God, he would have been unable to sin at all.

(3) For who is so crazy as to dare to say that the immutable and unchangeable nature which is God could sin in any sense? After all, the apostle says of him, *He cannot deny himself (2 Tm 2:13). Both of us, then, are opposed to Mani, when we say that Adam was not made by the good and just God so that it was necessary for him to sin and when we say that he, therefore, sinned because he willed to, though he could have not willed to. But in his offspring we see such great and such obvious evils, not voluntary evils of human beings, but evils with which they*

are born, and when you deny that they come from the origin corrupted by sin, your heresy certainly establishes Mani in a fortress in order to introduce the nature of evil, by mixture with which the nature of God is corrupted, and from that fortress the truth hurls down both him and you at the same time.

Everything Natural Is Necessary

55. JUL. All suffer this ignominy who declare war on the truth. Let us, then, sum up what we have inferred. The question is asked: Where has that first evil come from in the human being? We answer: From the act of the mind with nothing forcing it. The objection is raised: Has it appeared in the work of God? We agree that this is true. We are asked how it is that we do not reject this, since we deny natural sin. We answer: Because in the work of God this sin emerged as something possible, not as something necessary. Those things, then, which are necessary are natural, but those which are possible are voluntary.

AUG. There are also voluntary acts which are necessary; for example, we will to be happy, and it is necessary that we will this. There are also possible events which are natural; for example, it is possible that a woman conceives if she has intercourse with a man by means of their sexual organs, if neither she nor he is sterile, but it is not necessary. It can, of course, happen, but it is not necessary, and yet it is natural. Be quiet, I beg you. Your definitions are foolish, and your distinctions are not subtle, but childish.

Nature and Free Choice Do Not Cause the Will

56. JUL. And for this reason, as we attribute sin to the free act, so we attribute nature to the creator. Human nature, then, is a good work of God; freedom of choice, that is, the possibility of either sinning or acting correctly, is equally a good work of God. Both of these came to a human being as necessary; neither of these two things is the cause of evil. But up to this point they came as necessary. Now the will comes to be in them, but not from them. Nature and free choice are, of course, able to receive the will, but they are not filled with it, and they do not cause, but receive differences in merits.

AUG. (1) You are perfectly correct in admitting that nature and free choice are good works of God, but what could be said that is more insane than your claim that will comes to be in them, but not from them? Is it true, Julian, that the will of a human being does not come to be from a human being because a human being is the good work of God? Finally, could it have entered your heart that the will of a human being comes to be, but not from his free choice? Tell us, then, where it comes from if not from the nature, that is, not from the human being? If it does not come from his free choice, tell us, I beg you, from where the will of a human being comes to be. You said where it comes to be; tell us also from where it comes. Nature and free choice are good works of God. "The will," you say, "comes to be in them, but not from them." Where, then, does it come from? Tell us; let us hear and learn. Or show us that something has come to be somewhere, though it did not come from there.

(2) The world, of course, came to be from nothing, but with God as its maker. For if it did not have God as its maker, it could not have come to be from nothing at all. If, then, the will in a human being or in his free choice came to be out of nothing, who made it? Or if it was not made or did not come to be, who begot it? Or is it among the things which began to exist the only one made by no one, the only one sprung from nothing? Why, then, is a human being condemned on its account, since the evil will of which he was only the recipient, but not the cause, came to be in him without his willing it? But if, so that he was rightly condemned, the evil will came to be in him because he willed it, why do you deny that the will of that man came to be from him, when you do not deny that it came to be because he willed it and could not have come to be without his willing it? But since it has come to be from him, it has come to be from a nature, for a human being is a nature. And because he could also have not willed what he willed, it came to be from his free choice, which, as you admit, also pertains to nature.

(3) Why, then, do you deny with your eyes closed things that are evident, namely, that the will of a human being comes to be from the nature of the human being, while you are afraid that Mani will bring accusations against the author of that nature? What the Catholic truth preaches is sufficient for refuting that plague, namely, that human beings were created by the most good God so that they did not have a necessity to sin, and they would not have sinned if they had willed not to, since they could also, of course, have always willed not to. Who, then, would be so mentally blind as not to see that, as human beings were originally created, it was a great good of nature to be able not to sin, although it is a greater good not to be able to sin, and that it was arranged in a most orderly fashion that the former state should come first so that human beings might have merit from it and the latter should follow afterwards as the reward of their having merited well?

A Possibility for Good or Evil, but No Predetermination

57. JUL. (1) The good possibility, then, for doing good and evil does not force the will, but permits it to arise. No one, therefore, is good just because of having been given free choice. For there are many human beings equally free, but still very bad. But no one, therefore, is evil just because of having free choice. For there are many who equally share in this freedom and are still very good. Human beings, therefore, are neither good nor bad because they are free, but they could

not be either good or bad unless they were free. This possibility, then, which is indicated by the name of freedom, was established by the most wise God so that without it there does not exist that which is not forced to exist through it.

(2) For by the one capacity for contraries it is defended from a predetermination to either. That is, it cannot be called a cause and a necessity of either an evil will or of a good will, since it admits both in such a way that it does not compel either to exist. For necessary things there is, then, a single line and, so to speak, one thread, just like that geometrical length without breadth, nor can the single line be split into two. As long, then, as this line is extended in one direction, it preserves the power of its nature. But where it comes to the point at which it is split into different lines, that necessity is at that point ended. That is, the good God made human beings good.

AUG. (1) Why, then, did you say that human beings are neither good nor evil except by their own will, and that whatever they have from God they have as something necessary, not as something possible? You want us to understand that this comes from nature, not from the will, so that human beings are good by reason of themselves, not by reason of God, or at least are better by reason of themselves than by reason of God. These, after all, are your words. "No one," you said, "is good just because of having been given free choice." And a little later you said, "But no one is evil just because of having free choice." What are you saying by these words but that God made human beings neither good nor bad, but that human beings make themselves one of these when they use free choice in a good or a bad way?

Why is it, then, that you now say, "The good God made human beings good," if they are neither good nor bad by having the free choice which God produced in them, but by using it well, that is, when they themselves will in a good way, not when they have the possibility of willing in a good way? (2)And how will it be true that *God made human beings upright* (Eccl 7:30)? Or were they upright, though they did not have a good will, but only its possibility? They were, then, evil, though they did not have a bad will, but only its possibility? Then they have from themselves a good will, and scripture was incorrect to say: *The will is prepared by the Lord* (Prv 8:35 LXX), and *God also produces in you the willing* (Phil 2:13). And yet, you say that human beings do not have a good or a bad will from themselves, but that it comes to be in them, not from them. And so it turns out through your amazing wisdom that it was not God who made human beings upright, but human beings who could be upright if they willed to be, and that they do not make themselves upright, but are made upright by some chance or other, because the will by which they are made upright comes to be in them, not from them, but from an unknown source and in an unknown way. This is not the wisdom coming down from above, but earthly, unspiritual, and diabolical wisdom.[140]

Free Choice, Not Its Use, Is Necessary

58. JUL. And for a substance both its beginning and its beginning well are directed by the single line of the necessary. The substance also receives freedom of choice and is still equally held on the line of the necessary. But now there is an end of necessary elements; from here the wills are split into contraries. The nature of the division does not belong to the single line of the necessary. Thus we are forced to have the possibility, but we are not forced to make good or bad use of this possibility. And so it turns out that the possibility of sinning is also capable of good and of evil, but of voluntary good and evil, because it could not have been capable of its own good, unless it were capable of evil also.

AUG. (1) Say instead, if you want to speak the truth, that the nature of human beings was originally created capable of good and evil, not because it could not have been made capable of the good alone, but because it had to rise from this level in a fully orderly way so that, if it had not sinned when it could have sinned, it would have come to that beatitude in which it could not sin. For, as I have already said, each of these is a great good, though one is a lesser, the other a greater good. It is, after all, a lesser good to be able not to sin, but a greater one not to be able to sin. And it was fitting to come to the reward of the greater good by the merit of the lesser good.

(2) You say that human nature "could not have been capable of its own good, unless it were also capable of evil." Why, then, after piously living this life will it be capable of good alone and not of evil, removed, that is, not only from all will or necessity, but even from the possibility of sinning? Or will we perhaps have to fear that we might sin even when we will be equal to the holy angels?[141] Concerning the angels we must undoubtedly believe that they have received the inability to sin as a reward of their perseverance, because they stood firm when they too could have sinned, when the others fell. Otherwise, we would still have to fear that this world would have many new devils and their new bad angels.

(3) The life of the saints who have departed from their bodies will also be held suspect for us for fear that they may perhaps have sinned or may sin even there where they have arrived, if the possibility of sinning should remain in the rational nature, and if it cannot be capable of good unless it is also capable of evil. Since these ideas are highly absurd, this opinion must be rejected, and we must rather believe that this nature was originally created capable of both good and evil in order that, by choosing one of these, it would earn the recompense by which it would afterwards become capable of only good or only evil, in such a way, nonetheless, that, if it received everlasting damnation, it would be forced only to suffer evil and not be also allowed to do evil.

The Great Gap between Possibility and Necessity

59. JUL. (1) But there is a great a difference between necessity and possibility as there is between full and empty. For the possibility for that reality of which the substance is said to be receptive is empty, since, if it were not empty, it would not be capable of receiving anything. After all, what would receive what it already has? Necessity, however, does not indicate emptiness, but fullness. It cannot, of course, receive, as if it were empty what forces it to be as if it were full. There is, therefore, as great a difference between necessary things and possible ones as there is between filled things and empty ones. By the very reception of contraries it is, then, defended from a predetermination to either quality of which it is equally receptive. It has, then, a necessary good in nature insofar as it pertains to the honor of the creator. This is an innocence naturally mixed with no evil, receptive of its own work for the approval[142] of a good work and the accusation of an evil work. (2) Any sinners, then, can damage what comes to them from their own work, but they cannot spoil what they have received from the work of God.

There remains, then, even in evil human beings the value of the natural good, and it will never be evil to have been able to do good and evil. But it will not profit that person at all who certainly does not condemn the elements of his necessity, but has, nonetheless, compelled them not to benefit him. In that human being, then, in whom freedom has already been developed, we ascribe the evil to the will when he sins, but the nature to God, the author of creation. So too, if a little one who does not have use of its will and does not display anything but the elements of its nature is said to be full of wickedness and to have evil as something necessary, which the other receives as something possible, he who is the author of nature is undoubtedly proved to be the author of the sin.

AUG. (1) We clearly smash your rules in the case of adults so that you cannot apply them to little ones. It was not a little one who said, *I do not do the good that I will, but I do the evil that I do not will* (Rom 7:19). He did not have the emptiness of possibility; rather, he had the fullness of necessity—to speak about these matters in your fashion. He was not an emptiness able to receive evil, but full of the evil he had received. For he did not say: I can do both good and evil, a possibility which was not an evil of either human nature or of the will. Rather, he said, *I do not do the good that I will.* Not only that, but he also added: *But I do the evil that I do not will* (Rom 7:19). See, he owes the fact that he does not do good and the fact that he does do evil, not to possibility, as you yourself determine, but to his necessity, as he suffers it and admits it. He is, of course, weak for removing his own misery, but he is clearly a strong hammer to smash your rules. He wills, but does not do what is good; he does not will, but does what is evil. Where does this necessity come from?

(2) Catholic teachers, of course, know it; they understand that the apostle Paul said these things even about himself, and they do not doubt that it comes

from the law in the members which resists the law of the mind[143] and without which no human being is born. And they see that even saints say, *I do not do the good that I will, but I do the evil that I do not will* (Rom 7:19), precisely because they see how great a good it is not even to desire with the flesh those things which they reject with the mind. And they see that the saints will it and do not do it, and that it is evil, nonetheless, even to have such desires in the flesh, although the mind does not give its consent. They see that they do not will it and yet do it, without any condemnation because, once the guilt of this sin has been wiped out by rebirth, they resist with the mind so that they do not do what they desire with the flesh. But they are not without some evil of their own, because it is not a foreign nature mingled with theirs, but it is their own nature both in the mind and in the flesh.

(3) You refuse to accept this pious and true idea opposed to your darling, as if you might thereby prevent any charges coming not only from the scriptures, but also from the very conduct of human beings and the groans of the saints, from being read out against her despite your opposition in the court in which you defend her. And charges would be read out with such great evidence of the truth that there would remain, not your eloquence, but only your impudence, by which you could not defend her, though you would want to. What, after all, are you doing, when you try to spread clouds over clear issues with the tempest of your turbid verbosity?

The apostle cries out, *I do not do the good that I will, but I do the evil that I do not will* (Rom 7:19). He also cries out above, *It is no longer I who do it, but the sin that dwells in me, for I know that the good does not dwell in me, that is, in my flesh* (Rom 7:17-18). What does *I do what I do not will* mean? And what does, *It is no longer I who do it* mean? (4) What does it mean but what he goes on to explain? That is, in saying, *I do what I do not will* (Rom 7:16), he shows that he does it, and again in saying, *It is no longer I who do it* (Rom 7:17), he shows that it is not his consenting mind, but his desiring flesh that does it. The flesh, of course, acts through desiring, even if it does not pull the mind to consent. On this account he adds, *I know that the good does not dwell in me* (Rom 7:18). And in explaining why he says, *The good does not dwell in me*, he says: *That is, in my flesh* (Rom 7:18). But let these words be not the words of the apostle, as you would have it, but those of any human being weighed down by his own bad habits which cannot be overcome by the will.

Are these habits not so robust that with their strength they smash and crush your arguments about the possible and the necessary like childish and silly tablets? (5) For there is, though you do not admit it, not only the voluntary and the possible sin from which one is free to hold back, but also the necessary sin from which one is not free to hold back. This latter is not merely sin, but also the punishment of sin. Nor do you want to notice that what is produced in each individual by the force of habit—that which some learned people called a second nature—has been produced by the penal force of that greatest and most serious sin of the first man in all who were in his loins and were to come to be through his concupiscence when the human race is propagated, that is, the concupiscence which the sense of shame of the sinners covered in the area of their loins.[144]

The Evil Will Cannot Come from a Cause

60. JUL. (1) But why do we turn to the little ones, since the question of the Manichees implies that even an adult human being does not sin by the will? For if evil has come to be in human beings because they were made out of nothing and if human beings had it as something necessary that they were made out of nothing, they undoubtedly did not receive the evil as something possible, but as something necessary. Though this has already been destroyed by long argumentation, let us expand a little more on this same point so that it may become more and more clear by repetition.

(2) You ask, then, where the evil will in the first human being emerged from. I answer: From the act of the mind with nothing forcing it. You also ask where this act comes from. I answer: What are you asking? From where could it have come? Or from where was it compelled to come? If you say what you have also written: Or from where it was compelled to be, I will reply that you are making inconsistent and contradictory statements. For you are asking who has forced that which can only be if nothing forces it. And because it is undone by its own contradictoriness, the question has no rationality and, hence, has no force.

You are, then, asking most stupidly where the evil will comes from. For when you say, "From where?" you do not ask for the occasion of the evil will, but its origin, that is, its nature. But if, as has been shown above, it receives a nature, it loses its own definition which says, "with nothing forcing it." But if it holds onto its definition, it excludes a predetermination from its origin. The man, then, did not sin because he was made out of nothing, because he was made by God, because he was made out of the darkness, or because he was made with free choice. Rather, he sinned because he willed to; that is, he had an evil will precisely because he willed to.

AUG. (1) We say, or rather the truth says, that some adult human beings do evil by the will, some by necessity, or that the very same ones in some cases do evil by the will and in other cases by necessity. If you think this is not true, look at the one who cries out, *I do not do the good that I will, but I do the evil that I do not will* (Rom 7:19). He must be thrust in your face as often as, in saying these things, you either pretend that you do not see him or perhaps do not see him. Why do you wrap yourself in convoluted digressions? No one said to you: The human being had the necessity of sinning because he was made out of nothing; rather, you are saying this to yourself. He was, of course, made so that he had the possibility of sinning as something necessary, but sinning as something possible. He would, nonetheless, not have had even the possibility of sinning if he were the nature of God, for he would certainly have been immutable and unable to sin.

(2) He did not, therefore, sin, but he was able to sin, because he was made out of nothing. Between "He sinned" and "He could sin" there is a great difference; the former is guilt, while the latter is nature. Nor could everything that was made out of nothing sin, for trees and stones cannot sin. But the nature which could sin was, nonetheless, made out of nothing. Nor is it something great to be unable to sin, but it is something great to be unable to sin while one enjoys happiness. So too, it is not something great to be unable to be unhappy, because everything which cannot receive happiness is also unable to be unhappy. But it is something great for a nature to be happy in such a way that it cannot be unhappy. Although this latter is a greater good, the former is no small good, namely, that the nature of the human being was created in such happiness that, if it had willed, it would not have been unhappy.

(3) But it is said that all things were made out of nothing,[145] that is, out of things which were not, in order that we may understand that whatever was made out of that which was already in existence should be referred to the first origin. For flesh came from the earth, but the earth came from nothing. In this sense we say that all human beings are children of Adam because each is the child of one's own parent. All things, nonetheless, which were made, are mutable because they were made out of nothing; that is, they were not, and now they are, because God makes them. And they are good, for they were made by the good God, and those mutable good things would not exist at all, to the extent that they do exist, if there were not the immutable good by whom they were created.

(4) All evils, then, which are nothing but the privations of good things, have arisen from good things, though from mutable ones. And we can correctly say that the angel and the human being from whom evils arose are, of course, good natures, but we cannot correctly say that they are immutable. Those evils, nonetheless, could also not have arisen, if the angel and the human being had not willed to sin, since they could have willed not to sin. But God is so good that he makes good use even of the evils which his omnipotence would not have allowed to exist if he could not make good use of them by his supreme goodness, and for this reason he would rather seem weak or less good if he could not make good use of evil as well. Hence, you are not permitted to deny that he who says, *I do the evil that I do not will* (Rom 7:19), had already received an evil as something necessary, not as something possible. It is not true, as you claim, that every evil action comes, not from necessity, but from possibility. Rather, we find that some come from necessity. See now how your elaborate machine of war has collapsed.

(5) But to someone who asks from where the evil will in the first human being has emerged, you suppose that you reply with more caution: "From the act of the mind with nothing forcing it," as if you would not answer more quickly and easily: From the man himself. That addition, "with nothing forcing it," could also be added here by you, with no one opposing you. After all, who would oppose you speaking the truth, if you said: The evil will emerged in the first human being from the human being himself with nothing forcing him? But now, fearing to blame nature, as if any injury to it might reflect upon its author, you finally said what you wanted for a long time to say, and you have not gotten away from nature. For the mind is a nature, and in the constitution of the human being it is better than the body, though you said that the evil will emerged from its act with nothing forcing it. Do you see that what you cannot deny did not exist before it came to be could only have emerged from somewhere? What need is there to ask where the act of the mind comes from, since it is obvious enough that the act of the mind could only have emerged from the mind?

(6) If you deny this in a most impudent and foolish fashion, we still ask you where the evil will in the first human being came from, and we will not permit you to say: "From the act of the mind with nothing forcing it," because the very act of the mind with nothing forcing it is the will. Hence, to say: "The will comes from the act of the mind" is the same as to say: "The act of the mind comes from the act of the mind," or "The will comes from the will." Or do you say that this act arose from itself, not from the mind, for fear that for this reason the good nature, that is, the mind itself, would be blamed? Hence, it should not be condemned for this reason. (7) After all, who would tolerate the idea that the mind is rightly condemned because of that for which it cannot rightly be blamed?

But you say, "The man sinned because he willed to; he had an evil will precisely because he willed to." You say what is perfectly true, but if the brightest sunlight is not darkness, the evil will emerged from him because he willed it. After all, we do not say, as you slander us and as you falsely say that we wrote, "From where this act was compelled to be," but we say: From where it came to be with nothing compelling it. For that which did not exist before it came to be, nonetheless, did come to be with nothing compelling it, and it could not have come to be except from some source. If, then, the human being willed it, it came to be from the human being, and what was the human being before this act came to be from him but a good nature and good work of God? An evil human being is also a good nature and good work of God, insofar as he is a nature and a work of God.

Let Julian, then, be ashamed of his own folly, because Ambrose spoke the truth that evils have come to be out of good things.[146] Yet God is without blame, because nothing forces this. But because he permitted them to exist, he is praised in a more outstanding fashion for his just and good use of them.

No Virtue without the Possibility of Sin

61. JUL. (1) The will, then, which is nothing but the act of the mind with nothing forcing it, owes its possibility to nature, but its coming to be to itself. For it has come to be in a nature, but as something possible, not as something necessary. If at this point someone says: But it is an evil nature which could have an evil will, I reply: But it is a good nature which could have a good will. At one and the same time it will be called the best and the worst. But the nature of reality does not permit that at one and the same time one and the same reality is filled with merits of opposite character. (2) If, then, it should be thought evil because it could do evil, it should be considered good because it could do good. But why, he asks, was that which did the good able also to do evil? I answer: Because this good which is called virtue could not have had its special character, unless it were voluntary. But it would not have been voluntary if it had had the necessity for the good. It would, rather, have suffered under the necessity of the good, if it had not had the possibility of evil. In order, then, that responsibility for the good might be established, the possibility of evil was admitted.

AUG. (1) As I see it, you do not want to attribute even a good will to nature when the human being was originally created, as if God could not have made a human being with a good will. But God would not have forced him to remain in that will; rather, it would have lain in his choice whether he willed to continue in it always or not always. In this case his will would have changed itself into an evil will with nothing forcing it, as did in fact happen. After all, it is not true that Adam first did not have the will not to sin and that with the will to sin he began the life in which God created him upright,[147] certainly as such a human being as could already use reason. For who would tolerate his being said to have been made such as infants are now born? That perfection of the nature which was not given by age, but by the hand of God alone, could not fail to have a will and one that was not bad. Otherwise, scripture would not have said, *God made man upright* (Eccl 7:30).

(2) The man was, therefore, made with a good will, ready to obey God and obediently receiving the commandment which he would have kept without any difficulty, as long as he willed to, and which he would have abandoned, when he willed, without any necessity. Nor would he have done the former without reward, nor the latter with impunity. From this we infer with pious and sober thought that the first good will is the work of God; he, of course, made the human being upright with it. For no one is ever upright except by willing the right things. On this account the good will, once lost, is not restored except by him who created it. Nor should one suppose that the necessity of sinning can be healed in any other way than by the mercy of God by whose deep and just judgment this necessity has come upon the descendants of Adam who sinned without any necessity.

(3) Hence, after the apostle wept over the penal necessity of the sin dwelling in his flesh by which he was forced to do the evil he did not will, he immediately pointed to whom we must flee. He said, *Wretched man that I am, who will set me free from the body of this death? The grace of God through Jesus Christ our Lord* (Rom 7:24-25). You surely see how that possibility does not come to his rescue, though you think that by it you have found something great. It has, of course, already been lost when evil is done by necessity and the human being cries out under the necessary evil, *Wretched man that I am!* But he clearly comes to his rescue whose grace overcomes even those factors which you call necessary because they cannot be otherwise. For what is impossible for human beings is easy for God. For God it was not necessary that a camel could not enter through the eye of a needle; rather, it was possible for him that the camel did enter,[148] just as flesh and bones passed through the closed doors.[149]

(4) In vain, then, do you try to defend our damaged nature. If you are seeking to do something useful for it, work for its healing, not to excuse it. Allow the fact that it did to itself that for which it is rightly condemned. For whatever else you say about the source of the evil will, if you say that it did not arise from that nature, you claim that its condemnation is unjust. For what else do you say but: It did not do that for which it is condemned? What, then, is more unjust than that it should be condemned for what it did not do? But if it did it, why do you try to excuse it on the basis of the possible by which you are shown to accuse it more inexcusably? For you say that "the evil will, of course, has come to be in the nature, but as something possible, not as something necessary." (5) If this possibility lies outside the nature, it is rather this possibility from which the evil will arose that should be condemned, not the nature. But if the possibility pertains to the nature, nature rather produced for itself the evil will, because it could also not have produced it. For the definition of possibility which you endorsed proves this. No one says to you: Nature is evil because it could have an evil will. Certainly we, against whom you are now speaking, do not say this. Why do you delay over needless issues?

In your statement, "This good which is called virtue would not have been voluntary if it had had the necessity for the good. It would, rather, have suffered under the necessity of the good if it had not had the possibility of evil,"[150] you completely forgot about God, whose virtue is the more necessary to the degree that he wills it in such a way that he cannot not will it. (6) For you said in the first book of this work that "God cannot but be just."[151] If this must be called necessity, let it by all means be called that, provided that it is, nonetheless, admitted that there is nothing more felicitous than this necessity by which it is as necessary that God not live badly as it is necessary that he live always and most blessedly. Nor does such a necessity fear your words where you were unwilling to say: But it would have had "the necessity of the good," but preferred to say: It "would have suffered under the necessity of the good, if it had not had the possi-

bility of evil." In that way God might have seemed to have spared the human being so that he would not suffer under the necessity of the good, as if it were
something painful, if he did not have the possibility of evil.

This former is so great a good that it is reserved for the saints as their reward;
you forgot about them too, as you forgot about God. (7) After all, we shall not
then live without virtue when we shall be granted the inability to withdraw at
some time from God, because we will be unable to will it. In that way we shall
have as certain the good by which, as was promised, *we shall forever be with the
Lord* (1 Thes 4:16), so that we do not will and cannot will to withdraw from him.
Now, then, virtue would not exist[152] in us except on the condition that we do not
have an evil will, but could have such a will. But in accord with the merit of this
lesser virtue greater virtue will be given us as a reward so that we do not have an
evil will and also could not have such a will. O necessity that we should long for!
The truth will grant it in order that our security may be certain, for without it
there cannot exist that complete happiness of ours, to which nothing can be
added.

Neither Virtue Nor Vice Is Necessary

62. JUL. (1) But this argument can be turned to the contrary so that it says:
But nature was suited to evil. For, since evil could not be voluntary if there had
been a necessity of evil, the possibility of good was given in order that the responsibility for evil might be assigned. This is, of course, clever, but crazy. For
all things are evaluated from their better part. To this is added the dignity of the
author, that is, of God who did not make a free being on account of those actions
which he was going to punish, but who gave the possibility of contraries on account of those actions which he was going to reward.

I do not, nonetheless, want to quarrel over this point, but I accept some slander rather than to take anything away from the authority of the creator. It, nonetheless, follows necessarily that this possibility of doing good and evil is
removed by the coming to be of the good or the evil will. (2) And for this reason
neither the cause of virtue nor that of vice is proved to be something necessary.
Let us do this injustice to good people and say that, because they are seen to
struggle with the dishonest, the merit of the will is ascribed neither to that good
will nor to that evil will. It has, then, the testimony of its free-born condition that
it is innocent, because it is full of only the voluntary, not of either good or evil.
Attribute, then, the possibility of the will to nature, but do not attribute to nature
either the good or the evil will. It is irrefutably established that the evil will came
to be in the work of God, but as something possible, not as something necessary,
and that it cannot be ascribed to the one who gives the possibility, but to the one
who governs this possibility.

AUG. (1) You claim that neither the good will nor the evil will is ascribed to nature, but only the possibility of either a good will or an evil will, though both the angel and the human being are natures. If, as you say, the good or evil will is not to be ascribed to nature, then neither of them should either be honored for a good will or condemned for an evil will. What, after all, is more unjust than that we should judge that either should be condemned for an evil which is not to be ascribed to him? Or are the angel and the human being not natures? Who says this but someone who does not know what he is saying? What, then, is ascribed to an angel is ascribed to a nature; what is ascribed to a human being is ascribed to a nature, but to a nature which was created good by the good God and which was made evil by its own will.

(2) And for this reason it is perfectly correct not to ascribe to their creator the evil which is ascribed to these natures, because he did not create them, when he first created them, so that they would be under any necessity of having an evil will, but would only have the possibility of it. As a result their will would earn merit, and the good will in them, if not abandoned, would come to its reward, but, if abandoned, would come to its punishment. Why, then, do you try to excuse nature from the malice of the will, since to will or not to will belongs to the nature? For an evil will must belong to one who wills, either an angel or a human being, and we cannot for any reason say that they are not natures. Why, I ask, do you ascribe to human beings an evil will so that they can justly pay the penalty for the merit of their evil will, and yet you do not want to ascribe to a nature what you ascribe to a human being, as if a human being could in any way not be a nature?

(3) How much better it would be for you to speak sanely and say that the evil will of a human being must belong to some nature, because every human being is a nature, but this nature, when it first sinned, had an evil will, not as something necessary, but as something possible. For by these terms you like to distinguish these two. In one of them it is understood that what is necessary is done, but in the other it is understood that what can be, but is not necessary, is done, since it can also not be done.

This, after all, is said with perfect truth of the sin of the first human being or of the first human beings. But there remains that one who cries out, *I do not do the good that I will, but I do the evil that I do not will* (Rom 7:19). (4) He, of course, who does not will it and does it, does evil as something necessary; he breaks your rule which you framed with your rash wordiness, when you said, "Neither the cause of virtue nor that of vice is proved to be something necessary," since the cause of this evil is proved to be something necessary. For either the doing of evil is a vice, and not doing the good that one wills and not willing the evil and yet doing it is a necessity. Or, on the contrary, we will not have that blessed necessity of virtue, when our nature will be filled with such great grace and God will be all things in all,[153] so that our nature will not be able to will anything wrongly. Justice, of course, is a virtue, and we are promised a new heaven and a new earth in which justice shall dwell.[154]

(5) Or perhaps disturbed by this, you say that you framed this rule for the present life, not for the life to come. I do not argue with a man who has been defeated. You certainly do not deny that the other state pertains to this life in which you see human beings will the good, but not do it, and do not will evil and yet do it. And you are forced, contrary to your rule, to attribute this defect to necessity, not to the will. But from this necessity with which the little ones are also born, though it only begins to become evident with the increase in age, what will set the wretched man free except the grace of God through Jesus Christ our Lord?[155] You are enemies of this grace. You place your trust in your own virtue,[156] and with impious pride you argue against the words of God which condemn those who place their trust in their own virtue.[157]

The Passage of the Devil's Work through God's Work

63. JUL. (1) Let it stick in the mind of wise readers that there is a great difference between those things which come from what is possible and those which come from what is necessary. Let them ascribe all natural things to what is necessary, but voluntary ones to what is possible, and let them end all questions on the side from which they began. For if with a blind judgment they wander between the two of them, they fall into countless errors on almost every word. Since this has become clear enough, it is evident that you were utterly blinded when you said: As the evil which never existed could come to be in the work of God, so the evil, when it already existed, was also passed on through the work of God.[158] See, after all, the error in which you are tangled. You say that the sin which was conceived by the first will, a sin which came to be as something possible, was changed into something necessary so that, just as the act of the mind could come to be as free, it also passed without a free act into the necessity of natural things.

(2) But realize that the author of necessary things is God. If, then, God produces in natures what the mind produced in sins, it is necessary that he is just as guilty as the one whose will he blames. In fact, he is more guilty. It is more wicked to engender sin in someone than it is to commit sin to the extent that the necessary is more than the possible. Though the nature of reality does not admit this, I would, nonetheless, like to show here that your view of God is worse than Mani's. After all, wars, though ones he suffered, mutilated his God, but sins which are ancient and have been multiplied have corrupted your God. And for this reason you disagree with the Catholics not merely on the present question, but even about God. You do not worship the God we venerate in the Trinity as most just, absolutely omnipotent, and inviolable.

(3) Hence, something pertaining to the will could not be passed on through nature, and we were correct to say that the work of the devil is not permitted to pass through the work of God. For the work of the devil and of an evil human being is sin which can exist in no one without an act of the free will. This work has come and comes both to the devil and to the human being as something possible. But the work of God is a nature in which a human being exists, not as something possible, but as something necessary. This nature exists at many times without the will since its power is experienced only at a certain age. As long as the nature exists without the will, it is only the work of God, but this nature cannot have a sin which it has not committed. It is an irrefutable statement that the work of the devil is not permitted to pass through the work of God.

(4) Your statement, however, is no less false than godless: "The work of a work of God is passed on through the work of God."[159] This, after all, amounts to saying: God also sins, because the human being whom God made sinned. For sin never exists except in the work of a human being, and when a human being sins, nothing is added to his substance so that the sin is seen to protrude from it, but the evil work committed by the evil will only earns evil merit for the one by whom it was committed so that the person is called evil who produced the evil works. So too, if your God produced evil in his works, nothing was added to his substance, just as in the case of the human being. But he earns a monstrous merit so that he is called evil for doing evil.

(5) A little one, of course, is proved even in that case not to be guilty because it has its malice as something necessary, and if the devil did not have his malice as something possible, he could not be guilty. The God who is the true God of the Christians does not produce evil; a little one too has prior to the choice of its will only what God produced in him. No sin, therefore, can be natural. But since in our great concern we have broken into the caverns of the ancient error and since nothing has remained hidden on this question, let the careful readers hold onto the distinction between the possible and the necessary, and they will laugh no less at the stories of the Manichees than at those of the traducianists.

AUG. (1) Among those people who understand what they read so that they also understand what you say, you have accomplished nothing by repeating the same ideas in the same words with such great complexity, except that it is clear that, when you could not refute it, you chose to obscure our answer in my one book, which you undertook to refute in your eight books. But among those who do not understand these matters, you at least have brought them to think that you said something because they do not understand. Hence, they must meanwhile briefly be reminded of the issue with which we are now dealing so that, once the clouds of your wordiness have been removed, they may gaze upon that very statement of mine and see how it stands unrefuted.

For you said, "If nature is the work of God, the work of the devil is not permitted to pass through the work of God." To this I said, "What then do his words mean, 'If nature is the work of God, the work of the devil is not permitted to pass through the work of God'? (2) Did the work of the devil, when it first arose in the angel who became the devil, not arise in the work of God? Hence, if an evil which existed nowhere at all could come to be in the work of God, why could not an evil which already existed somewhere not pass through the work of God, especially since the apostle uses this very word, when he says, *And in that way it was passed on to all human beings* (Rom 5:12). Are human beings not the work of God? Sin, then, was passed on through human beings, that is, the work of the devil through the work of God. And to state this in other words, the work of a work of God through a work of God. And for this reason God is alone immutable and has an all-powerful goodness; before there existed any evil, he made all his works good, and from the evils which have arisen in the good things made by him he produces effects that are good in every way."[160]

(3) Upset by the evidence of these truths, you thought that you should darken the eyes of people with your long and inane discussion of the possible and the necessary, not so that you might withdraw your silly statement under the cover of this fog for fear that it might be refuted, but so that you might hide it for fear that it be seen to lie there refuted. What difference does it make to the question we are dealing with whether it came about from something necessary or from something possible? The angel and the human being certainly sinned. Either, then, dare to say that the angel and the human being are not natures, or, since you are not so crazy that you would dare to do so, it has been proved to you that, when the angel sinned, a nature sinned, that, when the human being sinned, a nature sinned. But, you say, they sinned as something possible, not as something necessary. This is true; the angel, nonetheless, sinned; the human being, nonetheless, sinned; a nature, nonetheless, sinned. And so, the work of God which the angel is, which the human being is, sinned, not with God forcing them, but by their own evil will, which they could also not have had. (4) The ignominy, therefore, belongs to the nature which, though it had been made well and was not forced to do evil, nonetheless did evil. But the glory belongs to God who both made the nature good and produces good out of the evil which he did not make.

By these and similar true and Catholic arguments, then, we can defend and proclaim God's creative nature, and we can accuse and blame our sinful nature. We can also praise our sinful nature insofar as God made it and blame it insofar as it fell away from him with no one forcing it and received in its descendants what it merited. The very same nature, of course, which sinned in the one man by the will is born in each individual without a will. Since this is so, who pushed you into saying, who pressed you to write: "If nature is the work of God, the work of the devil is not permitted to pass through the work of God"? Oh the deafness to the holy words! (5) Oh the blindness of your inventions! Is not sin the work of the devil? Has it not been passed on to all human beings who are the work of God? Is not death through sin the work of the devil, especially that death which you say was alone brought about through sin, that is, not the death of the body, but of the soul? Has it not been passed on to all human beings who are the work of God?[161]

But, you say, it was passed on by imitation. It was passed on, nonetheless, through human beings who are the work of God. But it was passed on as something possible, not as something necessary. Say whatever you want; it was, nonetheless, passed on through human beings who are the work of God. You, however, said without making any exception: "The work of the devil is not permitted to pass through the work of God." In order that you might become more foolish, you tried with so much wordiness, not to defend the obvious foolishness of this statement so that it might be acquitted, but to cover it over so that it would not be seen. (6) If the words of the apostle which would have prevented you from saying this had not come into your mind, why did you not notice, I ask you, that the fact that the work of the devil exists in the work of God is something more than that it passes through the work of God? Since, then, you admit the former, why do you deny the latter? Is it that what you wish to happen is possible, but what you do not wish is not possible? May God have mercy on you that you may cease to be foolish.

Mani, however, gladly embraces this statement of yours as favoring him and argues as follows: If the work of the devil is not permitted to pass through the work of God and is far less permitted to exist in the work of God, where does evil, then, come from, save from where we say? But we reply to him: Say this to Julian, not to us. The originator of this statement has been cast out;[162] heaven forbid that one who will be conquered by us with you—or rather one who has already been conquered with you—should be prejudicial to us.

Augustine's Claim That God Creates Evil Human Beings

64. JUL. (1) You, therefore, brought forth from your dull wits that other statement. You said, "God creates the evil, just as he feeds and nourishes the evil,"[163] because it is written in the gospel that he makes his sun rise over the good and the evil and he causes rain to fall upon the just and the unjust.[164] The ideas, after all, which you considered joined together are completely and entirely opposed. For the fact that God feeds even sinners and is good to the ungrateful and to the evil is testimony to his fidelity, not to his malice. For he does not will the death of those who die, but that they return and live.[165] Nor does he immediately punish those who go astray, and he does this for no other reason than that his goodness might grant them time for repentance. After all, this is what the apostle says: *Or are you not aware that the goodness of God draws you to repentance? But in accord with the hardness of your unrepentant heart you store up for yourself anger* (Rom 2:4-5). (2) Before the people of Lycaonia and at the Areopagus he argues that God did not fail to provide proofs of his providence in the times of past igno-

rance. *For he did not leave himself without testimony*, he says, *providing rain from heaven and times of harvest, filling their hearts with food and joy* (Acts 14:16).

This fact, then, that he causes rain to fall upon the good and upon the evil is a proof of his kindness which sustains and waits for those who go astray that they may return from evil and do good.[166] He wants sin not to be committed to the point that he feeds even the ungrateful out of a desire for human conversion. But[167] that is a proof of perfect fidelity, while your statement, "He creates the evil," is testimony to perfect injustice. See, then, how you do not know what you are saying, for from an example of mercy you wanted to prove his cruelty. (3) For it is good to feed even the evil so that, if they will, they may amend their lives, but it is criminal to make little ones evil so that those who cannot use their wills are forced, nonetheless, to be evil.

Generosity, then, shown to sinners draws them back from sins; it does not force them into sins. But the creation of evil persons does not draw them back from great evils, but drives both the work and its maker into all sorts of crimes. You are crazy when you say that God creates the evil, but you are more crazy when you try to support it by the testimony of the gospel—and by that testimony which contains a grand proof of God's goodness. Notice, then, how much more powerfully the argument is turned around: It is evident that God who feeds even the evil so that he may by his patience make them good does not create evil persons. (4) But if he creates evil persons, he does not love or reward the good, nor can he in the end have any good, because the power which creates not only possible evils but necessary ones harms more effectively and violently than any evil will.

Since this does not fit with the God of the Christians, that is, with the one who is called the father of mercy and the God of consolation,[168] all of whose judgments are proclaimed as just,[169] who is said to have made all things in his wisdom,[170] we have nothing in common with you as Manichees in the appreciation of our God. Your stupid stories and genital sins have carried you off to an entirely other maker whom you worship, one invented by the madness of Mani.

AUG. (1) I shall do what you have not done, and why should it be a concern of mine to say why you have not done it? Let the readers judge. For because of your statement that, according to our view, God makes human beings for the devil, I eventually arrived in my reply at these words from which you quoted what you wished. But I shall mention, even though you are unwilling, what you thought you ought to pass over. Among other things, therefore, all of which it would take too long to state, I said, "Does God feed the children of perdition, the goats on the left,[171] for the devil? Does he nourish and clothe them for the devil, because he *makes his sun rise over the good and the bad and sends rain upon the just and the unjust* (Mt 5:45). He, then, creates the evil, just as he feeds and nourishes the evil, because what he gave them in creating them pertains to the goodness of nature and the increase that he gives by feeding and nourishing them he certainly did not give to their malice, but as a good help to the same good nature that he created in his goodness. (2) After all, insofar as they are human beings, that pertains to the good of nature of which God is the author, but insofar as they are born with sin, destined to perish, if they are not reborn, that pertains to the seed cursed from the beginning[172] because of the defect from that early disobedience. He who makes the vessels of anger, nonetheless, makes good use of this defect, *in order to make known the riches of his glory toward the vessels of mercy* (Rom 9:23), so that, if any who pertain to that same lump are set free by grace, they do not attribute it to their own merits. Rather, *the one who boasts should boast in the Lord* (2 Cor 10:17)."[173]

To these words I added the following: "Along with the Pelagians this fellow abandons this apostolic and Catholic faith which is absolutely true and most solidly founded. For he does not want the newborn to be under the power of the devil so that little ones are brought to Christ to be rescued from the power of darkness and transferred into his kingdom.[174] (3) And so, he accuses the Church spread throughout the whole world, because everywhere in the Church all the little infants to be baptized undergo the rite of exsufflation[175] only so that the prince of this world might be driven out of them.[176] As vessels of anger they are necessarily held in his power, when they are born of Adam, if they are not reborn in Christ and transferred into his kingdom, after having been made vessels of mercy by his grace."[177]

Let those who want to and are able read or listen to the rest that is there. But after you left out these arguments by which those words you quoted are supported and defended, you thought that you should quote them so that, like a thief, you might attack them, as if they were left all alone with no one defending them. Hence, let those read these pages who want to know what you did. Or rather let them go back to a consideration of the same book from which I cited them again, and let them see that those ideas which you tried to knock down as if they were weak remain standing solidly.

(4) How, then, does it help you to have raised as objections against me those people whose conversion through repentance God's patience awaits? And for this reason he makes his sun rise and makes the rain fall upon them. For I raised as an objection to you the goats on the left.[178] God who foreknows all that will happen cannot fail to know that they will live in their impiety and sins without repentance up to the end and will, on this account, be punished with eternal punishment. And yet, he does not hold back the good of his creation from those for whom it would be better not to be born, nor does he hold back the good of nourishment and of his daily gift of life as long as he chooses from those for whom it would have been better to die as soon as possible.

Among these there are certainly very many who, if they were taken from this life as infants, would be removed, according to your heresy, from absolutely all

condemnation, but, according to the Catholic faith, from the most severe condemnation. (5) Why is it, then, that among these goats on the left destined for un-
ending fire in the foreknowledge of God which cannot be deceived there are
many who, after being washed by the bath of rebirth, either perish afterwards by
apostasy or live such sinful and wicked lives that they are undoubtedly assigned
to the left, and yet they are not carried off, like some, lest malice change their
mind?[179] God is not prevented by a fatal necessity so that he does not give them
so great a benefit, nor is he changed by partiality so that he gives it to others.
What do your possibility and your necessity, which you urge us to distinguish
carefully, do here where, though you do not know what you are saying, he knows
what he should do, for his judgments can be hidden, but cannot be unjust?

(6) It is not, then, unjust that good things are bestowed upon the evil, but it is
unjust that evils are imposed upon the good. Tell me, then, by what justice the little ones suffer such great evils which it annoys us to mention so often. But it does
not shame you to introduce these same evils into paradise, even if no one had
sinned. "Evil persons are not," you say, "created," that is, ones who contract
original sin. By what justice, then, are they weighed down by a heavy yoke from
the day they emerge from the womb of their mother?[180] In that yoke there is such
great misery that we can more easily bewail that misery than set it forth in words.

Sin, you say, cannot be changed from something possible into something
necessary, that is, from something voluntary into something non-voluntary, and
we have shown that this was possible in the case of the one who says, *I do the evil
that I do not will* (Rom 7:19). (7) You attribute this to the force of habit, not to the
chains of our damaged origin. You see, nonetheless, that sin could have been
changed from something possible into something necessary, and yet you do not
blush over your twisted and deceitful rules. You do not want that something of
the sort could have happened to the whole human race through the one human
being in whom all existed, and yet you do not deny that infants suffer so many
and such great punishments under the providence of the most omnipotent and
most just God, because the infants close your mouths and strike your eyes, if you
deny them. Do you not, then, notice whom you make unjust, when you see the
most obvious punishments and deny any evil merits of the little ones?

(8) You thought my words false and sacrilegious, "The work of a work of
God was passed on through the work of God."[181] For an angel is certainly a work
of God. The sin, then, which is the work of the angel, is a work of a work of God,
not a work of God himself. And on the basis of these words you accuse me, as if I
said, "God also sins because the human being whom God made sinned." I did not
say that. The works of God, that is, the angel and the human being, did, of course,
sin. But they sinned by their own work, not by the work of God. They themselves
are the good work of God, but their sin is their own evil work, not God's. But
what is worse? To say, "God also sins because the human being whom God
made sinned," which I did not say, or to deny original sin so that the unjust pun-

ishment of the little ones is nothing but God's sin? If sin cannot be found in God, the punishment, then, of the little one is just. But if it is just, it is punishment for sin. No one, therefore, can preach that God is just in so many and such great punishments of little ones, while denying original sin. (9) It, therefore,[182] would be testimony to God's injustice to create evil persons if he himself created the evil by which they are evil. But now, since it is human beings who are evil and since God himself creates that which human beings are and since their being evil results from their nature damaged by sin, what God creates is certainly good, even when he creates persons who are evil. For they are evil because of a defect which is not a nature, but he creates the nature which is not a defect, even if it is damaged. Bestowing the good of creation on the race that has been damaged and justly condemned is like bestowing the good of life and health even on evil human beings because they are human beings, not because they are evil.

But you say that "it is criminal to make little ones evil so that those who cannot use their will are forced, nonetheless, to be evil." Those who do not exist can by no means be forced into something. (10) But if they are not yet existing in the proper character of their own person and state, but are already existing by reason of the most hidden nature of the seed, as Levi was in the loins of Abraham,[183] they are already evil there because of a defect of nature coming from the sin of the first human being; those who cannot even use their will are not forced to be evil by God's creating them.

Consider the wonders of the grace of Christ of which you are wretched enemies. Look, the little ones who cannot use their will or cannot will either good or evil are forced, nonetheless, to be holy and righteous, when they are reborn by sacred baptism, though they at times fight back and cry out with tears. For, if they die before attaining the use of reason, they will undoubtedly be holy and righteous in the kingdom of God by that grace to which they came, not by their own possibility, but by necessity. And they will live their holy and righteous lives without end, while trampling and smashing your rules about the possible and the necessary. It is, however, undoubtedly something more to will not to do evil than neither to will nor not to will it, and yet that man did not will it and did it, who said, *I do the evil that I do not will* (Rom 7:19).

(11) And so, I am not crazy, nor do I say, "God creates evil." For he who even from our damaged nature does not create a defect, but a nature, creates something good. That nature, however, contracts a defect, not by God's working, but by his judgment. But if you are not completely crazy, see whether you are not crazy, when you say that God produces, not the evil of punishment which is just, but the evil which is called injustice. What else, after all, does he do, if he either inflicts or allows to be inflicted upon little ones guilty of no sin such great evils? But you should not be addressed and refuted by us; rather, you should, if it were possible, undergo exsufflation and exorcism by the whole Church which, you say, practices exsufflation and exorcism upon infants in vain.

Notes

1. See Heb 12:4.
2. Augustine cites the definition of wisdom which he found in Cicero's *Duties* (*De officiis*) 2, 5, a definition which he often cites from his very earliest works.
3. See Gn 2:19.
4. See Cicero, *Tusculan Disputations* (*Tusculanae disputationes*) I, 25, 62.
5. See Wis 9:15.
6. See Ps 144:4.
7. See Heb 11:25.
8. See Ps 145:13.17.
9. See Sir 40:1.
10. See Jb 14:4 LXX.
11. I have conjectured *"serio respondisset"* instead of *"se respondisse."*
12. Julian probably alludes to the decree of the emperor Honorius of 30 April 418 which sentenced Pelagius and Caelestius to exile.
13. See Sir 40:1.
14. Turbantius was one of the Pelagian bishops who initially refused to accept the letter "Tractoria," of Pope Zosimus; Julian dedicated to him his first work against the doctrine of original sin, which Augustine refuted in *Answer to Julian.*
15. Julian refers to his present work, *To Florus,* and to his previous work, *To Turbantius,* the relevant passage of the latter is cited in *Marriage and Desire* II, 12, 25.
16. See Gal 5:17.
17. See Gn 2:25.
18. See Gn 3:7.
19. See Ambrose, *Commentary on the Gospel of Luke* (*Expositio Euangelii secundum Lucam*) 7, 141: CCL 14, 263.
20. A passage excerpted from Julian's *To Turbantius*; it is cited in *Marriage and Desire* II, 12, 25.
21. The following sentence from Julian's *To Turbantius* was omitted in the excerpts to which Augustine replies in the second book of *Marriage and Desire.*
22. See Col 1:13.
23. See Mk 9:20.
24. *Marriage and Desire* II, 12, 45, with minor changes.
25. See Sir 40:1.
26. See Gal 5:17.
27. Augustine uses an untranslatable pair of rhymes: *"disputatione Pelagiana ... regeneratione Christiana."*
28. See Col 1:13.
29. See Rom 6:2-3.
30. See Gn 18:10-14.
31. Julian cites another passage from his *To Turbantius* which was omitted, it seems, from the excerpts which Augustine received.
32. A citation from Julian's *To Turbantius*; see *Marriage and Desire* II, 13, 26.
33. *Ibid.*
34. I have conjected *"adventu"* in place of *"adiutu."*
35. Vergil, *The Georgics* 3, 130-137.
36. See Wis 9:15.
37. See Gn 37–50.
38. See Heb 7:5-10.
39. See 1 Cor 15:53.
40. See Rom 7:24.
41. See Eccl 7:30.
42. See *Marriage and Desire* II, 14, 28.

43. *Ibid.*
44. I have followed here the conjecture in the NBA edition of *"juberet"* instead of *"liberet."*
45. *Marriage and Desire* II, 14, 29, with some changes.
46. Julian alludes to Vergil, *Georgics* I, 350.
47. It was commonly believed in the ancient world that lice were asexually generated from the bodies of animals; if the lice settled in the eyes, they caused blindness. See, for example, Aristotle, *History of Animals* V, 31, on the generation of lice.
48. Julian alludes to the myth of Cadmus who slew a dragon and buried its teeth from which there sprung up a race of fierce, armed men who killed one another.
49. The Myrmidons, a people of Thesally, were supposedly transformed from ants into human beings.
50. The PL and NBA texts have *"publicaria"* instead of *"pulicaria."*
51. See Ps 83:17.
52. See Gn 1:31.
53. See Gn 1:31 and Sir 39:21.
54. I have followed the conjecture in the NBA edition of *"praeverteret"* instead of *"perverteret."*
55. *Marriage and Desire* II, 14, 29.
56. *Ibid.*
57. I have conjectured *"munere"* instead of *"numero."*
58. See Gn 3:16.
59. See Sir 40:1.
60. See *Marriage and Desire* II, 15, 30.
61. See Gal 5:17.
62. See Wis 9:15.
63. See Eccl 7:30.
64. *Marriage and Desire* II, 20, 35.
65. Cicero, *Divination* (*De divinatione*) 1, 2.
66. See Gn 2:25.
67. *Marriage and Desire* II, 20, 35.
68. I have conjectured *"sed"* in place of *"si."*
69. See Gal 5:17.
70. See IV, 56.
71. Ambrose, *Commentary on the Gospel of Luke* (*Expositio Euangelii secundum Lucam*) 7, 141: CCL 14, 263.
72. *Marriage and Desire* II, 26, 43, with an omission.
73. *Marriage and Desire* II, 26, 43, with a sentence omitted.
74. Augustine plays with the Latin verbs: they read (*legunt*) the gospel; they neglect (*neglegunt*) you.
75. See Mt 8:12.
76. See Gal 3:11.
77. See Rom 10:17.
78. See Gal 5:17.
79. A quotation from the excerpts from *To Turbantius* which Augustine also cited in *Marriage and Desire* II, 26, 41.
80. See Mt 26:28.
81. Chrysippus of Soli (c. 380–c. 306) was a successor of Zeno of Citium and the great systematizer of Stoic philosophy.
82. See the Roman rule of law, "The mother is always certain; marriage shows who the father is," which is found in the jurist, Paulus, of the second or third century and taken up in the *Digest* of Justinian (II, 4, 5).
83. I have conjectured *"nuptiis"* in place of *"in nuptiis."*
84. The lesson in logic which Julian provides reflects the logic of Porphyry; see his *Isagoge* 3, 5-11; 7, 1-4 and 11-16.
85. I have conjectured *"obnoxia tenetur"* in place of *"obnoxiaretur."*

86. See above 21.

87. See Prv 19:14 LXX.

88. See Gal 5:17.

89. See *Marriage and Desire* II, 23, 38; Julian paraphrases Augustine's words.

90. The Latin has *"Patricius"* but I have taken Julian to refer to Patticius to whom Mani wrote *The Letter Known as "The Foundation."*

91. Melitides is mentioned in Aristophanes' *The Frogs* 989–991. He was apparently a legendary fool who was specially ignorant of sexual matters.

92. *Marriage and Desire* II, 13, 38.

93. See Rom 8:10.

94. Ambrose, *Penance* (*De poenitentia*) I, 3, 13: SC 179, 62.

95. See above 17; Julian refers to Mani as Augustine's teacher.

96. See *Marriage and Desire* II, 29, 49, where Augustine quotes the text from Julian's *To Turbantius.*

97. See *Marriage and Desire* II, 29, 40.

98. See I, 44, where Julian first cites this definition of sin which he took from Augustine's work, *Two Souls* 11, 15.

99. In Christian late antiquity and the Middle Ages, Epicurus' materialistic philosophy was viewed as a mere hedonism and Epicurus was considered as the anti-Christ. Here, however, Epicurus is mentioned because he was mistakenly thought to have been unfamiliar with either Platonism or Aristotelianism and, therefore, ignorant of logic.

100. See *Marriage and Desire* II, 28, 48, where Augustine cites these lines from Julian's *To Turbantius.*

101. Julian visited Carthage most probably after 408 when he received from Possidius a copy of the sixth book of Augustine's *Music* along with an invitation from Augustine to visit him; see Letter 101 to Memorius, Julian's father. In Africa Julian met Honoratus, a Manichean friend of Augustine, to whom he dedicated *The True Religion* and to whom he wrote Letter 140 in the winter of 411-412.

102. I have followed the reading in *Marriage and Desire* II, 28, 48 rather than the impossible *"opus Dei per opus operis Dei"* which is found in PL and NBA.

103. *Marriage and Desire* II, 28, 48, with two significant omissions. Augustine here quotes from Julian's *To Florus.*

104. *Marriage and Desire* II, 28, 48.

105. See III, 172 and following, especially 177, where Julian quotes from the Letter of Mani to his daughter, Menoch, the letter discovered and sent to Julian by Florus as proof that Augustine is really a Manichee.

106. See *Marriage and Desire* I, 23, 26 for the image of the fruit tree from which the devil plucks fruit.

107. *Marriage and Desire* I, 7, 8.

108. See Ps 148:5.

109. See Ambrose, *Penance* (*De poenitentia*) I, 3, 13; SC 179, 62.

110. See Gal 5:17.

111. See Ambrose, *Commentary on the Gospel of Luke* (*Expositio Euangelii secunduam Lucam*) 7, 141: CCL 14, 283.

112. See *Marriage and Desire* II, 28, 48.

113. See *Marriage and Desire* II, 28, 48, though Julian seriously misrepresents Augustine's thought.

114. See *Marriage and Desire* II, 28, 48, though the words Julian cites are not quite what Augustine said. For Augustine's exact words see his reply to this chapter.

115. *Marriage and Desire* II, 28, 48

116. See above 26.

117. See Rom 7:19.

118. See Eccl 7:30.

119. See *Marriage and Desire* II, 28, 48, though Julian again does not quote Augustine verbatim.

120. See above 24.

121. See *Marriage and Desire* II, 28, 48.

122. Ambrose, *Isaac and the Soul* (*De Isaac et anima*) VII, 60: CSEL 32/1, 685.

123. See *Answer to Julian* I, 9, 43, where Augustine quotes from the excerpts made from Julian's *To Turbantius*.

124. Julian reproduces with slight modifications Augustine's definition of sin from *Two Souls* 11, 15.

125. See above 26, where Julian quotes from his own *To Florus*. Augustine had already cited the sentence in *Marriage and Desire* II, 28, 48.

126. See Rom 5:12.

127. See Dn 3:72.

128. See 2 Mc 7:28, as well as various of the Greek Fathers.

129. See Rom 1:27.

130. I have followed the conjecture of *"quae"* in the NBA edition in place of *"qui."*

131. See Ex 21:28-32.

132. See Dt 22:8.

133. See Ps 51:19.

134. See *To Orosius in Refutation of the Priscillianists and Origenists* 5, 5–6, 7, where Augustine argues against the Origenist claim that even the devil will be saved. See also *Heresies* XLI and *The City of God* XXI, 17.

135. I have conjectured *"ut"* in place of the *"aut"* found in PL.

136. See Phil 1:19.

137. *Marriage and Desire* II, 28, 48.

138. See Ps 145:5. Julian runs through the declension of "nothing" in the preceding and following sentences, perhaps implying the weakness of Augustine's case from the weaker cases of the noun.

139. See Ps 145:5.

140. See Jas 3:15.

141. See Lk 20:36.

142. I have conjectured *"probatione"* instead of *"proprietate."*

143. See Rom 7:23.

144. See Gn 3:7.

145. See Sir 11:18.

146. See Ambrose, *Isaac and the Soul* (*De Isaac et anima*) 7, 60: CSEL 32/1: 685.

147. See Eccl 7:30.

148. See Mt 19:26.24.

149. See Jn 20:26.

150. Augustine omits parts of what Julian had said.

151. See I, 28.

152. I have followed the conjecture in the NBA edition of: "Nunc ergo aliter non esset" in place of "Non ergo aliter esset."

153. See 1 Cor 15:28.

154. See 2 Pt 3:13.

155. See Rom 7:25.

156. See Ps 49:7.

157. See Jer 17:5.

158. See *Marriage and Desire* II, 28, 48. Julian has changed Augustine's question into a statement.

159. *Marriage and Desire* II, 28, 48.

160. *Marriage and Desire* II, 28, 48, with part of one sentence omitted.

161. See Rom 5:12.

162. See Jn 12:31.

163. *Marriage and Desire* II, 17, 32.

164. See Mt 5:45.

165. See Ez 18:32.

166. See Ps 33:15.
167. I have conjectured "*at*" in place of "*ad.*"
168. See 2 Cor 1:3.
169. See Ps 119:75.
170. See Ps 104:24.
171. See Mt 25:32-33.
172. See Wis 12:11.
173. *Marriage and Desire* II, 17, 32.
174. See Col 1:13.
175. The rite of exsufflation, or "blowing out," was formerly a part of the ritual of baptism in the Catholic Church. The priest administering the sacrament would blow in the face of the person being baptized to symbolize the expulsion of the devil.
176. See Jn 12:31.
177. *Marriage and Desire* II, 18, 33.
178. See Mt 25:33.
179. See Wis 4:11.
180. See Sir 40:1.
181. *Marriage and Desire* II, 28, 48.
182. I have omitted "*inquit*" as a remnant from a repetition of "*iniquitatis.*"
183. See Heb 7:9.10.

BOOK SIX

Book Six

The Safety of the Road More Heavily Traveled

1. JUL. I have no doubt that up to now an opinion of this sort hovered over our conflict, namely, that it was believed to have to do with a question of detail rather than with the essence of the faith. Those who spend their time far from spiritual pursuits are disturbed merely by little breaths of rumor. Fearing the hostility of the times and not holding onto the bulwark of the truth which they have already discovered—as almost always in frightening matters one trusts no one less than oneself—they think the road safer which is more heavily traveled.

AUG. Our road is more heavily traveled to the extent that it is older, because it is Catholic, but yours is less traveled to the extent that it is, rather, newer because it is heretical.

Julian Identifies Two Causes

2. JUL. This, however, has happened at present for two reasons: because the view of the Manichees concerning the instigation of sins has been approved and because storms of persecutions that have been stirred up have turned those without spirit away from supporting the truth.

AUG. How can the road of the Manichees' view be more heavily traveled since they are only a very few in number? And how can you be suffering persecution for the truth when you take the little ones away from the savior?

The Masses Think the Traducianists and Catholics Agree

3. JUL. The side, then, concerned with pleasure and fear, accompanied by the peoples of the arena or of the circus or of the stage, aims because of its lustful desires to excuse all its outrageous actions under the pretext of necessity which always removes the odiousness of the sin committed, and this side aims to avoid by apostasy the thunderous roar of the world. These are, then, the reasons which cause the defense of the vices to have a better following. The majority from that mob has, nonetheless, as I have said, believed that the arguments of the traducianists and the Catholics are in agreement, even on God.

AUG. (1) The countless multitude of believers which was promised to Abraham[1] is scorned by you as a common mob, obviously because what you say can please the few whom you make Pelagians, that is, people sick with the poisons of this new plague. For you say that the very obvious misery of the human race, which is seen in the heavy yoke upon the children of Adam from the day they emerge from the womb of their mother,[2] does not come from the merit of the sin by which human nature was damaged in the first human being. (2) For this reason it follows that you are forced to say that, if no one had sinned, there would be in paradise not only so many and such great burdens of troubles which we see the little ones suffer, but also so many and such great defects of minds and bodies with which very many are born. In that place of happiness and rest you even locate your darling, sexual desire, by which the flesh has desires opposed to the spirit.[3] And with your eyes shut, you accuse us who make war against her as against a hostile defect, with the help of the spirit which has desires opposed to her; you accuse us, as if we were friends of pleasure and of lewd behavior into which no one falls sinfully and shamefully but one who consents to that darling of yours, which we blame, but you defend, with all her enticements and persuasions.

A Hope That Many of the Common Folk Will Be Corrected

4. JUL. But in the first and in the present debate[4] it became clear from the argumentation of Augustine that the God of the traducianists is not the God whom Christians venerate with a unanimous profession as just and as the creator of all. I, therefore, anticipate in my mind that, once these points have been recognized, very many of these people will be corrected, even those who have fallen through blind error.

AUG. On the contrary, once they have recognized these points which we make in reply to your fallacious nonsense in accord with the words of truth, only madness or stubbornness will keep anyone in the error of your heresy.

The Traducianist Is Mani's Heir and Offspring

5. JUL. In opposition to us Mani believes that mortals are driven by nature into crimes and outrages; he thinks that the original darkness provided material for bodies and for sins, that the pleasure of the sexes is a disease of the human race which asserts the rights of the devil and compels human beings into every disgrace. The traducianist having followed him in every respect, as his heir and offspring, testifies by his many discourses that sins are natural, that the eternal necessity of evil comes from the dark nothingness, that the desire destined for the senses pollutes all the saints and places the image of God in the kingdom of the devil.

AUG. (1) In opposition to the Catholic truth Mani creates with a singular insanity the myth of the nature of evil as a substance coeternal with the good God.

The Catholic truth, however, says that God alone is eternal without any beginning and that he is not only good, which Mani too admits, but is also immutable, which he denies. Against the madness of the Manichees, therefore, we preach this God who is supremely good and, for this reason, utterly immutable; no nature which is not what he is is coeternal with him, nor would it exist if it were not made, not out of him, but by him, that is, not out of his nature, but still by his power. We know and state that the nature which has been made is something good, and yet it could not have existed at all unless the omnipotent nature had made it, though not out of itself.

But it is not equal to its maker. (2) For God made all things very good,[5] but not supremely good, as he himself is. These goods, nonetheless, of whatever sort would not exist unless the supremely good God had made them. Nor would any mutable goods exist unless he who is immutably good had made them. And, for this reason, when the Manichees ask us where evil comes from, when they want to introduce an evil coeternal to God and do not know what evil is, but think that it is a nature and a substance, we answer them that evil does not come from God and is not coeternal with God, but that evil arose from the free will of the rational creature which was created well by the good creator, though its goodness is not equal to the goodness of its creator, because it is not God's nature, but his work. And for this reason it had the possibility, but not the necessity of sinning. But it would not even have this possibility if it were the nature of God who neither wills to be able to sin nor is able to will to sin. If, given this possibility of sinning, this rational nature, nonetheless, had not actually sinned when it could have sinned, it would have earned for itself great merit, and the reward of this merit would have been that due to a greater happiness it could not sin.

(3) But having heard this, Mani still goes on and says: If the evil comes from the free will of the rational nature, from where do these many evils come with which we see they are born who do not yet have the use of freedom of the will? From where does the concupiscence come by which the flesh has desires opposed to the spirit[6] and pulls one to commit sin, unless the spirit has even stronger desires opposed to it? From where does so great a discord come in a single human being between the two components from which one is composed? From where does the law in the members come which resists the law of the mind,[7] and without which no one is born? From where do so many and such great defects of minds and bodies come with which very many are born? From where do the hardships and woes of the little ones who do not yet sin with their will come? When they attain the use of reason, from where does so great a punishment of mortals come in learning grammar and other arts that to their painful efforts the torment of blows is added?

(4) Here we reply that even these evils take their origin from the will of a human nature and that, when this nature sinned greatly, it was damaged and condemned with the whole human race. Hence, the many natural goods of this

nature come from God's work, but evils come from God's judgment. The Manichees do not see that these evils are in no sense natures or substances, but are said to be natural because human beings are born with them, since the root, so to speak, of their origin was damaged.

But you new heretics contradict us; answer, therefore, the Manichees; say where so many and such great evils come from. For, if you deny that human beings are born with them, where is your sense of shame? If you admit that they are born with them, where is your heresy? (5) But argue that these evils are not evil, and fill paradise, not the true paradise, but your paradise, with hardships, pains, errors, groans, tears, and sorrows, even if no one had sinned. But if you do not dare to do so for fear that you would be laughed at even by children and would be judged in need of correction by rods, Mani concludes against you that these evils which you do not want to come from a good, but damaged nature come from our being mixed with evil. And he says that this evil is a nature coeternal with and opposed to God. And for this reason, when you try to be more distant from Mani, you become his helper.

Like Mani Augustine Accuses God

6. JUL. (1) But now the spears of accusations are hurled at God himself with a similar result, but with a dissimilar beginning. Mani, of course, says: The good God does not make evil, but he adds that he destines souls to eternal fire for natural sins, something which is the mark of obvious cruelty. And, for this reason, as the result of his view he defiles with clear injustice the God he had called good. But Augustine, as if trusting his patron to whom he writes,[8] scorns with a greater daring the cautiousness of his teacher and does not hesitate to begin where Mani ends up. He declares that God makes and creates evil, that is, sin, though it is clear that this God does not correspond to the God whom the faith of the Catholics worships.

(2) Let this most of all become fixed in the mind of the reader: No believer ever has had a greater reason than we do for fighting, and everyone who thinks that nature itself implies the necessity of sin has no fellowship in the worship of the God of the Christians. This has been frequently stressed, but the importance of the principal issue demanded its repetition. Let us now come to the discussion of those first human beings, for by blaming them the Numidian meets our battle line as if armed with a small shield.

AUG. (1) I would believe that you do not know what Mani says about the mixture of the good and evil substance if I did not know with certainty that you read what we wrote against that same error. For, from the book in which I refuted their opinion about the two souls found in a human being, of which one is said to be good and the other evil, you quoted certain testimonies, thinking that I contradicted myself.[9] Mani, therefore, maintained that in one human being there are two souls or spirits or minds, one proper to the flesh, and that this same soul is not evil because of a defect that comes upon it, but is evil and coeternal with God by nature, while the other is good by nature as a particle of God, but defiled by the mixture with the evil soul. And for this reason he wants the flesh, because of its evil soul, to have desires opposed to the spirit which is, of course, good, in order to hold the spirit in bonds, while the spirit has desires opposed to the flesh in order to be set free from that mixture. (2) But if it will not be able to be set free even by the final conflagration of the world, he says that it will be attached to the sphere of darkness and will be held for eternity in such punishment.

The God of Mani, then, does not, as you say, "destine souls to eternal fire for natural sins." Rather, because of their mixture with the alien evil nature, though he himself mixed them with that evil and could not set them free from it, he destines souls good by nature, not to eternal fire, but attaches them, as I said, to the eternal sphere of darkness in which the mind of darkness is enclosed. Mani, after all, does not think there is any eternal fire.

But you have abandoned the Catholic faith in order to found a new sect, clearly not one which attacks the Manichees, as you think or pretend, but rather one which helps them. When this Catholic faith hears or reads the words of the apostle, *The flesh has desires opposed to the spirit, but the spirit has desires opposed to the flesh, for these are opposed to each other so that you do not do what you will* (Gal 5:17), it does not think that two natures, that is, of good and of evil, were opposed to each other from eternity and mingled by a subsequent war, as the heretical Mani supposes. But as the Catholic teacher, Ambrose, knows, this discord between the flesh and the spirit was turned into our nature as the result of the transgression of the first human being.[10] As a result, this nature is not understood to be the nature of human beings as they were originally created, but the punishment of them once they were condemned that has been turned into their nature. (4) This faith is not a Numidian shield about which you insult us as if you were clever, but a genuine full shield of truth with which we extinguish, as the apostle urges us, all the flaming arrows of the evil one.[11]

When the illustrious Cyprian, not a Numidian, of course, but a Phoenician, had gone forth armed against you who were still to come, he was protected by this full shield, though your empty verbosity has also attacked us with this Phoenician name. Armed with this shield, I say, that illustrious Phoenician said in his book on the Lord's Prayer that, when we say, *Your will be also done on earth as in heaven* (Mt 6:10), we pray that with God's help harmony might be established between these two, that is, between the flesh and the spirit.[12] There the outstanding soldier of Christ extinguished the flaming spears of the evil one hurled both by the Manichees and by you. All heretics are soldiers for this evil one, and you think that his camps should be increased by your new troops.

(5) For by seeking the harmony between the spirit and the flesh, Cyprian teaches against the Manichees that both the natures of which we are composed are good if the evil of discord is healed by divine mercy. But he resists you, because you say that the concupiscence of the flesh is good though because of its attack there exists this discord which he asks to be healed. And it exists even when we act well so that we fight back with the help of the spirit which has desires opposed to the attacks of concupiscence of the flesh. For if we consent, there comes about not a desirable, but a blameworthy and even damnable harmony of the spirit with the flesh.

(6) Cyprian is also against you because you ascribe to free choice what he understands we must ask God to produce in a human being. But you, who without knowing what you are saying object to me that I say that God creates sin, stand up against Mani who says that in the discord between the flesh and the spirit are seen the two natures of good and evil which are opposed to each other. For there is one answer we should make in order that this plague may be conquered, namely, that this discord was turned into our nature through the transgression of the first human being. When you deny this, you try to make them conquer, and you are revealed well enough as the false attacker, but true helper of the Manichees.

The Incredibly Great Sin of Adam and Eve

7. JUL. (1) He, of course, repeats over and over in all his writings that Adam and Eve alone were created good by God, that is, enslaved to no natural sin, and that they sinned by free will, but sinned so greatly that they destroyed everything that God created in their nature. He says, "That sin which the devil inflicted was far greater and deeper than are these sins familiar to human beings. As a result, by that great sin of the first human being, our nature was at that point changed for the worse so that it not only became sinful, but also begot sinful offspring. And yet, this infirmity by which the strength to live well was lost is certainly not a nature, but a defect. That sin, then, which in paradise changed human beings themselves for the worse, because it is much more serious than we can judge, is contracted by every child that is born."[13]

(2) See how openly he expressed what he thought: Those first human beings, he said, had a good nature, but they committed so huge, so incalculable a sin that they destroyed the power to live good lives, they extinguished the light of free choice, they produced the necessity of sinning for those to come so that it would not be possible for anyone born of their lineage to try to attain the beauty of the virtues and to become possessors of holiness by having avoided the vices.

AUG. (1) You, or your Pelagian companions as well, think that you say something when, having abandoned divine authority, you exult in human vanity and oppose and shout against the truth of the holy scriptures by the arguments of your heart. For, surely, if with a Christian and Catholic mind you would pay attention to the words of the apostle, *The body is indeed dead on account of sin* (Rom 8:10), you would certainly understand that the first human being sinned so greatly that by that sin the nature, not of the one human being, but of the whole human race, was changed and, having fallen from the possibility of immortality, it was hurled down into the necessity of death. As a result, even those who turn back to God through the one mediator between God and human beings, the man Jesus Christ,[14] do not immediately obtain immortality of the body, but it is now promised to them by the Spirit of God who now dwells in them that it will be given later. (2) The same apostle explains this in the same passage as follows; he says, *If any do not have the Spirit of Christ, they do not belong to him. But if Christ is in you, the body is indeed dead on account of sin, but the spirit is life on account of righteousness. If, then, the Spirit of him who has raised Jesus from the dead dwells in you, he who raised Jesus Christ from the dead will also bring to life your mortal bodies through his Spirit dwelling in you* (Rom 8:9-11).

The body, then, is dead on account of sin because it carries about the necessity of death even among the living. But what sin is this if not that of the first man? For through the righteousness of the second man, that is, of Christ, the blessed gift of life will come to the same body which is now said to be dead. (3) For this reason Christ is called the second man and the second Adam,[15] though we see that so many generations of human beings have passed between Adam created as a man and Christ born as a man, and in the series of generations only Cain could be called the second man. But since there is first the death of the body which came about on account of the sin of Adam and in which this world runs its course, there is second the life of the body which will come to be on account of the righteousness of Christ. It has already come to be in the flesh of Christ, and in this life the world to come will last. Hence, the former is called the first Adam or man, but the latter is called the second.

(4) And you refuse to understand that the sin of that first man was so great that he begot this world of mortals, but that the righteousness of the second man was so great that he begot a world of immortals. And you raise as an objection to me the greatness of the sin of the first man which was the cause of so much evil for all human beings, as if I were the only one or the first one to say this. Listen to John of Constantinople, a priest of great renown. He said, "Adam committed that great sin and condemned the whole human race in common."[16] Listen also to what he says about the resurrection of Lazarus so that you may understand that the death of the body also came from that great sin. He said, "Christ wept because the devil made mortal those who could have been immortal."[17] Where, I ask you, did the devil make all human beings mortal except in that man upon whom he inflicted so great a sin of transgression that by it the human race was cast from the blessedness of paradise into the great misery which we see and

feel? (5) Not only the death of the body, but also so many and such great evils of the soul which the corruptible body weighs down,[18] as well as the heavy yoke upon the children of Adam from the day they emerge from the womb of their mother,[19] testify to this. Under this yoke there is also included what we read in the psalm, *Every living human being is complete vanity* (Ps 39:6).

When you refuse to attribute these evils to that great sin of the first human being, what do you accomplish but that you in fact introduce these evils into the paradise of that great happiness, as if they would also have been there if no one had sinned, while the Manichees attribute these evils to the nation of darkness, not embarrassed by your accusations, but relying on your help, unless they become run through along with you by the Catholic truth, as if by an invincible sword?[20] (6) But we do not say, as you pretend, that it is not possible for anyone born of the lineage of the first human beings "to try to attain the beauty of the virtues." For many in whom God also produces the willing[21] try to attain them, nor do they with his help try to attain them without succeeding in the attainment of them. But if the corruptible body did not weigh down the soul,[22] they would, of course, not struggle. And for this reason, if no one had sinned and there was not the heavy yoke upon the children of Adam,[23] they would in paradise easily and happily obey their God without effort.

The Charge That Free Choice Was Lost by Being Used

8. JUL. Augustine, then, thinks that the praise of those first human beings, that is, of the two alone, helps him to maintain the distinction between the Manichees and the traducianists. Hardly anything can easily be found either more crazy[24] or more impudent than this idea. Freedom of choice, he says, lost its strength after it began to be used. And as if turning to him, let us examine everything step by step. You admit, of course, that the first human being was endowed with free choice and was created good by God, unpolluted by any disease of sin from the beginning, but then, having transgressed with the freedom of his innocent condition, he introduced an inevitable compulsion to sin for all who were to come after him. This is certainly your teaching which we testify was squeezed from the filth of Mani who holds that even the nature of Adam himself is naturally evil, though it was mixed from the flower of the first substance and was much better than those that followed.[25]

AUG. (1) What was said above is sufficient proof that with regard to the first human beings and their descendants our teaching is Catholic and that your teaching is heretical. The former were created upright by God, but these others came to be, though made by the same creator, nonetheless from a nature damaged by sin and with the chain of sin, and they were cast down from the good health in which human beings were originally created into the weakness of disease and the necessity of death by the condition of their origin. On this account they need the help of the savior who first saves them by the forgiveness of all sins and afterwards by the healing of all their infirmities.[26]

For the apostle said to those who were already baptized and had already received the Holy Spirit: *The flesh has desires opposed to the spirit, but the spirit has desires opposed to the flesh, for these are opposed to each other so that you do not do what you will* (Gal 5:17). (2) You who deny that free choice lost its strength by sinning, that is, by making a bad use of itself, what will you reply here when you hear that, when the flesh has desires opposed to the spirit, even the faithful do not do what they will? What will you reply when you hear that even those whose sins have been forgiven in baptism do what they do not will, that those who the apostle says have received the Holy Spirit through the preaching of the faith[27] do not do what they will, and finally that those who the same teacher of the nations says were called into freedom[28] do not through free will do what they will?

Next, you yourself, so eloquent a defender of sexual desire, you who, as her illustrious patron, dare to do so much for your darling that you do not doubt that the concupiscence of the flesh by which it has desires opposed to the spirit existed even in paradise before the sin, do you not see that you are forced to say that in those first human beings free will was not even then able to fulfill its function? (3) For if the flesh then had desires opposed to the spirit, they certainly did not do what they willed. But because they undoubtedly did what they willed by free choice which then had its full strength, that is, because they observed the law of God not only with no impossibility, but also with no difficulty, your darling by which the flesh has desires opposed to the spirit did not exist there. Because of her, human beings who have already been even converted to God through faith, already baptized, made holy, and called into freedom do not do what they will in extinguishing that delight filled with vice.

That statement which the Catholic faith spoke through bishop Ambrose is most true: This defect by which the flesh has desires opposed to the spirit was turned into our nature by the transgression of the first human being.[29] By this inescapable and insuperable spear of the truth both Mani and you are slain. (4) On this issue, both of you, of course, are mistaken—figure out which of you is worse. You are mistaken because you claim that this disease is not an evil, but he is mistaken because he, of course, recognizes that it is an evil, but does not know where it comes from. And deprived of the Catholic faith he invents his myth full of lies and shamefulness concerning the mingling of the two natures, namely, of good and of evil.

Now, then, our righteousness consists in this: that having been justified through faith we have peace with God,[30] but we do battle against the concupiscence of the flesh which attacks us because by the help of God himself the spirit fights back. (5) The righteousness, then, of this life does not mean that we have no defect, but that we diminish our defects by not consenting to them and live in temperance, justice, and piety by resisting them. But to have no defect which we should resist belongs to the next life which is the reward of acting well in the present life. This will come about by the healing of our nature, not by its separation from an alien nature, as Mani, whose helper you are, so insanely thinks. There you have our teaching, not, as you charge, squeezed from the filth of Mani, and if you have not completely lost your mind, you see that by our teaching Mani has been crushed along with you.

The Insanity of Mixing Choice with the Seeds

9. JUL. (1) We must, then, at the present first expose the dullness of your mind; then we must show, as we have already often done, that you do not depart even by one step from the hovels and brothels of Mani. To begin with, then, it is completely insane to suppose that an act of choice is mixed in with the seeds and that functions of the will are embedded in babies so that, once the perfectly clear and vast difference between natures and actions has been removed, the will of the first parents is said to have reproduced itself in their descendants.

All of reality stands opposed to this error. Never have the children of the eloquent produced the beauty of their parents' art in their wailing, nor have the offspring of actors stretched out their hands in artful gestures to go with the words, nor have the children of warriors asked that the trumpet sound for the people. One could in this fashion run through examples of all people which resound in agreement louder than thunder. (2) The whole world will reply that the bounds of nature are other than the bounds of the will and that the conditions of the seeds cannot be influenced by the choices of actions. It has, therefore, been seen as most stupid and as the mark of a desperate insensibility to believe that what you admit is voluntary has been turned into our nature. But that other point is far, far more deformed, namely, that the possibility of acting was destroyed at the beginning of action, that is, that free choice, which is nothing but the possibility of sinning and of not sinning, which is not subject to any violence from either side, but which has the ability to move by its spontaneous judgment to the side which it wills, lost the ability to will both alternatives after it began to will one.

AUG. (1) But do you not see that in that way you support Mani, not knowingly, of course, but persistently, nonetheless, with this puffed up and foaming noise of your wordiness? For, if he asked us where evil comes from, the question by which they used to upset the hearts of the unlearned, we would reply that it arose from the free will of the rational creature. And he would say: Where, then, do these many evils come from, not the evils which befall those who are already born and, with their advance in age, are already making use of the choice of the will, but those evils with which either all or very many are born? Inborn in all, of course, is the concupiscence of the flesh by which the flesh has desires opposed to the spirit, even when the spirit has been filled with the correct faith and doctrine of piety. Also inborn in all is a certain slowness of mind; because of it even those who are called talented still have some difficulties and labors to learn any arts, even those which are called liberal, and to gain a richer knowledge of religion itself. (2) Some are also born with a body that is deformed and at times monstrous; many are born with poor memories, many slow to understand and dull, many prone to anger, and many lustful; some are even born completely stupid and feebleminded. What else would the Catholic faith answer but that all these evils arise from that nature which was damaged by the infection of sin from the time when the man sinned and was thrown out of paradise, that is, the place of happiness? For, if no one had sinned, neither such defects nor any others would have come to be in paradise.

If Mani heard this, he would recite for us your words, if he had them, where you say, "It is completely insane to suppose that an act of choice is mixed in with the seeds and that functions of the will are embedded in babies," and whatever else you added to this statement, when you tried to prove it from the fact that the children of the eloquent are not born eloquent, nor are the children of actors born actors, nor the children of warriors born warriors. (3) Mani makes use of your help to attack what we say, namely, that human nature was damaged by the sin of the first human being, even in his descendants who were in him in the nature of the seed[31] when he sinned through that great transgression. When Mani has attacked what we say, he would introduce the mixture of his two natures and claim that those evils with which human beings are born come to be from the mixture with the evil nature.

But you, in order to resist me, are forced to say something completely absurd and despicable, namely, that these evils of the newborn would have come to be even in paradise if no one had sinned. At this point Mani will push you to say where they came from. Here, you will be caught in great difficulties for, if you say that these evils would have come to be from the very natures of the newborn without any merit of their will, you will immediately blame the creator. To avoid doing that, you will have recourse to the merits of evil wills. (4) But he will ask: Of whose wills? For the seeds of newborn little ones do not have any will. If you want to escape and overcome Mani, what, then, will remain but to understand with us that even the seeds of the newborn are secretly involved in the hidden recesses of their origins along with the merits of their parents which come from an evil will, but that the sin of the first human being was so great that, to use the words of the saintly John, he condemned the whole human race in common.[32] And from this the conclusion is drawn that these evils would not have come about if no one had sinned and that they could not have existed in paradise from which those who sinned went forth before they had children.

(5) That Catholic teaching destroys what you thought you should add when you instructed us that no one is born with the art of his parents. For it is one thing to sin in terms of moral conduct by which one lives correctly; such a sin is usually punished either by the laws or by divine judgment. It is another thing to sin in the arts, whether they are respectable or shameful, when something is said to have been done contrary to the art. These sins are not blamed by God's law or punished by his severity, but are blamed and punished by those human beings to whose judgments they are subject and especially by the teachers of them, when they teach youngsters by the fear and pain of punishments. (6) On this topic we ought, nonetheless, to think that, if in paradise anything was to be learned that would have been useful to know for that life, the blessed nature would have acquired it without any toil or pain, either taught by God or by itself.

Hence, who would not understand that the torments of students in this life also pertain to the miseries of this world which has been propagated from the one for condemnation?[33] Here there is also this misery that wretched minds do not will what is good, or if the will has already been prepared by the Lord,[34] one who lives in this world still cries out, *I can will the good, but I cannot bring it to completion* (Rom 7:18). If you hold this, you will conquer the Manichees, but because you do not hold it, this faith conquers both of you.

The Atrocious State of Adam Destined to Fall

10. JUL. (1) Now, then, let us show what we said, namely, that your teaching differs in no way from the Manichees. There is absolutely no doubt that the nature of Adam himself was made completely evil if it was formed in such a condition that it had the necessity for evil, but not for good, that is, so that, even if sin was conceived by the will, it, nonetheless, became something natural in that condition in which goodness would not become natural. And Adam is falsely said to have sinned by the will if he labored under the obstacle of a completely evil condition. It is, after all, clear how he was bound[35] to evil if he was going to be filled with an inseparable sin. For what can I find worse than that substance which was made so that it could fall into iniquity, but could not pull back from iniquity? (2) If on the side of the good it had suffered this violence, even if [36] it had lost free choice, it would still not have amounted to an accusation against its author, because no one would raise a question for him about the abundance of his goodness. But when such dominion is located on the side of evil, it brings an accusation against no one more than the very creator of the man, and such a God is soothed by the utterly superfluous flattery of his accusers, namely, by your flattery, since he is proved the closest of friends to malice by the foulness of his creation. For who could be persuaded that the first man was not predestined for sins if God deprived him of the ability to correct himself, if he endowed him with

so evil a mind that his own error could not be displeasing to him, that he would have no path back to moral goodness, that he could not become better through experience? And in order that he would never perhaps feel the desire to recover his goodness, he took from him the very possibility of correcting himself.

(3) Certainly, if his condition was such that, as long as he was in this life, he lost by a single fall the ability to correct himself, he was created for no other reason than that he should fall. In fact, he is more truly said not to have fallen, but to have always been lying prostrate, if he is not allowed to rise up in terms of moral conduct. What, then, was that freedom which is supposed to have been bestowed on him at first, if of two contrary qualities he received the worse as something necessary and the better as something subject to change? In fact, once overcome by the tyranny of sin, he was stripped of the ability to come back to his senses. The state of the first man, then, was utterly atrocious from the very beginning if he was created by God so miserably that he was destined to fall into sin and would be bound by the perpetual necessity of sinning.

AUG. (1) You say things, and if you do not neglect to consider them at least when we admonish you, you should be embarrassed even in your own eyes, no matter how impudent you are. For why do you not notice that, if a nature was made completely evil which fell into evil by an unjust will, but cannot return to the good because of an unjust punishment, it is not merely human nature, which you raise as an objection to us, but also angelic nature which was made completely evil? Or perhaps you will say that even the devil who by his will fell away from the good, if he wills and when he wills, will return to the good which he abandoned. And in that way you will revive the error of Origen.[37] But if you do not do this, now that you have been admonished, correct what you said carelessly, and confess that the nature was created good which fell into the evil which it committed by its own will, not compelled by any necessity. (2) But it can be recalled to the good which it abandoned only by the grace of God, not by a will with the freedom which it lost by the merit of its sinfulness. Another person in error like you could, of course, say: What can I find worse than a substance which was created so that it could enter into eternal punishment and could not return from there? And almighty God can surely rescue it from the punishment from which he wills to rescue it, but he cannot lie who threatened that he would not do this when he said that this punishment would be eternal.

(3) But your definition deceives you so that you think nonsense on this topic; by this definition, to which we have already replied, you defined free choice in the previous paragraph, as you often do elsewhere. For you said, "Free choice is nothing but the possibility of sinning and of not sinning." By this definition you first of all took from God himself free choice, though you do not deny that he cannot sin, for you often say this too, and it is true. Next, the saints themselves will lose free choice in his kingdom where they will not be able to sin.

But here you must be warned about what you ought to think on this point with which we are now dealing, namely, that punishment and reward are to be seen as contrary to each other and that another pair of contraries are attached to these contraries. The inability, then, to act rightly is attached to punishment, just as the inability to sin will be attached to reward. Pay attention to the scriptures from which you wander off in pitiful fashion, and in your meandering you are tossed about by windy wordiness as if by a storm. See how scripture said, *Israel did not obtain what it was seeking, but the elect have obtained it. But the rest were blinded as scripture says: "God gave them a spirit of insensibility, eyes so that they would not see and ears so that they would not hear, up to the present day." And David says: "Let their table become for them a snare and a trap and a stumbling block and retribution. Let their eyes be darkened so that they do not see, and bend their backs forever* (Rom 11:7-10). (4) Also look at the passage in the Gospel; it says: *They were not able to believe because Isaiah again said: He blinded their eyes and hardened their heart in order that they would not see with their eyes and would not understand with their heart and be converted, and I would save them* (Jn 12:39-40).

I cited these words so that you might understand, if you can, that a punishment, which is undoubtedly just, causes human beings not to believe because of a heart that has been blinded, though mercy causes them to believe by free will. After all, who does not know that no one believes except by free choice of the will? But the will is prepared by the Lord,[38] nor is the will completely rescued from its evil servitude which is due to its merits except when it is prepared by the Lord through gratuitous grace. For if God did not make human beings willing from unwilling, we certainly would not pray that those who are unwilling to believe might will to believe. (5) Even the apostle showed that he did this for the Jews when he said, *Brothers and sisters, my heart's good will and prayer for them to God is for their salvation* (Rom 10:1). They, of course, could not have obtained this salvation except by a believing will; blessed Paul, then, prayed that they might have this will. And bishop Cyprian also understood the words of the Lord's Prayer, *Your will be also done on earth as in heaven* (Mt 6:10), in the sense that we were taught to pray even for our unbelieving enemies that, as we believe who are already heaven because we bear the image of the heavenly man, so they also might believe who are earth because they bear the image of only the earthly man.[39]

Freedom as the Possibility of Sinning Or Not Sinning

11. JUL. (1) There continues, of course, to be a pact between you and the Manichees in that they by public profession and you by argumentation claim that the nature of even the first human being was evil, though—to take up the first ex-

ample of righteousness after the sin of Adam, while passing over the legions of the saints—the admirable sanctity of Abel proves that this is full of silliness and lies. Though born of sinners, he showed that he did not lack the virtue to live well, even by the actual exercise of that virtue. I prefer, nonetheless, to pass over these points and to insist upon the statements of the traducianist tribe.

Of what sort, then, do you suppose free choice was which you admit was given to the first human beings? Certainly, it was such that they could change the acts of their mind either to do evil or to pull back from evil, either to abandon or to observe righteousness. (2) The will, then, to sin would not have existed unless the possibility of willing came first. After they began to make use of this free choice by their own will, that is, by the act of the mind with nothing forcing it, you say that they lost free choice. What could be thought crazier than that? For, to see clearly the force of your argument, you say that they perished on account of the will which was given them only on account of the will. Sin, of course, is nothing but bad will, but freedom was given solely for this purpose, that it would not force the will, but permit it to arise. But you say that this freedom lost its nature by the act of the will so that it is believed to have perished by that which alone, we see, causes it to flourish. A bad will, then, is not the fruit of freedom, but evidence of it. And freedom is nothing but the possibility of good and of evil, but of voluntary good and evil. (3) How, then, could it have happened that it perished through that on account of which it is shown to have been created, since bad will and good will are not the demise of freedom, but its heralds? And for this reason there is as great a difference between your opinion and the real nature of free choice, which you think has met with destruction from what are its praises, as there is between the functions of it and the grave dangers to it. What new factor or what unexpected factor came about when the man sinned that God's creation crumbled? Adam was created so that he could sin and not sin; when he sinned, he did what he, of course, ought not to have done, but he could, nonetheless, do it. How, then, did he lose this ability which was created in order that he could will or could not will what he wanted?

AUG. (1) You say the same things over and over, and the reader will clearly see that I already replied to them above. But since you persist on this point and claim that the freedom of acting well or badly cannot perish by its misuse, let blessed Pope Innocent, the bishop of the Church of Rome, also reply to you. In his official response on your case to the councils of African bishops, he said, "Once having made sad experience of free choice, when he unwisely made use of his own goods and, by falling, was plunged into the depths of his transgression, he found no way by which he could rise up from there; misled forever by his own freedom, he would have remained buried by the weight of his fall, if the coming of Christ had not later raised him up by his grace."[40]

Do you see what the Catholic faith thinks through its minister? Do you see that Adam had the possibility of standing and of falling in such a way that, if he fell, he would not rise up with the same possibility by which he had fallen, that is, because punishment followed upon the sin. On this account, the grace of Christ, toward which you are an ungrateful wretch, came to raise up the man who was lying flat. (2) In another official letter also, which he wrote to Numidia concerning you people, he said, "They, therefore, try to remove the grace of God which we must ask for, even when the freedom of our original state has been restored to us."[41]

You hear that our freedom is restored, and you argue that it had not perished. And content with the human will, you do not ask for the grace which our freedom, even when restored to its original state, understands to be necessary for it. But I ask you whether that man's freedom was already restored to its original state who says, *I do not do what I will, but I do what I hate* (Rom 7:15) and, *I can will the good, but I find that I cannot bring it to completion* (Rom 7:18). Or was it restored to those to whom he said, *The flesh has desires opposed to the spirit, and the spirit has desires opposed to the flesh, so that you do not do what you will* (Gal 5:17)? (3) I think that you are not so foolish as to say that the freedom of the original state is found in these people, and yet, if they had no freedom, they could not even have willed that which is holy and righteous and good. There are, after all, some who find such delight in sinning that they do not want or even hate righteousness, which a person cannot even want unless the will is prepared by the Lord[42] so that for carrying our righteousness the desire of the will comes first and afterwards little by little there is added to it the realization of the possibility, in some more quickly, in others more slowly, in each one as the Lord has given. For he alone can repair the salvation of a human being and increase it after it has been lost and also give the gift of its no longer being able to be lost.

In that number of those set free there is also included the saintly Abel whom you say did not lack the power to live well. He certainly did not lack it, but only after he began to have it. Before, however, who is clean from filth? Not even an infant who has lived one day on earth.[43] (4) Whoever, then, are redeemed are redeemed by him who came to seek what was lost[44] and who, even before he came in the flesh, redeemed people by the faith by which they believed that he would come. They are, however, redeemed into the everlasting freedom of beatitude where they can no longer be slaves to sin. For, if, as you say, freedom is only the possibility of voluntary good and evil, God does not have freedom since this possibility is not found in him. But if we look for the free choice of a human being that is inborn and absolutely unable to be lost, it is that by which all will to be happy, even those who do not will those things which lead to happiness.

Only an Evil Choice Destroys the Other Possibility

12. JUL. (1) Next, to continue along the crags of your thought, you argue that free choice was created in such a condition that it lost its strength because of the merit of the will which was followed and that it suffered from then on under the necessity of the quality it had chosen. On this point, then, pay attention to what we reply. Do you think that Adam was created so that he would be subject to this necessity of the quality he chose on both alternatives, that is, so that, if he had chosen the good, he would have been unable to sin thereafter, and so that, if he had chosen evil, he would have been unable to mend his ways? Or would it have been so that only the necessity of evil would follow upon the choice of evil, but nothing of the sort would happen if he had chosen the good, but he would be always exposed to the dangers of vacillation?

(2) Take whichever of these two you want: If you say that nature was created such that it would be subject only to the necessity of evil, no doubt will remain for anyone that it is defined most horribly if violence is attributed to it only for the worse alternative. Adam is also shown to have been created with an evil nature, and there will remain not even the shadow of voluntary sin under which you might hide. But if you declare that the same thing would also take place on the good alternative, that is, that, if he had willed the good, he would have been unable to sin thereafter, I reply: Why, then, did he sin? Why was he subject to no necessity toward the good so that he would be seen as impervious to the wiles of the devil, since at some time before he sinned, he is found to have been obedient to God?

(3) For he did not burn with the desire of a bad will from the time when the clay grew warm with the entrance of his soul. In fact, we read that, after he was introduced to paradise for its cultivation and preservation, he received the commandment from God to eat of all the fruits, but to abstain in obedience to God's word from the tree of the knowledge of good and evil. Before, therefore, the body of his woman was formed from his side, he remained obedient to the command, an innocent farmer of the lovely countryside. But after this he merited the help of a companion like himself. The trustworthy scripture, of course, taught these distinctions between the times. But after he saw the woman whom God had prepared for him, he observed the commandment of God as a zealous fulfillment of the duty to the point that he taught the law he had received to the woman as well. (4) Not only observing, but also teaching God's command, he trained Eve with regard to the reverence due to the source of the command, the manner of their servitude, and their grounds for fear. This is, of course, the reason why the woman also carefully resists the devil's approach, though God had given her no commandment, and she initially rejects the lies of the serpent and says that God did not command abstinence from all the trees, as the serpent had pretended, but had ordered them to avoid only one little bush, while permitting them all the

other fruits, and she says that God had imposed the fear of death which would justly overtake the transgressors. It is clear, then, that Adam observed the commandment not just for a short time, but also that Eve had even showed a concern for devotion which was destroyed by a love of knowledge and of godliness.

(5) Why, then, did that righteousness, that devoutness which flourished in Adam for a long time and in Eve for some time not remove the possibility of sinning so that the necessity of doing good would render them impervious to the evil means of persuasion? They were, then, obedient as long as they willed, and they did not, nonetheless, lose the ability to sin because of the merit of their devotion. Finally, they fell; it is clear, therefore, that, even after they sinned, they could not have lost the strength to correct themselves. And so, as everywhere, you have here lost the whole of what you put together, because that sin of the first human beings produced no necessity of any sins and did not turn into their nature, just as the righteousness which preceded did not impose any necessity of the virtues and did not claim for itself the paths of the seeds.

AUG. (1) The whole of what you said at such length and with such a great complexity of language can be briefly stated as follows. Why, you ask, did Adam lose by acting wrongly the possibility of acting rightly, but did not lose the possibility of sinning by previously acting rightly? And you want it to be understood that, if this is so, the man had not been created with a good, but with a bad nature, for an evil action had more force in him to make him unable to act rightly than a good action had to make him unable to act wrongly.

In this way you could say that human beings were badly created with eyes because, when they put their eyes out, there is produced in them the inability to see, but by seeing there was not produced in them the inability to put them out. Or you could say that the whole body of a human being was created badly because we have it in our power to kill ourselves, but do not have it in our power to bring ourselves back to life. And death produces in a person the inability to revive oneself, though life does not produce in one the inability to kill oneself. (2) But if you do not say this, because you see that it is stupid, why do you say that God created the nature of the man evil if an evil will made him unable to return to the good, although a good will did not make him unable to turn to evil?

For Adam was created with free choice so that he could not sin if he did not will to, not so that, if he willed to, he could sin with impunity. Why is it surprising, then, if by sinning, that is, by changing through perversity the uprightness in which he was created, there resulted along with the punishment the inability to act rightly? But as long as Adam remained standing in that uprightness in which he was able not to sin, he had not received the greater gift, namely, the inability to sin, because he did not will to remain in the good state he had up to the end, namely, the reward.

(3) For Adam would have received, without death intervening, what the saints will receive who will in the world to come be in a spiritual body. For, in

rising up from the state in which he was able not to die, he would have come to the state in which he was not able to die. And in rising up from the state in which he was able not to sin, he would have come to the state in which he was not able to sin. He was not, of course, created in a spiritual body, but in an animal body, though that body would not have been going to die, if he had not sinned. For, as the apostle says, *First there was not the spiritual body, but the animal body; the spiritual body came afterward* (1 Cor 15:46). For this reason blessed Ambrose says that Adam was created in the shadow of life from which he could fall, not by necessity, but by will.[45] If he had remained in it, he would, of course, have received the life of which that life was a shadow, the life which the saints will receive from which they will by no means be able to fall.

(4) On the other hand, Ambrose also understands this mortality in which this age runs its course as the shadow of death, but he recalls that death of which this death is a shadow, the death which is called second death,[46] from which no one will return who enters it. But whoever are set free from this shadow of death are prepared, not to return to the shadow of life, but to enter that life from which one can never depart. There Adam himself will also be, because it is correct to believe that, at the Lord's coming and descent into the lower regions, Adam was released from the bonds of the underworld so that the first creature God formed who had no father, but only God as his creator, and who was the first father of Christ according to the flesh, would remain no longer in bonds and would not perish in eternal punishment.

(5) But where mercy triumphs over judgment,[47] we should not think of merits, but of grace, whose depth is so great and so inscrutable and so unsearchable.[48] For, after that statement, *Anyone who is not reborn of water and the Spirit will not enter the kingdom of God* (Jn 3:5), we see that at times God does not grant to believers who have merited well that their children are with their parents in the kingdom of God. Rather, their little ones leave this life without being reborn, when, even though their parents at times ardently desire their rebirth and the ministers of the sacraments are making great haste, the most almighty and most merciful God does not postpone their death a little so that those born of Christian parents might leave this life reborn and not be lost to the kingdom of God and their parents. Rather, they expire before they are baptized, while at times the infant children of unbelievers and blasphemers against the grace of Christ are brought to the hands of Christians by God's marvelous governance, and they are given this grace so that, separated from their unbelieving parents, they enter the kingdom of God.

(6) Here, if you ask what sort of justice this is, you certainly will not find the answer in that dialectical and philosophical language in which you think that you have thoroughly discussed the justice of God. For the Lord knows that the thoughts of the wise are vain,[49] and hiding these mysteries from the wise and the prudent, he revealed them to the little ones,[50] that is, to the humble and to those

who put their trust, not in their own virtue,[51] but in the Lord—the sort of people whom you always or at least up to now refuse to be.

If, then, you ask where or when the inability to sin is granted to human beings, look for the rewards of the saints which it is right that they receive after this life. But if you do not believe that the free choice of the man by which he could have and ought to have acted rightly was lost because of the malice of sin, at least pay attention to the one who said, *I do not do what I will, but I do what I hate* (Rom 7:19), though you do not want him to suffer this because of his damaged origin, but because of the prevalence of bad habits. (7) And in that way, even you admit that free choice can be lost by being used badly, but you do not want free choice to have been able to be damaged in human nature by that sin that was so immense that it was greater and worse than every bad habit. You say that bad habits are so powerful for corrupting human nature that human beings cry out that they will to bring the good to completion, but cannot.[52] That freedom of the will, however, with which human beings were created and are created, remains unchangeable, for by it we all will to be happy, and we cannot not will this. But this freedom does not suffice for anyone to be happy nor for anyone to live rightly, which is the means to becoming happy. For the unchangeable freedom of the will by which one wills to act rightly and can act rightly is not inborn in a human being in the way that that freedom is inborn by which one wills to be happy, something that all will, even those who are unwilling to act rightly.

Augustine Is Confronted with a Difficult Dilemma

13. JUL. What, then, has been established? That one of the two is necessary: Either you must admit that Adam was created with a good substance and that his nature was not destroyed by the character of his will, and then you abandon natural sin, or you must maintain that he is, as you have held up to now, the cause of natural evils, and then you must declare that this man with the very worst substance belongs to your God, that is, yours and Mani's.

AUG. (1) Our previous response explains that there has not been established what you think has been established. For, when the question at issue between us was whether by the bad use of the free choice with which the man was created this freedom could be damaged so that one who had lived badly could not live rightly unless healed by the power of grace—to omit the very many other things which were said in that same response—we found the man who said with the highest authority of the scriptures, *I do not do the good that I will, but I do the evil that I do not will* (Rom 7:19). In these words it is clearly seen that free choice was damaged by its bad use. For, before the sin by which the man made bad use of free choice, when he was placed in the happiness of that paradise and endowed with a great facility for acting rightly, he could not say this.

(2) But you people do not attribute this to the human nature which was dam-aged in the first man, but to the bad habit of any person. And though they will to, people are unable to conquer this bad habit which has power over them, and when they do not find their freedom strong enough to carry out the good, they are forced to say these things—as if any but a weakened nature would suffer under the insuperable force of bad habit so that it would ask to be set free from it by the grace of God. For when the man who said these things came to those words where he said, *I see another law in my members that resists the law of my mind and holds me captive under the law of sin which is in my members* (Rom 7:23), he said, *Wretched man that I am! Who will set me free from the body of this death? The grace of God through Jesus Christ our Lord* (Rom 7:24-25). Inter-pret the body of this death however you will; with free choice weakened, the weakened nature, nonetheless, said this and longed to be set free by the grace of God from the body of this death in which it did not do the good which it willed, but did the evil which it hated.

(3) But you are defeated by an even clearer proof that the sin of the first man was so immense that it was greater and worse than all the violence of habit, when there are paraded before you the woes of children which would not, of course, have existed in paradise, if human nature had remained in that happiness of the uprightness in which it was created so that it would not have been driven out of paradise. For, to pass over in silence the sort of things which we have already mentioned in quite a few places and to omit not only untaught, but unteachable infancy, would not a child who receives from a teacher something to memorize and is willing, but unable to remember it, say with complete truth, if he could say it: "I see another law in my soul that resists the law of my will and holds me cap-tive under the law of the rods which threaten my members? *Wretched man that I am, who will set me free from the body of this death?* (Rom 7:24). *For the cor-ruptible body weighs down the soul* (Wis 9:15) so that what it wants to retain in memory it cannot."

(4) And who sets the soul free from this corruptible body but the grace of God through Jesus Christ our Lord, either when the soul has stripped off this body and is at rest, having been redeemed by the blood of Christ, or when this corruptible body has put on incorruptibility,[53] and when, after the trials of the body dead on account of sin, our mortal bodies will also be brought to life through the Spirit of Christ who dwells in us? Against his grace you defend the choice of the free will and the will which is a servant of sin. But we are far from Mani, for we confess both the defect of a good nature, whether in adults or in little ones, and its physi-cian.

Augustine Is Challenged to Show His Difference from Mani

14. JUL. (1) I have argued up to this point as the practice of our faith demanded. But not content with this role alone, I shall deal with you kindly and deliberately assume for myself the character of a person who seems to favor the views of your teacher. This will be done with the purpose that you are forced to attack Mani if you disagree with him. For by the fact that the traducianist does not find a way to oppose Mani, our claim will be proven to contain nothing devious. And so, it will be evident how great a conspiracy there is between you and how you look after everything to your mutual advantages since a quarrel cannot be stirred up between you. Let the reader bear in mind the plan with which, as I showed, I have taken this up. Let us now use the language of the character we are assuming.

(2) They who think that this composition of the body is capable of righteousness are utterly mistaken. The vile nature of flesh and blood resists every good pursuit. Whatever excitement there is for the seduction of the senses serves only for the disturbance, in fact for the overthrow of the mind which, cast down to this filth by some misfortune or other, loses its true brightness by its mixture with clay. To the extent it can, the mind strives to rise to its own place, that is, to the upper regions, but it is burdened by its earthly cell. Finally, when it wants to take flight to chastity, it experiences the glue and birdlime of obscene pleasure from its feverish organs. Even if the mind desires to be generous to the point of munificence, it is bound by the tightest shackles of greed which is covered over by the veil of frugality. But if it wants to stand in a certain balanced calm of constancy, it is overwhelmed at the same moment by the hail of fear and the storms of pain, and growing pale with fear in the face of everything doubtful, it is not permitted to remain in command of its own plan.

(3) Add to this the night of things unknown which surrounds it like a flood. What praiseworthiness shall we suppose in that living being which does not have eyes able to choose useful things and which is not able amidst the storms of desires and crises to count its shipwrecks? But let no one falsely claim that these evils befell a substance ruined by its will; the very creation of the first human beings is found subject to these woes. For, in order to prove this even by the testimony of Moses whom the Catholics venerate, the first human beings experienced the scourge of fear, and the threat of peril terrified them if they did not obey, and to the extent that one can measure by comparison, we believe that they were more filled with fear than their descendants, for they were troubled by a punishment which no one as yet had experienced. Why, after all, would they be shaken by the threat of death when they did not know the loss which their death would bring? They were surely disturbed by the mere suspicions of evils. In what peacefulness, then, would that mind have found itself which was upset by so bitter a winter of fear? (4) Moreover, how deep was the ignorance and how

harsh the condition of enduring it that the mind could not be set free from it save by transgression, for it would, of course, never have attained the knowledge of good and evil without a daring act worthy of condemnation.

The innate desire which the sweet charm of something forbidden aroused also rendered restless this blind and miserable animal. As if all this were not enough to express its unhappiness, the mind is exposed to the attack of a higher nature. Who, then, would be so foolish as to think that there is any good present where one admits that there were created the means for so many miseries. This flesh, then, with its most evil state and most evil nature, revealed in these first human beings its own character which it had from its beginning. A good God, however, could not fashion this evil substance. What, then, remains but to admit that the giver of the soul is other than the creator of the clay?

(5) Surely the battle line of Mani whose person I had donned stands in full array. You understand what we await, namely, that one who is opposed to him should show this by a subsequent attack. Let your teaching, then, do battle with him; it will be seen whether it can move even slightly without its own destruction. Mani has certainly declared not only that all are born sinful from the union of bodies, but also that Adam himself introduced the necessity of sinning from the formation of the inner organs and the slime of the earth from which he was formed. The nature of the flesh, he says, was evil in the first human beings; it enclosed, dampened, and extinguished the spark of the mind glimmering with the pursuit of goodness. The Catholics are, of course, foolish who resist the testimonies of sinners and are not satisfied with their own proofs , and though they see that they do not do the good that they will, but do the evil that they detest, they do not think that there is in the flesh the necessity of doing evil.

(6) Let the traducianist do battle against these hateful statements if he can; I, meanwhile, stand on the sideline as a spectator and await the outcome of your conflict. What, then, will you reply to one who swears that nature was evil even in the first human beings? Undoubtedly you will reply that God, who formed human beings, could not have made what he created something evil, and because God who does not produce evil produced human beings, they are proved to be not naturally evil at all. You said something and spoke the truth, but see whether you ought to have stated this while I was listening. For I do not care much about the power by which you strike Mani; you have in the meantime passed completely into my dominion. It is now a joy to mock you in captivity; I welcome with great applause your public statement, and I warn you to keep it in mind. Because of the dignity of their author, that is, God, who cannot produce something evil, you have declared that his works ought to be defended as good. Do you, then, think that all human beings begotten by the union of the sexes which was instituted by God are made by God or by the devil? (7) If by God, how do you dare to proclaim that they are guilty and evil, since you said that the single proof that Adam could not have been made with an evil nature is that he is shown to

have been created by God who is all good? If, then, there is a strong argument because of which we believe that the substance of the first human beings was not
created guilty, namely, the fact that God who we admit is good created it, that argument remains for the destruction of inherited sin. And the same testimony
proves that all those begotten of marriage cannot be created evil, because God
who we admit is good created them.

But if even after this, your rabid impudence persists in swearing that little
ones are created by God and that they are, nonetheless, naturally evil, these lies
certainly bring nothing prejudicial to the Catholic, just as they do not to our God.
It is clear, nonetheless, that you have not attacked Mani who gladly welcomes
your charges against God; he is content that you have lost the argument by which
you had tried to prove that Adam was created good.

AUG. (1) When you propose with eloquent blindness that I must enter into
battle with Mani while you look on, you bring ruin to your side through your lack
of foresight. And you have permitted even these people who are slow in their
wits to understand how by the plague-carrying wind of your teaching you help
that horrible scourge which a deadly error introduced into Mani. For, when any
people hear or read those things which you said in such abundance and with such
eloquence about the miseries of this mortal and corruptible life, they will recognize that you spoke the truth, not only from your words, but also from human
lives themselves. (2) It would, of course, have been nothing great or difficult for
Mani, into whose mouth you put words, as if they were against us, to see in this
mortal life, which was cast down and cast out of the happiness of paradise by the
merit of sin, these facts which you mentioned about it and to chatter away, either
like you or more fully and lavishly, about these same points. They are so obvious
that they are often read in the very many passages of the divine scriptures about
the burden of the corruptible body and about the weighing down of the soul coming from it.[54]

For this reason, even in the saints who struggle on the battlefield of this life,
*the flesh has desires opposed to the spirit, and the spirit has desires opposed to
the flesh* (Gal 5:17), when, as the most glorious Cyprian said, the spirit seeks
heavenly and divine things, while the flesh desires earthly and worldly things.[55]
From this there comes the conflict which the martyr we mentioned carefully and
eloquently explained in the book he wrote called *Mortality* where, among other
things, he said that we have a constant and difficult struggle with carnal vices
and worldly temptations.[56] (3) Indeed, blessed Gregory sets before our eyes this
battle which we have in the body of this death so that there are no athletes in this
contest who do not recognize themselves in his words as if in a mirror. He says,
"We are attacked within ourselves by our own vices and passions and are day
and night oppressed by the burning temptations of the body of this lowly state
and of the body of death. In it the snares of visible things entice and arouse us at
times in a hidden way and at other times quite openly, and the clay of these dregs

to which we cling breathes forth the foul odor of its filth though its larger passages. But the law of sin which is in our members also resists the law of the spirit, as it strives to take captive the royal image which is within us so that all that has been poured into us by the gift of our original and divine creation becomes his booty."[57]

(4) I quoted these words of the man of God both in the second book of those six which I published against your four and in this work[58] when I replied to your first volume where you thought that one should understand in a different sense the body of death from which the apostle says that he is being set free by grace.[59] And when Saint Ambrose said, "All of us human beings are born under the power of sin, and our very origin lies in guilt, as you have read where David says, *See, I was conceived in iniquities, and my mother bore me in sins* (Ps 51:7), he immediately added, "And so Paul's flesh was the body of death, as he himself says, *Who will set me free from the body of this death* (Rom 7:24)."[60]

(5) Why, then, is it surprising if Mani, who sees the evils of this life, including the body of this death which weighs down the soul,[61] and the discord between the flesh and the spirit,[62] and the heavy yoke upon the children of Adam from the day they emerge from the womb of their mother until the day of their burial in the mother of all,[63] says through your lips as if against us the sort of things which we see that Gregory said against you? From this it is clear that the Manichees as well as the Catholics admit the evils of this life which is a temptation upon earth.[64] For in the human race the world is filled with these evils on account of the heavy yoke upon the children of Adam from the day they emerge from the womb of their mother until the day of their burial in the mother of all.[65]

But it is also clear that about the source of these evils they do not both say the same thing and that there is a great difference between them. For the Manichees attribute them to an alien evil nature, while the Catholics attribute them to our own good nature, but a nature damaged by sin and deservedly punished. (6) But you who do not want to say what we say, what do you yourself say? How do you reply to the Manichee about the source of these evils with which human beings are born and which would not have come to be in paradise if no one had sinned and if our nature had remained there, not fallen, but upright, as it was created? If the defect is inborn because of which the flesh has desires opposed to the spirit and if it does not come from our nature which was damaged at its origin, tell us where it comes from. If the defect is inborn over which a human being cries out, *I know that the good does not dwell in me, that is, in my flesh, for I am able to will the good, but I find that I cannot bring it to completion* (Rom 7:18) and if it does not come from the nature damaged by the transgression of the first human being, tell us where it comes from. But if these defects are not inborn, tell us where they come from. From the habit of sinning, you will say, which each person builds up by free will. (7) Here you admit for the moment what you do not want to admit, namely, that freedom of the will could be lost by its own misuse, because by doing something evil it became less suited to do something good. But was anyone ever obtuse of heart because he willed to be? Was anyone ever forgetful because he willed to be? Was anyone ever feebleminded because he willed to be?

If you say that these and other defects of the mind and the spirit, with which no one has any doubt that human beings are born, do not come from our damaged origin, tell us where they come from. For you are never going to say that paradise could have included these evils if no one had sinned. Finally, the corruptible body weighs down the soul,[66] and under this miserable burden all who are not complete fools groan. Tell us where this comes from. For you are not going to say that the first human beings were created so that the soul of any of them would be weighed down by their corruptible body or that after that great sin of theirs anyone is born without such a body. (8) Why, then, do you with great wordiness introduce Mani speaking against us, since you could not answer him if you deny what we say?

Cyprian answers him, showing that the flesh and the spirit are in discord so that we must pray for the harmony of the two from God the Father.[67] Gregory answers him; he said about the flesh the sort of things which you made Mani say against us. But he testifies that both of them, that is, the spirit and the flesh, must be called back to God by God's mercy.[68] (9) Ambrose replies to him; he said that the flesh must be married to the judgment of the soul. He said, "It was such when it received the recesses of paradise as its dwelling before it knew the sacrilegious hunger after it was infected by the venom of the deadly serpent."[69]

By these statements, after all, the Catholic bishops have taught amply and clearly that the flesh does not have an evil nature, but a defect, and when this defect is healed, the flesh returns to the state in which, just as it was originally created, it will not weigh down the soul with any of its corruption and will have no discord with the spirit because it has desires opposed to it. For Mani was deceived by this discord so that he imagined that an alien evil substance was mixed in with us.

(10) If you were willing to follow with us the faith of these Catholic bishops, you would overthrow, not help the Manichees, but now you try not to destroy them, but rather to build them up. For, by denying the evils which newborn human beings contract from their damaged origin, you do not make us believe that there are no natural evils, because they are much too obvious, but you rather cause people to think that these evils come from an alien evil nature which, as the madness of the Manichean myth pretends, has been mixed in with us. Thus these evils are not shown to have come from our good nature that was damaged by the transgression of the first human being, as the sanity of the Catholics says.

(11) But Mani, you say, so detested even the very flesh of the first human being as it was before the sin that he tries to show that it is evil. You, of course, introduce him speaking in such a way that he imposes some sort of task of replying, not only upon me, but also upon you. For, where he says that the flesh

was made by an evil creator, we both answer that a creature so good that it was able not to sin if it did not will to sin, even though it would not equal its creator, could, nonetheless, have only have a good creator. But where he says that Adam was wretched even before he sinned because of the fear of death with which God threatened him if he sinned, we both answer that this man who was able never to sin, if he had never willed to sin, had a calm concern, not a violent fear of avoiding that punishment which would follow upon the sin.

(12) We can, of course, make this reply in common to our common enemy, as was said. But against Mani I increase the praises of that rational creature which was not only not tormented by any fear, but also enjoyed a great happiness, because he had it in his power to avoid suffering the evil of death which the hearts of all or almost all the faithful shrink from. Because your error by which you think that Adam would have died whether he sinned or did not sin is opposed to this faith of ours, what answer do you make here to Mani when he says that our nature was created wretched, because impending death tormented it with fear whether it sinned or did not sin? (13) For, if you say that it was created so that it did not fear death which would undoubtedly come at some point, you will surely admit that this nature which is found in his descendants is born wretched, since we see that the fear of death is so natural to it. For even these people who desire with a faith-filled hope the joys of the life to come still struggle in this life with the fear of death. They do not, after all, want to be stripped, but to be clothed over so that, insofar as it pertains to their will, this life would not be ended by death, but our mortal being would be swallowed up by life.[70]

The result is that, if you locate the fear of death in paradise before the sin, you are defeated by the Manichees who think and want others to think that even in the first human being human nature was created wretched. But if you reply that the fear of death by which the mind of mortals is pierced with misery did not exist before sin, you are defeated by us, because our nature would not have been changed for the worse if it were not damaged.

(14) Again, in what you make Mani say against us, namely, that "the innate desire which the sweet charm of something forbidden aroused also rendered restless that blind and miserable animal," recognize, Julian, the shipwreck of your teaching as if upon unavoidable rocks. For we say that in that blessedness there was no desire which would resist the will. But if those human beings desired something from which they willed rather to hold back, their desire undoubtedly resisted their will. You, therefore, made Mani say this through your words, not against me, but against yourself. For, if they were such persons that in them desire would resist the will, the flesh already had desires opposed to the spirit, and the spirit had desires opposed to the flesh. There the defect of the flesh is understood most clearly, on account of which the apostle said to believers, *For these are opposed to each other so that you do not do what you will* (Gal 5:17).

(15) There are, of course, no holy persons who would not will to make the flesh not to have desires opposed to the spirit, although they resist the desire of the flesh so that they do not carry it out by their consenting to it. For they hear the same apostle where he says, *But I say: Walk by the Spirit, and do not carry out the desires of the flesh* (Gal 5:16). He did not say: Do not have the opposing desires of the flesh, because he saw that perfect peace between the flesh and the spirit could not be realized in the body of this death. Rather, he said: *Do not carry out the desires of the flesh* (Gal 5:16). Here he rather proposed to us the battle which we ought to wage against the flesh with its opposing desires so that we do not carry out its desires by consenting, but overcome them by resisting.

But the peace in which we would not endure the opposition and resistance of these desires existed in the body of that life which we lost when the nature of the first human being was damaged by transgression. (16) For, if the peace between the flesh and the spirit did not exist there before the sin and if Ambrose's statement is false that the discord between the two was turned into our nature through the transgression of the first human being,[71] that statement will—heaven forbid!—be true which you made Mani say against us, namely, that "the innate desire which the sweet charm of something forbidden aroused also rendered restless the miserable animal," that is, the first human being when he was created.

(17) But we say that the first human being was so happy before the sin and had such free will that, while observing the commandment of God by the great strength of his mind, he did not suffer the flesh resisting him in any conflict, and he did not experience anything at all from any desire that he did not will, but that his will was first damaged by the poisonous enticement of the serpent so that desire came into being which would rather have followed upon the will than resisted it; but once sin had been committed, concupiscence fought back against the weakened mind as a punishment. And for this reason, if Adam did not first do what he willed by sinning, he would not have suffered what he did not will by desiring.

(18) See how we defeat Mani when he tries to introduce an evil creator for the nature of human beings. But you who, while Mani and I do battle, have for your acting as judge chosen for yourself the role of spectator, by what trick, I ask, or by what force will you dare to resist these words of yours which you thought you should give to Mani against us, especially you who say that the concupiscence of the flesh, the sort that now exists, which we see fights against the spirit, existed as such in paradise before the sin? We bring you down, whether you like it or not, from the seats in the stands into the arena, and we make you a combatant instead of a spectator. Enter the struggle, and defeat, if you can, our common opponent, for you also profess that you worship God as the creator even of the flesh. Defeat, then, the enemy who tries to persuade you that there is an evil god who made the

flesh whose concupiscence already resisted the spirit not yet become evil by transgression and which made the human being wretched by its conflict.

(19) Are you going to say: Of course, he had such concupiscence, and he was, nonetheless, not wretched? Is this to overcome the opponent, or is it rather to help Mani and rebel against the apostle? Have you utterly forgotten who said: *I see another law in my members that resists the law of my mind* (Rom 7:23), and after a few words added, *Wretched man that I am!* (Rom 7:24)? If Adam, then, was enticed by desire to eat the forbidden food when he willed to obey the commandment of God, and if concupiscence of the flesh, of the sort which you say he had even then, resisted the spirit with its contrary desires, would he not have spoken the complete truth if he chose to say: *I take delight in the law of God according to my interior self, but I see another law in my members that resists the law of my mind* (Rom 7:22-23)? How, then, was he not a wretched man since after such words the apostle said, *Wretched man that I am!* (Rom 7:24)? Finally, how was he not wretched and how did he have free will if, because the flesh had desires opposed to the spirit, as the apostle himself testifies, he certainly did not do what he willed?

(20) For, if you say that concupiscence of the flesh was before the sin as it is now, Mani will undoubtedly defeat you. Come over to my view, and let us both give our approval to Ambrose who says that discord between the flesh and the spirit was turned into our nature by the transgression of the first human being. In that way we will both defeat Mani. With your words which you composed as if Mani were going to recite them and to speak the words of another, a common practice in the schools of rhetoric, Mani said that Adam was created not merely miserable, but blind. Why was he created blind unless it was because he did not know sin, something which is said in praise of Christ?[72] After all, we are happy if we are ignorant of evils, whatever they are. which we do not know through wisdom, but through experience.

(21) But you perhaps say this along with me against Mani who speaks slanderously about the ignorance of the first human being. In accord, however, with what we have now answered you, seek what you should answer him about the death of the body and about the concupiscence of the flesh. For from these two most obvious facts it is clear that the condition of the first human beings who were not born from any line of parents was different from that of those who are created by God in such a way that they are also procreated by human beings. After all, they receive from God the manner of their creation; they receive from their parents the merit of their origin, and they owe their being formed to the work of the creator, their being bound to his judgment, and their being set free to his gift.

(22) When the Manichees see the evils with which human beings are born, they try to introduce an evil maker of human beings, the framework of whose

flesh—to say nothing of the soul which is the life of the flesh—testifies that God from whom all goods come, whether heavenly or earthly, is its maker. And it is such a good that the blessed apostle drew a comparison from the harmony of its members for the special praise of the love whose peaceful bond unites to one another good believers as members of Christ.[73] The result is that because of the perfectly obvious good of their nature only the good creator could create both those first human beings who were made without defect and their descendants who are born with an original defect.

Giving the Law Presupposes the Freedom to Observe It

15. JUL. (1) But for fear that we may press the first side of the controversy too much, let us allow you in the course of your thought to approve the nature of Adam as good. You say, of course: The just God would not impose on Adam the law of obedience if he knew that he was subject to the necessity of sinning. For, if he demanded righteousness of the will from him whose nature he knew was evil, he would not have held him guilty when he transgressed that law, but he would have revealed that he himself was an enemy of righteousness. The just God, however, imposed a law on Adam, and he promised he would punish him if he transgressed it.

It is, therefore, established that, as good by nature, Adam could sin only by the will. You see, of course, do you not, how legitimate is the conclusion I drew in your name? It is truly the gleaming sword in the hand of the Catholics which devastates the Manichees and the traducianists. (2) But I added too hastily[74] your name since I wanted the response in the present case to be seen as yours. Hence, the solid response has crushed only Mani. I follow up the august argument with fitting praises, but notice that the sword is sharpened against you with the help of the oil of this praise.

Repeat, therefore, I beg you, what you said. God, being just, you said, would not have imposed the law upon Adam if Adam was evil by nature. But he who is just did impose the law. It is clear now that Adam could have observed what the most just God commanded, because, unless he had the power to obey, the one who gave the command would never have had a just reason for giving the order. What a silly bit of nonsense![75] In the presence of me, as I look on, Augustine upholds on the basis of the justice of the lawgiver the goodness of the nature upon which the law is imposed, and he does not see that, before Mani feels a slight wound, he himself has brought destruction to the traducianists. (3) For, in order that you may understand that I take from you lying half-dead your bloody weapons, and in order that your dying eyes may carry with them the victorious truth,[76] I shall drive your own spears into you.

If the just God could not give a law to Adam unless he knew that, as free without any coercion from evil, he could observe what is just, undoubtedly, in the following times as well with the same gravity of justice there would not have been given to human beings a law which was also committed to writing, more extensive in its multiplicity, more explicit in its distinctions, and more revered because of the increased punishment, if they were born from the womb either too weak to do anything good and without the possibility of righteousness, or guilty, that is, evil. For, just as the pretext of necessity would excuse them in every transgression, so the excessiveness in the commandments, the ineffectiveness of the sanctions, and the injustice of the judgments would redound to the discredit of their author.

(4) And so, this second part comes to the same kind of conclusion as the first, namely, that you should confess that the justice of God could only have commanded what he considered his subjects could do, and the testimony of the first commandment destroys Mani, but the testimony of the commandments that followed afterwards destroys Mani and the traducianist. Or if impiety permits this idea, Mani, whom you have not struck even lightly, will show, with the whole world as witness, that he is your father and your leader and that he has along with you a single battle against us.

AUG. (1) This is, of course, what you have tried to achieve, not by clear speech, but by endless words, namely, that the first law which was given in paradise is evidence of a good nature which was created with free choice; otherwise, if Adam did not have free choice, the law would have been given most unjustly. Hence, the later law, you say, the law which was promulgated most extensively in writing, is also evidence of a good nature which is created from parents and is likewise without defect and with free choice. Arguing for this, you think you say something because you are following your own or merely human cleverness, but you do not care to read the words of God from which you think that you draw conclusions against us. Or, if you do care to read them, you do not want to understand them or you cannot. But if you should perhaps understand them because of our arguments, do not be the sort of person whom the scripture points out with the words: *Stubborn servants will not be corrected by words, for even if they understand, they will not obey* (Prv 29:19). (2) And yet, he could, if he wished, take from you even the stony heart because of which the words of God are not obeyed, even when they are understood, as he promised through the prophecy of the holy Ezekiel[77] to do for the stubborn people.

In paradise Adam, who was created upright, received the law so that he might learn that the sole or chief virtue of the rational creature is obedience. But by the transgression of the same law he made himself corrupt. And because he could damage himself, but could not heal himself, even afterwards at the time and the place when and where the wisdom of God judged that it should be done, human beings, though corrupt, received a law, not a law by which they could be corrected, but a law by which they would realize that they were evil and could not correct themselves, even after they received the law. And so, when sins did not cease because of the law, but were increased because of transgression, with their pride cast down and crushed, they would seek the help of grace with a truly humble heart, and they would be brought to life by the Spirit, after having been slain by the letter. (3) *For if a law had been given which could give life, righteousness would certainly have come from the law. But scripture enclosed all things under sin so that the promise might be given because of faith in Jesus Christ to those who believe* (Gal 3:21-22).

If you recognize the words of the apostle, you surely see either what you do not understand or what you do not care about, though you do understand them. The law, then, which was given in writing through Moses is not evidence of free will; for, if it were, he would not pertain to the law, who says, *I do not do the good that I will, but I do the evil that I hate* (Rom 7:15), though you claim that he was certainly not already under grace, but still under the law. Nor is the new law itself which was announced as the law that would go forth from Zion or as the word of the Lord from Jerusalem,[78] the law which we understand to be the holy gospel—not even this law, I say, is evidence of a will which is free, but rather of a will which needs to be set free. For in the new law it is written, *If the Son sets you free, then you will truly be free* (Jn 8:36).

(4) The Lord's Prayer testifies that this was said, not merely on account of past sins by the forgiveness of which we are set free, but also on account of the help of grace which we receive so that we do not commit sin. That is, we are made free so that, with God directing our journeys, every iniquity does not lord it over us.[79] For in the Lord's Prayer we say not only, *Forgive us our debts* (Mt 6:12), on account of the sins we have committed, but also, *Bring us not into temptation* (Mt 6:13), so that, of course, we do not commit sins. Hence, the apostle says, *We pray to God that you do nothing evil* (2 Cor 13:7). But if this were in their power as it was before the sin, before human nature was damaged, they would not, of course, ask for this by their prayers, but would rather hold onto it by their actions. (5) After that first fall, however, which was so grave that we fell into the misery of this mortality, God wanted us first to struggle, while he grants to us that we are led by his Spirit and put to death the works of the flesh and that, with him giving us victory through Jesus Christ our Lord, we reign with him afterwards in eternal peace. Hence, if God is not there to help, surely no one is fit to do battle with the vices so that we are not carried off by them without a fight or so that, if we are already fighting with them, we are not defeated in this conflict. (6) And so, in this contest God wanted us to do battle more with prayers than with our own forces, because he to whom we pray gives to those who fight even these forces to the extent that it is proper for us to have them in this life. If, then, these people whose spirit already has desires opposed to the flesh need the grace of

God for every single action so that they are not defeated, what sort of freedom of the will can those people have who have not yet been rescued from the power of darkness[80] where injustice reigns and who have not begun to fight or, if they wanted to fight, are defeated by the servitude of a will not yet set free?

The Goodness of Creatures Refutes the Traducianist

16. JUL. (1) I do not know, of course, whether, forced as you now are by necessity, you will here attempt something so foolish and so feeble as to say that you cannot teach by any arguments that Adam was created good by God, but that for believing this you are content with the authority of the passage alone which, after the formation of the man on the sixth day, says regarding all creatures, *And God saw all the things which he made, and behold, they were very good* (Gn 1:31). And since this was said, not in view of the dignity of the creator and not in consideration of his justice, but as a testimony which says generally that the things which were created were created good, you can also judge that Adam was not created unjust. But, though this strikes at Mani so slightly that he laughs, it, nonetheless, reveals to us the traducianist in chains. (2) In order not to gather people to this cause without any testimony of the divine scriptures, we invoke the authority of the apostle alone who, since he foresaw your foul error, pronounced against you in solemn tones, saying that *every creature of God is good* (1 Tm 4:4).

(3) If, then, in order to prove that the first human being was formed with a good nature, the words of Moses are sufficient, namely, that God created all things well, and if, for this reason, you maintain that Adam could not have been created by God with sin, since we read that he was created good along with all other things, we reply along the same lines that, for this reason, no one can be born with sin, since the apostle maintains that every creature of God is good.

What, then, has been accomplished by these arguments? Clearly that even the option of a war declared between you and Mani would make public what reason has discovered, namely that, when in the proposed battle you could not hurl even one spear at your teacher without your own destruction, it would be seen much more clearly that you and the Manichees have jelled into one body of impiety because of your obscene agreement. For what could be so closely united as that which is not separated even by the introduction of any distinctions? With every destruction of Mani the teaching of the traducianist dies as well. There is nothing that strikes him and leaves you unscathed. Your teachings are the same, your sacraments are the same, your perils are the same, and you complain if you are called the offspring of old Mani.

AUG. (1) You say that I cannot teach by any arguments that Adam was created good by God, as if I am in conflict with you on this point. Is it not true that it is not I alone, nor you alone, but both of us who say that Adam was created good? For we both say that it was a good nature that was able not to sin if it willed not to. But since I maintain that it was better than you do, because I say it could not have died if it had not willed to sin, why is it that you say that I could not teach by any arguments that Adam was created good by God, since my arguments show that he was better than yours do? My arguments, of course, show that he was not only able not to sin, if he did not will to, but was also able not to die, if he had not willed to sin. But your arguments show that he was created mortal so that, whether he sinned or whether he did not sin, he was going to die. (2) When this was raised as an objection to Pelagius in the episcopal court in Palestine, he himself condemned it so that he would not be condemned,[81] and he condemned himself, as the apostle says of a heretic.[82]

I also say that Adam did not fear death since it was in his power not to die, but you say that he was under the necessity of dying even if he was under no necessity of sinning. If you say that he feared death even before the sin, what are you saying but that he was created in misery? But if, in order that he would not be in misery, though death was coming, he still did not fear it, he undoubtedly at least begot his offspring in misery in whom he begot the fear of death. For who would deny that by nature human beings fear death so that it is a rare greatness of soul that makes scarcely a few not to fear it?

(3) Likewise, I add to the goodness of Adam's condition that in him the flesh did not have desires opposed to the spirit before the sin, but you say that concupiscence of the flesh such as it now exists would have existed in paradise if no one had sinned, and that such concupiscence existed in Adam even before he sinned. Thus you add to his condition even this misery through the discord between the spirit and the flesh. Since, then, I show by so many and such great arguments that Adam was created better and happier than you say, why did it seem good to you to rave with such madness as to say that I could teach by no arguments that Adam was created good by God, but that for believing this I was content with the authority of the passage alone because scripture said that God created all things very good?

(4) I am not, as your insults have it,[83] so much duller than a pestle that for refuting Mani I would raise as an objection the authority of a book by which he is not bound.[84] I raise this objection to you when the issue demands, because the authority is one common to me and to you. But I do not persuade Mani that these creatures are good because they are the work of God, something which he denies; rather, on the basis of their goodness I force him to admit that they have a good maker. But the Manichees claim to accept the apostle; hence, since it is clear about what creature he was speaking, his words, *Every creature of God is good* (1 Tm 4:4), would be valid testimony against them, if they did not maintain that certain false statements were introduced even into the canonical books which they accept. And for this reason they must always be pressed on the basis

of the goodness of creatures to admit that the good God is their author, the point which they deny.

(5) Moreover, all creatures are so good that reason demonstrates that even those which are created with defects are good, even from the testimony of their defects, because a defect is opposed to a nature. For, unless the nature itself were rightly a source of pleasure, its defect would in no way rightly be a source of displeasure. Against the Manichees who think that the defects themselves are natures and substances, this point is quite amply discussed in certain short works of ours,[85] and it is shown that a defect is not a nature and that, because it is contrary to a nature, it is, therefore, something evil, but that a nature, as a nature, is something good.

From this it is inferred that there is no creator of natures but the creator of good beings and that he is, for this reason, good. But he is better than his creatures by a great difference because of his supreme goodness, for he cannot be damaged at all, not because of the reception of grace, but because of the character of his nature. (6) Created natures, then, whether those which are without defect or those which become defective after birth or those which are born defective, can only have as their creator the creator of good beings because, insofar as they are natures, they are good, even those which are defective. Their creator, after all, is the author, not of their defects, but of their natures. For the author of their defects is himself good in respect to the nature which God made, but he became evil by the defect by which he turned away from his creator by an evil will.

And so, this true argument refutes the error of the Manichees who refuse to accept the authority of the scriptures, whether that which says, *God made all things, and behold they were very good* (Gn 1:31), when there as yet existed no evil, or that which says, *Every creature of God is good* (1 Tm 4:4), when this evil age already existed, since God is, of course, the creator of all ages.

(7) But you who accept this authority of the words of God so that you can rightly be pressured by them, why do you not notice in that book, where we read that God made all things very good, that paradise was planted as the best of all places? In it God willed that there be no evil to the point that he did not permit even his own image to be there after it sinned by its own will?[86] And yet, into a place of such great happiness and beauty where one should not believe that any defect could have existed or could exist, even a defect of a tree, or plant, or fruit, or of any crop or animal, you do not hesitate to introduce all the defects of human minds and bodies; over these defects with which human beings are born we allow you to feel sorrow, but we do not allow you to deny them.

(8) For it is necessary that you feel sorrow when you do not find any answer and you do not want to change your view which is so bad. For it forces you by an unavoidable necessity to locate in a place of such great happiness and beauty the blind, the one-eyed, those with inflamed eyes, the deaf, the mute, the lame, the

deformed, the crippled, the worm-infested, the lepers, the paralytics, the epileptics, and those suffering from all kinds of other defects, and at times monstrous because of a terribly ugliness and horrible strangeness in their members never seen before. What shall I say of the defects of minds because of which certain people are by nature lustful, others prone to anger, others timid, and still others forgetful, some insensitive, stupid, and so feebleminded that a person would prefer to live with some animals than with such human beings? Add the groans of mothers in childbirth, the wailing of the newborn, the pains of the suffering, the struggles of the ill, the many torments of the dying, and the many more dangers of the living.

(9) According to your error, but clearly against your sense of shame, you are forced, whether impudently or shamefacedly, to locate in the paradise of God all these and other such evils, or even worse ones. Who, after all, is able to mention them briefly with adequate words? And you are forced to say that they would have been there, even if no one had sinned! Say it, say it! Why, after all, are you afraid to dishonor with so many and such great defects and disasters a place from which you exclude yourselves by your unspeakable teaching? For, if you were planning to enter there at some point, you would never put such evils in that place. Or if a sense of shame wins out in your hearts and you are embarrassed, horrified, and dumbfounded at putting such evils in such a place, and if you still stubbornly cling to your error because of which you do not believe that human nature was damaged by the transgression of the first human being, answer the Manichees as to where these evils come from so that they do not conclude that they come from a mixture with an alien evil nature.

(10) For when we are asked about this, we reply that these evils do not come from a mixture with an alien nature, but from the transgression by our nature through the one who was cast down in paradise and cast out of paradise so that his condemned nature would not remain in the place of blessedness and so that the defects and punishments which were rightly going to come upon his descendants would not exist in that place where no evils are allowed to exist. But when you deny that these deformities or sufferings come from the merits of our damaged nature, you admit the mixture with an alien nature. And in your misery you are even forced to help the Manichees, and your error summons these evils back into paradise from which your sense of shame had removed them.

Augustine Ascribes a Matter of the Will to the Seeds

17. JUL. (1) But, on the contrary, see how genuine is our struggle against you and Mani and how swift is our triumph over you, for Mani's downfall always involves you. We circumscribe all those evils which he spewed forth in disparagement of God's work by the furrow of our first definition, and we force him to

explain what he considers sin to be. For it is clear that it is nothing but the will which desires that which justice forbids and from which one is free to hold back. Once this has been settled, all those brambles of words which attacked the formation of bodies are shown to have been pulled out by their roots and, as the author says, completely eradicated.[87]

But now the feeling of fear and the sense of pain, which he thought stirred up a storm for the shipwreck of human beings, are, we are taught, not only not coercions toward evil, but helps and incentives toward justice, once they have met the barrier of a good will. For who would dread the judgment if it were not for the warning of fear? (2) Who would be helped by the groans of penance if it were not for the expiatory power of pain and internal discomfort? What power would the severity of the judge have if the pain of inflicted torment did not punish voluntary sins? By the testimony of all these it is clear that sin is nothing else than free will which scorns the commandments of justice and that justice can be upheld only if it imputes as sin that from which it knows one was free to abstain. And for this reason no law can count those factors which are natural as sin, nor can anyone contract a serious sin unless one has committed it when one could avoid it. That power destroys Mani and the traducianist who, with the eyes of his intelligence gouged out, tries to ascribe a matter of the will to the seeds.

AUG. (1) We have already often replied to these errors of yours. Hence, those who read them and commit them to memory do not desire my answer wherever you repeat your verbosity. But lest anyone complain, I ought not to abandon even the slower folk, since those with quicker minds will forgive me. Look, here too I reply to you about the definition of sin which you suppose greatly helps you. This definition defines that which is a sin, but is not also the punishment of sin, when it says: Sin is the will that desires that which justice forbids and from which one is free to hold back. This definition applies especially to that man who by that great sin of his initiated the wretchedness of his descendants by that heavy yoke upon them from the day they emerge from the womb of their mother[88] and by the corruptible body which weighs down their soul.[89] (2) Having received a brief law, he, of course, knew what justice forbade, and he was certainly free to hold back from it, since the flesh did not yet have desires opposed to his spirit. On account of this evil, scripture said even to believers: *So that you do not do what you will* (Gal 5:17).

The blindness of heart, then, because of which one does not know that which justice forbids, and the violence of concupiscence, because of which even one who knows that from which one ought to hold back is overcome, are not merely sins, but also the punishment of sins. And, hence, they are not included in that definition of sin which defines only what is sin, not what is also the punishment of sin. For, when persons do not know what they should do and, for that reason, do what they ought not to do, they are not free to hold back from that from which they know that they should hold back. (3) So too, how is that person who is driven, as you say, not because of his origin, but because of habit, to cry out: *I do not do the good that I will, but I do the evil that I do not will* (Rom 7:15), free to hold back from that evil which he does not will but does, or even hates but does? If it were in the power of human beings to be without these punishments, they would not ask God's help both against blindness where scripture says to him, *Enlighten my eyes* (Ps 13:4), and against evil desire where it says to him, *Let every iniquity not lord it over me* (Ps 119:133). Moreover, if these too were not sins because one is not free to hold back from them, scripture would not say, *Do not remember the sins of my youth and of my ignorance* (Ps 25:7); it would not say, *You have sealed my sins in a sack, and you have noticed if I did anything unwillingly* (Jb 14:17 LXX).

(4) The Manichees are defeated by that definition, then, of a sin such as Adam committed, for he knew what justice forbade, but did not hold back from that from which he was free to hold back, but they are defeated by us who say that the origin of human evils with which we see even little ones are weighed down stems from this sin. And on account of this scripture also says when dealing with sins, *Not even an infant who has lived one day on earth is clean from filth* (Jb 14:4 LXX). But because you deny this, you try by your destructive defense of our nature to weigh down it even more so that in its misery it does not seek a deliverer.

When, however, the question arises where evil comes from, you allow Mani to introduce an alien nature coeternal with God. (5) For, in order to blame human nature, he does not appeal to the feeling of fear and the sense of pain, those two which you thought that you should praise in opposition to him, that is, because we are taught that fear and pain are "helps and incentives toward justice," when a person does not sin out of fear of the judgment or feels pain over having sinned because of the barbs of repentance.

This is not the question you are asked; rather, you are asked why there is the punishment of fear in little ones who do not flee from sins, and why are they afflicted with such great pains though they do not commit sins? You, of course, said, "What power would the severity of the judge have if the suffering of that inflicted torment did not punish voluntary sins?" By what justice, then, are the little ones who have no voluntary sins of their own punished by the pain of that inflicted torment? (6) In these surely it is clear how vain and foolish are your praises with which you extolled fear and pain. For these penalties are indeed grave, and the newly born and new images of God would not suffer them under the most just judgment and omnipotence of God, if they did not contract the merit of the original and ancient sin.

Finally, if no one had sinned in paradise and if the couple had offspring as a result of that true blessing of God, heaven forbid that anyone, whether an adult or a little one, should suffer there these torments. After all, not merely pain—which

is quite obvious—but also fear involves torment, as the divine scripture testifies.[90] Heaven forbid, then, that there should be any torments in the place of that
happiness. Hence, what would they fear at any age, if no one threatened them?
(7) What pain would they suffer, if no one injured them? But in this present evil
age into which we have been cast down from the paradise of delights in order to
live in our miseries, the suffering of fear and pain remains even in these people
whose sins have been forgiven in order that our faith concerning the age to come,
where there will be no such evils, may be tested not only in our sufferings, but in
those of our little ones. For we do not want them to be reborn in order that they
may not suffer these evils, but in order that they may be brought to that kingdom
in which such evils will not exist.

Since you reject this true and Catholic faith and try to refute it with the empty
noise from your lips, when Mani has raised the question where the evils of little
ones come from, all your wordiness will fall silent; since you deny original sin,
he will immediately strike you in the face and introduce an alien nature. (8) But
the Catholic faith has no fear about your idea that a matter of the will cannot be
ascribed to the seeds, since it listens to God who says that children will be punished for the sins of their parents to the third and fourth generation.[91] Certainly a
matter of the will, namely, the sin of the parents, is ascribed to the seeds when the
children are punished, and when the patriarch, Abraham, paid the tithe to
Melchizedek, he gave the tithe to that priest by his will, and yet sacred scripture
testifies that his children who were in his loins also paid the tithe at that time.[92]
This surely would not happen if a matter of the will could not be ascribed to the
seeds.

The Monstrous Stories Invented by the Phoenician

18. JUL. (1) By the faithfulness of our God and of human beings! That such
monstrous stories could have been invented so that with a great effort and with
energy expended they try to distort everything! For what is so monstrous as what
the Phoenician[93] says? Those factors, he says, which were natural were not lasting, and those which were taken up by choice clung to the first composition of
our members. Adam, he says, was created good and had a natural innocence;
also set above the other creatures by reason of his special dignity, he shone forth
in the likeness of the creator. (2) He received free choice in such a condition that
he could move by his own judgment in whichever direction he willed, and he obtained the ability either to move toward good or evil or to pull back from each of
them by the very condition of his creation by which he surpassed the rest. But
since he chose by his independent judgment an evil will of his free mind, he destroyed all those elements which were inborn, and only sin and the necessity of
sinning clung to him inseparably. That is what I called a monstrous story! It is, of

course, an unheard-of deformity to say: The living being was well made in which even natural goods were able to be lost, though even voluntary evils clung to it inseparably.

AUG. (1) When one says, "The living being was well made in which even natural goods were able to be lost, though even voluntary evils clung to it inseparably," you think that it is a monstrous story, and you are so strongly and deeply upset that we say these things that you appeal to the faithfulness of God and of human beings, as if you suffer violence because we said these things. But, please, set aside these terrible outbursts, and attend more calmly to what I say. If anyone blinds himself willingly, will he not lose a natural good, that is, sight, and will a voluntary evil, that is, blindness, not cling to him inseparably? Is the living being for this reason badly made for which the natural good was able to be lost and from which the voluntary natural evil is inseparable? Why, then, should not I rather cry out: By the faithfulness of our God and human beings! That these points which are so clear and set before the eyes are not seen by a human being who wants to be seen as very clever, as learned, as having pretensions of being a philosopher, and as a dialectician! (2) After all, if anyone willingly amputates any member, does that person not lose the natural good of bodily integrity and receive the inseparable evil of mutilation?

But you may perhaps say that this can happen in the goods of the body, but not in those of the mind. Why, then, when you mentioned "natural goods" or "voluntary evils," did you not add "of the mind," so that your hasty and unconsidered statement would not be destroyed because of the goods and evils of the body? Or did you perhaps forget? Let us grant this; it is only human. But there steps forth in our midst that man who cries out: *I do not do the good that I will, but I do the evil that I do not will* (Rom 7:15), and he shows you that some goods of the mind are lost through an evil will so that they cannot be restored by a good will, unless God does what a human being cannot do, for he can restore eyes willingly made blind and members willingly cut off. (3) Finally, what answer will you make about the devil himself who lost irreparably his good will? Or are you going to say that it can be recovered? Be so bold, if you can. Or are you rather going to admit that these things too did not come to your mind, and that forgetfulness of them made you rush into a rash statement? At least, then, when I remind you, correct yourself. Or does stubbornness not allow you to correct what ill-advised rashness said, and does the shame of correcting yourself reinforce the fall into error? We must, I see, pray to God on your behalf, the God to whom the apostle prayed for the people of Israel that he might heal them, when, not knowing the righteousness of God and wanting to establish their own righteousness, they were not subject to the righteousness of God.[94]

(4) You too, after all, are such people who want to establish your own righteousness which you yourselves produce for yourselves by your own free choice; you do not ask from God and receive from him the true righteousness

which is called the righteousness of God, not that by which God is righteous, but that which is given by God. In the same way, the Lord's salvation[95] is not that by which the Lord is saved, but that by which he saves us. For this reason the same apostle says, *That I may be found in him, not having my own righteousness which comes from the law, but that which comes from faith, the righteousness that comes from God* (Phil 3:9). This is the righteousness of God which the people of Israel did not know, and they wanted to establish their own righteousness which comes from the law. In destroying that righteousness, Paul did not, of course, destroy the law, but the pride of those who thought that the law was enough for them, as if they were fulfilling the righteousness of the law by free choice. They did not know the righteousness of God which is given by God in order that they might do with his help what the law commands, for his wisdom carries on its tongue the law and mercy:[96] the law because he commands and mercy because he helps us to do what he commands.

(5) Desire this righteousness of God, my son, Julian; do not place your trust in your own virtue. I repeat, desire this righteousness; may the Lord grant you the desire for it; may he even grant you the possession of it. Do not in your pride over your earthly origin[97] scorn this Phoenician who warns and admonishes you. Do not, after all, suppose that, because you are a son of Apulia, you must surpass the Phoenicians by your origin, though you cannot surpass them by your mind. Flee, rather, the punishments, not the Phoenicians.[98] For you cannot escape the Phoenician opponents as long as you take delight in placing your trust in your own virtue.[99] For blessed Cyprian was also a Phoenician, and he said, "We must boast over nothing when nothing is ours."[100]

The Loss and Restoration of Innocence

19. JUL. (1) Here someone might say: What then? Do you deny that the innocence in which Adam was created was corrupted by the commission of a voluntary sin? For, even if the possibility of returning to the good is not lost when the iniquity has been committed, it is, nonetheless, certain that the merit of innocence with which the human beginning starts off is lost by a defect of the will. But I do not deny that this is so; rather, that is what I want to illustrate by these examples, namely, that the condition of the qualities by which we are said to be good or evil was created such that they operate under the dominion of the will, and since this point is established with such validity that not even the innocence, which in accord with the dignity of our author precedes the act of the will and is natural, can preserve itself if any power in the mind resists it, this dominion has far more power on the side of evil, but only to the extent that a sin committed by the will receives no tyrannical rule to the destruction of reason. (2) And if the good quality with which the human being was made was not immutable—for it

would be false to say that a human being was free if he could not change his own acts—for even greater reason an evil quality could not be created as immutable and as belonging to reason; otherwise, that reason would suffer the loss of freedom on the side of evil, something that on account of its status it had not lost even on the side of the good.

AUG. (1) See, you too have discovered, and there has at long last come to your attention, though rather late, the reason why your rash view is destroyed. You said, of course, that a natural good, such as innocence, could be lost by a defect of the will, and in this way you have shown that this great good which belongs to the nature, not of the body, but of the mind itself, in such a way that God made the human being with this good, can be lost. If this had come to your attention before, you would not think that it was monstrous and terribly ugly to say: The living being was well made in which even natural goods were able to be lost. For you thought that either goods or evils, but only voluntary ones, could be lost, though you usually say that natural ones cannot be lost.

(2) You, after all, also say elsewhere that "natural characteristics last from the beginning of a substance up to its end,"[101] in order to maintain that free choice which God gave to human beings when he created them cannot be lost. And you especially claim that natural goods cannot be lost because of voluntary evils. And for this reason you say that we try to distort everything, as if we say that voluntary evils cannot be lost, but natural goods can be. We, of course, do not say this, for we say that both can be lost, but that the evils which are introduced by free will can be lost by God's forgiveness or by the human will, but only after it has been set free by God and prepared by the Lord. You, however, say that goods, voluntary goods, not natural ones, can be lost by an evil will. Look, you found one, and you yourself said that innocence, which is a natural good, can be lost by voluntary evil. (3) And innocence, if you pay close attention, is a greater good than free choice, for innocence belongs only to the good, while free choice belongs to both the good and the bad.

But whether innocence is lost by an evil will so that it can be recovered by a good will is a question that should not be scorned. For, if members of the body are amputated by the will, they are not likewise restored by the will. In the same way one must see whether in a different reality, that is, in the mind, something of the sort results from the loss of innocence, namely, that by an act of the will it can be lost, but cannot not be restored. For, if sacred virginity is lost by an act of an impure will, one can return to chastity, but not to virginity. Still one can reply that even the bodily integrity of virginity does not, of course, belong to the mind, but to the body. Yet, when one is discussing innocence, one is discussing something which belongs to the mind,[102] and one must, nevertheless, consider whether one who has sinned returns by the will to righteousness, not to innocence, just as that virgin returns to chastity, not to virginity. (4) For, just as righteousness is opposed to a lack of righteousness, so innocence is opposed as to its contrary, not to a lack of righteousness, but to guilt, and guilt is not removed by the will of a human being, though guilt is produced by one's will.

For one who thinks that penitents themselves remove their own guilt do not see the truth. Although God gives even repentance itself, as the apostle states, when he says, *Perhaps God may grant them repentance* (2 Tm 2:25), it is perfectly clear that God removes the guilt by granting a human being forgiveness, not the human being by doing penance. We ought, of course, to recall that man who did not find an opportunity for repentance though he asked for it with tears.[103] And in this way he both did penance and remained guilty, because he did not receive pardon. And those people who will say to one another, *while doing penance and groaning through the anguish of their spirit: What good did our pride do us?* (Wis 5:3.8), and so on, will indeed remain guilty for eternity without receiving pardon. Such was the one of whom the Lord said, *That person will not be forgiven it, but will be guilty of an eternal sin* (Mk 3:29).

(5) See, we have found innocence, a great good of a human being and one so natural that the first human being was created with it and, according to you, every human being is born with it, and yet it can be lost, but cannot be recovered by the will of a human being. And guilt is a great evil and the contrary of innocence, and the power of a human being can, nonetheless, bring it about, since it is voluntary, but the will cannot remove it. Do you see how your general rule is broken by which you thought that we cannot lose a natural good because of the will? For we have found that it is not only lost, but also that it cannot be restored by the will, at least by the human will. God, however, can take away the guilt and recall a human being to innocence.

(6) Why, then, do you not believe that the freedom of acting well could have been lost by the human will and cannot be restored except by the divine will? For you hear that man who says, *I do not do the good that I will, but I do the evil that I do not will* (Rom 7:19) and who cries out after such words, *Who will set me free?* and adds, *The grace of God through Jesus Christ our Lord* (Rom 7:24-25). But you claim, "It would be false to say that a human being was free if he could not change his own actions." You do not see that you take freedom away from God himself as well as from us, for, when we begin to live as immortal in that kingdom with him, it will not be possible for us change our actions, now toward good, now toward evil, and we shall, nonetheless, then be more happily free when we shall be unable to be slaves to sin, just as God cannot be. But we shall be unable because of his grace, while he is unable because of his nature.

Augustine Extols the Power of the Devil

20. JUL. (1) Finally, what toady has so extolled with flattery the might of a vainglorious soldier,[104] as the traducianist has done for the devil? This can be

seen from the weightiness of your feelings. God, of course, made the man, molding with a care deserving our veneration the very matter of the clay which would go on to be transformed into the shape of a human being under the hand of his author. The likeness had stood completed, but pale and lifeless, awaiting the spirit which would make it beautiful and alive. Then the soul which was created and breathed into it by the most august breath of its author filled and moved the members. At that moment all the senses were awakened to readiness for their proper functions. The indwelling soul entered and gave color to the flesh, warmth to the blood, strength to the members, and beauty to the skin.

(2) See what a task the divine goodness undertook in forming and giving life to the man. But this familiarity with the creator did not leave him once he was made. He is transferred to a more pleasant place, and the creator endows with riches the man he created with benevolence. Not content, nonetheless, to have bestowed these gifts, he enlightens him by entering into conversation with him. He gives him a commandment so that, in understanding his own freedom, he would see that he is offered the means of becoming a closer friend to the creator. This commandment does not extend to many details lest he should feel any burden from the multiplicity of the laws. Rather, by the prohibition of one small piece of fruit God sought evidence of the man's devotion. Afterward, so that he might also have a partner by whom he might become a father, he is honored once again by the touch of that hand by which he had been created. He is also favored and honored thereafter by conversation with God.

(3) These benefits, then, given by God, which were so long, so many, and so great—creation, gifts, commandments, conversations —produced in the man no necessity of doing good. But the devil, on the other hand, no less timidly than shrewdly spoke a few words with the woman, and they are said to have had such power that they were immediately turned into the condition of natural factors, even more, that they destroyed everything natural, produced the everlasting necessity of doing evil, and set the devil over the image of God as its lord and owner.

What, then, is stronger, what more excellent, what more magnificent than the power of the enemy if it accomplished more by a small chat than God could accomplish by his works and gifts? (4) It is evident, then, that you stand on the side of the one whose power you proclaim so excessively and that you have no share in the worship of our God whom we confess to be most just as well as most omnipotent. For he is powerful, and he has truth on his side; he brings down the proud like someone wounded,[105] that is, the devil and Mani and you, his disciples, who slander nature so that you need not admit that you sin freely. Our God himself, therefore, scatters his enemies in the might of his arm,[106] and on this account neither you nor the Manichees can produce anything that would not be shattered by the lightning bolt of his truth.

AUG. (1) We are not flatterers of the devil, nor as you insult us, do we with praise full of false flattery extol his power which is subject to the power of God. But would that you were not his soldiers, as all heretics are, whose teachings he casts like deadly spears through your tongues at whomever he can. The apostle says, *We thank the Father who makes us fit to have a share in the lot of the saints in the light; he has rescued us from the power of darkness and transferred us into the kingdom of his beloved Son* (Col 1:12-13), and you forbid us to offer these thanks for the little ones, when you claim that they are not under the power of the devil.

Why do you do this but so that they are not rescued from his power and so that the earnings of the devil might be not lessened? (2) Jesus, who in accord with his name saves his people from their sins,[107] says, *No one enters into the home of a strong man in order to steal his possessions unless he has first bound the strong man* (Mt 12:29), and you contend that the little ones are not included in this people of Christ whom he saves from their sins, since you hold that they are not bound by original sins, just as they are not bound by personal sins. When by your deceiving talk you lessen the strength of the one whom the Truth called strong, by your error you make him even stronger for gaining the little ones.

Jesus says, *For the Son of Man came to seek and to save what was lost* (Lk 19:10), and you answer him: You need not seek the little ones because they were not lost. And in that way when you ward off from them the savior's search, you increase against them the power of the one who wounded them. (3) Jesus says, *It is not the healthy, but those who are ill who need a physician; I have not come to call the righteous, but sinners* (Mt 9:12-13), and you say to him: The little ones do not need you, because they are not sinners either because of their own will or because of their human origin. When you forbid those who are not healthy to come to the physician in order to be healed, the plague of the devil exercises its dominion over them with greater power. How much more tolerable, then, would it be that you coddle the devil with false praises like his toadies and flatterers than that you help him with the lies of your teachings like his soldiers and henchmen!

With fulsome and ornate language you describe how God formed the man from the clay and brought him to life by breathing into him the soul, how he enriched him with paradise, helped him with the commandment, and had such great care not to burden him in some way that he did not extend that same commandment to many details so that the man whom he had created with such tenderness would not feel any burden from a multiplicity of laws. Why, then, does the corruptible body now weigh down the soul?[108] (4) Why, then, is there a heavy yoke upon the children of Adam from the day they emerge from the womb of their mother,[109] since he did not want to burden even Adam by a multiplicity of laws? You see, of course, that, if no one had sinned in paradise, the fecundity of the spouses would fill with the human race that place of such great felicity that the corruptible body would not weigh down the soul, that a heavy yoke would not press down upon the newborn human beings, and that toil and pain would not be the means of educating the poor little ones.

Where, then, do these evils come from? They certainly do not come from some evil nature which Mani imagines or believes, a nature alien to us and mixed into us. Where do they come from but from our own nature which was damaged by the transgression of the first human being? (5) But you, a clever and prudent fellow, are amazed, and you do not think that we should believe that the devil's few words of conversation with the woman could be said to have such power that they ruined all the natural goods, as if the words of the speaker did this, not the consent of the listener. After all, it is not true, as you say, that the few words of the serpent were turned into the condition of natural factors; rather, the will of the human being destroyed the good which could not be restored by the will of the human being, but can be restored by the will of God, when the most just, most powerful, and most merciful God will judge that it should be restored and to whom it should be restored. In the same way one's sight can, as we already said, be taken away by the will of a human being, and if that happens, there follows the blindness which necessity brings and which the will does not take away. And in the mind of a person the will can destroy its innocence and is not able to recover it.

(6) Look, rather, at the fact that the evils with which human beings are born, evils which could not have been born with human beings in the happiness of paradise, certainly would not have been born with them now unless their damaged nature had left paradise. Look at these evils, for they are obvious. The evils of mortals, after all, from the day the children of Adam emerge from the womb of their mother are not something at which we guess in the dark; rather, we see them in the brightest light. Since they do not come from being mingled with an alien evil nature, they undoubtedly come from the corruption of our own nature.

(7) Nor should you think it unfair that the image of God is subject to the devil. For this would not happen except by the judgment of God, nor can this condemnation be removed except by the grace of God. After all, we should not be surprised that one who by the excellence of his nature was made to the likeness of God so that he was the image of God has been made like a vanity by the corruption of his nature so that his days pass like a shadow.[110] But, you, tell me why countless images of God who commit no sins at their tender age are not admitted to the kingdom of God, if they are not reborn. For they have something because of which they merit to lie under the power of the devil, on account of which they do not merit to reign under the power of God. If you would cling to his light, you would not with such great arrogance compare your own words to a bolt of lightning.

Why Is the First Sin So Different from the Rest?

21. JUL. (1) It is, then, absolutely clear that Augustine differs in no way from his teacher, but that his arguments define the nature of other human beings, no less than that of Adam, as most evil. Finally, in order that we may discuss yet another point with this same person concerning these topics which we have treated, it is clear that you do not think that the first sin was also of the same in kind as the others. For, you say that the grave sins of the following eras could not pass into our nature, for example, so that the children born of an embezzler, of a murderer, or of someone incestuous are born subject to the sins of their parents, and you say that there is no sin which is mingled with the seeds except that one. In saying this, you clearly show that you do not think that the first disobedience was of the same kind as the rest.

(2) See, then, the great brevity and brilliance of our question. If the sin which Adam committed was contracted by the will and was able to become something natural, why are these sins which are committed daily, sins which a sinful will commits, not added to the deformity and detriment of the seeds? But if these sins which are as terrible as they are many cannot be inborn, by what law, by what condition, by what privilege is that first sin alone claimed to be inborn? If the sins which we know, which the law blames, and which justice punishes are of the same kind as that sin of the first human being which was committed by the will and punished with justice, why do we not come to know the character of these sins from that one or of that sin from these? Or if they cannot provide evidence for one another, by what impudence do you deny that the first transgression had another condition, that is, one produced not by the will, but by a natural decay?

(3) Finally, be so bold as to define any sin while defending inherited sin; I do not mean that first sin; rather, explain what definition these sins have, that is, even these sins which are at present committed, for example, sacrilege, scandalous behavior, or any evil action. You will undoubtedly say: Sin is the will which desires that which justice forbids and from which one is free to hold back. For, if there were not an evil will, sin could not exist. Pay attention to how reasonably we come to this point. Oh the stupidity! Oh the intolerable impudence! You define sin to be only the act of the will which is free and forbidden by justice, though the belief in natural evil demands that there is a non-voluntary sin with which a human being is born. (4) It is not, then, true that there is no sin except that which is freely committed, because there is a serious sin, even the very greatest sin, which is contracted, not freely, but by being born. Dismiss, therefore, the definition of sin which is welcome among the Catholics and does not visit you even with the rights of a guest, and once you have dismissed it, prove that you are not a fellow soldier of those who attack our very substance out of hatred for its depravity.

And to sum up what we have done, either one will teach that there is no voluntary sin if there is a natural sin, or there will be no natural sin, if every sin is defined as voluntary. From these we conclude that either you should deny that sin can come from birth and you should join the Catholic faith, or, if you continue to insist that not just any sin, but the greatest crime is contracted through nature without the will, you should submit your name to Mani to whom you offer full allegiance.

AUG. (1) You suppose that you stir up a great hatred for me when you say that I differ in no way from my teacher. But I take your insults as praise for me. I understand as I ought to understand, not your thoughts, but the words you speak, when you call me back to my faith. For you speak the truth, and you do not know it, like the priest Caiaphas, the persecutor of Christ, whose thoughts were full of crimes, but whose words, without his knowing it, spoke of salvation.[111]

With regard to this question at issue between us I am, of course, happy that I differ in no way from my teacher, first, because the Lord himself taught me that the little ones are dead unless he himself who died for all brings them to life. In explaining this, the apostle says, *All, then, have died, and he died for all* (2 Cor 5:14.15). But you contradict this, denying that the little ones are dead so that they are not brought to life in Christ, though you admit that Christ also died for the little ones. John, the apostle of the teacher of all, also teaches me this; he says that the Son of God came to destroy the works of the devil.[112] (2) But you say that these works are not destroyed in the little ones, as if he who came to destroy the works of the devil did not come on account of them.

I also ought not to deny my teachers who have helped me to understand this by the labor of their writings. Cyprian is my teacher; he says that an infant born in the flesh from Adam contracted by its first birth the contagion of the ancient death, and for this reason it approaches with greater ease to receive the forgiveness of sins, because the sins forgiven are not its own, but another's.[113] Ambrose is my teacher; I have not only read his books, but I even heard his words when he uttered them, and through him I received the bath of rebirth. I am far from being his equal in merits, but I confess and publicly declare that I differ in no way from my teacher on this issue. Heaven forbid that you should prefer Pelagius, your teacher, to him! (3) And yet, I hold Pelagius as a witness against you about Ambrose. For he said that not even an enemy dared to find fault with his faith and utterly flawless interpretation of the scriptures.[114] But you dare to find fault with him so that you maintain that his statement that the discord of the flesh was turned into our nature by the transgression of the first human being[115] and whatever else he thought or said about human nature which was damaged by Adam are Mani's false story.

You do, of course, observe in part the testimony of your teacher with regard to this great man, since you do not dare to find fault with him openly. But when you insult me by name with your vicious tongue and impudent heart, you surely accuse both him and other great and renowned teachers of the Catholic Church who have held and stated the same doctrine—and you do this more wickedly to the extent that you do so indirectly. Against you I, therefore, defend my faith and the faith of those whom you fear to have openly as your enemies and whom you are unwilling to tolerate as judges.

(4) Heaven forbid, however, that your arguments should have any effect before such judges; in those arguments you compare the sins of the following eras to that great sin, that is, to the transgression of the first human being, and you think that, if the nature of the human race was changed by the sin of the first human being, the sins of parents ought now also to have changed the nature of their children. For, when you say these things, you do not see that, after those sinners committed that great sin, they were both dismissed from paradise and forbidden with great severity access to the tree of life. Are the sinners of these times cast into some lower regions from this surface of the earth, when they commit these sins here, however great they may be? Are they forbidden access to the tree of life which is not at all found in this misery? Rather, there persists the human race's place and the life in which even very impious human beings live, though we see the place and life of those former sinners could not after their sin have continued, as it was before the sin.

(5) According to your opinion, however, the little ones bound by no guilt ought, as soon as they are born, to have been carried by the angels of God into the paradise of God as if they were innocent images of God. And they ought to have been raised there without any labor or pain so that, if any of them sinned, they would rightly be cast out from there so that sins would not increase by imitation. But now after that man alone who sinned in the happiness of paradise heard the words, *The earth will bring forth thorns and thistles for you, and it will be cursed in all your works. And in the sweat of your brow you will eat your bread* (Gn 3:18-19), we see no human being immune from the punishment of labor, though such labor would, of course, not have weighed down the blessed inhabitants of paradise. And after his wife alone heard, *In sorrow you will bear children* (Gn 3:16), we know that no woman is free from this punishment in giving birth.

Are you people, then, so crazy that you think that, if no one had sinned, human beings would have suffered these miseries in paradise? It is, after all, perfectly clear that God imposed these miseries only upon those human beings who transgressed at that time. Or are you so crazy that you deny their descendants exiled from paradise now suffer them and endure everywhere so many and such great miseries? Or are you going to say that people's fields will bring forth more thorns and thistles and that they will sweat more in their labors to the extent that they are more impious sinners? And are you going to say that a woman will suffer greater pains in giving birth to that extent that she is more sinful? (7) Just as, then, the punishments of human miseries which the children of Adam endure in common from the day they emerge from the womb of their mother are the common lot of all, because all have in common the parents from whose transgression they came, so the transgression of those two ought to be understood to be so great a sin that it could change for the worse the nature of all who are born of man and woman and could bind them with common guilt like a written list of an inherited debt.

If anyone, then, says that the condition of any sins which are now committed should have been the same as the condition of that sin which was committed in the great happiness of that life, when it was so easy not to sin, he ought also to make these two lives equal, namely, the life we are now leading and the life which was led in those holy and blessed delights. (8) But if you see that this is most stupid, stop trying to rule out on the basis of the sins of this present age that great sin's having its own singular power and merit. And yet, even in this life the omnipotent and just God who says, *I shall punish children for the sins of their parents* (Ex 20:5), shows quite clearly that descendants too are ensnared by the guilt of their parents. And, though the bondage is less harsh, they become debtors by inheritance unless, as we have argued in the previous parts of this book, they are released from the bonds of that proverb, which used to be spoken: *The parents ate sour grapes, and the teeth of their children were set on edge* (Jer 31:29), not by your argument, but by the new testament, not by the nature of birth, but by the grace of rebirth.

(9) But that definition of sin by which we understand the will which desires that which justice forbids and from which one is free to hold back is the definition of that sin which is only sin, not of the sin which is also the punishment of sin. I have no idea how many times I have replied to you on this point. The one, after all, who says, *I do not do the good that I will, but I do the evil that I do not will* (Rom 7:15), is not free to hold back from this evil, and he calls upon the deliverer precisely because he lost his freedom.

Either All Sins Are Voluntary Or God Is Unjust

22. JUL. (1) Time warns us to move on to other topics, but I am compelled to remain on the same passage for a while because of my anger. You dare, do you, to say that Adam sinned by the will? Where did you get that dream from? Because, you reply, it would have been unjust that God counted it as sin if he did not know that Adam was free to hold back from it. So what? Had that prince of darkness whom you worship for a moment conceded this justice to God, and has he, by demanding it back a little later, stripped this God of all justice? For this God, who understood in the beginning that an action was not to be counted as sin unless one was free to hold back from it, knew that through all the rest of time all the newborn would not be free to hold back.

Finally, where did you learn that it was just only in Adam's case that a sin could not be avenged unless it were voluntary, if you did not know that it is unjust to impute to anyone a sin which you admit was contracted without the will? (2) You will, then, suppose that the view of inherited sin is just so that it could agree with God's judgment when he imputes to a little one a sin which was not committed by its will, and you will also be forced to declare it to be just and in accord with the judgments of God that he imputed to Adam as a sin what he knew came from him, not because of the will, but because of the deformity of his substance. And in this way there will be no inherited sin, nor will nature be blamed as damaged by the agent's choice, but as created evil from the beginning, and you will admit that you are a Manichee. Or if you come to your senses and say that it is unjust that Adam should be held guilty for the sins of his nature, it follows irrefutably that it is utterly criminal if Abel, Enoch, Noah, and all the race of human beings are judged guilty of the original crime.

(3) If you ascribe this miscarriage of justice to your God, he alone will remain guilty instead of all, and it will be apparent, as always, that he is not the one whom we Catholics venerate in the Trinity as most just. But if you cease from your accusations against God, you condemn, like someone come back to life, the teaching of Manichean inherited sin by which you have up to now been fatally wounded.

AUG. (1) The reason you are greatly in error, the reason you are heretics, the reason you dare to put together by your human and vain arguments newfangled weapons against the Catholic faith which, while avoiding heretics, follows the words of God and is protected by them, is that you do not know, and you refuse to believe, since you cannot understand, what that which is linked to the seeds can do to succeeding generations. You do not understand or believe how great and how impenetrable by any thought are the natural laws of propagation in the creatures which God willed to be born, generation after generation according to their kind. Because of them there is implanted in the human race a desire so that all—to the extent it is up to them—want to be certain about their children. In the case of chaste women the fidelity of the marital covenant is conducive to this.

(2) On this account the philosopher Plato is rightly objectionable because he thought that women should be held in common in that city which in his dialogue he designed to be the best.[116] What else was he aiming at but that the adults should show toward all children that love which he saw that nature owes to one's own children? For each father would think that a child could be his own, if he saw the child to be of the right age that he might reasonably believe the child to have been born of his seed from some unidentified woman whom he had indiscriminately used. Why? Did not Cicero speak from the hearts of all fathers those words to his son to whom he said in writing, "You are the only one of all human beings by whom I would wish to be surpassed in all things."[117]

(3) We said that these natural laws of propagation were most hidden, though we know that it is quite believable that they have great influence. Did they not bring it about that the two twins who were not only not yet having children, but were not even born, were called two peoples when they were still in the womb of their mother?[118] The same natural laws of propagation make us say that Israel was a slave in Egypt,[119] that Israel left Egypt,[120] that Israel entered the promised land, that Israel acquired the goods and experienced the evils which God either bestowed or imposed on that people. Scripture also said of him, *He will come from Zion to remove and turn aside impiety from Jacob, and this will be for them a testament from me when I shall have taken away their sins* (Is 59:20.21). And yet, that man who first and alone received these two proper names, having died long before, did not see these goods or evils.

(4) These natural laws of propagation are the reason why the same people paid the tithe in the person of Abraham, precisely because that people was in his loins when he paid the tithe by his own will,[121] but that people paid the tithe, not by their own will, but by the natural law of propagation. Who, however, will explain in words, who will at least discover in thought how the same people was in the loins of Abraham, not only from his time up to the time mentioned in the Letter to the Hebrews, but from his time up to the present time and from now to the end of the world, as long as children of Israel are born, generation after generation? How, then, could there be in the loins of one man so countless a multitude of human beings?

(5) For if the seeds themselves from which so many human beings have been and are being and will be born up to the end were massed together, since they have a corporeal size, though the individual seeds from which each individual is born are small, they could not have been held in the loins of one man. Some sort of invisible and intangible power, then, is located in the secrets of nature where the natural laws of propagation are concealed, and on account of this power as many as were going to be able to be begotten from that one man by the succession and multiplication of generations are certainly not untruthfully said to have been in the loins of that father. They not only were there, but when he knowingly and willingly paid the tithe, they too paid the tithe, though not knowingly and not willingly, because they did not yet exist as persons who could have known and willed this.

But the author of that sacred Letter said this in order to teach the superiority of the priesthood of Christ over the Levitical priesthood, for the priest Melchizedek to whom Abraham paid the tithe prefigured the priesthood of Christ. The author of the Letter also taught that Levi himself, who was tithed by his brothers, that is, received tithes from them, paid in Abraham the tithe to Melchizedek. For Levi too was in the loins of Abraham, when Melchizedek was tithed, that is, received the tithe from him. And for this reason the author wants us to understand that Christ, to whom scripture said, *You are a priest forever according to the order of*

Melchizedek (Ps 110:4), did not pay the tithe so that he may rightly be held superior to the Levitical priesthood.[122] For Melchizedek received the tithe from Abraham; he did not pay the tithe, as Levi did in Abraham.

(7) But if someone asks how Christ did not pay the tithe since he too, as is clear, was in terms of the origin of his flesh in the loins of Abraham when that patriarch paid the tithe to Melchizedek, nothing comes to mind except that Mary, his mother, from whom he took his flesh, was born, of course, from the carnal concupiscence of her parents, but she did not conceive Christ in that way, since she became his mother, not by the seed of a man, but by the Holy Spirit. He, therefore, had nothing to do with the nature of the male seed by which those who according to the testimony of sacred scripture paid the tithe were in the loins of Abraham.

(8) The concupiscence of the flesh which causes the ejaculation of the carnal seeds either did not exist at all in Adam before the sin or was damaged in him by the sin. For either without it the sexual organs were able to be appropriately moved and the seed poured into the womb of his wife, if concupiscence did not then exist, or concupiscence was itself also able to obey at the least sign from the will, if it did exist. But if it were like that now, the flesh would never have desires opposed to the spirit. Either, then, it is a defect, if it did not exist before the sin, or it undoubtedly was damaged by the sin, and for that reason original sin is contracted from it. There was, then, in Mary's body the carnal material from which Christ took his flesh, but carnal concupiscence did not make her pregnant with Christ. Hence, he was born of the flesh and with flesh in the likeness of sinful flesh, not like other human beings in sinful flesh. For this reason he removed original sin in others by rebirth, but he himself did not contract it by birth. (9) Hence, the former was the first Adam, and the latter is the second Adam, because that one was created and this one was born without carnal concupiscence. But the former was only a man, while the latter is both God and man. And so, the former was able not to sin, while the latter was unable to sin.

In vain, then, do you try to make the sins of Adam's descendants, however great and horrible they may be, equal to or even greater than his sin. His nature fell more seriously to the extent that it stood more sublimely. That nature was such that it was able not to die if it refused to sin; that nature was such that it did not have within itself the discord between the flesh and the spirit; that nature was such that it did not struggle against any defects of its own, not because it yielded to them, but because there were no defects in it. You ought, then, to make the sins of his descendants equal to his sin, if you can find in them a nature like his, but you ought to declare those sins even greater if you can find in them a better nature than his.

(10) The fall of a rational nature is, of course, worse to the extent that its nature is better, and its sin is more worthy of condemnation to the extent it is more incredible. The fall of the angel was irreparable precisely because more is asked

from one to whom more is given.[123] The more the angel had in the goodness of its nature, the more it owed to willing obedience. Hence, the angel was punished for not doing what it ought so that, destined even for eternal punishments, it cannot now even will to do that. But in so many of his descendants that no one can count them, Adam is set free from everlasting punishment by the grace of God through Jesus Christ our Lord,[124] and he was set free in his own person, though so many thousands of years after his death, when Christ, having died for us, descended to the regions of the dead, not out of necessity, but by his power, and destroyed the pains of hell.[125] (11) For we should understand that in that way Wisdom delivered him from his sin,[126] for the Church rightly believes that through the holy flesh of the only Son of God of which he was the first parent, the father of the human race and, in that way, the father of Christ, who became a man for the salvation of human beings, was then set free from those chains, not by his merit, but by the grace of God through Jesus Christ our Lord.[127]

God, then, imputed to the first Adam this sin from which he was free to hold back, but the first Adam himself had so excellent a nature, because it was not damaged, that his sin was far greater than the sins of the others to the degree that he was far better than the others. Hence, his punishment, which immediately followed upon his sin, was also seen to be so great that he was immediately also held subject to the necessity of dying, though it had been in his power not to die. And he was immediately cast out from that place of great happiness and immediately forbidden access to the tree of life. (12) But when this happened, the human race was in his loins. Hence, in accord with those previously mentioned natural laws of propagation, which are quite hidden, but very powerful, it followed that those who were in his loins and were destined to enter this world through concupiscence of the flesh were condemned at the same time, just as it followed that those who were in the loins of Abraham by that law of propagation and by the nature of the seed paid the tithe at the same time.

All the children, then, of Adam were in him infected by the contagion of sin and bound by the condition of death. And for this reason, although they are little ones and do nothing either good or evil by their will, they, nonetheless, contract from him the guilt of sin and the punishment of death, because they have been clothed by that one who sinned with the will. In the same way the little ones who are clothed with Christ receive from him a share in righteousness and the reward of everlasting life, though they have done nothing good by their will. (13) In that way Christ is revealed to be by way of contrast the pattern of the one to come;[128] on this account the same apostle says, *Just as we have put on the image of the earthly man, so let us also put on the image of the one who comes from heaven* (1 Cor 15:49). Since this is so, let whoever dares to say that those who are reborn are not clothed with the righteousness and life of the second Adam say that those who are born are not clothed with the sin and death of the first Adam, even though these latter did not commit a sin from which they were free to hold back, and those former do not do works of righteousness which they are free to do.

How Could Adam's Sin Have Caused Such Harm?

23. JUL. (1) "That sin, then, which changed the man himself for the worse in paradise, because it is much greater than we can judge, is contracted by everyone who is born."[129] Who told you that the sin of Adam was much greater than that of Cain? Much greater than the sin of the people of Sodom? Much more monstrous, finally, than your sin and that of Mani? Surely there is no occasion for such nonsense in the history. The command was given that he should refrain from eating from one tree; a rustic, inexperienced, careless man, without experience of fear and without the example of righteousness, at the suggestion of the woman, he took the food whose sweetness and attractiveness had tempted him. Look, here is the transgression of the commandment. One transgression was committed from among the others which the desires of sinners carried out at different times. It was not something more than when the people of Israel ate forbidden animals. (2) The grounds for the accusation of the sin, after all, hardly lay in the quality of the apple, but in the transgression of the commandment. What, then, did Adam do that you charge that his sin exceeded the estimation of human beings? Or perhaps you suppose that Adam sinned gravely because by his eating the apple he injured the substance of your God, if you understand this sin too in accord with the mysteries of Mani. For Mani restrains people's hands from plucking apples and all growing things for fear of injuring a part of his God which he thinks is enclosed in barks and grasses.

Oh what madness! "Because that sin is much greater than we can judge," he says, "it is contracted by everyone who is born." (3) Was, therefore, eating the apple when it was forbidden a worse crime than to stab to death holy Abel out of fratricidal envy, a worse crime than to violate the laws of hospitality and of sexuality in Sodom, a worse crime than, when they were already under the law, to sacrifice their children to the demons, a worse crime, finally, than to subject innocents conscious of no act of the will, the newly made work of God, to the kingdom of the devil and to join them to his merits? Was it worse than to accuse God of injustice, than to ascribe the dignity of marriage to the prince of darkness, and, finally, to consider little ones worse than all the wicked, than all pirates, because they are brought to birth through the pleasure of their parents?

(4) I do not make this up, but simply infer it. You, of course, said that that sin was greater and grander than all crimes so that nothing could be equal to its guilt. You, however, claim that little ones arrive full of this evil which is so great that it outweighs all the vices. We have, therefore, understood quite well that they sur-

passed all criminals in their condemnation to the extent that they shared in a greater sin.

AUG. (1) You quoted my words from my book as if to refute them, if you could, where I said, "That sin, then, which changed the man himself for the worse in paradise, because it is much greater than we can judge, is contracted by everyone who is born."[130] On account of them you ask who told me that the sin of Adam was much greater than Cain's, much greater even than the sin of the people of Sodom. I, of course, did not express this in my words, but you understood them in that way. I said, after all, that that sin is greater than we can judge; I did not say that it was greater than the sin of Cain or of the people of Sodom. The wrongful taking of the forbidden apple, after all, undoubtedly exceeded all human judgments because it was punished so that the nature, which did not have to die, was subjected to the necessity of dying. (2) To eat the fruit forbidden by the law of God, of course, seems to be a slight sin, but from the greatness of the punishment one can see well enough how serious he judged it to be who cannot be mistaken.

The sin of Cain, his brother's killer, is seen by all as immense, and it is agreed that it is a horrible crime. And if it is compared through human judgment, as you do, to the fruit which it was wrong to pluck, the comparison will be judged ridiculous. The killer of his brother, although destined to die at some point, was not, nonetheless, punished by the death with which such crimes are often redressed by human judgments. God, of course, said to him, *You shall work the earth, and it will not continue to give you its strength; groaning and trembling you shall exist on the earth* (Gn 4:12 LXX). And when he heard that the earth would not give him its fruit in accord with his labor and that he would be miserable on it with groans and trembling, he was more shaken by the fear of death lest anyone should do to him what he had done to his brother. Hence, God put a mark on him so that no one who came upon him would kill him.[131]

(3) Here the sin was again great, and the punishment light, but this seems so in the judgments of human beings who do not know these mysteries and who cannot measure the sins of human beings with as clear and complete a judgment as God. The people of Sodom were surely destroyed by a punishment fitting their actions when fire came down from heaven upon that land.[132] But there were little ones in Sodom too, pure and free from all contagion of sin, according to your defense of them. And yet, the just and merciful God did not rescue beforehand through the ministry of the angels so many of his innocent images from the fire of Sodom, though it would have been quite easy for him, or he could have made the flames which consumed their parents harmless for them, just as the almighty did for those three young men in the furnace.[133]

(4) Consider these events; ponder them carefully and piously. And when you see in this world little ones along with adults equally subject to such miseries as could in no way have existed in the paradise of God if no one had sinned, ac-

knowledge original sin and the just yoke upon the children of Adam from the day they emerge from the womb of their mother.[134] Do not weigh them down more by your defense, by denying to the ill or to the dead Christ who heals and restores to life.

For, if you ask who told me how great a sin Adam committed, it is the same one who also spoke to you. But if you have ears to hear, you will hear him. You will, however, have them if you do not attribute those ears of yours to your choice, but receive them from the one who said, *I will give you a heart for knowing me and ears for hearing* (Bar 2:31). Who, after all, except one who lacks such ears, fails to hear the scripture speaking without any obscurity or ambiguity to the first human being: *You are earth, and you will return into the earth* (Gn 3:19)? (5) There it is clearly shown that he would not also have died in the flesh; that is, he would not have by the death of his flesh returned to the earth from which his flesh had been taken, if he had not merited to hear and suffer this on account of his sin. For this reason the apostle said afterwards, *The body is indeed dead on account of sin* (Rom 8:10).

Who except one who does not have such ears would fail to hear God speaking about Adam himself, *Let him not at some time stretch out his hand, take, and eat from the tree of life, and live forever* (Gn 3:22)? *And the Lord dismissed him from the paradise of pleasure* (Gn 3:23), where he would, of course, have lived forever without labor and pain. We should, of course, think of that pleasure of paradise, not in terms of shamefulness, but of blessedness, as you must admit if you have not already forgotten that you are Christians. (6) This, then, was the punishment which Adam merited, namely, that he would not live forever, and he was for this reason dismissed from the place of such great blessedness where, if he stayed and had not sinned, he would undoubtedly have lived forever. We ought to understand that the sin which deserved to be redressed by that punishment was as great as the punishment. What, then, are you doing, I ask, when you try to minimize the sin of Adam with such insistence, except accusing of brutal and horrible savagery God who punished this sin—I do not mean: with such severity, but with such cruelty? If it is unspeakable to think this of God, why do you not measure the magnitude of the sin, about which human beings cannot judge, by the greatness of the punishment, under the judgment of the incomparably just judge? And why do you not hold back your tongue from your sacrilegious wordiness?

(7) I, however, do not accuse God of injustice, for I say his yoke is just upon the children of Adam from the day they emerge from the womb of their mother.[135] But you, rather, make God unjust, for you suppose that they suffer this without any merit of any sin whatever. I say that those who are born of the first man are under the power of the enemy, not on account of the work which God produced, but on account of the defect which the same enemy implanted in them,

unless they are reborn in the second man. In their case you accuse the Catholic Church of the crime of lèse majesté if, as you say, the little ones are not rescued from the power of darkness when they are baptized and when, before they are baptized, the Church, nonetheless, subjects so many images of God to exorcism and exsufflation.

I do not ascribe the dignity of marriage to the prince of darkness, for I absolve it of all harm from sexual desire, if marriage makes good use of it for procreation. (8) But you do not shrink from locating in paradise the evil by which the flesh has desires opposed to the spirit, that is, in a place of such great peace, such great rest, such great goodness, and such great happiness. Nor do I judge that little ones who have only original sin are, as your slanders have it, worse than criminals and evildoers. It is, after all, one thing to be weighed down by a sin committed by oneself; it is quite another to be tainted by the infection of another's sin, however great. For this reason, little ones more easily approach the forgiveness of sins, as the Punic Cyprian, your punishment, says,[136] because they are forgiven, not their own sins, but the sins of another.[137] But when you say that little ones not only have not committed any sin by their own will—which we also say—but also that they have not contracted any sin from their origin, you undoubtedly make God unjust who imposed upon them a heavy yoke from the day they emerged from the womb of their mother.[138] We have already said this to you many times and must say even more often.

(9) In order, of course, that you may understand how the little ones born of Adam are both bound by a share in the sin of that man and are, nonetheless, not equal to him in guilt, pay attention to Christ who, as you read, is the pattern of the one to come,[139] and see how the little ones come to be reborn in him and partakers of his righteousness, though you do not dare to make them equal to him in merits. In the second book of this work of yours you too said that the pattern of sin in Adam was not the first, because Eve sinned before him, but was the greatest, just as in Christ the form of righteousness was not the first, but the greatest, because there were righteous persons even before him. If you had not forgotten that you had said this, you would not here minimize the sin of Adam, in whom you admitted the great pattern of sin existed.

Inherited Sin Attacks God as Well as Innocence

24. JUL. But why should anyone feel hatred for you because of your hostility toward innocence, since the impudent fury of your foul mouth is not bridled even by respect for the divinity? For you accuse the little ones, but accuse them along with God; you assail innocence, but do so with injury to justice. You deny the truth, but do so with criminal charges against him whom you call your God.

And for this reason, even if we were lacking the help of reason, the inheritance of sin would collapse readily enough because of the deformity of its supporters.

AUG. (1) Your abusive verbosity has raised as an objection against me the fury of a foul mouth. Do I defend and praise sexual desire? Have I dared to bestow even the possession of paradise on the concupiscence of the flesh by which the flesh has desires opposed to the spirit? Into that place of such beauty and peace you have introduced at once either the war by which one laudably resists this concupiscence when it impels one toward sin or the disgrace by which one shamefully yields to it. Why, then, do you rise up against me with such contempt and not see yourself? For I do not accuse God, but you do when you say that little ones upon whom God imposed a heavy yoke contract no sin from their origin. (2) Nor do I assail innocence along with injury to justice, but you do injury to justice, when you say that little ones have such great innocence, and yet, if justice knew what you hold were true, it would not punish them with a heavy yoke. I neither deny the truth, nor do I bring criminal charges against God; it is you, rather, who do so. After all, the apostle spoke the truth, *The body is dead on account of sin* (Rom 8:10), a point which you deny. But how do you not bring criminal charges against God, when you attribute to him the miseries of little ones which you cannot deny, though they have no original sin deserving of such misery? And for this reason your conclusion which attributes deformity to us does not follow from the truth of any reason.

More Sins against Understanding than Syllables

25. JUL. (1) But why do we think that we should follow the path of the truth all alone with our head so bowed, while the troops of our enemies rest their case upon the dangers of the world and rise up against us, defended by the support of sufferings? From the shame of intercourse, from the pain of childbirth, and from the sweat of labor, he, of course, wants to prove the transferral of sins and punishments into the seeds so that from these signs, namely, of difficult births, of sweating farmers, and of fields full of thorns, people would believe in natural sin, by whose merit the human race, which certain people think was made mortal by Adam's sin, is tested by so many difficulties. I said, "certain people," because Augustine, their leader, was in fact embarrassed to say this. Hence, he writes to Marcellinus that Adam is seen to have been created mortal, but with his customary eloquence he adds that death was the wages of sin, and he declares that Adam who he admits by nature was created mortal was not able to die.[140]

(2) Those statements found in Genesis by which Adam and Eve are chastised are, therefore, often brought forth against us, and it is now time to discuss them. Genesis says, *The Lord God said to the serpent: Because you did this, you will be cursed by all the cattle and by all the beasts which are on the earth. You will*

move on your chest and belly, and you will eat the earth all the days of your life. And I shall set enmities between you and the woman and between your seed and her seed. She will crush your head, and you will grasp her heel. But to the woman he said: I shall greatly multiply your sorrows and your groaning; in sorrow you shall bear children, and you will turn to your husband, and he will rule over you. But to Adam he said: Because you listened to the words of your wife and ate from the tree about which I commanded you that from it alone you should not eat, the earth will be cursed in your works. In sorrow you will eat from it all the days of your life; it will bring forth thorns and thistles for you, and you will eat the crops of your field. In the sweat of your brow you will eat your bread until you return to the earth from which you were taken, for you are earth and you will return to the earth (Gn 3:14-19).*

(3) You, then, take these sentences as evidence of inborn sinfulness, and you proclaim that women would not have suffered in childbirth if the sufferings of that fecundity were not passed on to them along with Eve's sin. You, therefore, want the very punishment to be a proof of the sin so that no woman is believed to experience without the same sinfulness what the first woman merited by her sin. For, you say, there would not be pain in childbirth if there were not sin in the newborn. I cannot easily measure how astonished I am to encounter these ideas. For your opinion on this passage has aroused such reaction that I scarcely deign to enter the fray; there are, of course, in these objections more sins against understanding than there are syllables.

AUG. (1) However glibly and cleverly you mock or pretend to mock the sufferings of the human race, they have driven you into such difficulties that you are forced to maintain that the paradise of God would have been filled with sufferings, even if no one had sinned. But even if out of shame you are unwilling to do this, you are pressed by your teaching to do so, and unless you have corrected yourself and cast aside this teaching, you will not escape these difficulties which overwhelm you and shove you over a horrible precipice. You are, after all, asked where you think these sufferings come from which we see in both adults and in little ones. According to your teaching you reply that the human race was created this way by God from its beginning. Your reply receives this response: They would have existed, then, in paradise if no sin had come to be there. At this point you will either fall headlong or change your teaching, either destroyed by your impudence or corrected in your thinking.

(2) For you will either fill the place of the most renowned happiness with a life of suffering, and then you will not find eyes with which you would dare to face any Christians. Or, having been hurled into more horrible pits, you will ascribe these sufferings of the human being to an alien nature mixed in with us, and then you will be swallowed up by the hellish depth of Mani. Or you will admit that this punishment of suffering has come from our damaged nature under the

judgment of God who imposes it, and then you will revive in the fresh air of the Catholic faith.

But you also say that "certain people think that the human race was made mortal by the sin of Adam," and you add that you said, "certain people," because I, their leader, would be embarrassed to say this, though I wrote to Marcellinus that Adam was seen to have been created mortal. Those who have read or read these words of yours and those of mine see, of course, if they are not Pelagians, how your tongue has committed itself to treachery. (3) For I never held, and I absolutely never said, as you people say, that Adam was created mortal and that he was destined to die whether he sinned or did not sin. These words were, of course, raised as an objection to Caelestius in the episcopal court in Carthage. These words were raised as an objection to Pelagius in the episcopal court in Palestine.[141] This is the question at issue between you and us, namely, whether Adam was going to die whether he sinned or did not sin. Who, after all, does not know that according to the definition by which a person is said to be immortal who cannot die, but is said to be mortal who can die, Adam was able to die, because he was able to sin, and he was, therefore, able to die by the merit of sin, not by the necessity of nature? But according to that definition by which a person is said to be immortal in whose power it is not to die, who would deny that Adam was created with this power? For one who had the power of never sinning certainly had the power of never dying.

(4) That, then, is what we say against you, namely, that this teaching of yours by which you suppose that Adam was going to die whether he sinned or did not sin is utterly false. Since this is so, how would I ever say what you falsely said that I said, namely, that Adam was created mortal by nature, as if he were burdened with the necessity of dying, though he could be forced into death only on account of sin? Or how do I declare that he had been unable to die, though I know that he did die, and he certainly would not have died if he had been unable to die? But I clearly declare that he was able not to die. It is, however, one thing not to be able to die, and quite another thing to be able not to die. The former is a greater form of immortality; the latter a lesser form. If you distinguish these two, you see both what you say about Adam and what we say in opposition to you. For you say: Whether he sinned or did not sin, he was going to die; we, however, say: As long as he did not sin, he was not going to die. And if he never had sinned, he would not have died.

(5) Next you quote those words from Genesis which are often cited against you, and concerning the pain of childbirth, the punishment by which Eve was first punished, you say something which you want people to think we say or which you think we say. For we do not say that women were not going to suffer the pains of childbirth, unless the suffering of that fecundity had been passed on to them along with Eve's sin. For there was passed on to them not the suffering of fecundity, but of sinfulness. For, although their fecundity became painful, it was

sinfulness, not fecundity that did this. The suffering of the mother in childbirth came from human sinfulness, but the fecundity came from the blessing of God.

(6) Or, if you did not want the suffering of fecundity to be understood in the sense that fecundity caused it, but in the sense that it received it, this is our position. But we do not say that even in paradise women would have suffered pain in giving birth; in fact, we infer that this pain is the punishment of sin from the fact that it would not have existed in that place where anyone who sinned would not be allowed to remain. You do not try to refute this without being forced, with your hand over your face and your eyes closed, to fill the paradise of God not only with the sexual desires, but also with the torments of human beings. But why is this a surprise? For you want to fill that place of memorable happiness even with the deaths of human beings, none or hardly any of which occur without some torment of the body. And though your teaching forces you to utter these monstrosities, you dare, moreover, to mock those who do not say these things—and heaven forbid that they should! For they hold instead the teaching of the Church of God handed down from antiquity which says, *The beginning of sin was caused by the woman, and on account of her we all die* (Sir 25:33). (7) Contrary to your knowledge and your conscience you insultingly call me their leader. For you are absolutely not unaware of how many great men, men who were taught in the Church and were teachers of the Church, said before us that the nature of the man was created by God so that, if he had not sinned, he would not have died. How, then, am I called the leader of these men whom I do not lead, but follow? But I do not say that you are the leader of those who claim that Adam was created mortal so that, whether he sinned or did not sin, he was going to die. And in that way these people try to fill with the torments of the dying, with the funerals of the dead, and with the grieving of mourners the paradise of holy pleasure where there was such great rest for soul and body. You are not their leader; Pelagius and Caelestius, who said these things first, hold the leadership in this unspeakable teaching. I wish that, as you do not lead them, so you would not follow them!

The Pains of Childbirth Are Natural, Not Penal

26. JUL. (1) How insane is your first statement that the pain of childbirth follows upon sin, since it so clearly has to do with the condition of the sexes rather than the punishment of sins! For all animals suffer these pangs and these groans in giving birth, though they are stained by no sin. From this it is clear that what can be found even without sin is not a proof of sin. Then you go on and raise another point far more foolish. A woman, you say, would not feel pain if she did not have a share in sins. But then you add there: This sin, however, on account of which the woman feels pain is not found in the mother, but in the newborn.

(2) For baptized women, as you say, live free from sin, but even they are afflicted with the difficulties of their bearing children because of the sinfulness of the children which they bear. According to this view the transmission of sin does not go from the mother to the child, but flows back upon the parents from the newborn. For, if a baptized woman feels pains because sins are found in the little one, the transmission of sin begins from below, not from above. Or[142] is she not tormented because her child has sin, but because she brought it along with her when she was born? You, however, said that this evil was taken from her by grace. If, then, the pain of childbirth was attached to the sin, the removal of the sin ought to have remedied the torment of childbirth. Or if this torment which is found in women even after baptism cannot exist without sin, their sinfulness is also not taken away by grace, and the ceremony of baptism has been cheapened. (3) If, however, there was in these mysteries that power and truth which we believe, not which you imagine, and if all sin has been taken away, though the pain still remains which is caused by the difficulty of giving birth, it is clear that these groans are a mark of nature, not of sin. For, as you agree, even those women suffer them who you admit were set free from the sin of the Manichees.[143]

Moreover, the same point is evident from concrete examples alone. But if we also look at the words of God's statement, it will surely dispel your clouds by a brightness more radiant than the rays of the sun. He, of course, did not say to the woman: Pains will come to be in you, or, I shall cause you groans, so that the experience of them would be seen to be produced after the sin. Rather, he said, *I shall greatly increase your sorrows* (Gn 3:16). He shows that there already exists in the plan of nature what he promises not to create, but to increase in the sinful person. Only things already existing are ever multiplied; before they exist, they are properly said to come to be, but it is too early to say that they are increased.

(4) Finally, so that you do not think this comes from us rather than from the truth itself, this order of the words is preserved in the case of all living beings. God says about the man before he was created, *Let us make man to our image and likeness* (Gn 1:26), and again of the woman, *God said: It is not good for the man to be alone; let us make him a helper like to him* (Gn 2:18). But after they were made, *He blessed them, saying: Increase and multiply, and fill the earth* (Gn 1:28). Before they were created, scripture did not say: Let them be multiplied, but: Let them be made. After they existed so that they could be increased, it logically adds: *Increase and multiply, and fill the earth* (Gn 1:28). (5) According to this order, then, the groans of childbirth, which had been created in accord with nature in the bodies of human beings as well as in animals, were not created in Eve, but increased, so that she was afflicted by the special greatness of the pains inflicted upon her. And yet, they would not affect the women of a later age except in a natural moderateness and in accord with their different bodies.

In Eve's case, then, the result of sin was not that the woman suffered pain in childbirth, but that she suffered excessively, just as we read that in different times bodily illnesses also happened to certain people because of sins, but that increase of miseries did not destroy the moderateness of the natural amount. And yet, not everything contained in that statement is included under the vigor of God's punishment. (6) But one part indicates merit; another points to duty. It says, *I shall greatly multiply your sorrows and your groaning; in sorrow you will bear children* (Gn 3:16). Up to this point there is the punishment which was merited, not by Eve's nature, but by her person. From here it simply indicates the function of the second sex; it says, *You will turn to your husband, and he will rule over you* (Gn 3:16). This certainly does not have to do with punishment, for, if it did, it would imply sin; that a wife is subject to her husband with proper affection is a matter of order, not a punishment. For, according to the apostle, *The man is the head of the woman* (Eph 5:23), because *the man was not created for the woman, but the woman for the man* (1 Cor 11:9). If, then, she shows respect for her head with proper reverence, she observes the laws of nature; she does not suffer the torments of sin. But if she rebels against that order, she is guilty. It does not, then, pertain to misery to carry out a duty, the neglect of which is wrong.

AUG. (1) We say that the pain of childbirth is the punishment of sin. For we know that God said this without any ambiguity and said it only to the transgressor of his commandment and said it only because he was angry that his commandment had been transgressed. But in order to render meaningless and frustrate this anger of God, you said that this is so far from being the punishment of sin that animals which have no sins suffer such pains and groans in giving birth. The animals did not tell you whether these mournful sounds were sounds of their singing or of their suffering. We see that chickens, of course, about to lay an egg seem to be singing rather than suffering, but after having laid an egg they often emit such sounds as they do in fear. But while they are laying an egg, they are in absolute silence, like doves and other birds, which are well known to the observant. (2) Who, then, knows with regard to speechless animals that cannot indicate what is happening in them whether at the time of giving birth their movement and their sounds not only do not involve any pain, but even involve some pleasure? But why is it up to me to search out the secrets of nature on this question, since our case does not depend on them? If, of course, speechless animals suffer no pain in giving birth, your argument comes to nothing, but if they do suffer, that itself is a punishment for the image of God to be set on a par with the animals. The punishment of the image of God, however, could not be just if sin did not come first.

Heaven forbid, however, that I should say what you thought you should refute as if I say this, namely, that, when a mother gives birth, she suffers pain, not because of her own merit, but because of that of the baby, and that for this reason, even after their sins have been forgiven, believing mothers suffer pain when the need to give birth is upon them. Heaven forbid, I repeat, that I should say this. (3) After all, does the fact that we say that death is the punishment of sin mean that we must say that it ought not to occur after the forgiveness of sins? These sufferings, which we call the punishments of sin in our nature damaged by transgression, remain even after the forgiveness of sins in order to test our faith which we hold about the world to come in which these evils will not exist. For we would not have faith if we believed because we would immediately be given the reward of having no suffering and of not dying. When this reason is given, that is, that the evils contracted by sin are left to us for the contest of faith, even though the guilt of the sins has been already removed by baptism, what power do your words have? You said, "If in the mysteries all sin has been taken away, though the pain still remains which is caused by the difficulty of giving birth, it is clear that these groans are a mark of nature, not of sin." (4) For you would not, of course, make this statement which has no power against us, if you either possessed or noticed the power of the faith which is mightier to the extent that we hope more for those things which we do not see and look forward to the fullness of happiness through the suffering of these miseries.[144]

But the very words of God, you say, where he did not say: "Pains will come to be in you, or: I shall cause you groans, so that the experience of them would be seen to be produced after the sin, but he said: *I shall greatly increase your sorrows* (Gn 3:16), show that there already existed in the plan of nature what he promises not to create, but to increase in the sinful person." And you add as a definitive and universal statement: "Only things already existing are ever multiplied; before they exist, they are properly said to come to be, but it is too early to say that they are increased."

(5) Here I ask you first of all how you can claim that the pains of Eve which she had not yet suffered were already in existence? How, I ask, did she who was suffering nothing already have pains? But if no pains existed in her, because she who was not suffering did not have them, even those pains which did not exist could be multiplied, and we understand the statement correctly, *I shall multiply your sorrows* (Gn 3:16), in the sense that I shall make them to be many. For this can be done whether something has already begun to exist or has not yet begun to exist. You, therefore, said to no point: "Only things already existing are ever multiplied," because, see, in Eve there were multiplied after the sin pains which did not exist at all before she sinned. (6) And for this reason God said, *I shall multiply your sorrows* (Gn 3:16), not because some sorrows had already begun to exist in her, but because they were going to be many once they began to exist.

"But they existed," you say, "in the plan of nature." If, then, there already exist in the plan of nature things which have not yet come to be, how do your words help you? You said, "God did not say: Pains will come to be in you, but, *I shall multiply your sorrows* (Gn 3:16), because they already existed in the plan of nature." For our answer to you is: He could have said: They will come to be in you, because he was going to multiply those pains which already existed in the plan of nature, but which had not yet come to be. Or are you perhaps going to say: They had, of course, already come to be in the plan of nature? (7) How much more clearly and credibly we say to you: The children of Adam were already existing in Adam in the plan of nature when, as blessed John the bishop says, "He committed that great sin and condemned all the human race in common,"[145] or as his colleague, Ambrose, says, "Adam existed, and we all existed in him; Adam perished, and all perished in him."[146]

For you dare to say not only: They already existed, but you also dare to say, something we do not dare to say of the children of Adam at the time the sin was committed: The pains of Eve had already come to be when God threatened that he would multiply them. Though it is necessary that mothers suffer pains in childbirth, Eve's pains, nonetheless, were not already in the plan of nature, because it was not necessary that she should suffer them when she began to give birth to children. They, of course, came upon her because of the condemnation of her sin, not because of the condition of nature. (8) In denying this what do you do but locate, even though no one sins, the torments of human beings in the place of that happiness where the human beings who already had to suffer torments were not permitted to be? I do not know the impudence with which you do this except that it somehow pleases you who are opposed to paradise to dwell opposite to it. For, when Adam was cast out of paradise, he too was placed opposite to it.[147]

Now, then, see with how much nonsense you argue against paradise, once you have been placed opposite to it. For you think that only those things which already exist to some degree are multiplied, while before they exist, you think that they should not be said to be multiplied, but come to be. No things come into being as multiple unless they are multiplied, that is, made multiple by additions. (9) And for this reason the Spirit who in Wisdom is said to be multiple,[148] though he did not begin to be, but was such from eternity, is not correctly called multiple, because no additions made him multiple.

Also, what are you going to say about God's reply to Abraham, where he says, *I shall greatly multiply your offspring like the stars of heaven* (Gn 22:17)? There we see that God multiplied the stars of heaven as he promised that he would multiply the offspring of Abraham. In order that the stars of heaven might be multiplied, did they, then, first begin to exist as fewer? And were they not created multiple in their number from the time they were created? Why, then, do you not in this sense accept the words, *I shall greatly multiply your sorrows* (Gn 3:16), as if God had said: I shall make your sorrows multiple? You are doing this only in order to introduce pains, if you can, into the paradise to which you are placed opposite and in order to preach that miseries were created in the place of such great happiness before the sin.

(10) For you call it a natural moderateness that Eve, as you claim, naturally received childbirth accompanied by pains before she sinned, and you do not want people to see that this natural moderateness was destroyed by that increase as a result of the penalty which was added to the woman as God's punishment when she had sinned. For these are your words: "But that increase of miseries did not destroy the moderateness of the natural amount." Hence, according to your teaching, the fact that women suffer moderate pains in childbirth is a natural moderateness, but what was added for Eve by the merit of sin is an increase of miseries.

You do not see, when you say these things, that, if her miseries were increased by sin, they were already established by nature, and the woman, whose miseries were increased by the merit of sin, was already naturally unhappy before the sin. (11) Though you say that she was moderately unhappy with a natural moderateness, you admit, nonetheless, whether you like it or not, that she was surely already unhappy before that increase when you say that an increase of miseries was added to her. See what human nature as originally created by God gains from you; see what the paradise of God gains from you. For cast out and placed opposite to it, you have in your opposition paid back such services that you said that in the place of happiness the miseries established by God did not begin to be, but were increased because of sins.

What are so opposite as unhappiness is to happiness and happiness to unhappiness? Or what does it mean that the sinner, having been excluded from paradise, is placed opposite to paradise, if not that he is placed in unhappiness which is opposite to happiness without anyone's opposition or doubt? And what does nature flee from as it flees from unhappiness? What does it desire as it desires happiness?

(12) Finally, the free choice which we have with regard to happiness is so naturally implanted in us that no unhappiness can take away from us the fact that we do not will to be unhappy and that we will to be happy. This is so true that even those who are unhappy because they live bad lives do, of course, will to live bad lives, but do not, nonetheless, will to be unhappy, but happy. This is the free choice unchangeably fixed in our minds, not that by which we will to act well, for we were able to lose this by human sinfulness and we are able to recover it by God's grace, but the free choice by which we will to be happy and do not will to be unhappy, and neither the unhappy nor the happy can lose it. We all, of course, want to be happy, as even the philosophers of this world and the Academics who doubt all things were forced to admit, as Tully their patron testifies;[149] they said that this is the only thing that does not need an argument because there is no one who does not desire it. (13) This free choice is helped by the grace of God so that by living well we can have what we naturally want, that is, to live happily.

And you say that miseries, though moderate ones, miseries, nonetheless, opposed to happiness, as no one denies, no one doubts, were established naturally in the first works of God without the sin of anyone coming first. As a result, the punishment of the sinful woman, on account of which it was said, *I shall greatly multiple your sorrows* (Gn 3:16), is not the beginning of miseries which, as you say, already existed in nature, but the increase of miseries which was added as a punishment.

Why should I deal with you now about the following words of God where, after he said what refers to punishment, *I shall greatly multiple your sorrows,* he added, *And you will turn to your husband, and he will rule over you* (Gn 3:16)? (14) What need is there for me to argue with you about whether this ruling of the husband is a punishment of the woman or the order of nature? God, nonetheless, did not mention this order when he created her, but when he punished her. But, as I said, what need is there for me to delay over this since, whichever is true, it does not hamper our case?

God, of course, would have suddenly turned from the punishment he inflicted upon the woman to commanding, and he would have said as a command, not as a condemnation, *You will turn to your husband, and he will rule over you* (Gn 3:16). (15) What does this have to do with the question we are discussing about the punishment of the sinful woman? I am dealing with you about the miseries which you, having been cast out of paradise and set opposite to it, try to locate in paradise, and you attribute them, not to the merits of sinners, but to God the creator of natures, as if he naturally established them, while your sense of shame perishes and your lips utter blasphemy. Tell me now what you are trying to persuade us of concerning the punishment of the man, since it is now clear enough how this woman who was naked and not ashamed has stripped you naked and put you to shame.

Adam Learns of the Comfort of Death's Coming

27. JUL. (1) But let this suffice concerning the woman; let us pass to the duties of the man. It says: *He said to Adam: The earth will be cursed in your works; in sorrow you will eat from it all the days of your life. It will bring forth thorns and thistles for you, and you will eat the crops of your fields. In the sweat of your brow you will eat your bread until you return to the earth from which you were taken, for you are earth and you will return to the earth* (Gn 3:17-19). Here it did not say: I shall multiply your thorns or your sweat. Rather, they are mentioned as if they were then first created. But God's hatred of the man is dispelled just as easily as that of his wife. To begin with, it is not the offspring of the man, but the soil that is cursed: *In your works,* it says, *the earth will be cursed* (Gn 3:17). Since the fields certainly could have nothing from Adam by way of inheritance,

how did they merit to receive the reproach of a curse for the sin of another's will? (2) Or was it in order to teach by the example of the very turf that there could be a curse where there was no guilt? For, if the sin is found in the man and the curse in the crops, it is clear that sins do not always go together with penalties. If, then, the earth is cursed in order that he who sinned may be afflicted, sinfulness is still not found where the curse is found.

Why would it not, nonetheless, follow, given that condition, that the newborn are not wretched because they are found guilty, even if we were taught that some sufferings of our nature were introduced after the sin of the first human being? Rather, by recalling the first sin, their subsequent affliction indicated to those whom it did not make guilty a warning against evil imitation. (3) For even the earth is shown to have borne the insult of a curse in order to denounce the evil of another's will, not to bring about a share in a sin of its own. Or are we perhaps to believe that the earth was dearer to God than innocence so that he does not allow the sod to be polluted by another's crime, but does permit that infancy be accused?

The curse, then, is directed toward the earth, nor does the curse itself remain veiled. For the scripture explains the goal toward which such a sentence is directed or the sense in which the earth is said to be cursed. It says, *In sorrow you will eat from it all the days of your life* (Gn 3:17). (4) Notice, then, how it is explained. The earth is said to be cursed, not so that someone might be able to take precautions against it; rather, this term reveals the opinion of a saddened state of mind. For, since he knew that the earth was barren on account of the merits of its cultivator, the weariness of the hungry worker ascribed to the earth what he had himself merited, and in his affliction he called it "cursed," though its richness was kept from him in order that that transgressor would admit that it was not his nature or the earth, but his own will and person which were subject to the curse.

God said, *It will bring forth thorns and thistles for you* (Gn 3:18). He was not content to say, *It will bring forth thorns and thistles,* but he added, *for you.* Among the other plants the earth had, of course, under God's command previously brought forth thornbushes, but at that point God promised that the earth would produce more thorns than usual so that the man would feel their pricks. This was able to chastise Adam greatly, since after the fountains and meadows of paradise even one thornbush could have offended him.

(5) *In the sweat,* however, *of your brow you will eat your bread.* I do not quite see how this pertains to suffering, since it is even a natural benefit that the limbs of workers are refreshed by sweat. But the passage itself testified that the work of farming was imposed on him before the sin. For it reads as follows: *And the Lord God took the man whom he made and placed him in paradise to work it and keep it* (Gn 2:15). If, then, even in paradise God did not want him to take his food entirely without work, but by the command to work stirred up the industry with

which he had endowed him, what new condition are we to believe befell him if he who experienced toil felt the sweat?

But there follows: *Until you return to the earth from which you were taken, for you are earth and you will return to the earth* (Gn 3:19). (6) This last part of his sentence, of course, like that of the woman, has to do with information, not punishment; on the contrary, as the facts indicate, it comforts the man with the promise of an end. After all, since it had previously mentioned the pains, labor, and sweat, which nature had experienced and which the person experienced in a greater amount, the indication of an end mitigates the suffering so that this would not seem to go on forever. It is as if it said: But you will not suffer this forever, but only *until you return to the earth from which you were taken, for you are earth and you will return to the earth* (Gn 3:19). Why, after God said, *until you return to the earth from which you were taken,* did he not add: Because you have sinned and transgressed my commandments? After all, he should have said this if the dissolution of our bodies is due to sins. But what did he say? *Because you are earth,* he said, *and you will return to the earth.* He revealed the reason why Adam was going to return to the earth: *Because you are earth,* he says. But God's previous words had disclosed in what sense he was earth; he said, *Because you were taken from the earth.* If, then, God said that this is the reason for returning to the earth, namely, that he had been taken from the earth and if, moreover, the fact that he was taken from it could not have to do with sin, it was undoubtedly not because of sin, but because of his mortal nature that he who was not eternal would face the dissolution of the body.

That barrenness, then, of the trees, that luxuriance of thorns, that increased difficulty of painful birth, were imposed upon human persons, not upon the human race. Then, when Cain and Abel were born, both of one nature, but with different wills, it did not help Cain who sinned voluntarily that the sins of his father did not weigh him down, nor did it harm Abel that his parents had sinned. Rather, each of them by his own judgment revealed by his different choice and different end that he had no natural predetermination either toward virtue or toward vice. (8) They fulfilled the office of priests and offered sacrifices to their God. But though their service was the same, their devotion was different. God's sentence upon them revealed this; for he found Abel's gift acceptable to him, but he disclosed the reason for his indignation toward Cain who was offended when he said that he offered the sacrifice well, but divided it wrongly. Without delay Cain's wicked mind blazed into anger, and crushed by the holiness of his brother, he indulged his hatred by killing his brother. In that way it was made clear at the first opportunity that death is not an evil, because a righteous person was the first of all to inaugurate it. And yet the audacity of the guilty mind did not escape the anger of God. He is questioned about his brother; he is convicted of his crime; he is condemned to punishment, and apart from the fear which hung over him in return for his remarkable cruelty, he was punished by a curse from the earth. (9) God said, *Cursed shall you be by the earth which opened its mouth to receive from your hand the blood of your brother, because you will work the earth, and it will not continue to give you its strength* (Gn 4:11-12).

See, once again the barrenness of the earth is imposed as punishment on its cultivator. Countless torments of this kind are promised in Deuteronomy. So what? Was it because of Cain's fratricide that the thickets of our lands sprung up so that the farmer armed with a sickle watches over them to cut them away? And because you think that every lord of a thorny farmland is subject to the sin which was punished by an abundance of thorns, will you say that all the little ones now have not only eaten apples, though they are born without teeth, but have also shed the blood of Abel? You surely see to what point of madness the inherited sin of the Manichees comes, and since that sin has nothing except insanity, the sobriety of the Catholics laughs at your arguments, but the affection of the same people deplores your downfall.

AUG. (1) Your long and belabored argumentation about the punishment of the first human being does nothing, of course, but minimize his sin by minimizing his punishment, for the sin was condemned by the infliction of this punishment. And you do this on account of those words of my book to which you are replying, the words which you quote as if you were going to refute them. In that book I said, "That sin, then, which changed the man himself for the worse in paradise, because it is much greater than we can judge, is contracted by everyone who is born."[150] In order, then, that the sin might not seem so great that it could change our nature for the worse, you maintain that the punishment which it merited is slight and almost nothing. (2) This is the reason that you twist the words about the earth which was cursed for the works of the transgressor into the depravity of your teaching; this is the reason that you claim that thorns and thistles were created even before the man sinned, though God did not name these among the things he originally created, but uses them as threats in the punishment of the sinner. This is the reason that, in order that it might not quite seem to pertain to suffering, you said that the sweat of the laborer is a natural benefit, namely, so that the limbs of workers might be refreshed by sweat, as if, when he said this, God was not imposing a punishment for sin, but even giving a reward. (3) And yet we would be correct to say this, if you were praising the sweat from labor, as if you were saying that it was created at that point. But now you claim that the man was placed in paradise even before the sin in such a way that he would not be without labor in working the earth, as if that strength without any weakness of the body could not have done work which could have brought delight, not only without labor, but even with the pleasure of the mind.

But you were unable to conceal why you said this; you, of course, speak most openly when you add, "What new condition are we to say befell him if he who experienced the toil felt the sweat?" (4) Has it given you so much pleasure to introduce into that most peaceful place of the blessed not only the sorrows of child-birth in women, but also the sweat of labor in men, that you say nothing new befell the one condemned, though God condemned him? Do you mock and scorn the severity of God so much that you maintain that what he imposed as a punishment was a gift of nature? If you say that nothing new befell the man to whom God said, *In the sweat of your brow you shall eat your bread* (Gn 3:19), deny that God said this while condemning him. Or are you going to say: He did indeed condemn the man with these words, but nothing new befell the man as a result of this? Did God, then, condemn him, but he was not condemned? Was the act of punishing foiled, as if God hurled a spear and was unable to strike the one he wanted? On the contrary, you say, he was condemned, and nothing new befell him.

Here it is difficult to control one's laughter. If, after all, he was condemned and nothing new befell him, he was, therefore, used to being condemned and, for this reason, used to sinning, for he would not have been unjustly condemned. (5) Or since no one doubts that he sinned first at that time, was he used to being un-justly condemned before? After all, you did not admit, as you said regarding the mother giving birth, that at least something new befell to the man so that, as the woman received the pain of childbirth, so the man received the sweat of labor. For in this way, by the addition of something which did not previously exist, you would have conceded that something new had befallen him. But when you say, "What new condition befell him?" whom you admit was condemned, what else do you claim than that he was used to being condemned? Or if we do not say "used to being done," unless we know it has been done repeatedly, you must surely grant that he was at least condemned in that way once before, if you main-tain that nothing new befell him because he was condemned in that way. (6) Here you see the cliffs to which you have drawn near. Pull back, then, from the head-long plunge of your laborious argumentation, and do not introduce labors and pains into the home of happy joys and into the place of ineffable repose.

Why do you also try to inject even the death of the body into paradise so that you say that it was promised, or rather made known, to the sinner as a benefit when God said, *You are earth and you will return to the earth* (Gn 3:19), as if the man did not know that he was created so that he was going to die, whether he sinned or did not sin, and as if God gave him this knowledge when he con-demned him for the sin he had committed? (7) Discussing these words of God, where he says, *In the sweat of your brow you will eat your bread all the days of your life, until you return to the earth from which you were taken, for you are earth and you will return to the earth* (Gn 3:19), you say, "This last part of his sentence, like that of the woman, has to do with information, not punishment; on the contrary, as the facts indicate, it comforts the man. After all, because it had previously mentioned the pains, labor, and sweat which nature had experienced and which the person experienced in a greater amount, the indication of an end mitigates the suffering so that this would not seem to go on forever. It is as if it said: But you will not suffer this forever, but only *until you return to the earth from which you were taken, for you are earth and you will return to the earth.*"

When you say these things, you try to persuade people that the man was, of course, created so that, even if he remained in the uprightness of life in which he was created, he would, nonetheless, have died at some point by the necessity of his mortal nature, but this was not made known to him except at the time of his condemnation so that he would take comfort from the promise of an end and would not think that his suffering would be eternal. Adam, then, would have thought that he was not going to die, if God had not made this known to him. But God would not have made this known to him, if it were not necessary that the sinner be condemned. He would, then, have remained in this error by which he believed that he was eternal or was never going to die, unless by the merit of the sin he had attained the wisdom by which a man knows himself. Do you understand what you are saying?

(9) Take another point. Adam undoubtedly did not know that he was going to die—something that he would, of course, not know unless he sinned, but if he had willed not to sin, he would, nonetheless, have been happy, even though he did not know this, and in believing the opposite of the truth, he would not have been unhappy. Do you hear what you say? Take a third point. If in the time of his righteousness Adam believed that he was not going to die even in the body if he did not violate the commandment of God, but learned that he was going to die when he violated it, we believe what he believed when he was righteous, but you believe what he only merited to know when he lost his righteousness. Our error, then, stands on the side of righteousness, and your wisdom stands on the side of sinfulness. Do you understand what you are saying?

(10) Take a fourth point too. If God did not make known to that man when he was happy and righteous the future death of his body, but made it known to him when he was unhappy and a sinner, it is more appropriate to believe that he wanted to torment him also by the fear of death, judging, of course, that he deserved this torment too. As nature itself cries out, death is feared more than labor; all human beings, of course, would labor in order not to die if such a choice should be presented to them that they would immediately die if they did not labor; how rarely a person is found who would prefer to die rather than to labor. Besides, Adam himself preferred to labor for so many years rather than to end his life and his labor together by not laboring and by dying of hunger.

(11) After all, by what other natural instinct did Cain too fear death more than labor? By what other instinct do judges punish, by judgments that are neither unjust nor inhuman, lesser crimes by work in the mines and greater ones by death? But why are the martyrs praised with such great glory for having died for righteousness, except that it takes greater virtue to scorn death than to scorn labor? On this account the Lord does not say, *No one has greater love* than to labor, but

than to lay down one's life for one's friends (Jn 15:13). If, then, it takes greater love to die than to labor for one's friends, who is so blind as not to see that labor involves a lesser punishment than death? Or if one ought to fear labor more than death, how is our very nature not wretched which fears death more than labor?

(12) And, without considering these points, you say that, when his death was made known to him, the man was consoled at the thought that his labor was not eternal, though, if your teaching were true by which you claim that Adam was going to die even if he did not sin, this ought not to have been made known to him before he began to suffer the punishment of condemnation so that God would not torture him with the fear of death before he sinned. But after he had sinned, when he judged him most deserving of punishment, he would make known to him that he was going to die so that the just God, as an avenger of a sin already committed, would increase the same punishment by the fear of death as well.

(13) Whoever, then, understand in accord with the Catholic faith these words of God by which Adam was punished when God said, *You are earth and you will return to the earth* (Gn 3:19), and do not want to introduce into paradise the death of the body, precisely so as not also to introduce diseases, by the wretched variety of which we see the dying are afflicted, and so as not to be forced to fill with pains, labor, and grief the paradise of holy pleasure and of spiritual and bodily happiness, to which you are not ashamed to be opposed, though you are forced to do this, and you do not find a way to escape as long as you refuse to change your teaching which is so impious. (14) Whoever, then, as I said, accept and understand these words of God in accord with the Catholic faith, just as they see the punishment of labor in the words, *In the sweat of your brow you will eat your bread* (Gn 3:19), so they also see the punishment of death in the words, *Until you return to the earth from which you were taken, for you are earth and will return to the earth* (Gn 3:19). And they accept this statement as if it said: I indeed took you from the earth, and I made you a human being, and I could, of course, have brought it about that the same earth which I made to live would never be forced to lose the life which I gave. But because you are earth, that is, you chose to live according to the flesh which was taken from the earth, not according to me who took you from the earth, you will labor on the earth until you return to it, and you will return to the earth because you are earth. And by a just punishment you will return to the earth out of which you were made because you did not obey the Spirit by whom you were made.

(15) This interpretation is recognized as sound and Catholic precisely because it does not force us to fill the land of the living with deaths and the land of the happy with all the very laborious and very grave evils which human beings suffer in this corruptible body, and when they do not bear them, they are forced to die. For you cannot say that human beings were going to die gentle deaths in paradise if no one had sinned, because this too is against you. For, if at that time

they would have died gentle deaths and now die difficult deaths, human nature was changed by the sin of Adam; when you deny this, you are logically forced to introduce precisely such deaths as now exist into the place of that great happiness and delight. And, for this reason, you are forced to introduce there countless kinds of diseases that are so grave and so intolerable that human beings are driven by them toward death.

(16) If this face of paradise drenches and confounds your faces with some shame, since you do not want to admit that our nature could have been changed by sin, change your views instead, and admit along with the apostle that the body is dead on account of sin.[151] Say along with the Church of God: *The beginning of sin was produced by the woman, and on account of her we all die* (Sir 25:33). Recognize along with the Church of God that *the corruptible body weighs down the soul* (Wis 9:15). For in paradise before the sin the body was not such that it weighed down the soul. Sing along with the Church of God: *Human beings have become like a vanity, and their days pass like a shadow* (Ps 144:4). For one who was made to the likeness of God would not except through sin become like a vanity so that by the passing of time and by the onslaught of death one's days pass like a shadow.

(17) Do not pour out the clouds of your error over the most bright light of the truth; the hearts of the faithful ought not to make bitter the paradise of God which they ought to love. Why does that memorable place of the blessed and of those at peace offend you? Why, I repeat, does it offend you so that with closed eyes, with an impudent face, with a most stubborn mind, and with a most verbose tongue you want to fill it with the deaths of human beings and, through these, to fill it with all the evils with which we see the agonies and needs of the dying abound? You do all this so that you are not forced to admit that through the very great sin of the first man human nature fell into these miseries with which we see the human race is filled from the wailing of little ones to the gasps of those worn out by age? (18) And since you see that it is unjust that the punishment of parents be passed on to their children without the guilt, admit that the guilt is passed on as well.

You tried to minimize, as much as you could, the fact that the guilt of the first man was the greatest, so that no one would think that human nature could have been changed by it. I, therefore, prove that that guilt was the greatest, not only by the miseries of the human race which begin from the cradles of infants, but also by you yourself. After all, in the second book of this work you placed the great pattern of sin in the first man so that, on the other hand, in Christ we might be shown the greatest pattern of righteousness.[152] You seem to me to have forgotten that you said this, for if you bore this in mind, you would, of course, never try to lessen the sin of Adam with so much talk. (19) I, however, prove that that sin was the greatest by the immensity of its punishment, for there is no greater punishment than to be cast out of paradise and to be excluded from the tree of life so that one does not live eternally and has the troubles of this life in addition so that one's days are filled with the groans of labor and pass like a shadow. Surely the hereditary disaster itself of the human race from infancy to old age bears witness to this, and these miseries would not have the character of punishment if they were not contracted by the contagion of sin. You stubbornly fight with us over this contagion, and in order that people do not believe in it, you minimize both the sin itself of the first man and his punishment, and you try to introduce into paradise by a most impudent and impious effort pains, labor, and death.

(20) You also say, "If the earth is cursed in order that he who sinned may be afflicted, sinfulness is still not found where the curse is found. Why would it not, nonetheless, follow, given that condition, that the newborn are not wretched because they are proved to be guilty, even if we were taught that some sufferings of our nature were introduced after the sin of the first human being? Rather, by recalling the first sin, their subsequent affliction indicated to those whom it did not make guilty a warning against evil imitation."

I see the difficulties in which you are caught. You are compelled to admit the miseries of the newborn because the evidence of the facts forces you to do so, since you are not permitted to deny that which lies before the eyes of all. But you want to maintain that these miseries of the newborn would have existed even in paradise if no one had sinned. Yet you see that you cannot persuade people of this if they have any mind at all. (21) It remains, then, for you to admit that the human race was made wretched on account of the sin of the first man, but because you are afraid to say this unconditionally, you say, "If we were taught that some sufferings have been inflicted upon our nature after the sin of the first man." What is this: "If we were taught that some"? Are we really not taught this perfectly obvious fact which you are also now compelled to see? Or must we go back to that point from which you plan to escape unnoticed by means of these words? For you understand the intolerable absurdity of believing that the miseries of the newborn would have also existed in paradise if no one had sinned. (22) But if you are horrified at saying this, since it is truly something very horrifying, why do you even say, "If we were taught," though we are without any doubt taught not that some suffering, but that all the sufferings of the newborn were inflicted upon our nature after the sin of the first man, in fact on account of the sin of the first man?

But you say, "The newborn are not wretched because they are proved to be guilty." I do not say: The newborn are wretched because they are proved guilty. Rather, I say: They are proved to be guilty because they are wretched. For God is just—something you constantly say against yourself without knowing it. God is, I repeat, just, and he would not allow the newborn to be born wretched or to become wretched if he did not know they were guilty. (23) For this reason the Catholic faith understands in no other way the words of the apostle: *Through one man sin entered the world, and through sin death, and in that way it was passed on to all human beings, in whom all have sinned* (Rom 5:12). Unwilling to apply this to the bond of our origin, you try to twist it to the example of our imitation.

As a result, we say to you: Why, then, in the first moments of the beginning of their life do infants who have sinned by no act of imitation bear witness to the miseries of the human race by their countless different woes? And, as if because of a very heavy and inescapable pressure on your stomach you would burst forth in this vomiting and say: The newborn are wretched, not because they are guilty, but in order that they may be warned by this misery and avoid imitating the sin of the first man. For I thought that I should in that way state more clearly and more simply what you said more obscurely and more complexly. (24) But however you say this, who would not see that out of a zeal to defend your own view you are absolutely unwilling to pay attention to what you say?

I ask you, were innocent human beings, then, to be punished with wretchedness, not because they had any sin, but in order that they might not have any sin? Eve, then, should have become wretched before she became guilty in order that by her wretchedness she would be warned not to consent to the serpent. Adam too should first have been punished by the evil of wretchedness in order that he might not agree with his wife who was seduced to the evil of sin. For you want that serious sins be avoided because of preceding punishments, not that they be punished by subsequent ones. And so, in the wrong order, not because there is sin, but in order that sin might not be, you would punish, not guilt, but innocence. Correct, I beg you, this perverted and reversed view, for you would surely correct your tunic if you dressed yourself with the right side on the left. (25) I said this because you want people to avoid having sins follow because of preceding penalties, though preceding sins are usually punished and ought to be punished by subsequent penalties.

Tell us, then, how we should warn infants subject to misfortunes to look upon their misery so that they do not imitate the sin of the first man, for they can neither imitate anyone nor receive as yet any warning. For the earth was cursed, and from this you took the example for your crazy idea, because in that way infants could be made wretched in order that they might avoid the sins of their parents, although they do not contract from them original sin, just as the earth was cursed on account of the punishment of the man, although it had no guilt. Why do you not notice that, as it has no guilt, so it does not have any punishment from the curse, but when the earth is cursed, it becomes the punishment of the man who sins?

(22) But when the newborn are wretched, they themselves feel their wretchedness. If, as you suppose, they contract no sin, they undoubtedly endure punishments that are, if this is so, unmerited, for they can as yet neither be warned, as I said, nor imitate the sin of the first man, which on account of they ought to be warned. Or are we to wait until they grow up and attain free choice when they perceive the warning and, by looking upon their own misery, they do not imitate

the guilt of another? But where shall we put those great multitudes who right up
to the day of their death do not know who Adam was, whether he existed, or what
he did? Where shall we put the multitudes who die before they come to the age at
which they might receive the warning? Where shall we put those who are born
with a mind so foolish and feeble that, even when grown up, they cannot be
warned of something like that with any result? (27) All of these, of course, are
punished by such great misery without any merit and without any benefit. Where
is the justice of God?

If you would bear that justice in mind, you would never believe that the newborn are so wretched without any merit of original sin. But you spoke with a condition, for you did not say: Because we are taught, but said: "If we were taught
that some sufferings were inflicted upon our nature after the sin of the first man."
Hence, you are ready, I think, to say: We are not taught. And for this reason there
remains for you to say that the evils which we see little ones suffer would have
existed even in paradise if no one had sinned in order that you need not admit that
they arose on account of the sin of the first man. (28) And so when you seek to escape these knots and to be able to slip from our hands, you stand immobile opposite to paradise to which you are so opposed that with a most audacious mouth
and a most wicked mind you bring into it the pains of mothers giving birth, the
labors of workers, the chills of the sick, and the diseases of the dying in order to
disturb its happiness and peace.

But you think that you have found something great to say in the praise of
death, namely, "It was made clear at the first opportunity that death is not an evil,
because a righteous person was the first of all to inaugurate it." Explain, then,
how the righteous Abel would only have had this death to inaugurate if the unjust
Cain had its temple built. The author and agent of that death was, of course, Cain,
not Abel. (29) Cain, then, who built its temple inaugurated it. For the death of the
good man was the evil work of the bad man. But Abel, who suffered evil for a
good cause, inaugurated, not death, but martyrdom, since he symbolized the one
who was killed by the people of the Jews as by an evil brother according to the
flesh.

Abel, therefore, is glorious, not because he derived something good from his
brother, but because by dying patiently for the sake of righteousness, he made
good use of that evil. For, just as transgressors are punished for making bad use
of the good of the law, so martyrs, on the other hand, receive their crowns for
making good use of the evil of death. Hence, if you do not refuse to say what I see
you do not know, death is an evil for all who die, but for some of the dead it is evil
and for some it is good. (30) Those who have put their praiseworthy discussions
on the good of death even into writing have followed this teaching.[153]

The death, then, of the righteous Abel who dwells in peace is not only not
evil, but is even good. But you have introduced into paradise, not the peace of the
good people who have died, but the torments of the dying so that there would not

be there the peace of the good. Or if you say: If no one had sinned, human beings would die in paradise without torment, at least, given the fact that hardly anyone dies outside of paradise without torment, admit at long last, now that you have been refuted and defeated, that human nature was changed for the worse by the sin of the first man.

The Need to Interpret the Curse upon the Serpent

28. JUL. (1) What, finally, shall we say about the serpent? Do you think that the devil or this common reptile was punished by that curse? That is, do you think that the sentence which was pronounced on the serpent, *You shall be cursed by all the cattle and by all the animals which are on the earth; you shall move on your chest and belly, and you shall eat the earth all the days of your life* (Gn 3:14), was carried out in the punishment of the devil or in that of this animal which is drawn out of its caverns by the warmth of spring? If you see it carried out in the punishment of this serpent whose form is stretched out in a smooth body and if you say that on account of the merit of that sin it was made into an eater of earth, the inheritance of sin, then, hangs over all the animals since you think that it can only be derived from the sexual desire of those having intercourse. The result is that you maintain that the sexual desire of serpents and also, for this reason, of irrational animals was implanted by the devil and that you intone for us a hymn of Mani, now that your view has been revealed.

(2) But if you declare that whatever is said to the serpent is in a spiritual sense carried out in the devil, you will undoubtedly agree that what is stated there as punishment is not a sign of guilty serpents at present and that the devil does not eat the earth in a proper sense. Rather, you will agree, even if he then made use of the services of a snake and if the severity of the Father afterwards crushed this spear, as it were, which the devil had used to wound the man, the sin, nonetheless, resided in the will of the agent alone. But food and thorns and sweat, which were first created as part of nature, and afterwards were increased in some cases by way of punishment, came down to our era without the addition of that sin.[154] The facts are so clear that they absolutely do not need a longer defense.

AUG. (1) Why is it that you twist even from the serpent your own viperous shrewdness? After all, who properly understands these words of the divine book which you quoted and does not see that that sentence was pronounced upon the devil who used the serpent, as he could, to the purpose he wanted rather than upon the animal itself, however earthy it is? But because the devil produced his seductive words, not through himself, but through the serpent, God spoke to the serpent since the serpent was suited to signify the malice of the devil and since the nature of the serpent was a symbol of the devil. Hence, God's words to the serpent, *You shall be cursed by all the cattle and by all the animals which are on the earth; you shall move on your chest and belly, and you shall eat the earth all the days of your life* (Gn 3:14), and so on, are understood and explained better to the extent that they are more appropriately interpreted as applying to the devil. (2) But since even in accord with the correct faith people interpret them in many ways and since which of them I choose to take is not now pertinent to the issue, it is enough that I answer you that the nature of the devil has absolutely nothing to do with the connection and succession of generation upon which the question of original sin rests.

But with regard to the thorns and the sweat of the laborer I believe that our previous response will convince the readers how impudently you maintain that they were created before sin was committed. You, of course, want to produce such a paradise that it would in no sense be called the paradise of God, but your paradise. When, nonetheless, you said that thorns were created before the sin, you did not dare to introduce them into paradise; in fact, you stated that they were not in paradise, though you wanted to locate labor there, the burden of which weighs one down, even if it does not prick one. If, nonetheless, even you do not think that thorns are fit for paradise, could it happen to human nature without any change from blessedness to misery that it first existed where there were no thorns and now exists where there are, and could this have happened without any merit of sin? At least such a punishment as you cannot deny should force you to acknowledge original sin, if you do not believe that God is unjust.

Julian's Afterthoughts on Childbirth and Labor

29. JUL. (1) Lest we seem, nonetheless, to have passed over anything in negligence, listen to another argument. It has been found that the pain of childbirth varies in accord with the bodies and strength of the mothers. The barbarian and shepherd women who have become hardened by exercise surely give birth in the midst of journeys with such great ease that they take care of their babies without interrupting the labor of travel and immediately carry them along, and without being weakened at all by the difficulty of giving birth, they transfer the burden of their belly to their shoulders. And, in general, the poverty of lower-class women does not require the work of midwives, while, just the opposite, the wealthy are softened by pleasures, and the more each one has caring for her, the more she learns to get sick and is happy to be sick and thinks she needs as many services as she receives.

(2) The hands of wealthy husbands, of course, never experience the suffering of the first man from the thorns; on the contrary, relying on their abundance, they think it beneath their dignity to spend a moment on prayers for fertility, and standing beyond the fear of even hunger by reason of the spread of their posses-

sions, they at times give the order, as the poet says, "Unhitch the oxen, provided you send us truffles."[155]

(3) If, then, the pain of those giving birth pertains to the laws of nature, as we are taught by the example of non-rational animals and by the proper meaning of God's sentence, if the loss of fruit and the sprouting of thorns was indeed created among the other things, though they, nonetheless, become more frequent and more troublesome for some persons, if, finally, like the difficulty of childbirth, the thorniness of the fields varies in accord with the bodies and regions, and if this anguish lasts in the organs of women after grace, though the luxury of the wealthy is completely unaware of it, and if it is explained why the dissolution of the body will ensue, tied more to our members than to our mistakes, it is seen here too that everything is in harmony with the truth of the Catholics and that neither the women nor the thorns profited you in any way.

AUG. (1) In discussing the punishment which God imposed upon the first sinners, you had long ago moved on from the woman so that you said, "Let this suffice concerning the woman."[156] Why have you, then, not kept faith with your promise? Look, after so much you return to her; look, what you had said should suffice concerning the woman is not sufficient for your wordiness. But unless you were such a verbose fellow, how would you fill eight books in reply to my one book? But say what you please; see, after the sufficiency you promised we patiently also listen to your superabundance. Why, after all, should you lose such fine ideas which came to your mind afterwards? And yet it also ought to have come to your mind that you should remove from your book, which was still in your hands awaiting completion, your words, "Let this suffice concerning the woman." In that way your readers would not find you so shamelessly going against your promise.

(2) But go on; set before us what you afterwards thought up contrary to your promise. Say that the labor of childbirth varies according to the bodies and strength of the mothers giving birth, and describe the barbarian and peasant women with their ease in giving birth so that they seem not to be in labor and, for this reason, seem to feel not a slight pain in giving birth, but none at all. If that is so, how does it help you? Are you not speaking against yourself, since you said that these pains are so natural that Eve could not have given birth without them, even if she had remained in paradise without any sin having been committed? Are you going to say that these barbarian and peasant women of yours are more fortunate in this respect than the first woman so that they bear children without pain in these lands filled with suffering, though Eve could not have done this if she had children in paradise? (3) As if in these women the feminine nature was changed into something better than it had been created and as if human exercise was more effective in changing it than the divine working was in creating it!

But if you do not want us to understand from your words that fierce and savage women bear children without pains and if you grant them a tolerable and easy childbirth so that you, nonetheless, admit that they have pain when they give birth, is this, then, no punishment because it is a lesser punishment? Whether, then, these women have less pain when they give birth or pain equal to that of other women or even pain greater than some and bear it remarkably because of the strength they have acquired through exercise and are not worn out and weakened by that torment, they do, nonetheless, suffer pain, and surely all who suffer pain, whether they suffer more or less, do undoubtedly suffer greater or lesser punishments, but punishments nonetheless. (4) If you, however, considered yourself—I do not say a Christian, but—any sort of human being, you would more easily maintain that there is no paradise of God than you would make it a place of punishment by your sacrilegious argumentation.

You, of course, elegantly defend wealthy men from the labor inherited from the first man, unaware or hiding your knowledge that the rich work harder with their minds than the poor with their bodies. By the term "sweat" sacred scripture, of course, signified labor in general, from which no human being is exempt, though some work at hard tasks, while others work with worrisome cares. To the same labors there also belong the studies of any who learn. And what earth brings forth these but this earth which its maker did not make burdensome when he created the first man? (5) But now, as scripture says, *the corruptible body weighs down the soul, and the earthly dwelling presses down the mind with many thoughts, and with difficulty we judge the things of earth, and with labor we discover things before our eyes* (Wis 9:15-16).

Whatever subjects a person strives to learn, whether useful ones or useless ones, it is necessary to labor because the corruptible body weighs down the soul. Hence, this earth brings forth thorns in this way too. Nor are the rich said to be exempt from these thorns, precisely because the divine teacher explained in the gospel that those thorns by which the seeds that are sown are choked off so that they do not come to maturity are the cares and concerns of this life.[157] He certainly calls not only the poor, but also the rich, when he says, *Come to me, all you who labor* (Mt 11:28). But why does he call them if not for the reason he gives a little later: *And you will find rest for your souls* (Mt 11:29). When will this be but when the corruption of our bodies which now weighs down our souls will no longer exist? (6) But now the poor labor; the rich labor; the righteous labor; the wicked labor; the adults labor; the little ones labor from the day they emerge from the womb of their mother until the day of their burial in the mother of all.[158]

This age is, of course, so evil that, if there were no departure from it, the rest promised us could not be attained. Though by the transgression of the first man labor came upon his descendants, even when the guilt of that transgression which we contracted has been removed, labor, nonetheless, remains for the struggle so that the testing of our faith may be carried out. For it is necessary that we do battle with our vices and labor in this struggle until we receive the gift of having no enemy. (7) Hence, in order that good warriors may be led to their rewards, their punishments are changed into battles. The labors of little ones also remain when the original guilt has been removed, although we are taught that these labors arose from this guilt, because it pleased God also to test in that way the faith of adults who offer the little ones to him for rebirth.

What sort of faith would there be in invisible things if the visible[159] reward immediately followed? Is it not better that, with the promised rest delayed, the task of faith should be carried out with the heart, not with the eyes? And in that way the age to come in which there will be no labors, something we do not as yet see, would be believed more sincerely and sought after with greater desire. For this reason with a wonderful goodness God turns our labors, that is, our punishments, into our benefits.

(8) In your desire to refute these ideas you labor in vain, for you labor in bringing forth thorns, not in uprooting them, but we labor to uproot your thorns to the extent that the Lord grants this. Or perhaps you boast that you do not labor because you compose so many books with the great facileness of your mind, and as those barbarian and peasant women give birth to their babies, so you too bring forth your thorns without any difficulty. But I think that you boast in vain of your facile mind; of course, you labor. For how can you intend not to labor, you who try to introduce labors even into paradise? For, certainly, the more impossible this task is shown to be, the greater and the more useless your labor is found to be.

The Laws of Nature versus the Rewards of Obedience

30. JUL. (1) I shall certainly not attack those who think that, if Adam had been obedient to the commandment, he could have been carried off to immortality as his reward.[160] We read, of course, that Enoch and Elijah were carried off so that they did not see death.[161] But the laws of nature are not the same as the rewards of obedience. The merit of a single person, after all, is not so great as to disturb everything that was established as part of nature. The inborn mortality, therefore, would have been the experience of the rest, even if that first man would have moved from longevity to eternity. This point does not rest upon a deniable conjecture, but upon a certain example, since the children of Enoch could not be removed from the condition of dying by the immortality of their father. (2) Nor should anyone think that this can happen, namely that, if not sinners, at least all the righteous, escape to immortality without the intervention of bodily dissolution. For Abel, the first of the righteous, Noah, Abraham, Isaac, Jacob, and all the crowds of the saints in both the old and new testaments have shown us their merit by their virtues and their nature by their death. The authority of Christ also confirms this point as absolutely certain. For the Sadducees had posed a question

about the example of the woman married seven times and asked: If one believes
in the raising of the dead, which husband would most of all claim her as his own?
And he answered, *You are mistaken, knowing neither the scriptures nor the
power of God, for in the resurrection they will neither marry nor be given in
marriage, for they will not die either* (Mt 22:29 and Lk 20:35-36).

(3) Mindful of his work, he stated why he instituted marriage, namely, so that
the birth of children would make up for the losses to death, but this marvelous fecundity was going to stop when greedy death ceased. If, then, by the testimony of
Christ who established it, fertility was created for the purpose of combating our
frailty and if this condition of marriage was established before the sin, it is clear
that mortality does not have to do with the transgression, but with the nature with
which we read that marriage also has to do. That law, then, which was promulgated, that is, *On whatever day you eat from the forbidden fruit you will surely
die* (Gn 2:17), is understood to be death as punishment, not death as bodily death,
to be death which poses a threat to sins, not to seeds, to be death which only
transgression incurs and only becoming better escapes. (4) But when scripture
says that it will be inflicted on the day of the sin, this is the custom of scripture
which often says that one who is already condemned will be condemned. This is
the reason for what the Lord says in the gospel: *Everyone who does not believe in
me is already condemned for not having believed in the name of the
only-begotten Son of God* (Jn 3:18), not that the unbelief which denies Christ is
going to be subjected to everlasting punishment before the day of judgment,
since all who come to the faith were first non-believers. Rather, in order to reveal
the censure of God who gave the commandment, sins are already said to be punishments. Finally, that book called Wisdom and the view of many people maintain that Adam himself was forgiven because of his subsequent repentance.[162]

AUG. (1) If you do not attack, as you say, those who think that Adam could
have been carried off to immortality as a reward, if he had been obedient to the
command, distinguish kinds of immortality, namely, a greater immortality and a
lesser one. For it is not unreasonabe also to call immortality that by which anyone is able not to die if one does not bring about the reason for which one should
die, though one could also do this. Adam existed in this immortality; he lost this
immortality by the merit of his transgression. This immortality was supplied to
him from the tree of life which was forbidden to him, not when he received the
good law that he should not sin, but when he sinned by an evil will. For he was
then cast out of paradise so that he would not stretch out his hand to the tree of
life and eat and live for eternity.[163]

(2) Hence, we should understand that Adam used to take from the tree of life a
sacrament, but from the other trees nourishment. For he was commanded not to
eat from only the tree which was called the tree of the discernment of good and
evil. Why, then, should he not be thought to have eaten from the tree of life since

it was far better than the rest and he had received the power to eat from all the trees except for that one by which he sinned? These are, after all, the words of God who gave the commandment: *From every tree which is in paradise you shall eat, but from the tree of the knowledge of good and evil you shall not eat from it* (Gn 2:16-17). Likewise, these are the words of God condemning him: *Because you listened to the words of your woman and ate from the tree about which alone I commanded you not to eat from it* (Gn 3:17). For what reason, then, would he not have taken care to eat mainly from the tree of life, since he was forbidden to eat only from that tree by the use of which he sinned? (3) In fact, if we are alert in understanding, just as he sinned by eating from the forbidden tree, so he would have sinned by not eating of the tree of life, because he would have denied himself the life which came from that tree.

But that immortality in which the holy angels live and in which we too are going to live is undoubtedly greater. For that immortality is not the sort in which one has in one's power not to die, as one has in one's power not to sin, though one could, nonetheless, also die because one can sin. Rather, that immortality is the sort in which everyone who is found in it or will be found in it will not be able to die, because everyone will also no longer be able to sin. The will to live well will then, of course, be as great as the will to live happily is even now, and we see that this will to live happily could not be taken from us even by our misery.

(4) If you say that as a reward for his obedience Adam could, without death intervening, have been transformed from that lesser immortality into this immortality which no one doubts is greater, you will say something which the correct faith ought not to disapprove. But if you praise this immortality so that you deny that former immortality, you are, of course, forced to fill the face of paradise with deaths and the diseases of the dying by which they are driven toward death because they cannot endure them, and you are forced to bring shame upon your own face to the point that you would want to flee from yourself if you could see your face in a mirror. For why would the descendants of the first man born in paradise, not only as good, but even as blessed, be forced to die if no guilt compelled them to leave paradise where there was the tree of life and the full power to live from it with no necessity of dying?

(5) From this necessity Enoch and Elijah were removed, for they were living in these lands where the tree of life did not exist, and for this reason the necessity of death common to all was pushing them toward the end of this life. For where are we to believe that they were carried off to if not to where there is the tree of life from which they have the power to live without any necessity of dying, just as those human beings in paradise would have had this power, if no will to sin arose in them which would not allow them to remain there where no justice would force them to die?

Hence, the examples of Enoch and Elijah help us rather than you. In these two, of course, God showed what he was going to give even to those whom he dismissed from paradise if they had not willed to sin. For these latter were cast out of the place to which those were carried off. (6) There we believe that this gift was also conferred upon them by the grace of God, namely, that they had no reason to say, *Forgive us our debts* (Mt 6:12). For in these lands where the corruptible body weighs down the soul,[164] they did battle with their vices in a great struggle so that, if they said that they had no sin, they would, nonetheless, have deceived themselves, and the truth would not have been in them.[165]

We believe that they will, of course, return to these lands for a short time in order that they too may do battle with death and pay the debt which the offspring of the first man owes. Hence, we should understand that those who would have had no sin and their children, if they had continued to be inhabitants of paradise in the same uprightness, would have rather remained in that former immortality until, without death intervening, they passed into a greater immortality, if we admit that such great longevity was given to those men, namely, Enoch and Elijah, who were righteous outside of paradise in these lands but could not say that they had no sin.

(7) But, you say, when the Lord was asked about that woman who was married seven times, he confirmed by his response that "marriage was instituted in order that the birth of children would make up for the losses to death, but that this marvelous fecundity was going to cease when greedy death ceased." You are absolutely wrong in thinking that marriage was instituted in order that the departure of the dead might be made up for by the subsequent birth of children. For marriage was instituted so that the chastity of the women would make fathers certain of their children and children certain of their fathers. For human beings could have been born from the promiscuous and indiscriminate intercourse with women, but there could not have been the certain relationship between fathers and children. (8) But if no one sinned and if, for this reason, no one died, this age in which there was the ability to sin and not to sin would have ended when the number of saints had been reached which was sufficient for the age to come. And it would have been replaced by that age in which no one could have sinned.

For, if souls stripped of their bodies can be either unhappy or happy, but cannot, nonetheless, sin, who of the faithful would deny that in the kingdom of God where there will be an incorruptible body which will not weigh down the soul, but add to its beauty, and which will no longer need nourishment, there will be such a disposition of soul that no one there could have any sin, not because of no will, but because of a good will which causes this? When the Lord said in speaking of the resurrection, *They will neither marry nor be given in marriage, for they will not die either* (Mt 22:30), he did not say this in order to show that marriage was instituted on account of the dying, but because, once the number of the saints was complete, there would be no need for anyone to be born where it would be necessary that no one die.

(9) But, you claim, Adam is said both in the Book of Wisdom and in the view of many people to have been freed from his sin after his subsequent repentance, and yet he died in order that we might know that death does not pertain to the punishment of that sin, but to the laws of nature. As if David did not wipe away those two grave sins, that is, adultery and murder, by doing penance so that the prophet himself who had struck terror into him testified that he received pardon! And yet we read that those penalties which God had threatened were carried out so that we might understand that that pardon was beneficial to the extent that the man who had committed such great evils would not be punished for them with an everlasting punishment.

(10) The first man, then, also had something to which his penance contributed, namely, that he suffered a long, but still not an eternal punishment. Hence, it follows that one is perfectly correct to believe that his son, that is, the Lord Jesus as man, released him from the bonds of the underworld when he descended into the lower regions. We should, after all, understand that according to the Book of Wisdom, Adam was then freed from his sin so that it is shown we understand that this book did not say that this was done, but foretold that it would be done, though it did so by a verb in the past tense. It said, Christ *freed him from his sin* (Wis 10:2) in the same way that by a verb in the past tense scripture said, *They pierced my hands* (Ps 22:17) and the other things which scripture says are still to come.

(11) And for this reason Adam paid the temporal punishment for sin even by the death of the body, and his penance did him some good in that he escaped everlasting punishment. In this case the grace of the deliverer was more effective than the merit of the penitent. There is no way for you to defend yourself against the onslaught of the truth by which you are struck down in the most brilliant daylight along with your machines of war, and you are not for any reason permitted to introduce into the paradise of God both deaths and countless diseases full of deadly torments. Believe God who says: *On whatever day you eat from it you will die the death* (Gn 2:17). They began to die on that day when they were separated from the tree of life which, as it was located in a bodily place, surely supplied life to the body, and thus they incurred the necessity of death and its condition.

(12) "The losses to death" and "greedy death" are certainly your words; these words which are so hard and horrible should at least have warned you to spare the paradise of God. Does that most celebrated place of the blessed offend you so much that you would send into it even death with its losses and greed? O enemies of the grace of God! O enemies of the paradise of God, how much further will you be able to go than to fill the sweetness of holy delights with the bitterest punishments and then to want paradise to be nothing but a lesser hell?

Julian's Interpretation of Our Death in Adam

31. JUL. (1) But we have now said enough about Genesis. Let us go on to the apostle Paul whom Mani and the traducianist think share their opinion. When he was discussing the resurrection of the dead, he said, *Just as all die in Adam, so too all will be brought to life in Christ* (1 Cor 15:22). You with whom we are in conflict used this testimony. But since you were silent about it, even if I can guess at it, I can, nonetheless, hardly be certain about what you thought you accomplished by it. After all, why does it have to do with inheritance if all are said to die in Adam, since Adam is the name of a man, but inheritance is a mark of sin and of the Manichean defilement? Or do you perhaps claim that Adam himself is nothing else and means nothing else but sin so that by this use of the name the apostle is seen to have declared that all die in sin? But this is obviously insane.

(2) Since by "Adam" the Hebrew language means nothing but "man," for this is what it says in translation, what is surprising, then, if the apostle said, *All die in Adam* and *all will be brought to life in Christ* (1 Cor 15:22), that is, those who die in accord with the nature of man are raised from the dead in accord with the power of Christ? Anyone who denies this statement is insane; by the power of the same author who created fecundity and mortality in this life, all will be raised up from the tombs in order that each may receive recompense for what he did in the body, whether good or evil.[166]

By this statement, then, of the apostle in which he says, *Just as all die in Adam, so too all will be brought to life in Christ* (1 Cor 15:22), do you think that he means the bodily death which is common to the just and the unjust or the punishment of death which is meant for the devil and the wicked? (3) If the apostle meant this simple, natural death, which is even precious in case of the saints,[167] and which is equally the lot not only of the good and the evil, but also of both human beings and the animals, if, I repeat, the apostle meant this death, it is clear that by the name "Adam" he indicated the nature of humanity and by the name "Christ" the power of God who creates and raises up. But if you want his words, *All die in Adam,* to be understood here in terms of sin, not of nature, there is at hand an explanation both clear and certain, namely, that he said, *Just as all,* that is, many, died by imitating Adam, *so too all,* that is, many, are saved by imitating Christ. Either, then, he spoke of the common death and meant nature, or he spoke of sin and blamed imitation. For, after a little he also added in the same way: *Just as we have borne the image of the earthly man, let us also bear the image of the heavenly man* (1 Cor 15:49). Surely the assumption of the image could not be commanded if one of the images was believed to be natural.

AUG. (1) Who is so negligent about the words of the apostle as not to see that the apostle was speaking about the resurrection of the body when he said, *Just as all die in Adam, so too all will be brought to life in Christ* (1 Cor 15:22)? But you introduce a question where there is no question in order to spread about, not your words, but your nonsense, and you ask me to which death the statement, *All die in Adam,* refers. That statement was, of course, made about the death of the body, this death, namely, by which the good and the bad must die, not that death because of which they are called dead who are evil because of that same death. The Lord included these two deaths in one short sentence when he said, *Let the dead bury their dead* (Mt 8:22).

(2) There is also the death which in Revelation is called the second death,[168] by which the soul and the body will be tormented by eternal fire. The Lord threatens this death when he says, *Fear him who has the power to destroy both the body and the soul in hell* (Mt 10:28). Although there are, then, many deaths found in the scriptures, there are two principal deaths, the first and the second. The first is the death which the first man introduced by his sin; the second is that which the second man will introduce by his judgment. In the same way many testaments of God are mentioned in the holy books, as those who read carefully can see, but there are, nonetheless, two principal ones, the old and the new. The first death, then, began to exist when Adam was cast out of paradise and separated from the tree of life; the second death will begin to exist when Christ will say, *Depart from me, you cursed ones, into eternal fire* (Mt 25:41).

(3) Since the apostle, then, was speaking of the resurrection, he said, *Through a man there came death, and through a man the resurrection of the dead, for just as all die in Adam, so too all will be brought to life in Christ* (1 Cor 15:21-22). We ought not, then, ask what death this passage deals with, for it is evident that it deals with the death of the body. But we ought instead to ask through whom this death with which it deals comes, whether it comes through God who created the man or through the man who by sinning became the cause of this death. But, as I said, we ought to notice this as something set before our eyes, not as if it were something hidden. For the apostle removed this question when he said with perfect clarity, *Through a man there came death* (1 Cor 15:21).

(4) And who is this but the first Adam? He is, of course, the one of whom it was said, *Through one man sin entered the world, and through sin death* (Rom 5:12); the second Adam, who is the pattern of the future,[169] is set opposite to him in contrast. For this reason it was said here, *Through a man there came death, and through a man the resurrection of the dead* (1 Cor 15:22). We should, then, interpret his words, *All die in Adam* so that we do not forget his words, *Through a man there came death. All,* then, *die in Adam* because death came through a man, just as they are brought to life in Christ because *through a man there came the resurrection of the dead.* A man, then, in both cases; just as, then, this latter is one, so the former is one. And, for this reason, because this latter is the second man, that other is the first man.

(5) We know, as you mentioned, that Adam means "man" in the Hebrew language, but this does not prove what you most impudently try to persuade us to

believe, namely, that in the words of the apostle, *All die in Adam,* the apostle meant that every man is mortal, that is, that we should think that all die, not in that first man, but insofar as they are mortal. Do not obscure what is clear; do not twist what is straightforward; do not complicate what is simple. All die in that one through whom death comes, just as all are brought to life in that one through whom the resurrection of the body comes. And who is this latter but the second man? And who is that other but the first man? Hence, who is this latter but Christ alone? Who is that other but Adam alone? (6) *And so, just as we have borne the image of the earthly man, so let us bear the image of the heavenly man* (1 Cor 15:49). The former is reported as a fact; the latter is given as a command. The former is, of course, already present; the latter is in the future. And so, we have borne the former image because of the condition of being born and because of the contagion of sin, but we bear this latter image because of the grace of being reborn. But we meanwhile bear it in hope; we shall bear it in reality as a reward when we shall rise and reign in blessedness and righteousness.

Since this is so, the death of the man who was created in that way and situated in that place so that he would not die if he did not sin is beyond doubt a punishment, but when God by his grace turns the evils of our punishment to a benefit for us, the death of his saints is precious in the sight of the Lord.[170] (7) Because of death they struggle, just as they struggle because of discipline, for as scripture says, *Discipline does not seem at the moment a cause of joy, but of sorrow, but afterwards it produces a richer fruit of righteousness for those who struggle because of it* (Heb 12:11).

But you who maintain that the death of the body would have existed even in paradise, even if no one sinned, are an enemy of the grace of God, an enemy of the saints whose death is precious and who struggle through death to enter and to make paradise their home. After all, you introduce, to the extent that you can, into the place of such great happiness and peace, not merely death alone, that is, the release from the body of the soul, which does not want to be stripped, but to be clothed over, so that the mortal body might be absorbed in life,[171] but you also introduce there all the diseases and every kind of evil which human beings cannot endure and, therefore, die. I see the great error that leads you to do this, but I do not know how you have the effrontery to do it.

The Full Context of Paul's Statement

32. JUL. (1) But let us set forth the whole context of this passage. It says, *If Christ is preached as having risen from the dead, how do some among you say that there is no resurrection of the dead? If there is no resurrection of the dead, Christ too has not risen. If Christ has not risen, our preaching is vain, and your faith is empty. We are also found to be false witnesses for God because we gave*

testimony against God that he raised up Christ whom he did not raise up. For if the dead do not rise, Christ too has not risen. But if Christ has not risen, your faith is vain because you are still in your sins, and those, therefore, who have fallen asleep in Christ have perished. (2) If we have hope in Christ only for this life, we are the most wretched of all human beings. But now Christ has risen from the dead, the first fruits of those who have fallen asleep, because through a man there came death, and through a man the resurrection of the dead. For, just as all die in Adam, so too all will be brought to life in Christ, but each in his own order: Christ as the first fruits; afterward, at his coming those who belong to Christ; finally, there will be the end (1 Cor 15:12-24).

AUG. You undertook to set forth this whole passage from the writings of the apostle on the resurrection of the body so that you might have the occasion to spread about your great wordiness in its abundant poverty, if one can say that, and so that you might obtain room for yourself to ramble in order to fill so many books. This will become clear in your endless and utterly pointless discussion.

The Flesh of Christ Is Not Separate from Ours

33. JUL. (1) This excellent teacher has most cleverly constructed his argument and brought us hope from our close connection with the mediator. For he claims that, to the extent that it has to do with the substance by which he is united to us, that man had excluded nothing and that the view stirred up by unbelief cannot fail to be as prejudicial to Christ as it is to us. Paul, therefore, unites the interests of Christ and of human beings so that it is necessary to believe of both of them what one judges concerning one of them. (2) At the same time people thought that there would not be a resurrection of the dead, but they, nevertheless, did not deny that Christ had risen. The teacher of the nations snatched up this point and declared that it is necessary that both be subject to the same judgment and that one must believe either that all human beings will rise or that Christ also has not risen. Surely the apostle would not have such force in his argumentation if in accord with the Manichees and their disciples, the traducianists, he separated the flesh of Christ from participation in our nature.

AUG. (1) The Manichees are not the ones who separate the flesh of Christ from participation in our nature; rather, they maintain that Christ had no flesh at all. And so, by linking to us the Manichees who are to be anathematized and condemned along with you, you make their crime less when you say that they separate the flesh of Christ from participation in our nature, as if they admit that Christ had flesh which they somehow distinguish from our flesh. Dismiss those people who differ much from us and differ much from you on this question about the flesh of Christ. Deal with us on the question at issue, for along with us you admit the flesh of Christ, though you do so with a difference.

For we do not exclude his flesh from participation in the substance and nature of our flesh, but from participation in sin. (2) Our flesh, after all, is sinful flesh; on this account his flesh was called, not the likeness of flesh, because it was true flesh, but the likeness of sinful flesh,[172] because it is not sinful flesh. If, then, our flesh were not sinful flesh, how, I ask you, could the flesh of Christ be the likeness of sinful flesh? Or are you so foolish as to say that something is like, but that there is nothing to which it is like? Listen to the Catholic bishop, Hilary, whom—whatever you may think of him—you surely cannot call a Manichee. When he was speaking of the flesh of Christ, he said, "When, therefore, he was sent in the likeness of sinful flesh, he did not have sin in the way he had flesh. But since all flesh comes from sin, that is, it is derived from the sin of our father Adam, he was sent in the likeness of sinful flesh, for there was in him not sin, but the likeness of sinful flesh."[173]

(3) What are you going to say to this, you most wicked, most wordy, most insulting, most slanderous fellow? Was Hilary a Manichee? But heaven forbid that I should refuse to accept your injuries, not only along with Hilary and the other ministers of Christ, but also along with the flesh of Christ to which you are not afraid to do such a great injury that you dare to make it equal to the remaining flesh of human beings, which is clearly sinful flesh, if the apostle did not lie when he said that Christ came in the likeness of sinful flesh.[174]

The Presuppositions of Paul's Argument

34. JUL. (1) If that were the case, the apostle would never have said, *If the dead do not rise, Christ also has not risen* (1 Cor 15:16). For one could reply to that: But because Christ was born of the Virgin, he has risen by way of exception; because, however, human beings are born of a diabolical union, they do not rise. Rather, the apostle would have immediately said: And what folly it was for him to rise if this was in preparation neither for our hope nor for his teaching! For what rationality was there in his teaching, and what seriousness was there in his example, if a nature in us unlike his lacked the hope of reigning with him and the power to imitate him? The faith of the apostle, then, is far, in fact very far, from this idea.

(2) Filled with the same spirit as Peter, he knows that Christ died for us in order to give us an example that we might follow in his footsteps.[175] And because he knows that the reason for so great a mystery was his sacrifice and his example, he does not hesitate to declare—in fact, he takes care to teach—that Christ as man did not undertake anything from which each of us is held back by the disadvantages of our nature. He says, *If there is no resurrection of the dead, Christ also has not risen. But if Christ has risen from the dead, how do certain people among you say that there is no resurrection of the dead?* (1 Cor 15:13.12). That

is, if you admit that he as man had the same nature as we have, for what reason do you think either that the resurrection did occur in his case or that it will not occur in the cases of the rest of us? Having set forth the conditions, he states their complete fulfillment: *But now,* he says, *Christ has risen from the dead* (1 Cor 15:20); therefore, the resurrection of the dead will take place.

AUG. (1) The apostle says to those who think that there is no resurrection of the dead and that Christ, nonetheless, has risen: *If there is no resurrection of the dead, Christ has also not risen* (1 Cor 15:13), because Christ rose in order to build up faith in the resurrection of the dead, showing that human beings will rise in the flesh just as he, having become a man, rose in the flesh. And for this reason it followed that those who did not believe that there was a resurrection of the dead should deny that Christ rose.

Hence, because these people with whom he was dealing could not deny the latter, they ought also to admit the former with all obfuscation removed. (2) For if, on account of some difference in Christ, people think that they are correct to deny the resurrection of the dead and yet not to deny the resurrection of Christ, they can mention many other things they find by which they might think that they defend their error. After all, what if when they hear, *If the dead do not rise, Christ has also not risen* (1 Cor 15:13), they reply and say: But he is not merely a man, but also God, unlike the rest of us? As man, he was born of the Holy Spirit and the Virgin Mary, unlike the rest of us; he had the power to lay down his life and to take it up again,[176] unlike the rest of us. Why, then, is it surprising if he could have risen from the dead, unlike what the rest of us will be able to do?

(3) If, then, they say these things, because they grant that Christ alone rose, but reject the resurrection of the rest, are we going to deny those very great differences of Christ from the rest of us so that we can persuade them of the resurrection also of the other dead on the basis of Christ's equality with them? And so, we do not, therefore, deny this difference because of which we say that only the flesh of Christ, unlike the flesh of the others, was not sinful flesh, but the likeness of sinful flesh, and we do not, nonetheless, maintain that his flesh alone rose and that the flesh of the others will not. And we maintain this so that we say what the apostle said, *If the dead do not rise, Christ has also not risen* (1 Cor 15:13). But Christ has risen; the dead, therefore, rise. (4) For it does not follow that, because in each flesh there are not the same merits from their origin, there is, therefore, not the same earthly and mortal substance. The likeness of sinful flesh, of course, has its difference by which it is distinguished from sinful flesh, but heaven forbid that Christ should by rising make himself unequal to those to whom he willed to make himself equal by dying.

We ought, therefore, not to make the likeness of sinful flesh equal to sinful flesh, insofar as it has to do with the difference in pertaining and not pertaining to sin, on the grounds that he who willed that there be no difference in dying and not dying willed that there be no difference in rising and not rising between each flesh. But how does the imitation which you support where there is no need help your case? Imitation is, of course, a matter of will, but when the will is good, as scripture says, *The will is prepared by the Lord* (Prv 8:35 LXX). (5) No one imitates anyone without willing to, but human beings die and rise, whether they will it or not. Imitation itself, however, does not always take place where there is the same nature in the one to be imitated and in the one who imitates. Otherwise, we could not imitate the righteousness and piety of the angels whose nature is different, and yet you yourself admitted[177] that we ask this of the Lord in prayer when we say, *May your will also be done on earth as it is in heaven* (Mt 6:10). Nor would we imitate God the Father whose nature is far different from ours; yet the Lord says, *Be like your Father who is in heaven* (Mt 5:48). And through the prophet we are told, *Be holy because I am holy* (Lv 11:44). It is not true, then, that we cannot imitate Christ because he was in the likeness of sinful flesh, while we are in sinful flesh.

Julian Turns Paul's Argument against Original Sin

35. JUL. (1) Let us apply the force of this argument to inherited sin and say: If Christ who became man did not have natural sin, how do certain people among you say that an innate evil lords it over the image of God? But if there is an evil in our nature, Christ who is found to be in the same nature was also situated under the reign of the devil. But if he is believed to be guilty, our preaching is vain, and your faith is empty. The apostles, however, are found to be false witnesses, because they gave testimony against God, namely, that he formed his own Son from the seed of David according to the flesh[178] innocent and holy, if the sin of the accused seed infected him.

(2) Moreover, if we place our hope in such a Christ, we are the most wretched of all human beings. Now, however, Christ, true man no less than true God, offspring of the family of Adam, born of a woman, born subject to the law,[179] committed no sin and, therefore, had no sin. Sin, then, is seen to be a matter of the will, not of the seed.

AUG. (1) Surely the whole structure of your argument arises, as if from its foundation, from this claim which you put first, "If Christ who became man did not have natural sin, how do certain people among you say that an innate evil lords it over the image of God?" Once this proposition is uprooted and destroyed, whatever you added to it subsequently is overthrown with a slight push. For it does not follow that, if Christ who became man did not have natural, that is, original sin, no innate evil lords it over the image of God, because it does not follow that, if the likeness of sinful flesh had no evil, that flesh to which it is like, that is, sinful flesh itself, has no evil. (2) On the contrary, it follows that, if there is the likeness of sinful flesh, there is also sinful flesh.

For everything that is like must be like to something. And if Christ alone had true flesh, just as the rest of us, but did not have sinful flesh itself, but the likeness of sinful flesh, it is not only necessary that there be another sinful flesh to which this flesh is like, but that all the rest of us have this sinful flesh. Hence, even if there is an evil in sinful flesh, it is not, nonetheless, found in Christ who came in true flesh, not, nonetheless, in sinful flesh, but in the likeness of sinful flesh, in order to heal sinful flesh. (3) He, therefore, is not believed to be guilty, but our guilt, both original guilt and that guilt we have added to it, is removed by him.

Hence, the preaching of the apostle is not vain, for he would not have preached the likeness of sinful flesh in Christ unless he knew that the others had sinful flesh. Nor is our faith empty, though it makes your heresy empty. Nor are the apostles found to be false witnesses, who distinguish the likeness of sinful flesh from sinful flesh, something your heresy does not do. And in the gospel they preach that Christ was born from the seed of David in such a way that they maintain that he was, nonetheless, born of the Holy Spirit and the Virgin Mary, but not from the concupiscence of the flesh. Hence, he had the likeness of sinful flesh, but could not have had sinful flesh. Nor are we the most wretched of all human beings when we believe this, but we believe with great wretchedness that the flesh of Christ was not distinct from the sinful flesh.

(4) Hence, you end your line of argument with a vain conclusion when you say, "It is, then, clear that sin is a matter of the will, not of the seed." You have inferred this in a completely foolish manner, for I have shown that the previous propositions from which you think it was deduced do not follow logically, and I have undoubtedly shown that, since they could not[180] have existed in paradise, no defects of the newborn would have existed after paradise unless the seeds of the first parents were also damaged by bad will.

Why, then—to use the same form of reasoning in a truthful manner which you used in a deceptive manner—do we not rather say to you: If Christ as man was sent to us human beings in the likeness of sinful flesh, how is it that not some of you, but all of you say that the other flesh to which his flesh is like is not sinful flesh? If there is no other sinful flesh, Christ did not have the likeness of sinful flesh.[181] (5) If Christ did not have the likeness of sinful flesh, the preaching of the apostle who said this is vain, and the faith of the Catholic Church which believed this is vain. The apostle, however, is also found to be a false witness who gave testimony against Christ, namely, that he had the likeness of sinful flesh which he did not have. If, however, we believe this, we are not in the society of believers. Now, however, Christ was sent in the likeness of sinful flesh because he alone had true flesh that was not sinful flesh, but its likeness. And for this reason we must admit that the flesh of the rest of us is sinful flesh which the true flesh, but not the sinful flesh, of Christ is like.

Adam Revealed Death As Christ Reveals the Resurrection

36. JUL. (1) The Manichees are, of course, fatally wounded who both believe in natural sin and deny the resurrection of the flesh. *But now,* the apostle says, *Christ has risen from the dead, the first fruits of those who have fallen asleep, for through a man there came death and through a man the resurrection of the dead* (1 Cor 15:20-21). Here the apostle is not speaking about the general resurrection in which the wicked, even sacrilegious people, will share, but only of the resurrection of those who will be transferred into glory. He, then, indicates the blessed resurrection by the simple term "resurrection," and he passes over that resurrection of the impious as if in comparison with the other it were not a resurrection at all.

(2) Here, then, the apostle is discussing, not merely the resurrection which is, as I said, common to the good and the evil, but the blessed resurrection, and though resurrection and blessed resurrection are not the same thing, just as resurrection and miserable resurrection are not the same thing, nonetheless, because eternal beatitude does not exist without resurrection, the term "resurrection" also signifies that happiness which makes rising something not to be regretted. Thus, if someone who was praising diligence, strength, and different aspirations wanted to indicate them by using the short expression "a life," he might, for example, call the life of that person learned, the life of this one elegant, and that of a third tireless. He would, of course, not destroy the distinction so that the life seems the same thing as diligence, as elegance, or as bravery. For to live is one thing and to be eager is another, and yet, unless you live, you will not be eager at all.

(3) So too, resurrection is not the same thing as blessedness; there is, of course, a miserable resurrection of the ashes; you will, nonetheless, not reign at all unless you rise. The death of the body, then, and the resurrection of the body stand as opposites. If, then, death were a general punishment, resurrection would also be a general reward. Now, however, resurrection is punishment for all who are destined for the eternal fires; hence, death is not penal, but natural. For, just as the death of the body does not bring it about in every case that one regrets having passed away, so resurrection does not bring it about in every case that one is pleased to return to life. Rather, the good of returning to life lies in the reward of those who rise, and the bitterness of the death of the body lies in the burning of those who are punished, and they attain each of these in accord with their merits.

(4) It is clear, then, that the apostle was not discussing natural death, but the death of the sinful which perpetual punishment makes unhappy, and he was not discussing the resurrection common to all, but that which everlasting glory makes blessed. Nor, when he discusses persons, does he introduce anything prejudicial to creatures, but with the distinctions always preserved and with the boundaries set between natures and wills, he at times interchanges the words so

that the particular character of what he is speaking about is not lost in confusion. *Through a man,* then, *there came death, and through a man the resurrection of the dead* (1 Cor 15:21). Here he does not declare that death was created by a man, but was revealed in a man, just as he does not say that the resurrection of the dead was produced by a man, that is, by Christ, but in a man, just as the same teacher says to the Philippians. He says, *He became obedient unto death, even the death of the cross; on this account God also exalted him and gave him a name above every name* (Phil 2:8-9). (5) The statement of Peter the apostle also concurs on this point: *People of Israel, listen. Through the hands of the wicked you put to death Jesus, a man among you approved by God, and God has raised him up, having freed him from the pains of the lower world* (Acts 2:22-24). Likewise, he said, *God has raised up this Jesus, and we all bear witness to him* (Acts 2:32).

In that case, then, as it properly pertained to the man to undergo death without injury to his deity, so it properly belonged to the divinity to raise up that man from the dead. But what God is said to do in the person of the Word, Christ himself also does. After all, he spoke as follows: *I have it in my power to lay down my life, and I have it in my power to take it up again* (Jn 10:18). Though there is, then, only one person of the Son, a legitimate distinction, nonetheless, assigns one thing to the flesh and another to the deity. (6) *Through a man,* then, *there came death, and through a man the resurrection of the dead* (1 Cor 15:21) is revealed, not created; rather, both were instituted by God, but in Adam there was seen the condition of death, while in the person of Christ the first fruits of the resurrection. Here, then, where the apostle says, *Through a man there came death,* if you say, Through his will, death does not pertain to nature; if you say, "Through nature," it has nothing to do with guilt. He set these men opposite to each other, the man of death and the man of resurrection, without wanting to subject the latter to the former.

And there follows, *Just as all die in Adam, so too all will be brought to life in Christ* (1 Cor 15:22). Does he, then, say these words of his, *All will be brought to life in Christ,* also of the non-believers or only of believers? (7) If he says of non-believers that all are brought to life in Christ, no one, then, is punished; if he says this of believers, not everyone, then, is brought to life in the faith of Christ, but only the believers, although absolutely all are raised up by the power of their creator. If, then, he says of the death of the body, *All die in Adam,* no one is shown to be guilty by this expression, since even Christ is found to have died in the same Adam. For the reality of the resurrection would not have followed if the reality of death had not come first. The apostle, therefore, declares that all die in Adam. If this death does not indicate anything other than the dissolution of the body, it certainly does not refer to natural sin, nor does it imply anything prejudicial to innocents, if they are said to die in Adam in whom even Christ has died. (8) But if you want his words, *All die in Adam,* to refer to the sin of the soul and not merely to death, but to a guilty and wretched death, that is, a death upon which there follows the punishment assigned to grave sinners, obviously neither Christ nor the saints could exist in that hell.

Nor does he, therefore, say anything prejudicial to the innocents who have no voluntary evil, as they have no voluntary good, but possess only what God made them to be. We consecrate them by the law of baptism so that he who made them good by creating them might make them better by renewing and adopting them. The words of the apostle, then, *Just as all die in Adam, so too all will be brought to life in Christ* (1 Cor 15:22), are as distant from this suspicion of Manichean inherited sin as Christ is distant from sin, and he had no sin, but also had nothing less of human nature.

AUG. (1) Why is it that in arguing against us you say, "The Manichees are fatally wounded who both believe in natural sin and deny the resurrection of the flesh"? Do we attribute sin to some other nature, as they do, or do we deny the resurrection of the flesh? Let the Manichees, of course, be fatally wounded by you for they are fatally wounded along with you by us, especially when they are helped by you. As a help to them you deny that the discord between the flesh and the spirit should be attributed to the sin of Adam. And so, when they seek or give a reason for this evil, they conclude that a foreign nature of evil coeternal with the good God has been mixed into us.

Next you explain the following lines where the apostle discusses the resurrection of the flesh, and you say that he is not speaking of the common resurrection, namely, of the good and the bad, but only of the resurrection of those who are transferred into glory. (2) That is, of course, so, but he is, nonetheless, speaking of the resurrection of the body. The death of the body, then, is opposed to this, and for them, that is, for the death of the body and for the resurrection, individual authors are assigned, namely, the two men: *Through a man there came death, and through a man the resurrection of the dead* (1 Cor 15:21). And these two men are even identified by their proper names in order that it might be clearly seen about whom he was speaking, and he added, *For just as all die in Adam, so too all will be brought to life in Christ* (1 Cor 15:22). He says: *All die;* he does not say, They will die. But in the other clause he does not say: They are brought to life, but *All will be brought to life.* For they die now as a punishment; they will then be brought to life as a reward.

He is not, therefore, now speaking about that death which is to come for those who will be tortured with body and soul in eternal fire; otherwise, he would have put the verb in the future tense in both clauses, and just as he said, *All will be brought to life,* he would have said: They will die. (3) When, however, he said, *All die,* which, of course, is now taking place, but *All will be brought to life,* which will take place then, he sufficiently indicated that by the words, *Through a man there came death,* he was dealing with that death which releases the soul from the flesh. And yet, those who do not remove by rebirth through Christ the guilt which they contracted by birth through Adam belong to that death to come which is called second death.

Now, then, he is speaking of the resurrection of the body which is to come and to which he opposes the death of the body which is now taking place, and these two contraries both have their own author, that is, death has Adam, and the resurrection of the dead has Christ. Hence, just as that resurrection is understood to be a reward, so this death should be understood to be a punishment. It is, of course, not nature, but punishment which is opposed to reward. (4) And, therefore, in this passage in which the resurrection of the body is opposed to the death of the body, the apostle is not dealing with the general resurrection which pertains to the just and the unjust, but rather with that resurrection in which there will be those who will be brought to life by Christ, not those who will be condemned by Christ. And yet, he will cause both groups to rise, for *all who are in the tombs will hear his voice, and those who have done what is good will go forth into the resurrection of life, but those who have done what is evil will enter into the resurrection of condemnation* (Jn 5:28-29).

As I said, then, he wanted[182] to commend that resurrection which has to do with the benefit Christ brings, not also that resurrection which has only to do with judgment. In that way, since the first of these resurrections pertains to our reward, he might show that the death of the body, which is opposed to it, also pertains to punishment. (5) For, just as death is opposed to life, so punishment is opposed to reward, and since the holy martyrs have struggled and conquered through this punishment, that is, through the death of the body, their death in which they now sleep *is precious in the sight of the Lord* (Ps 116:15), not by reason of its nature, but by reason of his gift. Even the punishments of the saints are undoubtedly precious, but just the fact that they are precious does not mean that they are not punishments, just as they are not precious because they are punishments, but because they were accepted for the sake of the truth or endured with piety.

If you had this sound and Catholic view, you would not inject into the paradise of God, that is, into the place of holy delights, not only the punishment of deaths, but also of fatal illnesses. But what is every punishment of a human being but a punishment of the image of God? And if it is imposed unjustly, he by whom it is imposed is certainly unjust. (6) Who, moreover, would doubt that a punishment is unjustly imposed on the image of God unless sin merits this? For only the mediator between God and human beings, the man Jesus Christ,[183] underwent punishment without sin in order that he might do away with our sin and punishment, not that punishment which was to be paid in this evil age, but that eternal punishment which was due to us. And, nonetheless, as death drew near, he assumed for himself our state of mind and said, *Father, if it is possible, let this chalice pass from me* (Mt 26:39). He, of course, had the power to lay down his life and to take it up again, but by these words that divine teacher showed that the death which, without any preceding sin, he accepted for us willingly, not out of necessity, is, nonetheless, a punishment, a punishment which he alone endured for our sinfulness without any of his own.

(7) If, then, this glorious mercy of Christ by which he endured for us punishment without sin is truly singular in the sense that he also died, not indeed in sinful flesh, but on account of the likeness of sinful flesh, but still died in Adam from whom there came sinful flesh, in this evil age which lies outside of paradise the other human beings undoubtedly suffer rightly and deservedly whatever punishments they suffer from birth to death. And among these punishments they, of course, also suffer, under the just and omnipotent God, death for their own sins either contracted by being born or added on by living badly. He, of course, without whose will not even a sparrow falls to the earth,[184] would not cause nor allow punishments to be inflicted upon his images unless he knew they were justly imposed. (8) And what does "justly" mean but because of the merit of sins or for the testing of virtues? In that way, even after sins have been forgiven, the pledge of eternal salvation which the reborn receive benefits them for the age to come, while they here pay whatever debt they must pay in the vanity and wickedness of this age of punishment.

What, then, does your statement mean that little ones are baptized so that God "who made them good by creating them might make them better by renewing and adopting them"? He certainly made them good because every nature, insofar as it is a nature, is good, but he would not unjustly have caused or allowed those whom he made good to be miserable. And yet, in saying that they are renewed, you also admit carelessly and unwittingly that they bring with them the oldness of the old self though they are, of course, new by birth. (9) You are, therefore, compelled to choose one of these three: either to fill paradise with the punishments of human beings, or to say that God is unjust in the punishments of his images which the innocence of the little ones suffers, or, because these two are hateful and damnable, to acknowledge original sin. And in that way you would understand that all who die bodily death die in Adam because death came through this man, that is, through his sin and punishment, and that all who are not condemned at the resurrection of the body, but are brought to life, are brought to life in Christ, because through this man there came the resurrection of the dead, that is, through his righteousness and grace. For, because the death of the body is a punishment, we see that the death of the body is opposed to the resurrection of the body insofar as it is only a reward, since there is the other resurrection which is a punishment.

The Destruction of Death, the Last Enemy

37. JUL. (1) *But each in his own order; Christ is the first fruits; afterward, at his coming, those who belong to Christ; finally, there will be the end* (1 Cor 15:23-24). The apostle says the same thing elsewhere: *He is the firstborn from the dead* (Col 1:18). *Then those who belong to Christ,* that is, the saints, are snatched up in the clouds.[185] After this, *there will be the end,* because these will enter into the eternal kingdom, but the wicked will enter into eternal fire,[186] *when he hands over the kingdom to God the Father, after he has destroyed every principality and every power and force. For he must reign until he has put all his enemies under his feet* (1 Cor 15:24-25). He, after all, makes all things subject to his feet, *but the last enemy to be destroyed will be death.* When the psalm says, *"All these things are made subject to him,"*[187] it is clear that he is excepted who subjected all things to him. *For when all things are subjected to him, then he himself will be subject to him who has subjected all things to him so that God may be all things in all* (1 Cor 15:26-28).

(2) The kingdom of God the Father means that, once the number of the saints which is contained in his foreknowledge has been made complete, every principality and all the forces of the enemy power will perish. It is necessary, of course, that this be the effect of so great a mystery, namely, that all the enemies of righteousness are placed under God's feet. This will take place when eternal death will see that it has been destroyed and conquered by all the saints. When, however, all those kinds of powers have been made subject to Christ and to his body by the revelation of the kingdom, all the glorified assembly of the saints will for much better reasons not cease to be subject to God, but the whole body worthy of the kingdom of the heavens, the body which is constructed under Christ the head, will cling to the divine will with a perfect love so that, when all desire for sins has been extinguished, God may both contain and fill all.

AUG. (1) In this part of your discussion you have brought forth almost nothing which pertains to the question at issue between us. After all, why did you think that this whole passage in which the apostle discusses the resurrection of the body should be inserted if it is not on account of his words, *Just as all die in Adam, so too all will be brought to life in Christ* (1 Cor 15:22)? That is, the reason is that you do not want to ascribe the death of the body to the sin of the first man, but to nature which you say was created in that first man so that, whether he sinned or did not sin, he was going to die.

On this point I think that I have replied to you sufficiently. (2) Hence, while omitting those points in the explanation of which you chose to delay needlessly, we perhaps should examine with regard to the apostle's words, *The last enemy to be destroyed will be death* (1 Cor 15:26), which death he spoke of. Was it this death which now exists by which the soul is compelled to leave the body or that death by which the soul is not allowed to leave the body so that both body and soul are tormented together by everlasting fire? This latter death does not, of course, exist as yet, but is to come, nor will it then be destroyed, but it will, rather, then begin to exist. Who has any doubt that this death does not yet exist at present?

But the death with which we are familiar in all who die bodily death, whose opposite is the resurrection of the body, is the death which the apostle was discussing so that he said all these things. This death, I repeat, which is occurring at present, common and well known to all, namely, the death of the body, will then be destroyed as the last enemy when this corruptible body will put on incorruptibility and this mortal body will put on immortality.[188] (3) We see that this was undoubtedly said about the resurrection of the body which will then occur in contrast with the death of the body which now occurs. Hence, if eternal death which has never existed cannot be destroyed at the point when it rather is beginning to be, and if it will never be destroyed because it will exist forever, it remains that this death which now exists, that is, this last enemy, will be destroyed in the end when the resurrection of the body will cause it not to exist. Moreover, how would it be an enemy if it were so natural that it was not a punishment? But it would in no way be a punishment under the just and omnipotent judge unless it occurred because of the merits of sin. Now at last, we beg you, correct your thinking, and purify the paradise of the blessed which you had defiled with the punishments of human beings.

(4) But I cannot tell you how much your words pleased me that in the kingdom of the heavens the result will be such that, "when all desire for sins has been extinguished, God may both contain and fill all." Oh, how I wish that you would correct yourself in accord with the admonition in this statement of yours! How I wish that you would not want to praise as something good, but rather to accuse as something evil, this desire for sins! For it does not cease to fight against us in our flesh at present, even when held in check, but it will then, as you most correctly admit, not exist when it has been extinguished. This desire is, after all, that darling of yours because of which the flesh has desires opposed to the spirit so that the spirit must have desires opposed to the flesh[189] if one is to avoid committing a sin which will bring condemnation. Ambrose, who was never a Manichee and not a helper of the Manichees, but their destroyer, proclaimed that this evil of discord between the two realities which are good and which were created by the good God, that is, the flesh and the spirit, was turned into our nature by the transgression of the first man.[190]

Baptism on behalf of the Dead

38. JUL. (1) The apostle says, *Otherwise, what will they accomplish who are baptized on behalf of the dead, if the dead do not rise at all? Why are they also baptized on behalf of them? Why are we also in danger at every hour? I die daily because of my pride in you which I have in the Lord. If as a man I fought the animals at Ephesus, what does it profit me, if the dead do not rise? Let us eat and drink for tomorrow we die* (1 Cor 15:29-32). If, he says, this hope of the future glory where God will be all things in all[191] is shaken by an impious disbelief and the resurrection of the dead is denied, what will those accomplish who are baptized on behalf of the dead? From this there arose the error of some people who think that at the very beginning of the gospel there was the custom that those present made the profession of faith on behalf of corpses and also poured the water of baptism over the members of the dead, and it is clear that this happened out of ignorance.[192] (2) For the words of the apostle, *They are baptized on behalf of the dead,* signify nothing else but what he said to the Romans: *We have been buried together with him through baptism into death* (Rom 6:4). That is, by what grace do we approach the reception of baptism in such a spirit that we mortify our members thereafter and live absolutely as if we were dead, if there is no hope that we shall live after death? But why, he says, do I also undergo daily danger, constantly facing the death which persecutors inflict, in order that I may be proud of your progress before God, if the dead do not rise? Why have I as a man also fought the animals at Ephesus, that is, why have I endured the bestial fury of the seditious, if it is still doubtful that the dead rise?

(3) *Do not be led astray; bad company corrupts good morals. For some in fact have no knowledge of God; I say this to embarrass you* (1 Cor 15:33.34). The love of sins, he says, leads you to have no faith about the future; you think that there is no judgment so that you sin with greater audacity. Those who deny the resurrection, he says, have absolutely no knowledge of how to think of God. You, therefore, deny not only the reward, but the power of the divinity, and you ought to be very ashamed of this. I say to embarrass you that certain people of that sort can be found among you.

AUG. And here too you have chosen to say absolutely nothing which pertains to the issue which is at stake in our discussion. Hence, I do not need to reply to your verbosity regarding the words of the apostle which you tried to explain in accord with your grasp of them, for what you said, though in some cases you were not faithful to the meaning of that author, is not, nonetheless, against the faith.

Adam Became a Living Soul, but a Mortal One

39. JUL. (1) *But someone will ask: How do the dead rise? In what sort of body will they come? Foolish fellow, what you sow does not come to life unless it first dies. Not all flesh is the same. There is one kind of flesh for human beings, another for animals, another for birds, and another for fish. There are heavenly bodies, and there are earthly bodies, but the brightness of heavenly bodies is different from that of earthly bodies. There is one brightness of the sun, another for the moon, and another for the stars. For one star differs from another in glory. And so it is with the resurrection of the dead. The seed is sown in corruption and rises in incorruption; it is sown in ignominy and rises in glory; it is sown in weakness and rises in power. An animal body is sown, and a spiritual body rises. Scripture also speaks that way: The first man, Adam, became a living soul,*[193] *but the last Adam became a life-giving spirit. The first man from the earth was earthly; the second man from heaven is heavenly. Those who are earthly are like the earthly man, and those who are heavenly are like the heavenly man. Just as we have borne the image of the earthly man, let us also bear the image of the heavenly man* (1 Cor 15:35-36.39-45.47-49).

(2) The apostle overcomes the difficulty of the question by examples, and he says that nothing is impossible when omnipotence promises the result. But just as he teaches the resurrection of bodies by a comparison with seeds, so he reveals the diversity of those who rise by the variety of creatures. He, nonetheless, says all this about the resurrection of the blessed. *The seed,* he says, *is sown in ignominy and rises in glory; it is sown in weakness and rises in power. An animal body is sown, and a spiritual body rises* (1 Cor 15:43-44). Surely this cannot be realized except in the saints; the non-believers, of course,[194] are not raised up into glory, but into everlasting shame, as the prophet says.[195]

(3) Here he appropriately distinguishes nature and grace and recalls the old testimony which said, *The first man, Adam, was made into a living soul,*[196] and he adds on his own: *The last Adam became a life-giving spirit* (1 Cor 15:45). And he shows that the gifts of immortality pertain to the life-giving spirit, but that the soul that is merely living pertains to the nature that dies at some time. The living one, then, is not the same as the life-giving one. The one who bestows immortality, which he attributes to Christ, is the life-giving one. But the one who simply lives his life, but does not exclude mortality, is the living one. He distinguished these two statements with the goal of showing that Adam became a living, but not immortal being, but that Christ became a spirit who not only is living, but who also brings a glorious resurrection to his own people, but eternal resurrection to all.

AUG. (1) Was Adam, then, going to die even if he had not sinned because he was created in an animal, not in a spiritual body? You are certainly mistaken if you think that it is necessary for us to fill the paradise of God with the deaths and punishments of the dying and, finally, with the ignominy, weakness, and corruption in which the animal bodies of human beings are now sown. For the tree of life, which God planted in paradise, protected even the animal body from death until because of the merit of continued obedience it would pass without the intervention of death into the spiritual glory which the righteous will have when they rise. (2) For it would have been just that the image of God which was darkened and soiled by no sin should be placed in such a body, though one created and formed from earthly matter, in order that the stability of life supplied to it from the tree of life would last. Thus it would live for a time because of the living soul which no necessity would separate from it, and then, because of its observance of obedience, it would attain the life-giving spirit. Hence, it would not lose this lesser life in which it was possible both to die and not to die, but it would gain that fuller life in which it would live without the benefit of any tree and would not be able to die.

For I ask you: In what sort of body do you think that Enoch and Elijah are now: An animal body or a spiritual body? If you say: An animal body, why do you not want to believe that, if they had not violated the commandment of God by any transgression, Adam and Eve and their descendants would have lived, though in an animal body, as these men now are living? For Adam and Eve were living in that place to which Enoch and Elijah were carried off, and these latter are living in that place from which the former were cast out in order that they might die. (3) The bodily tree of life was, after all, supplying life to their animal bodies, just as the spiritual tree of life, which is the Wisdom of God, supplies the life of salutary teaching to holy minds. For this reason even some Catholic commentators on the words of God preferred to present paradise as spiritual, but without rejecting the history which quite clearly shows that it was bodily.

But if you reply that Enoch and Elijah already have a spiritual body, why do you not admit that the animal body of those first human beings and of those who were born of them in succeeding generations would have been able to pass into a spiritual body without death's intervention, if no sin existed which would justly separate them from the tree of life? In that way you would not be forced to fill the paradise of God, that place of happy joys, with the punishments of deaths and of the dying and with the countless torments of death-bringing illnesses.

The Earthly Man and the Heavenly Man

40. JUL. (1) The apostle says, *But it is not the spiritual which came first, but the animal; afterward, there came the spiritual. The first man from the earth was earthly; the second man from heaven is heavenly. Just as we have borne the image of the earthly man, let us also bear the image of the heavenly man* (1 Cor

15:46-47.49). He, of course, clearly turns to conduct and wants there to be as great a difference between our past and our present way of living as there is between mortality and immortality. *The first man,* he says, *from the earth was earthly; the second man from heaven is heavenly;* by mention of the substances he indicates the difference in their intention. For Christ whom he calls the heavenly man did not bring down from heaven his flesh which he took from the offspring of David, from the offspring of Adam, and assumed within a woman and from a woman's flesh. By the terms "heavenly man" and "earthly man," then, he refers to virtues and vices.

(2) Next there follows: *Just as we have borne the image of the earthly man, let us also bear the image of the heavenly man.* In the same sense he writes to the Romans: *What I say to you is quite human on account of the weakness of your flesh. For, just as you offered your members to the service of impurity and of sinfulness for sinfulness, so now offer your members to the service of righteousness for sanctification* (Rom 6:19).

But continuing the tenor of the exhortation which he assumed, he adds something which, unless it is understood, will seem to undermine all that he has said: *I say this, brothers and sisters, because flesh and blood are not able to possess the kingdom of heaven, nor will the perishable possess perpetuity* (1 Cor 15:50). (3) In these passages, of course, in which he had worked at nothing but defending the resurrection of the flesh which he had said was going to take place in the glory of the kingdom, he now declares that *flesh and blood are not able to possess the kingdom.* If flesh does not possess it, if blood does not possess it, where is that which after its death the resurrection of the dead brings back to life? But in the manner of the scriptures he calls our vices, not our substance, "flesh and blood."

Then he explains this same point: *See, I tell you a mystery: all of us will indeed rise, but not all of us will be transformed* (1 Cor 15:51). The excellent teacher understood that he had above claimed the term "resurrection" only for future blessedness, and so that that point would not remain ambiguous, he concludes: *All of us will indeed rise;* there you see the general resurrection. *But not all of us will be transformed;* there you see the resurrection of the blessed. The transformation into glory, then, is only owed to those who merit not the anger of God, but his love.

In a moment he says, *in the blinking of an eye, at the last trumpet, the dead too will rise incorrupt, and we shall be transformed* (1 Cor 15:52). Finally, he turns to those saints whom that day will find in the flesh, and he says that in as brief a moment as the last sound of a note can be, both those who had died will also be raised up incorrupt, that is, whole and entire, and those who were found alive will be transformed into glory.

For this corruptible body must put on incorruptibility, and this mortal body must put on immortality. But when this mortal body has put on immortality, then there will be fulfilled the word of scripture: Death has been absorbed into your victory.[197] Where, death, is your sting? Where is your victory?[198] But the sting of death is sin, and the power of sin is the law (1 Cor 15:53-56). He showed, as he often did, that he was speaking only about the resurrection of the saints; hence, passing over that raising of the unbelievers, he declares that it is fitting that in bodies of the saints corruptibility should be swallowed up by the eternity of glory.

(5) But when this has been fulfilled, he says, then it will be permissible to mock the devil and everlasting death, which had made this natural corruption appear evil; then the joys of the saints will burst forth as they see that they have struck down the sting of death. And they will say, *Where, death, is your sting? Where is your victory? But the sting of death is sin, and the power of sin is the law* (1 Cor 15:55-56).

That is, you, O eternal death, had sin as your sting to wound by it those who abandoned righteousness, for, if you were not armed with this sting, that is, with voluntary sin, you would have harmed no one. You see that this sin and this sting have been crushed by the strength of the faith as our reward bears witness, the reward from which you were trying to draw us away. Sin was, of course, your sting, and the power of your sin was the law, because *where there is no law, there is no transgression either* (Rom 4:15).

(6) Though sin was your sting, this sting surely became stronger at least in the minds of transgressors after death was added to that law;[199] the law, however, was not given to sharpen the sting. For *the law is holy, and the commandment holy, just, and good, but in order that sin might be seen as sin, it produced death for me through the good so that sin might become sinful in excess through the commandment* (Rom 7:12-13). This power, then, which your sting obtained by the help of voluntary sinfulness in us, is shown to have been conquered and broken by the virtues of the faithful and so by the crowns of the faithful. We mock you, therefore, *as we give thanks to our God who has given us the victory through Jesus Christ our Lord* (1 Cor 15:57).

AUG. (1) We have above already sufficiently discussed the image of the earthly man and of the heavenly man, and we have answered you that the image of the heavenly man can now be borne by faith and by hope, but that it will be borne in reality, once it has been made present and given to us, when the body which is now being sown as animal rises as spiritual. He, of courses, ascribes these two images, namely, the one of the earthly man and the other of the heavenly man, to individual realities, namely, the former to an animal body, this latter to a spiritual body. After all, he said above: *But it is not the spiritual which came first, but the animal; afterward, there came the spiritual* (1 Cor 15:46); and he immediately added: *The first man from the earth was earthly; the second man from heaven is heavenly. Just as we have borne the image of the earthly man, let us also bear the image of the heavenly man* (1 Cor 15:46.49). Who is that former man but Adam through whom there came death? (2) And who is this latter but Christ through whom there came the resurrection of the dead? *Because through a man there came death, and through a man the resurrection of the dead. For, just as all die in Adam, so too all will be brought to life in Christ* (1 Cor 15:21-22), that is, whoever will be brought to life will be brought to life only in Christ, a topic on which we have already spoken above.[200]

There is certainly no ambiguity about the two realities to which these two images refer. For the former refers to death, the latter to resurrection. The former, therefore, refers to the death of the body because the latter refers to the resurrection of the body. The former refers to the animal body which is sown in ignominy, the latter to the spiritual body which will rise in glory. We are clothed with the former by being born; we are clothed with the latter by being reborn. Because we are born under the power of sin, but are reborn in the forgiveness of sins, he says: *Just as we have borne the image of the earthly man, let us also bear the image of the heavenly man* (1 Cor 15:49). He reminds us that the former has taken place; he exhorts us in order that the latter may take place. (3) For none of us can bring it about that we were not born in the punishment by which our body was sown in ignominy, but unless we have been reborn and persevere in what we have become by rebirth in grace, we will not attain the possession of a spiritual body which will rise in glory.

Why is it, then, that you say: "He, of course, clearly turns to conduct and wants there to be as great a difference between our past and our present way of living as there is between mortality and immortality"? For the apostle, rather, does not turn to something else, but continues what he had begun concerning the resurrection of the body, to which he sets directly opposite the death of the flesh. (4) He does not, therefore, want us to understand in this passage two ways of life, namely, a good and a bad way, but states that the resurrection of the flesh will come about through Christ, just as the death of the flesh came about through Adam. Allow the man of God to do what he is about; follow him; do not try to make him follow you. For he is not going to follow, no matter how much you try. He clearly sets the death of the flesh opposite to the resurrection of the flesh; he clearly assigns individual authors to these two realities, Adam to the death of the body, Christ to the resurrection of the body. In clearly comparing the two images, one of the earthly man, the other of the heavenly man, as opposed to each other, he attributes the former to the animal body which merited through Adam to be sown in ignominy and the latter to the spiritual body which will merit through Christ to rise in glory.

Christ was said to be the heavenly man even according to the flesh, not because he took his flesh from heaven, but because he raised it too up into heaven. (5) If good conduct and a good way of life cause one to come to the glorious resurrection, did evil conduct and an evil way of living this life which we live after we have been born and grow up cause us to be born in an animal body with the heritage of death? After all, who have by evil conduct or by any conduct gained for themselves a beginning in painful birth? Who have by an evil way of life made it necessary for themselves to die, however they have lived?

Clearly, if we want these two, that is, the image of the earthly man which pertains to the animal body and the image of the heavenly man which pertains to the spiritual body, also to refer to ways of life, just as we put the resurrection of the spiritual body on the side of righteousness, so we ought to put the death of the animal body on the side of sin. For, just as in the righteousness of Christ this resurrection will be brought about, so in the sinfulness of Adam that death was brought about. (6) If you understand this and agree with this perfectly clear truth, I grant what you say, namely, that the earthly man and the heavenly man refer to vices and virtues. For, just as the virtue of Christ will bring it about that the spiritual body will rise, so the vice of Adam brought it about that the animal body died.

That sentence, then, of the same apostle to the Romans, *For, just as you offered your members to serve impurity and to sinfulness for sinfulness, so now offer your members to serve righteousness for sanctification* (Rom 6:19), does not fit with this passage. There, after all, he was speaking about good and bad conduct, but here he is speaking about the resurrection of the body and the death of the body. (7) But because those who already have the use of reason cannot attain the glorious resurrection which will take place when the spiritual body will rise unless they both believe this and hope for this, he recalls that we have borne the image of the earthly man in which death comes through a man and exhorts us to bear the image of the heavenly man in which there comes through a man the resurrection of the dead. In that way, as we came through the sin of Adam to the death of the animal body, so we might come through Christ to the resurrection of the spiritual body.

Then the apostle adds: *I say this, brothers and sisters, because flesh and blood are not able to possess the kingdom of God* (1 Cor 15:50). (8) There we do not blame you for having believed that the expression "flesh and blood" signified the wisdom of the flesh, not the substance of the animal body, which is indeed sown in ignominy, but will still rise in glory and will undoubtedly possess the kingdom of God.[201] And yet, this can also be understood in another way so that in this passage the expression "flesh and blood" signifies the corruption which we now see in flesh and blood, for this corruption will certainly not possess the kingdom of God, because this corruptible body will be clothed with incorruptibility. Hence, when he said: *Flesh and blood are not able to possess the kingdom of God,* he added as if he were explaining what he meant by these terms so that we would not think of the very substance of the flesh: *Nor will corruption possess incorruptibility.* And he seems, rather, to weave together the other ideas in accord with this sense. (9) But whichever sense the author of these words wanted to signify by these same words, neither of them is contrary to the faith which is such that it has no doubt that the family of God gathered from all the nations will possess the kingdom of God in incorruptible flesh.

We, therefore, do not find fault with this interpretation which many Catholic commentators on the divine scriptures have also stated before us, namely, that "flesh and blood" can here be taken as human beings who are wise according to flesh and blood and, therefore, will not possess the kingdom of God. For the same teacher of the nations stated this same idea as follows: *To be wise according to the flesh is death* (Rom 8:6). (10) But you do not want the death of the animal body to have come about through the sin of the first man, though you hear the same apostle saying, *The body is dead on account of sin* (Rom 8:10), and though you do not dare to deny that the resurrection of the spiritual body, which is directly opposed to the death of the animal body, will come about through the righteousness of the second man. And you do not want this in order that you may fill paradise, the memorable place of blessed delights, with the bodies of the dead and, because of these, even with the torments of the dying. This we blame; this we detest; this we judge worthy of anathema.

For what death will be mocked in the end when there is said, *Where, death, is your victory? Where, death, is your sting?* (1 Cor 15:55), if not either the devil, who is also the author of bodily death, or the very death of the body which the resurrection of the body will swallow up? (11) For these words will then be realized when this corruptible body puts on incorruptibility and this mortal body puts on immortality. The apostle certainly says without ambiguity: *When the corruptible body puts on immortality, the words of scripture will be realized: Death has been swallowed up into victory. Where, death, is your victory? Where, death, is your sting?* (1 Cor 15:54-55). To what death will this be said if not to the death which will be swallowed up into victory? And what death is this if not the death which will be swallowed up when this corruptible and mortal body will be clothed with incorruption and immortality? The sting, therefore, of this bodily death is sin, because it will be said to this death: *Where, death, is your sting?* The apostle said that this sting is sin, the sting, that is, by which death comes about, not the sting which is caused by death.

(12) How, then, as you suppose, will not this death, but everlasting death be mocked? Will everlasting death be swallowed up into victory when this mortal body puts on immortality? Does it fight against the saints so that their struggle conquers the fear of that death which previously held them in bondage when they sinned because they feared it? Did not the Lord die to conquer it, and did he

not render powerless the one who held the power of death, that is, the devil? And did he not set free those who out of fear of death were subject[202] to slavery through their whole life?[203] Were they subject because of a fear of eternal death, though it is rather those who do not fear it who become subject to it? (13) In order that we would not fear this death of the body, the fear of which makes us subject, but would rather fear that everlasting death which makes us subject when we do not fear it, the Lord says most clearly: *Do not fear those who kill the body and afterwards can do nothing, but fear the one who has the power to destroy both body and soul in hell* (Lk 12:4-5).

This is certainly the second and perpetual death, and the saints do not battle against the fear of it, but against this temporal death of the body. For, in order to conquer this death, they fear that death, because, when they conquer this death in accord with piety and righteousness, they will not experience that other death. They will, therefore, mock this death, not that death, when they say, *Where, death, is your victory? Where, death, is your sting?* And elsewhere scripture has: *Where, death, is your struggle?* (Hos 13:14 LXX). Since, then, the sting of this death is sin, with what effrontery do you dare to say that the sin of the first man did not bring it about that in him we were separated from the tree of life and also punished by the death of the body? (14) Why is it, I ask, that you bark against the evidence of the words of God with such an incredible rabidness of foaming verbosity, as if your soul could not attain life in paradise unless you introduced into it the death of the body along with so many and such great bodily diseases, torturers, and precursors of death? Rather, take care of yourself so that by sending the punishments of the body into the place of holy delights, you yourself do not suffer in the place of perpetual sorrows punishments of both soul and body.

The Law Which Is the Power of Sin

41. JUL. (1) Augustine, of course, thinks that the sting of death in this passage is that ancient sin, for he does not understand what follows, that is, *The power of sin is the law* (1 Cor 15:56). He tries to maintain that the law is the commandment that was imposed on Adam. But that law was not the power of sin, but the origin of sin. For it is one thing to give power to something already existing and quite another to bring about that which does not yet exist. The eating, then, from that tree would not have been evil, if it had not been forbidden. But after the eating was forbidden and engaged in by transgression, sin came to be there as a result of God's prohibition and man's contempt for it, though the law was not given in order that transgression would be committed. Nonetheless, by doing the same act, that is, by eating from the tree, man would not have sinned, since the tree was good, if the tasting of it were not forbidden by the law. (2) Something, then, which is of itself evil, for example, parricide, sacrilege, or adultery, and is

recognized to be evil even without a law being given, is correctly said to acquire power through the law in the minds of transgressors who are made more desirous by the prohibition. But when something is not wrongly used unless it is forbidden, it is clear that in that case it properly receives its origin, not its strength from the occasion of the law.

But since I was on this point rather long-winded, at the end of this book I also advise my reader to notice carefully that no occasion for the Manichean infidelity is found in the law of God. If some passages are, however, thought to be ambiguous, the reader should have no doubt that they can be explained in accord with the rules of truth and reason and that they are compatible with justice. With the same vigor which befits the law of God we, therefore, condemn those who say that there will be no resurrection of the body through Christ and these who say—just as much in opposition to the apostle—that Christ did not have a body of our nature and, in this way, show their reverence for the doctrines of the Manichees.

AUG. (1) I never said that the apostle meant that law which was given in paradise when he said, *The power of sin is the law* (1 Cor 15:56). As if I had said this, you have, then, said many things against me in vain. For I have always understood the power of sin which still exists, though it now has less effect, to be that law of which the same apostle says, *What then shall we say? Is the law sin? Heaven forbid! But I would not have known sin except through the law. For I would not have known desire unless the law said, "You shall not desire." But having found the occasion, sin produced in me every desire through the commandment* (Rom 7:7-8). See how the law is the power of sin. For sin was less effective when it was not yet producing transgression because the law was as yet not given. *For where there is no law, there is no transgression* (Rom 4:15).

(2) There was as yet not *every desire* before desire was so increased by the prohibition and became so strong that it broke the chain of the prohibition by which it had increased. You showed that you knew this yourself by saying many things on this statement, though in order to show this, you preferred to use other testimonies from the apostle, not this one which I used—perhaps so that you would not have to admit that desire is sin. He most clearly showed that it is sin when he said the words I quoted: *I would not have known sin except through the law.* And as if we asked, "What sin?" he said, *For I would not have known desire unless the law said, "You shall not desire"* (Rom 7:7). (3) This desire, then, which is surely evil, this desire by which the flesh has desires opposed to the spirit,[204] did not yet exist before that great sin of the first human being. But it then began to exist, and it damaged human nature as if in its root from which it contracted original sin. Every human being is, of course, born with it, and the guilt of this concupiscence is not removed except in those who are reborn. And after this forgiveness no one is defiled by it unless one consents to it to carry out an evil

act, when the spirit does not have any desires opposed to it or does not have stronger desires opposed to it.

Sins which are committed by the personal will of sinners then add strength to that same desire, and so does the very habit of sinning, which is often not without reason called a second nature. But even then there is not *every desire.* For it still has room to grow, because it is less when the sin is committed not by one with knowledge, but by one in ignorance. (4) And so he did not say, "I would not have had," but, *I would not have known desire if the law did not say, "You shall not desire." But having found the occasion, sin produced in me every desire through the commandment* (Rom 7:7-8). For there exists *every desire* when forbidden things are desired more ardently and sins now known are committed more viciously because the excuse of ignorance is removed and the transgression of the law is added.

Hence, among those whom the grace of God does not help through the Lamb of God who takes away the sin of the world,[205] the law of God was not called the correction of the sinner, but rather the power of sin. And so, after he had said, *The law is the power of sin,* as if to answer the question, "What then shall we do if sin is not taken away by the law, but increased?" he went on to say where those who are struggling ought to find hope. He said, *Thanks be to God who has given us the victory*—or as other copies have it, as well as the Greek texts: *who gives us victory through our Lord Jesus Christ* (1 Cor 15:57). (5) That is, of course, most true. *For if a law had been given which could give life, righteousness would of course come from the law, but scripture enclosed all things under sin so that the promise might be given to those who believe on the basis of faith in Jesus Christ* (Gal 3:21-22).

For they are the children of the promise and the vessels of mercy to whom the promise has thus been given on the basis of faith in Jesus Christ, because they have obtained mercy so that they are believers, as the apostle also says of himself.[206] Hence, the faith from which we begin and to which there is referred whatever we do temperately, justly, and piously cannot be attributed to the choice of our will, as if it were not given to us by the mercy of God by whom the will itself is prepared, as scripture says.[207]

For this reason the holy Church prays by the lips of priests making supplication not only for the faithful so that they persevere in their piety and do not fall away in their belief, but also for unbelievers so that they believe. (6) For since the time when Adam committed that great sin through human free choice and condemned the whole human race in common,[208] all the human beings who are set free from this common condemnation are set free only by God's grace and mercy, and whatever the law commands is carried out only with the help, inspiration, and gift of him who commands. We pray to God that the faithful may remain, make progress, and be made perfect; we pray to God that unbelievers may begin to believe.

Those who in opposition to this grace of God extol rather than defend the choice of the human will so that they make it fall more seriously from on high desire to suppress and extinguish these holy prayers of the Church which are increasingly fervent throughout the whole world. (7) Among them you people either alone or most of all hold an intractable position, for you do not want Christ Jesus to be Jesus for the little ones whom you contend are infected with no original sin, though he was called Jesus precisely because he saved his people, not from bodily diseases which he often healed in a people not his own, but from their sins.[209]

The apostle, therefore, in his words, *The sting of death is sin,* clearly referred to that death which is opposed to the resurrection of the body about which he was speaking; that is, he referred to the death of the body. For that death will be swallowed up in victory, since it will no longer exist when the body rises as spiritual. For there will be an immortality even of the body, and it will not be able to be lost by any sin. Nonetheless, when he went on to add, *But the power of sin is the law,* he did not mean the law which was given in paradise, (8) for it could not be the power of sin, since there was as yet no sin. Rather, he called that law the power of sin which entered in so that sin might abound[210] and produce every desire, that is, not merely that desire which arose in paradise and brought death even to the body and with which every human being is born. Nor did it produce only that desire which increased as sins were added by the evil actions of each person. But it also produced that desire which was aroused more ardently by the commandment's prohibition and went so far as even to commit transgression. Thus the victory by which not only the desire to sin, but also the fear of bodily death might be conquered, and finally the weakness of its mortality might be swallowed up, was provided not by the law given through Moses, but by the grace brought through Christ.

(9) Therefore, the apostle said, *The sting of death is sin, but the power of sin is the law. Thanks be to God who gives us victory through our Lord Jesus Christ* (1 Cor 15:56-57), as if to say: The sting of death is indeed sin, because sin caused even this death of the body. To its author or to death itself it will be said in the end by those for whom death will be swallowed up when they rise in glory: *Where, death, is your victory? Where, death, is your sting?* (1 Cor 15:55). But the holy and righteous and good law could not take away this sting,[211] that is, the sin which entered through the one and was passed on to all human beings along with death and which was also made many by the addition of other sins. Rather, the law became its power when desire, once forbidden, burned more ardently and came to the peak of transgression. (10) What, then, was left but that grace should come to the rescue? Therefore, *thanks be to God who gives us the victory*

through our Lord Jesus Christ (1 Cor 15:57). By forgiving our debts and by not bringing us into temptation,[212] he brings us to the final victory by which the death even of the body will be swallowed up so that those who boast do not trust in their own virtue, but boast in the Lord.[213]

In the correct and Catholic faith we learn and hold that the death of the body was also produced by that sting which is sin. This faith is so different from the error of the Manichees—in fact, it is shown, rather, to be opposed to it—that they say with you rather than with us that Adam was created mortal so that he was going to die whether he sinned or did not sin. (11) We do not, nonetheless, call you Manichees because you also say this, but you do still not see that you ought not to call us Manichees because we and they say that the concupiscence by which the flesh has desires opposed to the spirit[214] is something evil. But on the very point which you hold in common with the Manichees, you disagree with them by an error, though a different one, for you do not attribute the death of the flesh, as they do, to that alien nature mixed into us, but you impose it upon our nature as undamaged by any sin. And thus you unhappily and indecently fill the paradise of most decent and most happy pleasures with funerals for the dead and torments of the dying.

(12) But though we say along with the Manichees that the concupiscence of the flesh by which the flesh has desires opposed to the spirit is an evil and does not come from the Father,[215] we differ from them, not by another error which, though different, is nonetheless heretical, but by the Catholic truth. For we do not say with the Manichees that this discord between these two desires of the flesh and of the spirit came to us through our being mixed with an alien evil nature coeternal with God. Rather, we say and claim against both of you with faith along with the Catholic Ambrose and his companions that this discord was turned into our nature through the transgression of the first human being,[216] and we preach the flesh of Christ, not no flesh at all, as they falsely claim, nor a flesh different from the nature of our flesh, as you falsely claim. Rather, we preach his flesh as free from this defect of ours by which the flesh has desires opposed to the spirit and as absolutely whole and entire. (13) But by denying that things which are evil are evil and by not attributing their origin to the sin of the first human being, you do not make them not to be evils, but to be thought to stem from the evil nature coeternal with the eternal good. With your detestable blindness you lend support to the Manichees, and you accuse them foolishly since you wretchedly offer them help.

Notes

1. See Gn 22:17.
2. See Sir 40:1.

3. See Gal 5:17.

4. Julian refers to his first work, *To Turbantius* to which Augustine replied in detail in his *Answer to Julian,* and to his *To Florus* to which Augustine is replying in this work.

5. See Gn 1:31.

6. See Gal 5:17.

7. See Rom 7:23.

8. Julian presumably alludes to Valerius for whom Augustine had written *Marriage and Desire.*

9. See Augustine, *The Two Souls* 11, 15.

10. See Ambrose, *Commentary on the Gospel of Luke* (*Expositio Euangelii secundum Lucam*) 7, 141: CCL 14, 263.

11. See Eph 6:16.

12. See Cyprian, *The Lord's Prayer* (*De oratione dominica*) 16: CCL 3A, 99-100.

13. See *Marriage and Desire* II, 34, 57-58; Julian changes the text and omits a good deal of Augustine's words.

14. See 1 Tm 2:5.

15. See 1 Cor 15:45.

16. John Chrysostom, Letter to Olympias (*Epistula ad Olympiadem*) 3, 3: PG 52, 574.

17. In *Answer to Julian* I, 6, 24, Augustine cites the same passage. The quotation is not from one of the homilies of John Chrysostom on the raising of Lazarus, but bears some similarity to the words of Potamius of Lisbon (✝. c. 360); see PL 8, 1414.

18. See Wis 9:15.

19. See Sir 40:1.

20. Augustine plays on the words: "*confusi, confisi* and *confossi,* embarrassed, relying on, and run through," as well as "*accusante* and *adjuvante,* accusing and helping."

21. See Phil 2:13.

22. See Wis 9:15.

23. See Sir 40:1.

24. I have followed the Maurists' suggestion of "*amentius,* more crazy" instead of "*eminentius,* more important."

25. See above III, 186 where Julian quotes from a letter of Mani to Patricius.

26. See Ps 103:3.

27. See Gal 3:2.

28. See Gal 5:13.

29. See Ambrose, *Commentary on the Gospel of Luke* (*Expositio Euangelii secundum Lucam*) 7, 141: CCL 14, 263.

30. See Rom 5:1.

31. Augustine uses the expression "*ratio seminalis*" which reflects a Neoplatonic doctrine which he used in *The Literal Meaning of Genesis* in order to account for the biblical statement that God created all things at once (Sir 18:1), though many things obviously arise in time one after another. He held that all things were originally created simultaneously in the "seminal reasons" from which they later developed. See *The Literal Meaning of Genesis* V, 23, 45.

32. John Chrysostom, Letter to Olympias (*Epistula ad Olympiadem*) 3, 3: PG 52, 574.

33. See Rom 5:16.

34. See Prv 8:35 LXX.

35. The manuscripts have "*iunctus,* joined" instead of "*uinctus,* bound."

36. I have conjectured "*et si*" instead of "*si.*"

37. Though Origen himself probably did not teach that everyone, including the devil, would ultimately be saved, he was generally accused of holding that view. See Augustine's *Heresies* 43, as well as his *To Orosius in Refutation of the Priscillianists and Origenists* 5, 5 and 6, 7.

38. See Prv 8:35 LXX.

39. See Cyprian, *The Lord's Prayer* (*De oratione dominica*) 16: CCL 3A, 99-100; see also 1 Cor 15:49.

40. Innocent, *In requirendis,* 27 January 417; Letter 181, 7 (among the Letters of Augustine).

41. Innocent, *Inter ceteras Ecclesiae Romanae,* 27 January 417; Letter 182, 4 (among the Letters of Augustine).

42. See Prv 8:35 LXX.

43. See Job 14:4 LXX.

44. See Lk 19:10.

45. Ambrose, *Paradise (De paradiso)* 5: CSEL 32/1: 285-286.

46. See Rev 20:6.

47. See Jas 2:13.

48. See Rom 11:33.

49. See Ps 94:11.

50. See Mt 11:25.

51. See Ps 49:7.

52. See Rom 7:18.

53. See 1 Cor 15:53.

54. See Wis 9:15.

55. See Cyprian, *The Lord's Prayer (De oratione dominica)* 16: CCL 3A, 99-100.

56. See Cyprian, *Mortality (De mortalitate)* 4: CCL 3A, 19.

57. Gregory Nazianzus, Sermon in Self-Defense *(Oratio apologetica)* 2, 91: PG 35, 494; in Rufinus' translation, *Apologeticus* 91: CSEL 46, 67-68.

58. See *Answer to Julian* II, 3, 7 and above I, 67.

59. See Rom 7:24-25.

60. Ambrose, *Penance (De poenitentia)* 1, 3, 13: SC 179, 64.

61. See Wis 9:15.

62. See Gal 5:17.

63. See Sir 40:1.

64. See Job 7:1 LXX.

65. See Sir 40:1.

66. See Wis 9:15.

67. Cyprian, *The Lord's Prayer (De oratione dominica)* 16: CCL 3A, 99-100.

68. Gregory Nazianzus, Sermon in Self-Defense *(Oratio apologetica)* 2, 91: PG 35, 494; in Rufinus' translation, *Apologeticus* 91: CSEL 46, 67-68.

69. Ambrose, *Commentary on the Gospel of Luke (Expositio Euangelii secundum Lucam)* 7, 142: CCL 14, 264.

70. See 2 Cor 5:4.

71. Ambrose, *Commentary on the Gospel of Luke (Expositio Euangelii secundam Lucam)* 7, 141: CCL 14, 263.

72. See 2 Cor 5:21.

73. See 1 Cor 12:12.

74. I have conjectured *"propere"* instead of *"propter."*

75. See Terence, *The Eunuch* 531.

76. See Vergil, *Aeneid* 10, 462-463.

77. See Ez 11:19 and 36:26.

78. See Is 2:3.

79. See Ps 119:133.

80. See Col 1:13.

81. See *The Deeds of Pelagius* 11, 24; 32, 57; 35, 60.

82. See Ti 3:10-11.

83. See, for example, 2, 117.

84. The Manichees rejected the whole of the Old Testament, but made the creation accounts of Genesis a particular target of their attacks.

85. Having been a member of the Manichean sect for at least nine years, Augustine argued in almost all of his early works up to the time of the *Confessions* against the Manichees, though the following nine works are often singled out as anti-Manichean: *The Catholic Way of Life*

and the Manichean Way of Life, Answer to Fortunatus, A Manichean Answer to Felix, A Manichean Answer to Adimantus, A Disciple of Mani, Answer to Secundinus, Answer to the Letter of Mani Known as "The Foundation," The Nature of the Good, The Two Souls, and *Answer to Faustus, A Manichean.*

86. See Gn 2:8 and 3:23-24.

87. Julian seems to refer to the use of *"eradicitus"* by an ancient author; if so, the term is rare, but found in Plautus' play, *The Ghosts* (*Mostellaria*) 1112.

88. See Sir 40:1.

89. See Wis 9:15.

90. See 1 Jn 4:18.

91. See Ex 20:5 and 34:7.

92. See Heb 7:9-10.

93. Again Julian uses "Phoenician" as a term of insult for Augustine.

94. See Rom 10:1.3.

95. See Ps 3:9.

96. See Prv 3:16 LXX.

97. Augustine's phrase, "earthly origin: *terrena propagine,*" carries a double meaning, referring to Julian's Apulian ancestry and his being a son of Adam.

98. Augustine brings the chapter to a close with a series of plays upon words: *"gente* people" and *"mente,* mind" and *"poenas,* punishments" and *Poenos,* Phoenicians."

99. See Ps 49:7.

100. Cyprian, *To Quirinus* (*Ad Quirinum*) 3, 4: CCL 3, 92.

101. See II, 76.

102. I have followed the suggestion of the NBA edition and have added: *"de re quae animi est disputatur."*

103. See Heb 12:17.

104. Julian alludes to the comedy of Plautus, *The Vainglorious Soldier* (*Miles gloriosus*), in which a toady plays an important role.

105. See Ps 89:9.11.

106. See Ps 89:11.

107. See Mt 1:21.

108. See Wis 9:15.

109. See Sir 40:1.

110. See Ps 144:3.

111. See Jn 11:49-52.

112. See 1 Jn 3:8.

113. See Cyprian, Letter to Fidus (*Epistula ad Fidum*) 64, 5: CSEL 3/2, 720. See *Answer to Julian* I, 3, 6, where Augustine quotes the words from this letter of Cyprian.

114. See Pelagius, *In Defense of Free Choice,* a text cited by Augustine fifteen times, but first in *The Grace of Christ and Original Sin* I, 43, 47.

115. See Ambrose, *Commentary on the Gospel of Luke* (*Expositio Euangelii secundum Lucam*) 7, 141: CCL 14, 263.

116. See Plato, *The Republic,* 457c, where he proposes the commonality of wives and children for the guardians of the ideal city.

117. The letter of Cicero to his son is not extant. See M. Testard, *Saint Augustin et Ciceron* (Paris: Études Augustiniennes, 1958) II, 87.

118. See Gn 25:23.

119. See Dt 16:12.

120. See Ex 14:30.

121. See Heb 7:9-10.

122. See Heb 7.

123. See Lk 12:48.

124. See Rom 7:25.

125. See Acts 2:24.

126. See Wis 10:2.

127. See Rom 7:25.

128. See Rom 5:14.

129. *Marriage and Desire II, 34, 58.*

130. *Marriage and Desire* II, 34, 58.

131. See Gn 4:12-15.

132. See Gn 19:1-25.

133. See Dn 3:49-50.

134. See Sir 40:1.

135. See Sir 40:1.

136. Again Augustine puns on "*Poenus,* Punic or Phoenician" and "*poena,* punishment."

137. See Cyprian, Letter to Fidus (*Epistula ad Fidum*) 64, 5: CSEL 3/2, 720.

138. See Sir 40:1.

139. See Rom 5:14.

140. Augustine adamantly denies saying this, but see *The Punishment and Forgiveness of Sins* I, 2, 2-3, 3, which may have occasioned Julian's attack.

141. See *The Deeds of Pelagius* 11, 23 and *The Grace of Christ and Original Sin* II, 3, 3-4.

142. The editors of the NBA edition conjecture that one should add: "*inquies*" while I have conjectured "*aut*" in place of "*at*" and made the sentence into a question.

143. Julian refers to original sin as the sin of the Manichees.

144. See Rom 8:25.

145. John Chrysostom, Letter to Olympias (*Epistula ad Olympiadem*) 3, 3: PG 52, 574.

146. Ambrose, *Commentary on the Gospel of Luke* (*Expositio Euangelii secundum Lucam*) 7, 234: CCL 14, 295.

147. See Gn 3:24 LXX.

148. See Wis 7:22.

149. See Augustine's *The Happy Life* II, 10 where he cites two fragments from Cicero's lost work, *Hortensius* Also see *The Trinity* XIII, 4, 7.

150. *Marriage and Desire* II, 34, 54; see above 23 where Julian cites the sentence.

151. See Rom 8:10.

152. See II, 189 and 190.

153. See Ambrose, *The Good of Death* (*De bono mortis*): CSEL 32/1, 703-753.

154. I have followed the conjecture of "*adiunctione*" in the notes of the NBA edition instead of "*admiratione*" which is found in PL.

155. Juvenal, *Satires* 5, 119.

156. See above 29.

157. See Mt 13:22.

158. See Sir 40:1.

159. I have conjectured "*visiblis*" instead of "*invisibilis.*"

160. See, for example, Rufinus the Syrian's *Faith* (*De fide*) 29-30, where he teaches this view.

161. See Sir 44:16, Heb 11:5, and 2 Kgs 2:11-12.

162. See Wis 10:1-2.

163. See Gn 3:22-23.

164. See Wis 9:15.

165. See 1 Jn 1:8.

166. See 2 Cor 5:10.

167. See Ps 116:15.

168. See Rv 2:11; 20:6; 21:8.

169. See Rom 5:14.

170. See Ps 116:15.

171. See 2 Cor 5:4.

172. See Rom 8:3.

173. This passage attributed to Hilary of Poitiers is also cited in *Answer to Julian* I, 3, 9. Jean Doignon has argued that the passage is a composite of passages from Hilary's *Trinity* (*De trinitate*) 10, 24-25 and his *Commentary on Matthew* (*Commentarium in Matthaeum*) 10:

23-24. See J. Doignon, "'Testimonia' d'Hilaire de Poitiers dans le 'Contra Iulianum' d'Augustin: Les textes, leur groupement, leur 'lecture,' " *Revue Bénédictine* 91 (1981) 7-19.

174. See Rom 8:3.

175. See 1 Pt 2:21.

176. See Jn 10:18.

177. See above II, 52.

178. See Rom 1:3.

179. See Rom 4:4.

180. I have conjectured the negative in this clause.

181. I have conjectured here the addition of: "*Christ non habuit similitudinem carnis peccati.*"

182. I have the suggestion of the NBA editors and read "*voluit*" instead of "*volui.*"

183. See 1 Tm 2:5.

184. See Mt 10:29.

185. See 1 Thes 4:17.

186. See Mt 25:46.

187. See Ps 8:8.

188. See 1 Cor 15:53-54.

189. See Gal 5:17.

190. See Ambrose, *Commentary on the Gospel of Luke* (*Expositio Euangelii secundum Lucam*) 7, 141: CCL 14, 263.

191. See 1 Cor 15:28.

192. The third Council of Carthage in 357 condemned the practice of baptism of the dead.

193. See Gn 2:7.

194. I have followed the conjecture in NBA of "*quippe*" instead of "*quoque.*"

195. See Jer 23:40.

196. See Gn 2:7.

197. See Is 25:8.

198. See Hos 13:14.

199. I have conjectured "*ei legi*" instead of "*ei legis.*"

200. See above 36 end.

201. Below Augustine explains that this interpretation of "flesh and blood" has been proposed by certain unidentified Catholic commentators on the scriptures.

202. The Latin "*reus*" can mean either "guilty" or "subject to punishment." I have translated it in this section as "subject" in order to preserve the connection in Augustine's thought.

203. See Heb 2:14-15.

204. See Gal 5:17.

205. See Jn 1:29.

206. See 1 Cor 7:25.

207. See Prov 8:37 LXX.

208. See *John Chrysostom,* Letter to Olympias (*Epistula ad Olympiadem*) 3, 3: PG 52, 574.

209. See Mt 1:21.

210. See Rom 5:20.

211. I have followed the conjecture in the NBA edition of "*multiplicatus, nec lege sancta et iusta et bona quivit auferri*" instead of "*multiplicatum, nec lex sancta et iusta et bona quivit auffere.*"

212. See Mt 6:12-13.

213. See 2 Cor 10:17.

214. See Gal 5:17.

215. See 1 Jn 2:16.

216. See Ambrose, *Commentary on the Gospel of Luke* (*Expositio Euangelii secundum Lucam*) 7, 141: CCL 14, 263.

INDEX OF SCRIPTURE

(prepared by Michael Dolan)

(The numbers after the scriptural reference refer to the section of the work)

1 Peter

2:12	IV, 123
2:21-22	IV, 85
2:22	IV, 85

2 Peter

2:19	I, 74; I, 107; I, 112

1 John

2:2	IV, 20
2:15-16	III, 170
2:15-17	IV, 20
2:16	IV, 18; IV, 20; IV, 21
2:16-17	IV, 22
3:1	III, 106
3:8	V, 47
3:9	II, 216; IV, 135
4:7	I, 95; III, 106
4:19	I, 131
5:19	IV, 18

INDEX

(prepared by Joseph Sprug)

Citations are to book [Roman number] and chapter.